I0891109

Sustainable Investments in Green Finance

Sanjay Taneja
Graphic Era University (Deemed), India

Pawan Kumar
Chandigarh University, India

Simon Grima
Department of Insurance, Faculty of Economics Management and Accountancy, University of Malta, Malta & Faculty of Business, Management and Economics, University of Latvia, Latvia

Ercan Ozen
Usak University, Turkey

Kiran Sood
Chitkara Business School, Chitkara University, India

A volume in the Advances in Finance, Accounting, and Economics (AFAE) Book Series

IGI Global
PUBLISHER of TIMELY KNOWLEDGE

Published in the United States of America by
IGI Global
Business Science Reference (an imprint of IGI Global)
701 E. Chocolate Avenue
Hershey PA, USA 17033
Tel: 717-533-8845
Fax: 717-533-8661
E-mail: cust@igi-global.com
Web site: http://www.igi-global.com

Library of Congress Cataloging-in-Publication Data

Names: Taneja, Sanjay, editor. | Kumar, Pawan (Professor of finance) editor. | Grima, Simon, editor.
Title: Sustainable investments in green finance / edited by Sanjay Taneja, Pawan Kumar, Simon Grima, Ercan Özen, Kiran Sood.
Description: Hershey, PA : Business Science Reference, [2024] | Includes bibliographical references and index. | Summary: "The book's evidence-based approach and analysis of successful green finance projects will elevate the quality of research in the field, fostering discussions on the effectiveness of different financing mechanisms, policy implications, and best practices for sustainable investments"-- Provided by publisher.
Identifiers: LCCN 2023040566 (print) | LCCN 2023040567 (ebook) | ISBN 9798369313886 (hardcover) | ISBN 9798369313893 (ebook)
Subjects: LCSH: Investments--Environmental aspects. | Social responsibility of business. | Finance--Environmental aspects.
Classification: LCC HG4515.13 .S878 2024 (print) | LCC HG4515.13 (ebook) | DDC 332.6/04--dc23/eng/20230831
LC record available at https://lccn.loc.gov/2023040566
LC ebook record available at https://lccn.loc.gov/2023040567

This book is published in the IGI Global book series Advances in Finance, Accounting, and Economics (AFAE) (ISSN: 2327-5677; eISSN: 2327-5685)

British Cataloguing in Publication Data
A Cataloguing in Publication record for this book is available from the British Library.

All work contributed to this book is new, previously-unpublished material. The views expressed in this book are those of the authors, but not necessarily of the publisher.

For electronic access to this publication, please contact: eresources@igi-global.com.

Advances in Finance, Accounting, and Economics (AFAE) Book Series

Ahmed Driouchi
Al Akhawayn University, Morocco

ISSN:2327-5677
EISSN:2327-5685

Mission

In our changing economic and business environment, it is important to consider the financial changes occurring internationally as well as within individual organizations and business environments. Understanding these changes as well as the factors that influence them is crucial in preparing for our financial future and ensuring economic sustainability and growth.

The **Advances in Finance, Accounting, and Economics (AFAE)** book series aims to publish comprehensive and informative titles in all areas of economics and economic theory, finance, and accounting to assist in advancing the available knowledge and providing for further research development in these dynamic fields.

Coverage

- Comparative Accounting Systems
- Economic Theory
- Field Research
- Public Finance
- Economics of Natural and Environmental Resources
- E-Finance
- International Economics
- Health Economics
- Economic Policy
- Applied Accounting

The Advances in Finance, Accounting, and Economics (AFAE) Book Series (ISSN 2327-5677) is published by IGI Global, 701 E. Chocolate Avenue, Hershey, PA 17033-1240, USA, www.igi-global.com. This series is composed of titles available for purchase individually; each title is edited to be contextually exclusive from any other title within the series. For pricing and ordering information please visit http://www.igi-global.com/book-series/advances-finance-accounting-economics/73685. Postmaster: Send all address changes to above address. ©

Titles in this Series

For a list of additional titles in this series, please visit: www.igi-global.com/book-series

Empowering Women Through Microfinance in Developing Countries
Yahaya Alhassan (University of Sunderland in London, UK) and Uzoechi Nwagbara (University of Sunderland in London, UK)
Business Science Reference • © 2023 • 281pp • H/C (ISBN: 9781668489796) • US $240.00

Management, Technology, and Economic Growth in Smart and Sustainable Cities
Jorge A. Ruiz-Vanoye (Universidad Politécnica de Pachuca, Mexico)
Business Science Reference • © 2023 • 341pp • H/C (ISBN: 9798369303733) • US $240.00

Enhancing Sustainability Through Non-Financial Reporting
Albertina Monteiro (ISCAP, CEOS, Polytechnic of Porto, Portugal) Ana Pinto Borges (ISAG - European Business School, Portugal & CICET-FCVC, Portugal & COMEGI, Portugal) and Elvira Vieira (ISAG - European Business School, Portugal & CICET-FCVC, Portugal & Polytechnic Institute of Viana do Castelo, Portugal & UNIAG, Portugal)
Business Science Reference • © 2023 • 313pp • H/C (ISBN: 9781668490761) • US $225.00

The Importance of Entrepreneurship in Fostering Economic Progress
Mohammed El Amine Abdelli (University of Brest, France) Naima Bentouir (Ain Temouchent University, Algeria) and Esra Sipahi Döngül (Aksaray University, Turkey)
Business Science Reference • © 2023 • 205pp • H/C (ISBN: 9781668471272) • US $240.00

Circular Economy Implementation for Sustainability in the Built Environment
Nicoleta Cobîrzan (Technical University of Cluj-Napoca, Romania) Radu Muntean (Transilvania University of Braşov, Romania) and Raluca-Andreea Felseghi (Technical University of Cluj-Napoca, Romania)
Business Science Reference • © 2023 • 330pp • H/C (ISBN: 9781668482384) • US $250.00

Optimizing Energy Efficiency During a Global Energy Crisis
Meltem Okur Dinçsoy (Trakya University, Turkey) and Hamit Can (Trakya University, Turkey)
Business Science Reference • © 2023 • 408pp • H/C (ISBN: 9798369304006) • US $240.00

Theory and Practice of Illegitimate Finance
Abdul Rafay (University of Management and Technology, Pakistan)
Business Science Reference • © 2023 • 389pp • H/C (ISBN: 9798369311905) • US $295.00

IGI Global
PUBLISHER of TIMELY KNOWLEDGE

701 East Chocolate Avenue, Hershey, PA 17033, USA
Tel: 717-533-8845 x100 • Fax: 717-533-8661
E-Mail: cust@igi-global.com • www.igi-global.com

Table of Contents

Detailed Table of Contents

The current study aims to examine the significant impact of entrepreneurial development programs (EDPs), the digital India mission, and sustainable finance in promoting and enhancing financial inclusion initiatives in IndiaEDPs facilitate the empowerment of people, enabling them to act as agents of entrepreneurship. Sustainable finance is enhanced by incorporating ethical investments and sustainability principles, fostering a more comprehensive integration of investments aligned with financial inclusion and sustainability goals. This research highlights the need for ongoing investment in digital literacy programs, infrastructure development, and regulatory harmonization in order to enhance the accessibility and effectiveness of financial inclusion initiatives. With the ongoing penetration of technology in rural regions and the increasing popularity of sustainable finance, India is positioned to harness the combined strength of these forces, leading to significant economic empowerment and social improvement.

To investigate the connection between sustainable talent management practices and their financial effect on firms, the researchers used a regression analysis. The results highlight the importance of investing in people, highlighting the link between good personnel management practices and financial benefit. In addition, the research reveals a strong link between sustainable practices and excellent financial consequences for businesses. The study's interacting effect is particularly noteworthy, as it suggests that focusing on people management and sustainability at the same time has a multiplier effect on financial impact. In conclusion, this chapter delivers a symphony of factual data showing that companies may amplify their financial performance by harmonizing talent management with sustainability strategies.

substances that deplete the ozone layer and other air pollutants. It is a new idea that offers individuals, organizations, and nations an alternative funding source for activities that are environmentally friendly and carbon-free. Businesses as members of society, have obligations to minimize carbon emissions and assist the government in doing so by implementing "green financing" for sustainable growth. Hence the chapter, examine the body of knowledge already in existence about green finance and Indian bank initiatives to support green financing.

This chapter seeks to address the ESG performance gap in the literature by examining the impact of board size, board independence, women on the board, incentive compensation in terms of sustainability, and CSR committee on the ESG performance. Using one of the largest datasets to date, consisting of an unbalanced dataset of 313 constant year observations from MENA region, spanning an eleven-year period (2007-2017), these results are several. First, the results indicate that board size is positively correlated with ESG performance. Also, the authors show that board independence and the percentage of women in the board are positively correlated with ESG performance.

The possibility of investment and movement of capital between the countries, and the simplification of tax and customs regulations for the expansion of business boundaries strengthen the role and value of non-financial information for stakeholders. The study examines global trends in non-financial reporting, its regulation, and the nature of its use among large and medium-sized enterprises. During the research, it was concluded that the Integrated Report is the most relevant report for a wide range of stakeholders, as evidenced by the active growth in demand for it. At the same time, the Integrated Report should be filled with relevant understandable information and answer key stakeholders` questions. Our research proves that accounts receivable is the important indicator, that makes possible to get an answer about the nature of the enterprise interaction with all types of capital.

The chapter explores the role of the central bank of Nigeria in greening the financial system. The author explores the ways in which the central bank can green the financial system. Some of the offered suggestions include disclosure requirements, establishing green finance labs, creating a green bank, and the use of differentiated cash reserve requirement based on environmental impact. The insights offered in this chapter are useful to bank supervisors and the monetary authority in understanding how financial and monetary decisions affect the environment.

management, enabling data-driven decisions and dynamic pricing strategies. Operational processes have been streamlined through AI, leading to improved efficiency and resource allocation. Furthermore, AI algorithms have leveraged guest data to deliver highly personalized experiences and customized offers, enhancing guest satisfaction and loyalty. In order to track the development of AI in the hotel industry, a bibliometric approach was used in this research. The study also seeks to pinpoint the crucial directions for further investigation. A systematic analysis of how artificial intelligence is changing the hotel business is offered as a perspective.

Sustainability and green finance both are totally intertwined. As the economies are developing, they are forgetting the basic purpose of sustainable development. To curb this, many regulatory institutions have framed the policies which are mandatory for the companies to oblige. The present study tried to explore the opportunities available in promoting green finance and challenges involved with it. Long term vision, technological risks, market and demand, reputational and social risks, and alignment with global trends are observed as the key working parameters to attain sustainable development with green finance. Disclosures for financial institutions to assess the risks assessing the actual and proposed vulnerability analysis for various sectors, stress testing, regulatory measures, and initiatives planned and implemented by the Indian regulators are considered. Research models are framed after understanding and observing the data. Market exploration for green products and services, carbon agenda 2070 are the few other challenges to be sorted by regulators for effective execution of green finance.

The proliferation of artificial intelligence (AI) evolved new business models through disruptive innovations. Recent technology developments and quicker data accessibility have moved it closer to commercial applications in financial industries. The study focused on exploring the significance and emergence of AI in the banking industry. This chapter depicting the adoption of AI in the banking sector also discusses the ground-level challenges in its large-scale implementation. Exploratory research was undertaken to examine the applications and factors that support and hinder the effective adoption of AI in the banking industry. Conventional banks are adopting AI due to the emergence of FinTech start-ups in their operations to improve productivity and customer services. The findings suggest that organizational resistance due to the high cost of implementation, skill, and lack of regulatory framework creates hurdles in its fuller adoption, and trust in financial technology is the critical indicator from the user's perspective.

Preface

Sustainable Investments in Green Finance is a remarkable journey through the ever-evolving landscape of sustainable finance, an exploration of the transformative power of green finance in paving the way towards a more sustainable and environmentally conscious future. As the editors of this reference book, we are honored to present to you a comprehensive compilation of real-world case studies that shed light on the success stories and challenges behind a diverse array of green finance initiatives from around the world.

Green finance, once considered a niche concept, has now emerged as a driving force for change. It encompasses a wide spectrum of financial instruments and mechanisms that aim to channel resources into projects and endeavors that yield environmental and societal benefits. These initiatives are pivotal in addressing the pressing global issues of climate change, resource depletion, and social inequality.

Within the pages of this book, you will embark on a journey through the inspiring landscapes of renewable energy, sustainable infrastructure, green bonds, and nature-based solutions, among other exciting areas of sustainable investments. Each case study offers a deep dive into the project's objectives, financing mechanisms, stakeholder collaborations, and the profound environmental impacts that have been achieved. The real-world examples you will encounter in this book highlight the tangible and positive outcomes that sustainable investments can bring about.

We invite you to discover how renewable energy revolutions are fueling a greener world and explore the innovation behind sustainable infrastructure transformations that are reshaping cities and communities. Unearth the potential of green bonds and climate finance in funding environmentally beneficial projects and reducing carbon emissions. Dive into the transformative potential of circular economy investments, where waste reduction and sustainable practices converge, leading us towards a regenerative future. Moreover, we explore socially responsible investing that addresses environmental and social issues hand-in-hand, unlocking a more equitable and inclusive pathway to sustainability.

While celebrating the successes, this book also candidly addresses the challenges that green finance initiatives face and uncovers the opportunities to overcome barriers and scale up sustainable investments. By analyzing supportive policies, regulations, and public-private partnerships, readers will gain a comprehensive understanding of the frameworks needed to foster and accelerate green finance on a global scale.

In this pivotal moment for our planet, "Sustainable Investments in Green Finance" serves as an essential resource, guiding us towards a greener and more resilient world. As we collectively strive for sustainable development, this book is an empowering compass, illuminating the path to a brighter future where finance becomes a potent force for positive environmental change.

This book is not just a reference for practitioners and policymakers; it is also a valuable resource for researchers, academicians, graduate and post-graduate students, post-doctoral and Ph.D. scholars, and professional practitioners. The rich and diverse set of real-world case studies presented here will make a significant impact on the research community. It bridges the gap between theoretical models and practical implementations, fostering discussions on the effectiveness of different financing mechanisms, policy implications, and best practices for sustainable investments.

The evidence-based approach and analysis of successful green finance projects in this book will elevate the quality of research in the field. It will encourage further exploration of the intricacies of green finance and contribute to the growing body of knowledge in this critical area of study. The insights drawn from these case studies will help shape future research agendas, paving the way for innovative and impactful studies in green finance and sustainable development.

ORGANIZATION OF BOOK

Chapter 1

This chapter dives into the pivotal role of Entrepreneurial Development Programs (EDPs), the Digital India Mission, and sustainable finance in promoting and enhancing financial inclusion in India. It explores how EDPs empower individuals to become agents of entrepreneurship and the integration of ethical investments and sustainability principles into sustainable finance. The study emphasizes the importance of investing in digital literacy programs, infrastructure development, and regulatory harmonization to improve the accessibility and effectiveness of financial inclusion initiatives. The ongoing technological penetration in rural areas, combined with the growing popularity of sustainable finance, positions India for significant economic empowerment and social improvement.

Chapter 2

This chapter delves into the connection between sustainable talent management practices and their financial impact on firms. Through regression analysis, it demonstrates the significance of investing in personnel management and sustainability practices in generating financial benefits. The study highlights the multiplier effect of concurrently focusing on talent management and sustainability, emphasizing how companies can harmonize these elements to amplify their financial performance.

Chapter 3

Amidst global challenges such as environmental variation, energy constraints, and financial crises, this chapter discusses the promise of Green Finance. It provides a comprehensive exploration of existing literature on green finance while shedding light on its potential in India. Green finance is depicted as a beacon of hope, guiding the path to a more environmentally conscious and resilient global economy.

Chapter 4

In a dynamic financial landscape influenced by FinTech, this chapter addresses the negative aspects associated with its growth. It explores the emergence of fraudulent practices enabled by technology's impact on finance, providing insights into the methods, risks, and consequences of these deceptive activities. The chapter emphasizes effective strategies and recommended approaches for safeguarding against FinTech-related harmful effects.

Chapter 5

This chapter employs technological acceptance models and perceived risk analysis to examine the variables influencing customer intentions to make online transactions in the Indian state of Haryana. The results reveal how perceived utility, risk, and ease of use influence online purchase intentions, while perceived risk apprehensions hinder them. The study offers a deep dive into the factors affecting online purchase intentions and highlights areas for future research.

Chapter 6

Exploring the potential of green banking and green finance within the tourism sector, this chapter reviews various green financing mechanisms and their advantages. It identifies the primary obstacles to expanding these practices and provides potential solutions. The chapter emphasizes the enhancement of green finance practices within the tourism sector, offering insights for sustainable development.

Chapter 7

This chapter analyzes the impact of rural media of communication on rural markets in Uttar Pradesh, India. The study highlights the role of various promotional sources, including Hindi dailies, posters, handbills, hoardings, banners, and television programs, in connecting with rural customers. It provides valuable insights into the effectiveness of different media vehicles in rural areas.

Chapter 8

This chapter explores Partially Balanced Incomplete Block (PBIB) Designs, using association matrices based on vertex incidence relations in a bipartite graph. The chapter presents a detailed examination of construction procedures, association schemes, P-matrices, efficiency factors, and total efficiency factors. It introduces new PBIB designs through the concept of juxtapositions in association matrices, offering a deeper understanding of these designs.

Chapter 9

This chapter addresses the demand for carbon offsets and their role in sustainable investments. It examines the use of carbon offset credits in various contexts and discusses mitigation deterrence and abatement approaches of firms. The study conducts a systematic literature review and synthesis of over 300 studies, shedding light on the demand for and use of carbon offsets in the context of sustainable investments.

Chapter 10

This chapter presents a comprehensive overview of green finance and its significance in addressing environmental issues. It delves into the tenets and practices of green finance, highlighting different financial tools and tactics that promote environmental sustainability. The chapter emphasizes the role of rules and policies in supporting green finance and accelerating the shift to a more resilient and sustainable economy.

Chapter 11

This chapter explores green finance and Indian bank initiatives aimed at promoting sustainable development. It discusses the challenges and opportunities associated with green financing, including long-term vision, technological risks, market demand, and alignment with global trends. The study also highlights the disclosures necessary for financial institutions to assess environmental risks and promote sustainability.

Chapter 12

This chapter examines the impact of board size, independence, gender diversity, incentive compensation for sustainability, and CSR committees on ESG performance. Using a large dataset spanning over a decade, the study reveals the relationships between board characteristics and ESG performance. It highlights the importance of certain board characteristics in driving positive ESG outcomes.

Chapter 13

This chapter delves into non-financial reporting and its relevance to understanding overdue receivables in Eastern European countries. The study analyzes statistical information to identify the critical role of accounts receivable and how its disclosure impacts different forms of capital interaction. The chapter suggests specific information related to receivables that should be included in Integrated Reports to reflect a company's commitment to sustainable development.

Chapter 14

This chapter explores the role of the central bank of Nigeria in greening the financial system. It suggests various strategies, including disclosure requirements, green finance labs, creating a green bank, and differentiated cash reserve requirements based on environmental impact. The insights provided are valuable for bank supervisors and monetary authorities in understanding the environmental impact of financial decisions.

Chapter 15

This chapter delves into the impact of green finance on the sustainability performance of Indian commercial banks. It examines how social, economic, and environmental aspects of green finance affect sustainability performance. The study gathers primary data through surveys and interviews, shedding light on the significant influence of green finance on social, economic, and environmental components.

Chapter 16

This chapter addresses the challenges and opportunities in sustainable investment practices through green finance. It highlights the global trends in green credit tools, including climate bonds and universal establishments. The chapter emphasizes the importance of overcoming challenges in sustainable investment practices, offering insights for promoting sustainable growth.

Chapter 17

This chapter explores the role of artificial intelligence (AI) in the hospitality industry, emphasizing its impact on tasks traditionally performed by humans. It discusses how AI-driven analytics, predictive modeling, and operational processes have optimized revenue management, enhanced personalized guest experiences, and improved efficiency. The chapter uses a bibliometric approach to track the development of AI in the hotel industry and identifies key directions for further research.

Chapter 18

This chapter explores the significance and emergence of artificial intelligence (AI) in the banking industry. It discusses how conventional banks are adopting AI to improve productivity and customer services, with a focus on its applications and the challenges hindering its full-scale implementation. The study sheds light on the hurdles faced by organizations due to the high cost of implementation, skill gaps, and a lack of regulatory framework.

Chapter 19

The final chapter explores the evolving concept of "Green Finance 2.0" and its role in aligning financial systems with sustainability and health outcomes. Building upon the guiding principles of the first version, this chapter recognizes the need for a comprehensive sustainability strategy and a broader range of environmental, social, and governance (ESG) factors. It highlights the latest developments and trends shaping a more sustainable and healthy future.

Chapter 20

In a world grappling with urgent challenges such as climate change, biodiversity loss, and public health concerns, the imperative to address these intertwined problems is undeniable. This chapter dives into the concept of "Green Finance 2.0," which has emerged as a powerful paradigm for realigning financial systems with sustainable development and health outcomes. It examines the ever-evolving landscape of green finance, shedding light on the significant developments and trends that form the bedrock for a more sustainable and healthier future. Building on the foundational principles of its predecessor, Green Finance 2.0 takes a giant stride by expanding its scope and ambition. It underscores the need for a comprehensive strategy for sustainability, incorporating a wider range of environmental, social, and governance (ESG) factors into the financial realm. This chapter serves as a forward-looking guide, steering us towards a future where finance plays a pivotal role in creating a world that is not only economically prosperous but also ecologically sustainable and socially healthy.

As editors, we extend our gratitude to the contributors of this book, who have shared their knowledge and experiences to make this project a reality. We hope that *Sustainable Investments in Green Finance* inspires you, empowers you, and provides a wealth of insights that will drive positive change in your own work and endeavors. Together, we can harness the power of green finance to create a more sustainable and equitable world.

Sanjay Taneja
Graphic Era University (Deemed), India

Pawan Kumar
Chandigarh University, India

Simon Grima
Department of Insurance, Faculty of Economics Management and Accountancy, University of Malta, Malta & Faculty of Business, Management and Economics, University of Latvia, Latvia

Ercan Özen
University of Usak, Turkey

Kiran Sood
Chitkara Business School, Chitkara University, India

Introduction

Inspirations and Insights

As the editors of *Sustainable Investments in Green Finance*, we take immense pride in introducing you to this comprehensive exploration of the transformative realm of green finance. In a world marked by the increasing urgency of climate change, dwindling resources, and pressing environmental issues, green finance emerges as a potent force for change. We are honored to present a compilation of real-world case studies from around the globe that reveal the success stories and challenges behind a diverse array of green finance initiatives.

Green finance, once a niche concept, has now become a catalyst for positive environmental and societal change. It encompasses a wide range of financial instruments and mechanisms designed to direct resources into projects that yield both financial and environmental benefits. These initiatives are central to addressing global challenges such as climate change, resource depletion, and social inequality.

This book takes you on a journey through the realms of renewable energy, sustainable infrastructure, green bonds, nature-based solutions, and much more. Each case study offers an immersive exploration of the project's objectives, financing mechanisms, stakeholder collaborations, and the profound environmental impacts achieved. These real-world examples highlight the tangible and positive outcomes that sustainable investments can bring about.

Explorations and Opportunities

Discover how renewable energy revolutions are reshaping our world and explore the innovations behind sustainable infrastructure transformations that are redefining cities and communities. Uncover the potential of green bonds and climate finance in funding projects that benefit the environment while reducing carbon emissions. Dive into the transformative potential of circular economy investments, where waste reduction and sustainable practices merge to lead us toward a regenerative future. Moreover, we explore socially responsible investing, a path that addresses environmental and social issues together, unlocking a more equitable and inclusive journey toward sustainability.

However, we do not shy away from addressing the challenges faced by green finance initiatives. We meet these challenges head-on, acknowledging their presence and providing a clear roadmap to surmount these hurdles. By analyzing supportive policies, thoughtful regulations, and the power of public-private partnerships, readers will gain a comprehensive understanding of the frameworks needed to foster and accelerate green finance on a global scale.

A Resource for Transformation

In this pivotal moment for our planet, *Sustainable Investments in Green Finance* serves as an essential resource, guiding us toward a greener and more resilient world. As we collectively strive for sustainable development, this book is an empowering compass, illuminating the path to a brighter future where finance becomes a potent force for positive environmental change.

This book is not just a reference for practitioners and policymakers; it is also a valuable resource for researchers, academicians, graduate and post-graduate students, post-doctoral and Ph.D. scholars, and professional practitioners. The rich and diverse set of real-world case studies presented here will make a significant impact on the research community. It bridges the gap between theoretical models and practical implementations, fostering discussions on the effectiveness of different financing mechanisms, policy implications, and best practices for sustainable investments.

The evidence-based approach and analysis of successful green finance projects in this book will elevate the quality of research in the field. It will encourage further exploration of the intricacies of green finance and contribute to the growing body of knowledge in this critical area of study. The insights drawn from these case studies will help shape future research agendas, paving the way for innovative and impactful studies in green finance and sustainable development.

We extend our gratitude to the contributors who have shared their knowledge and experiences to make this project a reality. We hope that *Sustainable Investments in Green Finance* inspires you, empowers you, and provides a wealth of insights that will drive positive change in your own work and endeavors. Together, we can harness the power of green finance to create a more sustainable and equitable world.

Sanjay Taneja
Graphic Era University (Deemed), India

Chapter 1
Assessing the Role of Entrepreneurial Development Programs, Digital India, and Sustainable Investments in Accelerating Financial Inclusion Initiatives

Mukul Bhatnagar
Chandigarh University, India

Nitin Pathak
Chandigarh University, India

ABSTRACT

The current study aims to examine the significant impact of entrepreneurial development programs (EDPs), the digital India mission, and sustainable finance in promoting and enhancing financial inclusion initiatives in IndiaEDPs facilitate the empowerment of people, enabling them to act as agents of entrepreneurship. Sustainable finance is enhanced by incorporating ethical investments and sustainability principles, fostering a more comprehensive integration of investments aligned with financial inclusion and sustainability goals. This research highlights the need for ongoing investment in digital literacy programs, infrastructure development, and regulatory harmonization in order to enhance the accessibility and effectiveness of financial inclusion initiatives. With the ongoing penetration of technology in rural regions and the increasing popularity of sustainable finance, India is positioned to harness the combined strength of these forces, leading to significant economic empowerment and social improvement.

DOI: 10.4018/979-8-3693-1388-6.ch001

INTRODUCTION

In a world characterised by a growing emphasis on economic development and technological innovation, ensuring fair and inclusive availability of financial resources has become critical (Kouladoum et al., 2022; Mao et al., 2023). The persistent financial inequity, seen on a global scale and within many communities, has continually impeded the opportunities available to millions of individuals, limiting their ability to engage in economic progress and advancement fully (Konou, 2023; Tufail et al., 2022). The severe difference is seen in several manifestations, including disparities between urban and rural areas and gender-based inequalities (Hu et al., 2023; Shen et al., 2023). Consequently, a substantial segment of the worldwide population lacks crucial financial services (Kien et al., 2023; Li et al., 2023).

Acknowledging the urgent need for financial inclusiveness and seeking to establish equitable conditions, the notion of financial inclusion has garnered momentum as a catalytic influence to bridge disparities and promote comprehensive prosperity. Financial inclusion, at its core, encompasses a fundamental objective: to broaden the accessibility of financial services to all segments of society, particularly those who have traditionally been marginalized from formal banking institutions. The objective is to dismantle obstacles and enable anyone to get and use a wide array of financial services regardless of their socio-economic status, geographical location, or demographic characteristics.

The importance of achieving financial inclusion in India cannot be overstated, as it is a critical step towards addressing the pervasive problem of uneven access to formal financial services within the country's multifaceted socio-economic context (Asif et al., 2023; Fu & Yi, 2023). Throughout history, a considerable segment of the populace, especially those residing in rural and remote regions, has faced exclusion from the official banking industry. Poverty has persisted and economic development has been stymied as a result of this exclusion. Access to vital financial resources is hampered by a number of circumstances, including physical distance, a lack of knowledge, inadequate infrastructure, and low income levels. India has a large population, a large urban-rural divide, and a wide range of socioeconomic statuses, all of which make the promotion of financial inclusion crucial to the country's economic development. Pradhan Mantri Jan Dhan Yojana (PMJDY) was launched in 2014 by the Indian government and regulatory authorities to promote financial inclusion through the use of the Aadhaar unique identification system in tandem with Microfinance Institutions (MFIs). Especially in underserved areas, the digital revolution has been crucial in expanding access to banking services (Bhatnagar, Pathak, et al., 2023).

In the context of India, the attainment of broad financial inclusion requires the implementation of a multidimensional strategy (Buenestado-Fernández et al., 2023; Daud & Ahmad, 2023). Entrepreneurial development programs (EDPs) are of paramount importance in promoting entrepreneurship and facilitating self-employment prospects, thereby establishing a favourable milieu for the advancement of financial inclusion. In contrast, Digital India, a prominent government program, utilizes advanced technology to improve the accessibility and effectiveness of financial services, thereby promoting greater inclusivity. Moreover, sustainable investments play a pivotal role in the establishment of a financially equitable society via their emphasis on fostering long-term economic development and advocating for responsible financial behaviours (Yang & Geng, 2022).

This chapter's main aim is to thoroughly examine the significance of EDPs, Digital India, and Sustainable Investments in expediting financial inclusion endeavours in India. In order to accomplish this aim, the chapter will explore the comprehension of financial inclusion activities in India, as well as the importance of the mentioned initiatives in promoting financial inclusion (Niu et al., 2022). The initiatives mentioned earlier also face several challenges in terms of effectively enhancing financial inclusion. Several ways are proposed to enhance financial inclusion in India via the implementation of EDPs, Digital India, and Sustainable Finance programs. The chapter will culminate by providing a summary of the principal findings and insights derived from the study, with a particular emphasis on the interconnectedness of these elements in expediting financial inclusion in India (Tang et al., 2023).

FINANCIAL INCLUSION IN INDIA

Since the early post-independence period, financial inclusion in India has been a major issue. Initially, banking services were mostly limited to metropolitan areas, resulting in a substantial portion of the population, especially those residing in rural regions, being excluded from participation in the official financial sector (Baber, 2017). The beginning of the nationalization of large banks in 1969 aimed to redirect banking services towards underserved and rural areas. One major impetus for these efforts was the 1969 introduction of the Lead Bank Scheme, which assigned a "lead bank" to each district for the purpose of coordinating banking activities with an emphasis on industries like agriculture and small business. Significant progress was made in the provision of credit and financial services to rural populations with the founding of Regional Rural Banks (RRBs) in 1975. These RRBs targeted small-scale farmers, agricultural labourers, and craftsmen (J. P. Singh, 2019). These businesses did wonders for the banking sector in rural India by making banking services more widely available and adaptable to local needs (Kunal & Sharma, 2022).

During the 1980s, novel methodologies such as Self-Help Groups (SHGs) and Microfinance Institutions (MFIs) saw increased acceptance, hence facilitating the establishment of microcredit and savings initiatives, which in turn empowered women and marginalized populations. The implementation of community-centric models has effectively promoted financial discipline and entrepreneurship at the grassroots level, hence fostering financial inclusion from a bottom-up approach.

In recent years, India has achieved notable progress in the realm of financial inclusion via the implementation of transformational programs. The Pradhan Mantri Jan Dhan Yojana (PMJDY) was initiated in 2014 with the aim of ensuring comprehensive accessibility to a range of financial services, including savings and deposit accounts, remittance, credit, insurance, and pension, for those who do not have access to banking services or have limited access to such services. Two insurance schemes were implemented to improve financial stability: the Pradhan Mantri Suraksha Bima Yojana (PMSBY), which provided coverage for accidental death and disability insurance, and the Pradhan Mantri Jeevan Jyoti Bima Yojana (PMJJBY) which provides life insurance coverage at a reasonable rate.

The Stand-Up India initiative, introduced in April 2016, was designed to foster entrepreneurial endeavours among marginalized groups like women, Scheduled Castes (SCs), and Scheduled Tribes (STs). The MUDRA Yojana was designed to assist micro-firms and entrepreneurs by facilitating the provision of financial goods and services. Its primary aim was to promote entrepreneurship and facilitate the availability of financing for enterprises. The cumulative effect of these endeavours has proven to be essential, as it has facilitated the inclusion of a substantial number of persons into the established financial sector, fostered a mindset of saving, bolstered financial stability via insurance programs, and stimulated entrepreneurial activities. These endeavours have significantly contributed to promoting economic expansion and mitigating financial susceptibility among marginalized segments of the population.

CURRENT STATUS OF FINANCIAL INCLUSION IN INDIA

The Financial Inclusion Index developed by the Reserve Bank of India (RBI) evaluates the level of accessibility, affordability, and availability of diverse financial goods and services for both individuals and enterprises (Mukul & Pathak, 2021a). The primary objective of this tracking mechanism is to assess the effectiveness of the financial services provided to the unbanked people inside the nation.

The measure spans from 0 to 100, where 0 denotes comprehensive financial exclusion, and 100 signifies comprehensive financial inclusion. The RBI monitors 97 indicators, which are categorised into three sub-indices: access, utilisation, and equality. These sub-indices are assigned weights of 35, 45, and 20, respectively. The index encompasses the areas of banking, investing, insurance, postal services, and pension, with the aim of monitoring the extent to which these sectors are used and accessed by the general public. The index assesses the government's capacity to distribute financial goods equitably across the populace and evaluates the accessibility and functionality of those items. Ensuring universal availability and accessibility of a product does not always imply uniform use across all segments of society. This is why the 'utilisation' index accounts for around 50% of the overall index weight.

RBI and the Indian government face significant challenges, with a value of 56.4. Although financial goods are generally available, as shown by the access sub-index of 73.3, the utilisation and equality indices negatively affect the total score. Consequently, some vulnerable groups and marginalised segments of society continue to have challenges in using banking, credit, and other financial services. The implementation of the JAM trinity, comprising Jan Dhan, Aadhaar, and Mobile, has facilitated the Indian government in enhancing the level of financial inclusion from 43.4% in 2017 to 56.4% in 2022. The aforementioned findings demonstrate the noteworthy impact of the Indian government's financial inclusion measures on enhancing the financial landscape of India.

ROLE OF ENTREPRENEURSHIP DEVELOPMENT PROGRAMMES IN BOOSTING FINANCIAL INCLUSION

Entrepreneurship Development Programs (EDPs) are strategic endeavours aimed at providing people with the essential competencies, expertise, and assets required to effectively engage in entrepreneurial activities and establish their own enterprises (Banna et al., 2022). These programs provide budding entrepreneurs with comprehensive coaching on several facets of entrepreneurship, including company planning, marketing strategies, financial management, and leadership skills. EDPs have the primary objective of cultivating an entrepreneurial attitude, enabling people to establish companies that generate money and ultimately positively impact economic development (Dou & Li, 2022).

India has initiated a strong endeavour to foster entrepreneurship and stimulate economic development via various strategic initiatives and programs. The Startup India program, introduced in 2016, is pivotal in cultivating a robust startup ecosystem throughout the country (A. Singh et al., 2023b). The flagship initiative covers the Startup India Action Plan, which provides businesses with various advantages, including tax breaks, streamlined rules, financial assistance, and guidance from experienced mentors (Bhatnagar, Taneja, et al., 2023). Furthermore, the Atal Innovation Mission (AIM), which was established by NITI Aayog, aims to foster innovation and entrepreneurship among young people by establishing a network of innovation hubs and Atal Tinkering Labs inside educational institutions (Kumar, Taneja, et al., 2023). The Stand-Up India initiative emphasises the empowerment of disadvantaged people and the promotion of economic development by providing loans to women, Scheduled Castes, and Scheduled Tribes to facilitate the establishment of enterprises. Additionally, the 'Skill India' effort seeks to provide the younger generation with skills that are pertinent to the sector, fostering entrepreneurship and self-employment via initiatives such as the Pradhan Mantri Kaushal Vikas Yojana (PMKVY). The aforementioned measures demonstrate India's dedication to fostering entrepreneurship, innovation, and economic growth, establishing the nation as a centre for burgeoning enterprises and generating employment opportunities (Bhatnagar et al., 2022; Dangwal, Taneja, et al., 2022).

These initiatives are crucial in promoting financial inclusion in India via a comprehensive strategy. The facilitation of capital access for people, particularly those from underprivileged populations, is achieved via initiatives such as the Stand-Up India initiative and Pradhan Mantri MUDRA Yojana (Jangir et al., 2023; Taneja, Jaggi, et al., 2022). These programs provide financial assistance and loans to entrepreneurs and micro-enterprises. This access is crucial in facilitating economic autonomy and diminishing dependence on informal finance channels. Furthermore, several programs such as Startup India, Skill India, and the Atal Innovation Mission emphasise the significance of technology and innovation (Dangwal, Kaur, et al., 2022; V. Singh et al., 2021). Through the promotion of digital literacy and the facilitation of the adoption of digital financial services, these entities effectively reduce geographical barriers, enhancing the accessibility of formal banking and financial services for persons and enterprises in distant regions. These initiatives serve not only to foster entrepreneurship and innovation but also to augment financial accessibility, therefore making a significant contribution towards the overarching objective of achieving financial inclusion in India (H. Kaur et al., 2023; Kumar, Mukul, et al., 2023).

ROLE OF DIGITAL INDIA IN BOOSTING FINANCIAL INCLUSION

The Digital India Mission, initiated by the Government of India in 2015, is a comprehensive endeavour to convert the country into a society enabled by digital technology and a knowledge-based economy (Nguyen et al., 2023). This comprehensive initiative incorporates several fundamental components, such as digital infrastructure, e-governance, and digital literacy, which all contribute to enhancing financial inclusion (Hodžić et al., 2023).

The diverse nature of Digital India's contribution to the advancement of financial inclusion is evident. To begin with, there has been a notable increase in the availability of digital financial services and online banking due to the implementation of programs like the Unified Payments Interface (UPI) and the Bharat Bill Payment System (BBPS). These platforms have expanded the reach of digital transactions and payments, enabling a wider range of individuals, especially those residing in distant and underserved regions, to access financial services. As a result, financial inclusion has been improved.

Furthermore, the incorporation of Digital India into governmental initiatives such as the PMJDY and Aadhaar has facilitated the efficient linkage of bank accounts with biometric IDs. The establishment of this connection facilitates the effective distribution of subsidies, direct transfer of benefits, and provision of diverse financial services to people across the nation, with a special focus on underprivileged populations (Kumar et al., 2021). In addition, the mission's focus on promoting digital literacy and raising awareness via campaigns has been essential in providing individuals with the necessary abilities to effectively traverse the digital financial realm. Digital India has effectively increased consumers' capacity to access, comprehend, and effectively use online financial services through the provision of digital information (Bansal et al., 2023; Taneja, Bhatnagar, Kumar, & Rupeika-Apoga, 2023).

The Digital India initiative has played a crucial role in facilitating the progress of financial inclusion via the expansion of digital connectivity, the optimization of financial procedures, and the promotion of digital literacy. The reduction of obstacles to financial access has successfully facilitated greater inclusivity and accessibility of financial services, hence promoting economic empowerment and boosting overall development.

ROLE OF SUSTAINABLE INVESTMENTS IN BOOSTING FINANCIAL INCLUSION

Sustainable finance, also referred to as responsible or ethical finance, is an investment strategy that integrates environmental, social, and governance (ESG) variables into decision-making frameworks. The objective is to produce not just financial rewards but also to create beneficial social and environmental consequences (A. Singh et al., 2023a; Taneja, Gupta, et al., 2023). Sustainable investments cover a diverse array of financial instruments and programs that aim to foster sustainability, uphold ethical principles, and facilitate equitable economic development (Gupta, Arora, et al., 2023; Taneja, Grima, et al., 2023).

Sustainable investments play a crucial role in enhancing financial inclusion (Taneja & Ozen, 2023). These investments often focus on firms and programs that specifically cater to disadvantaged and marginalised groups. Sustainable finance facilitates the allocation of financing towards enterprises that prioritise solving the financial requirements of underserved sectors, hence promoting and improving overall financial inclusion (Kumar, Verma, et al., 2023; Taneja, Kaur, et al., 2022).

The implementation of sustainable finance has the potential to facilitate the development of ethical microfinance practices. It assists microfinance institutions that uphold ethical lending practices and promote the financial inclusion of those with low incomes and those residing in rural regions (Taneja, Bhatnagar, Kumar, & Grima, 2023; Taneja & Sharma, 2023). These establishments serve a crucial role in facilitating the availability of financial services, including micro-loans and savings accounts, promoting the expansion of financial inclusion among those who have traditionally faced exclusion from the conventional banking sector. In addition, sustainable investments promote the expansion of firms that prioritise social responsibility and environmental sustainability. By allocating money towards enterprises that emphasise financial inclusion and sustainability, these investments effectively integrate economic expansion with the long-term welfare of society and the environment (Kumar, Özen, et al., 2023; Reepu et al., 2023).

The promotion of sustainable finance in India has the capacity to facilitate financial inclusion via the encouragement of firms that cater to excluded groups, the backing of responsible microfinance institutions, and the cultivation of socially and ecologically responsible businesses (Gupta, Taneja, et al., 2023). The concept encompasses a comprehensive approach to financial matters, which yields economic profits and contributes to the overarching objective of fostering a more equitable and sustainable society (Mukul et al., 2023; Mukul & Pathak, 2021b).

CHALLENGES FACED IN ACCELERATING FINANCIAL INCLUSION BY LEVERAGING EDP'S, DIGITAL INDIA MISSION AND SUSTAINABLE FINANCE

Several challenges must be addressed to improve financial inclusion via the use of EDPs- Entrepreneurial Development Programs, the Digital India mission, and sustainable financing. Despite the admirable endeavours of the Digital India initiative, the enduring digital gap continues to pose a substantial impediment. The limited availability of digital resources, such as smartphones and dependable internet connection, remains a significant obstacle to the widespread adoption of digital financial services, especially in distant and disadvantaged regions. The act of bridging this barrier is of utmost importance in order to provide fair and equal access to possibilities for financial inclusion.

The confluence of these endeavours may encounter obstacles due to the intricate nature of regulations and challenges related to compliance (Chien, 2023; Gopalan & Rajan, 2022; Lee et al., 2022; Lu et al., 2023). The regulatory structure in India's financial industry sometimes hinders entrepreneurial endeavours and investment, necessitating a regulatory system fostering innovation while protecting consumer interests. Furthermore, sustainable finance projects encounter obstacles pertaining to the monitoring of their effect and the reporting of their sustainability efforts. The process of defining and measuring the social and environmental effects of investments may be complex, leading to possible uncertainty over their efficacy (Ali & Ghildiyal, 2023; Khan et al., 2023; Soro & Senou, 2023). Using standardized metrics and effect assessment frameworks is essential in providing guidance for sustainable finance endeavours.

Furthermore, with the increasing prevalence of digital financial services, it becomes imperative to prioritize implementing strong cybersecurity measures and rigorous data privacy safeguards. The preservation of sensitive financial data from cyber threats and protecting people's financial transaction privacy are crucial in maintaining trust and confidence in digital financial services. Moreover, the inadequate levels of financial literacy in several locations, namely in rural and socioeconomically disadvantaged areas, impede the efficient use of digital financial services. The lack of adequate understanding about financial decision-making and digital transaction management contributes to the ongoing distrust and limited adoption of these services.

Infrastructure deficiencies, such as inconsistent energy supply and inadequate network connection in geographically isolated areas, persistently hinder the smooth operation of digital financial services, hence underscoring the need for infrastructure enhancement. Furthermore, the problem persists in enabling the participation of all members of society, especially disadvantaged populations and those with restricted access to adequate identification, in digital financial services.

To effectively tackle these complex difficulties, it is imperative that governments, financial institutions, technology providers, and civil society collaborate in a concerted manner. Their collective efforts are essential in establishing an inclusive, sustainable, and safe financial ecosystem in India, benefiting all residents.

SUGGESTED STRATEGIES TO OVERCOME THE CHALLENGES FACED

In order to effectively tackle the challenges encountered in enhancing financial inclusion via the use of EDPs, the Digital India Mission, and sustainable finance, it is imperative to adopt a comprehensive strategy. To begin with, implementing customized training programs may play a pivotal role in enhancing digital literacy among people, particularly those residing in distant regions. This approach equips them with the necessary competencies to engage with digital financial services proficiently. It is imperative that these programs be made readily available and purposefully constructed to elucidate the intricacies of digital platforms, guaranteeing inclusivity and equitable participation for all individuals throughout the digital revolution. Additionally, regulatory reform has significant importance. Engaging in partnerships with politicians and regulatory entities may provide a conducive regulatory framework that fosters innovation while protecting consumers and companies. Implementing streamlined laws across many sectors would reduce compliance obligations, facilitating the smooth integration of EDP systems, digital initiatives, and sustainable finance.

The establishment of standardized measures to assess the effectiveness of sustainable finance projects is of utmost importance. These measurements facilitate transparency, enabling investors to evaluate their investments' social and environmental consequences appropriately. Standardization is crucial in promoting consistency, reliability, and comparability in impact assessment, hence improving the process of making sustainable financial decisions. Furthermore, it is of utmost importance to address the dangers associated with cybersecurity and the issues around data privacy. Maintaining substantial investments in cybersecurity measures and data protection technologies is vital to ensure the safety of digital financial services. Concurrently, it is essential to implement a thorough user education program on online security measures to guarantee the secure and responsible use of digital financial instruments.

The construction of infrastructure continues to be a fundamental aspect of promoting financial inclusion. Sustained allocations for digital infrastructure, including network connection and dependable power provision, are necessary, especially in rural and distant areas, to guarantee equitable accessibility to digital financial services. Furthermore, it is essential to build customized financial products and services that are designed to meet the distinct requirements and preferences of various demographic segments. This strategy guarantees that financial inclusion efforts effectively connect with the intended audiences, promoting the acceptance and use of such initiatives.

The active involvement of the community and the establishment of partnerships are crucial factors in promoting and increasing knowledge about the concept of financial inclusion. Local leaders, self-help groups, and community-based organizations have the potential to serve as intermediates, playing a crucial role in enabling financial literacy initiatives and promoting active engagement in financial services. In addition, it is essential to develop unambiguous sustainability reporting standards for sustainable financing efforts to augment the levels of openness, accountability, and comparability of impact data.

Financial inclusion is best achieved via a collaborative framework encompassing several stakeholders, including government agencies, financial institutions, fintech businesses, civil society groups, and international actors. This approach promotes a comprehensive and coordinated strategy towards enhancing financial inclusion. The collaborative ecosystem facilitates the exchange of resources, optimal methodologies, and firsthand knowledge, fostering enhanced efficacy and long-term viability. Ultimately, the incorporation of resilient monitoring and evaluation methods guarantees that endeavours towards financial inclusion have a foundation rooted in empirical evidence and the ability to adapt to changing circumstances. The regular evaluation of the effect enables stakeholders to make well-informed choices and adjust tactics in order to attain the overarching objective of achieving complete financial inclusion across all sectors of the population.

Programmes that help aspiring business owners get started have become an effective way to broaden access to banking services. We help people become financially independent by providing them with the tools they need to start their own businesses, including training, coaching, and access to capital. From what we've seen, initiatives like this also boost personal savings and impart useful financial knowledge to participants. The ambitious drive towards digitization by Digital India has changed the face of financial inclusion in the country. More people now have easier access to financial services because of the widespread use of the internet and smartphones. Managers could take advantage of this trend by introducing accessible digital platforms for banking and payments, allowing even those living in rural areas to easily utilise these services. Sustainable investments may alter approaches to broadening access to credit. We aim for long-term economic prosperity by investing in programmes that help disadvantaged populations and foster lasting change. The key to our success has been forming partnerships with impact investors that put a premium on initiatives aimed at reducing poverty. In conclusion, progress in financial inclusion efforts relies heavily on managers' grasp of the full implications of programmes for fostering entrepreneurship, of Digital India, and of investments in the long-term. Including these factors in our plan will help us have a long-lasting impact and decrease the income gap in India.

Our efforts to promote financial inclusion in India via initiatives like Digital India and sustainable investment have far-reaching societal ramifications. These measures are more than just economic tactics; they will also have significant effects on society as a whole. Programmes that encourage entrepreneurship let people take control of their own lives. When people in a community have better access to information and tools, they may not only establish enterprises but also improve the lives of others around them. As a result of this empowerment, economic disparity decreases, living standards rise, and social cohesiveness strengthens. Previously inaccessible banking options are now widely available in Digital India. The ripple effect of this is that more people, especially women and those living in rural areas, are able to take part in the formal economy. Improved health, education, and general well-being among economically included persons improves communities. An ethical component may be added to financial inclusion via sustainable investing. Prioritising initiatives that improve environmental and social conditions helps make our society more resilient and fair. Cleaner environments, more employment options, and better infrastructure all contribute to a feeling of community pride and shared responsibility. In conclusion, our efforts to broaden access to financial services will have far-reaching and positive effects on society. They help people become self-reliant, unite communities, and advance long-term prosperity, all of which contribute to India being a more cohesive and equitable nation.

The government might use the findings from studies on financial inclusion programmes in a number of crucial ways. First, it offers a solid basis upon which to build policies. The government may get a more nuanced knowledge of which policies are most successful in increasing financial inclusion by analysing the impact of multiple components, such as entrepreneurial development programmes, Digital India, and sustainable investments. By using a data-driven approach, Indian policymakers may develop plans that are better equipped to meet the unique requirements and difficulties of the country.

Furthermore, this study may aid in the distribution of available means. Budget and resource limits are common in government, making effective use of available resources crucial. In order to effectively allocate resources, it is important to know which components of financial inclusion efforts provide the greatest results. If studies show that programmes encouraging entrepreneurship have a significant beneficial impact, for instance, policymakers may decide to invest more resources in expanding such initiatives so that they may benefit a wider demographic.

In addition, the study enables regular checks and balances. In order to determine how successful financial inclusion projects are, they must be constantly evaluated. The government may utilise the research's key performance indicators (KPIs) and benchmarks to evaluate the effectiveness of its programmes. Policymakers can make immediate modifications, hone their tactics, and make sure their projects are still on track because of this continuous feedback loop.

The government stands to gain both economically and socially, and not only in the short term. Reducing income inequality, encouraging social cohesion, and promoting economic growth are only some of the larger implications of financial inclusion. Access to formal financial services by people and enterprises boosts economic development, increases employment, and decreases poverty. Long-term governance and societal well-being rely on social stability and cohesiveness, which are bolstered by this.

In sum, the Indian government may gain a lot from the findings of the studies conducted on financial inclusion programmes. It gives decision-makers the information they need to make better-informed decisions about policy, resource allocation, and maintaining progress over time. In addition, it helps achieve national objectives for social and economic growth, which benefits everyone.

CASE STUDY

Rang De: Empowering Entrepreneurs Through EDPs and Digital India for Financial Inclusion

Rang De, a peer-to-peer lending platform predominantly functioning in India, was established in 2008 by Ramakrishna NK and Smita Ram, marking a significant milestone in the field. Rang De represents the amalgamation of EDPs and the Digital India initiative, aiming to foster financial inclusion by providing inexpensive and easily accessible loans to those from economically disadvantaged backgrounds. Many aspiring entrepreneurs face considerable challenges when seeking loans from traditional financial institutions as a result of lacking credit history, collateral, or formal documents.

Rang De operates by establishing connections between marginalized persons and a network of socially conscious investors prepared to provide financial resources at equitable interest rates. The platform essentially facilitates the democratization of the loan process by establishing a direct connection between investors and borrowers. This technique surpasses the conventional obstacles encountered by underprivileged populations and empowers both the borrowers and the investors.

One of the critical accomplishments of Rang De is its success in mitigating the financial disparity faced by those striving to become entrepreneurs. The platform facilitates a direct connection between borrowers and investors, supplying the required funds and enabling people to actively pursue their entrepreneurial ambitions. The empowerment also encompasses the investors, who are able to see the concrete effects of their contributions on grassroots entrepreneurship.

The influence of Rang De is seen in several areas, including agriculture, small companies, and handmade crafts. Entrepreneurs with limited access to financial resources from conventional channels have effectively used the platform to get funding for their enterprises. Rang De exemplifies the successful synergy between Entrepreneurial Development Programs and the Digital India initiative, showcasing its potential to enable persons from economically disadvantaged backgrounds to engage in entrepreneurial pursuits. Rang De effectively tackles the issue of financial inclusion and fosters entrepreneurial endeavours among underrepresented groups by offering accessible loan opportunities via a digital platform. This unique strategy serves as evidence of the significant impact that entrepreneurial development and digital infrastructure have in promoting financial empowerment and fostering economic growth at the grassroots level.

CONCLUSION

The chapter thoroughly analyses the significant contributions made by EDPs, the Digital India Mission, and sustainable finance in expediting efforts to promote financial inclusion in India. The interdependence of these three pillars is apparent as they collaborate harmoniously to address the disparities and surmount the obstacles in attaining comprehensive financial inclusion.

EDPs have the capacity to empower people by fostering entrepreneurial abilities and digital competencies, enabling them to assume the roles of both job creators and catalysts for financial inclusion. When included in the Digital India framework, these empowered entrepreneurs are vital intermediaries in facilitating digital financial services to marginalized people. The Digital India Mission has effectively mitigated the digital gap and facilitated the provision of financial services to distant villages via its ambitious development of digital infrastructure. By incorporating government initiatives such as the PMJDY, the Digital India campaign has effectively facilitated the provision of formal financial services to even the most socioeconomically disadvantaged families. In contrast, sustainable finance programs aim to direct resources towards enterprises that value financial inclusion and sustainability. This method guarantees that investments not only provide economic profits but also contribute to beneficial social and environmental outcomes.

Nevertheless, it is important to recognize the enduring obstacles and impediments that exist, such as the disparity in access to digital resources, intricate legal frameworks, the assessment of effects, vulnerabilities in cybersecurity, and deficiencies in financial literacy. Addressing these difficulties necessitates a collaborative endeavour involving several stakeholders, including governmental entities, financial institutions, fintech pioneers, and civil society groups.

The interdependent association of EDPs, the Digital India Mission, and sustainable finance presents a prospective trajectory towards fostering a financial ecosystem in India that is both inclusive and sustainable. Through the acknowledgement and resolution of existing obstacles, India may persist in its pursuit of achieving all-encompassing financial inclusion. This endeavour will enable every individual to engage in and reap the advantages of the nation's expanding digital economy. This research highlights the significance of cooperation, creativity, and a collective dedication to attaining financial inclusion as a fundamental aspect of India's economic advancement and societal growth.

REFERENCES

Ali, J., & Ghildiyal, A. K. (2023). Socio-economic characteristics, mobile phone ownership and banking behaviour of individuals as determinants of digital financial inclusion in India. *International Journal of Social Economics*, *50*(10), 1375–1392. doi:10.1108/IJSE-10-2022-0673

Asif, M., Khan, M. N., Tiwari, S., Wani, S. K., & Alam, F. (2023). The Impact of Fintech and Digital Financial Services on Financial Inclusion in India. *Journal of Risk and Financial Management*, *16*(2), 122. doi:10.3390/jrfm16020122

Baber, H. (2017). Risk mitigation practices in banking: A study of hdfc bank. In Risk and Contingency Management: Breakthroughs in Research and Practice (pp. 453–468). IGI Global. doi:10.4018/978-1-5225-3932-2.ch023

Banna, H., Hassan, M. K., Ahmad, R., & Alam, M. R. (2022). Islamic banking stability amidst the COVID-19 pandemic: The role of digital financial inclusion. *International Journal of Islamic and Middle Eastern Finance and Management*, *15*(2), 310–330. doi:10.1108/IMEFM-08-2020-0389

Bansal, N., Bhatnagar, M., & Taneja, S. (2023). Balancing priorities through green optimism: A study elucidating initiatives, approaches, and strategies for sustainable supply chain management. In *Handbook of Research on Designing Sustainable Supply Chains to Achieve a Circular Economy*. IGI Global., doi:10.4018/978-1-6684-7664-2.ch004

Bhatnagar, M., Özen, E., Taneja, S., Grima, S., & Rupeika-Apoga, R. (2022). The Dynamic Connectedness between Risk and Return in the Fintech Market of India: Evidence Using the GARCH-M Approach. *Risks*, *10*(11), 209. doi:10.3390/risks10110209

Bhatnagar, M., Pathak, N., & Taneja, S. (2023). Tech-Optimists and Financial Education - A Research on the Efficacy of Communication Mediums of Government Economic Policies. *International Journal of Sustainable Development and Planning*, *18*(7), 2245–2252. doi:10.18280/ijsdp.180729

Bhatnagar, M., Taneja, S., & Rupeika-Apoga, R. (2023). Demystifying the Effect of the News (Shocks) on Crypto Market Volatility. *Journal of Risk and Financial Management*, *16*(2), 136. Advance online publication. doi:10.3390/jrfm16020136

Buenestado-Fernández, M., Ramírez-Montoya, M. S., Ibarra-Vazquez, G., & Patiño, A. (2023). Digital competency as a key to the financial inclusion of young people in complex scenarios: A focus groups study. *Citizenship. Social and Economics Education*, *22*(1), 48–62. doi:10.1177/14788047231170083

Chien, F. (2023). The Impact of Green Investment, Eco-Innovation, and Financial Inclusion on Sustainable Development: Evidence from China. *The Engineering Economist*, *34*(1), 17–31. doi:10.5755/j01.ee.34.1.32159

Dangwal, A., Kaur, S., Taneja, S., & Taneja, S. (2022). A Bibliometric Analysis of Green Tourism Based on the Scopus Platform. In J. Kaur, P. Jindal, & A. Singh (Eds.), *Developing Relationships, Personalization, and Data Herald in Marketing 5.0* (Vol. i, pp. 1–327). IGI Global., doi:10.4018/978-1-6684-4496-2.ch015

Dangwal, A., Taneja, S., Özen, E., Todorovic, I., & Grima, S. (2022). Abridgement of Renewables: It's Potential and Contribution to India's GDP. *International Journal of Sustainable Development and Planning*, *17*(8), 2357–2363. doi:10.18280/ijsdp.170802

Daud, S. N. M., & Ahmad, A. H. (2023). Financial inclusion, economic growth and the role of digital technology. *Finance Research Letters*, *53*, 103602. Advance online publication. doi:10.1016/j.frl.2022.103602

Dou, D., & Li, L. (2022). *Does sustainable financial inclusion and energy efficiency ensure green environment? Evidence from B.R.I.C.S. countries*. Economic Research-Ekonomska Istrazivanja., doi:10.1080/1331677X.2022.2032785

Fu, Y., & Yi, Z. (2023). Multi-province comparisons of digital financial inclusion performance in China: A group ranking method with preference analysis. *China Economic Review*, *80*, 102014. Advance online publication. doi:10.1016/j.chieco.2023.102014

Gopalan, S., & Rajan, R. S. (2022). Does digital financial inclusion moderate or exacerbate output volatility? *Applied Economics Letters*, *29*(19), 1804–1809. doi:10.1080/13504851.2021.1963400

Gupta, M., Arora, K., & Taneja, S. (2023). Bibliometric analysis on employee engagement and human resource management. In *Enhancing Customer Engagement Through Location-Based Marketing*. IGI Global. doi:10.4018/978-1-6684-8177-6.ch013

Gupta, M., Taneja, S., Sharma, V., Singh, A., Rupeika-Apoga, R., & Jangir, K. (2023). Does Previous Experience with the Unified Payments Interface (UPI) Affect the Usage of Central Bank Digital Currency (CBDC)? *Journal of Risk and Financial Management*, *16*(6), 286. doi:10.3390/jrfm16060286

Hodžić, S., Šikić, T. F., & Dogan, E. (2023). Green environment in the EU countries: The role of financial inclusion, natural resources and energy intensity. *Resources Policy*, *82*, 103476. doi:10.1016/j.resourpol.2023.103476

Hu, D., Fang, X., & DiGiovanni, Y. M. (2023). Technological progress, financial constrains, and digital financial inclusion. *Small Business Economics*. doi:10.100711187-023-00745-7

Jangir, K., Sharma, V., Taneja, S., & Rupeika-Apoga, R. (2023). The Moderating Effect of Perceived Risk on Users' Continuance Intention for FinTech Services. *Journal of Risk and Financial Management*, *16*(1), 21. doi:10.3390/jrfm16010021

Kaur, H., Singh, K., Kumar, P., & Kaur, A. (2023). Assessing the environmental sustainability corridor: An empirical study of Renewable energy consumption in BRICS nation. *IOP Conference Series. Earth and Environmental Science*, *1110*(1), 012053. doi:10.1088/1755-1315/1110/1/012053

Khan, Z., Badeeb, R. A., Zhang, C., & Dong, K. (2023). Financial inclusion and energy efficiency: Role of green innovation and human capital for Malaysia. *Applied Economics*, 1–16. doi:10.1080/00036846.2023.2206109

Konou, C. M. (2023). Entrepreneurial Risk and Digital Financial Inclusion: A Cross-Country Analysis. *Economic Papers*, *42*(3), 267–281. doi:10.1111/1759-3441.12399

Kouladoum, J.-C., Wirajing, M. A. K., & Nchofoung, T. N. (2022). Digital technologies and financial inclusion in Sub-Saharan Africa. *Telecommunications Policy*, *46*(9), 102387. doi:10.1016/j.telpol.2022.102387

Kumar, P., Khurana, A., & Sharma, S. (2021). Performance evaluation of public and private sector banks. *World Review of Entrepreneurship, Management and Sustainable Development*, *17*(2–3), 306–322. doi:10.1504/WREMSD.2021.114436

Kumar, P., Mukul, Kaur, D., & Kaur, A. (2023). Green Infrastructure- A Roadmap Towards Sustainable Development. *IOP Conference Series. Earth and Environmental Science*, *1110*(1), 012060. doi:10.1088/1755-1315/1110/1/012060

Kumar, P., Özen, E., & Vurur, S. (2023). Adoption of blockchain technology in the financial sector. In *Contemporary Studies of Risks in Emerging Technology, Part A*. Emerald Group Publishing Ltd., doi:10.1108/978-1-80455-562-020231018

Kumar, P., & Taneja, S. Mukul, & Ozen, E. (2023). Digital transformation of the insurance industry - a case of the Indian insurance sector. In The Impact of Climate Change and Sustainability Standards on the Insurance Market. Wiley.

Kumar, P., Verma, P., Bhatnagar, M., Taneja, S., Seychel, S., Todorović, I., & Grim, S. (2023). The Financial Performance and Solvency Status of the Indian Public Sector Banks: A CAMELS Rating and Z Index Approach. *International Journal of Sustainable Development and Planning*, *18*(2), 367–376. doi:10.18280/ijsdp.180204

Kunal, & Sharma, T. (2022). An empirical study of customer satisfaction and customer loyalty intentions for payment banks. In *Digital Marketing Outreach: the Future of Marketing Practices*. Taylor and Francis. doi:10.4324/9781003315377-4

Lee, C.-C., Wang, F., & Lou, R. (2022). Digital financial inclusion and carbon neutrality: Evidence from non-linear analysis. *Resources Policy*, *79*, 102974. doi:10.1016/j.resourpol.2022.102974

Li, G., Lv, X., & Han, X. (2023). Digital financial inclusion and household debt in China. *Applied Economics Letters*, *30*(19), 2862–2866. doi:10.1080/13504851.2022.2110560

Lu, X., Lai, Y., & Zhang, Y. (2023). Digital financial inclusion and investment diversification: Evidence from China. *Accounting and Finance*, *63*(S2), 2781–2799. doi:10.1111/acfi.13043

Mao, F., Wang, Y., & Zhu, M. (2023). Digital financial inclusion, traditional finance system and household entrepreneurship. *Pacific-Basin Finance Journal*, *80*, 102076. doi:10.1016/j.pacfin.2023.102076

Mukul, T. S., Özen, E., Plaha, R., & Zammit, M. L. (2023). Banking, Fintech, BigTech: Emerging challenges for multimedia adoption. In Intelligent Multimedia Technologies for Financial Risk Management: Trends, Tools and Applications. Institution of Engineering and Technology.

Mukul, & Pathak, N. (2021a). Are the financial inclusion schemes of India developing the nation sustainably? *E3S Web of Conferences, 296*, 06011. doi:10.1051/e3sconf/202129606011

Nguyen, T. T., Quynh, M. P., Van, H. N., Le Thi, H., Van, L. N., Nguyen, T. D., & Van, D. N. (2023). The Role of Availability of Financial Institutions and Financial Innovation on the Financial Inclusion: Does Digital Finance Moderate this Linkage? *Cuadernos de Economía (Santiago, Chile)*, *46*(130), 11–20. doi:10.32826/cude.v1i130.1002

Niu, G., Jin, X., Wang, Q., & Zhou, Y. (2022). Broadband infrastructure and digital financial inclusion in rural China. *China Economic Review*, *76*, 101853. doi:10.1016/j.chieco.2022.101853

Reepu, R., Taneja, S., Ozen, E., & Singh, A. (2023). A globetrotter to the future of marketing: Metaverse. In *Cultural Marketing and Metaverse for Consumer Engagement*. IGI Global. doi:10.4018/978-1-6684-8312-1.ch001

Shen, H., Luo, T., Gao, Z., Zhang, X., Zhang, W., & Chuang, Y.-C. (2023). Digital financial inclusion and the urban–rural income gap in China: Empirical research based on the Theil index. *Ekonomska Istrazivanja*, *36*(3), 2156575. doi:10.1080/1331677X.2022.2156575

Singh, A., Sharma, S., Singh, A., Unanoğlu, M., & Taneja, S. (2023a). Cultural Marketing and Metaverse for Consumer Engagement. In *Cultural Marketing and Metaverse for Consumer Engagement*. IGI Global. doi:10.4018/978-1-6684-8312-1

Singh, A., Sharma, S., Singh, A., Unanoğlu, M., & Taneja, S. (2023b). Preface. In *Cultural Marketing and Metaverse for Consumer Engagement*. IGI Global. doi:10.4018/978-1-6684-8312-1

Singh, J. P. (2019). Development finance 2.0: Do participation and information technologies matter? *Review of International Political Economy*, *26*(5), 886–910. doi:10.1080/09692290.2019.1616600

Singh, V., Taneja, S., Singh, V., Singh, A., & Paul, H. L. (2021). Online advertising strategies in Indian and Australian e-commerce companies:: A comparative study. *Big Data Analytics for Improved Accuracy, Efficiency, and Decision Making in Digital Marketing*, 124–138. doi:10.4018/978-1-7998-7231-3.ch009

Soro, K., & Senou, M. M. (2023). Digital financial inclusion and income inequality in WAEMU: What causality for what heterogeneity? *Cogent Economics & Finance*, *11*(2), 2242662. doi:10.1080/23322039.2023.2242662

Taneja, S., Bhatnagar, M., Kumar, P., & Grima, S. (2023). A Panel Analysis of the Effectiveness of the Asset Management in Indian Agricultural Companies. *International Journal of Sustainable Development and Planning*, *18*(3), 653–660. doi:10.18280/ijsdp.180301

Taneja, S., Bhatnagar, M., Kumar, P., & Rupeika-Apoga, R. (2023). India's Total Natural Resource Rents (NRR) and GDP: An Augmented Autoregressive Distributed Lag (ARDL) Bound Test. *Journal of Risk and Financial Management*, *16*(2), 91. doi:10.3390/jrfm16020091

Taneja, S., Grima, S., Kumar, P., & Ozen, E. (2023). Special Issue: 'Green Asset and Risk Management for Promoting Sustainable Entrepreneurship in the Building of the Green Economy.'. *International Journal of Technology Management & Sustainable Development*, *22*(2), 127–130. doi:10.1386/tmsd_00071_7

Taneja, S., Gupta, M., Bhushan, P., Bhatnagar, M., & Singh, A. (2023). Cultural marketing in the digital era. In *Cultural Marketing and Metaverse for Consumer Engagement*. IGI Global. doi:10.4018/978-1-6684-8312-1.ch008

Taneja, S., Jaggi, P., Jewandah, S., & Ozen, E. (2022). Role of Social Inclusion in Sustainable Urban Developments: An Analyse by PRISMA Technique. *International Journal of Design & Nature and Ecodynamics*, *17*(6), 937–942. doi:10.18280/ijdne.170615

Taneja, S., Kaur, S., & Özen, E. (2022). Using green finance to promote global growth in a sustainable way. *International Journal of Green Economics*, *16*(3), 246–257. doi:10.1504/IJGE.2022.128930

Taneja, S., & Ozen, E. (2023). Impact of the European Green Deal (EDG) on the Agricultural Carbon (CO2) Emission in Turkey. *International Journal of Sustainable Development and Planning*, *18*(3), 715–727. doi:10.18280/ijsdp.180307

Taneja, S., & Sharma, V. (2023). Role of beaconing marketing in improving customer buying experience. In *Enhancing Customer Engagement Through Location-Based Marketing*. IGI Global. doi:10.4018/978-1-6684-8177-6.ch012

Tang, T., Ran, G., & Ran, X. (2023). Analyzing the effect of digital financial inclusion on urban private sector employment in China. *Applied Economics Letters*, 1–5. doi:10.1080/13504851.2023.2206614

Tufail, M., Song, L., Umut, A., Ismailova, N., & Kuldasheva, Z. (2022). Does financial inclusion promote a green economic system? Evaluating the role of energy efficiency. *Ekonomska Istrazivanja*, *35*(1), 6780–6800. doi:10.1080/1331677X.2022.2053363

Van Kien, P., Ou, J. P., Sadiq, D. M., Nguyen, T. T. H., Huy, P. Q., & Tran, T. K. (2023). What role financial inclusion, green trade and natural resources utilization play in ASEAN economic growth: Evidence from post COVID era. *Resources Policy*, *85*, 103884. doi:10.1016/j.resourpol.2023.103884

Yang, L., & Geng, Z. (2022). Impact of Digital Financial Inclusion on Optimization of Employment Structure: Evidence from China. *Applied Economics*, *54*(57), 6625–6638. doi:10.1080/00036846.2022.2078779

Chapter 2
Sustainability's Symphony: Orchestrating Talent Management for Creating Financial Impact

Mitushi Singh
https://orcid.org/0000-0001-7344-9691
Jaypee Institute of Information Technology, India

Mukul Bhatnagar
Chandigarh University, India

ABSTRACT

To investigate the connection between sustainable talent management practices and their financial effect on firms, the researchers used a regression analysis. The results highlight the importance of investing in people, highlighting the link between good personnel management practices and financial benefit. In addition, the research reveals a strong link between sustainable practices and excellent financial consequences for businesses. The study's interacting effect is particularly noteworthy, as it suggests that focusing on people management and sustainability at the same time has a multiplier effect on financial impact. In conclusion, this chapter delivers a symphony of factual data showing that companies may amplify their financial performance by harmonizing talent management with sustainability strategies.

INTRODUCTION

The term "Sustainability's Symphony" is a metaphor that brings together the ideas of sustainability and a symphony orchestra to highlight the importance of living in harmony with nature and human civilization. "Sustainability" is providing for current needs without jeopardizing future generations' capacity to do the same (Taneja, Bhatnagar, Kumar, and Rupeika-Apoga 2023; Bansal, Bhatnagar, and Taneja 2023). Creating a sustainable system entails balancing economic, social, and environmental concerns (Taneja, Grima, et al. 2023; Kaur et al. 2023; Kumar, Mukul, et al. 2023; Taneja, Grima, et al. 2023). A "symphony" is an orchestral work that has many musical sections that build upon one another to form a

DOI: 10.4018/979-8-3693-1388-6.ch002

cohesive whole. A symphony is successful because all of the individual parts work together to create a whole that is greater than the sum of its parts. Combining these ideas, the term "Sustainability's Symphony" emphasizes that a concerted effort among multiple factors (economic, social, and environmental) is necessary to achieve sustainability. To preserve the long-term health of the planet and its people, many facets of society, the economy, and the environment must function in tandem, much like the instruments in a symphony (Taneja and Ozen 2023; Dangwal, Kaur, et al. 2022; Dangwal, Taneja, et al. 2022; Taneja, Kaur, and Özen 2022). Because of the interrelated and interdependent nature of the world's many parts, "Sustainability's Symphony" essentially stresses the significance of working together in harmony to accomplish sustainability objectives.

The term "orchestrating talent management" is figurative, referring to the complex and deliberate balancing of several elements necessary for efficient human resource management. Like a conductor conducting an orchestra, effective talent management requires coordinating many tactics to produce a unified, productive staff that boosts the company's bottom line (Ardichvili and Zavyalova 2019). Fundamentally, this idea stresses the need of taking a strategic and value-driven approach to personnel management (Valentin and Valentin 2019). Organizations need a clear vision for their talent management processes, just as a conductor sees the big picture and leads the musicians to perform in harmony. Talent management initiatives are not siloed but rather incorporated into the bigger organizational goals thanks to the close ties between this vision and the company's overarching business plan. The whole employee lifetime, from hiring to leaving the company, may be orchestrated through talent management (Fang 2019). It's important for businesses to find and hire people whose talents and interests complement the company's overall vision, like picking the perfect instruments for a symphony. Employees, like musicians, need regular practice and constructive criticism to hone their skills and advance in their careers (Kantrowitz, Grelle, and Lin 2019). This evolving procedure encourages progress toward excellence and helps build a workforce that can quickly adjust to new requirements. In the same way that a conductor watches over the whole orchestra, businesses require performance management systems to establish standards, disseminate information, and assess employees' efforts. These systems guarantee that employees are working toward the same objectives as the company and that their efforts are being properly acknowledged and directed (Psychogios and Prouska 2019). Another crucial part is succession planning, which resembles the way orchestras train up-and-coming performers to take on leadership responsibilities. A company may guarantee a smooth transition and reduce skill shortages if its future leaders are identified and developed. In addition to the practical considerations, organizing talent management involves much more (Hernandez, Zatarain, and Barron 2019). It promotes a culture where workers feel appreciated, appreciated, and devoted to their jobs. Employees repaint their best work when they feel valued, appreciated, and appreciated by their employers, and their needs are taken into account. The values of diversity and acceptance are also central to this symphony. The same way that using a wide variety of instruments improves the quality of a song, encouraging diversity and inclusiveness in the workplace strengthens an organization's ability to think outside the box and adapt to change (Deters 2019). A varied set of viewpoints helps with problem solving and flexibility in today's complex corporate environment. Simply said, orchestrating talent management highlights the interdependence of the many factors needed to develop a workforce that not only improves an organization's bottom line but also supports ethical and environmentally responsible activities. Organizations may compose a symphony of talent that resounds with success, growth, and ongoing relevance by integrating recruiting, training, performance management, leadership development, and cultural factors.

The notion of sustainability has developed as a crucial paradigm driving human pursuits in a society defined by fast globalization, technological developments, and heightened environmental awareness (V. Singh et al. 2021). Ultimately, the goal of sustainability is to provide for the needs of the present without jeopardizing the capacity of future generations to provide for their own (Taneja et al. 2022). Orchestrating efficient personnel management procedures that not only foster the workforce but also provide big financial benefit is at the core of this multidimensional endeavour (Jangir et al. 2023). The coordination of talent management within the larger framework of sustainability is analogous to the orchestration of a symphony, where different instruments work in concert to create an entrancing piece of music. This allegory highlights the idea that the synergy between human capital development and financial results is critical for attaining sustainable growth and resilience in today's complex socio-economic milieu, much to how a symphony flourishes when each instrument performs its distinct function. Management of human resources has a direct bearing on a company's bottom line. Talent management techniques that include sustainable practices provide their adopting companies a leg up in the marketplace and lay the groundwork for long-term financial success. Thus, the significance of this study rests on the complicated interaction between encouraging the development of a competent and invested workforce and promoting economic growth (Mukul et al. 2023).

In today's competitive corporate environment, the study "Sustainability's Symphony: Orchestrating Talent Management for Creating Financial Impact" is very important (Benitez-Amado, Javier Llorens-Montes, and Fernandez-Perez 2015). A research with this name unites the seemingly unrelated fields of sustainability and talent management into a coherent whole, with implications for a wide range of interested parties (Bhastary et al. 2023). The importance of this study is borne up by the many insights it provides. This study represents the synthesis of many different fields (Swailes, Downs, and Orr 2014). The research takes a risk by merging two relatively uncharted fields: people management and environmental management (A. G. Khan et al. 2021). This multidisciplinary strategy not only improves our theoretical knowledge, but also more accurately reflects the complexity of actual business practices (Anlesinya and Amponsah-Tawiah 2020). This study investigates the possibility of concordance between profitability and responsibility at a time when businesses are struggling to strike this balance.

The findings are especially important in the fast-paced commercial environment of today. The research's focus on sustainability rings true at a time when corporate social and environmental responsibility is under growing scrutiny (A. Singh et al. 2023b; Gupta, Arora, and Taneja 2023; Taneja and Sharma 2023). It demonstrates a road where ethical concerns and financial rewards are not mutually incompatible by highlighting the possible financial benefits that emerge from adopting sustainable practices. The study highlights the real-world results that might result when companies adopt global sustainability targets. The study's real-world relevance is similarly impressive (Reepu et al. 2023). The research provides useful information to decision-makers by demonstrating the connection between people management and financial effect in the field of sustainability (A. Singh et al. 2023a). It provides a holistic strategy that propels both financial success and ethical business practices by enabling managers to build plans that nourish human capital while aligning with sustainability goals (Dahiya, Taneja, and Özen 2023). Moreover, the study adds to the business landscape strategic landscape. "Sustainability's Symphony" is a perfect metaphor for the life-changing path that companies might take. The findings highlight the orchestration required to generate financial impact through talent management and sustainability, much like the collaboration required to perform a symphony (Gupta et al. 2023). This point of view transforms talent management from a necessary evil into a valuable strategic asset, increasing the likelihood of monetary success for sustainability efforts (Sharma and Kumar 2021).

For this reason, the study's—"Sustainability's Symphony: Orchestrating Talent Management for Creating Financial Impact"—stands out as a beacon of understanding that brings together vital aspects of contemporary business. Its impact goes well beyond the academy, influencing real-world organizational practices. This study foresees a future in which ethical practices create the song of financial success by bringing together sustainability, talent management, and profit.

LITERATURE REVIEW

The literature review in the research paper "Sustainability's Symphony: Orchestrating Talent Management for Creating Financial Impact" provides a comprehensive overview of the existing research and scholarly discussions pertinent to the relationship between talent management practices, sustainability initiatives, and financial outcomes within organizations.

Management of Talent and Its Economic Consequences

Numerous studies have stressed the importance of efficient personnel management techniques to an organization's bottom line (Visvizi 2022). **Pinnington et al. (2015)** found that when employees are both knowledgeable and invested in their job, businesses see gains in efficiency, creativity, and profitability (Pinnington et al. 2015). An organization's bottom line may be positively impacted by a highly engaged workforce via improved productivity and lower attrition rates (Kafetzopoulos, Psomas, and Bouranta 2022).

Economic Success and Environmental Responsibility

There is now a pressing need for companies to adopt environmental practices. It has been argued by academics (Alparslan and Saner 2020; E. Khan, Mubarik, and Shahid 2021; Mousa and Ayoubi 2019) that businesses who implement sustainability initiatives see an improvement in their company reputation, customer loyalty, and risk management. Long-term financial stability and a competitive edge are benefits of these qualities. **Taneja and Özen** both found that sustainable practices, such as responsible resource management and social responsibility, have a favorable effect on financial performance (Taneja and Özen 2023).

Sustainability and Talent Management

Academics have started paying attention to the ways in which talent management and sustainability are converging (Shikweni, Schurink, and van Wyk 2019). **Noreen and Imran 2021** highlight the need of aligning personnel strategy with sustainability goals for businesses. Businesses that prioritize environmental and social responsibility in their hiring and management processes are more likely to succeed in their pursuit of socially aware workers (Noreen and Imran 2021). Alignment of environmental and financial objectives promotes a culture of accountability and creativity (Gardas et al. 2019).

Disparities and Prospects

While talent management and sustainability themselves have been shown to have an effect on financial results, there has been very little study of their combined impact. There is a dearth of research that thoroughly examines the benefits and drawbacks that come when businesses put equal emphasis on fostering talent and implementing sustainable practices in order to boost their bottom line. Because of this knowledge vacuum, it is crucial to study how these two factors might be orchestrated as one integrated strategy to have economic benefit.

The literature study demonstrates the interdependence of talent management, sustainability, and business results. Evidence suggests that businesses need to adopt sustainable people management as a strategy for long-term financial success because it integrates the growth of human capital with sustainability goals. This research aims to expand on these understandings by providing a clearer picture of how the harmonious integration of these three practices—talent management, sustainability, and financial impact—can lead to greater organizational performance.

RESEARCH OBJECTIVES

To help steer the inquiry and provide a sense of purpose to the research process, the authors of a study titled "Sustainability's Symphony: Orchestrating Talent Management for Creating Financial Impact" developed a set of research goals. The study's main aims may be summed up as follows: investigate the connections between talent management methods, sustainability efforts, and their combined effect on financial results. Here are some concrete goals for the study:

- To Analyze the Connection Between Talent Management Practices and Organizational Financial Outcomes The major purpose of this research is to examine the connection between talent management practices and organizational financial outcomes. This study employs rigorous quantitative approaches to answer the question of whether or not good personnel management strategies lead to financial success.
- To learn how sustainable initiatives affect bottom-line results is another important goal. The purpose of this research is to determine whether and how much more profitably businesses may operate when they adopt sustainable practices.
- Third, we want to evaluate the impact of talent management on sustainability on financial performance. The study's overarching goal is to learn more about the complex relationship between personnel management and long-term viability. To achieve this goal, we need to determine whether these two variables interact with one another in a way that has a multiplicative effect on the financial outcomes rather than an additive one.
- Maximizing Financial Impact via Talent Management and Long-Term Sustainability, Part 4: Developing Managerial Strategies. This goal tries to provide actionable management methods for maximizing financial impact, building on the insights acquired from the analysis. The study's primary objective is to provide practical suggestions that businesses can use to capitalize on the symbiotic relationship between personnel management and environmental initiatives.
- To Add to Our Knowledge of the Complex Interactions Between Environmental Stewardship, Human Resource Management, and Financial consequences This study aims to add to our knowl-

edge of the complex interplay between environmental stewardship, human resource management, and financial consequences. The study's overarching goal is to contribute to the growth of knowledge in the disciplines of management and sustainability via the empirical exploration of these interconnections.

In conclusion, "Sustainability's Symphony: Orchestrating Talent Management for Creating Financial Impact" seeks to investigate the interplay between talent management strategies, sustainability programs, and the impact they have on financial results. These aims serve as a road map for the research as it moves toward its ultimate goal of contributing to theoretical development and practical decision making in organizations.

RESEARCH METHODOLOGY

To investigate the connection between sustainable talent management practices and their financial effect on firms, the researchers behind the report "Sustainability's Symphony: Orchestrating Talent Management for Creating Financial Impact" used a regression analysis. The Statistical Package for the Social Sciences (SPSS) was the major statistical instrument used for this investigation. To investigate and quantify the correlations between variables, a quantitative research approach will be used in this study. The study used a regression analysis to determine the relationship between sustainable talent management practice differences and monetary result variations. In order to gather information for this research, a questionnaire will be sent out to employees at different companies. In order to measure opinions on people management techniques, sustainability efforts, and the financial effect, the questionnaire will contain Likert-scale questions. The demographic data gathered will include job titles, industries worked in, and years of experience. Regression analysis in SPSS will be used to examine the data. Independent variables (talent management practices, sustainability efforts, etc.) will be analyzed using multiple regression to determine their capacity to predict the dependent variable (financial effect). By doing this study, we can learn how much of a role these factors have in the final financial results. The power and direction of the associations between the independent factors and the dependent variable may be evaluated by multiple regression analysis. Regression coefficients will be calculated to show how much each independent variable affected the dependent variable after adjusting for other variables in the study. Data will be analyzed using SPSS, the Statistical Package for the Social Sciences. The associations and correlations between the variables in this research are well suited to SPSS, a well-known and effective tool for performing statistical studies. All aspects of the study will be conducted ethically. All replies from participants will be kept strictly secret, and participation is entirely optional. Prior to any data acquisition, informed permission will be asked. Only aggregated, anonymous data utilized for research purposes will be provided. Though it may provide light on correlations between variables, causality cannot be determined by regression analysis. The results of the research may also be specific to the companies and industries that were questioned. The aforementioned study approach aims to dissect the dynamic bond between long-term personnel management strategies and bottom-line results. Utilizing SPSS regression analysis, this research tries to demonstrate the link between well-orchestrated people management strategies and long-term financial performance for businesses.

Reliability Testing

Table 1 gives insights into how the data was handled and processed throughout the analysis of the research study may be found in the "Case Processing Summary" table. Cases are the individual data points or respondents that were included in the analysis, and this table gives an overview of the cases and explains how they were classified based on their appropriateness for the study's aims. For the total number of instances that qualified to be included in the study, see the "Cases Valid" column. All required information was present, and the instances were appropriate for the study variables being studied.

Table 1. Case processing summary

		N	%
Cases	Valid	100	100.0
	Excluded[a]	0	0.0
	Total	100	100.0

Table 2. Reliability statistics

Cronbach's Alpha	Cronbach's Alpha Based on Standardized Items	N of Items
.837	.835	9

The "Reliability Statistics" table (Table 2) provides information on the consistency and reliability of the study's survey. Cronbach's alpha is the primary statistic used in this table to evaluate the consistency of survey questions that measure the same concept. The coefficient of internal consistency dependability known as Cronbach's alpha has seen extensive application. The reliability and validity of a measurement system is evaluated by looking at how well a collection of items that are all supposed to measure the same construct do so in practice. Cronbach's alpha = 0.837, as seen in the following table. This score represents the level of agreement between the survey items used to gauge a given construct. In addition, we provide a value of 0.835 for "Cronbach's Alpha for Items That Have Been Standardized." After standardization, this number takes into account how well the objects match up with one another, which may assist reduce the impact of problems like inconsistent scales or measuring units.

Figure 1. Item statistics

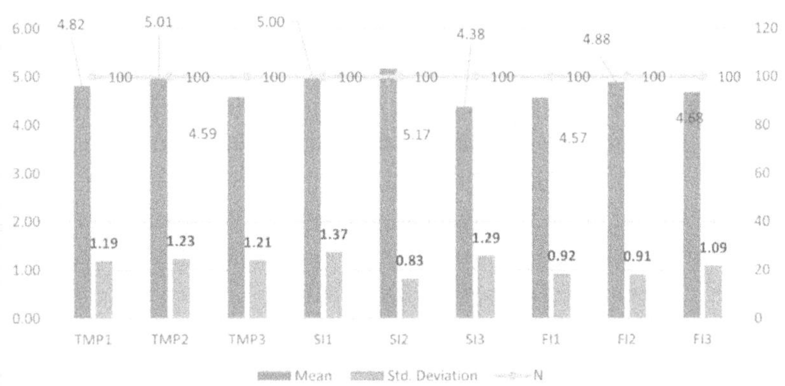

The "Item Statistics" figure 1 provides an in-depth summary of how respondents rated each question on the survey used in the study. These descriptive statistics provide light on the mean and standard deviation of responses, painting a more complete picture of the respondents' thoughts and feelings. Looking at the "TMP1" item, for instance, we might infer that participants had a relatively good view of the talent management feature being examined by this item (given that the mean answer was 4.82). There was considerable discordance in replies, with some people expressing more enthusiastic agreement and others displaying more restraint (as shown by the standard deviation of 1.19). A total of one hundred people's answers were taken into account for this particular question, as shown by the sample size (N). The mean replies to things like "SI2" and "FI2" are 5.17 and 4.88, respectively. These more positive averages suggest that respondents had a more positive outlook on the respective components of sustainability activities and financial effects. While the "SI2" standard deviation is lower than the "FI2" standard deviation (0.91 vs. 0.83), it signifies that respondents were more or less in agreement. On the other hand, the average for "SI3" is just 4.38, while other products have even lower mean values. This indicates that people were a little less enthusiastic about this facet of sustainability projects on average. There was more variation in replies, as shown by the larger standard deviation of 1.29, suggesting that respondents had a variety of viewpoints. Using these descriptive data, researchers may learn more about how survey respondents felt about certain questions.

Table 3. Inter-Item correlation matrix

	TMP1	TMP2	TMP3	SI1	SI2	SI3	FI1	FI2	FI3
TMP1	1.000	.337	.524	.352	.215	.530	.259	.435	.429
TMP2	.337	1.000	.403	.298	.038	.194	.225	.261	.137
TMP3	.524	.403	1.000	.653	.353	.496	.520	.486	.352
SI1	.352	.298	.653	1.000	.489	.558	.415	.258	.358
SI2	.215	.038	.353	.489	1.000	.128	.202	.241	-.029
SI3	.530	.194	.496	.558	.128	1.000	.544	.501	.581
FI1	.259	.225	.520	.415	.202	.544	1.000	.537	.253
FI2	.435	.261	.486	.258	.241	.501	.537	1.000	.438
FI3	.429	.137	.352	.358	-.029	.581	.253	.438	1.000

The study's "Inter-Item Correlation Matrix," shown in Table 3, shows the connections between survey questions. To have a better grasp of the possible patterns and correlations among the constructs being assessed, it is essential to consult the correlation matrix between the survey questions. The rows and columns of the matrix contain the identical data, making it symmetrical. A correlation coefficient, which measures the degree and direction of the association between any two given elements, is stored in each cell of the matrix. There is perfect negative correlation (-1) when there is no correlation (-0) and perfect positive correlation (+1) where there is no correlation (+1). Taking "TMP1" and "TMP2" as an example, the r=0.337 between these two items indicates a favorable relationship between these two talent management techniques. Participants' agreement with one item suggests some degree of agreement with the other. An further pair of variables that have a negative correlation is "SI2" and "FI3," with a value of -0.029. This weak association between sustainability initiatives and financial outcomes is indicative of a lack of causality between the two. Several of the matrix's correlation coefficients are very high and positively skewed; for example, the association between "TMP3" and "SI1" has a value of 0.653. Thus, these two features of talent management approaches are positively correlated with sustainability endeavors. As a counterexample, the matrix also contains negative correlations, such as the negative correlation between "SI2" and "SI3" (coefficient: -0.128). This data points to a little inverse relationship between these two aspects of the sustainability project. The "Inter-Item Correlation Matrix" summarizes the replies of the participants to provide light on the relationships between the various components of talent management practices (TMP), sustainability initiatives (SI), and financial impact (FI).

Table 4. Inter-Item covariance matrix

	TMP1	TMP2	TMP3	SI1	SI2	SI3	FI1	FI2	FI3
TMP1	1.422	.497	.754	.576	.213	.817	.285	.473	.558
TMP2	.497	1.525	.600	.505	.039	.309	.257	.294	.185
TMP3	.754	.600	1.456	1.081	.353	.774	.579	.536	.463
SI1	.576	.505	1.081	1.879	.556	.990	.525	.323	.535
SI2	.213	.039	.353	.556	.688	.137	.155	.182	-.026
SI3	.817	.309	.774	.990	.137	1.672	.650	.592	.820
FI1	.285	.257	.579	.525	.155	.650	.854	.453	.255
FI2	.473	.294	.536	.323	.182	.592	.453	.834	.436
FI3	.558	.185	.463	.535	-.026	.820	.255	.436	1.189

Table 5. Summary item statistics

	Mean	Minimum	Maximum	Range	Maximum / Minimum	Variance	N of Items
Item Means	4.789	4.380	5.170	.790	1.180	.064	9
Item Variances	1.280	.688	1.879	1.191	2.731	.170	9
Inter-Item Covariances	.465	-.026	1.081	1.107	-41.797	.064	9
Inter-Item Correlations	.360	-.029	.653	.682	-22.857	.026	9

Table 5, "Summary Item Statistics," summarizes important statistical factors from the study's survey replies. These metrics show survey question response distribution, relationships, and fluctuation, illuminating data dynamics. The "Item Means" section shows survey question averages. The mean item mean of 4.789 showed that respondents liked the constructs under examination. Participants' responses were consistent across questions (mean range: 4.380–5.170). The "Range" score of 0.790 highlights the median dispersion, indicating that viewpoints were diverse. The "Maximum / Minimum" ratio of 1.180 demonstrates the diversity of opinion, with the highest mean 1.18 times the lowest mean. The "Variance" score of 0.064 suggests limited response variability around the averages. The "Inter-Item

Covariances" section shows item correlations. The mean covariance value of 0.465 showed that the components positively co-varied. The covariance range of -0.026 to 1.081 shows the variability of these interactions. The "Maximum / Minimum" ratio of -41.797 is surprisingly negative due to negative co-variance values, which reflect opposing trends between certain pairs of elements. The "Variance" score of 0.064 suggests a narrow covariance range across items. Finally, "Inter-Item Correlations" explains item-to-item relationships. The relatively positive connection across questions (mean correlation value of 0.360) indicates respondents' domain-aligned responses.

Table 6. ANOVA with Friedman's test

		Sum of Squares	df	Mean Square	Friedman's Chi-Square	Sig
Between People		494.778	99	4.998		
Within People	Between Items	51.449[a]	8	6.431	59.042	.000
	Residual	645.662	792	.815		
	Total	697.111	800	.871		
Total		1191.889	899	1.326		
Grand Mean = 4.7889						
a. Kendall's coefficient of concordance W = .043.						

Table 6 shows Friedman's test analysis of variance (ANOVA) to assess whether participant responses vary significantly across items and groups. The table provides crucial information for this evaluation and helps explain the statistical significance of these inconsistencies. The table's "Between People" column shows responses differences. The total of squares, degrees of freedom (df), and mean square may indicate study participant variance. The mean square number of 4.998 represents the average diversity between participant responses, revealing how much perspectives differ or agree. The research then examines within-person variance in survey replies in the "Within People Between Items" section. The amount of squares for this group shows that participants answered questions differently. The df, mean square, and Friedman's Chi-Square value of 59.042 reveal statistically significant differences in survey responses. Given that a Sig of.000 indicates statistical significance at the more common.05 level, item differences must be assessed. The "Residual" section describes variability not caused by participant or item differences. This unexplained variance may be evaluated using sum of squares and df values to determine how other factors affect participant responses. A residual variance of.815 indicates unaccounted-for data variability. The "Total" portion shows participant, item, and residual variability. Sum of squares, df, and variance numbers show dataset variability. The "Total" section restates the sum of squares, df, and variance values for the complete analysis to emphasize the study's comprehensive variability examination. The Grand Mean is beneficial since the median response across all topics and items is 4.7889. The notation "a. Kendall's coefficient of concordance W =.043" explained the degree of agreement or concordance among participants' rankings or responses for the items. Coefficient values closer to 1 suggest more agreement, while values closer to 0.043 indicate less unanimity. The Friedman's test ANOVA is fully described in Table 6, offering a deep dive into the significance of differences in survey question responses between individuals. By giving a more nuanced interpretation of data variability, statistics let researchers draw conclusions from the study's findings.

Figure 2. Hotelling's T-squared test

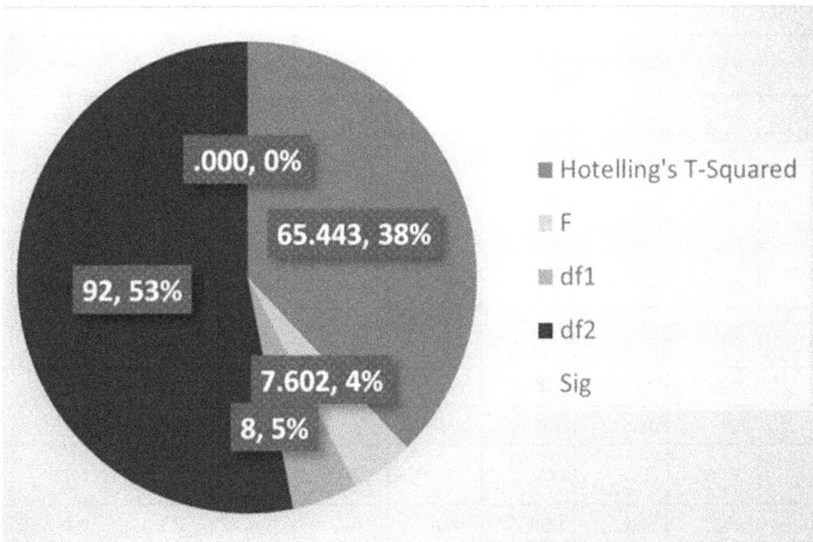

Hotelling's T-Squared Test (Figure 2) is a common statistical test for statistically significant differences between multivariate data points. This test excels at averaging several factors. The table's statistical data helps explain and assess these disparities. The "Hotelling's T-Squared" test statistic for comparing the two groups is 65.443. This value strongly determines whether group differences are statistically significant. 7.602 is the "df1" value, which represents the variables' degrees of freedom. Hotelling's T-Squared Test counts the number of independent variables. The study's variables are deducted from the sample size to yield the "df2" value, which is 8. This value indicates the statistical analysis residuals' degrees of freedom. The test statistic's "Sig" value of.000 should be accorded significant weight. Figure 2 shows substantial group differences with a value of.000. In conclusion, Figure 2 shows Hotelling's T-Squared Test findings. The statistical data suggests significant group differences. The test excels at finding significant differences across multivariate data, helping researchers analyze data trends and outliers.

Table 7. Validity testing

		TMP1	TMP2	TMP3	SI1	SI2	SI3	FI1	FI2	FI3	Total
TMP1	Pearson Correlation	1	.337**	.524**	.352**	.215*	.530**	.259**	.435**	.429**	.699**
	Sig. (2-tailed)		.001	.000	.000	.032	.000	.009	.000	.000	.000
	N	100	100	100	100	100	100	100	100	100	100
TMP2	Pearson Correlation	.337**	1	.403**	.298**	.038	.194	.225*	.261**	.137	.508**
	Sig. (2-tailed)	.001		.000	.003	.709	.054	.024	.009	.173	.000
	N	100	100	100	100	100	100	100	100	100	100
TMP3	Pearson Correlation	.524**	.403**	1	.653**	.353**	.496**	.520**	.486**	.352**	.815**
	Sig. (2-tailed)	.000	.000		.000	.000	.000	.000	.000	.000	.000
	N	100	100	100	100	100	100	100	100	100	100
SI1	Pearson Correlation	.352**	.298**	.653**	1	.489**	.558**	.415**	.258**	.358**	.758**
	Sig. (2-tailed)	.000	.003	.000		.000	.000	.000	.009	.000	.000
	N	100	100	100	100	100	100	100	100	100	100
SI2	Pearson Correlation	.215*	.038	.353**	.489**	1	.128	.202*	.241*	-.029	.413**
	Sig. (2-tailed)	.032	.709	.000	.000		.206	.044	.016	.778	.000
	N	100	100	100	100	100	100	100	100	100	100
SI3	Pearson Correlation	.530**	.194	.496**	.558**	.128	1	.544**	.501**	.581**	.779**
	Sig. (2-tailed)	.000	.054	.000	.000	.206		.000	.000	.000	.000
	N	100	100	100	100	100	100	100	100	100	100
FI1	Pearson Correlation	.259**	.225*	.520**	.415**	.202*	.544**	1	.537**	.253*	.648**
	Sig. (2-tailed)	.009	.024	.000	.000	.044	.000		.000	.011	.000
	N	100	100	100	100	100	100	100	100	100	100
FI2	Pearson Correlation	.435**	.261**	.486**	.258**	.241*	.501**	.537**	1	.438**	.673**
	Sig. (2-tailed)	.000	.009	.000	.009	.016	.000	.000		.000	.000
	N	100	100	100	100	100	100	100	100	100	100
FI3	Pearson Correlation	.429**	.137	.352**	.358**	-.029	.581**	.253*	.438**	1	.604**
	Sig. (2-tailed)	.000	.173	.000	.000	.778	.000	.011	.000		.000
	N	100	100	100	100	100	100	100	100	100	100
Total	Pearson Correlation	.699**	.508**	.815**	.758**	.413**	.779**	.648**	.673**	.604**	1
	Sig. (2-tailed)	.000	.000	.000	.000	.000	.000	.000	.000	.000	
	N	100	100	100	100	100	100	100	100	100	100

**. Correlation is significant at the 0.01 level (2-tailed).

*. Correlation is significant at the 0.05 level (2-tailed).

Validity Testing

Pearson correlation coefficients were used to determine the results of the validity tests shown in Table 7. When evaluating the reliability of a measuring tool or exploring the connections between survey questions, this table is invaluable. Linear connections between two variables may be measured by calculating the Pearson correlation coefficient. The table displays a correlation matrix between all survey items and the overall score. Each survey question's correlation with every other item, including itself, and the overall score is shown in a detailed table. In order to see whether these connections are in line with theoretical predictions and hypotheses, we need to look at their strength and significance. Examine the connection, for instance, between "TMP1" and "TMP2." A positive association between these two variables was found at the 0.01 level, as shown by a Pearson correlation value of 0.337**. This indicates that respondents who rated "TMP1" highly were more likely to also rate "TMP2" highly. Also, "SI2" and "FI3" have a negative correlation of -0.029, which is not statistically significant. This indicates that the replies to these items are not linearly related to one another. In addition, the correlations between each item and itself form the matrix's diagonal, which is always 1. This ensures that the data and the measuring device are trustworthy. Total score, which reflects participants' aggregate reaction to all items, is likewise correlated. How effectively each item contributes to the overarching construct being examined may be gleaned from the correlations between items and the total score. Table 7 is essential for establishing validity since it shows how the many survey questions relate to one another and to the concept as a whole. Correlations are statistically significant at the ** and * levels, where ** represents the 0.01 level and * represents the 0.05 level. This table provides researchers with a more nuanced assessment of the correlations within the data and helps them evaluate the convergent and discriminant validity of their measuring instrument.

DATA ANALYSIS

The demographics of research study participants are shown in Table 8. The table shows participant distribution across demographic categories to help understand the sample's composition and how various qualities may affect research results. The table's "Organizational Role" column shows participants' organizational roles. It demonstrates that 26.3% of respondents were senior executives, 22.9% HR professionals, 25.6% middle managers, and 13.3% non-management personnel. A lesser number of respondents stated "5.00" and "6.00," suggesting more company jobs. The "Work Experience" column divides the sample by individuals' years in the workforce. Nearly 20% of respondents had less than a year of experience, while 40% had one to three years. In addition, 30.2% had 4–6 years of job experience, while 10.0% had 7 or more years. The "Industry Type" section highlights the survey responders' diverse disciplines. 14.4% worked in manufacturing, 28.1% in technology, 22.7% in healthcare, 14.6% in finance, and 10.1% in energy. Ten percent more used "Other," which may contain several firms not on the main list. The "Demographic Profile" in Table 8 is essential to understanding the study's sample. This table summarizes participants' organizational positions, career experience, and industry ties to assist researchers understand the study's findings. It identifies sample variability and helps identify demographic differences, similarities, and trends. This diverse group of subjects and situations enhances the study's findings and generalizability.

Table 8. Demographic profile

		Frequency	Percent	Valid Percent	Cumulative Percent
Organisational Role	Executive Leadership	115	26.3	26.3	26.3
	Human Resources	100	22.9	22.9	49.2
	Middle Management	112	25.6	25.6	74.8
	Non-Management Employee	58	13.3	13.3	88.1
	5.00	26	5.9	5.9	94.1
	6.00	26	5.9	5.9	100.0
	Total	437	100.0	100.0	
Work Experience	Less than 1 year	86	19.7	19.7	19.7
	1-3 years	175	40.0	40.0	59.7
	4-6 years	132	30.2	30.2	89.9
	7 or more years	44	10.1	10.1	100.0
	Total	437	100.0	100.0	
Industry Type	Manufacturing	63	14.4	14.4	14.4
	Technology	123	28.1	28.1	42.6
	Healthcare	99	22.7	22.7	65.2
	Financial Services	64	14.6	14.6	79.9
	Energy	44	10.1	10.1	89.9
	Other	44	10.1	10.1	100.0
	Total	437	100.0	100.0	

Table 9. Descriptive statistics

		Statistic	Bootstrap[a]			
			Bias	Std. Error	95% Confidence Interval	
					Lower	Upper
Financial Impact	Mean	4.3402	-.0022	.0434	4.2548	4.4256
	Std. Deviation	.88434	-.00077	.03149	.82087	.94433
	N	437	0	0	437	437
Talent Management Practices	Mean	4.8993	-.0008	.0503	4.8009	4.9954
	Std. Deviation	1.04683	-.00245	.04658	.95052	1.13115
	N	437	0	0	437	437
Sustainability Practices	Mean	4.7948	-.0025	.0434	4.7109	4.8794
	Std. Deviation	.93049	-.00240	.03249	.86317	.99207
	N	437	0	0	437	437

a. Unless otherwise noted, bootstrap results are based on 1000 bootstrap samples

Table 9 describes Financial Impact, Talent Management Practices, and Sustainability Practices extensively. These measurements of central tendency, variability, and trustworthiness show the data's category distribution. The first portion of the table shows each group's mean respondent ratings.

The average Financial Impact score is 4.3402. This amount is the median participant-reported monetary impact. The bootstrap sample bias is -0.0022, indicating that random fluctuation in the samples underestimates the mean. A bootstrap standard error of -0.00077 indicates sample distribution variability, while a standard deviation of 0.88434 indicates dispersion around the mean. The true population mean is most likely between 4.2548 and 4.4256, the 95% confidence range. Participants awarded Talent Management Practices an average rating of 4.8993. The -0.0008 bootstrap bias indicates a little mean shift due to sample variances. Standard deviation (1.04683) implies a wider range of values than in Financial Impact. Bootstrapping standard error of -0.00245 highlights the mean estimate's accuracy. The 95% confidence interval of 4.8009–4.9954 matches the expected population mean.

Respondents gave sustainable behaviors a median score of 4.7948. A small mean adjustment suggests sample variability with a bootstrap bias of -0.0025. The bootstrap standard error of -0.00240 and standard deviation of 0.93049 indicate response variability and mean accuracy, respectively. The 95% CI for the population mean is 4.7109–4.78794, suggesting a respectable mean value. The category statistics were compiled from 437 observations (the "N" number). Since the bootstrap conclusions are based on 1000 bootstrap samples, the table emphasizes the research's trustworthiness. The trustworthy approach of bootstrap sampling can estimate a statistic's distribution and uncertainty. In conclusion, Table 9 helps explain financial effect, talent management, and sustainability practices distributional characteristics, biases, variability, and confidence intervals. These statistics illuminate the selected measures' correctness and reliability and enhance the data's qualities.

Financial Impact, Talent Management Practices, and Sustainability Practices are examined in Table 10. Several relationships and statistical metrics are provided for each of these three factors. Pearson's correlation coefficient is used extensively throughout the table to measure the magnitude and direction of these associations. To begin, the major diagonal of the table depicts the correlations of each variable with itself; unexpectedly, all of them are 1.000, since there is a perfect connection between any two variables. After shifting to non-diagonal plot components, relationships between variables become more clear. As an example, a 0.388 estimated correlation between Financial Impact and Talent Management Practices indicates a somewhat good association between these two variables. Similarly, there is a substantial positive relationship between Financial Impact and Sustainability Practices (r=0.532). There is a strong positive association between Talent Management Practices and Sustainability Practices, with a correlation of 0.635.

In order to assess whether these relationships are statistically significant, the table includes "Sig. (1-tailed)" values. All of these correlations have a value of 0.000, which indicates that they are very significant statistically and are thus highly unlikely to have happened by coincidence. Regarding the sample size, denoted by "N," all correlations use the same 437 observations as their basis. This uniformity guarantees that the observed relationships are real. Also included in the table are the bootstrap-calculated biases, standard errors, and confidence ranges for the correlations. 1000 bootstrap samples are used to obtain the bootstrapped findings. Each correlation's bootstrap bias, standard error, and confidence interval provide light on the range of possible outcomes and the precision of the estimates. Table 10 summarizes the statistical measurements of Financial Impact, Talent Management Practices, and Sustainability Practices, including their correlation coefficients, statistical significance, and associated metrics. The coefficients show the quantitative relationship between the variables. Statistical significance and confidence intervals are included in the table to strengthen the validity and consistency of the reported relationships. The table helps to better understand the interaction between these crucial factors by displaying both the intensity of connections and the accuracy of the measurements.

Model regression data is in Table 11. Financial_Impact" is the dependent variable, and the table compares "Sustainability Practices" with "Talent Management Practices". Look at the regression model's accuracy with the multiple correlation coefficient, or "R" value, of 0.536. This coefficient demonstrates the linear link between Financial_Impact, Sustainability, and Talent Management Practices.

Table 10. Correlations

Pearson Correlation	**Financial Impact**	**Financial Impact**	**1.000**
		Talent Management Practices	.388
		Sustainability Practices	.532
	Talent Management Practices	Financial Impact	.388
		Talent Management Practices	1.000
		Sustainability Practices	.635
	Sustainability Practices	Financial Impact	.532
		Talent Management Practices	.635
		Sustainability Practices	1.000
Sig. (1-tailed)	Financial Impact	Financial Impact	
		Talent Management Practices	.000
		Sustainability Practices	.000
	Talent Management Practices	Financial Impact	.000
		Talent Management Practices	
		Sustainability Practices	.000
	Sustainability Practices	Financial Impact	.000
		Talent Management Practices	.000
		Sustainability Practices	
N	Financial Impact	Financial Impact	437
		Talent Management Practices	437
		Sustainability Practices	437
	Talent Management Practices	Financial Impact	437
		Talent Management Practices	437
		Sustainability Practices	437
	Sustainability Practices	Financial Impact	437
		Talent Management Practices	437
		Sustainability Practices	437

Table 10. Continued

Bootstrap for Pearson Correlation[a]	Bias	Financial Impact		Financial Impact	0.000
				Talent Management Practices	-.001
				Sustainability Practices	.002
		Talent Management Practices		Financial Impact	-.001
				Talent Management Practices	0.000
				Sustainability Practices	-.002
		Sustainability Practices		Financial Impact	.002
				Talent Management Practices	-.002
				Sustainability Practices	0.000
	Std. Error	Financial Impact		Financial Impact	0.000
				Talent Management Practices	.043
				Sustainability Practices	.033
		Talent Management Practices		Financial Impact	.043
				Talent Management Practices	0.000
				Sustainability Practices	.033
		Sustainability Practices		Financial Impact	.033
				Talent Management Practices	.033
				Sustainability Practices	0.000
	95% Confidence Interval	Lower	Financial Impact	Financial Impact	1.000
				Talent Management Practices	.301
				Sustainability Practices	.468
			Talent Management Practices	Financial Impact	.301
				Talent Management Practices	1.000
				Sustainability Practices	.563
			Sustainability Practices	Financial Impact	.468
				Talent Management Practices	.563
				Sustainability Practices	1.000
		Upper	Financial Impact	Financial Impact	1.000
				Talent Management Practices	.473
				Sustainability Practices	.598
			Talent Management Practices	Financial Impact	.473
				Talent Management Practices	1.000
				Sustainability Practices	.694
			Sustainability Practices	Financial Impact	.598
				Talent Management Practices	.694
				Sustainability Practices	1.000

a. Unless otherwise noted, bootstrap results are based on 1000 bootstrap samples

Table 11. Regression statistics

Model	R	R Square	Adjusted R Square	Std. Error of the Estimate	Change Statistics					Durbin-Watson
					R Square Change	F Change	df1	df2	Sig. F Change	
1	.536[a]	.287	.284	.74834	.287	87.437	2	434	.000	1.220
a. Predictors: (Constant), Sustainability Practices, Talent Management Practices										
b. Dependent Variable: Financial_Impact										

The "R Square" score of 0.287 shows how much of the dependent variable's variation is explained by the model's predictor variables. This scenario's Financial_Impact variance is 28.7% due to sustainability and talent management. The "Adjusted R Square" score of 0.284 depends on the number of predictor factors. This adjustment prevents overestimating the model's explanatory power by accounting for additional predictors. The residuals' standard deviation is 0.74834, the "Std. Error of the Estimate". The model's Financial_Impact forecasting accuracy is the average difference between predicted and actual values. Besides "Stats," the table shows "Change Statistics," including R Squared deviation. The predictor factors increase Financial_Impact variation with a change value of 0.287.

After adding predictor variables, the model's "F Change" statistic, 87.437, demonstrates relevance. Compared to the model without predictors, assesses model fit. The F Change statistic has 2 and 434 "df1" and "df2" degrees of freedom. The F statistic's importance relies on these degrees of freedom. The final "Durbin-Watson" statistic is 1.220. This statistic measures residual autocorrelation and correlation at various regression analysis stages. Autocorrelation around 2 is unlikely. In conclusion, Table 11's regression findings show how Sustainability and Talent Management Practices affect Financial_Impact. Statistical significance and fit show the model's performance and how predictor variables affected Financial_Impact.

Table 12. Bootstrap for model summary

Model	Durbin-Watson	Bootstrap[a]			
		Bias	Std. Error	95% Confidence Interval	
				Lower	Upper
1	1.220	-.468	.069	.614	.891
a. Unless otherwise noted, bootstrap results are based on 1000 bootstrap samples					

Bootstrapping regression analysis model summary is in Table 12. Durbin-Watson, bootstrap bias, standard error, and 95% confidence range are shown in the table. The "Durbin-Watson" value, 1.220, reveals regression model residual autocorrelation. When close to 2, residuals are not consistently correlated and have no autocorrelation. The table in the model summary now has 1000 bootstrap replicates. The "Bias" score of -0.468 shows sample variance underestimates Durbin-Watson.

The bootstrap samples' Durbin-Watson statistic's "Std. Error" sampling distribution standard deviation is 0.069. This chart illustrates sample-level statistic changes. The "95% Confidence Interval" gives us a Durbin-Watson population statistic's certainty range. The confidence interval is 0.614 to 0.891, demonstrating the population's Durbin-Watson range. The model summary is improved by Durbin-Watson statistic bootstrap analysis in Table 12. Bootstrap findings provide extra information by accounting for sample variability, while Durbin-Watson determines autocorrelation. By improving the regression model's robustness and dependability, bootstrap bias, standard error, and confidence intervals enhance the study and provide a more complete picture.

Table 13. ANOVA

Model		Sum of Squares	df	Mean Square	F	Sig.
1	Regression	97.932	2	48.966	87.437	.000[b]
	Residual	243.047	434	.560		
	Total	340.979	436			
a. Dependent Variable: Financial_Impact						
b. Predictors: (Constant), Sustainability Practices, Talent Management Practices						

Table 13 shows a detailed ANOVA for a regression model that analyzes "Financial_Impact" in connection to "Sustainability Practices" and "Talent Management Practices." This table shows variation, predictor contributions, and model significance. First, the "Regression" component of the ANOVA breaks down Model 1's variables' explained variance. "Sum of Squares" for the regression section is 97.932, which is the variance in "Financial_Impact" due to observable predictors. The "Mean Square" with 2 degrees of freedom is 48.966, demonstrating predictor variance. Critical F-statistic is 87.437, indicating how much the model improves over a null model. A relatively tiny Significance value of.000b shows that predictors significantly improve model fit.

The Residual examines "Financial_Impact."'s unanticipated change. The variability after adjusting for variables is 243.047 in the residual squared sum. The mean square value of 434 degrees of freedom random variation is 0.560. The Total section describes the dependent variable's total variance lastly. In "Financial_Impact," 340.979 sum of squares and 436 degrees of freedom represent the total number of observations. Table 13 provides valuable ANOVA and regression model results for study. It assesses the model's significance using the F-statistic and relevance value and explains predictor contributions to explained and unexplained variability. This research shows how well the model fits the data and how well the predictor factors explain dependent variable changes.

Regression model coefficients are shown in Table 14. This table's dependent variable is financial effect, whereas Talent Management and Sustainability Practices are independent. The coefficients illustrate how original and adjusted predictor factors impact the dependent variable.

This section lists initial regression model coefficients. The constant coefficient standard error is 0.199 and 1.811. The "t" value coefficient estimate is 9.093 standard deviations off the mean. The.000 Sig. value clearly shows the constant is not zero. The constant's 1.419–2.202 confidence interval confirms population number location.

Table 14. Coefficients[a]

Model		Unstandardized Coefficients		Standardized Coefficients	t	Sig.	95.0% Confidence Interval for B		Correlations			Collinearity Statistics	
		B	Std. Error	Beta			Lower Bound	Upper Bound	Zero order	Partial	Part	Tolerance	VIF
1	(Constant)	1.811	.199		9.093	.000	1.419	2.202					
	Talent Management Practices	.071	.044	.085	1.612	.108	-.016	.158	.388	.077	.065	.597	1.674
	Sustainability Practices	.455	.050	.478	9.120	.000	.357	.553	.532	.401	.370	.597	1.674

a. Dependent Variable: Financial Impact

Strategic Talent Management Coefficient 0.071, standard error 0.044. Each standard deviation shift in "Talent Management Practices." changes "Financial Impact" by 0.085. Given the much higher significance threshold of 0.108 (Sig.), the "t" value of 1.612 implies this coefficient estimate is not statistically significant. The confidence range for population coefficients is -0.016 to 0.158.

Green methods have 0.455 coefficients and 0.050 margins. "Financial Impact" standard deviations alter with "Sustainability Practices." The typical beta is 0.478. "t" values of 9.120 are statistically significant (Sig. =.000). The population coefficient is reasonable within the confidence interval of 0.357 to 0.553. The predictive factors and independent variable ("Financial Impact") are correlated in the table. These are r=0.388 for "Talent Management Practices" and r=0.532 for "Sustainability Practices." Finally, collinearity statistics indicate predictor variable relationships. The tolerance value is the proportion of predictor variable volatility not explained by other predictors. Variance Inflation Factor assesses predictor variable correlation. With a VIF score of 1.674, this table has no multicollinearity issues. Table 14 continues with thorough regression coefficient analysis. It provides statistical significance, confidence intervals, correlations, and collinearity of predictor variables' effects on the dependent variable. This coefficient may show how variables impact the model's prediction power.

Table 15 examines regression model coefficients using bootstrap techniques to assess their significance and reliability. The table below lists these coefficients' biases, standard errors, significance levels, and confidence ranges.

Table 15. Bootstrap for coefficients

Model		B	Bootstrap[a]				
			Bias	Std. Error	Sig. (2-tailed)	95% Confidence Interval	
						Lower	Upper
1	(Constant)	1.811	-.010	.197	.001	1.416	2.205
	Talent Management Practices	.071	.000	.047	.135	-.025	.166
	Sustainability Practices	.455	.003	.049	.001	.359	.552

a. Unless otherwise noted, bootstrap results are based on 1000 bootstrap samples

A Model 1 constant coefficient calculation returns 1.811. A bootstrap bias of -0.010 means random sampling may underestimate or exaggerate the genuine coefficient. The bootstrap standard error of 0.197 shows the coefficient's fluctuation between bootstrap samples. The constant coefficient is not statistically significant at 0.197. The 95% confidence interval (1.416–2.2205) indicates the most probable range for the true population coefficient. The Talent Management Practices coefficient bootstrap bias is 0.000, which is low. The bootstrap standard error for the coefficient, 0.135, reflects this uncertainty. This coefficient may affect the dependent variable since it is statistically significant at 0.047. The population coefficient is likely between -0.025 and 0.166, the 95% confidence interval. The Sustainability Practices coefficient bootstrap bias is 0.003. The standard error of 0.049 shows that bootstrap samples vary the coefficient. The coefficient's marginal statistical significance (0.049) suggests it affects the dependent variable. The population coefficient might be anywhere in the 95% confidence interval (0.359–0.552). These coefficients' relevance and reliability are best appreciated using bootstrap results. The table calculates biases, standard errors, significance levels, and confidence ranges to evaluate coefficients. This research increases our comprehension of the regression model by revealing predictor variable statistical significance and their probable influence on the dependent variable.

Table 16 details regression model coefficient correlations, covariances, and bootstrap results. This table examines "Sustainability Practices" and "Talent Management Practices," predictor factors, and bootstrapping techniques to assess their robustness. Model 1 coefficient covariances and correlations are below. This section gives the predictor variable correlations. The correlation between "Sustainability Practices" is 1.000 because variables always correlate. The inverse connection between "Sustainability Practices" and "Talent Management Practices" is -0.635. Similar to how "Sustainability Practices" connects negatively with "Talent Management Practices," -0.635. Exactly as expected, "Talent Management Practices" self-correlates 1.00. The predictors' covariances are noted in their own section. Overall, "Sustainability Practices" has a 0.002 covariance with itself, whereas "Talent Management Practices" has -0.001. Similar to "Sustainability Practices," "Talent Management Practices" has a -0.001 covariance with itself and 0.002.

The bootstrap correlations are shown here. Bootstrapping bias = 0.000, showing negligible sampling error bias in "Sustainability Practices" correlation. A 0.002 positive bias exists between "Sustainability Practices" and "Talent Management Practices." A slight positive bias (r=0.002) exists between "Talent Management Practices" and "Sustainability Practices." There is no bias when comparing "Talent Management Practices" against itself. The bootstrap standard error is 0.000 for "Sustainability Practices" and itself and 0.033 for "Talent Management Practices." For the correlation between "Talent Management Practices" and "Sustainability Practices" (0.033) and themselves (0.000), standard error is roughly the same. The 95% confidence intervals provide the population values for correlations. The CI for this correlation is 1.000 because "Sustainability Practices" and itself are perfectly correlated. Between "Sustainability Practices" and "Talent Management Practices," the correlation is -0.694 to -0.563. The correlation between "Talent Management Practices" and "Sustainability Practices" is (-0.694, -0.563). Finally, "Talent Management Practices" correlates precisely 1.000 with itself. Table 16 presents bootstrap sample and regression model coefficient correlations and covariances results. The bootstrap results help us understand predictor variable correlations and covariances' consistency and error potential. The table helps explain predictor variable linkages and implications.

Table 16. Coefficient correlations[a]

Model						
1	**Correlations**			**Sustainability Practices**	**Sustainability Practices**	**1.000**
					Talent Management Practices	-.635
				Talent Management Practices	Sustainability Practices	-.635
					Talent Management Practices	1.000
	Covariances			Sustainability Practices	Sustainability Practices	.002
					Talent Management Practices	-.001
				Talent Management Practices	Sustainability Practices	-.001
					Talent Management Practices	.002
	Bootstrap for Correlations[b]	Bias		Sustainability Practices	Sustainability Practices	0.000
					Talent Management Practices	.002
				Talent Management Practices	Sustainability Practices	.002
					Talent Management Practices	0.000
		Std. Error		Sustainability Practices	Sustainability Practices	0.000
					Talent Management Practices	.033
				Talent Management Practices	Sustainability Practices	.033
					Talent Management Practices	0.000
		95% Confidence Interval	Lower	Sustainability Practices	Sustainability Practices	1.000
					Talent Management Practices	-.694
				Talent Management Practices	Sustainability Practices	-.694
					Talent Management Practices	1.000
			Upper	Sustainability Practices	Sustainability Practices	1.000
					Talent Management Practices	-.563
				Talent Management Practices	Sustainability Practices	-.563
					Talent Management Practices	1.000

a. Dependent Variable: Financial_Impact

b. Unless otherwise noted, bootstrap results are based on 1000 bootstrap samples

In Table 17, we see the results of a thorough investigation of collinearity diagnostics for a regression model including the predictor variables "Talent Management Practices" and "Sustainability Practices." This table is an attempt to evaluate the likelihood of multicollinearity problems resulting from the interplay of various factors. The collinearity diagnostics for Model 1 are described in this subsection. The eigenvalues quantify the significance of correlations between independent variables used as predictors. With a value of 1.000, the first eigenvalue clearly holds the most weight. The decreased size of the second eigenvalue (0.023) indicates a much lesser effect. With a value of 0.014, the third eigenvalue continues this trend of diminishing significance. To determine how severe model multicollinearity is, one might utilize the condition index. High multicollinearity is indicated by a condition index greater than 30. The low value of 2.963 for the first condition index indicates that this part of the model does not suffer from excessive multicollinearity. The proportions of the variation attributable to the various predictors and the constant are provided in the next section. The variance of the first eigenvalue can be fully explained by the constant. The "Constant," "Talent_Management_Practices," and "Sustainability_Practices" account for 89%, 39%, and 4% of the variation in the second eigenvalue, respectively. In the case of the third eigenvalue, the same sources explain 11%, 61%, and 96% of the variation. Table 17 sums together all the information you need to know about the collinearity diagnostics of the regression model. Potential multicollinearity effects resulting from interactions between predictor variables may be evaluated using the eigenvalues, condition index, and variance proportions. This study helps in determining how well the model performs in conditions of multicollinearity.

Table 17. Collinearity diagnostics[a]

Model		Eigenvalue	Condition Index	Variance Proportions		
				(Constant)	Talent_Management_Practices	Sustainability_Practices
1	1	2.963	1.000	.00	.00	.00
	2	.023	11.460	.89	.39	.04
	3	.014	14.502	.11	.61	.96
a. Dependent Variable: Financial_Impact						

Table 18. Casewise diagnostics[a]

Case Number	Std. Residual	Financial Impact	Predicted Value	Residual
205	-3.143	1.67	4.0186	-2.35193
209	-3.198	2.00	4.3930	-2.39305
352	-3.143	1.67	4.0186	-2.35193
356	-3.198	2.00	4.3930	-2.39305
a. Dependent Variable: Financial Impact				

Case-by-case diagnostics for the regression model are provided in Table 18, allowing for an in-depth analysis of the model's efficacy on specific instances within the dataset. This table explores the precision and consistency of the model's predictions for individual observations, with a focus on the dependent variable "Financial Impact."

The following are the case-by-case diagnostics for Model 1:

By assigning a unique case number to each person, we are able to link diagnostic data with specific patient records. The Std. Residual provides a numerical measure of the gap between the model's projected value and the actual observed value for "Financial Impact." A positive number indicates that the model overestimated the effect, whereas a negative value suggests that the model underestimated the effect. The observed values for the dependent variable are shown in the Financial Impact column so that they may be compared with the model's predictions. The Predicted Value displays, for each individual example, the values projected by the regression model, demonstrating how well the model fits the actual results. The Residuals, which show the absolute disparities between the predicted values and the actual observed values for each example, are perhaps the most illuminating. When the residual is positive, the model has overstated the monetary effect, and when it is negative, the model has underestimated it.

Case-by-case analysis in this table provides granular insight into the model's overall performance. This study reveals how well the model fits the observed data by comparing the standardized residuals, actual values, projected values, and residuals. These diagnostics provide important details about the model's performance and any anomalies or trends that might affect its predictions.

Table 19. Residuals statistics[a]

		Statistic	Bootstrap[b]			
			Bias	Std. Error	95% Confidence Interval	
					Lower	Upper
Predicted Value	Minimum	2.9905				
	Maximum	5.4926				
	Mean	4.3402	-.0022	.0434	4.2548	4.4256
	Std. Deviation	.47394	.00295	.03792	.40138	.55652
	N	437	0	0	437	437
Residual	Minimum	-2.39305				
	Maximum	1.46413				
	Mean	.00000	.00000	.00000	.00000	.00000
	Std. Deviation	.74662	-.00358	.02703	.69134	.79690
	N	437	0	0	437	437
Std. Predicted Value	Minimum	-2.848				
	Maximum	2.432				
	Mean	.000	.000	.000	.000	.000
	Std. Deviation	1.000	.000	.000	1.000	1.000
	N	437	0	0	437	437
Std. Residual	Minimum	-3.198				
	Maximum	1.956				
	Mean	.000	.000	.000	.000	.000
	Std. Deviation	.998	.000	.000	.998	.998
	N	437	0	0	437	437
a. Dependent Variable: Financial_Impact						
b. Unless otherwise noted, bootstrap results are based on 1000 bootstrap samples						

The properties and distribution of residuals are illuminated by Table 19's in-depth study of residual statistics within the context of a regression model. Residuals, which show discrepancies between predicted and observed values, are important measures of a model's efficacy. The table below breaks down residuals into their component parts, including predicted value residuals, residuals, standardized predicted value residuals, and standardized residuals.

The table below displays a complete set of residual statistics for Model 1 with their related bootstrap results:

Residuals Based on Anticipated Value

The range of discrepancies between projected and actual values is highlighted by the table's lowest and maximum residual values. The computed mean of these residuals is 4.3402, with a little bootstrap bias of -0.0022. The feasible range for the population mean is shown by the 95% confidence interval for the mean, which extends from 4.2548 to 4.4256. The residuals are dispersed with a standard deviation of 0.47394. Bootstrap findings provide a 95% confidence range for the standard deviation of 0.40138 to 0.55652, with a standard error of 0.00295. There are 437 observations available for these residuals, providing a sizable data set for study.

Similar Insights May Be Found in the Residuals Section

The residual range is the lowest and highest values and shows how far the model's predictions are from reality. Overestimations and underestimations are about evenly distributed based on the mean of these residuals. The biases, standard errors, and 95% confidence intervals for the mean and standard deviation in bootstrap analyses are all small, confirming this consistency. The confidence range for the residuals is 0.69134-0.79690, with a bootstrap standard error of -0.00358. The residuals standard deviation is 0.74662. With a sample size of 437, we may be confident in the validity of our statistical analysis of these residuals.

The table also includes comparable statistics and bootstrap findings for Std. Predicted Value Residuals and Std. Residuals.

Table 19 concludes our exploration of residual statistics by revealing the distribution, central tendency, variability, and resilience of several residuals inside the regression model. The supplied data gain credibility and trustworthiness when bootstrap findings are included. This in-depth analysis helps shed light on how well the model's predictions match up with real data and where possible sources of variability lie.

MANAGERIAL IMPLICATIONS

Several crucial management inferences may be made from the analysis's reported results. These ramifications are meant to give decision-makers and managers with useful takeaways:

Place a premium on talent management and long-term planning, since this research shows a positive relationship between "Talent Management Practices" and "Financial Impact," indicating that money put into efficient personnel management techniques may lead to better financial results. More importantly, the correlation between "Sustainability Practices" and "Financial Impact" demonstrates the potential monetary gains from incorporating sustainable practices into corporate operations (Kumar, Özen, and Vurur 2023). Managers should think about how they might improve talent management and sustainability simultaneously.

The research found that both "Talent Management Practices" and "Sustainability Practices" significantly affected "Financial Impact." This finding highlights the need of prioritizing balanced approaches. This suggests that a corporate plan that takes into account both human capital management and environmental issues might provide desirable financial results. Managers shouldn't prioritize one area over another, but rather look for ways to improve both simultaneously (Kumar, Khurana, and Sharma 2021).

Decisions based on empirical evidence: Relationships between variables may be better understood with the use of a regression analysis. Businesses may use this information to make smarter choices. When managers examine the coefficients, they may see how much weight each predictor variable carries in determining financial results. Managers may make more informed decisions and focus on the areas with the most potential for financial success when they have access to relevant data (Taneja, Gupta, et al. 2023).

Casewise diagnostics draw attention to specific instances in which the model's predictions differ from actual values during monitoring and optimization. Managers should pay close attention to situations with large discrepancies and determine whether or not they represent outliers. With the use of this method of monitoring and optimization, managers may fine-tune their plans, operations, and policies to be more in line with actual results (Taneja, Bhatnagar, Kumar, and Grima 2023).

Organizations may take a diversified approach to sustainability because of the favorable association between sustainability initiatives and financial effect. Sustainable practices, waste reduction, energy efficiency improvements, and social responsibility programs are all examples of what this may include. In addition to the financial benefits, these measures highlight the company's dedication to environmental and social causes (Kumar, Verma, et al. 2023).

While this research shows modest multicollinearity across predictor factors, managers should nevertheless exercise caution in light of the possibility of interactions between variables. Predictions may be improved, and errors in interpreting correlations between variables reduced, if multicollinearity is taken into account. It might be helpful to get advice from professionals and use methods like regularization (Mukul Bhatnagar et al. 2022).

The outcomes of the research highlight the dynamic nature of corporate settings, highlighting the need of continuous learning and adaptation. Managers should participate in ongoing learning and adaptation as the associations between predictor factors and financial effect change over time (M Bhatnagar, Taneja, and Rupeika-Apoga 2023). If managers don't keep up with the latest developments in their fields, their plans will quickly become obsolete.

In conclusion, the analysis's managerial implications provide practical guidance for businesses that want to boost their bottom line by improving their personnel management and sustainability policies. Positive financial effect may be produced while simultaneously contributing to larger social and environmental objectives when managers prioritize a balanced approach, use data-based decision-making, and maintain flexibility.

CONCLUSION

This study illuminates the relationship between "Talent Management Practices," "Sustainability Practices," and "Financial Impact." This work has broad significance outside academia and is relevant on many levels. The study's main conclusions are crucial for academics and professionals. This study used regression analysis and a variety of diagnostic methods to reveal the subtle relationships between these critical elements. The findings contribute to management and sustainability literature and aid policymakers in several domains. This research emphasizes the necessity for a balanced approach to management. Results indicate that excellent human management and sustainability efforts work together to achieve financial success. Managers may now use the synergy between these activities to create a more complete plan that supports economic success and social responsibility. This study promotes social sustainability beyond institutions. This study's favorable correlation between "Sustainability Practices" and "Financial

Impact" encourages corporations to embrace greener and more socially aware strategies. Businesses that incorporate sustainability into their operations may help the world become more sustainable. There are several benefits for readers and others. More data on this dynamic connection in the real world helps scholars. The study's methodological rigor and analytical accuracy guide future research, helping us understand similar interactions in various environments. Practitioners may get insights outside academic frameworks. Management implications turn the findings into meaningful guidance that may benefit businesses and society. This knowledge allows managers to steer their organizations to financial success while promoting ethical and environmental principles. Finally, this research's journey shows its broad ramifications for the domains of scholarship, business, and daily life. Deconstructing "Talent Management Practices," "Sustainability Practices," and "Financial Impact," the research creates a narrative of integrated management, virtuous action, and game-changing societal contributions. This study may guide companies toward a future where they can succeed while conserving the environment and supporting their communities.

REFERENCES

Alparslan, A., & Saner, T. (2020). The Influence of Sustainable Talent Management on Job Satisfaction and Organizational Commitment: Moderating Role of In-Service Training. *Revista de Cercetare si Interventie Sociala*, *69*(June), 96–121. doi:10.33788/rcis.69.6

Anlesinya, A., & Amponsah-Tawiah, K. (2020). Towards a Responsible Talent Management Model. *European Journal of Training and Development*, *44*(2/3), 279–303. doi:10.1108/EJTD-07-2019-0114

Ardichvili, A., & Zavyalova, E. (2019). TALENT MANAGEMENT AND DEVELOPMENT IN THE RUSSIAN FEDERATION. In K. M. Dirani, F. M. Nafukho, and B. J. Irby (eds.) Global Issues And Talent Development: Perspectives From Countries Around The World, 41–56. International Higher Education.

Bansal, N., Bhatnagar, M., & Taneja, S. (2023). *Balancing Priorities through Green Optimism: A Study Elucidating Initiatives, Approaches, and Strategies for Sustainable Supply Chain Management. Handbook of Research on Designing Sustainable Supply Chains to Achieve a Circular Economy*. IGI Global. doi:10.4018/978-1-6684-7664-2.ch004

Benitez-Amado, J., Llorens-Montes, F., & Fernandez-Perez, V. (2015). IT Impact on Talent Management and Operational Environmental Sustainability. *INFORMATION TECHNOLOGY \& MANAGEMENT, 16*(3), 207–20. . doi:10.1007/s10799-015-0226-4

Bhastary, M. D., Lubis, A. R., Utami, S., & Meldi Kesuma, T. (2023). Implementation Of Talent Management as An Effort to Realize Sustainable Performance of The Palm Oil Industry in Indonesia. *Quality - Access to Success*, *24*(195), 255–262. doi:10.47750/QAS/24.195.30

Bhatnagar, M., Özen, E., Taneja, S., Grima, S., & Rupeika-Apoga, R. (2022). The Dynamic Connectedness between Risk and Return in the Fintech Market of India: Evidence Using the GARCH-M Approach. *Risks*, *10*(11), 209. doi:10.3390/risks10110209

Bhatnagar, M., Taneja, S., & Rupeika-Apoga, R. (2023). Demystifying the Effect of the News (Shocks) on Crypto Market Volatility. *Journal of Risk and Financial Management*, *16*(2), 136. doi:10.3390/jrfm16020136

Dahiya, K., Taneja, S., & Özen, E. (2023). *To Analyse the Impact of Multi-Media Technology on the Rural Entrepreneurship Development. Contemporary Studies of Risks in Emerging Technology, Part A.* Emerald Group Publishing Ltd., doi:10.1108/978-1-80455-562-020231015

Dangwal, A., Kaur, S., Taneja, S., & Ozen, E. (2022). *A Bibliometric Analysis of Green Tourism Based on the Scopus Platform. Developing Relationships, Personalization, and Data Herald in Marketing 5.0.* IGI Global., doi:10.4018/978-1-6684-4496-2.ch015

Dangwal, A., Taneja, S., Özen, E., Todorovic, I., & Grima, S. (2022). Abridgement of Renewables: It's Potential and Contribution to India's GDP. *International Journal of Sustainable Development and Planning*, *17*(8), 2357–2363. doi:10.18280/ijsdp.170802

Deters, J. (2019). Global leadership talent selection as an integrated acquisition process. Advances in Global Leadership. Emerald Group Publishing LTD. doi:10.1108/S1535-120320180000011003

Fang, T. (2019). A Tale of Two Strategies: Economic Growth Strategy and Talent Management Strategy in China. In H Wang and L Miao (eds.) Handbook On China And Globalization, 393–412. Edward Elgar Publishing LTD.

Gardas, B. B., Mangla, S. K., Raut, R. D., Narkhede, B., & Luthra, S. (2019). Green Talent Management to Unlock Sustainability in the Oil and Gas Sector. *Journal of Cleaner Production*, *229*(August), 850–862. doi:10.1016/j.jclepro.2019.05.018

Gupta, M., Arora, K., & Taneja, S. (2023). *Bibliometric Analysis on Employee Engagement and Human Resource Management. Enhancing Customer Engagement Through Location-Based Marketing*. IGI Global., doi:10.4018/978-1-6684-8177-6.ch013

Gupta, M., Taneja, S., Sharma, V., Singh, A., Rupeika-Apoga, R., & Jangir, K. (2023). Does Previous Experience with the Unified Payments Interface (UPI) Affect the Usage of Central Bank Digital Currency (CBDC)? *Journal of Risk and Financial Management*, *16*(6), 286. doi:10.3390/jrfm16060286

Hernandez, Y., Zatarain, R., & Barron, L. (2019). A Talent Management Model for Innovation and Competitiveness in Complex Domains: A Case Study in the Latin American Energy Sector. In G. Cortes-Robles, J. L. Garcia-Alcaraz, and G. Alor-Hernandez (eds.) Managing Innovation In Highly Restrictive Environments: Lessons From Latin America And Emerging Markets. Springer. doi:10.1007/978-3-319-93716-8_6

Jangir, K., Sharma, V., Taneja, S., & Rupeika-Apoga, R. (2023). The Moderating Effect of Perceived Risk on Users' Continuance Intention for FinTech Services. *Journal of Risk and Financial Management*, *16*(1), 21. doi:10.3390/jrfm16010021

Kafetzopoulos, D., Psomas, E., & Bouranta, N. (2022). The Influence of Leadership on Strategic Flexibility and Business Performance: The Mediating Role of Talent Management. *Management Decision*, *60*(9), 2532–2551. doi:10.1108/MD-10-2021-1310

Kantrowitz, T. M. (2019). Applying Adaptive Approaches to Talent Management Practices. In R. N. Landers (ed.) Cambridge Handbook Of Technology And Employee Behavior. Cambridge Univ Press.

Kaur, H., Singh, K., Kumar, P., & Kaur, A. (2023). Assessing the Environmental Sustainability Corridor: An Empirical Study of Renewable Energy Consumption in BRICS Nation. In *IOP Conference Series: Earth and Environmental Science*. Institute of Physics. 10.1088/1755-1315/1110/1/012053

Khan, A. G., Banik, S., Uddin, M. A., & Moudud-Ul-Huq, S. (2021). Unlocking the Relationship Between Talent Management Practices and Performance Sustainability in the Sports Industry. *International Journal of Asian Business and Information Management*, *12*(3), 366–380. doi:10.4018/IJABIM.20210701.oa22

Khan, E., Mubarik, M. S., & Shahid, Z. A. (2021). In the Pursuit of Green in COVID-19: Harnessing the Existing Talent to Pursue Green Corporate Entrepreneurship. *Frontiers in Psychology*, *12*(October), 751961. Advance online publication. doi:10.3389/fpsyg.2021.751961 PMID:34759871

Kumar, P., Khurana, A., & Sharma, S. (2021). Performance Evaluation of Public and Private Sector Banks. *World Review of Entrepreneurship, Management and Sustainable Development*, *17*(2–3), 306–322. doi:10.1504/WREMSD.2021.114436

Kumar, P., & Mukul, D. (2023). Green Infrastructure- A Roadmap Towards Sustainable Development. In *IOP Conference Series: Earth and Environmental Science*. Institute of Physics. 10.1088/1755-1315/1110/1/012060

Kumar, P., Özen, E., & Vurur, S. (2023). *Adoption of Blockchain Technology in the Financial Sector. Contemporary Studies of Risks in Emerging Technology*. Emerald Group Publishing Ltd. doi:10.1108/978-1-80455-562-020231018

Kumar, P., Verma, P., Bhatnagar, M., Taneja, S., Seychel, S., Todorović, I., & Grim, S. (2023). The Financial Performance and Solvency Status of the Indian Public Sector Banks: A CAMELS Rating and Z Index Approach. *International Journal of Sustainable Development and Planning*, *18*(2), 367–376. doi:10.18280/ijsdp.180204

Mousa, M., & Ayoubi, R. M. (2019). Inclusive/Exclusive Talent Management, Responsible Leadership and Organizational Downsizing A Study of Academics in Egyptian Public Business Schools. *Journal of Management Development*, *38*(2), 87–104. doi:10.1108/JMD-11-2018-0325

Mukul, S. Taneja, E. Özen, R. Plaha, M., & Zammit, L. (2023). *Banking, Fintech, BigTech: Emerging Challenges for Multimedia Adoption. Intelligent Multimedia Technologies for Financial Risk Management: Trends, Tools and Applications*. Institution of Engineering and Technology.

Noreen, U., & Imran, R. (2021). Impact of Talent Management Practices on Financial Performance: Evidence from GCC Banking Sector. *Middle East Journal Of Management*, *8*(2–3), 113–124. doi:10.1504/MEJM.2021.113977

Pinnington, A., Alshamsi, A., Karatas-Ozkan, M., Nicolopoulou, K., Ozbilgin, M., Tatli, A., & Vassilopoulou, J. (2015). Early Organizational Diffusion of Contemporary Policies: Narratives of Sustainability and Talent Management. In E. Gimzauskiene, K. Duoba, X. Pavie, A. Pinnington, & M. Vilka, 20th International Scientific Conference - Economics And Management. Elesvier. doi:10.1016/j.sbspro.2015.11.480

Psychogios, A., & Prouska, R. (2019). Human Resource Management Practices in SMEs. In Managing People In Small And Medium Enterprises In Turbulent Contexts. Routledge. doi:10.4324/9781315102610-2

Reepu, R., Taneja, S., Ozen, E., & Singh, A. (2023). *A Globetrotter to the Future of Marketing: Metaverse. Cultural Marketing and Metaverse for Consumer Engagement*. IGI Global, doi:10.4018/978-1-6684-8312-1.ch001

Sharma, M., & Kumar, P. (2021). *Adoption of Blockchain Technology: A Case Study of Walmart. Blockchain Technology and Applications for Digital Marketing*. IGI Global, doi:10.4018/978-1-7998-8081-3.ch013

Shikweni, S., Schurink, W., & van Wyk, R. (2019). Talent Management in the South African Construction Industry. *SA Journal of Human Resource Management*, *17*(May). doi:10.4102ajhrm.v17i0.1094

Singh, A., Sharma, S., Singh, A., Unanoğlu, M., & Taneja, S. (2023a). *Cultural Marketing and Metaverse for Consumer Engagement. Cultural Marketing and Metaverse for Consumer Engagement*. IGI Global. doi:10.4018/978-1-6684-8312-1

Singh, A., Sharma, S., Singh, A., Unanoğlu, M., & Taneja, S. (2023b). *Preface. Cultural Marketing and Metaverse for Consumer Engagement*. IGI Global. doi:10.4018/978-1-6684-8312-1

Singh, V., Taneja, S., Singh, V., Singh, A., & Paul, H. L. (2021). *Online Advertising Strategies in Indian and Australian E-Commerce Companies: A Comparative Study. Big Data Analytics for Improved Accuracy, Efficiency, and Decision Making in Digital Marketing*. IGI Global. doi:10.4018/978-1-7998-7231-3.ch009

Swailes, S., Downs, Y., & Orr, K. (2014). Conceptualising Inclusive Talent Management: Potential, Possibilities and Practicalities. *Human Resource Development International*, *17*(5), 529–544. doi:10.1080/13678868.2014.954188

Taneja, S., Bhatnagar, M., Kumar, P., & Grima, S. (2023). A Panel Analysis of the Effectiveness of the Asset Management in Indian Agricultural Companies. *International Journal of Sustainable Development and Planning*, *18*(3), 653–660. doi:10.18280/ijsdp.180301

Taneja, S., Bhatnagar, M., Kumar, P., & Rupeika-Apoga, R. (2023). India's Total Natural Resource Rents (NRR) and GDP: An Augmented Autoregressive Distributed Lag (ARDL) Bound Test. *Journal of Risk and Financial Management*, *16*(2), 91. doi:10.3390/jrfm16020091

Taneja, S., Grima, S., Kumar, P., & Ozen, E. (2023). Special Issue: 'Green Asset and Risk Management for Promoting Sustainable Entrepreneurship in the Building of the Green Economy.'. *International Journal of Technology Management & Sustainable Development*, *22*(2), 127–130. doi:10.1386/tmsd_00071_7

Taneja, S., Gupta, M., Bhushan, P., Bhatnagar, M., & Singh, A. (2023). *Cultural Marketing in the Digital Era. Cultural Marketing and Metaverse for Consumer Engagement*. IGI Global. doi:10.4018/978-1-6684-8312-1.ch008

Taneja, S., Jaggi, P., Jewandah, S., & Ozen, E. (2022). Role of Social Inclusion in Sustainable Urban Developments: An Analyse by PRISMA Technique. *International Journal of Design & Nature and Ecodynamics*, *17*(6), 937–942. doi:10.18280/ijdne.170615

Taneja, S., Kaur, S., & Özen, E. (2022). Using Green Finance to Promote Global Growth in a Sustainable Way. *International Journal of Green Economics*, *16*(3), 246–257. doi:10.1504/IJGE.2022.128930

Taneja, S., & Ozen, E. (2023). Impact of the European Green Deal (EDG) on the Agricultural Carbon (CO2) Emission in Turkey. *International Journal of Sustainable Development and Planning*, *18*(3), 715–727. doi:10.18280/ijsdp.180307

Taneja, S., & Özen, E. (2023). To Analyse the Relationship between Bank's Green Financing and Environmental Performance. *International Journal of Electronic Finance*, *12*(2), 163–175. doi:10.1504/IJEF.2023.129919

Taneja, S., & Sharma, V. (2023). *Role of Beaconing Marketing in Improving Customer Buying Experience. Enhancing Customer Engagement Through Location-Based Marketing*. IGI Global. doi:10.4018/978-1-6684-8177-6.ch012

Valentin, M. A., & Valentin, C. (2019). TALENT MANAGEMENT BEST PRACTICES Harnessing the Dragon for Competitive Advantage. In K M Dirani, F M Nafukho, and B J Irby, (eds.) Global Issues And Talent Development: Perspectives From Countries Around The World. Information Age Publishing.

Visvizi, A. (2022). Sustainability in International Business: Talent Management, Market Entry Strategies, Competitiveness. *Sustainability (Basel)*, *14*(16), 10191. Advance online publication. doi:10.3390u141610191

APPENDIX

Table 20. Questionnaire

Section 1: Demographic Information	
1. What is your current role within the organization?	
A	Executive Leadership
B	Human Resources
C	Middle Management
D	Non-Management Employee
E	Other (please specify): ___________
2. How long have you been with the organization?	
A	Less than 1 year
B	1-3 years
C	4-6 years
D	7 or more years
3. What industry does your organization operate in?	
A	Manufacturing
B	Technology
C	Healthcare
D	Financial Services
E	Energy
F	Other (please specify): ___________
Section 2: Talent Management Practices	
4. Our organization effectively recruits and selects employees who align with our strategic goals.	
5. Our organization invests in regular training and development programs to enhance employee skills.	
6. Performance expectations for employees are clearly communicated and consistently measured.	
Section 3: Sustainability Initiatives	
7. Our organization has a well-defined sustainability strategy.	
8. Sustainability practices are integrated into our organization's daily operations.	
9. Sustainability initiatives positively influence our organization's reputation.	
Section 4: Financial Impact	
10. Effective talent management practices have positively impacted our organization's financial performance.	
11. The alignment between talent management strategies and financial goals is evident in our organization.	
12. Integrating sustainability principles with talent management practices is crucial for achieving long-term financial success.	

Chapter 3
Green Finance:
An Integral Pathway to Achieving Sustainable Development

Vikas Sharma
https://orcid.org/0000-0002-2447-7773
Chandigarh University, India

Sanjay Taneja
https://orcid.org/0000-0002-3632-4053
Graphic Era University (Deemed), India

Kshitiz Jangir
https://orcid.org/0000-0001-9823-0039
Manipal University, India

Kirti Khanna
https://orcid.org/0000-0002-0093-9451
MRIIRS, India

ABSTRACT

Amidst rapid computerized progression, the universal economy faces three significant encounters: environmental variation, energy restraints, and financial crises. The pursuit of pecuniary progress often comes at the disbursement of environmental degradation. Green finance is a promising solution to strike a harmonious balance between the economy and nature. This chapter delves into a comprehensive exploration of existing literature on green finance while shedding light on the future potential of green finance in India. By promoting and investing in environmentally conscious projects, green finance is key to fostering sustainable development while addressing pressing ecological concerns. It is a beacon of hope, guiding the path toward a greener and more resilient global economy.

DOI: 10.4018/979-8-3693-1388-6.ch003

1. INTRODUCTION

During this 21st century, the significance of green financing has grown exponentially, encompassing the business realm and environmental science (Abbas et al., 2020). Developed and developing nations must actively strive for green financing, with projections indicating that global investment in green set-up could spread a staggering $40 trillion between 2012 and 2030 (Dobbs et al., 2016). Green finance operates on eco-friendly credit, entailing regulatory measures that mandate commercial banks and financial institutions to undertake research and development initiatives to create pollution treatment facilities and engage in ecological preservation and restoration efforts (Udeagha & Muchapondwa, 2023).

Moreover, green finance fosters the creation and utilization of new energy resources, focusing on economic growth, green product manufacturing, and environmentally conscious agricultural practices(Zhang et al., 2021). It extends financial support through credits to facilitate relevant projects and institutions, implementing concessional low-interest rates(Chen, 2020). However, it also discourages new investments in polluting ventures by subjecting them to punitive interest rates(McMullen & Warnick, 2016).

1.1 Objectives of the Chapter

This Chapter provides a comprehensive depiction of green financing, highlighting various aspects. Given the strong connection between business and the environment, green financial products and services are crucial for maintaining sustainable relationships. The primary objectives of this study revolve around establishing green financing at the grassroots levels of the nation, aiming to foster sustainable practices and promote environmental stewardship(Dörry & Schulz, 2018).

1.2 Methodology

The current study primarily relies on secondary findings from researchers on global green financing(Larsen, 2022). our research endeavors to explore the initiatives of green money in a evolving economy like India. In every society, green funding plays a crucial role in supporting eco-friendly businesses(Aneja et al., 2023). As the world's population overgrows, green finance becomes increasingly essential to ensure a sustainable environment for all living creatures(Barnosky et al., 2014). Our work aims to shed light on the significance of green finance in fostering a harmonious coexistence between humanity and nature(Hugé et al., 2013).

2. REVIEW OF LITERATURE

(Sunil & Momany, 2020) discovered that stockholders in the capital market are progressively ecologically cognizant, favoring industries that adhere to contamination norms. (Schaltegger & Wagner, 2011) Highlighted the unanswered requirement for universally acceptable and applicable accounting and reporting standards with relevant indicators across all industries. They argued that social and environmental reporting should progress hand in hand. (Weber et al., 2008) surveyed UNEP and non-UNEP banks, revealing that environmental risk analysis was integrated mainly during the loan application's due diligence phase, neglecting other aspects like the controlling stage (Jangir et al., 2022). They concluded that banks lack a comprehensive considerate of the impression of ecological perils on their lend ranges. (Verma et al., 2012) emphasized that several matters hinder the growth of green fiscal avenues.

Green products still face challenges in establishing themselves as economically viable options due to the presence of lower-cost alternatives in the market. Unlike Europe's growing need for green financial products and services, the global market is in its early stages, lacking clear boundaries and distinct characteristics that set it apart from traditional industries. Financial institutions, especially banks, are crucial in developing a robust and thriving low-carbon economy(P. Sharma et al., 2023). They can achieve this by incorporating environmental information into their credit extension and investment decisions, proactively enhancing their ecological act, and generating long-term business value (V. Sharma, Jangir, et al., 2023).

Businesses with larger carbon footprints could be perceived as riskier in the future, which would discourage banks from providing finance for them. Instead, financial institutions may invest in new technology answers; help detention or cut down carbon discharges. (Aleksić et al., 2012) define "green finance" as fiscal stashes focused towards justifiable expansion initiatives, environmental products, and policies that promote the emergence of a more maintainable economy (Gupta et al., 2023).

These monetary investments also include measures to minimise greenhouse gas emissions (GHGs), manage industrial pollution, and save biodiversity. Green finance, according to Pricewaterhouse Coopers Consultants (PWC 2013), refers to financial products and services that take environmental factors into account during the decision-making, monitoring, and risk management processes.(V. Sharma, Gupta, et al., 2023). These products are intended to support and advance low-carbon technology, projects, industries, and businesses while also encouraging investments that are environmentally responsible.

(Lindenberg, 2014) further expands on the concept of green finance, outlining three key components:

1. We finance green investments in environmental products and services to prevent ecological and climate damage.
2. It is funding communal green initiatives that encourage implementing environmental projects and initiatives.
3. We are establishing a green financial system that handles and facilitates environment friendly stashes.

(Jha & Bhome, 2013) steered an experiential study was conducted to analyse different persons related to banking industry to judge understanding of green banking practises. They gathered primary data from 13 bank managers, 60 staff, and 45 available consumers. According to the findings, numerous green banking tactics are frequently used with good understanding(P. Sharma et al., 2023).

(Chowdhary et al., 2013) elaborated on the notion and profits of "green banks" in this paper. Researcher also examined the green funding practices of prominent Indian banks, including some public and private banks. The study provided valuable insights into green banking practices, offering tips on online banking, waste management, maintaining fresh and disinfected environments, implementing green funding in rustic divisions, and introducing green credit cards and loans (M. Sharma & Choubey, 2022). Goel (2016) found that India has a robust latent to build the green organization required for this financing (Nawaz et al., 2021). Overcoming barriers and raising awareness among corporate citizens would be essential to achieve this goal. IFC (2016) conducted an analysis demonstrating the progress made by various stakeholders in incentivizing and measuring green finance. The study showed that estimating green finance flows through private financial institutions is feasible, providing a foundation for further advancements in sustainable finance.

Nevertheless, the present analysis underscores the necessity for greater accountability and transparency in green finance. The bond market is a well-developed example with clear definitions and effective tracking mechanisms that could serve as a model for other sectors. In the banking sector, there is room for improvement in tracking processes for loans, while institutional investors must establish well-defined approaches to transition from mindfulness to applied application(Sobti et al., 2023).

A complete grasp of the current condition of environmentally friendly funding is required for thorough assessments versus policy aims. Multinational organisations, countrywide administrations, regulators, private financial sectors, data suppliers, and standard setters can all benefit from such an understanding. An exemplary model comes from China, where regulations require banks to disclose their green loan data regularly. Countries considering similar measures can benefit from learning from China's policy implementation and the insights from the collected data.

Outlined below are precise achievement points for each stakeholder cluster to enhance the future tracking and development of green finance, capitalizing on existing sources of green finance information. (Li et al., 2016) conducted a study for asserting that this finance represents an advanced fiscal approach that aims to protect the environment and promote sustainable resource utilization. Assuming a rational market mechanism for green finance, it can effectively guide fund flows, manage environmental risks, and optimize the allocation of green and social resources. They also emphasize that well-regulated policies can prevent information asymmetry and mitigate moral hazards.

Existing literature on green finance suggests that a significant portion of green investments is funded through banks. Banks can proactively accomplish the hazards allied with loaning to poisoning sectors by including environmental considerations into their decision-making processes, which boosts the financial system's overall resilience. In India, the banking sector is expected to facilitate the necessary resources for driving green transformation(Mohd & Kaushal, 2018).

However, it is concerning that there is a lack of substantial evidence regarding the state of green finance in India. Despite theoretical discussions, there is a shortage of empirical research to elucidate the reasons for this underperformance(V. Sharma, 2022). Additionally, limited knowledge prevails regarding green finance, green finance products, and their operational mechanisms in the Indian context.

2.1 System of Green Finance

The term "green financing" lacks a universally standardized definition. However, it generally refers to financial support for environmentally friendly projects significantly reducing greenhouse gas emissions and air pollutants. Green development, characterized by the harmonious economic and environmental relationship, is fostered through such financing. Investing in industrial and financial advancements while dipping greenhouse gas productions and other environmental pollutants aligns with the principles of green finance. Notably, green development solves three global economic threats. Consequently, green finance poses a comprehensive challenge to traditional financial regulations in every country.

"Green finance encompasses a broad spectrum, involving financial investments directed towards sustainable development projects, eco-friendly products, and solutions that contribute to building a more sustainable economy(Singh et al., 2022). While climate finance is part of it, green finance goes beyond and includes various other environmental objectives. It encompasses both mitigation and adaptation efforts concerning climate change. In the context of mitigation, financial flows are directed towards investments and initiatives that aim to reduce or prevent greenhouse gas emissions (GHGs), while in adaptation, financial flows focus on investments that help decrease vulnerability to the impacts of climate change(Aleksić et al., 2012).

3. HISTORICAL BACKGROUND OF GREEN FINANCE

UNEP linked with a assemblage of viable banks in 1992 to advance environmental awareness inside the financial sector, UNEP FI was established. The UNEP Finance Initiative is a special collaboration between UNEP and the financial industry that established the idea of Green Finance. With time, this programme grew to involve more financial organisations, such as commercial and banking institutions, insurance firms, and fund managers, and it helped to create fruitful discussions about how to combine safeguarding the environment with sustainable economic growth. The main goal is to include environmental factors into current financial services and procedures.

Approximately 195 financial institutions have joined this initiative, with over 40 countries endorsing the UNEP FI statement. As signatory institutions, they gain access to a network that provides insights into the latest trends and follows to leverage green occasions for development and actively contribute to shaping the agenda for sustainable finance in their respective contexts(Hřebíček et al., 2011).

4. THE STRUCTURE OF EQUATOR PRINCIPLES (SEPS)

A number of top international banks, including Citigroup Inc., The Royal Bank of Scotland, and Westpac Banking Corporation, initially accepted the structural equator principles (SEPs) when they were first announced in 2003. According to Bhattacharyya et al. (2008), the SEPs are a voluntary set of guidelines for different dealings in project finance.The International Financial Initiatives (IFC) and the World Bank Group's Environmental, Health, and Safety principles served as the foundation for the construction of the SEPs. They establish a common benchmark and framework for Equator Principles Financial Institutions (EPFIs), the entities adopting the principles, to develop their sociao economic policies, approaches, and criteria for project financing. EPFIs commit not to provide loans to projects that do not adhere to the canons outlined in the SEPs. Simultaneously, EPFIs are responsible for ensuring that borrowers are aware of these principles and guiding them on integrating the standards into their planned projects. Furthermore, they require their clients to comply with the SEPs' standards if they wish to continue seeking project financing.

These principles are applicable to new developments with total capital costs equal to or exceeding US$10 million, regardless of whether they are nationally or internationally located. As of now, nearly 70 financial institutions globally have adopted and implemented SEPs. Unlike the UNEP FI report, the SEPs expressly offer industry-specific guidelines that let EPFIs independently monitor and oversee their practises. It's important to keep in mind that the SEPs smear to plan backing and subsidiary advisory services, making this a relatively small portion of the financial industry.

4.1 UN Global Worldwide Compact

Ten voluntarily accepted principles make up the UN Global Compact (UNGWC). Banks pledge to uphold human rights, follow labour laws, fight corruption, and protect the environment by signing the UNGWC.

Regarding its particular sector focus, the UNGWC (2011) emphasises that enterprises should adopt a responsible approach to environmental concerns, launch campaigns to encourage larger ecological accountability, and support the development and dissemination of naturally approachable skills.

4.2 Project on Carbon Disclosure

The Project on Carbon Disclosure (PCD) is a nonprofit organisation that promotes disclosure of greenhouse gas (GHG) emissions from operations and evaluation of potential dangers related to climate change. PCD enables participants to understand their climate impacts through its climate change reporting system. For banks, this initiative allows for a precise calculation of the portion of GHG emissions attributed to their financing of specific companies. However, it is essential to note that the PCD lacks standardized criteria to address the direct effects of bank financing on companies that do not disclose their carbon emissions (Villarini et al., 2011).Despite this limitation, many banks worldwide have embraced these initiatives, leading to improved sustainability practices and enhanced environmental risk management within the banking sector(H. Kaur et al., 2023).

4.3 How it Works

Green industries and inventions occur at different stages of expansion, which necessitates varying stages of subsidy from diverse capital sources. While domestic public finance refers to cash provided directly by a government, international public finance refers to funds provided by multilateral development banks and other international institutions. The private sector, however, receives money from both domestic and foreign sources. Through different investment methods, there are numerous ways to arrange green financing.

Figure 1. Green finance interface
Source: Computed by authors

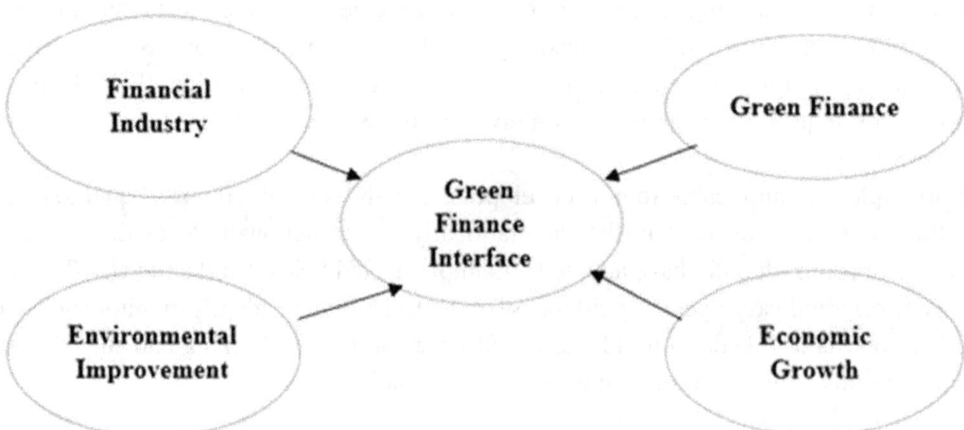

The green deposit is vital in facilitating low-carbon green development as it bridges the gap between the financial industry, environmental sustainability, and economic growth (Figure 1). One significant challenge in transitioning to a green industry is the missing link between knowledge and action, essentially "green finance." Implementing green initiatives in industries incurs costs, and many of these business models are untested or unconventional. Consequently, traditional financing may find supporting these green industrial proposals challenging or financially unattractive(Kang et al., 2009).

Figure 2. Green finance products
Source: Compiled by author

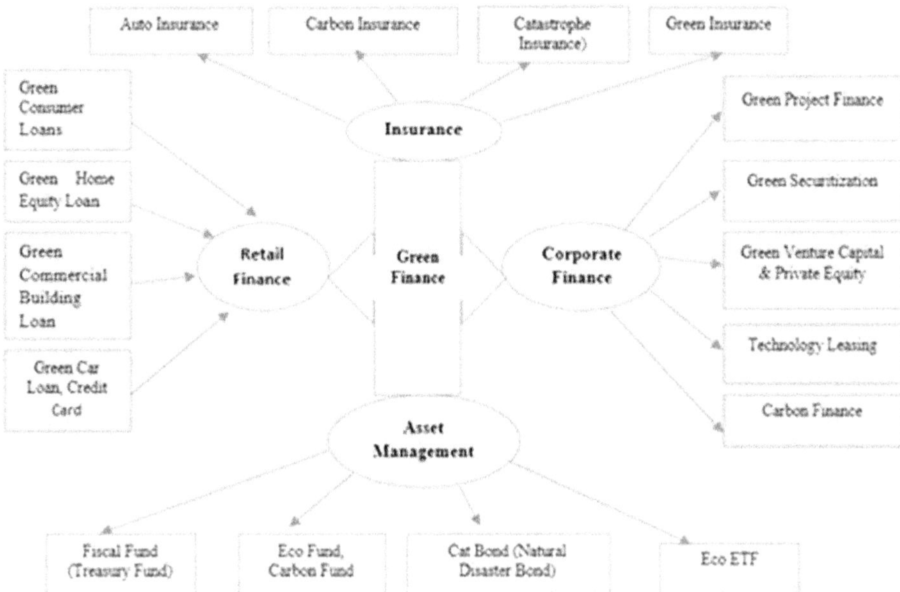

Green funds can be classified into three categories: the framework of green financing, financial support for industries or firms, and financial markets. It addresses climate change by supporting mitigation and adaptation projects. However, many private investors perceive environmentally sustainable projects as lacking sufficient returns on investment. Public financing mechanisms can alter this perception by enhancing profitability, such as offering private banks soft loans or credit guarantees. By doing so, public funding can stimulate private investment in green initiatives. International organizations are strives to promote a supportive framework for financing an inclusive and environmentally sustainable future(Han Oh et al., 2010).

5. BOOSTING SUPPORT FOR SUSTAINABLE FINANCING

The concept of sustainability has gained significant attention in India. Predominantly, it concerning the financial markets and banking system, where it has been associated with malicious and authoritarian actions. To address this issue, the Reserve Bank of India (RBI) introduced its guidelines in 2007 to foster the development and better management of accounts while promoting transparency and adherence to best practices.

Since the release of these guidelines, substantial progress has been made in the following manner. The Companies Act of 2013 explicitly incorporated Corporate Social Responsibility (CSR) provisions, effective from April 1 2014, among other progressive initiatives taken in this direction. This move seeks to encourage companies to be more responsible towards society and the environment, reflecting the growing importance of sustainability in the corporate landscape.

Table 1. Sustainability initiatives in India's financial sector

Years	Sustainability Creativities
2007	"RBI circular"(researchgate.net)
2008	"Launch of the S&P ESG India Index"(researchgate.net)
2012	"SEBI's mandate for inclusion of business responsibility reports as part of the listed entity's annual reports. Launch of the S&P BSE CARBONEX" (researchgate.net)
2013	Launch of the MSCI ESG India Index
2014	The Companies Act of 2013 mandates 2% of profits towards CSR
2015	"Inclusion of renewable energy under Priority Sector Lending. Miniratna status granted to IREDA. IBA's guidelines on responsible banking. Exim Bank of India issued a five-year US$500 million green bond. YES, Bank issued the first INR-denominated green bond"(researchgate.net)
2016	SEBI proposed new norms for issuance and listing of green bonds
2023	"Green Debt Securities of the Operational Circular for issue and listing of Non-Convertible Securities (NCS), Securitised Debt Instruments (SDI), Security Receipts (SR), Municipal Debt Securities and Commercial Paper (CP) dated August 10, 2021 (hereinafter referred to as the 'NCS Operational Circular'), as amended from time to time." https://www.sebi.gov.in/legal/circulars/feb-2023/revised-dis closure-requirements-for-issuance-and-listing-of-green-debt-securities_67837.html

Source: compiled by authors

Companies, whether private or public, with total assets exceeding INR 5 billion (equivalent to US$95.9 million), a turnover surpassing INR 15 billion (equivalent to US$224.7 million), or a net profit exceeding INR 62 million (equivalent to US$0.9 million), are required to allocate a minimum of two percent of their average net profit from the immediate preceding three financial years for Corporate Social Responsibility (CSR) initiatives. Notably, businesses can consider sustainability-linked financing as an alternative, as stated by FICCI in April 2021.

6. BUILDING A SUSTAINABLE FUTURE IN INDIA THROUGH GREEN FINANCE

Amidst India's impressive economic growth, the nation has faced environmental hurdles like pollution and deforestation, impacting health and progress. Nonetheless, the government is proactively seeking sustainable remedies to address these concerns. This encompasses the strategic embrace of green finance, a key approach to curbing the country's carbon footprint and propelling it toward a more environmentally conscious future.

Green financing is venturing into a mission of forging inventive and enduring frameworks. As fintech endeavors to automate financial services and refine operations, the realm of green fintech in India centers on diminishing emissions and advocating biodiversity.

In its essence, green finance denotes financially sustainable and socially responsible investments. This form of funding is progressively recognized as a potent instrument for addressing climate change and fostering sustainable growth. In India, it has gained substantial momentum recently, with the government initiating multiple endeavors to promote eco-friendly investments.

Green financing embarks on a quest to create ingenious and enduring structures. As fintech endeavors to mechanize financial services and optimize procedures, the sphere of green fintech in India is dedicated to curbing emissions and advancing biodiversity(A. Kaur et al., n.d.). This novel lineage is devoted to harnessing technology to steer environmental sustainability and nurture a healthier planet.

Leading the way toward a sustainable future, green finance in India provides crucial financial support to eco-friendly projects. The collaboration of government actions, private sector involvement, and advancing technological optimization drives the growth of green finance. Embracing green finance offers India multiple benefits, including promoting sustainable development, reducing carbon emissions, and improving energy security. India's steadfast dedication to prioritizing green finance is foreseen to endure, propelling resolute progress toward a sustainable and environmentally aware future.

The Companies Act of 2013 mandates that larger corporations are required to allocate a minimum of 2% of their profit after tax for initiatives related to CSR activities. These initiatives encompass, among other things, the following:

- Fostering preventative healthcare and sanitation, as well as ensuring access to safe drinking water.
- "Ensuring environmental sustainability, ecological balance, protection of biodiversity, animal welfare, agroforestry, conservation of natural resources, and maintaining the quality of soil, air, and water" (rbi.org).
- Donations or resources provided to innovation incubators located within academic institutions; and projects focused on rural development.

6.1 Sustainable Financial Products and Services

6.1.1 Green Bond

Towards the end of 2007, a consortium of Swedish pension funds indicated their desire to invest in environmentally advantageous projects. Breaking ground in November 2008, the World Bank pioneered the issuance of Green Bonds, aiming to attract fixed-income security investors to provide funds for qualified projects dedicated to tackling climate-related challenges. Since that time, more than 50 nations have emulated this approach, issuing their own Green Bonds, with the United States taking the lead in terms of the total volume of Green Bond offerings.

In 2015, Yes Bank achieved a milestone as the first institution in India to introduce a Green Bond. Through three separate tranches, the bank successfully secured Rs. 1645 crores in funding, with subscriptions from the IFC which is the private sector arm of the World Bank. Subsequently, these bonds were traded by the IFC on the London Stock Exchange, significantly enhancing the global visibility of Yes Bank's bonds. This development opened avenues for other Indian companies to also issue offshore

Green Bonds. By December 2022, the collective value of Green Bonds issued by Indian entities had surged to $19.17 billion, constituting approximately 3.8% of India's overall outstanding corporate bonds.

6.1.2 Green Insurance

The global challenge of climate change-induced global warming brings forth a multitude of economic, environmental, and societal complexities. The international community is actively engaged in addressing these complexities(Wang et al., 2017) with the insurance industry emerging as a key player in these efforts. Inherent in their operations, insurance companies operate within certain limitations regarding insurability. Nevertheless, they possess the capacity to contribute by adjusting pricing, terms, and conditions to encompass climate-related risks and distribute the burden of losses(Mills, 2009). However, insurers face vulnerabilities and at times confront data gaps that hinder informed decision-making. Consequently, they encounter challenges in safeguarding clients against natural catastrophes while ensuring sufficient coverage(Belozyorov & Xie, 2021). In response, insurance firms are formulating advanced strategies that factor in the climate change threat, and among these strategies is the emergence of green insurance products.

6.1.3 Green Loan Initiative

Analogous to a green bond, a green loan functions to secure funding for projects adhering to environmentally conscious criteria. Nevertheless, a green loan typically takes the form of a smaller, privately conducted lending arrangement, as opposed to the larger scope and potential exchange listing associated with green bonds. Green bonds often involve higher transactional complexities and may either be publicly traded or privately placed. It's noteworthy that both green loans and green bonds adhere to distinct yet matched ethics: the Green Credit Philosophies and the Green Bond Principles (GBP) established by the International Capital Market Association (ICMA). These devices underscore the requirement that the entirety of the raised funds must be allocated exclusively to activities meeting established green criteria(Gilchrist et al., 2021).

6.1.4 Green Financing in India's Future

As India navigates its environmental challenges, the trajectory of green financing in its future holds significant promise. The nation is increasingly focusing on sustainable practices and responsible allocation of resources. The adoption of green financing mechanisms, including innovative instruments like green bonds, green loans, and others, is on the brink of acceleration. These avenues are set to empower enterprises, institutions, and governmental entities to fund and bolster eco-friendly projects, renewable energy endeavors, and infrastructure built to withstand climate impacts.

India's commitment to international accords such as the Paris Agreement reinforces the imperative of transitioning toward a low-carbon economy. This commitment aligns seamlessly with the objectives of green financing, as addressing environmental degradation remains a priority.

7. RECENT GOVERNMENT INITIATIVES AND GREEN FINANCING BENEFITS IN INDIA

Following are the recent governmental policies and initiatives that have expanded the landscape of green financial products in India:

- National Action Plan on Climate Change (NAPCC): Enacted in 2008, the NAPCC outlines India's strategy for mitigating and adapting to climate change. It includes eight national missions focused on different sectors related to these initiatives.
- Jawaharlal Nehru National Solar Mission (JNNSM): Launched in 2010, this mission aims to promote the adoption of solar energy through incentives, subsidies, and policy support. It has set ambitious targets for increasing solar capacity in the country.
- National Mission for Enhanced Energy Efficiency (NMEEE): Under NMEEE, initiatives like the Perform, Achieve, and Trade (PAT) scheme encourage industries to improve energy efficiency. This involves setting energy consumption norms and allowing trading of energy-saving certificates.
- National Smart Grid Mission: This initiative focuses on modernizing the power distribution system by integrating renewable energy sources, improving grid efficiency, and enhancing demand-side management.
- Green Energy Corridors: The government is investing in building transmission infrastructure to facilitate the smooth integration of renewable energy into the grid.
- FAME India Scheme: The Faster Adoption and Manufacturing of Hybrid and Electric Vehicles (FAME) scheme offers incentives for electric vehicle adoption to promote eco-friendly transportation.
- Renewable Purchase Obligation (RPO): State electricity regulators mandate that a certain percentage of power procured by distribution companies must come from renewable sources, incentivizing the adoption of renewable energy.
- Goods and Services Tax (GST) Benefits: Certain renewable energy equipment and technologies enjoy reduced GST rates, making them more affordable and encouraging adoption.
- Green Bonds: The Securities and Exchange Board of India (SEBI) has introduced regulations and guidelines for issuing and listing green bonds, promoting investments in sustainable projects.
- Corporate Social Responsibility (CSR) Rules: The Companies Act mandates that a portion of CSR spending should be directed towards environmental sustainability, creating an incentive for businesses to support green initiatives.

8. CONCLUSION

The significance of green finance has amplified as a worldwide imperative within the sphere of sustainable economic and financial advancement. Countries across the globe are displaying heightened concerns regarding environmental shifts and pollution. To facilitate sustainable progress, several pivotal actions must be undertaken: identifying feasible green projects and affirming their eco-friendly attributes; financing initiatives that curtail waste generation or transform waste into valuable resources; augmenting investments for environmenral ventures; disseminating cognizance at the ordinary level amid bucolic societies; establishing and propagating replicable green endeavors; fostering afforestation; incentivizing the construction of environmentally conscious buildings; supporting financing for eco-friendly products; extending microfinance with minimal interest rates to encourage the production of ecologically conscious goods; and investing in rainwater harvesting and renewable energy sources like solar power.

This study delves comprehensively into the exploration of green financing, accentuating its indispensable role in a nation's progression. The global predicaments induced by global warming, ascribed to greenhouse gas emissions, are underscored. The research underscores the potential of green financing to considerably mitigate these emissions, thereby fostering a reduction in environmental ramifications. The study concludes by affirming India's ability to establish the requisite green infrastructure for sustainable finance, advocating for the surmounting of hurdles and heightening awareness among corporate entities. The expectation is that the prominence of green finance will continue to escalate across societies worldwide in the foreseeable future.

REFERANCES

Abbas, Q., Nurunnabi, M., Alfakhri, Y., Khan, W., Hussain, A., & Iqbal, W. (2020). The role of fixed capital formation, renewable and non-renewable energy in economic growth and carbon emission: A case study of Belt and Road Initiative project. *Environmental Science and Pollution Research International, 27*(36), 45476–45486. doi:10.100711356-020-10413-y PMID:32794094

Aleksić, J., Alvarez, E. A., Antonelli, L. A., Antoranz, P., Asensio, M., Backes, M., Barrio, J. A., Bastieri, D., González, J. B., & Bednarek, W. (2012). Performance of the MAGIC stereo system obtained with Crab Nebula data. *Astroparticle Physics, 35*(7), 435–448. doi:10.1016/j.astropartphys.2011.11.007

Aneja, R., Kappil, S. R., Das, N., & Banday, U. J. (2023). Does the green finance initiatives transform the world into a green economy? A study of green bond issuing countries. *Environmental Science and Pollution Research International, 30*(14), 42214–42222. doi:10.100711356-023-25317-w PMID:36645606

Barnosky, A. D., Brown, J. H., Daily, G. C., Dirzo, R., Ehrlich, A. H., Ehrlich, P. R., Eronen, J. T., Fortelius, M., Hadly, E. A., Leopold, E. B., Mooney, H. A., Myers, J. P., Naylor, R. L., Palumbi, S., Stenseth, N. C., & Wake, M. H. (2014). Introducing the scientific consensus on maintaining humanity's life support systems in the 21st century: Information for policy makers. *The Anthropocene Review, 1*(1), 78–109. doi:10.1177/2053019613516290

Belozyorov, S. A., & Xie, X. (2021). China's green insurance system and functions. *E3S Web of Conferences, 311*, 3001.

Bhattacharyya, M., Chaudhary, A., & Yadav, G. (2008). Conditional VaR estimation using Pearson's type IV distribution. *European Journal of Operational Research, 191*(2), 386–397. doi:10.1016/j.ejor.2007.07.021

Chen, M. (2020). Beyond donation: China's policy banks and the reshaping of development finance. *Studies in Comparative International Development, 55*(4), 436–459. doi:10.100712116-020-09310-9

Chowdhary, R., Jore, S., & Khandewal, S. (2013). Income Consumption Relationship in Indore City, An Application of Engel's Law. *PRERNA: Journal of Management Thought and Practice, 5*(1), 1–13.

Dobbs, R., Manyika, J., & Woetzel, J. (2016). No ordinary disruption: The four global forces breaking all the trends. Hachette UK.

Dörry, S., & Schulz, C. (2018). Green financing, interrupted. Potential directions for sustainable finance in Luxembourg. *Local Environment*, *23*(7), 717–733. doi:10.1080/13549839.2018.1428792

Gilchrist, D., Yu, J., & Zhong, R. (2021). The limits of green finance: A survey of literature in the context of green bonds and green loans. *Sustainability (Basel)*, *13*(2), 478. doi:10.3390u13020478

Gupta, M., Taneja, S., Sharma, V., Singh, A., Rupeika-Apoga, R., & Jangir, K. (2023). Does Previous Experience with the Unified Payments Interface (UPI) Affect the Usage of Central Bank Digital Currency (CBDC)? *Journal of Risk and Financial Management*, *16*(6), 286. doi:10.3390/jrfm16060286

Han Oh, J., Hoon Kim, S., Kang, J. Y., Hee Oh, C., & Gong, H. S. (2010). Effect of age on functional and structural outcome after rotator cuff repair. *The American Journal of Sports Medicine*, *38*(4), 672–678. doi:10.1177/0363546509352460 PMID:20357401

Hřebíček, J., Soukopová, J., Štencl, M., & Trenz, O. (2011). Integration of economic, environmental, social and corporate governance performance and reporting in enterprises. *Acta Universitatis Agriculturae et Silviculturae Mendelianae Brunensis*, *59*(7), 157–177. doi:10.11118/actaun201159070157

Hugé, J., Waas, T., Dahdouh-Guebas, F., Koedam, N., & Block, T. (2013). A discourse-analytical perspective on sustainability assessment: Interpreting sustainable development in practice. *Sustainability Science*, *8*(2), 187–198. doi:10.100711625-012-0184-2

Jangir, K., Sharma, V., Taneja, S., & Rupeika-Apoga, R. (2022). The Moderating Effect of Perceived Risk on Users' Continuance Intention for FinTech Services. *Journal of Risk and Financial Management*, *16*(1), 21. doi:10.3390/jrfm16010021

Jha, N., & Bhome, S. (2013). A study of green banking trends in India. *International Monthly Referred Journal of Research in Management and Technology*, *2*, 127–132.

Kang, L., Wang, J., Zhang, Y., Kou, Z., & Gao, S. (2009). iPS cells can support full-term development of tetraploid blastocyst-complemented embryos. *Cell Stem Cell*, *5*(2), 135–138. doi:10.1016/j.stem.2009.07.001 PMID:19631602

Kaur, A., Kumar, P., & Sharma, V. (n.d.). *Probabilistic Assessment To Measure Insolvency Risk Of Indian Public Sector Banks For Sustainable Financial Health*. Research Gate.

Kaur, H., Sood, K., Yadav, U. S., & Grima, S. (2023). Sustainable Solutions for Insurance and Risk Management. *The Impact of Climate Change and Sustainability Standards on the Insurance Market*, 359.

Larsen, M. L. (2022). Driving global convergence in green financial policies: China as policy pioneer and the EU as standard setter. *Global Policy*, *13*(3), 358–370. doi:10.1111/1758-5899.13105

Li, X.-F., Li, Q.-K., Cheng, J., Liu, L., Yan, Q., Wu, Y., Zhang, X.-H., Wang, Z.-Y., Qiu, Q., & Luo, Y. (2016). Conversion of dinitrogen to ammonia by FeN3-embedded graphene. *Journal of the American Chemical Society*, *138*(28), 8706–8709. doi:10.1021/jacs.6b04778 PMID:27383680

Lindenberg, N. (2014). *Definition of green finance*. SSRN.

McMullen, J. S., & Warnick, B. J. (2016). Should we require every new venture to be a hybrid organization? *Journal of Management Studies*, *53*(4), 630–662. doi:10.1111/joms.12150

Mills, E. (2009). A global review of insurance industry responses to climate change. *The Geneva Papers on Risk and Insurance. Issues and Practice*, *34*(3), 323–359. doi:10.1057/gpp.2009.14

Mohd, S., & Kaushal, V. K. (2018). Green finance: A step towards sustainable development. *MUDRA: Journal of Finance and Accounting*, *5*(1), 59–74. doi:10.17492/mudra.v5i01.13036

Nawaz, M. A., Seshadri, U., Kumar, P., Aqdas, R., Patwary, A. K., & Riaz, M. (2021). Nexus between green finance and climate change mitigation in N-11 and BRICS countries: Empirical estimation through difference in differences (DID) approach. *Environmental Science and Pollution Research International*, *28*(6), 6504–6519. doi:10.100711356-020-10920-y PMID:32997248

Schaltegger, S., & Wagner, M. (2011). Sustainable entrepreneurship and sustainability innovation: Categories and interactions. *Business Strategy and the Environment*, *20*(4), 222–237. doi:10.1002/bse.682

Sharma, M., & Choubey, A. (2022). Green banking initiatives: A qualitative study on Indian banking sector. *Environment, Development and Sustainability*, *24*(1), 293–319. doi:10.100710668-021-01426-9 PMID:33967597

Sharma, P., Sharma, V., Jangir, K., Gupta, M., & Pathak, N. (2023). In A. Khosla & M. Kolhe (Eds.), *Unfolding the Emerging Trends in Non-performing Assets with Special Reference to the Energy Sector in Banking Industry BT - Renewable Energy Optimization, Planning and Control* (pp. 411–422). Springer Nature Singapore.

Sharma, V. (2022). A Pragmatic Study on Management with Autocratic Approach and Consequential Impact on Profitability of the Organization. In P. K. Mallick, A. K. Bhoi, A. González-Briones, & P. K. Pattnaik (Eds.), *Electronic Systems and Intelligent Computing* (pp. 121–130). Springer Nature Singapore. doi:10.1007/978-981-16-9488-2_10

Sharma, V., Gupta, M., Jangir, K., Chopra, P., & Pathak, N. (2023). The Impact of Post-Use Consumer Satisfaction on Smart Wearables Repurchase Intention in the Context of AI-Based Healthcare Information. In *Enhancing Customer Engagement Through Location-Based Marketing* (pp. 77–101). IGI Global. doi:10.4018/978-1-6684-8177-6.ch007

Sharma, V., Jangir, K., Chowhan, S. S., & Pathak, N. (2023). Key Factors Influencing Electric Vehicle Purchase Decisions by Consumers: An Empirical Study of Indian Consumers. In *Renewable Energy Optimization, Planning and Control: Proceedings of ICRTE 2022* (pp. 449–464). Springer.

Singh, N., Bathla, G., & Sharma, V. (2022). Task Scheduling Algorithm Based on Load Balancing and Activity based Costing Method in Cloud Computing. *2022 11th International Conference on System Modeling & Advancement in Research Trends (SMART)*, 429–432.

Sobti, N., Sharma, V., & Khanna, K. (2023). A Systematic Literature Review on Factors Affecting Customer Engagement in Mobile Applications. *Cultural Marketing and Metaverse for Consumer Engagement*, 12–25.

Sunil, A., & Momany, M. T. (2020). Impact of green finance on the economy of developing countries. [IJM]. *International Journal of Management*, *11*(8), 1112–1120.

Udeagha, M. C., & Muchapondwa, E. (2023). Green finance, fintech, and environmental sustainability: Fresh policy insights from the BRICS nations. *International Journal of Sustainable Development and World Ecology*, *30*(6), 1–17. doi:10.1080/13504509.2023.2183526

Verma, A. K., Dash, R. R., & Bhunia, P. (2012). A review on chemical coagulation/flocculation technologies for removal of colour from textile wastewaters. *Journal of Environmental Management*, *93*(1), 154–168. doi:10.1016/j.jenvman.2011.09.012 PMID:22054582

Villarini, G., Smith, J. A., Serinaldi, F., & Ntelekos, A. A. (2011). Analyses of seasonal and annual maximum daily discharge records for central Europe. *Journal of Hydrology (Amsterdam)*, *399*(3–4), 299–312. doi:10.1016/j.jhydrol.2011.01.007

Wang, C., Nie, P., Peng, D., & Li, Z. (2017). Green insurance subsidy for promoting clean production innovation. *Journal of Cleaner Production*, *148*, 111–117. doi:10.1016/j.jclepro.2017.01.145

Weber, O., Fenchel, M., & Scholz, R. W. (2008). Empirical analysis of the integration of environmental risks into the credit risk management process of European banks. *Business Strategy and the Environment*, *17*(3), 149–159. doi:10.1002/bse.507

Zhang, D., Mohsin, M., Rasheed, A. K., Chang, Y., & Taghizadeh-Hesary, F. (2021). Public spending and green economic growth in BRI region: Mediating role of green finance. *Energy Policy*, *153*, 112256. doi:10.1016/j.enpol.2021.112256

Chapter 4
Unveiling the Shadows:
Understanding and Combating Fraudulent Services in the FinTech Landscape

Preet Kanwal
University of Quebec in Montreal, Canada

ABSTRACT

In an ever-evolving financial landscape, where FinTech is making commendable progress, one must be aware of the negative drawbacks that come with it as the opportunities for unscrupulous actors to exploit vulnerabilities and engage in fraudulent practices have expanded concurrently. This chapter discusses the negative influence of FinTech and explores various fraudulent services that have arisen due to technology's impact on finance. The aim is to examine the methods employed, associated risks, and outcomes of these deceptive activities while emphasizing effective strategies and recommended approaches for safeguarding ourselves against their harmful effects.

INTRODUCTION

Overview of the Transformation in Financial Technology and Its Influence on the Domain of Financial Services

A concise overview of the transformation in FinTech and its influence on financial services is presented. FinTech, short of financial technology, has brought profound changes in how people acquire and avail themselves of financial solutions. Specifically, FinTech refers to finance-related solutions that capitalize on advancements in information systems technology (Arner et al., 2015). Over time, there have been three distinct periods that distinguish different advancements in financial technology and alterations in the provision of financial services. The first era, known as FinTech 1.0 and from 1866 to 1987, witnessed substantial progress in technological infrastructure within the finance realm (Arner et al., 2015). This progress was instrumental in establishing global interconnectedness but relied heavily on traditional means to deliver financial services with only limited technology implementation. FinTech 2.0 emerged

DOI: 10.4018/979-8-3693-1388-6.ch004

between 1987 and 2008 and represented a significant shift toward digitizing processes involved in providing financial services (Arner et al., 2015). Computerized systems and electronic networks became popular during this period, bringing enhanced efficiency to operations within financial institutions that recognized the value of incorporating technology. Subsequently, after the global economic crisis of 2008 came FinTech 3.0—the current phase characterized by startups and tech-driven companies challenging conventional finance routes (Giglio, 2022); these enterprises leverage advanced technologies like artificial intelligence, and blockchain solutions, referencing specific instances when advances such as mobile applications for money matters were introduced innovation into highly efficient ways demanding them wholly (Khan et al., 2018). The advancements brought about by the FinTech revolution have fundamentally transformed financial services. By combining Finance with cutting-edge technology, FinTech has opened access to financial solutions for individuals previously excluded from traditional banking channels. These innovations have led to the development of reliable and cost-effective digital platforms that empower anyone to seamlessly avail themselves of diverse financial services (Nathan et al., 2020).

Financial technology (FinTech) boosts financial inclusion by providing credit and financing to those who didn't have access before. FinTech has expanded credit availability through alternative and peer-to-peer lending platforms, enabling those previously excluded from traditional banking systems to obtain funding (Nathan et al., 2020). Nevertheless, the swift growth of FinTech has presented challenges for regulators and market participants alike. The advent of fresh approaches and business models in FinTech has sparked concerns regarding consumer protection, data privacy, and systemic risks (Arner et al., 2015). Regulators are responsible for promoting innovation and ensuring stability and integrity within the financial system.

To sum up, the realm of FinTech has brought about a revolution in the world of financial services through the sophisticated utilization of technology to provide inventive and reachable financial solutions. This groundbreaking transformation has unfolded throughout three distinct periods, with the present phase marked by the ascent of startups and tech-savvy businesses in this domain. FinTech has not only broadened financial inclusion and enhanced credit accessibility but has also posed significant challenges for regulators tasked with managing risks and securing consumers.

Introduction to the Rise of Fraudulent Services in the FinTech Ecosystem

The emergence of FinTech has brought forth a plethora of advantages and advancements in the realm of financial services. Though, it has also given rise to deceptive schemes that exploit weaknesses within the FinTech ecosystem. Fraudulent activities in the FinTech domain present substantial hazards for consumers, financial institutions, and overall financial system stability. One particular technology that has played a dual role as both an instigator of innovation and a target for scams is blockchain. Serving as the foundation for numerous FinTech applications, blockchain technology offers transparency, immutability, and decentralization. However, it remains susceptible to security threats and attacks. Examining the safety measures employed by blockchain systems brings to light various vulnerabilities and documented instances of assaults directed at extensively used blockchains (Leong et al., 2017). These assaults encompass double-spending attacks, 51% attacks, and intelligent contract susceptibilities.

Understanding these security risks is crucial when developing resilient security measures to mitigate the dangers of fraudulent activities in the FinTech industry. In financial technology, deceitful services can take on various disguises. Identity theft, a prevalent form of fraud, involves crafty individuals stealing personal data to assume someone else's identity, gain unauthorized access to financial resources, or engage in deceitful practices. Investment scams are another type of fraud that entice victims with promises of great returns but ultimately lead to monetary losses. Moreover, there are instances where borrowers fall prey to deceptive lending platforms that make false commitments and impose exorbitant interest rates. To counteract the increasing presence of fraudulent services in the world of FinTech, it is imperative to implement a range of proactive measures. First and foremost, laying down robust security protocols becomes paramount in safeguarding user information while deterring any attempts at unlawful penetration. Such measures encompass implementing rigorous authentication procedures, employing advanced encryption methods, and conducting regular security assessments (James et al., 2023).

In addition, it is imperative to set up regulatory structures that guarantee the adherence of FinTech companies to stringent compliance standards and regulations for consumer protection. This encompasses performing extensive investigations on FinTech companies before granting them licenses to operate and consistently monitoring their operations to identify and prevent any instances of fraudulent behavior. Moreover, raising public awareness and promoting education plays a vital role in safeguarding individuals against the perils associated with deceptive services. By enlightening consumers about the potential risks of FinTech and offering guidance on recognizing and evading deceitful schemes, individuals can become empowered to make well-informed choices and shield themselves from financial fraud.

In summary, the emergence of deceitful services within the FinTech environment presents notable dangers to consumers and the financial sector. Comprehending the security risks and weaknesses associated with innovations like blockchain is imperative to devise comprehensive protective measures. To effectively combat fraudulent endeavors in FinTech, it becomes crucial to rigorously implement security protocols, establish appropriate regulatory frameworks, and prioritize public awareness through education initiatives. By engaging these pivotal strategies, we can fortify our defenses against illicit practices prevalent in this realm while empowering individuals with knowledge about plausible vulnerabilities.

Different Categories of Fraudulent Practices in Financial Technology (FinTech)

Fraudulent activities within the FinTech industry can manifest in various ways, posing substantial risks to consumers and the financial system. One form of fraud pertains to digital currencies like Bitcoin failing to meet the standards of legitimate money due to its lack of stability, low transaction volume, and pronounced volatility (Sapuric et al., 2013). Moreover, Bitcoin is exposed to hacking and theft dangers while lacking access to a banking system that offers deposit insurance coverage. Furthermore, it is limited to consumer credit or loan agreements (Wronka, 2023). Highlighting how Bitcoin's design principles and characteristics make it less amendable for regulatory supervision, Pournader et al. (2020) illustrate how this situation creates opportunities for fraudulent practices. Another fraudulent service prevalent in FinTech relates specifically to lending platforms. In one case study discussed by Una & Prabowo (2022), strategies were implemented to prevent fraud within FinTech lending setups. These strategies involve promoting financial literacy education among users, establishing a digital complaint service where individuals can report suspected fraud cases conveniently, and publishing information regarding legal versus illegal financial services on these platforms (Una & Prabowo, 2022). Additionally, supporting evidence from Najaf et al.'s research in 2020 signals that portfolios held by FinTech firms possess higher financial risk compared to those held by non-FinTech companies, thereby highlighting potential susceptibility to fraudulent activities within the FinTech lending sector itself (Najaf et al.,2020).

In addition, using machine learning and big data techniques in FinTech applications presents an opportunity to identify and prevent fraudulent activities. An article published in 2021 explores the use of machine learning to identify abnormalities within FinTech applications and anticipate future instances of fraud (Stojanović et al., 2021). Similarly, a study conducted by Liao et al. (2022) suggests employing a nonlinear activated beetle antennae search algorithm for detecting fraud in public trading companies, thereby emphasizing the significance of computational Finance approaches in identifying fraudulent financial behaviors (Liao et al., 2022). It should be noted that fraudulent activities present within FinTech encompass various forms, such as deception with digital currencies or deceptive lending platforms. To tackle this issue, measures including financial literacy education, complaint services, and implementing advanced technologies like machine learning can be vital in preventing and identifying fraudulent activities within the FinTech industry (Bhatnagar et al., 2022a, 2022b,2023a, 2023b; Dangwal et al., 2022a, 2022b; Kumar et al., 2023a, 2023b; Özen et al., 2022, Singh et al., 2021; Taneja et al., 2022a, 2022b; 2023a, 2023b, 2023c, 2023d, 2023e 2023f; Gupta et al. 2023; Dahiya 2023; Bansal 2023; Reepu 2023;).

TACTICS EMPLOYED BY FRAUDSTERS

Methods and Techniques Employed by Fraudsters to Exploit Vulnerabilities in FinTech Systems and Deceive Users

Fraudsters utilize various methods and strategies to exploit vulnerabilities in FinTech systems and deceive unsuspecting users. One commonly employed tactic is known as phishing, which involves deceitfully sending out emails or messages that appear to be from reputable financial institutions or FinTech platforms. These deceptive communications often contain links to fraudulent websites that mimic the layout and design of legitimate platforms, tricking users into providing their login credentials or personal information (Hu et al., 2019). Another technique utilized by fraudsters is malware and hacking. By developing malicious software or exploiting weak points within FinTech systems, these scammers gain unauthorized access to user accounts or steal sensitive data. This can entail using keyloggers to record user keystrokes, employing ransomware that encrypts user data until a payment is made, or employing remote access tools to allow manipulation of devices owned by individuals (Hassan, 2019). Fraudsters also employ social engineering tactics wherein they manipulate users psychologically by assuming identities trusted by targets. They use persuasive techniques to deceive individuals into revealing confidential details or performing actions advantageous to the criminals. Examples include impersonating customer support representatives via phone, requesting personal information over telephonic communication channels, and leveraging social media platforms to gather targeted information for future attacks (Jaccard et al., 2019).

Fraudsters take advantage of the vulnerabilities in FinTech systems' security and privacy. Because FinTech relies heavily on technology, it becomes susceptible to targeted attacks due to data storage, network infrastructure, and application security weaknesses. For instance, fraudsters exploit data-oriented safety shortcomings, facility and equipment protection loopholes, application security deficiencies, or service model insecurities to gain unauthorized access or manipulate information (Aklilu et al., 2021). FinTech companies employ diverse security measures to combat these fraudulent activities. These measures encompass multi-factor authentication techniques, encryption, and robust identity verification procedures.

Besides, continuous observation and examination of user behavior and transactions make it possible to identify suspicious activities and patterns that may indicate fraudulent actions. Employing machine learning and artificial intelligence algorithms makes it feasible to recognize abnormalities and recurring trends that suggest potential fraudulent behavior (Hu et al., 2019). In summary, individuals engaged in fraud employ diverse techniques to exploit vulnerabilities within FinTech systems to deceive users. These tactics comprise phishing, malware attacks, hacking endeavors, social engineering schemes, and taking advantage of security weaknesses and privacy gaps. Financial technology companies must adopt robust security measures while utilizing cutting-edge technologies for detecting and preventing fraudulent actions to safeguard users' financial interests effectively.

The instances of fraud related to financial technology have been witnessed in real-life situations across various contexts, underscoring the necessity for strong security measures and regulatory supervision. To illustrate, fraudulent practices during fund collection and misappropriation of assets have been detected in China's equity crowdfunding industry (Hua & Huang, 2020). These occurrences serve as valuable lessons for the sector by emphasizing the significance of implementing regulatory policies and safeguarding the interests of investors. In the United States, concerns regarding potential deception underpinned discussions surrounding FinTech lending platforms amidst the COVID-19 pandemic within the Paycheck Protection Program (PPP). Griffin et al. (2023) investigated how FinTech lenders facilitated PPP fraud cases and determined that suspicious loans were being forgiven at rates comparable to regular ones (Gfiffin et al., 2023). This highlights the crucial need for adequate surveillance systems centered on risk management and identification of fraudulent activities throughout FinTech lending operations. It is essential to recognize that instances of financial fraud extend beyond conventional financial institutions alone and seep into cloud-based FinTech systems. Criminal acts such as credit card information theft occur frequently, perpetuating economic loss alongside other forms of damage (Roberts et al., 2013).

Implementing robust security measures to safeguard user information and prevent illegal transactions cannot be emphasized enough. While machine learning algorithms have shown potential in detecting fraud, identifying fraudulent transactions can still pose a challenge due to the limited number of fraudulent cases compared to legitimate ones (Valavan & Rita, 2023). Nevertheless, employing predictive analysis and boosting classifiers can enhance fraud detection capabilities within FinTech applications. The implications of FinTech on accounting practices also give rise to concerns regarding fraud management. FinTech advancements, such as artificial intelligence (A.I.) and big data analysis, can enhance risk monitoring and identifying fraudulent activities (Bonsu et al., 2023).

However, integrating these progressions also leads to challenges that require proper focus to guarantee adequate control of deceptive practices. To sum up, actual manifestations of fraud related to financial technology emphasize the significance of enforcing robust security protocols, overseeing regulatory measures, and deploying efficient mechanisms for identifying fraudulent behavior. The dynamic nature of FinTech calls for consistent endeavors in outwitting deceitful actions and safeguarding users and the monetary framework.

VULNERABILITIES IN FINTECH PLATFORMS

Examination of the Vulnerabilities and Weaknesses in FinTech Platforms That Fraudsters Can Exploit

Fraudsters have the potential to exploit inherent vulnerabilities and weaknesses in FinTech platforms, which in turn pose risks for users. Various sources reveal insights into these vulnerabilities and their impact on FinTech platforms: According to (Tang et al., 2022), perceived risk factors such as financial risk, legal risk, and operational risk can hurt users' intention to utilize FinTech platforms. This indicates that individuals may be reluctant to adopt FinTech services due to concerns about potential financial losses, legal complications, and operational failures. Ng et al. (2022) emphasize the distinctive characteristics of FinTech platforms, including their vulnerability to public scrutiny and the need for cognitive legitimacy. FinTech platforms often cater to vulnerable segments of society and consequently attract greater attention from the public eye. This suggests that fraudsters could exploit these vulnerabilities to deceive users while undermining the legitimacy of FinTech platforms themselves. The dynamic regulatory landscape and competitive actions of market incumbents also present challenges for FinTech companies (Ng et al., 2023). Fraudsters might seize opportunities arising from regulatory gaps or engage in competitive acts by exploiting weaknesses within the regulatory framework, ultimately leading to fraudulent activities. In certain regions like Indonesia, where adequate regulations concerning consumer data protection are lacking, this poses an increased risk associated with FinTech payments (Afif et al., 2021).

Weak regulations in the FinTech industry can allow fraudsters to carry out cybercrime or launch cyberattacks, thus posing a threat to the security of payment systems. Concerns over security risks, such as the possible exposure of personal information and loss of control, may discourage individuals from adopting FinTech services (Despotovic et al., 2023). Fraudsters might illicitly obtain user data or commit identity theft by exploiting these vulnerabilities. FinTech platforms should enforce robust security measures, comply with regulatory standards, and enhance user understanding and awareness regarding potential dangers to counteract this risk.

Moreover, through consistent monitoring and diligent assessment of potential risks, we can effectively pinpoint and alleviate vulnerabilities that fraudsters may exploit. To sum up, it is crucial to acknowledge that the intrinsic susceptibilities and deficiencies present in FinTech platforms - encompassing perceived risks, regulatory hurdles, and security loopholes - are prone to exploitation by individuals engaging in fraudulent activities. Consequently, comprehending these weaknesses and implementing suitable measures to rectify them becomes imperative to uphold security and reliability surrounding FinTech platforms.

Discussion of How the Fast-Paced Nature of FinTech Innovation Can Sometimes Outpace Security Measures

FinTech innovation is known for its rapid pace, but sometimes this speed leaves security measures behind. As a result, FinTech platforms become exposed to exploitation by fraudsters. Various sources shed light on these susceptibilities and their consequences. Gomber et al. (2018) emphasize the significant security risks inherent in FinTech innovation, stressing the importance of information systems research in establishing strategies for effectively adopting and implementing FinTech innovations. Allen et al. (2021) discuss the regulatory challenges that arise for FinTech platforms and highlight the need to develop technology platforms that not only meet minimum regulatory requirements but also remain flexible enough to support additional requirements arising from the innovative nature of the business model. There is a necessity for efficient, secure, and reliable payment systems in FinTech, and examines how financial technology affects monetary and overall financial system stability (Ducas & Wilner, 2017). Finally, Alexandri et al. (2023) mention cybersecurity risks, regulatory issues, and customer trust as hurdles encountered during FinTech adoption in the banking industry; they stress the importance of understanding how FinTech innovation impacts investment decision-making processes.

Morgan (2022) stress the importance of implementing security and control measures to mitigate the risks connected with FinTech, underscoring how FinTech companies can face significant losses without adequate security measures. Varma et al. (2022), on their part, analyze FinTech innovation, examining its impact on business transformation and the issues surrounding security and investor trust. Their objective is to explore the disruptive potential of FinTech within the financial industry. Moreover, Irimia-Diéguez et al. (2023) delve into a discussion regarding perceived risks associated with FinTech innovation encompassing financial, legal, and security-related concerns along with operational risks and how these affect the adoption of FinTech solutions. In summary, the rapid pace of FinTech innovations can generate vulnerabilities within FinTech platforms that malevolent individuals may exploit for illegal purposes. Addressing these vulnerabilities requires a comprehensive approach involving robust security protocols, compliance with regulations, and continual monitoring while adapting to emerging risks in this ever-evolving landscape.

IMPLICATIONS OF FRAUDULENT SERVICES

Exploration of the Consequences of Falling Victim to FinTech-Related Fraud for individuals and the industry

Experiencing FinTech-related fraud can have significant ramifications for individuals and the industry. On an individual level, falling victim to scams associated with FinTech can manifest as direct financial losses, potential civil or criminal liabilities, and a loss of trust in FinTech platforms (Ng & Kwok, 2017). Such victims might face financial hardship while struggling to retrieve their stolen funds. Moreover, certain jurisdictions' lack of legal protection for borrowers can intensify the impact on individuals (Qadri et al., 2022). On a larger scale, the industry could endure consequences from fraudulent activities that erode public faith and confidence in FinTech platforms (An et al., 2021). Fraud incidents can negatively impact the industry's reputation and growth. Governments may impose stricter regulations to address the systemic risks associated with FinTech and improve consumer protection (Bouheni et al., 2023).

Besides, financial inclusion efforts can be hindered by the consequences of fraud. FinTech can enhance financial capability and provide access to financial services for individuals and small businesses (Panos & Wilson, 2020). Nevertheless, trust can be eroded, hindering the adoption of FinTech payment services and reducing the potential benefits for promoting financial inclusion (Coffie et al., 2021).

Moreover, becoming a target of fraud associated with FinTech can impact the willingness to use and embrace FinTech services. People may view certain risks related to Finance and fraudulent activities as deterrents in their decision-making process when utilizing FinTech platforms (Anshari et al., 2021). Consequently, this reluctance may cause a slowdown in the adoption rate of FinTech services and impede the sector's potential for expansion. To mitigate the repercussions of falling victim to FinTech-related fraud, implementing robust security measures, strengthening regulatory frameworks, and fostering financial literacy and awareness among users have become pivotal (Panos & Wilson, 2020). Establishing trustworthiness and instilling confidence in the reliability of FinTech platforms are crucial steps towards maintaining integrity within this field while simultaneously fostering its continuous growth.

Economic and Reputational Impact on Consumers, Businesses, and FinTech Providers

Individuals can face various economic repercussions as a result of fraud. These include direct monetary losses, potential legal fees, and the need to invest time and resources into recovering stolen funds (Gottschalk, 2010). Such financial setbacks can severely impact individuals' overall financial well-being and create ongoing financial challenges. The effects of fraudulent activities are not limited to personal finances; they also have significant implications for businesses and FinTech providers regarding reputation. When businesses fall victim to fraud, their customers may lose their trust and confidence. This loss of faith can translate into a decline in sales and damage the company's reputation (Guiso, 2010). FinTech providers specifically rely heavily on establishing trustworthiness with their customer base. Instances of fraud within the industry have the potential to erode that crucial trust factor, resulting in decreased consumer adoption and usage of FinTech services (Elsaid, 2021). The consequences go beyond individual incidents as they affect the entire industry. High-profile cases of fraud not only tarnish individual reputations but also negatively impact the perception people hold about the entire FinTech sector. Consequently, this kind of negative publicity may prompt increased regulatory scrutiny and lead to potential changes in regulatory frameworks (Panos & Wilson, 2020). Ultimately such changes entail additional compliance costs and burdensome regulations for those operating within FinTech services.

Moreover, the advancement of the FinTech industry can be hindered by occurrences of fraudulent activities. Such incidents can discourage prospective and venture capitalists from investing in FinTech startups. As a result, these startups need more access to capital, impeding their ability to innovate effectively (Roszkowska, 2021). Furthermore, a negative perception of fraud risks can slow organizations' and individuals' adoption of FinTech services. This curtails the industry's capacity to drive economic growth and facilitate financial inclusion (Ryu, 2018). Individuals and businesses must implement robust security measures to mitigate economic and reputational consequences from fraud in the FinTech sector. Solid authentication protocols and encryption technologies are vital factors that mitigate fraudulent activities related to FinTech (Mehrban, 2020). FinTech providers must prioritize security measures and efforts to prevent fraud to cultivate customer trust and instill confidence. Additionally, regulatory authorities play an essential role in upholding consumer protection regulations within the boundaries of the FinTech industry. Their active involvement ensures safeguarding consumers and maintaining integrity throughout this innovative financial technology space (Ahiabenu, 2022).

The Role of Regulation and Compliance

The issue of addressing FinTech-related fraud is complex, with various regulatory challenges that demand holistic solutions. The sources cited offer valuable insights into these challenges: FinTech firms face difficulties due to regulatory uncertainty and the absence of clear guidelines as they struggle to determine if their activities require specific approvals or licenses (Davis et al., 2017). Lacking definite regulatory frameworks can introduce ambiguity and hinder regulators' capacity to tackle fraud risks effectively. For smaller startups, compliance costs can be exorbitant (Florin et al., 2017). Such expenses strain resources and inhibit investment in robust measures for preventing fraudulent practices. Regulatory authorities encounter obstacles when combating cross-border FinTech activities (Cumming, 2023). Given the global reach of FinTech ventures, international cooperation becomes essential for harmonizing regulatory frameworks and efficiently addressing fraud risks.

The ever-changing landscape of FinTech innovation and the rapid emergence of novel technologies present a constant challenge for regulators to keep up with evolving fraud risks (Stewart & Jürjens, 2018). Regulators must continuously revise their frameworks to account for new types of fraud enabled by emerging technologies. Collaboration among regulatory authorities, financial institutions, and FinTech providers is vital in addressing fraud risks (Stojanović et al., 2021). Establishing effective communication lines and promoting information sharing can enhance the ability to detect and prevent fraudulent activities. Additionally, regulators and the industry face challenge from the reputational impact of fraudulent incidents. Balancing consumer protection with fostering innovation and growth in the FinTech sector is crucial for regulators. It is, therefore, necessary to establish comprehensive regulatory frameworks that provide clear guidance for FinTech firms while ensuring consumer protection (Ringe et al., 2020). Furthermore, regulatory authorities should encourage stakeholder collaboration and facilitate information sharing to strengthen efforts to detect and prevent fraud.

Mitigating FinTech-Related Fraud

To proactively identify and mitigate fraud risks, FinTech companies can employ several strategies:

1. It is of immense importance to incorporate resilient systems for identifying fraudulent activities. This involves employing advanced measures such as machine learning, data analytics, and artificial intelligence to pinpoint abnormalities and unravel trends that may indicate potential fraud (Gunasegaran et al., 2018).
2. FinTech firms must develop strong internal controls and implement risk management measures to detect and avert fraud. They should conduct periodic evaluations of potential risks, establish segregation of responsibilities, and enforce adequate procedures for authorization and approval processes (Wanyama, 2022).
3. Working collaboratively and exchanging information with professionals in the industry and regulatory authorities can significantly bolster efforts to prevent fraud. FinTech organizations can actively participate in forums dedicated to their field, allowing them to stay informed about the latest developments in fraudulent activities and preventive measures (Ng & Kwok, 2017). Additionally, forming alliances with cybersecurity firms can offer valuable access to specialized knowledge and advanced tools to thwart fraud attempts.
4. The timely detection of suspicious activities can be facilitated through continuous monitoring and real-time analysis of transactions.

FinTech companies can effectively address possible fraud incidents by utilizing technologies to monitor real-time transactions and analyze the data (Awotunde et al., 2021). To proactively manage fraud risks, these companies must adopt an approach that combines advanced technologies with robust internal controls, encourages collaboration, and promotes continuous monitoring.

Educating Users and Raising Awareness

Promoting responsible usage of FinTech services involves educating consumers about potential risks and red flags. A significant concern that affects their inclination to use such services is the perceived risks associated with them, including issues like misuse of personal information and privacy concerns (Pentury, 2023). When consumers are well-informed about these risks in FinTech, they tend to exercise caution and develop a skeptical attitude towards using such services. Hence, awareness plays a significant role in shaping their perception. Trust holds immense significance when adopting FinTech solutions, as it significantly impacts consumers' willingness to engage with these services (AlHajjaj & Ahmad, 2022). Within this context, FinTech companies are essential in raising awareness and promoting responsible usage by addressing key areas such as trust-building strategies, cyber-security threats, and privacy concerns (Peong & Tan, 2021). FinTech entities must prioritize certain aspects to maximize consumer adoption rates and encourage favorable usage behavior. These include focusing on interface characteristics that enhance user experience and engaging users through value co-creation practices while positioning marketing efforts strategically (Peong & Tan, 2021). Their collective impact can help establish long-lasting relationships with customers. To summarize, imparting knowledge regarding potential threats posed by FinTech services is vital for fostering responsible usage among consumers. Correspondingly, it becomes incumbent upon FinTech firms themselves to address these concerns effectively while building trust throughout their interactions with clients.

Collaborative Efforts: Industry, Government, and Consumers

Effectively combating fraud related to FinTech necessitates a collaborative technique that includes the participation of FinTech companies, regulatory agencies, law enforcement personnel, and consumer organizations. This collaboration addresses the risks associated with FinTech, such as fraud, security breaches, and privacy violations (Ryu, 2018). FinTech companies play a critical role by implementing strong security measures and internal procedures to minimize operational risks and safeguard customer data (Ryu, 2018). Regulatory bodies are responsible for creating and implementing regulations ensuring FinTech services' reliability and security (Ryu, 2018). Law enforcement agencies investigate fraudulent activities within the FinTech sector and bring perpetrators to justice (Stojanović et al., 2021). Consumer groups contribute significantly by raising awareness among users about potential risks while advocating for their rights (Stojanović et al., 2021). Successful initiatives have already been witnessed where these stakeholders have come together; one example is using machine learning algorithms to detect fraud in various FinTech applications (Stojanović et al., 2021). Through collaboration and sharing knowledge, resources, and information amongst themselves, matters about FinTech-related fraud can be effectively addressed, resulting in a more secure ecosystem that promotes safety for all involved parties.

CONCLUSION

Amidst the ever-changing world of financial technology (FinTech), where innovation drives convenience and accessibility, there is a constant threat: fraudulent services. These insidious practices hinder the transformative potential that technology possesses. This section has shed light on the intricacies surrounding financial tech fraud, exposing both the tactics employed by criminals and the vulnerabilities they exploit. The range of dangers extends from phishing scams to deceptive investment platforms. However, within these challenges emerges a glimmer of hope as industry entities, governments, and consumers unite in collaborative efforts. Just as FinTech solidifies its presence in society, countermeasures also evolve to combat illicit activities. Regulatory frameworks adapt to keep up with changing technologies while individuals' awareness grows. Nevertheless, this battle against fraudulent practices still persists. The widespread implications of FinTech-related deceit deeply impact economies and people's lives– a poignant reminder of the pressing need for understanding, prevention, and proactive measures. By staying vigilant and internalizing the critical insights from this chapter, stakeholders can lay down sturdy foundations for a future where FinTech attains its full potential while safely warding off dishonest elements at a distance. As we journey further into an ever-evolving landscape shaped by

FinTech advancements, the knowledge imparted within this chapter acts as our guiding light towards safeguarding against the darker side of nefarious innovations. Equipped with an understanding of fraud strategies, vulnerabilities, and effective countermeasures, take pride in building a more secure, fraud-resistant ecosystem that fosters trust.

REFERENCES

Afif, N., & Purwantini, A. H. (2022, December). The Paradox of Perceived Risk and Trust on Intention to Use Fintech Payment: Evidence in MSMEs. In *3rd Borobudur International Symposium on Humanities and Social Science 2021 (BIS-HSS 2021)* (pp. 645-648). Atlantis Press.

Ahiabenu, K. (2022). A Critical Analysis of the Regulatory Framework for the Financial Technology (FinTech) Sector in Ghana. *African Journal of Business & Economic Research, 17*(2), 109–128. doi:10.31920/1750-4562/2022/v17n2a5

Aklilu, Y. T., & Ding, J. (2021). Survey on blockchain for smart grid management, control, and operation. *Energies, 15*(1), 193. doi:10.3390/en15010193

Alexandri, M. B., Usman, I., Narimawati, U., & Taryana, A. (2023). Unraveling the Fintech Landscape: A Systematic Mapping Study on the Impact of Financial Technology Innovation on Investment Decision-Making in ASEAN Banking. *Khazanah Sosial, 5*(1), 113–124. doi:10.15575/ks.v5i1.24555

AlHajjaj, H. Z., & Ahmad, A. M. K. (2022). Drivers Of the Consumers Adoption Of FinTech Services. *Interdisciplinary Journal of Information, Knowledge, and Management, 17*, 259–285. doi:10.28945/4971

Allen, F., Gu, X., & Jagtiani, J. (2021). A survey of fintech research and policy discussion. *Review of Corporate Finance, 1*(3-4), 259–339. doi:10.1561/114.00000007

An, Y. J., Choi, P. M. S., & Huang, S. H. (2021). Blockchain, cryptocurrency, and artificial intelligence in finance. In *Fintech with artificial intelligence, big data, and blockchain* (pp. 1–34). Springer Singapore. doi:10.1007/978-981-33-6137-9_1

Anshari, M., Almunawar, M. N., Masri, M., & Hrdy, M. (2021). Financial technology with ai-enabled and ethical challenges. *Society, 58*(3), 189–195. doi:10.100712115-021-00592-w

Arner, D. W., Barberis, J., & Buckley, R. P. (2015). The evolution of Fintech: A new post-crisis paradigm. *SSRN, 47*, 1271. doi:10.2139srn.2676553

Awotunde, J. B., Adeniyi, E. A., Ogundokun, R. O., & Ayo, F. E. (2021). Application of big data with fintech in financial services. In *Fintech with Artificial Intelligence, Big Data, and Blockchain* (pp. 107–132). Springer Singapore. doi:10.1007/978-981-33-6137-9_3

Bansal, N., Bhatnagar, M., & Taneja, S. (2023). Balancing Priorities Through Green Optim000ism: A Study Elucidating Initiatives, Approaches, and Strategies for Sustainable Supply Chain Management. In *Handbook of Research on Designing Sustainable Supply Chains to Achieve a Circular Economy* (pp. 60–81). IGI Global. doi:10.4018/978-1-6684-7664-2.ch004

Ben Bouheni, F., Tewari, M., Sidaoui, M., & Hasnaoui, A. (2023). An econometric understanding of Fintech and operating performance. *Review of Accounting and Finance*, *22*(3), 329–352. doi:10.1108/RAF-10-2022-0290

Bhatnagar, M., Özen, E., Taneja, S., Grima, S., & Rupeika-Apoga, R. (2022a). The Dynamic Connectedness between Risk and Return in the Fintech Market of India: Evidence Using the GARCH-M Approach. *Risks*, *10*(11), 209. doi:10.3390/risks10110209

Bhatnagar, M., Taneja, S., Kumar, P., & Özen, E. (2023a). Does Financial Education Act as a Catalyst for SME Competitiveness. *International Journal of Education Economics and Development*, *1*(1), 1. doi:10.1504/IJEED.2023.10053629

Bhatnagar, M., Taneja, S., & Özen, E. (2022b). A wave of green start-ups in India—The study of green finance as a support system for sustainable entrepreneurship. *Green Finance*, *4*(2), 253–273. doi:10.3934/GF.2022012

Bhatnagar, M., Taneja, S., & Rupeika-Apoga, R. (2023b). Demystifying the Effect of the News (Shocks) on Crypto Market Volatility. *Journal of Risk and Financial Management*, *16*(2), 136. doi:10.3390/jrfm16020136

Bu, D., Hanspal, T., Liao, Y., & Liu, Y. (2022). Cultivating self-control in FinTech: Evidence from a field experiment on online consumer borrowing. *Journal of Financial and Quantitative Analysis*, *57*(6), 2208–2250. doi:10.1017/S0022109021000314

Chen, L., Tong, T. W., Tang, S., & Han, N. (2022). Governance and design of digital platforms: A review and future research directions on a meta-organization. *Journal of Management*, *48*(1), 147–184. doi:10.1177/01492063211045023

Coffie, C. P. K., Hongjiang, Z., Mensah, I. A., Kiconco, R., & Simon, A. E. O. (2021). Determinants of FinTech payment services diffusion by SMEs in Sub-Saharan Africa: Evidence from Ghana. *Information Technology for Development*, *27*(3), 539–560. doi:10.1080/02681102.2020.1840324

Cumming, D., Johan, S., & Reardon, R. (2023). Global fintech trends and their impact on international business: A review. *Multinational Business Review*, *31*(3), 413–436. doi:10.1108/MBR-05-2023-0077

Dahiya, K., Taneja, S., & Özen, E. (2023). To Analyse the Impact of Multi-Media Technology on the Rural Entrepreneurship Development. In Contemporary Studies of Risks in Emerging Technology, Part A (pp. 221-240). Emerald Publishing Limited. doi:10.1108/978-1-80455-562-020231015

Dangwal, A., Kaur, S., Taneja, S., & Taneja, S. (2022a). A Bibliometric Analysis of Green Tourism Based on the Scopus Platform. In J. Kaur, P. Jindal, & A. Singh (Eds.), *Developing Relationships, Personalization, and Data Herald in Marketing 5.0* (Vol. i, pp. 1–327). IGI Global. doi:10.4018/978-1-6684-4496-2.ch015

Dangwal, A., Taneja, S., Özen, E., Todorovic, I., & Grima, S. (2022b). Abridgement of Renewables: It's Potential and Contribution to India's GDP. *International Journal of Sustainable Development and Planning*, *17*(8), 2357–2363. doi:10.18280/ijsdp.170802

Davis, K., Maddock, R., & Foo, M. (2017). Catching up with Indonesia's fintech industry. *Law and Financial Markets Review, 11*(1), 33–40. doi:10.1080/17521440.2017.1336398

Despotović, A., Parmaković, A., & Miljković, M. (2023). Cybercrime and Cyber Security in Fintech. In *Digital Transformation of the Financial Industry: Approaches and Applications* (pp. 255–272). Springer International Publishing. doi:10.1007/978-3-031-23269-5_15

Ducas, E., & Wilner, A. (2017). The security and financial implications of blockchain technologies: Regulating emerging technologies in Canada. *International Journal (Toronto, Ont.), 72*(4), 538–562. doi:10.1177/0020702017741909

Elsaid, H. M. (2021). *A review of literature directions regarding the impact of fintech firms on the banking industry.* Qualitative Research in Financial Markets. doi:10.1108/QRFM-10-2020-0197

Florin, M. V., & Bürkler, M. T. (2017). *Introduction to the IRGC risk governance framework* (No. REP_WORK). EPFL.

Giglio, F. (2022). Fintech: A literature review. *International Business Research, 15*(1), 80–85. doi:10.5539/ibr.v15n1p80

Gomber, P., Kauffman, R. J., Parker, C., & Weber, B. W. (2018). On the fintech revolution: Interpreting the forces of innovation, disruption, and transformation in financial services. *Journal of Management Information Systems, 35*(1), 220–265. doi:10.1080/07421222.2018.1440766

Gottschalk, P. (2010). Categories of financial crime. *Journal of Financial Crime, 17*(4), 441–458. doi:10.1108/13590791011082797

Griffin, J. M., Kruger, S., & Mahajan, P. (2023). Did fintech lenders facilitate PPP fraud? *The Journal of Finance, 78*(3), 1777–1827. doi:10.1111/jofi.13209

Guiso, L. (2010). *A trist-driven financial crisis. implications for the future of financial markets.*

Gunasegaran, M., Basiruddin, R., Abdul Rasid, S. Z., & Mohd Rizal, A. (2018). The case studies of fraud prevention mechanisms in the Malaysian medium enterprises. *Journal of Financial Crime, 25*(4), 1024–1038. doi:10.1108/JFC-05-2017-0034

Gupta, M., Arora, R., & Taneja, S. (2023). Bibliometric Analysis on Employee Engagement and Human Resource Management. In *Enhancing Customer Engagement Through Location-Based Marketing* (pp. 185–205). IGI Global. doi:10.4018/978-1-6684-8177-6.ch013

Hassan, N. (2019). *Ransomware revealed.* Apress. doi:10.1007/978-1-4842-4255-1

Hu, Z., Ding, S., Li, S., Chen, L., & Yang, S. (2019). Adoption intention of fintech services for bank users: An empirical examination with an extended technology acceptance model. *Symmetry, 11*(3), 340. doi:10.3390ym11030340

Hua, X., & Huang, Y. (2021). Understanding China's fintech sector: Development, impacts and risks. *European Journal of Finance, 27*(4-5), 321–333. doi:10.1080/1351847X.2020.1811131

Irimia-Diéguez, A., Velicia-Martín, F., & Aguayo-Camacho, M. (2023). Predicting FinTech innovation adoption: The mediator role of social norms and attitudes. *Financial Innovation*, *9*(1), 1–23. doi:10.118640854-022-00434-6 PMID:36687792

James, E., & Rabbi, F. (2023). Fortifying the IoT Landscape: Strategies to Counter Security Risks in Connected Systems. *Tensorgate Journal of Sustainable Technology and Infrastructure for Developing Countries*, *6*(1), 32–46.

Jang-Jaccard, J., & Nepal, S. (2014). A survey of emerging threats in cybersecurity. *Journal of Computer and System Sciences*, *80*(5), 973–993. doi:10.1016/j.jcss.2014.02.005

Khan, M. A., & Salah, K. (2018). IoT security: Review, blockchain solutions, and open challenges. *Future Generation Computer Systems*, *82*, 395–411. doi:10.1016/j.future.2017.11.022

Kumar, P., Taneja, S., Özen, E., & Singh, S. (2023b). Artificial Intelligence and Machine Learning in Insurance: A Bibliometric Analysis. In Smart Analytics, Artificial Intelligence and Sustainable Performance Management in a Global Digitalised Economy (pp. 191-202). Emerald Publishing Limited. doi:10.1108/S1569-37592023000110A010

Kumar, P., Verma, P., Bhatnagar, M., Taneja, S., Seychel, S., Todorović, I., & Grim, S. (2023). The financial performance and solvency status of the indian public sector banks: A CAMELS rating and Z index approach. *International Journal of Sustainable Development and Planning*, *18*(2), 367–376. doi:10.18280/ijsdp.180204

Leong, C., Tan, B., Xiao, X., Tan, F. T. C., & Sun, Y. (2017). Nurturing a FinTech ecosystem: The case of a youth microloan startup in China. *International Journal of Information Management*, *37*(2), 92–97. doi:10.1016/j.ijinfomgt.2016.11.006

Mehrban, S., Nadeem, M. W., Hussain, M., Ahmed, M. M., Hakeem, O., Saqib, S., & Khan, M. A. (2020). Towards secure FinTech: A survey, taxonomy, and open research challenges. *IEEE Access: Practical Innovations, Open Solutions*, *8*, 23391–23406. doi:10.1109/ACCESS.2020.2970430

Mirza, N., Elhoseny, M., Umar, M., & Metawa, N. (2023). Safeguarding FinTech innovations with Machine Learning: Comparative Assessment of Various Approaches. *Research in International Business and Finance*, *66*, 102009. doi:10.1016/j.ribaf.2023.102009

Morgan, P. J. (2022). Assessing the risks associated with green digital finance and policies for coping with them. In *Green Digital Finance and Sustainable Development Goals* (pp. 51–68). Springer Nature Singapore. doi:10.1007/978-981-19-2662-4_3

Najaf, K., Schinckus, C., & Yoong, L. C. (2020). VaR and market value of fintech companies: An analysis and evidence from global data. *Managerial Finance*, *47*(7), 915–936. doi:10.1108/MF-04-2020-0169

Nathan, J., & Jacobs, B. (2020). Blockchain consortium networks: Adding security and trust in financial services. *Journal of Corporate Accounting & Finance*, *31*(2), 29–33. doi:10.1002/jcaf.22428

Ng, A. W., & Kwok, B. K. (2017). Emergence of Fintech and cybersecurity in a global financial centre: Strategic approach by a regulator. *Journal of Financial Regulation and Compliance*, *25*(4), 422–434. doi:10.1108/JFRC-01-2017-0013

Ng, E., & Pan, S. L. (2022). Competitive strategies for ensuring Fintech platform performance: Evidence from multiple case studies. *Information Systems Journal*, isj.12406. doi:10.1111/isj.12406

Ng, E., Tan, B., Sun, Y., & Meng, T. (2023). The strategic options of fintech platforms: An overview and research agenda. *Information Systems Journal*, *33*(2), 192–231. doi:10.1111/isj.12388

Osei-Assibey Bonsu, M., Wang, Y., & Guo, Y. (2023). Does fintech lead to better accounting practices? Empirical evidence. *Accounting Research Journal*, *36*(2/3), 129–147. doi:10.1108/ARJ-07-2022-0178

Özen, E., & Sanjay, T. (2022a). Empirical Analysis of the Effect of Foreign Trade in Computer and Communication Services on Economic Growth in India. *Journal of Economics and Business Issues*, *2*(2), 24–34.

Panos, G. A., & Wilson, J. O. (2020). Financial literacy and responsible finance in the FinTech era: Capabilities and challenges. *European Journal of Finance*, *26*(4-5), 297–301. doi:10.1080/1351847X.2020.1717569

Pentury, F. (2023). The Role Of Knowledge and Penetration Of FinTech Services In Improving Msmes Of Fishermen And Marine Farmers In Remote Small Islands Region. *Jurnal Manajemen Teori Dan Terapan [Journal of Theory and Applied Management]*, *1*(16), 23-37. doi:10.20473/jmtt.v16i1.43743

Peong, K. K. & Tan, K. (2021). Behavioural Intention Of Commercial Banks' Customers Towards Financial Technology Services. *GATR Journal of Finance and Banking Review*, *5*(4), 10-27. doi:10.35609/jfbr.2021.5.4(2)

Pournader, M., Shi, Y., Seuring, S., & Koh, S. L. (2020). Blockchain applications in supply chains, transport and logistics: A systematic review of the literature. *International Journal of Production Research*, *58*(7), 2063–2081. doi:10.1080/00207543.2019.1650976

Qadri, R. A., Nabilah, I., & Ambarwati, R. D. (2022). Black-or-White of Online Lending in Indonesia: Conventional Platform or Sharia Scheme (A Netnography Study). *Jurnal Ilmiah Akuntansi dan Bisnis*, *17*(2), 184-200.

Reepu, R., Taneja, S., Ozen, E., & Singh, A. (2023). A Globetrotter to the Future of Marketing: Metaverse. In *Cultural Marketing and Metaverse for Consumer Engagement* (pp. 1–11). IGI Global. doi:10.4018/978-1-6684-8312-1.ch001

Ringe, W. G., & Christopher, R. U. O. F. (2020). Regulating Fintech in the EU: The Case for a Guided Sandbox. *European Journal of Risk Regulation*, *11*(3), 604–629. doi:10.1017/err.2020.8

Roberts, L. D., Indermaur, D., & Spiranovic, C. (2013). Fear of cyber-identity theft and related fraudulent activity. *Psychiatry, Psychology and Law*, *20*(3), 315–328. doi:10.1080/13218719.2012.672275

Roszkowska, P. (2021). Fintech in financial reporting and audit for fraud prevention and safeguarding equity investments. *Journal of Accounting & Organizational Change*, *17*(2), 164–196. doi:10.1108/JAOC-09-2019-0098

Ryu, H. (2018). Understanding Benefit and Risk Framework Of FinTech Adoption: Comparison Of Early Adopters And Late Adopters. *Proceedings of the 51st Hawaii International Conference on System Sciences*. Scholar Space. 10.24251/HICSS.2018.486

Ryu, H. S. (2018). *Understanding benefit and risk framework of fintech adoption: Comparison of early adopters and late adopters*.

Sapuric, S., Kokkinaki, A., & Georgiou, I. (2022). The relationship between Bitcoin returns, volatility and volume: Asymmetric GARCH modeling. *Journal of Enterprise Information Management*, *35*(6), 1506–1521. doi:10.1108/JEIM-10-2018-0228

Singh, V., Taneja, S., Singh, V., Singh, A., & Paul, H. L. (2021). Online advertising strategies in Indian and Australian e-commerce companies:: A comparative study. *Big Data Analytics for Improved Accuracy, Efficiency, and Decision Making in Digital Marketing*, 124–138. doi:10.4018/978-1-7998-7231-3.ch009

Stewart, H., & Jürjens, J. (2018). Data security and consumer trust in FinTech innovation in Germany. *Information and Computer Security*, *26*(1), 109–128. doi:10.1108/ICS-06-2017-0039

Stojanović, B., Bozic, J., Hofer-Schmitz, K., Nahrgang, K., Weber, A., Badii, A., Sundaram, M., Jordan, E., & Runevic, J. (2021). Follow the Trail: Machine Learning For Fraud Detection In FinTech Applications. *Sensors (Basel)*, *5*(21), 1594. doi:10.339021051594 PMID:33668773

Stojanović, B., Božić, J., Hofer-Schmitz, K., Nahrgang, K., Weber, A., Badii, A., Sundaram, M., Jordan, E., & Runevic, J. (2021). Follow the trail: Machine learning for fraud detection in Fintech applications. *Sensors (Basel)*, *21*(5), 1594. doi:10.339021051594 PMID:33668773

Taneja, S., Bhatnagar, M., Kumar, P., & Grima, S. (2023c). A panel analysis of the effectiveness of the asset management in Indian agricultural companies. *International Journal of Sustainable Development and Planning*, *18*(3), 653–660. doi:10.18280/ijsdp.180301

Taneja, S., Bhatnagar, M., Kumar, P., & Rupeika-apoga, R. (2023b). India ' s Total Natural Resource Rents (NRR) and GDP : An Augmented Autoregressive Distributed Lag (ARDL) Bound Test. *Journal of Risk and Financial Management*, *16*(2), 91. doi:10.3390/jrfm16020091

Taneja, S., Gupta, M., Bhushan, P., Bhatnagar, M., & Singh, A. (2023f). Cultural Marketing in the Digital Era. In *Cultural Marketing and Metaverse for Consumer Engagement* (pp. 109–122). IGI Global. doi:10.4018/978-1-6684-8312-1.ch008

Taneja, S., Jaggi, P., Jewandah, S., & Ozen, E. (2022b). Role of Social Inclusion in Sustainable Urban Developments: An Analyse by PRISMA Technique. *International Journal of Design & Nature and Ecodynamics*, *17*(6), 937–942. doi:10.18280/ijdne.170615

Taneja, S., Kaur, S., & Özen, E. (2022a). Using green finance to promote global growth in a sustainable way. *International Journal of Green Economics*, *16*(3), 246–257. doi:10.1504/IJGE.2022.128930

Taneja, S., & Özen, E. (2023a). To analyse the relationship between bank's green financing and environmental performance. *International Journal of Electronic Finance*, *12*(2), 163–175. doi:10.1504/IJEF.2023.129919

Taneja, S., & Ozen, E. (2023d). Impact of the European Green Deal (EDG) on the agricultural carbon (CO2) emission in Turkey. *International Journal of Sustainable Development and Planning*, *18*(3), 715–727. doi:10.18280/ijsdp.180307

Taneja, S., & Sharma, V. (2023e). Role of Beaconing Marketing in Improving Customer Buying Experience. In *Enhancing Customer Engagement Through Location-Based Marketing* (pp. 176–184). IGI Global. doi:10.4018/978-1-6684-8177-6.ch012

Una, B. K., & Prabowo, H. Y. (2022). Fintech lending fraud prevention strategy: A case study. *Journal of Contemporary Accounting*, 37-52.

Valavan, M., & Rita, S. (2023). Predictive-Analysis-based Machine Learning Model for Fraud Detection with Boosting Classifiers. *Computer Systems Science and Engineering*, *45*(1), 231–245. doi:10.32604/csse.2023.026508

Varma, P., Nijjer, S., Sood, K., Grima, S., & Rupeika-Apoga, R. (2022). Thematic Analysis of Financial Technology (Fintech) Influence on the Banking Industry. *Risks*, *10*(10), 186. doi:10.3390/risks10100186

Wanyama, D., & Mwikya, J. (2022). *Internal Control Measures On Fraud Detection and Prevention in Fintech Companies in Kenya.* Kirinyaga University

Wronka, C. (2023). Financial crime in the decentralized finance ecosystem: New challenges for compliance. *Journal of Financial Crime*, *30*(1), 97–113. doi:10.1108/JFC-09-2021-0218

Chapter 5
Perceived Risks With Technology Acceptance Model in Online Shopping

Kapil Sharma
https://orcid.org/0000-0001-8244-8009
Chandigarh University, India

Yogesh Kumar
Chandigarh University, India

Rajiv Khosla
DAV College, India

Sanjay Taneja
https://orcid.org/0000-0002-3632-4053
Graphic Era University (Deemed), India

ABSTRACT

Based on technological acceptance models and perceived risks, this study examines and assesses the variables affecting customer intentions to make online transactions in Indian state Haryana. Three hundred-eight valid responses were obtained from the poll, which was performed online. The Smart PLS 3.0 application and structural equation modeling methods were used to examine the data. The results showed that perceived utility, danger, and simplicity of use all positively affected online purchase intentions. In contrast, perceived risk apprehensions have a detrimental impact on plans to make purchases online. The study focused on how online purchase intentions are impacted by perceived usability, perceived risk, along with perceived ease of use. Future research has to take other factors into account.

DOI: 10.4018/979-8-3693-1388-6.ch005

INTRODUCTION

More than 4 billion people will utilize the internet by the year 2020, according to Internet World Stats (2015). The majority (50.3%) of internet users are from the Asian area. Second on the list, among the nations behind China, is India. With a presentation of achieved 692 million subscribers, India placed second in Asia's greatest considerable internet use presentation, according to Annur (2019). It is impossible to distinguish the growing number of internet users in India from those who conduct online transactions. An estimated 1.8 billion people made online purchases in 2018 around the globe. Internet sales have reached $2.8 billion due to the average number of users globally, and they are expected to reach $4.8 billion by 2021. (Statista, 2019).

According to Statista (2019), online business transactions are available everywhere there is an internet connection, including at home, at the workplace, in a public space, and on devices like PCs, cellphones, and tablets (Ariffin et al., 2018). Nowadays, it is a commonplace to utilize an online shopping system to buy things like airline tickets, hotel bookings, movie tickets, clothes, and cosmetics. Travel-related items, which had an overall score of 82.2 percent among the things customers bought online, were followed by general goods (59%) and books (69%) (Ariffin et al., 2018). E-commerce has changed how consumers think about getting products and services. Scholars and marketers have focused their attempts on better comprehending online purchase behavior as online transactions and clients have grown in popularity (Lim, 2015). Businesses engaged in e-commerce need to monitor the expansion of online spending and understand the elements influencing buyers' choice to make a purchase online (Marron & Steel, 2000; Lohse & Spiller, 1998). One of the 2 major features that influence the behavior of a customer while shopping is their desire to buy (Mayer et al., 1995; Muncy & Wilkie, 1987).

In studies on the elements that affect consumers' online shopping decisions, several models are used. The adoption of new technologies has often been assessed utilizing the TAM ("Technology Acceptance Model"). To comprehend the elements of acceptance of IT or driving user adoption, Davis (1985) created the TAM. These elements are utility and usability. The literature studies have effectively used the technology acceptance model to look at people's intentions and behavior when they purchase online (Pavlou, 2003; Gefen et al., 2003a; b). A technological acceptance model was proposed in the earlier investigation to assess the elements affecting the adoption of e-shopping technologies (Mpinganjira, 2016). Investigators have deemed e-shopping to accept the usage of IT systems since it revolves around utilizing mobile apps and web apps to buy goods as well as services. The technological acceptance model may help in understanding e-commerce adoption since it has been applied to online transactions.

Among the most important elements that influence customer inclination to purchase online is perceived risk. Given that buyers do not personally contact sellers or the products in question while making an online purchase, the risk for customers is increased (Jarvenpaa et al., 2000; Pavlou, 2003). Product risk and financial risk are 2 potential dangers that internet shoppers may encounter (Bhatnagar et al., 2000). Perceived risk's impact on online purchase intentions has been studied extensively. Nevertheless, the outcomes of certain investigations varied. Perceived risk is a characteristic that influences online purchasing intentions adversely, according to earlier research (Chiu, 2014; Almousa, 2011; Ha et al., 2020; Ariffin, 2018; Clement, 2019; Pires et al., 2006; Singh & Srivastava, 2018; Prayag et al., 2009). Gefen et al. (2003) discovered that there is no correlation between the desire to purchase online and perceived risk. As per Ventre & Kolbe (2020), intentions for online purchases were unaffected by perceived risk. Therefore, to analyse customer intentions in Indian online buying, this research integrates perceived risk with the technological acceptance model.

Through the technological acceptance model and perceived risk, the theoretical models presented in this study contribute to the existing body of information by encouraging consumer adoption intentions and by offering helpful information that will advance standard practice. The next part provides the research's theoretical framework. The notion that follows contains a model of technical adoption as well as perceived dangers that have been examined for their influence on online purchase intentions. Research hypotheses are developed in accordance with the given literature. Along with the results, the study's methodology is also discussed. Finally, this study evaluates the limits, future research paths, as well as practical and theoretical implications.

LITERATURE REVIEW

Technology Acceptance Model

The TAM stigmatizes customers who utilize information technology by using behavioral theory concepts (Lee et al., 2011). PU (Perceived utility), PEOU ("Perceived Ease of Use"), attitude (ATT), as well as intention utilized as endogenic key elements, are exogenous crucial words (Zhang et al., 2017). As per Davis (1985), PEOU denotes an individual's perception of the simplicity of using technology. PEOU makes someone think that using such systems doesn't need much work (Davis, 1985). The TAM includes PEOU. The TAM hypothesis places a strong emphasis on convenience and advantages for its consumers, and this ease element is connected to how operational transactions occur online. As per Davis, PU is known as the extent to which a user feels that applying a certain technique would strengthen their task and productivity (1985). According to Kim (2016), ATT refers to someone who develops a positive/negative attitude towards adopting a specific technology, which results in the goal to utilize that technology and the determination of that technology (Wang et al., 2012). Davis (1985) created the TAM to forecast user acceptance of the technology they utilize. The study's grand theory for the technological adoption paradigm was the TRA ("Theory of Reason Action"). The theory examines people's actions and attitudes. The TRA model's elements are included in the technology acceptance model as distinct information technology domains (Bhatnagar et al., 2022a, 2022b,2023a, 2023b; Dangwal et al., 2022a, 2022b; Jangir et al. 2023, Kumar et al., 2023; Özen et al., 2022a 2022b; Singh et al., 2021; Taneja et al., 2022a, 2022b; Taneja et al., 2023a, 2023b, 2023c, 2023d, 2023e, 2023f, 2023g, 2023h, 2023i, 2023j, 2023k). The positioning of attitude components from TRA, however, is what makes (TAM and TRA) distinct from one another. The PU and PEOU variables are introduced by the TAM to forecast user adoption of computer technology.

Perceived Risk (PR)

As per Schierz (2010), PR is a prediction of losses. Customers will be exposed to a higher degree of risk the more loss is possible. PR is defined by Laroche (2005) as an adverse view of unforeseen and unpredictable results from acquired items. A buyer's perception of modifications and negative effects associated with the acquisition of a product and service is defined as perceived risk, according to Ko (2004). This idea consists of two parts: uncertainty and consequence. Indecision is used to express the potential for a negative outcome, while loss's importance is used to explain it as a result (Laroche et al., 2005). PR includes safety, time, psychological hazards, financial, social, as well as performance, according to Pavlou and Featherman (2003). In addition, Garner (1986) identified six more elements of PR: time, performance, financial, social, and psychological hazards. Physical danger, operational risk, financial risk, and psychological risk are the four characteristics of PR in purchasing intentions, according to Bhukya & Singh (2015). Products, finances, privacy, social security, time, and psychology are some of the perceived multi-dimensional hazards in the setting of the online market, with an online shopping framework that is more intense than other aspects (Han & Kim, 2017). Product, security, and financial risks are the most significant, according to Almousa (2011). In this study, we quantify the effects of six different sources of potential danger on consumers' propensity to shop online: time risk, financial risk, security risk, product risk, psychological risk, & social risk (Ariffin et al., 2018).

Online Purchase Intention (OPT)

It is a variable that predicts how consumers will behave while utilizing the Internet to complete transactions (Wagner Mainardes 2019). In addition, OPT is often believed to result from a number of motivational aspects that consumers experience (Pappas et al., 2017; Diallo & Siqueira, 2017). A shopping cart, a search function, a price comparison sheet, website confidence, and an online payment mechanism are all available on an e-commerce website. It is believed that a customer is more likely to purchase from a nearby shop (Liao & Wong, 2008). Therefore, the significance of each connected component plays a crucial function in drawing customers and sustaining sales. Buyer attitude along with subjective criteria are the 2 main factors that affect behavioral intentions with regard to personality traits (Chen & Yang, 2019). OPT refers to a buyer's propensity to depict a fixed activity (like purchasing) in a fixed setting (like online retailers) (Ventre & Kolbe, 2020).

HYPOTHESIS

When adopting a technology, people should take into account variables that might eventually affect how they feel about their desire to use the technology (Li et al., 2019). As per Davis (1985), PEOU, as well as PU, have a direct effect on intentions. Previous studies have looked at aspects of the TAM in different circumstances and discovered that PEOU and PU had a favorable impact on attitudes (Li 2019; Dutot 2019). Other research indicates that mindset has a substantial impact on OPT (Dutot et al., 2019). So, the following are the research's hypotheses:

H_1: PU has been a positive impact on ATT.
H_2: PU has been a positive impact on OPT.
H_3: PEOU has been a positive impact on ATT.
H_4: PEOU has been a positive impact on OPT.
H_5: ATT has been a positive impact on OPT.

PR has a strong influence on consumers' intentions to make purchases. The way consumers perceive risk influences their actions and choices significantly (Ko et al., 2004). When making an online purchase, customers perceive a greater level of risk than when making a physical store purchase. Customers who are more at risk are less likely to make online purchases of goods and services (Tan & Lee, 2003). It is inferable that buyers' intentions to make online purchases are adversely affected by PR (Liu & Wei,

2003). According to Kim (2016), client buying propensities decrease as online business risk increases. Perceived risks undermine customers' aspirations to make online purchases. According to the consumers' propensity to make online purchases decreases as they become aware that the transaction is risky (Ahmed & Akhlaq, 2015) (Fig 1). Adu (2020)'s study investigates if PR has an adverse effect on attitudes and OPT. Thus, researchers propose the hypothesis mentioned below.

H_6: PR has been a negative impact on ATT.
H_7: PR has been a negative impact on OPT.

Figure 1. Conceptual framework
Source: Researchers Concept

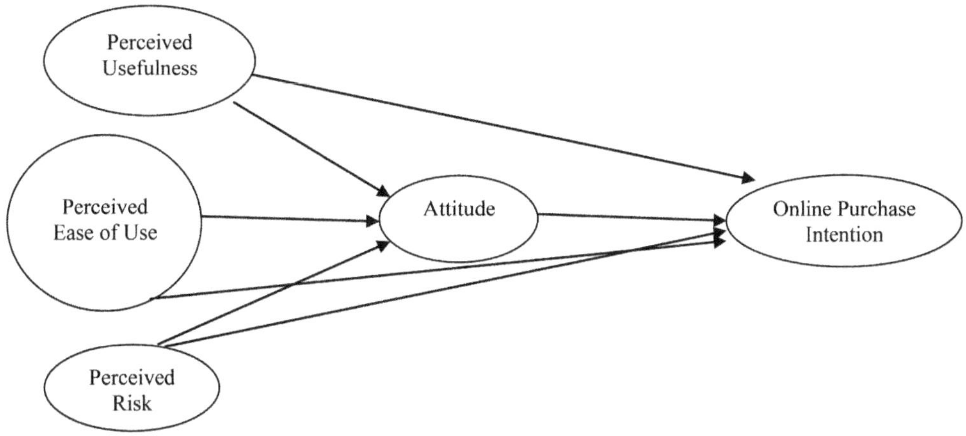

RESEARCH METHODS

Internet users in various major Indian cities, including Ambala, Karnal, Faridabad, Rohtak, Hisar, and Gurgaon, have received 338 surveys. Respondents are given questionnaires as part of the data collection process. A Likert scale was used as the measurement in this experiment. The Likert scale used a 1 (strongly agree) to a 5 scale (strongly disagree). Prior to now, assessing things for perceived utility (4 items) and perceived usability (4 items) (Davis, 1985). In the research, six perceived risk items were used (Ariffin et al., 2018). In this assessment, the attitude was measured by 3 items (Taylor & Todd, 1995). 3 elements were finally modified from Pappas (2017). It is utilized to assess internet shopping intentions. Partial Least Square (PLS) analysis was employed in this work, and data processing technologies, specifically Smart PLS programs, were utilized.

RESULTS

Demographic Profile

A representative demographic profile from the research is shown in Table 1. Male respondents made up 24.7% of the sample, compared to female respondents, who made up 75.3%. 80.4% of respondents were between the ages of 21 and 30; 10.4% were under 20; 5.2% were between the age 31 and 40; & 3.9% were above 41. Regarding income, 20.7 percent participants earned in between Rs. 1,500,000 to Rs. 1,999,999, 25.6% of respondents earned between Rs. 2,000,000 to Rs. 2,499,999, 29.8 percent earned between Rs. 2,500,000 to Rs. 2,999,999, and 23.7 percent earned between Rs. 3,000,000. Housewives make up 4.5 percent of total employment, followed by civil servants at 13.6 percent, private employees at 35.7 percent, self-employed workers at 30.5 percent, employees of cafés at 5.8 percent, consultants at 7.14 percent, and pharmacy assistants at 3.89 percent.

Table 1. Demographic profile

	N	%
Gender		
Woman	232	75.3
Man	76	24.7
Age		
<20 years	32	10.5
21 to 30 years	246	80.4
31 to 40 years	18	5.2
>41 years	12	3.9
Income		
Rs. 1.500.000 to Rs. 1.999.999	64	20.7
Rs. 2.000.000 to Rs. 2.499.999	79	25.6
Rs. 2.500.000 to Rs. 2.999.999	92	29.8
> Rs. 3.000.000	73	23.7
Work		
Civil Servants	42	13,6
Housewife	14	4.5
Private Employees	110	35.7
Cafe Employees	18	5.8
Self-employed	94	30.5
Pharmacist's Assistant	12	3.89
Consultants	22	7.14

Source: Output Descriptive Analysis

Evaluation of Measurement Model (Outer Model)

The link between the contract and the indicator is evaluated as part of the measurement model assessment. When using data analysis methods with Smart PLS, the 3 criteria utilized to evaluate outer models are composite reliability, convergent validity, and discriminant validity. Table 2 reveals that all of the study's indicators had outer loading values greater than 0.7. Chin (1998) states that the loading value has to be greater than or equivalent to 0.7 in order to be valid for convergence. As a result, the variables examined in this research have been approved as practicable or reliable for use in research and may be used in further studies.

In this part, the results of the discriminant validity tests will be reported. In order to assess the discriminant validity, a cross-loading value is utilized. A measure is considered to have discriminant validity only if its cross-loading value is greater than that of other variables (Ghozali, 2013). The cross-loading value for every sign on the research factor has the most significance in comparison to the cross-loading value for other variables, and it can be inferred from Table 3 that this is the case. It follows logically from the findings that the indicators utilized in this research had exceptional discriminant validity when they were used to create the relevant variables. CR ("Composite reliability"), AVE ("Average variance"), as well as Cronbach's Alpha, were the reliability metrics used in this study (Fornell & Larcker, 1981; Chin, 1998; Hair, 2014). The results show that Cronbach's Alpha and CR values were greater than 0.7 and that the values of AVE for every variable were greater than 0.5, respectively. The study findings in Table 2 may be accepted.

Structural Model Testing (Inner Model)

Once the measurement model has passed all relevant tests, the structural model will next be put to the test. In this research, the structural model (inner model) test will be examined in connection to the path coefficient test and conclusions of the goodness of fit path coefficient test. The path coefficient test illustrates how strongly independent factors have an impact on dependent variables. The endogenous variable's influences are found using the coefficient determination (R-Square) method.

The R2-dependent latent variable is utilized to evaluate the Goodness of Fit model (Chin, 1998). The influence of exogenous factors on endogenous variables (which are impacted) is shown by endogenous latent variables in structural models having a 0.67 R-Square value or above, which falls into the excellent category. The result is categorized as medium if it is between 0.33 & 0.67, and it is categorized as weak if it is between 0.19 & 0.33. The R^2 value for the ATT variable was 0.684, as per the study's findings. According to value acquisition, PR, PU, and PEOU accounted for 68.4% of the degree of customer attitude. Consequently, the OPT variable of 0.852 is used, given the obtained R-Square value. The figure illustrates how an ATT of 85.2% would explain the prevalence of OPT.

Table 2. Model measurement results

Construct	Items	Mean	Outer Loading	AVE	CR	Cronbach's Alpha
Perceived	PU1	4.500	0.729	0.645	0.879	0.821
Usefulness	PU2	4.503	0.788			
	PU3	3.867	0.839			
	PU4	4.065	0.850			
Perceived	PEOU1	3.912	0.871	0.735	0.917	0.880
Ease of Use	PEOU2	3.802	0.823			
	PEOU3	4.049	0.875			
	PEOU4	4.065	0.861			
Perceived	PR1	3.838	0.735	0.641	0.914	0.886
Risk	PR2	3.951	0.718			
	PR3	3.802	0.729			
	PR4	3.903	0.864			
	PR5	3.899	0.896			
	PR6	3.763	0.842			
Attitude	ATT1	3.873	0.902	0.645	0.868	0.770
	ATT2	3.318	0.794			
	ATT2	4.049	0.786			
Online	OPT1	3.873	0.846	0.773	0.911	0.854
Purchase	OPT2	3.318	0.904			
Intention	OPT3	3.458	0.886"			

Source: Output SPSS

Hypothesis Test

Table 4 displays the analysis findings, and it can be shown that PU significantly and positively affects ATT and OPT with p-values of 0.013 and 0.001, respectively. The first and second hypotheses were accepted in light of this finding. This finding suggests whether the third and fourth hypotheses are accepted since PEOU has a substantial positive influence on ATT with 0.004 p-values and OPT with 0.012 p-values. Attitude is adversely impacted by PR with a -0.031 p-value, while OPT is negatively impacted with a -0.014 p-value. The 6th hypothesis, as well as the point, are accepted as a consequence of this finding, which supports the research hypothesis that was used in the prior study. With a p-value of 0.002, the attitude does, nonetheless, have a significant and advantageous effect on the decision to make an online purchase. These results suggest that the potential risks of e-commerce adoption negatively affect consumers' inclinations to make purchases online.

Table 3.

	PEOU	PR	PU	ATT	OPT
A1.1	0.546	0.522	0.729	0.388	0.737
A1.2	0.531	0.585	0.788	0.463	0.876
A1.3	0.657	0.643	0.839	0.653	0.993
A1.4	0.861	0.708	0.850	0.704	0.883
A2.1	0.871	0.728	0.717	0.608	0.473
A2.2	0.823	0.654	0.583	0.651	0.563
A2.3	0.875	0.667	0.697	0.786	0.525
A2.4	0.861	0.708	0.850	0.704	0.583
A3.1	0.613	0.735	0.607	0.636	0.589
A3.2	0.641	0.718	0.554	0.615	0.491
A3.3	0.633	0.729	0.593	0.505	0.440
A3.4	0.641	0.864	0.639	0.596	0.545
A3.5	0.699	0.896	0.705	0.647	0.571
A3.6	0.614	0.842	0.613	0.584	0.561
B3.1	0.669	0.652	0.732	0.602	0.646
B3.2	0.483	0.553	0.762	0.694	0.704
B3.3	0.470	0.547	0.743	0.608	0.586
C.1	0.669	0.652	0.632	0.902	0.846
C.2	0.483	0.553	0.462	0.794	0.704
C.3	0.675	0.667	0.697	0.786	0.525

Source: Output SPSS

Table 4. Hypothesis test

Hypothesis	Influence	T-Statistics	*P-Values*	Result
H_1	PU – ATT	3.248	0.013	Accepted
H_2	PU – OPT	5.361	0.001	Accepted
H_3	PEOU – ATT	9.491	0.004	Accepted
H_4	PEOU – OPT	7.523	0.012	Accepted
H_5	ATT – OPT	8.820	0.002	Accepted
H_6	PR – ATT	5.954	- 0.031	Accepted
H_7	PR – OPT	4.001	- 0.014	Accepted

Source: Output Smart PLS

DISCUSSION

The research's main objective was to integrate the technological acceptance model with other theories, such as PR, to evaluate the influence of online buying intentions. The technology adoption model is frequently utilized in studies to look at how people utilize new technologies (Li et al., 2019; Kim, 2016). It is crucial for PR to influence customers' intentions to make purchases. The degree to which consumers perceive risk affects both their behavior and their purchasing decisions (Ko et al., 2004). The mentality of high-risk customers will affect how they accept new technologies (Li et al., 2019). To assess the impact of PR on OPT, the research incorporates PR into the technology acceptance model hypothesis.

According to this research, high PEOU and PU strongly affect customers' attitudes toward online purchase intents. This suggests that high PEOU, as well as PU have a favorable impact on intention and attitude to make an online purchase. This shows that customers think that online buying is advantageous to them when they complete transactions fast and easily using websites or mobile apps for e-commerce (Saving time, for instance, may be done anywhere and at any time.). As a result, customers are more inclined to utilize and have a good view of online transactions. However, e-shopping businesses must use specific tactics to raise PU and PEOU if they want to persuade people to purchase online through the Internet or e-shopping apps. For instance, to make it simpler to use, the e-shopping interface has to be more beautiful. E- commerce platforms should be run with professionalism and in the 21st century to help customers purchase online. Additionally, as a result of globalization, customers purchase online both inside and outside of their own nation. Websites must thus support a variety of languages to better serve their diverse audience of users. To get the word out about the advantages of internet purchasing, certain campaigns must be conducted. The results are consistent with earlier research that examined the TAM in a range of technology adoption scenarios (Li 2019; Dutot 2019).

In the survey, it was also shown that ATT and users' inclinations to make online transactions were significantly impacted (Chiu, 2014; Almousa, 2011; Ariffin, 2018; Ha, 2020; Singh & Srivastava, 2018). Though, prior research has shown that PR has no impact (does not act as a barrier) on online sales (Ventre & Kolbe, 2020). These findings are the consequence of the respondents being students, who are thought to have greater expertise and familiarity with internet purchasing. Additionally, other research indicates that the desire to purchase online has no clear correlation (Gefen et al., 2003). The study analyzed OPT utilizing a large sample using the technology acceptance model in response to some of these and revealed that PR negatively affects both OPT and ATT, validating prior study that also demonstrated that PR negatively affects both OPT and ATT (Singh & Srivastava, 2018; Almousa et al., 2011; Ariffin 2018; Ha et al., 2020; Chiu 2014). With the use of these statistics, it is reasonable to conclude that people will have a negative attitude about online shopping when they perceive the risk as being significant, even though they may still do so or make minor purchases. Companies that provide online purchasing have various options for lowering customer risk. Rules and regulations may be created, for example, to govern online transactions and payments. Modern security technologies make it possible for third parties to leak and steal personal information. In order to reduce the danger of products not being delivered even after payment has been completed, e-commerce businesses may use COD payment options or payments via 3rd parties.

CONCLUSION

E-Shopping trends are growing in popularity as people look at how people may use this technology while taking into account important variables. The study's strategy combined perceived risk with the theory of the TAM to produce results that were either novel or corroborated by earlier research. The research discovered that an individual's propensity to make an online buy is mostly influenced by perceived utility, perceived risk, along with perceived ease of use. Particularly, a customer's propensity and attitude to purchase online are favorably influenced by perceived utility and convenience of use. PR has a detrimental effect on users' views and online shopping inclinations. E-commerce businesses should concentrate on perceived usability, perceived risk, as well as perceived ease of use when encouraging people to purchase online. Potential repercussions have been investigated in light of these results.

RESEARCH IMPLICATIONS

Firstly, participants in this research were polled by handing out questionnaires in many important Indian cities, including Ambala, Karnal, Faridabad, Rohtak, Hisar, and Gurgaon. Thus, it is anticipated that the survey area will be expanded by the subsequent investigation. Additionally, it is essential to conduct surveys using other channels and techniques to broaden the variety of the sample population. Secondly, the research aimed at the impact of perceived usability, perceived risk, along with perceived ease of use on the intention to make an online purchase. Future research has to take other factors into account.

REFERENCES

Adu, E., Zhang, Y. D., Liu, D., & Tontiwachwuthikul, P. (2020). Parametric process design and economic analysis of post-combustion CO2 capture and compression for coal-and natural gas-fired power plants. *Energies*, *13*(10), 2519. doi:10.3390/en13102519

Akhlaq, A., & Ahmed, E. (2015). Digital commerce in emerging economies: Factors associated with online shopping intentions in Pakistan. *International Journal of Emerging Markets*.

Almousa, M. (2011). Perceived risk in apparel online shopping: A multi-dimensional perspective. *Canadian Social Science*, *7*(2), 23–31.

Annur, C.M. (2019). *APJII Survey: Internet user penetration in Indonesia reaches 64.8%*. Datadata.co.en.

Ariffin, S. K., Mohan, T., & Goh, Y. N. (2018). Influence of consumers' perceived risk on consumers' online purchase intention. *Journal of Research in Interactive Marketing*.

Bansal, N., Bhatnagar, M., & Taneja, S. (2023i). Balancing Priorities Through Green Optim000ism: A Study Elucidating Initiatives, Approaches, and Strategies for Sustainable Supply Chain Management. In *Handbook of Research on Designing Sustainable Supply Chains to Achieve a Circular Economy* (pp. 60–81). IGI Global. doi:10.4018/978-1-6684-7664-2.ch004

Bhatnagar, A., Misra, S., & Rao, H. R. (2000). On risk, convenience, and Internet shopping behavior. *Communications of the ACM*, *43*(11), 98–105. doi:10.1145/353360.353371

Bhatnagar, M., Özen, E., Taneja, S., Grima, S., & Rupeika-Apoga, R. (2022a). The Dynamic Connectedness between Risk and Return in the Fintech Market of India: Evidence Using the GARCH-M Approach. *Risks*, *10*(11), 209. doi:10.3390/risks10110209

Bhatnagar, M., Taneja, S., Kumar, P., & Özen, E. (2023a). Does Financial Education Act as a Catalyst for SME Competitiveness. *International Journal of Education Economics and Development*, *1*(1), 1. doi:10.1504/IJEED.2023.10053629

Bhatnagar, M., Taneja, S., & Özen, E. (2022b). A wave of green start-ups in India—The study of green finance as a support system for sustainable entrepreneurship. *Green Finance*, *4*(2), 253–273. doi:10.3934/GF.2022012

Bhatnagar, M., Taneja, S., & Rupeika-Apoga, R. (2023b). Demystifying the Effect of the News (Shocks) on Crypto Market Volatility. *Journal of Risk and Financial Management*, *16*(2), 136. doi:10.3390/jrfm16020136

Bhukya, R., & Singh, S. (2015). The effect of perceived risk dimensions on purchase intention: An empirical evidence from Indian private labels market. *American Journal of Business*, *30*(4), 218–230. doi:10.1108/AJB-10-2014-0055

Bourlakis, M., Papagiannidis, S., & Fox, H. (2008). E-consumer behaviour: Past, present and future trajectories of an evolving retail revolution. [IJEBR]. *International Journal of E-Business Research*, *4*(3), 64–76. doi:10.4018/jebr.2008070104

Burke, T. J., & Segrin, C. (2014). Examining diet-and exercise-related communication in romantic relationships: Associations with health behaviors. *Health Communication*, *29*(9), 877–887. doi:10.1080/10410236.2013.811625 PMID:24295060

Chen, L., & Yang, X. (2018). Using EPPM to evaluate the effectiveness of fear appeal messages across different media outlets to increase the intention of breast self-examination among Chinese women. *Health Communication*. PMID:30080982

Chin, W. W. (1998). The partial least squares approach to structural equation modeling. *Modern Methods for Business Research*, *295*(2), 295–336.

Chiu, C. M., Wang, E. T., Fang, Y. H., & Huang, H. Y. (2014). Understanding customers' repeat purchase intentions in B2C e-commerce: The roles of utilitarian value, hedonic value and perceived risk. *Information Systems Journal*, *24*(1), 85–114. doi:10.1111/j.1365-2575.2012.00407.x

Clement, J. (2019). E-commerce worldwide-Statistics & Facts. *Statista. Recuperado el, 5.*

Dahiya, K., Taneja, S., & Özen, E. (2023g). To Analyse the Impact of Multi-Media Technology on the Rural Entrepreneurship Development. In Contemporary Studies of Risks in Emerging Technology, Part A (pp. 221-240). Emerald Publishing Limited. doi:10.1108/978-1-80455-562-020231015

Dangwal, A., Kaur, S., Taneja, S., & Taneja, S. (2022a). A Bibliometric Analysis of Green Tourism Based on the Scopus Platform. In J. Kaur, P. Jindal, & A. Singh (Eds.), *Developing Relationships, Personalization, and Data Herald in Marketing 5.0* (Vol. i, pp. 1–327). IGI Global. doi:10.4018/978-1-6684-4496-2.ch015

Dangwal, A., Taneja, S., Özen, E., Todorovic, I., & Grima, S. (2022b). Abridgement of Renewables: It's Potential and Contribution to India's GDP. *International Journal of Sustainable Development and Planning*, *17*(8), 2357–2363. doi:10.18280/ijsdp.170802

Davis, F. D. (1985). *A technology acceptance model for empirically testing new end-user information systems: Theory and results.* [Unpublished doctoral dissertation, Massachusetts Institute of Technology].

Diallo, M. F., & Siqueira, J. R. Jr. (2017). How previous positive experiences with store brands affect purchase intention in emerging countries: A comparison between Brazil and Colombia. *International Marketing Review*, *34*(4), 536–558. doi:10.1108/IMR-07-2014-0224

Dutot, V., Bhatiasevi, V., & Bellallahom, N. (2019). Applying the technology acceptance model in a three- countries study of smartwatch adoption. *The Journal of High Technology Management Research*, *30*(1), 1–14. doi:10.1016/j.hitech.2019.02.001

Fornell, C., & Larcker, D. F. (2012). Equation algebra unobservable error: Variables. *JMR, Journal of Marketing Research*, *18*(3), 382–388. doi:10.1177/002224378101800313

Garner, S. J. (1986). Perceived risk and information sources in services purchasing. *The Mid-Atlantic Journal of Business*, *24*(2), 49–58.

Gefen, D., & Straub, D. (2005). A practical guide to factorial validity using PLS-Graph: Tutorial and annotated example. *Communications of the Association for Information Systems*, *16*(1), 5. doi:10.17705/1CAIS.01605

Ghozali, I. (2013). *Multivariate Analysis Application with IBM and SPSS Programs* (5th ed.). BP Universitas Dipenogoro.

Gupta, M., Arora, R., & Taneja, S. (2023e). Bibliometric Analysis on Employee Engagement and Human Resource Management. In *Enhancing Customer Engagement Through Location-Based Marketing* (pp. 185–205). IGI Global. doi:10.4018/978-1-6684-8177-6.ch013

Ha, N. (2020). The impact of perceived risk on consumers' online shopping intention: An integration of TAM and TPB. *Management Science Letters*, *10*(9), 2029–2036. doi:10.5267/j.msl.2020.2.009

Han, M. C., & Kim, Y. (2017). Why consumers hesitate to shop online: Perceived risk and product involvement on Taobao. com. *Journal of Promotion Management*, *23*(1), 24–44. doi:10.1080/10496491.2016.1251530

Jangir, K., Sharma, V., Taneja, S., & Rupeika-Apoga, R. (2023). The Moderating Effect of Perceived Risk on Users' Continuance Intention for FinTech Services. *Journal of Risk and Financial Management*, *16*(1), 21. doi:10.3390/jrfm16010021

Jarvenpaa, S. L., Tractinsky, N., & Vitale, M. (2000). Consumer trust in an Internet store. *Information Technology and Management*, *1*(1), 45–71. doi:10.1023/A:1019104520776

Kim, J. S. (2016). An extended technology acceptance model in behavioral intention toward hotel tablet apps with moderating effects of gender and age. *International Journal of Contemporary Hospitality Management*, *28*(8), 1535–1553. doi:10.1108/IJCHM-06-2015-0289

Ko, H., Jung, J., Kim, J., & Shim, S. W. (2004). Cross-cultural differences in perceived risk of online shopping. *Journal of Interactive Advertising*, *4*(2), 20–29. doi:10.1080/15252019.2004.10722084

Kumar, P., Taneja, S., Özen, E., & Singh, S. (2023h). Artificial Intelligence and Machine Learning in Insurance: A Bibliometric Analysis. In Smart Analytics, Artificial Intelligence and Sustainable Performance Management in a Global Digitalised Economy (pp. 191-202). Emerald Publishing Limited. doi:10.1108/S1569-37592023000110A010

Kumar, P., Verma, P., Bhatnagar, M., Taneja, S., Seychel, S., Todorović, I., & Grim, S. (2023). The financial performance and solvency status of the indian public sector banks: A CAMELS rating and Z index approach. *International Journal of Sustainable Development and Planning*, *18*(2), 367–376. doi:10.18280/ijsdp.180204

Laroche, M., Yang, Z., McDougall, G. H., & Bergeron, J. (2005). Internet versus bricks-and-mortar retailers: An investigation into intangibility and its consequences. *Journal of Retailing*, *81*(4), 251–267. doi:10.1016/j.jretai.2004.11.002

Lee, K. S., & Tan, S. J. (2003). E-retailing versus physical retailing: A theoretical model and empirical test of consumer choice. *Journal of Business Research*, *56*(11), 877–885. doi:10.1016/S0148-2963(01)00274-0

Lee, Y. H., Hsieh, Y. C., & Hsu, C. N. (2011). Adding innovation diffusion theory to the technology acceptance model: Supporting employees' intentions to use e-learning systems. *Journal of Educational Technology & Society*, *14*(4), 124–137.

Li, J., Wang, J., Wangh, S., & Zhou, Y. (2019). Mobile payment with alipay: An application of extended technology acceptance model. *IEEE Access : Practical Innovations, Open Solutions*, *7*, 50380–50387. doi:10.1109/ACCESS.2019.2902905

Liao, Z., & Wong, W. K. (2008). The determinants of customer interactions with internet-enabled e-banking services. *The Journal of the Operational Research Society*, *59*(9), 1201–1210. doi:10.1057/palgrave.jors.2602429

Liu, X., & Wei, K. K. (2003). An empirical study of product differences in consumers' E-commerce adoption behavior. *Electronic Commerce Research and Applications*, *2*(3), 229–239. doi:10.1016/S1567-4223(03)00027-9

Lohse, G. L., & Spiller, P. (1998). Electronic shopping. *Communications of the ACM*, *41*(7), 81–87. doi:10.1145/278476.278491

Marron, D. B., & Steel, D. G. (2000). Which countries protect intellectual property? The case of software piracy. *Economic Inquiry*, *38*(2), 159–174. doi:10.1111/j.1465-7295.2000.tb00011.x

Mayer, R. C., & Davis, J. H. (1999). The effect of the performance appraisal system on trust for management: A field quasi-experiment. *The Journal of Applied Psychology*, *84*(1), 123–136. doi:10.1037/0021-9010.84.1.123

Mpinganjira, M. (2016). An investigation of customer attitude towards online stores. *African Journal of Science, Technology, Innovation and Development*, *8*(5), 447–456. doi:10.1080/20421338.2016.1222752

Muncy, J. A., & Wilkie, W. (1987). Consumer behavior. In *Journal of Marketing, 51(3)*. Dryden. doi:10.2307/1251656

Özen, E., & Sanjay, T. (2022a). Empirical Analysis of the Effect of Foreign Trade in Computer and Communication Services on Economic Growth in India. *Journal of Economics and Business Issues*, *2*(2), 24–34.

Özen, E., Taneja, S., & Makalesi, A. (2022b). Critical Evaluation of Management of NPA / NPL in Emerging and Advanced Economies : a Study in Context of India GelişenveGelişmişEkonomilerde NPA / NPL YönetimininEleştirelDeğerlendirmesi : HindistanBağlamında Bir Çalışma. *YalovaSosyalBilimlerDergisi, 12*(2), 99–111.

Pappas, I. O., Kourouthanassis, P. E., Giannakos, M. N., & Chrissikopoulos, V. (2017). Sense and sensibility in personalized e-commerce: How emotions rebalance the purchase intentions of persuaded customers. *Psychology and Marketing*, *34*(10), 972–986. doi:10.1002/mar.21036

Pavlou, P. A. (2003). Consumer acceptance of electronic commerce: Integrating trust and risk with the technology acceptance model. *International Journal of Electronic Commerce*, *7*(3), 101–134. doi:10.1080/10864415.2003.11044275

Pavlou, P. A., & Featherman, M. S. (2003). Predicting e-services adoption: A perceived risk facets perspective. *International Journal of Human-Computer Studies*, *59*(4), 451–474. doi:10.1016/S1071-5819(03)00111-3

Pires, P. J. (2006). Winning through innovation: A practical guide to leading organizational change and renewal. *RAC. Revista de Administração Contemporânea*, *10*(1), 177–177. doi:10.1590/S1415-65552006000100013

Prayag, G. (2009). Tourists' evaluations of destination image, satisfaction, and future behavioral intentions-The case of Mauritius. *Journal of Travel & Tourism Marketing*, *26*(8), 836–853. doi:10.1080/10548400903358729

Reepu, R., Taneja, S., Ozen, E., & Singh, A. (2023j). A Globetrotter to the Future of Marketing: Metaverse. In *Cultural Marketing and Metaverse for Consumer Engagement* (pp. 1–11). IGI Global. doi:10.4018/978-1-6684-8312-1.ch001

Schierz, P. G., Schilke, O., & Wirtz, B. W. (2010). Understanding consumer acceptance of mobile payment services: An empirical analysis. *Electronic Commerce Research and Applications*, *9*(3), 209–216. doi:10.1016/j.elerap.2009.07.005

Singh, S., & Srivastava, S. (2018). Moderating effect of product type on online shopping behaviour and purchase intention: An Indian perspective. *Cogent Arts & Humanities*, *5*(1), 1495043. doi:10.1080/23311983.2018.1495043

Singh, V., Taneja, S., Singh, V., Singh, A., & Paul, H. L. (2021). Online advertising strategies in Indian and Australian e-commerce companies:: A comparative study. *Big Data Analytics for Improved Accuracy, Efficiency, and Decision Making in Digital Marketing*, 124–138. doi:10.4018/978-1-7998-7231-3.ch009

Stats, I.W. (2015). *Internet usage statistics: World internet users and population stats.*

Taneja, S., Bhatnagar, M., Kumar, P., & Grima, S. (2023c). A panel analysis of the effectiveness of the asset management in Indian agricultural companies. *International Journal of Sustainable Development and Planning, 18*(3), 653–660. doi:10.18280/ijsdp.180301

Taneja, S., Bhatnagar, M., Kumar, P., & Rupeika-apoga, R. (2023b). India's Total Natural Resource Rents (NRR) and GDP : An Augmented Autoregressive Distributed Lag (ARDL) Bound Test. *Journal of Risk and Financial Management, 16*(2), 91. doi:10.3390/jrfm16020091

Taneja, S., Gupta, M., Bhushan, P., Bhatnagar, M., & Singh, A. (2023k). Cultural Marketing in the Digital Era. In *Cultural Marketing and Metaverse for Consumer Engagement* (pp. 109–122). IGI Global. doi:10.4018/978-1-6684-8312-1.ch008

Taneja, S., Jaggi, P., Jewandah, S., & Ozen, E. (2022b). Role of Social Inclusion in Sustainable Urban Developments: An Analyse by PRISMA Technique. *International Journal of Design & Nature and Ecodynamics, 17*(6), 937–942. doi:10.18280/ijdne.170615

Taneja, S., Kaur, S., & Özen, E. (2022a). Using green finance to promote global growth in a sustainable way. *International Journal of Green Economics, 16*(3), 246–257. doi:10.1504/IJGE.2022.128930

Taneja, S., & Özen, E. (2023a). To analyse the relationship between bank's green financing and environmental performance. *International Journal of Electronic Finance, 12*(2), 163–175. doi:10.1504/IJEF.2023.129919

Taneja, S., & Ozen, E. (2023d). Impact of the European Green Deal (EDG) on the agricultural carbon (CO2) emission in Turkey. *International Journal of Sustainable Development and Planning, 18*(3), 715–727. doi:10.18280/ijsdp.180307

Taneja, S., & Sharma, V. (2023f). Role of Beaconing Marketing in Improving Customer Buying Experience. In *Enhancing Customer Engagement Through Location-Based Marketing* (pp. 176–184). IGI Global. doi:10.4018/978-1-6684-8177-6.ch012

Taylor, S., & Todd, P. A. (1995). Understanding information technology usage: A test of competing models. *Information Systems Research, 6*(2), 144–176. doi:10.1287/isre.6.2.144

Ventre, I., & Kolbe, D. (2020). The impact of perceived usefulness of online reviews, trust and perceived risk on online purchase intention in emerging markets: A Mexican perspective. *Journal of International Consumer Marketing, 32*(4), 287–299. doi:10.1080/08961530.2020.1712293

Wagner Mainardes, E., de Almeida, C. M., & de-Oliveira, M. (2019). e-Commerce: An analysis of the factors that antecede purchase intentions in an emerging market. *Journal of International Consumer Marketing, 31*(5), 447–468. doi:10.1080/08961530.2019.1605643

Wang, Y. S., Wu, S. C., Lin, H. H., Wang, Y. M., & He, T. R. (2012). Determinants of user adoption of web''Automatic Teller Machines': An integrated model of'Transaction Cost Theory and Innovation Diffusion Theory'. *Service Industries Journal, 32*(9), 1505–1525. doi:10.1080/02642069.2010.531271

Zhang, S., Xu, C., Larrimore, K. E., & Ng, D. T. (2017). Slp1-Emp65: A guardian factor that protects folding polypeptides from promiscuous degradation. *Cell, 171*(2), 346–357. doi:10.1016/j.cell.2017.08.036 PMID:28919078

Chapter 6
Challenges and Sustainability of Green Finance in the Tourism Industry:
Evidence From Bangladesh

Sanjeev Kumar
https://orcid.org/0000-0002-7375-7341
Lovely Professional University, India

Mohammad Badruddoza Talukder
https://orcid.org/0000-0001-7788-2732
Daffodil Institute of IT, Dhaka, Bangladesh

Firoj Kabir
Daffodil Institute of IT, Dhaka, Bangladesh

Fahmida Kaiser
Daffodil Institute of IT, Dhaka, Bangladesh

ABSTRACT

A country's tourism sector is a vital component of economic growth. It can benefit from 'green finance' by raising the bar for service and increasing its sense of social responsibility. Banks and other non-bank financial entities worldwide have participated in green finance initiatives for developing the tourism industry. Based on reviews of secondary sources (such as academic papers, reports on sustainability from different economic and organizations that support the environment, and printed materials of the Bangladesh bank), this chapter aims to highlight the difficulties and potentials of green banking as well as the various types of green financing (such as green mortgages, green credit cards, and green bonds), as well as the advantages of green finance in the tourism sector in Bangladesh. In addition to describing existing green finance techniques in the tourism industry, this chapter identifies the primary obstacles to expanding such practices and offers potential solutions. Enhancing green finance practices within the tourism sector are highlighted in this chapter.

DOI: 10.4018/979-8-3693-1388-6.ch006

BACKGROUND

Many banks and other financial intermediaries worldwide have recently decided to alter people's focus from maximization of profits to consideration of the broader community (Hailiang et al., 2023). Financial institutions (FIs) and banks offer cutting-edge "green" products covering a range of financial services supporting environmentally safe activities. These environmentally friendly financial institutions are sometimes known as "ethical banks," "socially responsible banks," or "sustainable banks." However, because these terms encompass generalized actions and ideas, people's precise meanings may vary (Gao et al., 2022). Green banking and financing contain various environmental causes, from stopping climate change to preventing water pollution, soil erosion, and species extinction. Degradation of the atmosphere includes things like air pollution, changes in the climate, rising levels of greenhouse gases, and depletion of the ozone layer. 'Green Financing/Banking' is an ideology that promotes businesses that minimize adverse effects on people, the environment, and profits (Ren et al., 2020). Banks and other financial institutions are crucial to each country's economic growth and prosperity. Financial institutions (FIs) that adopt green finance and banking practices raise both people's own and other businesses' social accountability. Financial institutions (FIs) and banks conduct most people's interactions with the money of others. However, people cannot shirk their responsibility to people transact with financial institutions (FIs), and banks that prioritize environmental sustainability need not sacrifice profits to do so. Institutions of financial intermediation (FIs) and banking institutions (banks) are for-profit businesses (Tvaronavičienė, 2023).

Every dollar a bank mobilizes comes with a cost. Therefore, profits are required to pay depositors and cover administrative and other expenses. The banking and financing sector may reject environmental policies that are too expensive to implement. Green finance in tourism refers to using financial resources to promote ecologically and socially responsible business activities. Investment decisions about the tourism industry can now include environmental, social, and governance (ESG) factors. Green financing in tourism aims to maximize the positive social and economic effects of tourism while reducing its adverse environmental impact. Green finance in tourism is a subset of sustainable tourism financing that prioritizes the planet's and its inhabitants' welfare (Shang et al., 2023). It entails keeping locations financially viable while supporting activities that improve people's ecological and social conditions. Hospitality organizations, financiers, and financial institutions can all benefit from this type of financing because it takes factors related to the environment, society, and governance, or ESG, into account. Investment in environmentally conscious infrastructure, funding for projects to lessen the tourism industry's environmental impact, and backing efforts that put the well-being of local people first are all examples of the processes and approaches that make up "green finance" in the tourism industry. It promotes eco-friendly behavior by advocating for changes that result in less waste, less energy use, and less pollution.

INTRODUCTION

In order to reduce carbon emissions and their harmful health effects, build climate-resilient infrastructure for cities, and assure environmental sustainability, green finance is crucial for financing renewable and green energy projects (Taghizadeh-Hesary & Yoshino, 2020).

The expansion rate in this industry has not been without challenges, either. Examples include the need to balance the trade-off between economic growth and social priorities like environmental protection, as well as questions about the primary objective function of businesses, what they should concentrate on, and how to balance profitability with more general sustainability issues relevant to the entire community. A substantial and expanding body of literature is devoted to various aspects of the asset class, including whether or not the capitalist financial system is the best place to start when considering ecological sustainability. The structures of social investment and the opinions surrounding their development and operation are also diverse and complex (Gilchrist et al., 2021).

Businesses that cater to eco-tourists and adapt to shifting consumer tastes might benefit from green finance, which offers financial incentives for developing sustainable tourism. Investors and other stakeholders can evaluate tourism enterprises' social and environmental impacts using ESG reporting and accreditation systems, which are emphasized. Green finance in the tourism industry also encourages cooperation between governments, banks, enterprises, and neighborhoods. The stakeholders can tackle environmental concerns like climate change and build more substantial destinations. Additionally, the funding helps to spread environmentally conscious tourism practices that value and protect local communities' histories, customs, and landscapes (Wang et al., 2023). Essentially, tourism green finance acts as an engine for beneficial improvements within the travel and tourism sector by channeling investment dollars toward initiatives that not only produce economic value but also aid in the preservation of ecosystems, the lessening of carbon dioxide emissions, and the emancipation of local communities at popular tourist hotspots.

LITERATURE REVIEW

Any organized financial activity to preserve the environment is called "green finance." This program includes a variety of loans, funding tools, and investments to encourage the development of environmentally friendly projects or to reduce more traditional ones' climatic impact (Bhatnagar et al., 2022). Government financial inclusion schemes are popping up everywhere as proof of this. However, the growth of any country on earth should not come at the expense of the environment. Indeed, there are significant links between climate change and sustainable growth. Over the past few decades, global temperatures have risen mainly due to fossil fuel burning (Bhatnagar & Pathak, 2021). Since the implementation of the SDGs in 2015, several governments have started to focus on environmental issues, including air pollution, sanitation problems, and severe damage to natural resources and forests (PEREIRA-ROMEIRO et al., 2021). Governments have also started to focus on green finance to address environmental issues (see Bhatnagar, 2022b). Poor environmental conditions are a threat to human health and economic well-being. (See Tallis et al., 2008). All aspects of human well-being (including health, environment, and physical capital) and approaches to water, food, and land are vulnerable to climate change. These concerns have led to a worldwide movement to fight climate change (Taghizadeh-Hesary & Yoshino, 2020).

In order to advance the goals of sustainable development, there should be an increase in financial flows (banking, microcredit, insurance, and investment) from the public, private, and non-profit sectors (Desalegn & Tangl, 2022). Thus, green finance plays a crucial role in fulfilling the objectives of sustainable development goals that consider green growth. Because inclusive green financing helps to reduce and increase resilience to the adverse effects of climate change, it can be used to create equitable green growth (LEE, 2020). By marketing green goods in savings, credit, insurance, money transfers, and new digital delivery channels, financial institutions must offer those finances crucial support to those navigating an uncertain climate (Zhang et al., 2022). The goal of green finance codes, taxonomies, regulations, guidelines, safeguards, and catalogs (henceforth referred to as "standards") is to assist governments, corporations, and other involved stakeholders in channeling funding and investments into environmentally friendly economic development, such as in renewable energy, sustainable transportation, or sustainable agriculture (Nedopil et al., 2021).

Types of Green Financing

Green finance may be the following forms, which are discussed below. Such are:

Green Mortgages

Lenders can offer more favorable conditions to buyers of environmentally sustainable homes or people who agree to improve the property's environmental performance (Alharbi et al., 2023).

Green Loans

These financing options help green ventures get off the ground, whether installing solar panels at home, buying an electric car, improving energy efficiency, or something else entirely.

Green Credit Cards

When a customer uses a green credit card, such as the Aspirations Zero card, the company plants a tree in the consumer's honor. The bankers enable consumers to channel people's money into green finance, which has a positive and long-lasting effect on the planet.

Green Banks

Green banks are financial institutions like conventional banks, except people use public funding to encourage private investment in green technologies and practices.

Green Bonds

The majority of green finance comes from green bonds. Funding for things like renewable energy, sustainable transportation, and conservation comes from the interest and principal of bond investments (Chan et al., 2022).

Benefits of Green Finance

Green finance helps disseminate technologies and promotes eco-friendly infrastructure. Governments in emerging nations invest in the infrastructure required to manage resources over the long run, boost national competitiveness, and direct private capital into domestic green markets.

Adds Business Value

A low-carbon green development may be forced to switch from a voluntary to a mandatory strategy in response to growing threats from climate change and other environmental and economic difficulties. When environmental rules become more stringent, boosting green financing will give travelers an edge (Zhou & Zhang, 2023).

Enhances Economic Prospects

Increasing (and boasting about) a company's involvement in green financing is a great way to boost the value of a portfolio. It gives people a competitive advantage in the environmentally conscious marketplace.

To protect populations from resource depletion, governments that encourage green financing help. People achieve this by expanding into lucrative new markets and bolstering existing ones for renewable energy (Guang-Wen & Siddik, 2022).

Critical Components of Tourism Green Finance

1. One form of "green finance" in the tourism industry is investing in sustainable infrastructure development and improvement initiatives. Hotels, transit networks, waste reduction technologies, and water conservation programs could all benefit from such expenditures (Soundarrajan & Vivek, 2016).
2. Financial institutions and investors may incentivize eco-friendly activities, such as lower credit rates or more favorable conditions, to tourism enterprises. Responsible water management, trash reduction and recycling initiatives, and energy-efficient operations are all examples of such procedures.
3. Additionally, disclosure of environmental, social, and governance (ESG) performance may be required of tourism enterprises seeking green financing. This openness aids investors, and other stakeholders judge the company's dedication to social responsibility and environmental preservation.
4. Green tourism funding can also be linked to third-party certifications and standards that attest to an organization's commitment to eco-friendly operations. If hotels were to become certified as "green" or "eco-friendly," people might be eligible for special tax breaks.
5. Bonds and loans designed exclusively for green initiatives are called "green bonds" and "green loans," respectively. These could fund initiatives that increase a destination's energy efficiency, decrease its carbon footprint, or improve its sustainability for tourists (Zheng et al., 2021).
6. Partnerships and collaboration between governments, financial institutions, and tourism industry stakeholders are joint in green finance. The tourism industry can benefit significantly from public-private collaborations encouraging environmentally responsible practices.
7. Green financing can aid tourism businesses in identifying and reducing exposure to climate change and other environmental concerns. Companies can better withstand disruptions if people invest in robust infrastructure and adaptation mechanisms.
8. Funds for Tourism Development Eighth, in some cases, governments set aside money specifically to promote tourism. Businesses and projects that adhere to the tenets of green finance can receive funding from these pools of capital (Falcone, 2020).

Green finance in tourism essentially works to coordinate the sector's monetary operations with broader environmental objectives. Green finance helps ensure that the tourism industry can thrive in the long run by rewarding and enabling activities that are good for the environment and society.

Products of Green Finance

Figure 1. Products of green finance
Source: Authors compilation

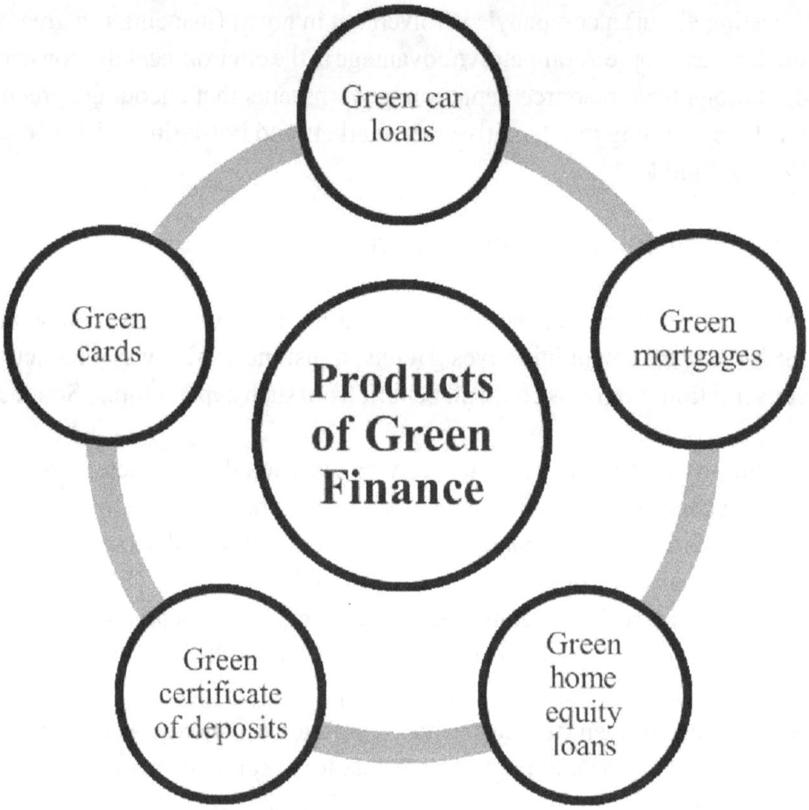

CHALLENGES AND OPPORTUNITIES

Challenges Regarding Green Financing

Transitioning to a carbon-free economy in light of the tourism sector in Bangladesh will require a substantial investment of resources. The private sector must actively participate in these vital investments. Private investments can transform from risk management methods into drivers of innovation and new opportunities by incorporating ESG (environmental, social, and governance) factors into people's decision-making processes. In turn, these openings provide lasting benefits to enterprises as well as society at large. However, several microeconomic hurdles have hampered the cash flow towards green initiatives in the travel industry. The mismatch between short-term and long-term green investments is a significant cause for alarm. Investors' inclination for short-term horizons exacerbates the problem of capital mobilization towards sustainable projects.

Similarly uncommon is the combination of fiscally and ecologically sound methods. Developing a unified concept of "green" and a taxonomy detailing environmentally responsible actions is essential. Such transparency is critical for helping businesses and individuals in the financial sector allocate people's resources effectively and make well-considered decisions. To combat 'green washing' and support genuine sustainable efforts, it is critical to define the parameters of green funding (He et al., 2019).

The tourism industry needs a standardized set of essential sustainable finance criteria to evaluate industries, control risks, and establish standards. By establishing such standards, people can more reliably refocus financial resources on environmentally responsible initiatives. The stock of green financial assets can be bolstered even further by easing disclosure regulations and norms. Implementing and monitoring green finance concepts and standards across asset classes is critical. These standards are voluntary, but people are supported by legislative incentives, highlighting the importance of coordinating investment with ecological and environmentally friendly methods in Bangladesh's booming tourism sector (Lan et al., 2023).

There Are Various Obstacles in the Way of a Green Financing Policy Being Put Into Action

It will be challenging for the central banks to formulate appropriate rules, such as splitting sectors based on hazard or environmental risk because people will be up against powerful corporate groups (Dong et al., 2023).

- **Lack of financial institutions concern**
  - Facilitating a standardized approach to green banking and finance across all financial institutions.
  - Raise the amount of money put into green banking and finance programs.
  - Financial institutions should have the moral fortitude to put people's money into environmentally friendly initiatives (Chen et al., 2022).
  - Financial institutions (FIs) should provide customers with eco-friendly options. Encourage people to rideshare.
  - Some investors and financial institutions may view green projects as riskier than others due to people's perceived novelty or the inherent economic viability questions people raise. Potential investors may be dissuaded from participating in green finance initiatives due to people's perception of increased risk.
- **Lack of governmental concern**
  - Environmentally harmful industries should be forced to relocate to less populated locations with the help of enforcement from the relevant authorities.
  - There is a need for strict enforcement to get legacy industries to implement ETP.
  - Making sure government employees from the appropriate departments are overseeing projects.
- **Lack of environmental concern**
  - Adding new characteristics concerning green activities to the CAMELS rating motivates the FIs.

- The most dangerous industries, such as brickmaking, will have people's dedicated monitoring cells.
- Simplifying and reducing the cost of renewable energy technology setup and upkeep.
- Significant up-front investments in environmentally friendly infrastructure, technology, and operational adjustments are typically necessary for successful green practice implementation. This can be a substantial barrier to entry for many tourism organizations and tiny and medium-sized businesses (SMEs) when it comes to implementing sustainable practices.

- **Lack of educational research and awareness**
    - Supporting government and university efforts to do research.
    - Improve knowledge to better craft policies for specific financial institutions/banks. A bank that has adopted green banking principles should provide its employees with opportunities for physical training (Mozib Lalon, 2015).
    - A failure to inform and educate the public about green finance's benefits and significance in the tourist industry. This includes firms, investors, and consumers. Sustainable methods benefit both the planet and the bottom lines of tourism companies, so there needs to be an educational push to get the word out (Hafner et al., 2020).
- **Lack of financial support**
    - Provide funding for medium-sized businesses, public works, and other endeavors with positive social returns but low private profits.
    - Provide Money for Public Investments despite Competing Priorities
    - Deal with the many obstacles and inefficiencies evident even in "efficient" financial markets.
    - Getting people's hands on green finance can be challenging —the money and resources people need to implement environmentally friendly tourism projects. Since the profitability and viability of green projects are questionable, financial institutions may be unwilling to provide financing or capital for such endeavors.
- **Lack of public awareness**
    - A failure to inform and educate the public about green finance's benefits and significance in the tourist industry. This includes firms, investors, and consumers. Sustainable methods benefit both the planet and the bottom lines of tourism companies, so there needs to be an educational push to get the word out (Hafner et al., 2020).
    - Investors may find it challenging to evaluate the credibility and efficacy of projects due to the absence of established metrics and reporting frameworks for monitoring the environmental and social effects of green efforts in tourism. This lack of openness may hamper the availability of green financing.
    - Focusing on short-term profits has historically characterized the tourism industry, which can cause enterprises to put short-term benefits ahead of long-term viability. The only way to get stakeholders to embrace an environmentally friendly and ethical strategy is to convince people that doing so is profitable.
    - Confusion for businesses and investors can result from inconsistent or confusing policies and regulations about green practices and tourism finance. Implementation of green finance initiatives may be slowed by a lack of uniformity between different areas or countries (Taghizadeh-Hesary & Yoshino, 2020).
    - The achievement of sustainable finance in tourism hinges on consumers' propensity to embrace and pay more for environmentally friendly goods and services. Businesses may be

cautious about investing in environmentally friendly products if there is a lack of demand for people.

- There is a wide variety of players in the tourist business, from multinational conglomerates to independent travel agencies. Standardizing green finance initiatives across this diverse terrain and coordinating sustainable practices can be challenging (Madaleno et al., 2022).
- Guaranteeing green finance initiatives' social and environmental advantages depends on robust measuring, monitoring, and verification systems. It is not easy to show the results of these efforts without solid infrastructure.

Opportunities of Green Financing in Tourism

Many opportunities exist for green banking and green financing in the tourism industry of Bangladesh. These suggestions aim to encourage multi-sector collaboration toward ecologically responsible tourism practices. These parties are crucial to developing Green Banking (GB) practices in several important ways. These ways include ecological governance, risk mitigation, internal performance, proactive efforts, and transparent reporting.

The tourism business in Bangladesh can benefit significantly from green funding, described in detail below.

1. **Renewable Energy Projects:** Green finance may help fund the growth of renewable energy projects, including wind, solar, and hydroelectric power. Renewable energy systems to power hotels and other tourist infrastructure can be established with this funding. This method aids in creating a more environmentally friendly vacation by reducing carbon emissions and using fossil fuels (Mirza et al., 2023).
2. **Improving Energy Efficiency:** Businesses catering to tourists can reduce people's energy use and associated costs by investing in energy-efficient modifications made possible through grants and loans. LED lighting, smart thermostats, and energy-efficient appliances are all examples of energy-saving techniques that could be used to reap economic and environmental rewards.
3. **Carbon Offsetting and Sequestration:** Eco-friendly hotels, hiking trails, and landfills are all examples of tourism-friendly infrastructure that could benefit from an influx of green finance. These measures help sustain tourism expansion while minimizing the adverse effects on local ecosystems (Du & Wang, 2023).
4. **Waste Management and Recycling:** Reforestation and other carbon sequestration initiatives can be funded through green finance, allowing tourism-focused businesses to reduce people's carbon footprint. Aligning tourism with the environment, this financial commitment helps counteract the carbon footprint caused by tourism activities.
5. **Effective Garbage Management and Recycling:** The detrimental effects of tourism-related garbage on the environment can be mitigated by investing in waste disposal and recycling programs in popular tourist areas. This method supports the ideas behind the "circular economy" and reduces the environmental impact of trash (Wang et al., 2023).
6. **Ecotourism Development:** Water conservation efforts, such as installing effective drainage systems, water-saving devices, and wastewater treatment plants in tourist hotspots, can all benefit from green finance.

7. **Promoting Ecotourism:** Ecotourism projects that aim to protect and enhance local ecosystems can access money through green finance mechanisms. These initiatives improve the regional economy while protecting precious natural resources (Liu et al., 2023).
8. **Transportation Upgrades:** Green avenues are a funding source for environmentally friendly modes of transportation like electric and hybrid cars, bike-sharing schemes, and enhanced public transportation systems. These actions significantly lessen the environmental impact of getting to and from locations.
9. **Environmental Certifications:** Green financing can assist tourism businesses in obtaining and maintaining environmental certifications like LEED and Green Key. Conscious vacationers will appreciate that these certificates attest to the hotel's commitment to eco-friendly policies.
10. **Community Engagement:** Sustainable and environmentally friendly tourism growth is aided by investing in community engagement in planning and decision-making processes and the fair distribution of tourism's economic advantages (Qin et al., 2023).
11. **Research and Education:** Funding Research and Education Sustainable tourism practices raise understanding among visitors, businesses, and communities about protecting natural and cultural resources (Talukder et al., 2023).
12. **Partnerships and Collaborations:** Collaboration Catalyst Green Finance drives new partnerships between the public and private sectors, non-governmental organizations, and financial backers. By working together, all involved parties may more effectively achieve people's goals for sustainable tourism and its sound effects (Talukder, 2021).

Together, these suggestions can boost Bangladesh's tourism industry while protecting the country's natural and cultural resources to improve the power of green funding and banking practices.

Green Banking in the Tourism Industry of Bangladesh

Considering the negative impacts of climate change and the need for progressive action worldwide, Bangladesh Bank (the central bank of Bangladesh) has demonstrated a solid commitment to the vision of a green world through its green initiatives. In this regard, Bangladesh Bank seems to be a model for the financial sector, as it has implemented some green banking initiatives for its headquarters and branch office management. These initiatives signal the financial institutions that Bangladesh Bank is serious about the green movement (Islam et al., 2023).

Specific action measures:

- Installation of solar power system at headquarters on the roof of the building
- Environmentally harmful burning of uncountable damaged currency notes will be abolished and crushing instead.
- Timed target for carbon dioxide emissions reduction within the internal work (Kunhibava et al., 2019).

Network Expansion Initiatives (Bukhari et al., 2021)**:**

- Merger of BB headquarters and subsidiaries computer (LAN/WAN)
- BB brought into business an online store

- Web-based electronic bidding system
- Online salary and necessary advice, office orders, and so on.

Office automation (Sun et al., 2014)**:**

- Bangladesh Automated Check Processing System
- Bangladesh Electronic Money Transfer Network (BEFTN),
- Company resources Planning (ERP),
- Credit information Office web services Mobile banking service Establishment of a State tax Switch (NPS) and Company Information Warehouse (EDW)

Green Financing: A Tool for Promoting Sustainable Tourism

The continued effects of the Coronavirus outbreak have severely impacted the tourism business. There is a rising movement to reorganize the tourist industry such that it has a more positive impact on both people and the environment following the Sustainable Development Goals (SDGs). Providing the availability of environmentally friendly financing for small and medium-sized enterprises (SMEs) in Bangladesh is an essential step toward achieving this transformation. It demonstrates the critical role played by the financial sector in propelling the country toward a low-carbon, equitable, and sustainable developmental trajectory (Krahnen et al., 2023).

In line with the goals of the Sustainable Tourist Bangladesh (STB) program, several small and medium-sized enterprises (SMEs) in Bangladesh's tourist sector have identified access to financing as a significant impediment to implementing sustainable practices. High interest rates, cumbersome application processes, and stringent collateral requirements have all been noted as problems. In reaction, the STB program hosted webinars and workshops specifically for SMEs. Green Finance was introduced, and participants were given the skills to incorporate it into people's business practices, ultimately leading to more sustainable expansion (Krahnen et al., 2023).

A Participatory Symposium on Investment in a Sustainable Bangladesh was a significant part of the wrap-up events for the STB program. Approximately forty top-level delegates from financial institutions met to discuss how to best invest in an environmentally friendly tourism landscape, how to help small and medium-sized enterprises (SMEs) access green finance, and what the next phase of tourism in Bangladesh might look like. The Sustainable Tourism Bangladesh program received funding from the European Commission's Switch Asia Green program. This project's primary objective has been to help Bangladesh realize its target of being a certified Green Tourism Destination by 2030 (Talukder et al., 2023).

Figure 2. Sustainability of green finance in the tourism industry
Source: Authors Compilation

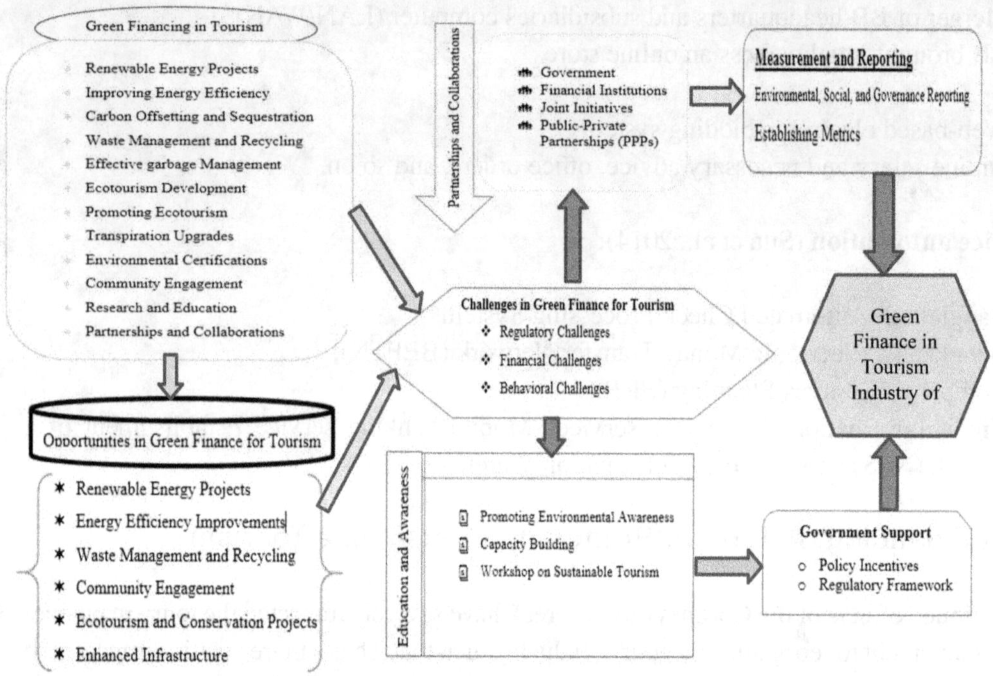

CONCLUSION AND FUTURE STUDY

In conclusion, sustainable finance is a powerful tool for fostering environmentally responsible tourism methods in Bangladesh, mitigating the effects of the current epidemic while meeting the need to protect the planet's natural resources. This transformation from banking that prioritizes profits over people to banking that prioritizes people is a watershed moment. To engage with environmentally conscious initiatives in the tourism industry, financial institutions have created "green" products. These methods highlight the significance of environmental risk management, accountability, and social responsibility. Although there has been progress, there are still obstacles to overcome, such as defining "green," emphasizing short-term profits, overcoming regulatory hurdles, and accurately reporting environmental, social, and governance factors. Cooperation between governments, financial institutions, tourism businesses, and local people is essential for overcoming these challenges. The promise of green finance lies in its potential to drive ecotourism and boost economic and social well-being. Businesses succeed, investors see long-term returns, and communities prosper when resources are allocated in a way that considers environmental concerns. Ultimately, green finance promotes a better tourist future by investing in projects that boost the economy, protect the environment, give locals more power, and positively impact the world.

REFERENCES

Alharbi, S. S., Al Mamun, M., Boubaker, S., & Rizvi, S. K. A. (2023). Green finance and renewable energy: A worldwide evidence. *Energy Economics*, *118*, 106499. doi:10.1016/j.eneco.2022.106499

Bhatnagar, M., & Pathak, N. (2021). Are the financial inclusion schemes of India developing the nation sustainably? *E3S Web of Conferences, 296*, 06011. doi:10.1051/e3sconf/202129606011

Bhatnagar, M., Taneja, S., & Özen, E. (2022). A wave of green start-ups in India—The study of green finance as a support system for sustainable entrepreneurship. *Green Finance*, *4*(2), 253–273. doi:10.3934/GF.2022012

Bukhari, S. A. A., Hashim, F., & Amran, A. (2021). Green banking: A conceptual framework. *International Journal of Green Economics*, *15*(1), 59. doi:10.1504/IJGE.2021.117682

Chan, C.-S., Chang, T. C., & Liu, Y. (2022). Investigating Creative Experiences and Environmental Perception of Creative Tourism: The Case of PMQ (Police Married Quarters) in Hong Kong. *Journal of China Tourism Research*, *18*(2), 223–244. doi:10.1080/19388160.2020.1812459

Chen, Z., Mirza, N., Huang, L., & Umar, M. (2022). Green Banking—Can Financial Institutions support green recovery? *Economic Analysis and Policy*, *75*, 389–395. doi:10.1016/j.eap.2022.05.017 PMID:35694019

Desalegn, G., & Tangl, A. (2022). Enhancing Green Finance for Inclusive Green Growth: A Systematic Approach. *Sustainability (Basel)*, *14*(12), 7416. doi:10.3390u14127416

Dong, C., Wu, H., Zhou, J., Lin, H., & Chang, L. (2023). Role of renewable energy investment and geopolitical risk in green finance development: Empirical evidence from BRICS countries. *Renewable Energy*, *207*, 234–241. doi:10.1016/j.renene.2023.02.115

Du, Y., & Wang, W. (2023). The role of green financing, agriculture development, geopolitical risk, and natural resource on environmental pollution in China. *Resources Policy*, *82*, 103440. doi:10.1016/j.resourpol.2023.103440

Falcone, P. M. (2020). Environmental regulation and green investments: The role of green finance. *International Journal of Green Economics*, *14*(2), 159. doi:10.1504/IJGE.2020.109735

Gao, Q., Liu, Y., Ayub, B., & Hussain, M. (2022). Does Health Crises Effect Tourism: Role of Financial Inclusion for Green Financial Development. *Frontiers in Public Health*, *10*, 896894. doi:10.3389/fpubh.2022.896894 PMID:35719629

Gilchrist, D., Yu, J., & Zhong, R. (2021). The Limits of Green Finance: A Survey of Literature in the Context of Green Bonds and Green Loans. *Sustainability (Basel)*, *13*(2), 478. doi:10.3390u13020478

Guang-Wen, Z., & Siddik, A. B. (2022). Do Corporate Social Responsibility Practices and Green Finance Dimensions Determine Environmental Performance? An Empirical Study on Bangladeshi Banking Institutions. *Frontiers in Environmental Science*, *10*, 890096. doi:10.3389/fenvs.2022.890096

Hafner, S., Jones, A., Anger-Kraavi, A., & Pohl, J. (2020). Closing the green finance gap – A systems perspective. *Environmental Innovation and Societal Transitions*, *34*, 26–60. doi:10.1016/j.eist.2019.11.007

Hailiang, Z., Chau, K. Y., & Waqas, M. (2023). Does green finance and renewable energy promote tourism for sustainable development: Empirical evidence from China. *Renewable Energy*, *207*, 660–671. doi:10.1016/j.renene.2023.03.032

He, L., Liu, R., Zhong, Z., Wang, D., & Xia, Y. (2019). Can green financial development promote renewable energy investment efficiency? A consideration of bank credit. *Renewable Energy*, *143*, 974–984. doi:10.1016/j.renene.2019.05.059

Islam, K., Akhther, N., & Seeger, M. W. (2023). Variability in Media Content of Public Health Outbreak Coverage: A Crisis Communication Approach. *Communication Studies*, *74*(2), 113–130. doi:10.1080/10510974.2023.2183516

Krahnen, J., Rocholl, J., & Thum, M. (2023). A Primer on Green Finance: From Wishful Thinking to Marginal Impact. *Review of Economics*, *74*(1), 1–19. doi:10.1515/roe-2023-0019

Kunhibava, S., Ling, S. T. Y., Rahman, N. F. A., & Ruslan, M. K. (2019). Green banking frameworks in Asia with an in-depth focus on Bangladesh and China. *Asia Pacific Journal of Environmental Law*, *22*(1), 93–116. doi:10.4337/apjel.2019.01.05

Lan, J., Wei, Y., Guo, J., Li, Q., & Liu, Z. (2023). The effect of green finance on industrial pollution emissions: Evidence from China. *Resources Policy*, *80*, 103156. doi:10.1016/j.resourpol.2022.103156

Lee, J. W.LEE. (2020). Green Finance and Sustainable Development Goals: The Case of China. *The Journal of Asian Finance. Economics and Business*, *7*(7), 577–586. doi:10.13106/jafeb.2020.vol7.no7.577

Liu, Z., Zheng, S., Zhang, X., & Mo, L. (2023). The Impact of Green Finance on Export Technology Complexity: Evidence from China. *Sustainability (Basel)*, *15*(3), 2625. doi:10.3390u15032625

Madaleno, M., Dogan, E., & Taskin, D. (2022). A step forward on sustainability: The nexus of environmental responsibility, green technology, clean energy and green finance. *Energy Economics*, *109*, 105945. doi:10.1016/j.eneco.2022.105945

Mirza, N., Afzal, A., Umar, M., & Skare, M. (2023). The impact of green lending on banking performance: Evidence from SME credit portfolios in the BRIC. *Economic Analysis and Policy*, *77*, 843–850. doi:10.1016/j.eap.2022.12.024

Mozib Lalon, R. (2015). Green Banking: Going Green. *International Journal of Economics. Finance and Management Sciences*, *3*(1), 34. doi:10.11648/j.ijefm.20150301.15

Nedopil, C., Dordi, T., & Weber, O. (2021). The Nature of Global Green Finance Standards—Evolution, Differences, and Three Models. *Sustainability (Basel)*, *13*(7), 3723. doi:10.3390u13073723

Qin, M., Zhang, X., Li, Y., & Badarcea, R. M. (2023). Blockchain market and green finance: The enablers of carbon neutrality in China. *Energy Economics*, *118*, 106501. doi:10.1016/j.eneco.2022.106501

Ren, X., Shao, Q., & Zhong, R. (2020). Nexus between green finance, non-fossil energy use, and carbon intensity: Empirical evidence from China based on a vector error correction model. *Journal of Cleaner Production*, *277*, 122844. doi:10.1016/j.jclepro.2020.122844

Shang, Y., Zhu, L., Qian, F., & Xie, Y. (2023). Role of green finance in renewable energy development in the tourism sector. *Renewable Energy*, *206*, 890–896. doi:10.1016/j.renene.2023.02.124

Soundarrajan, P., & Vivek, N. (2016). Green finance for sustainable green economic growth in India. [Zemědělská Ekonomika]. *Zemedelská Ekonomika*, *62*(1), 35–44. doi:10.17221/174/2014-AGRICECON

Sun, Y., Zhang, J., Xiong, Y., & Zhu, G. (2014). Data Security and Privacy in Cloud Computing. *International Journal of Distributed Sensor Networks*, *10*(7), 190903. doi:10.1155/2014/190903

Taghizadeh-Hesary, F., & Yoshino, N. (2020). Sustainable Solutions for Green Financing and Investment in Renewable Energy Projects. *Energies*, *13*(4), 788. doi:10.3390/en13040788

Talukder, M., Kabir, F., Muhsina, K., & Das, I. R. (2023). Emerging Concepts of Artificial Intelligence in the Hotel Indusatry: A Conceptual Paper. *International Journal of Research Publication and Reviews.*

Talukder, M. B. (2021). An assessment of the roles of the social network in the development of the Tourism Industry in Bangladesh. *International Journal of Business, Law, and Education*, *2*(3), 85–93. doi:10.56442/ijble.v2i3.21

Talukder, M. B., Kumar, S., Sood, K., & Grima, S. (2023). Information Technology, Food Service Quality and Restaurant Revisit Intention. *International Journal of Sustainable Development and Planning*, *18*(1), 295–303. doi:10.18280/ijsdp.180131

Tvaronavičienė, M. (2023). Towards Renewable Energy: Opportunities and Challenges. *Energies*, *16*(5), 2269. doi:10.3390/en16052269

Wang, Z., Yao-Ping Peng, M., Anser, M. K., & Chen, Z. (2023). Research on the impact of green finance and renewable energy on energy efficiency: The case study E−7 economies. *Renewable Energy*, *205*, 166–173. doi:10.1016/j.renene.2022.12.077

Zhang, A., Wang, S., & Liu, B. (2022). How to control air pollution with economic means? Exploration of China's green finance policy. *Journal of Cleaner Production*, *353*, 131664. doi:10.1016/j.jclepro.2022.131664

Zheng, G.-W., Siddik, A. B., Masukujjaman, M., Fatema, N., & Alam, S. S. (2021). Green Finance Development in Bangladesh: The Role of Private Commercial Banks (PCBs). *Sustainability (Basel)*, *13*(2), 795. doi:10.3390u13020795

Zhou, B., & Zhang, C. (2023). When green finance meets banking competition: Evidence from hard-to-abate enterprises of China. *Pacific-Basin Finance Journal*, *78*, 101954. doi:10.1016/j.pacfin.2023.101954

Chapter 7
Rural Communication Media: Its Impact on the Rural Markets

K. K. Kishore Mishra
https://orcid.org/0000-0001-6466-0575
Chandigarh University, India

Swati Priya
BBDNIIT, India

Syed Sajid Hussain
Chandigarh University, India

Swati Gupta
Chitkara University, India

ABSTRACT

The chapter aims at analyzing the impact of rural media of communication, which is a blend of conventional rural-centric media and modern mass media, on the rural markets of Uttar Pradesh, India. An interview schedule as a survey instrument was conducted administered for a sample of 1200 respondents in central Uttar Pradesh from February to June 2021. The data analysis of the study was carried out in IBM SPSS Statistics 27.0. The study concluded that buyers respond maturely to the various promotional sources investigated. Hindi dallies, both national and local, play an important role in raising awareness about various items. The most successful media vehicles for connecting with clients in rural areas are posters, handbills, hoardings, banners, and television programs. Mobile vans, newspapers, and e-displays and advertisements plastered on public transportation are all very successful advertising tools.

DOI: 10.4018/979-8-3693-1388-6.ch007

1. INTRODUCTION

Rural media (Gupta, 2012) are now no more conventionally rural-centric media, but, are a good blend of modern mass media (Othman, 2020; Gangwani,2022) and traditional rural media or traditional media of communication (Gajanad, Ashok and Karthik, 2017) which are reaching millions of people across rural India, but creating a significant positive impact on the rural market is still an uphill task (Thalladi, 2022). The enormous potential of the rural markets of India provides businesses with considerable prospects, and it is now even larger than the urban equivalent for most categories. (Gujrati, 2016)".

But, varying media reach, habits and comprehension abilities, low literacy, language and cultural diversity, the vast geographical spread of the market and feudalism pose major challenges to the market's communication (Kashyap, 2012). There are 22 scheduled "Languages Included in the Eighth Schedule of the Indian Constitution" and 1800 (Census of India, 2011) vernacular languages in India which are dialect-specific in different regions of the country, e.g., Awadhi in central Uttar Pradesh and Bhojpuri in eastern Uttar Pradesh.

Modern mass media, which reaches millions of people in rural markets, includes mobile internet, e-Suvidha Kendra, television, radio, print, electronic hoardings, and direct mailers, whereas traditional rural media, which is old and deeply rooted, includes paintings on walls, video vans, folk drama, video raths, folklore, folk song, village market (Jain & Rathod 2005), and dance, among other things (Kediehor & Odiepiye, Chimezie,2019). Radio reaches people regardless of their geographic location or area of residence, literacy levels, or geography (Kashyap, 2012).

The proliferation of FM radio stations has effectively transformed radio into a rural communication medium ("Proliferation of radio stations: Social impacts and need for rededication" 2021). In rural India, television is the fastest-growing, most popular, and most powerful mass medium. In recent years, rural India has seen a tremendous increase in DTH connections ("Money life Foundation Report" 2010)

In rural areas, however, newspapers constitute an important part of the print media (Julie, 2019).

With low literacy levels in rural areas, the print media continues to struggle in terms of reach and accessibility in rural markets. Another form of mass communication that allows for the dissemination of product information through brief advertisements, films, and cinema is cinema (Kashyap, 2012).

According to research by "the Internet and Mobile Association of India (IAMAI) Kantar ICUBE 2020", India's active internet users (AIU) are expected to increase by 45 per cent by 2025 compared to 2020. From roughly 622 million in 2020, the number of AIU in the country is expected to rise to 900 million by 2025. The poll also reveals that even while urban areas have more than twice as many internet users as rural ones, in 2020, rural users are anticipated to grow at a faster rate year over year due to a higher adoption rate ("Internet Adoption in India ICUBE 2020", June 2021). Rural marketers face huge problems in expressing their message to rural consumers because their customers are dispersed across a broad geographic area across the country (Pande, 2022).

The bulk of India's villages is still out of the reach of traditional media because of their broad geographic dispersion (Census of India, 2011, Uttar Pradesh). There are approximately 650000 villages in India (Rural Energy Access/ Reach the World, 2021). Even using nontraditional media makes it nearly impossible for a marketer to reach out to a geographically dispersed rural population. The challenge is exacerbated by the fact that the consumers are diverse in terms of the languages they speak. The country's 22 scheduled languages plus 19500 dialect-specific vernacular languages, such as Awadhi in central Uttar Pradesh and Bhojpuri in eastern Uttar Pradesh, make interacting with rural consumers extremely difficult ((Bhatnagar et al., 2022a, 2022b,2023a, 2023b; Dangwal et al., 2022a, 2022b; Kumar et al.,

2023a, 2023b; Özen et al., 2022, Singh et al., 2021; Taneja et al., 2022a, 2022b; 2023a, 2023b, 2023c, 2023d, 2023e 2023f; Gupta et al. 2023; Dahiya 2023; Bansal 2023; Reepu 2023).

Only one-fifth of people in rural areas have matriculated or higher degrees, and about two-fifths of the population, there is illiterate, (Statistical Diary Uttar Pradesh, 2020). This demonstrates the wide range of literacy levels among rural residents. Furthermore, literacy levels vary greatly between states. Kerala, for example, has a literacy rate of 95%, whilst Bihar has a literacy rate of only 52%. These differences make it difficult for all types of rural audiences to understand the message simply and clearly. To effectively communicate with the less educated, it is crucial to concentrate on creating a clear communication message using self-explanatory visuals like flip charts, storyboards, and role-plays ("Challenges in Rural Communication", 2018-23).

Due to regional and state differences as well as the limited reach of mass media in rural areas, it is impossible to develop a single strategy for interacting with rural consumers. According to a 2016 BARC broadcast survey ("Television viewership in India up by 12%" 2016) In rural India, television has the highest penetration rate (59%) followed by cable and satellite (32.6%), radio (15.9%), the press (22%), the cinema (2%), and the internet (0.8%). The following are the research project's objectives:

Objective 1- To look into how consumers in central Uttar Pradesh's rural markets respond to various media vehicles.

Objective 2- To investigate the impact of rural communication on rural markets in Central Uttar Pradesh.

2. LITERATURE REVIEW AND HYPOTHESES DEVELOPMENT

2.1 Response of customers toward promotional sources

The study examines how consumer product trial and repurchase behaviour is impacted by sales promotion strategies such as coupons, price discounts, free samples, bonus packs, and in-store displays. Price reductions, free samples, bonus offers, and in-store displays all correlate with product trials, according to data research. Trialling a product is not much impacted by coupons. Trial influences repurchase decisions and mediate the link between sales promotions and subsequent purchases. Fear of looking bad dramatically modifies the link between product trial and in-store presentation. (Ndubisi, et al, 2005). The usage of ever-larger budgets has increased the importance of the field of sales promotions. For effective sales promotion techniques and other associated components of the communications-mix require, it is crucial to understand how consumers react to promotions (Meryl and Roger.,1984). Promotional materials can only persuade a customer to try a new product or buy more (Jain, 2012). Therefore, a marketer cannot benefit long-term from a sale campaign alone unless and until consumers associate a product's purchase with value and quality. If a marketer doesn't overlook the quality and value that consumers perceive, sales promotion can assist marketers to reach both their short- and long-term goals, ("Consumer responses to promotional tools in hotels", 01 Jul. 2016). According to the article on Consumer response toward native advertising, a micro-social celebrity's social media tweets regarding experiential native advertising generated more information-sharing attributions than those from a mainstream celebrity. However, one way to boost a product's sales is through promotional offers. Companies struggle with deciding how much money to devote to sales promotions vs other initiatives (Cotton & Babb, 1978). Keeping these reviews in view, six promotional sources have been identified for the study and the first hypothesis is suggested accordingly as under-

H1- The responses of the respondents for the six promotional sources mentioned above are not identical.

2.2 Effectiveness of Dailies in Creating Brand Knowledge or Awareness

In every nation, newspapers are a vital medium for communication (Sama,2019). Newspapers are an essential form of communication in India because they are available in every part of the nation. On a daily circulation basis, newspapers in India have a market of over 330 million readers. (Nayak & Shah, 2015). Newspaper advertising offers a wealth of information on daily events in the state or neighbourhoods (Henry, 1970). Newspapers and periodical journals in England throughout the 17th and 18th centuries became a significant source of ads after the invention of the printing press. (Nayak & Shah, 2015). The author stresses that newspaper advertisements have an impact on brand development and marketing and also help consumers make purchasing decisions. People like reading newspapers daily and find them to be dependable, despite other forms of advertising and technological advances (Mishra, 2015). Daily publications, according to Nayak and Shah, build trust in the minds of readers (Raju & Devi, 2012) similarly found advertisements in dailies to be more trustworthy. Press advertisements are more influential among those who look for certified advertisements and the presentation of this advertisement in dailies such as captions and colour effects capture the minds of customers. In his study, (Sama, 2019) noted that dailies have a notable impact on consumers' awareness, interest, conviction, purchase, and post-buy behavior.

The study by Mallou, J. V., et. al. (2001) conducted in Spanish national daily markets shows that brand i.e. the name of the newspaper has a significant influence on consumer preferences rather than other attributes such as price, daily pullout, and Sunday supplement. For those customers, who have access to only one source of information, newspaper advertisements are a primary informative source (Kakkad,2016).

Another study by Ashram, M. (2018) states that due to the low literacy rate and poor reading habits, dailies are not so popular medium of communication in rural areas. However, the low-priced dailies in the local language are more popular in rural areas where people read newspapers on Fridays and Sundays. In his research, Siddiqui (2021) discovers that literacy rates are rising in rural areas and that more people there are subscribing to newspapers to learn about the goods on the market. His study mentions advertisement have a major influence on the on-purchase decisions of consumers and the most favored means of advertising is television, newspaper and word of mouth.

Nobin, (2016) explored in his study the association between community newspapers and brand building in the digital age, even in the digital age, due to lack of communication with neighbours, newspapers are much more needed. The brand building through dailies shows that print and digital media are companions. Another study by Ghachem, (2011) mentions that in the era of digital newspapers, online news is becoming a necessity and their websites are the most visited. Dailies are a tool for advertisement which wide and easy circulation and where all marketers can advertise their products and services. Keeping these reviews in view, the second hypothesis is suggested accordingly as an under-

H2- The respondents' responses for the various media vehicles mentioned above are not identical.

2.3 TV Programs Attracting the Attention of Customers

TV is a good and successful form of media because it provides a number of significant advantages, such as economical access to a big audience, sound and moving visuals, high appeal, and attention-getting.

The largest influence on viewers comes from television, which also motivates people to start buying. (Ansari & Joloudar, 2011).

There are three key advantages of using television as a marketing tool. To begin with, it significantly affects customers' views and preferences. It is also a cheap approach to getting in front of a big audience. Thirdly, the audio and visual content evoke strong feelings. (2007) Ramalingam et al.

You can give the audience the details they require to learn more about the product and spark their interest in purchasing it by grabbing their attention. (Chithra and Kothai, 2015).

Recognize that analyzing sales is one way to gauge the effectiveness of advertising. While determining the extent to which advertising dollars are producing the highest return on investment, it's important to take into account how well television programmes can grab and hold viewers' attention as well as how likely it is that they will engage viewers' cognitive processes to the same extent as objectives (Perreault and McCarthy, 2000).

The aim of consumer purchasing behavior is to identify the elements that lead a customer to behave a certain way in a variety of situations. (Ayanwale et. al, 2005). In light of these data, we suggest that hypothesis three be as follows:

H3- The responses of the respondents for the various TV programs discussed above are not identical.

2.4 Effectiveness of Mass Media Sources in Creating Awareness

Advertising and marketing push potential customers more quickly and easily than ever before because of the business communication that media has made available ("Federal Communications Commission" 2016).

Mass media campaigns have the power to influence huge populations' health-related habits positively or negatively, both directly and indirectly. A study indicated that it is challenging to isolate the independent effects of mass media efforts. However, substantial evidence supporting the idea that mass media campaigns can alter population health habits has been gathered from study designs that, taken individually, are less than traditionally outstanding. (Wakefield, B Loken, and Hornik, 2010).

Since the participants admitted using media websites for health awareness throughout the course of four weeks, Rehman et al. F (2021) found that knowledge gains connected to COVID-19 were often influenced in a positive way. This increase in knowledge encourages the practice of healthy behaviors and stops all undesirable conduct among the study subjects. The investigation also emphasized the participants' media preferences. During the coronavirus pandemic, there was a huge increase in the number of people using social and electronic media.

Nelson et al, (2016) observed that the primary method for enhancing women's access to breast cancer care was through messaging in the media. This is critical because health-related behaviors of women in South-West Nigeria might change positively or negatively as a result of messages in the media.

In order to tell a large portion of the general public about the Corona Virus Pandemic sickness, Dmour et al., (2022) found that public awareness campaigns are the most efficient and successful mode of communication.

Mass media interventions that aim to indirectly affect people by making positive changes in the places (or settings) in which people live and work are currently understudied, despite the fact that they have an equal or even greater potential to encourage positive changes in population health behaviors (Abroms and Maibach, 2008). Keeping these reviews in view, the following hypothesis is suggested-

H4- The respondents' responses to the various mass media sources mentioned above are not identical."Auraiya district -

3. RESEARCH METHODOLOGY

3.1 Data Collection

Present research work is conducted through a face-to-face interview schedule, to collect responses from 21 districts of Uttar Pradesh (India). In the present research work, cluster and convenience sampling methods were used for deciding upon the sample size and sample units to collect their responses in view of the objectives and hypotheses developed. Out of 21 districts; "Auraiya, Banda, Baranbanki, Chitrakoot, Etawah, Farrukhabad, Fatehpur, Hamirpur, Hardoi, Jalaun, Jhansi, Kannauj, Kanpur Dehat, Kanpur Nagar, Lakhimpur Kheri, Lalitpur, Lucknow, Mahoba, Rae Bareli, Sitapur, and Unnao", (Paul and Christo, 2022), of central Uttar Pradesh, 4 districts- Barabnki, Hardoi, Sitapur and Rae Bareli were clustered based on the socio-economic factors ("India Stat districts", 2019) for development as these districts are found to be fast developing. Based on convenience, rurban (semi-urban) markets of each of the two Tehseels from each the of four districts were selected and visited to administer the interview schedules, both in English and Hindi, to collect the responses of the respondents (age group 18-35) during February to June 2021. Thus, a total of 1200 respondents were approached and data analysis is done based on the entire sample of 1200.

Questionnaire Distribution

Table 1. Sample collection from district wise villages

ZONE	DISTRICT	VILLAGE/ Tehsil	SAMPLE
Central Uttar Pradesh Total sample= 1200	Sitapur= 300 sample	Mahmoodabad	150
		Misrikh	150
	Barabanki= 300 sample	Nawabganj	150
		ramnagar	150
	Raebareily= 300 sample	Bachhrawan	150
		Lalganj	150
	Hardoi= 300 sample	Sandila	150
		Shahabad	150

3.2 Univariate Statistics

The data analysis of the study was conducted in IBM SPSS Statistics 27.0. To understand the basic descriptive statistics such as frequency, mean, and standard deviation related to promotional sources, Language wise Newspapers, TV programs, and various mass media sources are calculated.

3.3 Assessment of Association

To test the significance between factors like promotional sources, language-wise newspapers, TV programs, various mass media sources and the rating given by 1200respondentst is calculated by means of chi- a square test at a 95% confidence interval.

4. DATA ANALYSIS

4.1 Responses of Customers Toward Six Promotional Sources

H1-The responses to the six promotional sources – mobile vans, paintings on the walls, advertising in halls, roadshows, newspapers and journals, and commercials on public transportation – differ.

From Table - 4.1, it is apparent that mobile vans, news publications and magazines, advertising pasted on public transportation, and paintings on the walls are the most desired and effective promotional sources, listed from 1 to 4. Hall commercials and roadshows are less successful promotional methods. The average awareness (μ) of the six promotional sources understudy is 3.07, with a standard deviation (∂) of 0.44.

Except for classified ads in halls and avenues suggests, all of the promotional resources fall in the variety of variations of μ from standard deviation σ (μ ± σ), which covers two 1/3 (68.27% of the place) of the observations, while classified ads in halls and roadshows fall inside μ ± 2σ (i.e., Ninety-five. 45% of the region), that's inside the left facet of the location. The coefficient of variation is 14.3% which is notably variable and for this reason less uniform.

This implies that all of the factors are less effective, but four out of six observations fall within two-thirds of the region, indicating that they are a more reliable and preferable promotional source.

At a 5% level of significance, the predicted values of χ2 exceed the 9.48 value in the table. Therefore, the alternative hypothesis is accepted and the null hypothesis is disproved: the respondents' responses for the six promotional sources – mobile vans, paintings on the walls, commercials in halls, roadshows, newspapers, periodicals, and commercials on public transportation – differ.

4.2 Effectiveness of Dailies in Creating Brand Knowledge or Awareness

H2-The respondents' reactions to increasing awareness about different FMCG products through different regional, national, and local Hindi daily varies.

From Table – 4.2, it is clear that the regional daily, local daily in Hindi, and national daily in Hindi are ranked frrst to third respectively, hence, are extremely effective media vehicles in creating awareness about the products amongst the customers of rural markets. National dailies in English are ranked fourth and fifth respectively, and hence, are fewer effective media vehicles for creating awareness about the products amongst the customers of rural markets. In this case, the mean awareness (μ) is 3.42 with a standard deviation (∂) 0 .24.

National daily in Hindi, Local daily in English and Hindi fall in the range of variation of μ from standard deviation σ (μ ± σ), which covers 1/3 (sixty-eight. 27% of the area) of the observations, while the nearby every day and countrywide daily in English fall inside μ ± 2σ (i.e., Ninety-five. 45% of the place) inside the right and left sides of the region respectively.

Table 2. Promotional sources attracting you most, rated from one to five

Factors / Rating	Not at all effective	Not very effective	Somewhat effective		Very effective	Extremely effective	Total	Weighted Average	Rank	Mean of WA (μ)	SD (∂)	Range (μ±∂)	CV	χ^2 Calculated Value	χ^2 Table Value at 5% d.f.-4	Null Hypothesis Rejected / Accepted
Mobile van promotion	160	168	236		296	340	1200	3.41	1	3.07	0.44	2.62 to 3.51	14	480.7	9.48	Rejected
Paintings on the walls	170	178	246		322	284	1200	3.31	4					513.7		
Commercials in halls	436	268	168		168	160	1200	2.46	5					956.5		
Roadshows	440	256	186		176	142	1200	2.44	6					919.8		
Newspapers and Periodicals	158	156	196		422	268	1200	3.41	2					206.7		
Commercials posted on public transport	168	176	216		288	352	1200	3.4	3					102.9		

Source: Author's calculation

Table 3. Effectiveness of the dailies creating the maximum brand knowledge or awareness, rated from one to five

Factors Rating	Strongly disagree	Disagree	Somewhat agree	Agree	Strongly agree	Total	Weighted Average	Rank	Mean of WA (μ)	SD (∂)	Range (μ±∂)	CV	χ^2 Calculated Value	χ^2 Table Value at 5% d.f.-4	Null Hypothesis Rejected / Accepted
National daily in English	236	208	188	278	290	1200	3.15	5	3.42	0.24	3.18 to 3.67	7.018	32	9.48	Rejected
National daily in Hindi	218	196	152	196	438	1200	3.37	3					213.7		
Local daily in English	188	214	236	286	276	1200	3.21	4					28.3		
Local daily in Hindi	158	170	118	224	530	1200	3.67	2					461.9		
The regional daily	136	156	122	236	550	1200	3.76	1					532.9		

Source: Author's calculation

The coefficient of variation is 7.02 per cent, which indicates that the data is less varied and thus more consistent. This implies that regional, local, and national Hindi dailies are the most effective media vehicles for raising product awareness in rural areas.

At a 5% level of significance, the predicted values of $\chi 2$ exceed the 9.48 value in the table. As a result, the null hypothesis is rejected, and the alternate hypothesis, that there are differences in respondents' replies in raising awareness about different FMCG items through various regional, national, and local Hindi newspapers, is accepted.

4.3 TV Programs Attracting the Attention of Customers

H3-Respondents' responses to various TV programs in terms of attracting them varied.

From Table – 4.3, It is evident that Krishi Jeevan, movies, detective series, film songs, and programmes about the environment are listed from 1 to 5 sequentially. As a result, these TV shows are incredibly successful at drawing viewers in rural regions.

The rest of the serials stated above are ranked from 6 to nine respectively, and subsequently, are much less attractive programs to the clients of rural markets. Mean awareness (μ) of the above four kinds of opinion leaders beneath consideration is three.14 with a trendy deviation (∂) 0 .47. Saas Bahu serials, movie songs, tele purchasing, environment-associated programs, and video games and contests fall within the variety of variations of μ from preferred deviation σ ($\mu \pm \sigma$), which covers third (sixty-eight. 27% of the area) of the observations, while films, Krishi Jeevan, caricature films and detective serials fall within $\mu \pm 2\sigma$ (i.e., 95. Forty-five % of the vicinity) inside the right and left facets of the region respectively.

The coefficient of variation is 15%, which indicates that the data is more varied and thus less uniform. This implies that Krishi Jeevan, films, detective serials, film songs, and environmental-related programs are particularly effective TV shows for luring clients in rural regions.

At a 5% level of significance, the estimated values of $\chi 2$ are bigger than the table value of 9.48. The alternative hypothesis, that there is a difference in the respondents' replies in attracting different TV shows, is therefore accepted, and the null hypothesis is rejected.

4.4 Effectiveness of Mass Media Sources in Creating Awareness

H4- The respondents' responses to the various mass media sources mentioned above are identical.

4- H1-The responses of the respondents to posters and banners are different.

From Table- 4.4, It is obvious that banners and posters rank first and second, respectively, and are therefore very successful media outlets for raising consumer awareness in rural marketplaces. Stickers and handbills are less effective media outlets for raising consumer awareness in rural markets because they are ranked third and fourth, respectively.

The mean recognition (μ) of the above four kinds of opinion leaders beneath consideration is 3.25 with a well-known deviation (∂) zero .29. Handbills and banners fall in the range of variants suggesting μ from widespread deviation σ ($\mu \pm \sigma$), which covers a third (sixty-eight. 27% of the region) of the observations, while posters and stickers fall inside $\mu \pm 2\sigma$ (i.e., 95.45% of the vicinity) in the proper and left sides of the place respectively.CV of 8.92%, which is a substantially lower and hence more uniform coefficient of variation This suggests that manufacturers of FMCG items should rely more on banners and posters to increase consumer awareness of their products in rural marketplaces.

Table 4. TV programs attracting the attention of the customers, rated from one to five

Factors / Rating	Not at all effective	Not very effective	Somewhat effective	Very effective	Extremely effective	Total	Weighted Average	Rank	Mean of WA (μ)	SD (∂)	Range (μ±∂)	CV	χ^2 Calculated Value	χ^2 Table Value at 5% d.f.-4	Null Hypothesis Rejected / Accepted
Films	124	164	142	332	438	1200	3.66	2	3.14	0.47	2.67 to 3.62	14.97	318.7	9.48	Rejected
Saas Bahu Serials	164	436	288	180	132	1200	2.73	7					257.3		
Krishi Jeevan	138	90	156	238	578	1200	3.86	1					642.5		
Filmi Songs	122	236	176	244	422	1200	3.51	4					213.2		
Cartoon Films	264	464	152	170	150	1200	2.57	9					297.9		
Teleshopping	278	318	228	212	164	1200	2.72	8					59.3		
Environment-related programmes	210	334	230	236	190	1200	2.89	5					51.4		
Games/ contests	234	352	218	230	166	1200	2.79	6					77.6		
Detective serials	132	176	168	256	468	1200	3.63	3					304.9		

Source: Author's calculation

Table 5. Effectiveness of mass media sources in creating awareness, rated from one to five

Factors / Rating	Not at all effective	Not very effective	Somewhat effective	Very effective	Extremely effective	Total	Weighted Average	Rank	Mean of WA (μ)	SD (∂)	Range (μ±∂)	CV	χ^2 Calculated Value	χ^2 Table Value at 5% d.f.-4	Null Hypothesis Rejected / Accepted
Handbills & Booklets	164	236	352	236	212	1200	3.08	3	3.25	0.29	2.96 to 3.55	8.923	79.7	9.48	Rejected
Posters	104	152	196	436	312	1200	3.58	1					299		
Stickers	210	270	352	202	166	1200	2.87	4					88.6		
Banners	118	172	210	386	314	1200	3.51	2					196.6		

Source: Author's calculation

At a 5% level of significance, the estimated values of $\chi 2$ are bigger than the table value of 9.48. This disproves the null hypothesis, and as a result, the alternative hypothesis—that there are differences in the responses of the responders to posters and banners—is accepted.

5. CONCLUSION

After the research, it can be concluded that buyers respond maturely to the various promotional sources investigated. Hindi dallies, both national and local, play an important role in raising awareness about various items. The most successful media vehicles for connecting with clients in rural areas are posters, handbills, hoardings, banners, and television programs. Mobile vans, newspapers and journals, and advertisements plastered on public transportation are all very successful advertising tools. Overall, it can be argued that, while we may have a national strategy, we must think and act locally in any type of rural communication. The need for targeted communication aimed at the rural market should not be overlooked. This necessitates creativity and significant adjustments in marketing methods. The study in future can provide theoretical for analyzing the impact of new rural media which could be a blend of current rural media as discussed in the research paper and social media and digital media marketing (Sultana, 2018)". A further investigation can be necessitated to assess the impact of social media marketing and digital marketing in the rural markets of the state and country which is having huge market potential. A further investigation shall be required to observe the same. The study offers practical implications for rural media to investigate the effectiveness of social media and digital marketing because it is based on empirical data gathered from the survey.

REFERENCES

Abroms, L. C., & Maibach, E. W. The Effectiveness of Mass Communication to Change Public Behavior. *Annual Reviews*. https://www.annualreviews.org/doi/pdf/10.1146/annurev.publhealth.29.020907.090824

Akanbi, A., & Adeyeye, C. (2011). The Association between Advertising and Sales Volume. *Journal of Emerging Trends in Economic and Management Sciences*. www.jetems.scholarlinkeresearch.org

Al-Dmour, H., Ra'ed Masa'deh, A. S., Al-Dmour, R., & Abuhashesh, M. (2022). The Role of Mass Media Interventions on Promoting Public Health Knowledge and Behavioral Social Change Against COVID-19 Pandemic in Jordan. *SAGE Open*, *12*(1). doi:10.1177/21582440221082125

Ansari, M., & Joloudar, E. (2011). An investigation of TV advertisement effects on customers' purchasing and their satisfaction. *International Journal of Marketing Studies*, *3*(4), 175.

Ayanwale. (2005). The Influence of Advertising on Consumer Brand Preference. *Journal of Social Science*, *10*(1), 9–16.

Ayesha, Meryem, M., Vaneeza, R., & Anjum. (2020). *Role of Mass Media and Public Health Communications in the COVID-19 Pandemic*. doi:10.7759/cureus.10453

Badugu, D., & Chanhan, S. (2011). Understanding the Indian Rural Market Potential. *International Journal of Multidisciplinary Research, 1*(6), 68–82. https://www.researchgate.net/publication/312161872_UNDERSTANDING_THE_INDIAN_RURAL_MARKET_POTENTIAL

Bansal, N., Bhatnagar, M., & Taneja, S. (2023). Balancing Priorities Through Green Optim000ism: A Study Elucidating Initiatives, Approaches, and Strategies for Sustainable Supply Chain Management. In *Handbook of Research on Designing Sustainable Supply Chains to Achieve a Circular Economy* (pp. 60–81). IGI Global. doi:10.4018/978-1-6684-7664-2.ch004

Bernadette, J. & Goddard, C. (2002), *Australian Institute of Family Studies.* AIFS. https://aifs.gov.au/resources/policy-and-practice-papers/role-mass-media-facilitating-community-education-and-child

Bhatnagar, M., Özen, E., Taneja, S., Grima, S., & Rupeika-Apoga, R. (2022a). The Dynamic Connectedness between Risk and Return in the Fintech Market of India: Evidence Using the GARCH-M Approach. *Risks, 10*(11), 209. doi:10.3390/risks10110209

Bhatnagar, M., Taneja, S., Kumar, P., & Özen, E. (2023a). Does Financial Education Act as a Catalyst for SME Competitiveness. *International Journal of Education Economics and Development, 1*(1), 1. doi:10.1504/IJEED.2023.10053629

Bhatnagar, M., Taneja, S., & Özen, E. (2022b). A wave of green start-ups in India—The study of green finance as a support system for sustainable entrepreneurship. *Green Finance, 4*(2), 253–273. doi:10.3934/GF.2022012

Bhatnagar, M., Taneja, S., & Rupeika-Apoga, R. (2023b). Demystifying the Effect of the News (Shocks) on Crypto Market Volatility. *Journal of Risk and Financial Management, 16*(2), 136. doi:10.3390/jrfm16020136

Census of India. (2011). *Uttar Pradesh.* CDN. https://cdn.s3waas.gov.in/s34c5bde74a8f110656874902f07378009/uploads/2016/09/2018022381.pdf

Challenges in Rural Communication. (2018-23). Brainkart. https://www.brainkart.com/article/Challenges-in-Rural-Communication_6095/

Chithra, V., & Kothai, S. (2015). Television viewing behavior of consumers and television advertisement's impact on consumer purchase decision. *International Journal of Research in Commerce & Management, 6*(10).

Cotton, C., & Babb, M. (1978). Consumer Response to Promotional Deals. *Journal of Marketing, 42*(3), 109–113. doi:10.2307/1250544

Customer's Perception towards Promotional Tools of IMC. Retrieved from https://www.academia.edu/38955514/Customers_Perception_towards_Promotional_Tools_of_IMC

Dahiya, K., Taneja, S., & Özen, E. (2023). To Analyse the Impact of Multi-Media Technology on the Rural Entrepreneurship Development. In Contemporary Studies of Risks in Emerging Technology, Part A (pp. 221-240). Emerald Publishing Limited. doi:10.1108/978-1-80455-562-020231015

Dangwal, A., Kaur, S., Taneja, S., & Taneja, S. (2022a). A Bibliometric Analysis of Green Tourism Based on the Scopus Platform. In J. Kaur, P. Jindal, & A. Singh (Eds.), *Developing Relationships, Personalization, and Data Herald in Marketing 5.0* (Vol. i, pp. 1–327). IGI Global. doi:10.4018/978-1-6684-4496-2.ch015

Dangwal, A., Taneja, S., Özen, E., Todorovic, I., & Grima, S. (2022b). Abridgement of Renewables: It's Potential and Contribution to India's GDP. *International Journal of Sustainable Development and Planning*, *17*(8), 2357–2363. doi:10.18280/ijsdp.170802

Department of Official Language. (n.d.). *Languages Included in the Eighth Schedule of the Indian Constitution.* Ministry of Home Affairs GoI. https://rajbhasha.gov.in/en/languages-included-eighth-schedule-indian-constitution

Money Life. (2010). Digital TV growth in India driven by the rural market. *Money Life.* https://www.moneylife.in/article/digital-tv-growth-in-india-driven-by-rural-market/5287.html

Federal Communications Commission, Broadcast Station Totals as of September 30, 2016, on the internet retrieved from https://apps.fcc.gov/edocs_public/attachmatch/DOC-341807A1.pdf

Gajanad, A. & Karthik. (2017). *Role of traditional media in rural development.* BioTech Articles. https://www.biotecharticles.com/Agriculture-Article/Role-of-Traditional-Media-in-Rural-Development-4099.html

Gangwani, N. (2022). How Rural Communication Has Evolved: The Journey of Media In Rural India. *Rural Marketing Association of India (RMAI).* https://armworldwide.com/how-rural-communication-has-evolved-the-journey-of-media-in-rural-india/

Ghachem L. (2011). *Communications of the IBIMA.* IBIMA Publishing. . doi:10.5171/2011.489627

Gujrati (2016). An emerging Indian rural market: Challenges and opportunities. *International Journal of Multidisciplinary Research and Development*, *3*(7) 334-340 https://www.researchgate.net/publication/333131633_An_emerging_Indian_rural_market_Challenges_and_opportunities

Gupta, M., Arora, R., & Taneja, S. (2023). Bibliometric Analysis on Employee Engagement and Human Resource Management. In *Enhancing Customer Engagement Through Location-Based Marketing* (pp. 185–205). IGI Global. doi:10.4018/978-1-6684-8177-6.ch013

Gupta, T. (2012). Rural Marketing: Looking Ahead. *International Journal of Management Research and Review*, *2*(1), 186–191. https://www.proquest.com/scholarly-journals/rural-marketing-looking-ahead/docview/1418665021/se-2

ETV Bharat. (2021). *India's active Internet population to hit 900M by 2025: Report.* ETV Bharat National. https://www.etvbharat.com/english/national/science-and-technology/indias-active-internet-population-to-hit-900m-by-2025-report/na20210606053027467

Indian Express. (2018). More than 19,500 mother tongues spoken in India: Census. *Indian Express.* https://indianexpress.com/article/india/more-than-19500-mother-tongues-spoken-in-india-census-5241056/

Jain, A. (2012). Brand Awareness and Customer Preferences for FMCG Products in Rural Market of Garhwal Region. *VSRD-IJBMR*, *2*(8), 434-443. https://www.scribd.com/document/142534349/Brand-Awareness-Consumer-Preference

Jain, A., & Rathod, R. (2005). Distribution and Retailing Trends in Rural Markets - A Study in Villages of Gujarat. *Indian Journal of Marketing*, *35*(9), 1–10. https://www.indianjournalofmarketing.com/index.php/ijom/article/view/34243/0

Julie, T. (2019). The Role of Newspapers in Rural Minnesota. *Rural Minnesota.* https://www.ruralmn.org/the-role-of-newspapers-in-rural-minnesota/

Kakkad, R. (2016). A study on effect of newspaper advertisement on consumer buying behavior of two wheelers. *Philica*, *2*, 35.

Kashyap, P. (2012). *Rural Marketing. Pearson* (3rd ed.).

Kediehor, O. & Chimezie. (2019). The Effectiveness of Rural Communication Modes on Modern Mass Media. *Transatlantic Journal of Rural Research*, *1*(3), 1-16. https://www.transatlanticj.com/tjrr/. doi:10.5281/zenodo.3402105

Kothari, C. R. (2020). *Research Methodology* (2nd ed.). New Age International Publishers.

Kumar, P., Taneja, S., Özen, E., & Singh, S. (2023b). Artificial Intelligence and Machine Learning in Insurance: A Bibliometric Analysis. In Smart Analytics, Artificial Intelligence and Sustainable Performance Management in a Global Digitalised Economy (pp. 191-202). Emerald Publishing Limited. doi:10.1108/S1569-37592023000110A010

Kumar, P., Verma, P., Bhatnagar, M., Taneja, S., Seychel, S., Todorović, I., & Grim, S. (2023). The financial performance and solvency status of the indian public sector banks: A CAMELS rating and Z index approach. *International Journal of Sustainable Development and Planning*, *18*(2), 367–376. doi:10.18280/ijsdp.180204

Kumar & Dangi. (2013). Rural Marketing in India: Challenges and Opportunities, International. *Journal of Management and Social Sciences Research*, *2*(8), 93–100. https://citeseerx.ist.psu.edu/viewdoc/download?doi=10.1.1.403.7838&rep=rep1&type=pdf

Macarthy, E. & McDaniel, C. (2000). *Basic Marketing.* University Book Stall.

Mallou, V., Boubeta, R., & Tobío, B. (2001). Consumer Preferences and Brand Equity Measurement of Spanish National Daily Newspapers: A Conjoint Analysis Approach. *The Spanish Journal of Psychology*, *4*(1), 48–54. doi:10.1017/S1138741600005643 PMID:11705342

Meryl, P., & Roger, A. (1984). Consumer Response to Promotions: Some New Perspectives. Advances in Consumer Research, 11, 420-425. Agro- Economic Research Centre University of Allahabad.

Mishra, B. (2003). *Rural Non-Farm Employment in Uttar Pradesh.* Agro- Economic Research Centre University of Allahabad. https://allduniv.ac.in/ckfinder/userfiles/files/Rural_Non-Farm_Employment_in_Uttar_Pradesh.pdf

Mishra, (2015). An empirical analysis of the marketing of services in rural Uttar Pradesh. *IMPACT: International Journal of Research in Business Management, 3*(2), 23-34 https://citeseerx.ist.psu.edu/viewdoc/download?doi=10.1.1.684.600&rep=rep1&type=pdf

Nayak, K., & Shah, B. (2015). The effectiveness of newspaper prints ads. *Indian Journal of Applied Research, 5*(2), 328–331.

Ndubisi, N., & Moi, C. (2005). Customers behavioral responses to sales promotion: The role of fear of losing face. *Asia Pacific Journal of Marketing and Logistics, 17*(1), 32–49. https://www.researchgate.net/publication/241699350_Customers_behaviourial_responses_to_sales_promotion_The_role_of_fear_of_losing_face. doi:10.1108/13555850510672278

Nelson, O., & Salawu, A. (2016). Effective Use of Media Awareness Campaigns for Breast Cancer Care among Women: A Comparative Study. *Journal of International Women's Studies, 17*(4), 160–173. https://vc.bridgew.edu/jiws/vol17/iss4/12

Nobin, E. (2016). *Exploring community newspapers and brand building in the digital age* [Doctoral dissertation, The IIE].

Othman, H. (2020). Ambient Ads as Unconventional Media Approach. *International Design Journal, 10*(2), 269-278. https://idj.journals.ekb.eg/article_81142.html doi:10.21608/idj.2020.81142

Özen, E., & Sanjay, T. (2022a). Empirical Analysis of the Effect of Foreign Trade in Computer and Communication Services on Economic Growth in India. *Journal of Economics and Business Issues, 2*(2), 24–34.

Pande. (2022). Rural Marketing: Problems & Strategies. *International Journal For Administration in Management, Commerce and Economics*, 123-128, https://www.researchgate.net/publication/361901564_Rural_Marketing_Problems_Strategies

Paul & Christo. (2022). *Central Uttar Pradesh Region.* Encuclopedia. https://encyclopedia.adventist.org/article?id=AJB2#:~:text=Territory%3A%20The%20following%20districts%20in,Bareli%2C%20Sitapur%2C%20and%20Unnao

Oduntan, T. (2021). Proliferation of radio stations. *Daily Trust.* https://dailytrust.com/proliferation-of-radio-stations-social-impacts-and-need-for-rededication

Raju, A., & Devi, S. (2012). Means of advertisement impact on consumer buying behavior with reference to health drinks in Kuppam. *International Journal of Management and Social Sciences Research, 1*(2), 31–35.

Ramalingam, V., Palaniappan, B., Panchnatham, N., & Palanivel, S. (2006). Measuring Advertising Effectiveness - A Neural Network Approach. *Journal of Business Research, 31*, 159–160.

Reepu, R., Taneja, S., Ozen, E., & Singh, A. (2023). A Globetrotter to the Future of Marketing: Metaverse. In *Cultural Marketing and Metaverse for Consumer Engagement* (pp. 1–11). IGI Global. doi:10.4018/978-1-6684-8312-1.ch001

Rehman, A. U., Zakar, R., Zakar, M. Z., Hani, U., Wrona, K. J., & Fischer, F. (2021). Role of the Media in Health-Related Awareness Campaigns on Perception of COVID-19: *A Pre-post Study in the General Population of Pakistan. Frontiers in Public Health*, *9*, 779090. doi:10.3389/fpubh.2021.779090 PMID:34869191

Rural Energy Access. (2021). Reach the World. https://www.reachtheworld.org/karans-journey-india/nations/rural-energy-access)

Sama, R. (2019). Impact of Media Advertisements on Consumer Behavior. *Journal of Creative Communications*, *14*(1), 54–68. doi:10.1177/0973258618822624

Siddiqui, S., Johri, A., Shoeb, A., Saxena, K., Siddiqui, J. H., & Usmani, K. (2021). A study on the influence and impact of advertising to consumer purchase behavior in rural areas of India. *Academy of Strategic Management Journal*, *20*(5), 1–22.

Singh, V., Taneja, S., Singh, V., Singh, A., & Paul, H. L. (2021). Online advertising strategies in Indian and Australian e-commerce companies:: A comparative study. *Big Data Analytics for Improved Accuracy, Efficiency, and Decision Making in Digital Marketing*, 124–138. doi:10.4018/978-1-7998-7231-3.ch009

Srinvasrao, G. (2002). *Rural Marketing in India- A Case Study*. Anmol Publication P. Ltd.

Sultana. (2018). Analyzing the Impact of Social Media. *Global Journal of Management and Business Research: E Marketing*, *18*(2), 1-9 https://www.researchgate.net/profile/Nahida-Sultana-3/publication/326327402_Analyzing_the_Impact_of_Social_Media_A_Study_on_Online_Shoppers_of_Apparel_Companies_in_Bangladesh/links/5b46146a458515b4f663dd84/Analyzing-the-Impact-of-Social-Media-A-Study-on-Online-Shoppers-of-Apparel-Companies-in-Bangladesh.pdf

Taneja, S., Bhatnagar, M., Kumar, P., & Grima, S. (2023c). A panel analysis of the effectiveness of the asset management in Indian agricultural companies. *International Journal of Sustainable Development and Planning*, *18*(3), 653–660. doi:10.18280/ijsdp.180301

Taneja, S., Bhatnagar, M., Kumar, P., & Rupeika-apoga, R. (2023b). India ' s Total Natural Resource Rents (NRR) and GDP : An Augmented Autoregressive Distributed Lag (ARDL) Bound Test. *Journal of Risk and Financial Management*, *16*(2), 91. doi:10.3390/jrfm16020091

Taneja, S., Gupta, M., Bhushan, P., Bhatnagar, M., & Singh, A. (2023f). Cultural Marketing in the Digital Era. In *Cultural Marketing and Metaverse for Consumer Engagement* (pp. 109–122). IGI Global. doi:10.4018/978-1-6684-8312-1.ch008

Taneja, S., Jaggi, P., Jewandah, S., & Ozen, E. (2022b). Role of Social Inclusion in Sustainable Urban Developments: An Analyse by PRISMA Technique. *International Journal of Design & Nature and Ecodynamics*, *17*(6), 937–942. doi:10.18280/ijdne.170615

Taneja, S., Kaur, S., & Özen, E. (2022a). Using green finance to promote global growth in a sustainable way. *International Journal of Green Economics*, *16*(3), 246–257. doi:10.1504/IJGE.2022.128930

Taneja, S., & Özen, E. (2023a). To analyse the relationship between bank's green financing and environmental performance. *International Journal of Electronic Finance*, *12*(2), 163–175. doi:10.1504/IJEF.2023.129919

Taneja, S., & Ozen, E. (2023d). Impact of the European Green Deal (EDG) on the agricultural carbon (CO2) emission in Turkey. *International Journal of Sustainable Development and Planning*, *18*(3), 715–727. doi:10.18280/ijsdp.180307

Taneja, S., & Sharma, V. (2023e). Role of Beaconing Marketing in Improving Customer Buying Experience. In *Enhancing Customer Engagement Through Location-Based Marketing* (pp. 176–184). IGI Global., doi:10.4018/978-1-6684-8177-6.ch012

Livemint. (2016). *Television viewership in India up by 12% since: Barc study*. Live Mint. https://www.livemint.com/Consumer/mHADAtpTFzfZ3UnC54oyDI/Television-viewership-in-India-up-by-12-since-2016-Barc-st.html

Thalladi. (2022). Rural Communication. *International Journal of Research*, *9*(2), 371-389. https://www.ijrjournal.com/index.php/ijr/article/view/377

Wakefield, A., Loken, B., & Hornik, C. (2014). *Use of mass media campaigns to change health behavior*. NCBI. https://www.ncbi.nlm.nih.gov/pmc/articles/PMC4248563/

Chapter 8
Pattern of PBIB Design Having Higher Associated Class by Juxtapositions in Association Matrices

Gurinder Pal Singh
Chandigarh University, India

Amandeep Singh
https://orcid.org/0000-0002-0970-5467
Chitkara Business School, Chitkara University, India

ABSTRACT

This chapter represents two new series of partially balanced incomplete block (PBIB) designs. Association matrices based on incidence relation of vertices of a bi-partite graph of order s (s>=3) are being taken as base design. The foundation series of given PBIB designs are used to construct two more series of PBIB patterns, having three and four associated class, respectively, through promoting an idea of juxtapositions in association matrices of base design. To better comprehend the construction procedures, association schemes, P – matrices, efficiency factors of all types, as well as total efficiency, factors have been examined with examples from above series.

INTRODUCTION

As we are aware of some statistical techniques such as sampling, probability theory, statistical inference as well as a partially balanced incomplete block (PBIB) design plays an important role in modern statistics having wide applications in agricultural experimentation, medical research, population studies, and other relative fields. Intently, observations and data collection, based on sampling techniques, experimenter faces the difficulties to study the characters/ features of the study and the target population based on selected sampling units for a particular purpose based on objectives of defined problem, because of the

DOI: 10.4018/979-8-3693-1388-6.ch008

heterogeneity nature of given population units. Another best approach to study the problem/situation by using an appropriate incomplete block design. But, sometimes the existing Balanced Incomplete Block(BIB) designs as well as two associate class PBIB designs in the available literature are either unable to interpreted the problem or not to fit for a particular parametric situation under study. So, there is a need to develop higher associate class PBIB designs. For this purpose, an analytical approach of reviewing the construction methodologies of following PBIB designs to develop new series of higher associate class PBIB designs.

"Doubly Linked Block Association Scheme" based on their intersection number of treatment in given blocks for some combinatorial is defined by Meitei(2015). Sharma and Garg (2017) presented the construction methodology of three associate PBIB designs using some sets of initial blocks. Agrawal.et.al (2019) gives the construction method of α-resolvable group divisible (GD) designs based on dualisation of certain known affine resolvable balanced incomplete block designs. Kaur & Garg (2020) constructed Tm – type and Tm – assisted PBIB designs. Some higher associate class PBIB Designs using method of Duality, Juxtapositions and Literals of K – Maps were developed by Garg and Gurinder (2011,2014, 2022).

In the continuation of juxtaposition of association matrices of existing/ base design, two new series of higher associate class PBIB designs have been explored along with their association schemes in generalized form is presenting in research work.

General Introduction of Base Series-1 of Higher Associate Class PBIB Designs

This section presents an introduction to base series of three associate class partially balanced incomplete block designs by choosing bi – partite graph $K_{s,s}$, where s (>=3) constructed by the authors. In general, first and second kind of parameters of base-series of PBIB design are given as

$$v = 2s,\ b = s(s-1)/2,\ r = s-1,\ k = 4,\ \lambda_1 = s-1,\ \lambda_2 = \lambda_3 = 1,\ n_1 = 1,\ n_2 = n_3 = s-1 \text{ where } (s>=3) \tag{1}$$

P matrices are

$$P_1 = \begin{bmatrix} 0 & 0 & 0 \\ 0 & 0 & s-1 \\ 0 & s-1 & 0 \end{bmatrix} \quad P_2 = \begin{bmatrix} 0 & 0 & 1 \\ 0 & 0 & s-2 \\ 1 & s-2 & 0 \end{bmatrix} \quad P_3 = \begin{bmatrix} 0 & 1 & 0 \\ 1 & s-2 & 0 \\ 0 & 0 & s-2 \end{bmatrix}$$

Construction Methodology

The construction methodology of a series of three associate class symmetric PBIB designs as well as series of PBIB designs having four associate classes, both based on the concept of juxtapositions of ith (i=0,1,2,3) association matrices of series-1 to develop the incidence matrices of new series.

Treatment structure matrix of new series satisfied all axioms of block design and hence, the new patterned matrix representing two more series of three and four associate class PBIB designs along with their association schemes in the following theorems respectively. The expressive study of construction methodologies, association schemes and numerical illustrations of existing series have been deliberated in detail in the following sub–sections:

Theorem2.1: Given that B_0, B_1, B_2, and B_3 are association matrices of a series of three associate class PBIB designs having parameters defined in equation (1), then the patterned matrix N* = [$B_0 + B_2$] of order v is observed as an incidence matrix of a series of three associate class symmetric PBIB designs having parameters defined as below.

$v = 2s = b,\ r = s = k,\ \lambda_1 = 2,\ \lambda_2 = s\text{-}2,\ \lambda_3 = 0,\ n_1 = s\text{-}1 = n_2, n_3 = 1$ for (s>=3).

Proof: As B_0 and B_2 both have the same order, firstly, compute the addition of both association matrices, say $B_0 + B_2$ and generate a patterned matrix say N* = [$B_0 + B_2$] of order v. Since all entries of B_0 and B_2 are either zeros or ones, it is observed that the row and column sum of patterned matrix N* is equal.

Also, the product of patterned matrix N* and its transpose, say N* N*/ proves the following results.

a) Row and Column Sums of N* N*/are unique.
b) Diagonal elements of N* N*/are also unique.

Based on the above results, product N* N*/be stated as a treatment structure matrix of a PBIB design. Hence, it proves that patterned matrix N* is called an incidence matrix of a PBIB design with parameters given as

$v = 2s = b,\ r = s = k,\ \lambda_1 = 2,\ \lambda_2 = s\text{-}2,\ \lambda_3 = 0,\ n_1 = s\text{-}1 = n_2,\ n_3 = 1$ for (s>=3)

Association scheme: An association scheme of the above-constructed series of PBIB designs is defined as below.

Here the generalized parametric values of constructed series of PBIB design are given as v(number of treatments)= 2s = b(number of blocks), r(replication of a treatment)= s= k (block size). Select a particular treatment say 'θ'.

Treatment pair, says (θ, φ) occurs twice in constructed blocks and observe that there are 's-1' such treatment pairs exist are called 1st associates of a particular treatment 'θ'.

Another type of treatment pair says (θ, μ) occurs 's-2' times in constructed blocks and observed that 's-1' such treatment pairs exist are called 2nd associates of a particular treatment 'θ.

Remaining a particular treatment say 'δ' not linked with 'θ' in any block or treatment pair (θ, δ) does not exist and is called 3rd associate of a particular treatment 'θ'.

P matrices

$$P1 = \begin{bmatrix} 0 & s-2 & 0 \\ s-2 & 0 & 1 \\ 0 & 1 & 0 \end{bmatrix} \quad P2 = \begin{bmatrix} s-2 & 0 & 1 \\ 0 & s-2 & 0 \\ 1 & 0 & 0 \end{bmatrix} \quad P3 = \begin{bmatrix} 0 & s-1 & 0 \\ s-1 & 0 & 0 \\ 0 & 0 & 0 \end{bmatrix}$$

Theorem 2.2: Given that B_0, B_1, B_2, and B_3 are association matrices of a series of three associate class PBIB designs having parameters defined in equation (1), then patterned matrix N*= [$\dfrac{B_{1d}}{B_{2d}}$] of order v x b is denoted as an incidence matrix of a series of PBIB designs having four associate classes with parameters

$v= 4s, b=2s, r =s, k = 2s, \lambda_1 = s, \lambda_2 = 2,\lambda_3 = s-2, \lambda_4 = 0, n_1 = 1, n_2 = 2s-2= n_3, n_4 = 2$

where$B_{1d} = [B_0 + B_2]$ $B_{2d} = [B_1 + B_3]$ for ($s \geq 3$).

Proof: Given that all association matrices B0, B1, B2 and B3 have the same order, therefore B0 + B2, B1 + B3 both exist and denoted as B_{1d} and B_{2d} respectively.

Generate a patterned matrix say $N^* = [B_{1d} \mid B_{2d}]'$ of order v x b.

As elements of all association matrices are either zero or one, it is observed that the row and column sum of patterned matrix N* is equal. Also, the product of patterned matrix N* and its transpose, say N* N*′ proves the following results.

a) Row and Column Sums of N* N*′are unique.
b) All diagonal elements of N* N*′are 's'(unique).

Based on the above results, product N* N*′be stated as a treatment structure matrix of a PBIB design. Hence, it proves that patterned matrix N* is called an incidence matrix of a series of four associate class PBIB designs with parameters given as

$v= 4s, b=2s, r =s, k = 2s, \lambda_1 = s, \lambda_2 =2, \lambda_3= s-2, \lambda_4=0, n_1 = 1, n_2 = 2s-2= n_3, n_4 = 2$ where ($s \geq 3$)

Association scheme: An association scheme of the above-constructed series of PBIB designs is defined as below.

Here the generalized parametric values of constructed series of PBIB designs are given as v(number of treatments)= 4s, b(number of blocks) = 2s, r(replication of a treatment)= s and k (block size) = 2s. Select a particular treatment say 'θ'.

A treatment pair, says (θ, φ) occurs exactly 's' times in constructed blocks is called 1st associates of a treatment 'θ' and $n_1 = 1$.

Another type of treatment pair, says (θ, μ) occurs twice in constructed blocks and observed that there are '2s-2' such treatment pairs exist are called 2nd associates of a particular treatment 'θ and $n_2 = 2s - 2$. Similarly, treatment pairs of type (θ, ε) occur 's-2' times in these blocks are 3rd associates of a particular treatment 'θ and $n_3 = 2s - 2$.Lastly, a particular treatment pair says (θ, δ) does not exist in any block or unpaired treatments are called 4th associates of a treatment 'θ' and $n_4 = 2$.

P matrices are

$$P_1 = \begin{bmatrix} 0 & 0 & 0 & 0 \\ 0 & 2s-2 & 0 & 0 \\ 0 & 0 & 2s-2 & 0 \\ 0 & 0 & 0 & 2 \end{bmatrix} \quad P_2 = \begin{bmatrix} 0 & 1 & 0 & 0 \\ 1 & 0 & 2s-4 & 0 \\ 0 & 2s-4 & 0 & 2 \\ 0 & 0 & 2 & 0 \end{bmatrix}$$

$$P_3 = \begin{bmatrix} 0 & 0 & 1 & 0 \\ 0 & 2s-4 & 0 & 2 \\ 1 & 0 & 2s-4 & 0 \\ 0 & 2 & 0 & 0 \end{bmatrix} \quad P_4 = \begin{bmatrix} 0 & 0 & 0 & 1 \\ 0 & 0 & 2s-2 & 0 \\ 0 & 2s-2 & 0 & 0 \\ 1 & 0 & 0 & 0 \end{bmatrix}$$

Illustrations

This section elaborate the conceptual structure and methodologies of above mentioned series of PBIB designs.

Demonstration of Base Design

Let draw a bi – partite graph $K_{5,5}$

Figure 1. Demonstration

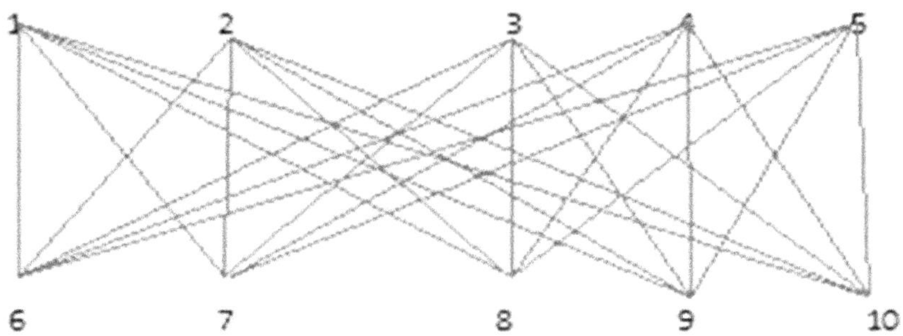

By choosing s = 5 in equation (1), the parametric values of base design are

$v = 2s$, $b = s(s-1)/2$, $r = s-1$, $k = 4$, $\lambda_1 = s-1$, $\lambda_2 = \lambda_3 = 1$, $n_1 = 1$, $n_2 = n_3 = s - 1$ where (s>=3)

$v = 10$, $b=10$, $r= 4$, $k = 4$, $\lambda_1 =4$, $\lambda_2 =\lambda_3 = 1$, $n_1 = 1$, $n_2 = n_3 = 4$

and the blocks of this designs are

(1,6,2,7) (1,6,3,8) (1,6,4,9) (1,6,5,10) (2,7,3,8)

(2,7,4,9) (2,7,5,10) (3,8,4,9) (3,8,5,10) (4,9,5,10)

P matrices are

$$P_1 = \begin{bmatrix} 0 & 0 & 0 \\ 0 & 0 & 4 \\ 0 & 4 & 0 \end{bmatrix} \quad P_2 = \begin{bmatrix} 0 & 0 & 1 \\ 0 & 0 & 3 \\ 1 & 3 & 0 \end{bmatrix} \quad P_3 = \begin{bmatrix} 0 & 1 & 0 \\ 1 & 3 & 0 \\ 0 & 0 & 3 \end{bmatrix}$$

Verification of Theorem 2.1

By substituting s=5, parametric values of PBIB design defined in theorem 2.1are

$v = 10 = b,\ r = 5 = k,\ \lambda_1 = 2,\ \lambda_2 = 3,\ \lambda_3 = 0,\ n_1 = 4 = n_2,\ n_3 = 1$

Since B0 and B2 both matrices have same order 10 x 10, then adding B0 + B2 and get a square matrix say N* = [B0 + B2] of order 10

$$N^* = \begin{bmatrix} 1000001111 \\ 0100010111 \\ 0010011011 \\ 0001011101 \\ 0000111110 \\ 0111110000 \\ 1011101000 \\ 1101100100 \\ 1110100010 \\ 1111000001 \end{bmatrix}$$

Also, N*N*′ = [B0 + B2] [B0 + B2]′ is also a square matrix of order 10 proves the following results.

a) Row and Column sums of N*N*′are exactly 5.
b) Diagonal elements of N*N*′ are also 5.

Hence, it proves that N* N*′ be stated as a treatment structure matrix and patterned matrix N* is called an incidence matrix of a PBIB design with parameters

$v = 10 = b,\ r = 5 = k,\ \lambda_1 = 2,\ \lambda_2 = 3,\ \lambda_3 = 0,\ n_1 = 4 = n_2,\ n_3 = 1$ for s=5 and developing blocks are given below

(1,7,8,9,10) (2,6,8,9,10) (3,6,7,9,10) (4,6,7,8,10) (5,6,7,8,9) (2,3,4,5,6) (1,3,4,5,7) (1,2,4,5,8) (1,2,3,5,9) (1,2,3,4,10)

Association Scheme: Here, the total 10 treatments are present in total 10 blocks of sizes 5 with replication5 in these blocks. Choose a particular treatment say '1'.

Treatment pairs such as (1,7) (1,8) (1,9) (1,10) occur twice in these blocks are called 1st associates of a particular treatment '1'i.e $\lambda_1 = 2$ and $n_1 = 4$.

Treatment pairs such as (1,2) (1,3) (1,4) (1,5) occur thrice in above blocks are called 2nd associates of a particular treatment '1'i.e $\lambda_2 = 3$ and $n_2 = 4$.

Remaining, a particular treatment '6' not generated a pair with '1' in any block is called 3rd associate of a particular treatment '1' i.e $\lambda_3 = 0$ and $n_3 = 1$.

P matrices are $P_1 = \begin{bmatrix} 0 & 3 & 0 \\ 3 & 0 & 1 \\ 0 & 1 & 0 \end{bmatrix}$ $P_2 = \begin{bmatrix} 3 & 0 & 1 \\ 0 & 3 & 0 \\ 1 & 0 & 0 \end{bmatrix}$ $P_3 = \begin{bmatrix} 0 & 4 & 0 \\ 4 & 0 & 0 \\ 0 & 0 & 0 \end{bmatrix}$

Verification of Theorem 3.2

Putting n =5, the parametric values of PBIB designs defined in theorem 2.2 are

v= 20, b=10, r =5, k = 10, $\lambda_1 = 5$, $\lambda_2 = 2$, $\lambda_3 = 3$, $\lambda_4 = 0$, $n_1 = 1$, $n_2 = 8 = n_3$, $n_4 = 2$

Here $B_{1d} = [B_0 + B_2]$ $B_{2d} = [B_1 + B_3]$.

Since B_0, B_1, B_2 and B_3 have same order of order 10, therefore addition $B_0 + B_2$& $B_1 + B_3$both exist and generate the matrices B_{1d} and B_{2d}respectively.

Here $B_{1d} = [B_0 + B_2]$ $B_{2d} = [B_1 + B_3]$.

Construct a patterned matrix the $N^* = [B_{1d} \mid B_{2d}]'$of order 20 x 10 given as below.

N* = [(1 0 0 0 0 0 1 1 1 1
0 1 0 0 0 1 0 1 1 1
0 0 1 0 0 1 1 0 1 1
0 0 0 1 0 1 1 1 0 1
0 0 0 0 1 1 1 1 1 0
0 1 1 1 1 1 0 0 0 0
1 0 1 1 1 0 1 0 0 0
1 1 0 1 1 0 0 1 0 0
1 1 1 0 1 0 0 0 1 0
1 1 1 1 0 0 0 0 0 1
0 1 1 1 1 1 0 0 0 0
1 0 1 1 1 0 1 0 0 0
1 1 0 1 1 0 0 1 0 0
1 1 1 0 1 0 0 0 1 0
1 1 1 1 0 0 0 0 0 1
1 0 0 0 0 0 1 1 1 1
0 1 0 0 0 1 0 1 1 1
0 0 1 0 0 1 1 0 1 1

0 0 0 1 0 1 1 1 0 1
0 0 0 0 1 1 1 1 1 0)]

The elements of every association matrix are either zero or one. As a result, product of patterned matrix and its transposed matrix say $N^*N^{*/} = [B0 + B2]\,[B0 + B2]^{/}$ is a square matrix of order 20 proves the following results.

a) $N^*\,N^{*/}$has a unique row and column sum
b) Diagonal elements of $N^*\,N^{*/}$are also unique say '10'

Hence, it proves that $N^*\,N^{*/}$be stated as a treatment structure matrix and patterned matrix

N* denotes the incidence matrix of a series of four associate class PBIB designs with parameters for s =5 are

$v= 20, b=10, r =5, k = 10, \lambda_1 = 5, \lambda_2 = 2, \lambda_3 = 3, \lambda_4 = 0, n_1 = 1, n_2 = 8= n_3, n_4 = 2$

and the constructed blocks are given as

(1,7,8,9,10,12,13,14,15,16) (2,6,8,9,10,11,13,14,15,17)
(3,6,7,9,10,11,12,14,15,18) (4,6,7,8,10,11,12,13,15,19)
(5,6,7,8,9,11,12,13,14,20) (2,3,4,5,6,11,17,18,19,20)
(1,3,4,5,7,12,16,18,19,20) (1,2,4,5,8,13,16,17,19,20)
(1,2,3,5,9,14,16,17,18,20) (1,2,3,4,10,15,16,17,18,19)

Association scheme: Here, total 20 treatments are arranged in a total of 10 blocks of sizes 10 with replication 5 as presented in the above N* incidence matrix.

To elaborate an association scheme, consider a particular treatment say '1'.

A treatment pair (1,16) occurs exactly 5 times in above blocks are 1st associates of treatment '1' and n_1 = 1.Treatment pairs such as (1,7) (1,8) (1,9) (1,10) (1,12) (1,13) (1,14) (1,15) appear twice in exactly 10 blocks are 2nd associates of a particular treatment '1' and n_2 = 8.Treatment pairs such as (1,2) (1,3) (1,4) (1,5) (1,17) (1,18) (1,19) (1,20) occur thrice in these blocks are 3rd associates of a particular treatment '1' and n_3 = 8. The remaining, two treatments '6' and '11' not paired with a treatment '1' in any block are 4th associates of a particular treatment '1' and n_4 =2.

P matrices are

$$P_1 = \begin{bmatrix} 0 & 0 & 0 & 0 \\ 0 & 8 & 0 & 0 \\ 0 & 0 & 8 & 0 \\ 0 & 0 & 0 & 2 \end{bmatrix} \quad P_2 = \begin{bmatrix} 0 & 1 & 0 & 0 \\ 1 & 0 & 6 & 0 \\ 0 & 6 & 0 & 2 \\ 0 & 0 & 0 & 2 \end{bmatrix} \quad P_3 = \begin{bmatrix} 0 & 0 & 1 & 0 \\ 0 & 6 & 0 & 2 \\ 1 & 0 & 6 & 0 \\ 0 & 2 & 0 & 0 \end{bmatrix} \quad P_4 = \begin{bmatrix} 0 & 0 & 0 & 1 \\ 0 & 0 & 8 & 0 \\ 0 & 8 & 0 & 0 \\ 1 & 0 & 0 & 0 \end{bmatrix}$$

Tabulation of Newly Constructed Designs

In this section, PBIB designs based on above mentioned construction methodologies are listed in below tables.

Table 1. Series of symmetric three associate class PBIB designs based on theorem 2.1

S.No	Graph	v	b	r	k	λ_1	λ_2	λ_3	n_1	n_2	n_3	E_1	E_2	E_3	E
1	$K_{3,3}$	6	6	3	3	2	1	0	2	2	1	85.10	71.42	63.49	74.34
2	$K_{4,4}$	8	8	4	4	2	2	0	3	3	1	85.71	85.71	75	84
3	$K_{5,5}$	10	10	5	5	2	3	0	4	4	1	85.49	91.30	79.05	88.70
4	$K_{6,6}$	12	12	6	6	2	4	0	5	5	1	85.10	94.11	80.80	88.53
5	$K_{7,7}$	14	14	7	7	2	5	0	6	6	1	85.37	95.74	81.63	86.66

Table 2. Series of PBIB designs having four associate classes based on theorem 2.2

S.No	Graph	v	b	r	k	λ_1	λ_2	λ_3	λ_4	n_1	n_2	n_3	n_4	E_1	E_2	E_3	E_4	E
1	$K_{3,3}$	12	6	3	6	3	2	1	0	1	4	4	2	1	91.95	83.33	77.66	86.44
2	$K_{4,4}$	16	8	4	8	4	2	2	0	1	6	6	2	1	92.30	92.30	85.71	91.83
3	$K_{5,5}$	20	10	5	10	5	2	3	0	1	8	8	2	1	92.27	95.45	88.30	93.52
4	$K_{6,6}$	24	12	6	12	6	2	4	0	1	10	10	2	1	91.95	95.38	89.38	93.50
5	$K_{7,7}$	28	14	7	14	7	2	5	0	1	12	12	2	1	91.71	97.82	89.88	94.48

CONCLUSION

Finally, two new series of PBIB designs having three and four associate classes have been constructed by juxtaposition the association matrices of a series of three associated classes PBIB designs by using a bipartite graph taken as a base design in this research.

The purpose of construction of new series is to eliminate the additional restriction of base design that is the block size in base series is exactly 4 and it is observed that all kinds of efficiencies, as well as the overall efficiency factor of base designs, are continuously declined after increasing the number of treatments and blocks for large value of 's'. But all kinds of the parameter are varies in both series of PBIB designs and arise a strong comparison with base design as well as some already existing PBIB designs in the available literature.

Also, the parametric range $6 < v<14$, $12< v< 28$ with $3<r<7$ and $6<b<14$ of the above series are easily adjustable and useful from particular parametric combinations and practical points of view.

REFERENCES

Agrawal, B., Awad, R., & Banerjee, S. (2019). Construction of α Resolvable 2-Associates PBIB Designs. *International Journal of Applied Social Science*, *6*(1), 166–170.

Garg, D. K., & Singh, G. P. (2011). Construction of Three and Four Associate Class PBIB Designs using Method of Duality. *International Journal of Agricultural and Statistics Sciences*, *7*(2), 579–587.

Garg, D. K., & Singh, G. P. (2014). Construction of Three Associate Class PBIB Designs using Method of Juxtapositions. *Indian Journal of Research*, *4*(5), 616–618.

Kaur, P., & Garg, D. K. (2020). Construction of Tm – type and Tm – Assisted PBIB Designs. *Revista de Statistica*.

Meitei, K. K. S. (2015). Doubly Linked Block Association Schemes. *International Journal of Innovative Research in Engineering & Management (IJIREM) ISSN: 2350-0557*, *2*(6), 101- 104.

Sharma, K. & Garg, D. K. (2017). Construction of Three Associate PBIB Designs using Some Sets of Initial Blocks. [IJASS]. *International Journal of Agricultural and Statistics Sciences*, *13*(01), 55–60.

Singh, G. P., & Garg, D. K. (2022). Modified Partially Balanced Incomplete Block Designs Having Higher Associate Classes by using the Literals of K-Maps. *Far East Journal of Theoretical and Applied Sciences*, *1*, 25–32.

Chapter 9
Carbon Offsets and Green Finance:
Understanding Corporate Demand for Carbon Offsets and Mitigation – A Global Literature Review

Andre Poyser
University of Otago, New Zealand

ABSTRACT

Understanding corporate demand for carbon offsets is a critical component of sustainable investments in green finance. It reflects companies' and investors' commitment to environmental sustainability, contributes to emissions reduction, supports the development of green financial instruments, and aligns with broader global sustainability objectives. In recent years, the use of carbon offset credits has increased alongside the voluntary carbon offset market with concerns being raised about the cobra effect of offsets vis-à-vis the investment required for abatement and a reduction in gross emission in keeping with the mitigation hierarchy concept. As the demand for sustainable investments continues to grow, carbon offsets will play an increasingly significant role in shaping the landscape of green finance. This chapter conducts a global systematic literature review and synthesis of 303 peer-review studies and grey publications on the demand for and use of carbon offsets, mitigation deterrence, and abatement approaches of firms.

INTRODUCTION

Growth in the use of offset credits has increased concerns that firms may be foregoing opportunities to abate their emissions. The drivers of a firm's decision to offset or abate their emissions are not well understood by policy makers. To consolidate knowledge and provide policy perspectives on offsetting and abatement decisions being made by firms, we conduct a global literature review drawing from a collection of peer-review studies and grey publications on the demand for and use of carbon offsets, miti-

DOI: 10.4018/979-8-3693-1388-6.ch009

gation deterrence and abatement approaches. First, we conducted a systematic search across the Scopus and Web of Science databases using carbon offsets, mitigation deterrence and abatement approaches as search terms, obtaining a collection of 303 articles after grey literature was added and duplicates and false positives were removed. Secondly, we organized the collection into three main themes and reviewed the high citation articles under each theme.

The specific objectives of the review included: (a) identifying the drivers of a company's decision to offset, inset or abate (b) understanding the costs of and approaches to abatement of gross emissions.

Through our review, we highlight the major drivers of offset demand and supply discussed by the literature. We also provide a summative description of current industry-specific and cross-industry abatement approaches which are proposed or already being implemented. Finally, we review the policy considerations around the concept of mitigation deterrence and the proposed policy solutions.

We review the literature to tease out issues and identify applications and policy implications in helping firms to meet their emissions reduction goals. The remainder of the chapter is structured as follows: section 2 provides a background to the issues section 3 outlines the protocol for the literature search, section 4 details the results section and 5 concludes with a summary of the findings and literature synthesis.

BACKGROUND

The Political Economy of Carbon Offset Credits

International scrutiny around the use of carbon offset credits has increased in recent times as industry giants seeking to make good on their net zero pledges have ramped up the use of offsets as part of their carbon management strategies and as a means of marketing themselves to be net zero or on track to achieve their net zero targets. An analysis of 35 multinationals found that 66% of them are relying on offsetting to fulfil their net zero pledges (Arnold and Toledano,2021). This demand from corporations no doubt led to the growth of the global carbon offset market from US$0.6 billion in 2019 to US$1 billion in 2020 with the overall carbon credits market projected to be valued at around US$50 billion in 2030 (Blaufelder et al.,2021). This proliferation in the use of carbon credits has raised questions about the credibility of voluntary carbon offsetting schemes and the propensity of cheaply available carbon credits to create a disincentive for firms to make the required investment for decarbonization and carbon abatement within their own operations (Canham,2021). Guidance released by the Science Based Targets initiative (SBTi) argued strongly for abatement as the primary means for companies to achieve net-zero emissions and for the use of neutralization methods only as a means to balance residual emissions when companies have reached the technological limits of abatement. The SBTi guidance has however raised questions around the level of abatement required before companies could be granted a "social license to offset" and whether and how companies will be rewarded for going beyond abatement (Keohane and Seymour, 2021).

Carbon offsetting can take place in either mandatory carbon offset markets (MCM) or Voluntary carbon offset markets (VCM) and has been established as a mechanism to achieve net neutrality. A carbon offset refers to a reduction in GHG emissions (e.g., through carbon capture and storage associated with planting trees) that compensates for emissions from other sources (Broekhoff et al.,2019). Offsets are possible because of the scientific understanding that greenhouse house (GHGs) have a uniform impact on the atmosphere thereby resulting in the same benefit of emissions reduction regardless of where it has taken place (Mckinsey,2009). Companies and individuals generally utilize offsets to "balance or cancel out" their own emissions (Macfarlane, 2022).

Internationally, offsetting schemes have their genesis in The Clean Development Mechanism (CDM) and the Joint Implementation (JI), the primary international offset schemes operationalized in 2006 by the United Nations under Article 12 of the Kyoto Protocol, the forerunner to the Paris Climate Agreement. The CDM, an MCM, allows developed countries to earn tradable certified emission reduction (CER) credits, each equivalent to one tonne of CO2, for financing emission-reduction projects in developing countries while the JI rewards credits for projects in developed countries (Gillenwater and Seres,2011). The CERs were used to count towards the meeting of Kyoto targets before the protocol was replaced by the Paris Agreement. As at June 2022 the CDM has issued 2.2 billion CERs for 7,846 emissions reduction projects and 55 million CERs for 359 programmes of activities (POAs) registered with the CDM (Clean Development Mechanism, 2022). The growth of Voluntary offset schemes has, in part, been propelled by the sale of offset projects which do not meet CDM requirements in voluntary markets. Changes to the CDM mechanism following the Paris Climate agreement created a high bar for projects to be registered as legitimate offset projects. The growth of voluntary markets has also been driven by uncertainty around the post-2020 future of the CDM given the expiration of the Kyoto Protocol; the Sustainable Development Mechanism (SDM) has been proposed as the successor of the CDM under Article 6 of the Paris Agreement but is not yet operational (Clean Development Mechanism,2022)

The CDM excludes agriculture, forestry and Reducing Emissions from Deforestation and Degradation (REDD) projects, as such VCMs have become an enabling and alternative source of investment capital for these types of projects. Voluntary carbon credits known as Verified Emission Reductions (VERs) or Verified Carbon Units (VCUs) are purchased in VCMs directly from project developers, companies that act as intermediaries between projects and firms or from carbon funds such as the World Bank BioCarbon Fund. Private companies have dominated VCMs as they seek to purchase carbon credits mostly for purposes relating to corporate social responsibility and public relations (Seeberg-Elverfeldt,2010. 2021 is considered a watershed year for the voluntary carbon market as this was the year a surge in demand, from companies seeking to action their net zero pledges, made the market a seller's market as demand outstripped supply for the first time (Environmental Finance, 2022). This trend has continued as preliminary data for 2022 indicates that as of August, an estimate of US$748 million in transactions were conducted in voluntary markets (Ecosystem Marketplace,2022).

A significant challenge being faced by the voluntary markets is the verification of offset projects and the fact that these markets are unregulated. The market's response to this problem has been the establishment of governance bodies and standards organizations such as the Integrity Council for the Voluntary Carbon Market (IC-VCM), the Taskforce on Scaling Voluntary Carbon Markets (TSVCM) and the International Carbon Reduction and Offset Alliance (ICROA), which together are building systems to police standards for emissions reduction projects aimed at ensuring high-quality carbon credits are traded in the voluntary market. Some of the industry-based certification standards that have emerged include the American Carbon Registry standard, the Climate Action Reserve standard, Climate, Community & Biodiversity Standard, Gold Standard, ISO-14064 standard, the Social Carbon standard and the Verified Carbon Standard. Assurance bodies such as EPIC Sustainability Services, SGS and Verra; trading platforms such as the London Stock Exchange's Voluntary Carbon Market, the CBL market operated by Xpansiv, futures contracts; daily price reporting by S&P Global and other data providers are all part of the emerging ecosystem of the VCM. These developments point to developed, liquid spot and futures markets with instituted benchmarks, settlement mechanisms, and freely available market data, all of which support the view that VCMs have matured into established commodity markets (Environment and Finance,2022).

The minimum rules underling carbon credit standards are additionality, permanence, avoidance of leakage, measurability, verifiability and transparency (Seeberg-Elverfeldt,2010). The US Securities and Exchange Commission (SEC) and the European Union have signalled their intensions to introduce disclosure and enforcement mandates based on these rules (Macfarlane,2022).

Carbon Offset Credits and Green Finance

The dynamics driving a firm's decision to make use of carbon offset credits to manage their carbon footprint as opposed to insetting or abating are not well understood by policy makers. In recent years, the use of carbon offset credits has increased alongside the voluntary carbon offset market with concerns being raised about the cobra effect of offsets vis-à-vis the investment required for abatement and a reduction in gross emission in keeping with the mitigation hierarchy concept (Bhatnagar et al., 2022).

Understanding corporate demand for carbon offsets is of paramount importance in the context of addressing climate change and achieving sustainability goals. Carbon offsets play a crucial role in mitigating greenhouse gas emissions by allowing organizations to invest in projects that reduce or capture an equivalent amount of carbon dioxide or other greenhouse gases from the atmosphere. Comprehending corporate demand for carbon offsets is significant because Carbon offsets enable companies to take immediate action to offset their emissions while they work towards implementing more sustainable practices. This is especially important given the urgent need to reduce global emissions and limit global warming to safe levels. Furthermore, Many companies recognize their role in contributing to climate change and want to demonstrate their commitment to environmental responsibility. Understanding their demand for carbon offsets can help gauge the level of seriousness companies attach to addressing their carbon footprint. Carbon offsets can be an essential tool for companies as they transition to more sustainable operations. While the long-term goal should be to reduce emissions directly, offsets provide an interim solution to neutralize their impact. As the demand for carbon offsets increases, it can create a more robust market for emissions reduction projects. This, in turn, can incentivize the development of innovative and impactful projects that can drive broader environmental benefits beyond carbon reduction. In regions with carbon pricing mechanisms or emissions reduction targets, understanding corporate demand for offsets can shed light on companies' efforts to comply with regulations and meet carbon reduction goals. Customers, investors, and employees are increasingly conscious of a company's environmental practices. Meeting or exceeding carbon offset targets can enhance a company's reputation and foster positive relationships with these stakeholders. Greater corporate demand for carbon offsets can lead to increased investment in sustainable technologies and practices. This can spur innovation in sectors such as renewable energy, afforestation, and carbon capture and storage. Addressing climate change requires collaboration between governments, industries, and individuals. Corporate demand for carbon offsets can indicate a willingness to participate in collective efforts to combat climate change on a global scale. Companies face risks associated with climate change, such as supply chain disruptions, regulatory changes, and reputational damage. By investing in carbon offsets, companies can mitigate these risks and demonstrate adaptability. Understanding corporate demand for carbon offsets provides insights into how seriously companies are integrating sustainability into their long-term strategies. It can reflect a commitment to long-term environmental and social well-being.

Carbon offsets are considered green assets in the realm of sustainable investments. Investors can purchase carbon offsets as a way to directly contribute to emissions reduction and environmental preservation. This aligns with the principles of green finance, which aims to allocate capital to projects and activities that have positive environmental impacts. Companies and investors can channel funds into emission reduction projects, such as renewable energy installations, reforestation, methane capture, and other initiatives that generate carbon offsets. These projects not only contribute to sustainability goals but also offer financial returns, making them attractive investment options within the realm of green finance. Carbon offset projects can be financed through climate bonds and sustainable bonds. These financial instruments raise capital specifically for environmentally friendly projects, including those that generate carbon offsets. Investors who purchase these bonds are essentially supporting projects that contribute to reducing carbon emissions and mitigating climate change. Environmental, Social, and Governance (ESG) considerations are a cornerstone of green finance and sustainable investments. Companies that invest in carbon offsets can improve their ESG performance by demonstrating their commitment to environmental stewardship. This, in turn, can attract ESG-focused investors and positively influence the company's valuation. Sustainable investments often involve assessing the environmental impact of a company's operations and investments. Understanding corporate demand for carbon offsets provides insights into a company's efforts to integrate sustainability criteria into its business practices, making it a valuable metric for green finance evaluation (Taneja, 2023a; 2023b).

Green finance seeks to balance financial returns with positive environmental outcomes. Carbon offsets contribute to risk mitigation by helping companies and investors manage their carbon footprint and adapt to changing regulatory and market conditions. This aligns with the risk-conscious approach of sustainable investments. Sustainable investments in green finance are closely aligned with global sustainability goals, such as the United Nations Sustainable Development Goals (SDGs) and the Paris Agreement. Carbon offsets directly contribute to achieving these goals by reducing greenhouse gas emissions and combating climate change. Corporate demand for carbon offsets can drive innovation and development in the green finance market. As companies invest in carbon reduction projects, new financial products and investment opportunities may emerge, fostering a more vibrant and dynamic green finance ecosystem. Understanding corporate demand for carbon offsets is therefore a critical component of sustainable investments in green finance (Taneja, 2022). It reflects companies' and investors' commitment to environmental sustainability, contributes to emissions reduction, supports the development of green financial instruments, and aligns with broader global sustainability objectives. As the demand for sustainable investments continues to grow, carbon offsets will play an increasingly significant role in shaping the landscape of green finance. The systematic literature review and synthesis proposed in the chapter will enrich the understanding of sustainable investments in green finance by providing valuable insights into corporate demand for carbon offsets, mitigation approaches, challenges, and opportunities. This knowledge can guide investors, policymakers, and companies toward more effective and impactful sustainable investment decisions and practices.

METHODOLOGY

The systematic literature review was conducted with the aim of synthesizing the available knowledge on the drivers of demand for offsets and how these interact with abatement approaches and mitigation deterrence. For the purposes of further scoping and efficiency, the most relevant studies are those with the highest number of citations. We extracted data from Elsevier's Scopus and Web of Science databases, two of the leading databases for scientific publication. Two separate searches were conducted. The first search was conducted using the following Boolean search query: TITLE-ABS-KEY ("offset demand" OR "forest offset" OR "abatement approaches") AND SUBJAREA ("All") AND DOCTYPE ("AR"); this search yielded 101 articles from Scopus and 41 from Web of Science. The second search was conducted using the following search query: TITLE-ABS-KEY ("mitigation deterrence") AND SUBJAREA ("ALL") AND DOCTYPE ("AR"); this search yielded 107 articles from Scopus and 90 articles from Web of Science. The search syntax captured all 'academic articles' containing the search terms in either their titles, abstracts and/or among their keywords, within all the subject areas of indexed by Scopus and Web of Science. The combined searches yielded 339 results which were extracted and uploaded to a bibliographic management software where 18 grey literature reports were added and 54 duplicates and false positives were removed resulting in a final collection of 303 articles. The steps for the literature search are summarized in the diagram below.

Figure 1. Showing overview summary of literature search and article selection process

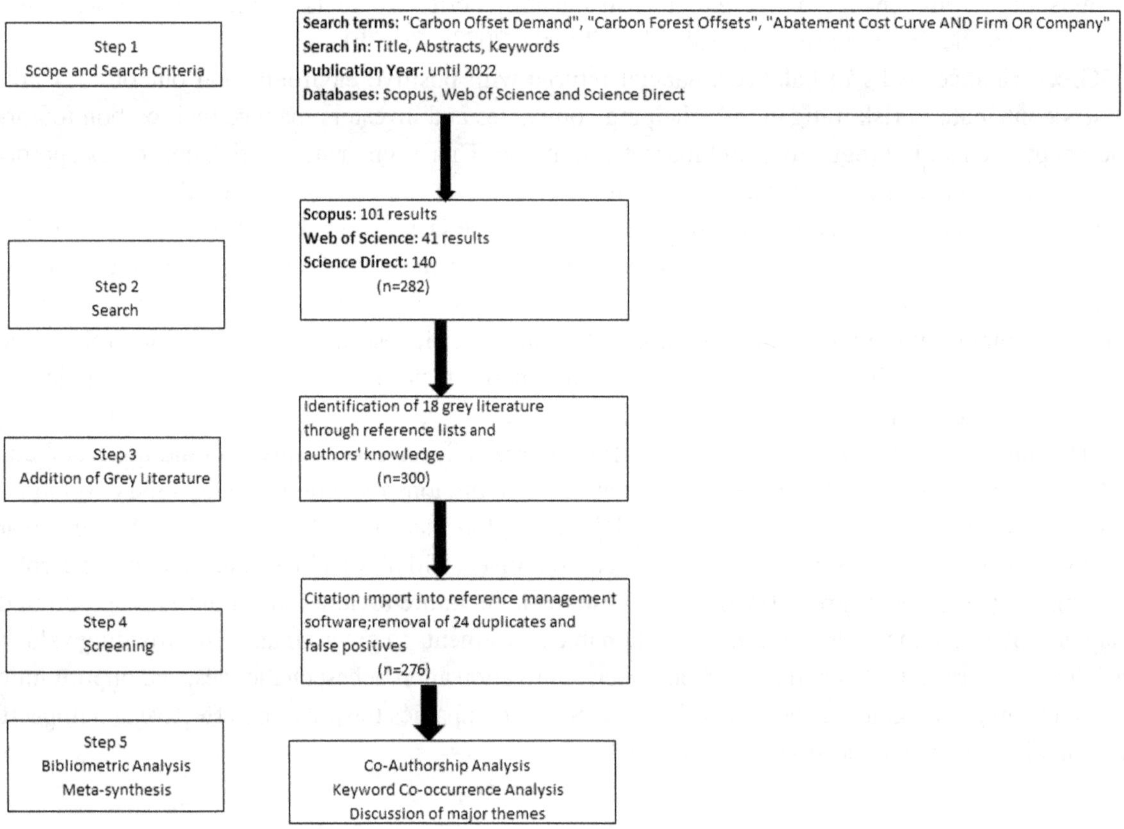

SEARCH RESULTS

General Descriptive Statistics

The 303 articles which formed the final collection of articles produced by the Scopus and Web of Science searches have been published in 124 journals and authored by 423 authors. The articles were published within a 50-year timespan between 1972 and 2022 with an annual growth rate of 3.97%. The average number of citations per article is 17.3 and the average age of the articles is 13.3 years. The Annual publication output did not exceed three articles until 1999, with the highest number being produced in 2021 (13). The period 2012-2022 represents the period of highest publication output with 47.3% of the articles being published within this time span indicating increased academic interest in offsetting and abatement within the last ten years. Figure 2 shows a chart of the annual scientific production.

Figure 2. Showing annual scientific production of publications

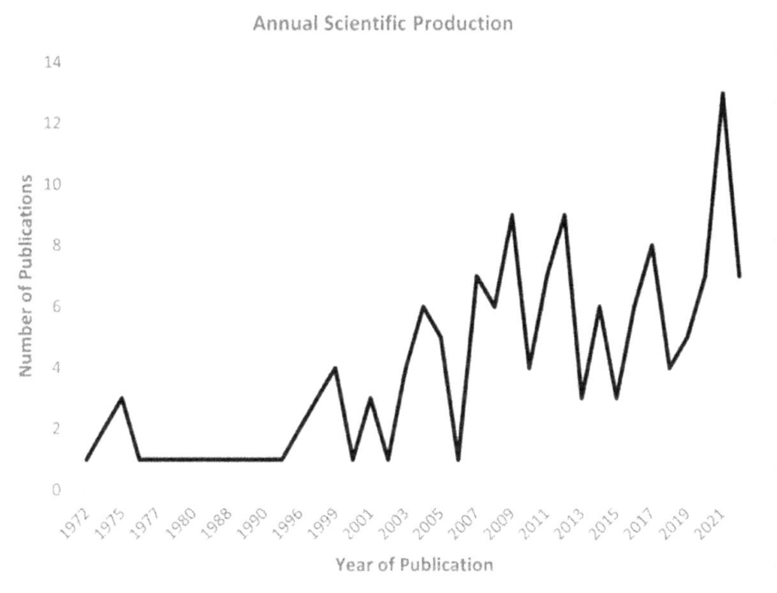

Major Themes for Thematic Analysis

A review of the articles with the highest number of citations generated the following consolidated themes:

1. Demand, Supply and Markets for Offsets
2. How and Why Firm Make Abatement Decisions
3. Mitigation Deterrence and Abatement Approaches of Firms

A synthesis of the high citation articles within each theme follows.

Table 1. Showing articles with the highest number of citations under each major theme

Major Themes	Number of Articles	High Citation Articles Selected for Thematic Analysis
Demand, supply and markets for offsets	103	Dormandy & Englander (2016) Miller, Snyder & Kilgore (2012) Badgley et al. (2022) Lee, Kim & Kim (2018) Van Kooten & Johnson (2016) McPherson E.G. (1998) Galik C.S. and Jackson R.B. (2009) Kerchner, C.D.,Keeton, W.S. (2005) Martinson et al. (2022) Blum et al. (2021) Richardson-Barlow et al. (2022) Choi and Qi (2019) McKenney B.A., Kiesecker J.M. (2010)
How and why firms make abatement decisions	123	Blanco, Caro & Corbett (2020) Ulrich, Trench & Hagerman (2022) Martinson et al. (2022) Guo et al. (2022) Wei,Zhu and Tan (2022)
Mitigation deterrence and abatement approaches of firms	77	Goulder L.H., Parry I.W.H., Williams III R.C., Burtraw D. (1999) Damert et al. (2017) Miller,S.A.,John,V.Pacca,S. and Horvath,A.(2018) Busch,P., Kendall, A.,Murphy, C.W.,and Miller,S.A. (2022) Ruud Mark D., Mitchell John W., Klein Sanford A. (1990) Markusson N., McLaren D., Tyfield D. (2018) McLaren D. (2016) McLaren,D.,Willis,R.,Marcuson,N.(2021) Taylor M.R. (2012) Carton,W., Lund,J.F. and Dooley,K. (2021) Asayama,S. (2021)

THEMATIC ANALYSIS AND LITERATURE SYNTHESIS

Demand, Supply, and Markets for Offsets

The drivers influencing decision around offsetting are not only driven by cost considerations as the literature also indicates that environmental and social values also playing a role. On the supply side, surveys of forest landowners' decision to participate in carbon offset programmes found that the decision was influenced by program characteristics, owner characteristics and land characteristics. Results from a survey of 2,200 family forest owners in the United States found in the category of landowner characteristics that landowner attitudes towards both non-market forest amenities (e.g., improved water and soil quality, forest aesthetics, wildlife habitat) and climate change are positively related to the willingness to sell forest carbon credits, in the programme characteristics category the payment amount was the most significant predictor of participation, while the land characteristic positively related to carbon market participation was the total acreage owned; landowners with more forest lands were more likely to participate (Miller, Snyder and Kilgore,2012). Further survey studies in the Appalachian region which contain about 20% of US forestland found that offsets provided a greater payoff than incentive payment approaches for forest-based carbon sequestration (Cho et al.,2018; Latta et al.,2011); surveys of private forest owners also found that revenue from offsets is the driving motivation for participation in California's carbon offset market which operates as compliance offset programme under the California ETS (Kelly, Gold and Di Tommaso,2020)

Dormady and Englander (2016) suggest that offsets and allowances behave as imperfect substitutes and that much of the divergence in demand for allowances and offsets can be attributed to the structural design of emissions trading schemes. They further argued that the main demand drivers of offsetting are price spreads, procedural cost, institutional capacity, offset limit, banking, Ex post invalidation risk, reversal risk, regulatory uncertainty, economic growth, fuel price and weather (Dormady and Englander,2016). According to Dormady and Englander (2016) procedural costs, offset limit and reversal risk all decrease offset demand. Procedural costs refer to the costs to develop and gain approval for offset projects, offset limit refers to any cap on the quantity of offsets a firm is able to purchase while reversal risk refers to the risk that sequestered $CO2$ emissions are released (Dormady and Englander,2016). Factors which increase demand for offsets include a positive spread between allowance and offset price, economic growth, decrease in the fuel price of high-carbon fuels and extreme temperatures (Dormady and Englander, 2016). Dormady and Englander (2016) also suggest that uncertainty in government regulation can either increase or decrease demand for offsets depending on the particularities of any anticipated regulatory changes.

A significant challenge with offsets is the issue of permanence. The state operator of the California offset programme has sought to address this issue through the introduction of a buffer pool, the purpose of which is to insure against loss of permanence; When offset projects earn credits, a percentage is held in the buffer pool in the event of unintentional carbon loss/reversals from the project. When an event of unintentional reversal has occurred (e.g., a forest fire), credits from the pool are surrendered to account for the carbon loss. Actuarial analysis of the buffer pool mechanism conducted by Badgley et al. (2022) indicates that the pool is undercapitalized due to depletion from wildfires in California, highlighting the impact of extreme temperatures in increasing offset demand as highlighted by Dormady and Englander (2016).

Government's role in setting policy for the use of offsets is one which is emphasized in the literature. In reviewing biodiversity offset policy frameworks from the US, EU, Australia and Brazil, McKenney and Kiesecker (2010) highlight similarities across the countries and best practice for the development of offset policy. The policy frameworks were assessed on three main dimensions: policy goals, mitigation approach and implementation. In the area of policy goals, the study found that the policy goals ranged from net gain to nature/biodiversity to no net loss. When assessed for how well the polices adhered to the mitigation hierarchy of avoiding impacts, minimizing impacts and offsetting/compensating for residual impacts, the review found that all the polices reflected these principles (McKenney and Kiesecker,2010). In the area of implementation, the key issues highlighted by the study were equivalence, location of offset relative to impact, additionality, timing, offset duration and management and ensuring offset units compensate for project impacts. Significant differences were found across all of these criteria, highlighting the difficulties of implementing offset projects (McKenney and Kiesecker,2010).

On the demand side, analysis of offset markets indicates that offset credits from forestry projects are the most popular type of offset credit available globally because they offer better value for money and generate co-benefits (such as biodiversity conservation) that are more visible than climate change mitigation; co-benefits can help explain why forest offset projects are preferred over others (Graton et al.,2021;Hamick and Gallant,2017a;Goldstein and Ruef,2016). Hamrick and Gallant (2017a) conducted a review of 148 forest carbon projects in 2016 and showed that all of the projects assessed had at least one type of co-benefit. The most common co-benefits of forest-based carbon offset projects were additional employment and/or training opportunities – 147 projects (98%), followed by community benefits – 75 projects (50%) and then biodiversity – 70 projects (47%). Many projects reported multiple co-benefits; 60% of projects reported at least two, 33% reported at least four, and 8% reported six co-benefits (Hamrick and Gallant, 2017a).

A key question on the demand side which the literature has grappled with is the efficiency and viability of offsets in competing with abatement as a climate strategy. From a climate policy perspective, the right balance has to be struck between reduction of gross emissions and offsetting given that the United Nations' Intergovernmental Panel on Climate Change has argued that the use of carbon removals is unavoidable for hard-to-abate emissions in the mission to achieve net-zero (Intergovernmental Panel on Climate Change,2022). The management literature, via the managerial opportunism hypothesis, suggests that there is tension between managerial ambitions to invest in emissions reductions and the need to increase financial performance, particularly when executive compensation is linked to financial performance (Bragdon and Marlin,1972; Friedman,1970; Preston and O'Bannon,1997). Broadly speaking results on the impact of carbon risk on firm value are mixed (Wang, Wu, Zhang,2022). Misani and Pogutz (2015) argue,however, that while a firm invests in carbon mitigation technologies, its competitors may still benefit from avoiding such expenditures. Additionality, Brammer and Millington (2008) observe that stakeholders may not immediately notice such improvements and, thus, it takes time for the benefits of differentiation to materialize. Delmas and Montiel (2009) further argue that cost savings that are attributed to better carbon performance largely depend on savings from liability and compliance costs, which can barely be realized in the short term.

While not specifically addressing abatement, early evidence from the European Union Emissions Trading System (EU ETS) shows that the EU compliance market has induced carbon emission reductions in the order of -10% between 2005 and 2012 all while having no negative impact on the economic performance of participating firms (Dechezleprêtre, Nachtigall and Venmans,2018). While there are limited studies on the impact of abatement activity on the financial performance of a company managers may be overlooking profitable abatement projects (King and Lennox,2002) and may also be ignoring the rapid pace of at which new decarbonization technologies are advancing (Cutler,2022). As firms evaluate their options for abatement related CAPEX and OPEX, demand for offsets is expected to increase, particularly forest carbon offsets which are perceived to be more cost-effective than other offset projects such as carbon storage and capture (Shrestha et al.,2022).

Of interest to policy makers seeking to utilize climate policy to dampen demand for offsets and influence firm behaviour towards abatement is evidence emerging from China, which indicates that climate policy uncertainty does not have a significant impact on corporate investments in the high-level range, which is where most abatement investment would sit in the capital budgeting portfolio of a firm (Ren,Shi and Jin,2022).

How and Why Firms Make Abatement Decisions

Extensive investments are needed to achieve the global ambitions of net zero carbon emissions by 2050. The International Renewable Energy Agency (IRENA) estimates that USD 4.4 trillion must be invested annually by 2050 for a 1.5°C climate pathway (IRENA,2021). The ability of firms to beat the abatement cost curve appears to be a daunting prospect. While there are a few companies which are taking significant steps towards decarbonization, the investment that firms will be required to engage to eliminate emissions from their value chains serves as an inhibitor for most to take real action towards reducing their gross emissions (Blum et al.,2021). For many sectors the available abatement options are costly, resulting in a high-cost abatement cost curve for firms. See Blanco (2022) for classification of carbon abatement opportunities.

When firms are faced with an increased pressure to reduce emissions, they can either abate or offset their emissions. Studies which model these choices, and their relationship with the price of carbon and other climate policy tools are beginning to emerge. Wei,Zhu and Tan (2022) employ an agent-based model analysis (computer simulation of actions and interactions of individuals and organizations) of 351 thermal power firms in China and found that regulatory pressure increases the adoption of low-carbon technology and that increases in the carbon price drives significant investment in low carbon technology; these findings supports their hypothesis that higher regulatory intensity (whether through reduction of free allowances or changing settings in the ETS) increases the role that an ETS has in incentivizing technology innovation and investment in abatement technology at the firm level (Wei,Zhu and Tan,2022). Assessment of the EU Emission Trading System (ETS), the oldest and currently the largest carbon market in the world found a positive correlation between firm's trading profits on the ETS and the reduction in their emissions (Guo et al., 2020). Similar work from Sweden provides the most convincing evidence on the impact of carbon pricing on emissions reduction at the firm level; using panel regressions on 4,000 firms with data spanning 26 years, Martinson et al. (2022) show that carbon pricing has resulted in the reduction of carbon emissions from Swedish manufacturing. The study is significant as it is the first to quantify the carbon pricing elasticity of firms based on their abatement cost; firms with lower abatement costs have higher carbon pricing elasticity (Martinson et al.,2022). The authors of the study conceptualize carbon pricing elasticity as a measure of how a firm's abatement expenditure changes in response to changes in the price of carbon. Using industry-level Pollution Abatement Costs Expenditures (PACE) estimates as a proxy for marginal abatement costs (MAC), Martinson et al. (2022) calculate carbon pricing elasticity as the ratio of industry PACE to industry sales divided by the percentage change in the price of carbon. The result of this formula is interpreted in the standard microeconomic fashion. A firm or industry with a higher carbon pricing elasticity is more responsive to changes in the price of carbon and will have greater abatement expenditure at lower carbon prices.

Ulrich,Trench and Hagerman (2022) in studying 177 gold mines across 35 countries investigated the cost impact of carbon pricing on the relative cost competitiveness and emissions reduction potential of gold mining companies. Utilizing a carbon price of US$50-100/t CO_2-e the study showed that the mines could absorb this cost and would still be profitable while continuing investments in renewable energy and low emission technology that they have already started; the study was based on the premise that a carbon price of at least US$50–100/t CO2-e by 2030 is needed to induce behaviours towards a low carbon economy (Ulrich, Trench and Hagermann,2022).

The global collapse of carbon prices in 2013 highlighted the importance of a suitable price level of carbon and effective carbon policy initiatives to influence the behaviour of polluting firms; the introduction of carbon price floors, carbon price support and greater harmonization of carbon prices between industries and among countries have been among the resulting policy responses that have emerged from the period of low carbon prices. Richardson-Barlow et al. (2022) in analysing the impact of these policy responses examined green steel making (hydrogen direct reduction of iron (H_2-DRI) using green hydrogen produced with water electrolysis, along with electric arc furnaces) in the United Kingdom (UK) and found that green steelmaking was at a price disadvantage because of the introduction of a Carbon Price Support (CPS) policy by the UK government in response to the collapse of carbon prices.

The CPS was introduced as an added cost to ETS allowances for electricity generators and was aimed at increasing the price of carbon above the Carbon Price Floor (CPF) set by the UK Government. Richardson-Barlow et al. (2022) found that firms involved in green steel making faced higher costs than those involved in traditional blast furnace steel making because higher CPS costs were being passed on to them from electricity generators. Green steel making requires a significant amount of electricity, making it a major cost centre for green steel makers. Richardson-Barlow et al. (2022) argue that the continuation of the CPS policy in a period when the ETS price has far exceeded the CPF established by the UK Government is a barrier to the decarbonization of steel production in the UK. Putting the influence of government regulation aside, we now discuss how the literature addresses the approach firms take when making abatement decisions.

Understanding the particular analytical tools that firms are using to make abatement investment decisions is also important for policy makers as they seek to influence these decisions through the mechanisms of carbon pricing. The literature argues that firms should make abatement decisions by equating marginal costs and benefits and selecting projects which are most economical. Blanco, Caro and Corbett (2020) point out that in practice firms do not follow this theoretical prescription but rather utilize simpler investment decision making tool such as payback period. Their study of global payback periods for carbon abatement projects found that between 2010-2016 average payback period for 20,930 emission reduction projects being implemented by 1,400 firms were relatively flat at an average of 2 years indicating that a a higher price of carbon is needed to incentivize firms toward carbon abatement projects (Blanco, Caro and Corbett,2020). The weaknesses of the payback period as an investment decision making tool are well document but its use in industry continues to prevail (Lin,2010). This dominance of the payback period highlighted by Blanco, Caro and Corbett (2020) is a component of the abatement puzzle policy makers will need to interrogate so that more comprehensive capital budgeting tools such as the net present value and the marginal abatement cost curve can be promoted among firms making assessment of abatement projects.

Mitigation Deterrence and Abatement Approaches of Firms

Supply chain decarbonization remain an expensive venture for firms and has been shown to negatively impact supply chain performance (Hua,2016). Despite these factors more firms are being pushed towards decarbonization because of the demand drivers of new market opportunities, regulatory risk, increasing energy prices, social responsibility and consumer preferences (Olatunji et al.,2019). The approaches being taken by firms to decarbonize include product development innovation, green procurement, environmental regulation conformity, green packaging and distribution, integration of carbon compliance throughout the manufacturing process, measurement of supply chain emission, carbon reporting and climate-related financial disclosure, collaboration among firms on emissions reduction strategies through the formation of industry groups and green technology financing schemes (Olatunji et al.,2019). A formal model of a firm's overall approach to abatement was conceptualized by Damert et al. (2017) in the corporate carbon strategy framework which included three main strategic objectives: carbon governance, carbon reduction and carbon competitiveness. The framework also outlines ten related corporate activities these firms have been pursing under each objective. Under the carbon reduction objective, the main focus of this review, the main strategies are carbon measurement and policy, product improvement, process improvements and carbon compensation (Damert et al., 2017). While carbon compensation, which involves the practices of offsetting and in-setting, could be considered as forms of mitigation deterrence, the literature argues that compensation is a legitimate pathway to net-zero for companies in hard to abate sectors (Pinkse and Busch,2013). In their empirical analysis of the carbon governance, reduction and competitiveness of a sample of 79 companies, Damert et al. (2017) found that carbon governance had a non-significant relationship with carbon reduction because while firms had made commitments to decarbonize at the board level, they had not yet built the capacity to actually do so at the production and operational level. Furthermore, the analysis found that investment in carbon competitiveness had a negative impact on financial performance in the short term due to high compliance costs, but found that investment in carbon reduction was strongly correlated with long-term financial performance in support of findings by Alvarez, Segura and Martinez-Ferrero (2013). A significant finding of the Damert et al. (2017) study is that no significant relationship was found between carbon reduction and long-term carbon performance (decrease in carbon intensity), which the authors argued could be explained by the disconnect between carbon governance and carbon reduction and legitimacy-seeking behaviour which may prompt firms to demonstrate efforts on climate mitigation without emphasizing the actual results of these actions. Goulder et al. (1999) provide insights into the impact of taxation policy on mitigation costs that could perhaps explain the dissonance between the stated carbon reduction intensions and actions of firms and their actual carbon performance. Using a general equilibrium framework for cap and trade policy (CTP), low carbon subsidy policy, carbon taxes,performance standards, technology mandates and other policy instruments, they showed that pre-existing taxes increase the abatement cost under all of the policy instruments which were modelled; thereby creating a disincentive for firms to undertake deep carbonization and drive increased carbon performance. The policy instrument which experienced the highest cost impact under the model was the cap-and-trade policy; further modelling showed that the cost effectiveness of a cap-and-trade policy could be significantly improved by using revenue from the cap-and-trade programme to fund tax cuts of pre-existing taxes (Goulder et al,1999). Stackelberg game modelling provides insights into the collaboration strategy firms may be engaging to overcome the high cost of abatement as it indicates that a joint emissions strategy was profitable under conditions of cap-and-trade regulations and low-carbon consumer preferences (Ji, Zhang and Yang, 2017).

The pathway towards decarbonization for several industries often begins with cost-neutral activities such as packaging- and waste-reduction efforts, energy reduction and logistics optimization, representing about a third of the decarbonization that firms have to undertake. The strategic choices firms have to make on decarbonization activities will see them following, sharing or leading (Spiller, 2021). Assessment of firm abatement behaviour in CTP markets for sulphur dioxide and nitrogen oxide in the United States can provide insights into how firms are approaching abatement under carbon compliance markets. Taylor (2012) studied firm abatement strategies under the sulphur dioxide and nitrogen oxide cap and trade programmes and found that firms which had started investing in clean technology installations cancelled these investments when they recognized that the cost of compliance under the CTP was less than the investment being made in the clean technology. This recognition led to a practice of increased banking of allowance units for future use in the CTP and the observation that CTPs may be limited in their ability to stimulate clean technology investment in the private sector (Taylor,2012).

The abatement approaches of the global cement industry feature prominently in the literature on abatement approaches. A review of 37 studies on cement and concrete decarbonization by Busch et al. (2022) identified improving energy efficiency, fuel switching, carbon capture and storage and reduction of clinker-to-cement ratio as the main abatement approaches within the industry. The reduction of clinker-to-cement ratio approach aligns with a study by Miller et al. (2018) which assessed the carbon reduction potential of using clinker, gypsum and limestone as alternative materials in cement production and found that clinker provided the greater emissions reduction potential. Another highly cited paper on abatement approaches by Rudd, Mitchell and Klein (1990), closely related to the cement industry, investigates the use of thermal mass (heat absorbing and conducting capacity of building materials) to reduce cooling energy. Common materials used for thermal mass include concrete or filled concrete block, stone or masonry usually used in floors or walls. The experiment conducted by Rudd, Mitchell and Klein (1990) on a large commercial building in Florida found that there was a 18% reduction in cooling energy after the implementation of building thermal mass materials.

An emerging approach which some firms have been taking to the carbon competitiveness component of their corporate carbon strategy (Damert et al.,2017) is pioneering of negative emissions technologies (NETs) which they have been promoting as legitimate offsetting mechanisms. Markusson et al. (2018) in their analysis of NETs posit the view that NETs, if not regulated effectively present a significant risk for mitigation deterrence. Similar mitigation deterrence concerns around solar radiation management (SRM), another emerging technological approach which seeks to offset some human-induced warming by reflecting solar energy back into space, and biodiversity offsets have also been raised (McLaren, 2016; McKenney and Kiesecker,2010).

McLaren, Willis and Markusson (2021) define mitigation deterrence as delay or avoidance of action to reduce emissions as a result of reliance on unproven or uncertain greenhouse gas removal technologies and methods. Through focus group workshops with 66 climate and greenhouse gas removal experts, McLaren, Willis and Markusson (2021) theorize that the main drivers and mechanisms of mitigation deterrence include the attractions of delay, exaggeration and psychological power of promises and rational substitution. Attractions of delays refers to reasons why businesses and governments may want to delay climate action; the main reason that was identified was the deeply entrenched economic and structural power of fossil fuel in human activity. Exaggeration and the power of promises was highlighted through the exaggeration of the potential of green-house gas removal to effectively address the climate crisis while rational substitution was described as the false equivalence attributed between emissions reductions and offsetting (McLaren, Willis and Markusson,2021). The solutions, proposed by McLaren, Willis and Markusson (2021) to address mitigation deterrence include restriction and regulation of voluntary markets, challenging the power of the fossil fuel industry, increasing accountability of greenhouse gas removal promises and instituting separate accounting for emissions reductions and removals.

Asayama (2021) provides further insights into the entrenched nature of fossil fuels as a driver of mitigation deterrence. Technically described as carbon lock-in or fossil-fuel lock, the reluctance to abandon fossil-fuels limits the extent to which low-carbon alternatives can be introduced and adopted (Asayama,2021). Asayama (2021) points out that there is a growing literature on the causes, types and dynamics of carbon lock-in since the term was first introduced in 2000 by Dr. Gregory Unruh, Arison Endowed Professor of Values Leadership at George Mason University. The main types of carbon lock-in identified in the literature are infrastructural, institutional, behavioural and cognitive (Asayama,2021). Carbon Storage and Capture (CSS) and Carbon Dioxide Removal (CDR) technologies have been suggested as possible solutions to address carbon lock-in, Asayama (2021) argues however that CSS poses an inherent risk of deepening carbon lock-in because of the enabling role it plays in continued fossil fuel production and that CDR poses the risk of false equivalence raised by Carton, Lund and Dooley (2021) which has lead to the practice of substituting carbon removals for abating carbon emissions.

Carton, Lund and Dooley (2021) argue that the practice of mitigation deterrence has resulted from the false equivalence of emissions reductions and emissions removals in carbon accounting. Carbon accounting, they argue has been built on the assumptions of carbon equivalence, geographical equivalence and temporal equivalence; assumptions which they believe are not robust enough to justify their continued use. Carbon equivalence refers to the treatment of fossil fuel carbon and the carbon sequestered through land use, land use change and forestry (biotic carbon) as the same type of carbon. According to Carton, Lund and Dooley (2021) fossil fuel and biotic carbon are fundamentally different because fossil fuel carbon has permanence in terms of its storage in fossil carbon sinks while biotic carbon has a more temporary storage characteristic because of its role in short-term carbon cycles. Given that Carbon accounting practices does not truly account for the risk of reversal associated with biotic carbon, offsetting emissions through land use, land use change and forestry is problematic (Carton, Lund and Dooley,2021). Geographical equivalence assumes that carbon emissions which have occurred in a particular location can be accounted for by carbon emissions removed in another geographic location. Carton, Lund and Dooley (2021) challenge the concept of geographical equivalence by pointing out that locations in the global South where offsetting occurs through afforestation projects have unique socio-political and biological characteristics which are often not considered in carbon accounting. As it relates to temporal equivalence, Carlton, Lund and Dooley (2021) define this concept as equating present mitigation action with mitigation action proposed to undertake in the future. They argue that temporal equivalence is problematic because the risks of the future are not as well known as the risks of the present and also because of the uncertainty around what future climate tipping points and characteristics will be.

Various forms of mitigation deterrence were characterized by McLaren (2020) as substitution and failure (type 1), rebounds, multipliers and side effects (type 2) and imagined offsets (type 3). McLaren (2020) defined type 1 mitigation and deterrence as the potential for carbon emissions removal mechanism and technologies, permitted to substitute for at source decarbonization, to fail; type 2 was defined as emissions removal activity which result in indirect and unintended production of additional emissions (for example carbon emissions from soils converted to biomass) while type 3 was defined as mitigation foregone by the moral hazard created by unrealized carbon removals promised by offsetting. Using climate models, McLaren (2020) estimated that 50-229 $GtC0_2$ from type 1 mitigation deterrence is at risk of failure, 23-134 $GtC0_2$ is at risk from type 2 and 182-297 $GtC0_2$ from type 3.

CONCLUSION

In this study, we provide a comprehensive review of the academic literature on the demand for and use of carbon offsets, mitigation deterrence and abatement approaches at the firm level. Our global systematic literature review produced 303 articles which we categorized into three main themes: demand, supply and markets for offsets; how and why firms make abatement decisions; and mitigation deterrence and abatement approaches of firms. We reviewed and provided literature synthesis for the articles with the highest number of citations under each theme.

From the review of the high citation articles under the demand, supply and markets for offsets theme we learnt that the main demand drivers of offsetting are price spreads, procedural cost, institutional capacity, offset limit, banking, Ex post invalidation risk, reversal risk, regulatory uncertainty, economic growth, fuel price and weather. We also learnt that on the supply side, owners of offset projects are strongly motivated by the potential earnings they are able to obtain from their offset project, this is particularly true of forest owners who may be considering utilizing their forest for offsetting. Analysis of the offset market indicates that offset credits from forestry projects are the most popular type of offset credit available globally because they offer better value for money and generate co-benefits (such as biodiversity conservation) that are more visible than climate change mitigation.

The key take-away from the articles under the how and why firms make abatement decisions theme is the insight from the literature that the price of carbon influences a firm's abatement actions. Furthermore, we learnt that the payback period is the most widely used tool used by firms to make decisions on which abatement projects to implement despite the fact that theory suggests that they should make abatement decisions by equating marginal costs and benefits and selecting projects which are most economical.

The practice of firms in using a short-term tool such as payback period to make abatement decisions underscore the challenges that policy makers face with the issue of mitigation deterrence explored under the mitigation deterrence and abatement approaches of firms theme. From the articles reviewed under this theme we learnt that despite the availability of current technology to abate emissions, many firms are engaging in mitigation deterrence through the use and promotion of carbon storage and capture, negative emissions technology and carbon dioxide removals. We gained insights into the fact that firms may be embracing mitigation deterrence because of the attractions of delay, exaggeration and psychological power of promises and rational substitution. Embedded in these reasons is what the literature describes as carbon lock-in whereby fossil-fuel use is deeply entrenched in human activity and as such limits accelerated adoption of low-carbon alternatives.

REFERENCES

Arlinghaus, J. (2015). *Impacts of Carbon Prices on Indicators of Competitiveness: A Review of Empirical Findings.* (OECD Environment Working Papers, No. 87). OECD Publishing, Paris. doi:10.1787/19970900

Arnold, J., & Toledano, P. (2021). *Corporate Net-Zero Pledges: The Bad and the Ugly*. Columbia Centre on Sustainable Investment.

Asayama, S. (2021). The Oxymoron of Carbon Dioxide Removal: Escaping Carbon Lock-In and yet Perpetuating the Fossil Status Quo? *Frontiers in Climate*, *3*, 673515. doi:10.3389/fclim.2021.673515

Badgley, G., Chay, F., Chegwidden, O., Hamman, J., Freeman, J., & Cullenward, D. (2022). California's forest carbon offsets buffer pool is severely undercapitalized. *Frontiers in Forests and Global Change*, *5*, 930426. doi:10.3389/ffgc.2022.930426

Benjaafar, S., Li, Y., & Daskin, M. (2013). Carbon footprint and the management of supply chains: Insights from simple models. *IEEE Transactions on Automation Science and Engineering*, *10*(1), 99–116. doi:10.1109/TASE.2012.2203304

Bhatnagar, M., Taneja, S., & Özen, E. (2022b). A wave of green start-ups in India—The study of green finance as a support system for sustainable entrepreneurship. *Green Finance*, *4*(2), 253–273. doi:10.3934/GF.2022012

Blanco, C. (2020). (Forthcoming). A Classification of Carbon Abatement Opportunities of Global Firms. *Manufacturing & Service Operations Management*.

Blanco, C., Caro, F., & Corbett, C. (2020). Do carbon abatement opportunities become less profitable over time? A global firm-level perspective using CDP data. *Energy Policy*, *138*, 111–252. doi:10.1016/j.enpol.2020.111252

Blaufelder, C., Levy, C., Mannion, P., & Dickon, P. (2021). *A blueprint for scaling voluntary carbon markets to meet the climate challenge*. McKinsey and Company.

Blum, P., Helmcke, S., Heuss, R., Hundertmark, T., Marlier, S., Somers, K., & Pinner, D. (2021). *Net zero or bust: Beating the abatement cost curve for growth*. McKinsey and Company. https://www.mckinsey.com/capabilities/operations/our-insights/net-zero-or-bust-beating-the-abatement-cost-curve-for-growth

Bragdon, J. H., & Marlin, J. A. T. (1972). Is pollution profitable? *Risk Management*, *19*(4), 9–18.

Brammer, S., & Millington, A. (2008). Does it pay to be different? An analysis of the relationship between corporate social and financial performance. *Strategic Management Journal*, *29*(12), 1325–1343. doi:10.1002mj.714

Broekhoff, D., Gillenwater, M., Colbert-Sangree, T., & Cage, P. (2019). Securing Climate Benefit: A Guide to Using Carbon Offsets. Stockholm Environment Institute & Greenhouse Gas Management Institute. Busch,P.,Kendall,A.,Murphy,C.W., Miller,S.A. (2022). Literature Review on policies to mitigate GHG emissions for cement and concrete. *Resources, Conservation and Recycling*, *182*, 106278.

Busch, T., Bassen, A., Lwandowski, S., & Sump, F. (2022). Corporate Carbon and Financial Performance Revisited. *Organization & Environment*, *35*(1), 154–171. doi:10.1177/1086026620935638

Canham, C. (2021). *Rethinking forest carbon offsets. Cary Institute of Ecosystem Studies*. Cary Institute. https://www.caryinstitute.org/news-insights/feature/rethinking-forest-carbon-offsets

Cao, K., Xu, X., Wu, Q., & Zhang, Q. (2017). Optimal production and carbon emission reduction level under cap-and-trade and low carbon subsidy policies. *Journal of Cleaner Production*, *167*, 505–513. doi:10.1016/j.jclepro.2017.07.251

Cardwell, H. (2022). *Govt unlikely to prevent pine and exotic forest owners from earning under ETS*. Radio New Zealand. https://www.rnz.co.nz/news/national/471839/govt-unlikely-to-prevent-pine-and-exotic-forest-owners-from-earning-under-ets

Carton, W., Lund, F. J., & Dooley, K. (2021). Undoing Equivalence: Rethinking Carbon Accounting for Just Carbon Removal. *Frontiers in Climate*, *3*, 664130. doi:10.3389/fclim.2021.664130

Carver, T., Dawson, P., & Kerr, S. (2017). *Including Forestry in an Emissions Trading Scheme: Lessons from New Zealand.* (Motu Working Paper 17-11). Motu Economic and Public Policy Research.

Childs, P. D., Ott, S. H., & Triantis, A. J. (1998). Capital Budgeting for Interrelated Projects: A Real Options Approach. *Journal of Financial and Quantitative Analysis*, *33*(3), 305–334. doi:10.2307/2331098

Choi, Y., & Qi, C. (2019). Is South Korea's Emission Trading Scheme Effective? An Analysis Based on the Marginal Abatement Cost of Coal-Fueled Power Plants. *Sustainability (Basel)*, *11*(9), 2504. doi:10.3390u11092504

Clean Development Mechanism. (2022). *CDM Executive Board 114th meeting: meeting report*. United Nations Framework Convention on Climate Change.

Climate Change Commission. (2022). *Advice on NZ ETS unit limits and price control settings for 2023-2027*. CCC. https://ccc-production-media.s3.ap-southeast-2.amazonaws.com/public/ETS-advice-July-22/PDFs/NZ-ETS-settings-2023-2027-final-report-web-27-July-2022.pdf

Climate Change Committee. (2022). *Voluntary Carbon Markets and Offsetting*. Climate Change Committee, United Kingdom. https://www.theccc.org.uk/publication/voluntary-carbon-markets-and-offsetting/

Cutler, Z., Huizenga, T., Kuvshinikov, M., & Westney, R. (2022). *Transforming capital projects to deliver net-zero emissions*. McKinsey & Company. https://www.mckinsey.com/capabilities/operations/our-insights/global-infrastructure-initiative/voices/transforming-capital-projects-to-deliver-net-zero-emissions

Damert, M., Paul, A., & Baumgartner, R. (2017). Exploring the determinants and long-term performance outcomes of corporate carbon strategies. *Journal of Cleaner Production*, *160*, 123–138. doi:10.1016/j.jclepro.2017.03.206

Daugaard, D. (2019). Emerging new themes in environmental, social and governance investing: A systematic literature review. *Accounting and Finance*, *60*(2), 1501–1530. doi:10.1111/acfi.12479

Dechezleprêtre, A., Nachtigall, D., & Venmans, F. (2018). The joint impact of the European Union emissions trading system on carbon emissions and economic performance. (OECD Economics Department Working Papers, No. 1515). OECD Publishing, Paris. doi:10.1787/18151973

Delmas, M., & Montiel, I. (2009). Greening the supply chain: When is customer pressure effective? *Journal of Economics & Management Strategy*, *18*(1), 171–201. doi:10.1111/j.1530-9134.2009.00211.x

Delmas, M., Nairn-Brich, N., & Lim, J. (2015). Dynamics of environmental and financial performance: The case of greenhouse gas emissions. *Organization & Environment*, *28*(4), 374–393. doi:10.1177/1086026615620238

Department of the Environment. (2016). *Modelling and analysis of Australia's abatement opportunities. Government of Australia*. DCCEEW. https://www.dcceew.gov.au/sites/default/files/documents/modelling-and-analysis-australias-2030-abatement-opportunities.pdf

Dormady, N., & Englander, G. (2016). Carbon allowances and the demand for offsets: A comprehensive assessment of imperfect substitutes. *Journal of Public Policy*, *36*(1), 139–167. doi:10.1017/S0143814X14000336

Elgin, B. (2022). This Timber Company Sold Millions of Dollars of Useless Carbon Offsets. *Bloomberg News*. https://www.bloomberg.com/news/articles/2022-03-17/timber-ceo-wants-to-reform-flawed-carbon-offset-market?leadSource=uverify%20wall

Environment and Finance. (2022). *Transparency, liquidity and integrity in the voluntary carbon market*. Field Gibson Media. https://www.environmental-finance.com/content/analysis/transparency-liquidity-and-integrity-in-the-voluntary-carbon-market.html

Gallego-Alvarez, I., Segura, L., & Matinez-Ferrero, J. (2015). Carbon emission reduction: The impact on the financial and operational performance of international companies. *Journal of Cleaner Production*, *103*, 149–159. doi:10.1016/j.jclepro.2014.08.047

Gibson, E. (2022). *Government proposes banning pine carbon farms from the ETS*. Stuff. https://www.stuff.co.nz/environment/climate-news/127946385/government-proposes-banning-pine-carbon-farms-from-the-ets?rm=a

Gillenwater, M., & Seres, S. (2011). *The Clean Development Mechanism: A review of the first international offset program*. Pew Centre on Global Climate Change.

Goldstein, A., & Ruef, F. (2016). State of Forest Carbon Finance 2016 - View from the Understory. *Ecosystem Marketplace, Forest Trends*. https://www.forest-trends.org/publications/view-from-theunderstory/

Goulder, L. H., Parry, I. W. H., Williams, R. C. III, & Burtraw, D. (1999). The cost-effectiveness of alternative instruments for environmental protection in a second-best setting. *Journal of Public Economics*, *72*(3), 329–360. doi:10.1016/S0047-2727(98)00109-1

Guo, J., Gu, F., Liu, Y., Liang, X., Mo, J., & Fan, Y. (2020). Assessing the impact of ETS trading profit on emission abatements based on firm-level transactions. *Nature Communications*, *11*(1), 2078. doi:10.103841467-020-15996-1 PMID:32350279

Hamrick, K., & Gallant, M. (2017a). Fertile Ground - State of Forest Carbon Finance 2017. *Ecosystem-Marketplace, Forest Trends.* https://www.forest-trends.org/publications/fertile-ground/

Hamrick, K., & Gallant, M. (2017b). Unlocking Potential - State of the Voluntary Carbon Markets 2017. *Ecosystem Marketplace, Forest Trends*. https://www.forest-trends.org/publications/unlockingpotential/

Hua, S. Y. (2016). Logistic suppliers' decarbonization practices and prioritization. *International Journal of Environmental, Cultural, Economic and Social Sustainability*, *12*(1), 1–16. doi:10.18848/1832-2077/CGP/1-16

Intergovernmental Panel on Climate Change. (2022). Climate Change 2022: Mitigation of Climate Change. *IPCC Sixth Assessment Report. Intergovernmental Panel on Climate Change 2022*. IPCC. https://report.ipcc.ch/ar6/wg3/IPCC_AR6_WGIII_Full_Report.pdf

Iwata, H., & Okada, K. (2011). How does environmental performance affect financial performance? Evidence from Japanese manufacturing firms. *Ecological Economics*, *70*(9), 1691–1700. doi:10.1016/j.ecolecon.2011.05.010

Ji, J., Zhang, Z., & Yang, L. (2017). Carbon emission reduction decisions in the retail-/dual-channel supply chain with comsumers' preference. *Journal of Cleaner Production*, *141*, 852–867. doi:10.1016/j.jclepro.2016.09.135

Keohane, N., & Seymour, F. (2021). *Forests and International Carbon Markets: Climate and Forests 2030.* The Climate and Land Use Alliance. https://www.climateandforests2030.org/app/uploads/2021/10/CARBON-MARKETS_Forests-and-International-Carbon-Markets_KeohaneSeymour.pdf

King, A., & Lenox, M. (2002). Exploring the Locus of Profitable Pollution Reduction. *Management Science*, *48*(2), 289–299. doi:10.1287/mnsc.48.2.289.258

Lee, K.-H., Min, B., & Yook, K.-H. (2015). The impacts of carbon (CO2) emissions and environmental research and development (R&D) investment on firm performance. *International Journal of Production Economics*, *167*, 1–11. doi:10.1016/j.ijpe.2015.05.018

LinH.-J. (2010). Why Should Managers Like Payback Period? SSRN. https://ssrn.com/abstract=1688730

Linnenluecke, M., Marrone, M., & Singn, A. (2020). Conducting systematic literature reviews and bibliometric analyses. *Australian Journal of Management*, *45*(2), 175–194. doi:10.1177/0312896219877678

Lu, M., Xu, H., & Wang, X. (2021). Impact of carbon markets on industrial competitiveness: An analysis of selected industries in Beijing. *Energy Reports*, *7*, 1601–1611. doi:10.1016/j.egyr.2021.09.063

Macfarlane, M. (2022). Assessing the State of the Voluntary Carbon Market in 2022. *Carbon Direct Blog*. https://www.carbon-direct.com/insights/assessing-the-state-of-the-voluntary-carbon-market-in-2022

Manero, A., Taylor, K., Nikolakis, W., Adamowicz, W., Marshall, V., Spencer-Cotton, A., Nguyen, M., & Grafton, Q. (2022). A systematic literature review of non-market valuation of Indigenous peoples' values: Current knowledge, best-practice and framing questions for future research. *Ecosystem Services*, *54*, 101–147. doi:10.1016/j.ecoser.2022.101417

Manley, B. (2013). Deforestation Survey 2012. *MPI Technical Paper 2013/02*. Ministry for Primary Industries.

Manley, B. (2014). Deforestation Survey 2013, Final Report. *MPI Technical Paper 2014/02*. Ministry for Primary Industries. https://www.mpi.govt.nz/document-vault/4131

Manley, B. (2015). Deforestation Survey 2014. *MPI Technical Paper 2015/02*. Ministry for Primary Industries. https://www.mpi.govt.nz/document-vault/6355

Manley, B. (2016a). *Afforestation Responses to Carbon Price Changes and Market Certainties*. University of Canterbury School of Forestry. https://www.mfe.govt.nz/publications/climatechange/afforestation-responses-carbon-price-changes-and-market-certainties

Manley, B. (2016b). *Deforestation Intentions Survey 2015*. Ministry for Primary Industries. https://www.mpi.govt.nz/document-vault/11776

Manley, B. (2019). *Impacts of carbon prices on forest management*. Ministry for Primary Industries. https://www.mpi.govt.nz/dmsdocument/46561-Impacts-of-carbon-prices-on-forest-management

Manley, B. (2021). *Afforestation and Deforestation Intentions Survey 2021*. Ministry for Primary Industries. https://www.mpi.govt.nz/dmsdocument/52405-Afforestation-and-Deforestation-Intentions-Survey-2021

Marketplace, E. (2022). *The art of integrity- state of the voluntary carbon markets 2022 Q3*. Forest Trends.

Markusson, N., McLaren, D., & Tyfield, D. (2018). Towards a cultural political economy of mitigation deterrence by negative emissions technologies (NETs). *Global Sustainability*, *1*(e10), 1–9. doi:10.1017us.2018.10

MartinssonG.StrombergP.SajtosL.ThomannC. (2022). *Carbon Pricing and Firm-Level CO2 Abatement: Evidence from a Quarter of a Century-Long Panel.* (Finance Working Paper No. 842) European Corporate Governance Institute. https://ssrn.com/abstract=4206508 or doi:10.2139/ssrn.4206508

Mather-Gratton, Z. J., Larsen, S., & Bentsen, N. S. (2021). Understanding the sustainability debate on forest biomass for energy in Europe: A discourse analysis. *PLoS One*, *16*(2), e0246873. doi:10.1371/journal.pone.0246873 PMID:33596217

McKenney, B. A., & Kiesecker, J. M. (2010). Policy Development for Biodiversity Offsets: A Review of Offset Frameworks. *Environmental Management*, *45*(1), 165–176. doi:10.100700267-009-9396-3 PMID:19924472

McLaren, D. (2016). Mitigation deterrence and the "moral hazard" of solar radiation management. *Earth's Future*, *4*(12), 596–602. doi:10.1002/2016EF000445

Mclaren, D. (2020). Quantifying the potential scale of mitigation deterrence from greenhouse gas removal techniques. *Climatic Change*, *162*(4), 2411–2428. doi:10.100710584-020-02732-3

McLaren, D., Willis, R., Szerszynski, B., Tyfield, D., & Markusson, N. (2021). Attractions of delay: Using deliberative engagement to investigate the political and strategic impacts of greenhouse gas removal technologies. *Environment and Planning. E, Nature and Space*, *0*(0).

Media, S. (2022). Planting Forests That Are Good For Nature, Climate, And The Economy. *Scoop News Website.* https://www.scoop.co.nz/stories/PA2210/S00032/planting-forests-that-are-good-for-nature-climate-and-the-economy.htm

Milne, P. (2021). The potential for using forestry offsets to meet University of Canterbury's net-zero carbon emissions targets: a case study. [Unpublished Dissertation. New Zealand School of Forestry].

Ministry for Primary Industries. (2021). *National Exotic Forest Description.* MPI. https://www.mpi.govt.nz/dmsdocument/43540/direct

Ministry for Primary Industries. (2022). *Managing exotic afforestation incentives: A discussion document on proposals to change forestry settings in the New Zealand Emissions Trading Scheme.* (MPI Discussion Paper No:2022/02). MPI. https://www.mpi.govt.nz/dmsdocument/50206-Managing-exotic-afforestation-incentives-Proposals-to-change-forestry-settings-in-the-NZ-Emissions-Trading-Scheme

Ministry for the Environment. (2018). *Emissions pricing impact on innovation and competitiveness.* Wellington: Ministry for the Environment. https://environment.govt.nz/assets/Publications/Files/Innovation-and-competitiveness-review-FINAL.pdf

Ministry for the Environment. (2020). *Guidance for voluntary carbon offsetting –updated and extended until 31 December 2021.* Wellington: Ministry for the Environment. https://environment.govt.nz/assets/Publications/Files/guidance-for-voluntary-carbon-offsetting-updated-and-extended-until-31-December-2021.pdf

Ministry for the Environment. (2020). *Marginal abatement cost curves analysis for New Zealand: Potential greenhouse gas mitigation options and their costs.* Wellington: Ministry for the Environment. https://environment.govt.nz/assets/Publications/Files/marginal-abatement-cost-curves-analysis_0.pdf

Ministry for the Environment. (2020). *Marginal abatement cost curves analysis for New Zealand: Potential greenhouse gas mitigation options and their costs.* Cabinet Briefing, Wellington: Ministry for the Environment. https://environment.govt.nz/assets/publications/Cabinet-papers-briefings-and-minutes/2020-b-06369-publication-of-marginal-abatement-cost-curves-report.pdf

Ministry of Agriculture and Forestry. (2012). *Interaction between the voluntary carbon market, New Zealand's accounting under the Kyoto Protocol and the New Zealand Emissions Trading Scheme*. Wellington: Ministry for Agriculture and Forestry. https://www.mpi.govt.nz/dmsdocument/5140/direct

Misani, N., & Pogutz, S. (2015). Unraveling the effects of environmental outcomes and processes on financial performance: A non-linear approach. *Ecological Economics*, *109*, 150–160. doi:10.1016/j.ecolecon.2014.11.010

Morton, J. (2021). Covering climate now: is NZ getting forestry right? *New Zealand Herald*. https://www.nzherald.co.nz/nz/covering-climate-now-is-nz-getting-forestry-right/5J2IA4YVDQO2K4YEEIFKHBCQIQ/

Naucler, T., & Enkvist, P. (2009). *Pathways to a Low-Carbon Economy: Version 2 of the Global Greenhouse Gas Abatement Cost Curve*. Mckinsey & Company.

New Zealand Forest Service. (2022). *Emissions Trading Scheme for Forestry as at 30 June 2022*. Ministry for Primary Industries. https://www.mpi.govt.nz/dmsdocument/45232-Emissions-Trading-Scheme-for-Forestry-land-statistics-

New Zealand Productivity Commission. (2018). *Low-emissions economy: Final report*. New Zealand Productivity Commission. www.productivity.govt.nz/low-emissions

Olatunji, O., Akinlabi, S. A., Ayo, O., Madushele, N., Adedeji, P. A., & Fatoba, S. O. (2019). Drivers and barriers to competitive carbon footprint reduction in manufacturing supply chain: A brief review. *Procedia Manufacturing*, *35*, 992–1000. doi:10.1016/j.promfg.2019.06.047

Pinkse, J., & Busch, T. (2013). The emergence of corporate carbon norms: Strategic directions and managerial implications. *Thunderbird International Business Review*, *55*(6), 633–645. doi:10.1002/tie.21580

Preston, L. E., & O'Bannon, D. P. (1997). The Corporate Social-Financial Performance Relationship: A Typology and Analysis. *Business & Society*, *36*(4), 419–429. doi:10.1177/000765039703600406

Ren, X., Shi, Y., & Jin, C. (2022). Climate policy uncertainty and corporate investment: Evidence from the Chinese energy industry. *Carbon Neutrality*, *1*(1), 14. doi:10.100743979-022-00008-6

Richardson-Barlow, C., Pimm, A., Taylor, P., & Gale, W. (2022). Policy and pricing barriers to steel industry decarbonization: A UK case study. *Energy Policy*, *168*, 1–12. doi:10.1016/j.enpol.2022.113100

Rudd, M. D., Mitchell, J. W., & Klein, S. (1990). Use of building thermal mass to offset cooling loads. *1990 Annual Meeting of the American Society of Heating, Refrigerating and Air-Conditioning Engineers, Technical and Symposium Papers, Conference Proceedings*. NREL.

U.S. Securities and Exchange Commission. (2022). *Factsheet: Enhancement and Standardization of Climate-Related Disclosures*. US Securities and Exchange Commission.

Seeberg-Elverfeldt, C. (2010). *Carbon finance possibilities for agriculture, forestry and other land use projects in the smallholder context*. Natural Resources Management and Environment Department, Food and Agriculture Organization.

Shrestha, A., Eshpeter, S., Li, N., Li, J., Nile, J. O., & Wang, G. (2022). Inclusion of forestry offsets in emission trading schemes: Insights from global experts. *Journal of Forestry Research*, *33*(1), 279–287. doi:10.100711676-021-01329-5

Spiller, P. (2021). *Making supply-chain decarbonization happen*. McKinsey and Company. https://www.mckinsey.com/capabilities/operations/our-insights/making-supply-chain-decarbonization-happen

Taneja, S., Kaur, S., & Özen, E. (2022). Using green finance to promote global growth in a sustainable way. *International Journal of Green Economics*, *16*(3), 246–257. doi:10.1504/IJGE.2022.128930

Taneja, S., & Özen, E. (2023a). To analyse the relationship between bank's green financing and environmental performance. *International Journal of Electronic Finance*, *12*(2), 163–175. doi:10.1504/IJEF.2023.129919

Taneja, S., & Ozen, E. (2023b). Impact of the European Green Deal (EDG) on the agricultural carbon (CO2) emission in Turkey. *International Journal of Sustainable Development and Planning*, *18*(3), 715–727. doi:10.18280/ijsdp.180307

Taylor, M. R. (2012). Innovation under cap-and-trade programs. *Proceedings of the National Academy of Sciences of the United States of America*, *109*(13), 4804–4809. doi:10.1073/pnas.1113462109 PMID:22411797

Ulrich, S., Trench, A., & Steffen, H. (2022). Gold mining greenhouse gas emissions, abatement measures, and the impact of a carbon price. *Journal of Cleaner Production*, *340*, 130851. doi:10.1016/j.jclepro.2022.130851

Unruh, G. C. (2000). Understanding carbon lock-in. *Energy Policy*, *28*(12), 817–830. doi:10.1016/S0301-4215(00)00070-7

van Kooten, C., & Johnston, C. (2016). The Economics of Forest Carbon Offsets. *Annual Review of Resource Economics*, *8*(1), 227–2246. doi:10.1146/annurev-resource-100815-095548

Wakelin, S., Paul, T., & Manley, B. (2021). *The potential contribution from increased sequestration in pre1990 forests to New Zealand's Paris Agreement 2030 target.* (MPI Technical Paper No: 2021/28). Ministry for Primary Industries. https://www.mpi.govt.nz/dmsdocument/47980-The-potential-contribution-from-increased-sequestration-in-pre-1990-forests-to-New-Zealands-Paris-Agreement-2030-target

Wang, L., Li, S., & Gao, S. (2014). Do greenhouse gas emissions affect financial performance? An empirical examination of Australian public firms. *Business Strategy and the Environment*, *23*(8), 505–519. doi:10.1002/bse.1790

Wang, Y., Wu, Z., & Zhang, G. (2022). Firms and climate change: A review of carbon risk in corporate finance. *Carbon Neutrality*, *1*(1), 6. doi:10.100743979-022-00005-9

Wannan, O. (2022). Start-up CarbonCrop pauses new carbon offsets after questions raised. *Stuff*. https://www.stuff.co.nz/environment/climate-news/129091128/startup-carboncrop-pauses-new-carbon-offsets-after-questions-raised?rm=a

Wei, Y., Zhu, R., & Tan, L. (2022). Emission trading scheme, technological innovation, and competitiveness: Evidence from China's thermal power enterprises. *Journal of Environmental Management*, *320*, 115874. doi:10.1016/j.jenvman.2022.115874 PMID:35947908

Zhang, X. (2014). Reference-dependent electric vehicle production strategy considering subsidies and consumer trade-offs. *Energy Policy*, *67*, 422–430. doi:10.1016/j.enpol.2013.12.028

Chapter 10
Green Finance: Addressing Environmental Challenges Through Sustainable Investments

Kapil Kumar Aggarwal
https://orcid.org/0000-0002-2752-9495
Chandigarh University, India

Rumit Kaur
Chandigarh University, India

Girish Lakhera
Graphic Era University (Deemed), India

ABSTRACT

In order to address environmental issues through sustainable investments, this chapter will examine the idea of green finance. The report gives a general outline of the environmental problems that are now plaguing the world, and emphasises how crucial sustainable investments are to resolve these problems. It goes into the tenets and practices of green finance, looking at different financial tools and tactics used to advance environmental sustainability. The chapter also examines the advantages and difficulties of green finance, including how rules and policies from the executive branch have aided in its expansion. The significance of green financing is emphasised as a key factor in the conclusion as a means of accelerating the shift to a more resilient and sustainable economy.

INTRODUCTION

In recent years, green finance has drawn a lot of attention as a strategy for addressing the urgent environmental issues that the world is currently experiencing. The critical need to move towards a more sustainable and low-carbon economy has been underscored by the growing awareness of climate change, resource depletion, and biodiversity loss.

DOI: 10.4018/979-8-3693-1388-6.ch010

Historically, traditional financial systems have prioritised short-term profit maximisation over long-term effects on society and the environment. However, the effects of these unsustainable practises are starting to show themselves more and more, with ecological degradation, extreme weather, and rising global temperatures all posing serious threats to economic stability.

Green finance, a specialised area of finance with the goal of incorporating environmental considerations into financial decision-making processes, has evolved in response to these difficulties. It includes a broad range of financial tools, goods, and services that fund green and sustainable ventures, enterprises, and innovations.

Any financial instruments or investments, including grants, purchases, debt, sales, and risk management tools (covering insurance products, investment guarantees, commodities, credit or interest rate derivatives, etc.), issued under contract to a company, facility, person, project, or agency, public or private, in exchange for the delivery of positive environmental externalities that are actual, verified, and additional to any other benefits that the recipient may receive, are referred to as "green finance."

According to:

- Organisation for Economic Co-operation and Development (OECD): "Green Finance is finance for "achieving economic growth while reducing pollution and greenhouse gas emissions, minimising waste and improving efficiency in the use of natural resources".
- People's Bank of China: "Green finance policy refers to a series of policy and institutional arrangements to attract private capital investments into green industries such as environmental protection, energy conservation and clean energy through financial services – including lending, private equity funds, bonds, shares and insurance."

Green finance is significant because it has the potential to reroute capital towards environmentally friendly endeavours, stimulate the development of clean technology, and encourage resource conservation. Green finance works to reduce environmental hazards, promote sustainable economic growth, strengthen corporate social responsibility, and contribute to the accomplishment of the Sustainable Development Goals (SDGs) established by the United Nations.

In order to close the significant funding gap needed for the shift to a low-carbon and resilient economy, green finance has the potential to mobilise private sector investments as well as supplement public sector support. It provides chances for investors to make good returns while funding initiatives that benefit the environment, resulting in a situation where both financial and environmental goals are met.

Overall, the importance of green finance resides in its capacity to trigger a systemic transition towards sustainable and climate-resilient economies, fostering resource allocation that is both effective and ensures the long-term wellbeing of the earth and future generations.

REVIEW OF LITERATURE

(Kharade, 2021) indicates that green finance should be utilized for the long-term investment. It should not only include the domestic investors but also the foreign investors, which could promote the more growth.

(Jain, 2020) included in his study that if the private sector and public sector and asset managers are designed with their roles effectively then definitely the economy will achieve the sustainability in financial system.

(Reddy, 2018) suggests that government of India is trying their best in order to achieve the sustainability, but the private sector is actively participating in the sustainable development of an economy.

(Wang & Zhi, 2016) finds out the utility of green money for the concept of renewable energy and finds out that insufficiency is there. The attention should be paid towards the market development and the formulation of the policy. He tries to make the understanding towards internal conflicts between the concept of green finance and conservation of an environment as they are spontaneously proposed for achieving balance environmental.

(de Carvalho Ferreira et al., 2016) studies about the different types of concepts being adopted in order to gain the knowledge related the finance and sustainability with the help of different methods being adopted through the availability of different journals.

(S. Vadrale, 2016) study tells us about the steps taken by the different private sector and public sector banks in order to encourage the green finance and bring the sustainability which is being admired and taken over by many people including internal and external environment.

(Parvadavardini & Nagarajan, 2015) suggests the suitability about the green finance in Indian industries and how they cope up to establish a healthy environment.

(D.Kandavel*, 2013)Suggests that the green finance initiative is being taken well. As in order to guide the citizens about this many seminars, green projects and even green loans etc are being designed. So, that the importance of green finance should be well communicated. This is being done not in the urban areas but also the rural areas.

(Haigh, 2012) the study shows the increase impact of finance and sustainability. The Journal of Sustainable Finance & Investment (JSF&I), the effect of green Finance in different sectors. The effect of Green finance can be seen in both the economy and the society.

OBJECTIVES

1. To assess the need for and effectiveness of incorporating green finance into the financial system in solving environmental issues.
2. To evaluate the potential advantages and disadvantages of implementing green finance.
3. To examine current environmental, financial, and global sustainability activities in order to comprehend the framework in which green finance operates.
4. To identify the main issues and problems encountered while incorporating green finance into the current framework.
5. To offer policy suggestions and methods for implementing green finance successfully and removing obstacles.

RESEARCH METHODOLOGY

The secondary data is being used for this research. The research data has been gathered with the help of Websites, reports, Research Articles and Research papers.

The Need for Green Finance: Environmental Challenges and Climate Change

Environmental Challenges and the Climate Crisis

Climate change is one of the most urgent environmental problems that the world is now experiencing. According to the Intergovernmental Panel on Climate Change (IPCC), human activities, especially the burning of fossil fuels, have greatly increased greenhouse gas (GHG) emissions, which has led to global warming and its corresponding effects on the climate.

Ecosystems, biodiversity, and human health are all seriously threatened by climate change. It causes temperature increases, a rise in sea level, changes in rainfall patterns, and an increase in the frequency and severity of extreme weather events (including hurricanes, droughts, and floods). Economic stability and social welfare are in danger as a result of these changes, which also have significant effects on agriculture, water resources, coastal regions, and public health.

By mobilising funding for climate mitigation and adaptation initiatives, green finance plays a critical role in solving these environmental concerns. It makes investments possible in fields like waste management, sustainable transportation, energy efficiency, and renewable energy. Green finance assists in lowering GHG emissions, minimising negative environmental effects, and increasing climate resilience by channelling financial resources towards low-carbon and climate-resilient enterprises.

Furthermore, green finance is essential for achieving the goals set out in the Paris Agreement, an international agreement aimed at limiting global warming to well below 2 degrees Celsius above pre-industrial levels. To achieve the ambitious targets outlined in the agreement, significant investments are needed to transition to a low-carbon economy and support developing countries in their climate action efforts. Green finance provides the necessary financial mechanisms to facilitate these investments and support the implementation of sustainable projects worldwide.

Sustainable Development Goals

Green finance plays a crucial role in attaining sustainable development's more general goals, as specified by the Sustainable Development Goals (SDGs) of the United Nations, in addition to combating climate change. The SDGs offer a thorough framework for international development initiatives with the goals of eradicating poverty, safeguarding the environment, and ensuring prosperity for all.

By encouraging investments in industries that advance sustainable development, green money directly contributes to the achievement of many SDGs. The following are some significant ways that green money supports the SDGs:

1. Access to clean, affordable energy (SDG 7): Green financing makes it possible to invest in renewable energy sources like solar, wind, hydropower, and geothermal energy. Additionally, it backs initiatives to improve energy efficiency, which lowers overall energy use and carbon emissions..
2. Sustainable cities and communities (SDG 11): Green financing aids in funding sustainable urban infrastructure, such as eco-friendly structures, public transit options, and trash disposal techniques. It helps to create liveable and inclusive urban places by fostering compact, efficient, and resilient cities.
3. Responsible consumption and production (SDG 12): Green finance promotes investments in resource efficiency, waste reduction, and sustainable production methods. The implementation of

circular economy ideas, which seek to reduce waste production and increase resource utilisation, is encouraged.

4. Climate action (SDG 13): Green finance is essential for financing climate mitigation and adaptation projects, assisting nations in the transition to low-carbon economies and increasing their capacity to withstand the effects of climate change. It backs projects including reforestation, climate-smart agriculture, and building climate-resilient infrastructure.
5. Life below water and life on land (SDGs 14 and 15): Ecosystems on land and in the ocean can be protected and restored with the help of green finance. In order to protect natural resources and ecosystems, it promotes sustainable fishing, the preservation of biodiversity, and investments in sustainable land management techniques.
6. Partnerships for the goals (SDG 17): Collaboration between the governmental and corporate sectors, as well as between global organisations and civil society, is promoted by green financing. It encourages collaboration in order to mobilise funds, exchange information, and enable the dissemination of green technology for sustainable development.

Green finance assists in directing investments towards initiatives that have positive social, environmental, and economic consequences by coordinating financial flows with the SDGs(Aggarwal & Aggarwal, 2021). It offers the required funding for programmes and projects that help achieve sustainable development goals, ensuring a more just and prosperous future for all communities across the world.

The Role of Finance in Transitioning to a Green Economy

In order to move to a green economy, where economic growth is unrelated to environmental damage, finance is essential. Green financing makes it easier to reallocate capital to environmentally friendly and sustainable projects, enabling the transformation of entire industries and fostering the adoption of sustainable behaviours(Poonam & Aggarwal, 2023). The following examples will help you understand why green finance is necessary for the transition to a green economy:

1. Investment in sustainable infrastructure: Sustainable infrastructure projects, such as renewable energy installations, energy-efficient buildings, sustainable transportation networks, and robust water and waste management systems, can be financed with the help of green finance. These investments contribute to the reduction of carbon emissions, the improvement of resource efficiency, and the establishment of a green economy.
2. Fostering innovation and the use of clean technology: Green finance helps with the investigation, creation, and use of clean technologies. It offers funding to companies and startups developing cutting-edge solutions for waste management, sustainable agriculture, energy storage, renewable energy, and other problems. Green financing encourages investments in these technologies, which promotes innovation and quickens the shift to a green economy.
3. Reducing financial risks and fostering long-term value: Businesses and investors face financial risks from climate change and environmental deterioration. By encouraging investments in robust and sustainable assets, green financing aids in risk management. It promotes long-term value creation and strengthens the financial resiliency of organisations by encouraging the consideration of environmental issues in risk assessment and investment decision-making.

4. Promoting economic growth and job creation: The shift to a green economy presents several prospects for both of these. Green financing encourages investments in environmentally friendly businesses and initiatives, which boosts jobs and the economy. It encourages the growth of environmentally friendly industries including green technologies, eco-tourism, sustainable agriculture, and renewable energy, which benefits both the economy and the environment.
5. Enhancing corporate sustainability and responsibility: Sustainable business practises and the incorporation of environmental concerns into daily operations are encouraged by green finance. By encouraging businesses to cut their carbon footprint, increase resource efficiency, and embrace environmentally friendly business models, it fosters corporate sustainability. Since firms are increasingly expected to demonstrate their commitment to sustainable development, green money also strengthens corporate social responsibility.
6. Attracting investment opportunities: Green finance offers the potential for investors to get involved in moral and sustainable enterprises. It receives money from socially and environmentally conscious investors who aim to have both profitable business ventures and positive environmental effects. By expanding the range of investment options, green finance encourages a larger shift towards sustainable investing practises and helps raise additional funds for sustainable activities.

In conclusion, green finance plays a crucial role in the shift to a green economy by facilitating investments in sustainable infrastructure, encouraging innovation, lowering financial risks, boosting economic growth, improving corporate sustainability, and luring socially conscious investments. It accelerates the transition to a more sustainable and inclusive economy by combining financial activities with environmental aims.

BENEFITS OF GREEN FINANCE

Reducing Environmental Dangers

Green money offers various benefits by lowering environmental hazards and promoting sustainable practises. Some notable benefits include:

- Lower greenhouse gas emissions: Green financing makes investments in energy efficiency and renewable energy as low-carbon alternatives. Reduced greenhouse gas emissions and the development of energy-efficient practises are made possible with the help of green finance, which helps address climate change and the dangers it poses.
- Conservation of natural resources: Investing in water conservation, ethical forestry practises, and sustainable land management all contribute to the preservation of natural resources. Green finance provides funding for initiatives that promote resource efficiency, cut waste generation, and ensure the sustainable use of natural resources.
- Preserving biodiversity: Green financing enables investments in plans and programmes that safeguard and replenish biodiversity. It promotes conservation initiatives, environmentally friendly farming methods, and the preservation of natural environments. Green finance supports ecological balance and the long-term health of ecosystems by preserving biodiversity.

Promoting Long-Term Economic Growth

By encouraging investments in environmentally friendly sectors, green finance plays a critical role in promoting sustainable economic growth. The advantages include:

- Job creation: Investing in sustainable companies, energy-efficient infrastructure, and renewable energy sources results in job openings. Green finance helps to create jobs in industries like sustainable agriculture, green construction, and the production of clean technologies, which promotes economic growth and lowers unemployment.
- Economic resilience: Green finance encourages investments in sustainable practises and infrastructure that is resistant to climate change. It contributes to greater economic stability and lessens the susceptibility of communities and companies to the effects of climate change by enhancing infrastructure resilience to hazards associated to climate change, such as flooding or extreme weather events.
- Cost savings: Green financing promotes investments in environmentally friendly practises and energy-efficient technologies, which translates into long-term cost savings for both consumers and enterprises. Buildings that use less energy, for instance, use less energy and cost less to operate. Sustainable agriculture methods optimise productivity, minimise resource inputs, and cut expenses associated with production. These financial savings boost economic competitiveness and efficiency.

The Promotion of Corporate Social Responsibility

By encouraging companies to incorporate sustainability into their operations, green financing promotes corporate social responsibility. The advantages include:

- Positive brand perception: Green finance enables companies to show their dedication to sustainable growth. Businesses can improve their brand image and reputation and draw in environmentally concerned customers and investors by investing in environmentally friendly projects and implementing sustainable practises.
- Stakeholder engagement: Companies are encouraged by green financing to interact with stakeholders and take into account their environmental concerns. Businesses can improve ties with communities, clients, staff, and investors by incorporating stakeholders in decision-making procedures and applying sustainable practises.
- Environmental law observance: Green finance encourages observance of environmental laws and norms. Businesses can avoid fines and damage to their reputation associated with non-compliance by financing initiatives that do not violate environmental requirements.

Attracting Investment Opportunities

Green finance creates investment opportunities for investors seeking both financial returns and positive environmental impact. The benefits include:

- Diversification: Green finance broadens the range of investment options available to investors. It provides opportunities to invest in sectors such as renewable energy, sustainable infrastructure, clean technologies, and green bonds. By diversifying their investment portfolios, investors can reduce risks and potentially achieve attractive returns.
- Long-term value creation: Green finance encourages investments in sustainable projects with long-term value creation potential. By considering environmental factors, businesses can identify and capitalize on emerging opportunities associated with the transition to a green economy. Investors can participate in these sustainable investments, aligning their financial interests with long-term environmental and social goals.
- Risk mitigation: Green finance takes into account environmental risks and helps investors manage their exposure to climate-related risks. By integrating environmental considerations into investment decisions, investors can better assess the risks associated with their portfolios and make informed choices that align with their risk appetite and long-term sustainability objectives.

Obstacles of Using Green Finance

Despite the advantages and significance of green finance, there are a number of obstacles to overcome in its implementation. To ensure the successful integration of green finance into the financial system, several issues must be resolved. Some major difficulties include:

Unstandardized Metrics and Definitions

Lack of standardised definitions and measures for identifying and measuring green investments is one of the major obstacles to adopting green financing. It can be challenging to tell the difference between true green investments and greenwashing, where investments are misrepresented as environmentally benign, due to the lack of precise and widely acknowledged criteria. It is difficult for investors and financial institutions to evaluate the environmental impact and sustainability of their investments because consistency prevents openness and comparison.

To address this issue, the world needs definitions and frameworks that are broadly accepted. Examples include sustainability standards and green taxonomies, which offer precise criteria and metrics for categorising and evaluating green investments. Such standards are now being developed through industry-led initiatives and the Sustainable Finance Taxonomy of the European Union. The mainstreaming of green finance would be made easier by standardisation, which would also improve transparency and allow for better risk assessment.

Financial Uncertainty and Dangers

The application of green financing may be hampered by specific financial risks and uncertainties. These dangers include long-term investment perspectives, technology hazards, policy and regulatory uncertainties, and market volatility. The financial viability of green projects, for instance, can be considerably impacted by changes in government policies and regulations relating to subsidies for renewable energy sources or carbon pricing. The development and application of novel and emerging green technologies is accompanied by technological risks since these technologies may not always be effective, scalable, or economically viable.

Establishing stable and predictable policy and regulatory frameworks that offer clarity and long-term assurance for green investments is essential to addressing these concerns.. To stimulate investments in green initiatives, governments and financial institutions must collaborate to provide supportive regulations, incentives, and risk-sharing arrangements. Additionally, boosting research and development initiatives, public-private sector cooperation, and the use of cutting-edge financial tools can assist in reducing technological risks and facilitating the implementation of green technologies.

Frameworks for Regulations and Policies

A major obstacle to the deployment of green finance is the lack of comprehensive and supportive regulatory and legislative frameworks. There may be contradictions or competing agendas among various regulatory authorities, and in many jurisdictions, current laws and policies do not properly take into account or encourage green investments. For investors and financial organisations wishing to participate in green finance initiatives, this raises restrictions and uncertainties.

To address this issue, authorities must create thorough, unified regulatory frameworks that formally support and encourage green finance. This entails setting precise regulations for the issue of green bonds, coming up with tax breaks and financial aid for eco-friendly investments, and taking environmental concerns into account when determining risk tolerance and disclosing information. In order to unify legal frameworks and create an environment that is favourable to green finance, coordinated efforts at the national and international levels are required.

Limited Capacity Building and Awareness

The implementation of green finance has difficulties due to stakeholders' limited knowledge and skills, including financial institutions, investors, legislators, and the general public. The concepts, options, and products related to green finance may not be well known or understood by many stakeholders. The mainstream acceptance of green finance may be hampered, and its potential influence may be constrained by this lack of awareness.

There is a need for extensive awareness-raising and capacity-building initiatives to tackle this problem. These initiatives ought to educate and teach a variety of stakeholders on green finance concepts, tactics, and investment possibilities. To raise awareness and develop the necessary skills and knowledge, financial institutions and industry groups can play a significant role in organising workshops, training sessions, and information campaigns.

In conclusion, despite the fact that green finance has a lot of potential for addressing environmental issues and promoting sustainable development, there are still issues that need to be resolved. These consist of a lack of uniform definitions and measures, risks and uncertainties related to money, regulatory and policy frameworks, and a lack of knowledge.

The financial institutions from the public and private sectors, government support, mutual funds agencies, etc. collaborate and coordinate green finance. To alleviate the stress of receiving capital at various levels of maturity, all units are attempting to demonstrate that they are better. Utilising the most up-to-date technologies, they aim to transform scarce resources into priceless ones. Here are some case studies that highlight effective green finance efforts and the lessons that can be drawn from them:

1. Green Bonds: As a successful green finance programme, the issuing of green bonds has gained momentum. For instance, in 2017 the French Republic issued the first sovereign green bond ever. The bond raised €7 billion and provided funding for initiatives in the fields of sustainable transport, energy efficiency, and renewable energy. The success of green bonds shows that investor interest in sustainable investing is rising. Lessons learnt include the necessity for strong frameworks and standards to define qualified green projects as well as the significance of clear reporting and tracking methods to make sure the funds are used for the intended green initiatives..
2. Financing for Renewable Energy: The Indian Renewable Energy Development Agency (IREDA) has been crucial in helping India finance renewable energy projects. Solar, wind, biomass, and small hydropower projects are all eligible for low-interest loans and financial support from IREDA. IREDA has effectively recruited private investment in renewable energy through its financing programmes, helping India meet its lofty renewable energy ambitions. The most important takeaway from this programme is how important it is for specialised financial institutions to provide targeted funding for renewable energy projects at a competitive price.
3. Energy Efficiency Financing: In Germany, the KFW Bank Group's Energy Efficiency Financing Programme has been successful in encouraging energy efficiency improvements in residential buildings. The programme offers homes grants and low-interest loans for energy-saving renovations including solar panels, insulation, and energy-efficient heating systems. In addition to lowering greenhouse gas emissions and generating jobs in the construction industry, the effort has increased demand for energy efficiency upgrades. The program's accomplishments demonstrate the value of easily available and inexpensive financing options for energy efficiency improvements, together with public awareness efforts to encourage energy-saving practises.
4. Green Investment Banks: The UK Green Investment Bank (GIB), a division of Macquarie Group today, was founded in 2012 to encourage private investment in environmentally friendly initiatives. Projects involving renewable energy, such as offshore wind farms, waste-to-energy facilities, and energy-efficient infrastructure, were crucially financed in part because to GIB. It leveraged public funding, drew private investment, and proved that green projects could be financed. The GIB's experience serves as a reminder of the significance of organisations specifically devoted to green finance and the necessity of public-private collaborations to promote investments in sustainable initiatives.
5. Green Mortgage Programmes: A number of banks and financial organisations have introduced green mortgage programmes that give homeowners financial incentives for energy-efficient homes. For instance, Rabobank launched a green mortgage programme in the Netherlands that offers lower interest rates for houses that use less energy. The programme encourages homebuyers to make investments in energy-saving technologies and supports green building techniques. By adding environmental factors into loan products, financial institutions have the potential to influence sustainable behaviour, as shown by the success of green mortgage programmes.

The necessity of supportive policy and regulatory frameworks, collaboration between the public and private sectors, targeted financial incentives, capacity building, and awareness-raising initiatives to engage stakeholders are just a few of the lessons learned and best practises from these initiatives.

THE DILEMMA OF GREEN FINANCE

Implementisustainability anditiatives often involves navigating a dilemma between balancing financial returns and environmental impact, addressing trade-offs between short-term gains and long-term sustainability, and ensuring inclusivity and social equity. Let's explore these dilemmas in more detail:

Balancing Financial Returns and Environmental Impact

One of the dilemmas faced in green finance is striking a balance between financial returns and environmental impact. While green investments contribute to environmental sustainability, there may be concerns about their financial viability and profitability compared to conventional investments. Investors and financial institutions may hesitate to allocate resources to green projects if they perceive them as less financially lucrative or riskier.

To address this dilemma, it is essential to demonstrate that green investments can generate competitive financial returns while delivering positive environmental outcomes. Robust risk assessment frameworks, reliable data on the financial performance of green investments, and transparency in reporting environmental impact can help build investor confidence. Additionally, financial incentives such as tax breaks, subsidies, and green investment funds can help bridge the financial gap and encourage investment in green projects.

Trade-Offs Between Short-Term Gains and Long-Term Sustainability

Another dilemma arises from the trade-offs between short-term gains and long-term sustainability. Green finance initiatives often require significant upfront investments and may have longer payback periods compared to conventional investments. This can create a tension between immediate financial returns and the long-term benefits of sustainability.

To overcome this dilemma, it is crucial to emphasize the long-term value and resilience associated with green investments. By considering environmental risks and opportunities in investment decision-making, investors can factor in the potential costs and benefits over the investment's lifespan. Incorporating environmental, social, and governance (ESG) criteria into investment analysis can help assess the long-term viability and sustainability of projects. Policymakers can also provide incentives and regulatory support that encourage long-term thinking and reward sustainable investments.

Ensuring Inclusivity and Social Equity

Green finance initiatives must address the challenge of ensuring inclusivity and social equity. There is a risk that the benefits of green investments may not reach all segments of society equally, exacerbating existing social and economic inequalities. For example, low-income communities may face barriers in accessing green financing or may not have the means to adopt sustainable practices.

To address this dilemma, it is crucial to promote inclusive green finance models that ensure equal access to sustainable investments and benefits for all. This can be achieved through targeted financing programs for underserved communities, affordable financing options, and capacity-building initiatives to enhance awareness and knowledge about green finance. Collaborations between public and private sectors, civil society organizations, and community stakeholders can help design and implement inclusive green finance strategies that prioritize social equity and ensure that no one is left behind in the transition to a green economy.

POLICY RECOMMENDATIONS FOR GREEN FINANCE

To promote and accelerate the adoption of green finance, policymakers should consider implementing the following policy recommendations:

Strengthening Regulatory Frameworks

- Develop comprehensive and consistent regulatory frameworks that incentivize green investments and integrate environmental considerations into financial decision-making processes.
- Establish clear guidelines and criteria for identifying and categorizing green investments, such as green taxonomies or sustainability standards.
- Implement mandatory disclosure requirements for financial institutions and companies to report their environmental risks, impacts, and sustainability practices.
- Encourage the alignment of financial regulations with sustainability goals and promote the integration of environmental, social, and governance (ESG) factors into risk assessment and decision-making processes.

Enhancing Transparency and Reporting Standards

- Establish standardized and transparent reporting frameworks for green investments, ensuring consistency and comparability of environmental impact assessments.
- Encourage the adoption of internationally recognized reporting standards, such as the Global Reporting Initiative (GRI) or the Task Force on Climate-related Financial Disclosures (TCFD).
- Facilitate the development of green finance data platforms and information-sharing networks to enhance transparency and enable investors and financial institutions to access reliable and up-to-date information on green investments.
- Support research and development efforts to improve methodologies for measuring and quantifying the environmental impact of green investments.

Promoting Collaboration and Knowledge Sharing

- Foster collaboration between public and private sectors, including financial institutions, governments, and international organizations, to develop shared goals and strategies for green finance.
- Establish platforms and networks for knowledge sharing, best practices exchange, and capacity building among stakeholders involved in green finance.
- Encourage the formation of partnerships between financial institutions, businesses, and civil society organizations to drive innovation, share expertise, and support the development of green projects.
- Support the establishment of green finance centres or hubs that serve as knowledge and resource centres, facilitating information dissemination, research, and training on green finance.

Encouraging Innovation and Green Investment Products

- Provide financial incentives, such as tax breaks, subsidies, or grants, to encourage the development and adoption of green technologies, projects, and infrastructure.
- Promote the issuance of green bonds and other green investment products, providing investors with opportunities to support sustainable projects while earning financial returns.
- Facilitate the creation of green investment funds and vehicles that focus on financing green projects and companies.
- Foster innovation in financial instruments and mechanisms, such as green insurance, green leases, or green guarantee programs, to address specific challenges and risks associated with green finance.

By implementing these policy recommendations, policymakers can create an enabling environment for green finance, incentivize investments in sustainable projects, and accelerate the transition to a more sustainable and resilient economy. These policies should be tailored to specific national or regional contexts while considering international best practices and collaboration. Continuous monitoring and evaluation of policy effectiveness will also be essential to ensure the desired outcomes are achieved.

CONCLUSION

In conclusion, green finance has emerged as a crucial tool in addressing environmental challenges, promoting sustainable development, and transitioning to a green economy. This research paper has examined the need for green finance, its benefits, challenges, and policy recommendations. Here is a recap of the key findings:

- Green finance is an urgent requirement of the system due to environmental challenges, climate change, and the pursuit of sustainable development goals.
- Green finance offers various benefits, including mitigating environmental risks, fostering sustainable economic growth, enhancing corporate social responsibility, and attracting investment opportunities.
- Implementing green finance faces challenges such as lack of standardized definitions and metrics, financial risks and uncertainties, regulatory and policy frameworks, and limited awareness and capacity building.
- Policy recommendations include strengthening regulatory frameworks, enhancing transparency and reporting standards, promoting collaboration and knowledge sharing, and encouraging innovation and green investment products.

Implications for the Financial System

Green finance presents significant implications for the financial system. It encourages financial institutions to consider environmental factors in their decision-making processes, integrate sustainability into risk assessment frameworks, and allocate resources towards green investments. This shift can lead to the reallocation of capital from environmentally harmful sectors to sustainable projects, driving the transition to a low-carbon and resource-efficient economy. It also opens up new investment opportunities, stimulates innovation in financial products and services, and enhances the resilience of the financial system to environmental risks.

Future Prospects and Challenges

The future of green finance holds promising prospects. As the awareness of environmental issues grows and sustainability becomes a priority for governments, businesses, and society, the demand for green finance is expected to increase. Governments and international organizations are working towards developing standardized frameworks and regulations, enhancing transparency and reporting standards, and fostering international cooperation to facilitate the growth of green finance.

However, the lack of harmonized definitions and metrics, financial risks and uncertainties, regulatory barriers, and limited awareness and capacity building continue to hinder the widespread adoption of green finance. Overcoming these challenges requires ongoing efforts from policymakers, financial institutions, investors, and other stakeholders to strengthen regulatory frameworks, improve data transparency, promote collaboration, and enhance knowledge and awareness.

In conclusion, green finance is an urgent requirement of the system, offering a pathway to address environmental challenges while fostering sustainable economic growth. By implementing the policy recommendations outlined in this research paper and addressing the challenges, the financial system can play a pivotal role in driving the transition to a more sustainable and resilient future.

By examining the urgency and complexity of integrating green finance into the existing financial system, this research paper aims to contribute to the ongoing discussions surrounding sustainable finance and its implications for global economic and environmental stability.

REFERENCES

Aggarwal, K. K., & Aggarwal, S. (2021). Is Green banking an Adequate Initiative for Environment Sustainability. In New India: Emerging Trends in Indian Business Scenario (Vol. 1, pp. 87–97). Notion Press.

de Carvalho Ferreira, M. C. R., Sobreiro, V. A., Kimura, H., & de Moraes Barboza, F. L. (2016). A systematic review of literature about finance and sustainability. *Journal of Sustainable Finance \& Investment, 6*(2), 112–147. doi:10.1080/20430795.2016.1177438

de Kandavel. (2013). Green Banking Initiatives of Commercial Banks in India. *SIT Journal of Management, 3*(2), 213–225.

Haigh, M. (2012). Publishing and defining sustainable finance and investment. *Journal of Sustainable Finance & Investment, 2*(2), 88–94. doi:10.1080/20430795.2012.688797

Jain, S. (2020). Financing India's Green Transition. *Observer Research Foundation, 338.*

Kharade, M. (2021). *Green Finance for Sustainable Development- study on the Indian context, 18*(10), 2459–2466.

Parvadavardini, S., & Nagarajan, V. (2015). A study on the agricultural value chain financing in India. *Zemedelská Ekonomika, 61*(2), 31–38. doi:10.17221/38/2014-AGRICECON

Poonam, & Aggarwal, K. K. (2023). Analysis of the impact of COVID-19 on the stock market and capability of investing strategies. *AIP Conference Proceedings, 2782*. doi:10.1063/5.0154174

Reddy, A. S. B. (2018). Green Finance-Financial Support for Sustainable Development. *International Journal of Pure and Applied Mathematics*, *118*(20), 645–652.

Vadrale, S. K. (2016). *Green Banking Initiatives By Indian Public and Private Sector Banks. 9*(February), 1–14. https://www.researchgate.net/publication/305547284

Wang, Y., & Zhi, Q. (2016). The Role of Green Finance in Environmental Protection: Two Aspects of Market Mechanism and Policies. *Energy Procedia*, *104*, 311–316. doi:10.1016/j.egypro.2016.12.053

Chapter 11
Green Finance:
A Path to Sustainability

Kanika Thapliyal
Graphic Era University (Deemed), India

Chandan Gupta
Graphic Era University (Deemed), India

Priya Jindal
Chitkara Business School, Chitkara University, India

Amar Mishra
Graphic Era University (Deemed), India

ABSTRACT

Nature nurtures us constantly and provides for us from the moment we are born. However, in response to these natural blessings, humans are damaging the environment in various ways, including by polluting the resources and testing nuclear energy as a representation of scientific growth and the industrial revolution. Green finance is the solution to establishing a deal between economic growth and ecology. Green financing is viewed as monetary backing for environmentally friendly growth that eliminates the emission of substances that deplete the ozone layer and other air pollutants. It is a new idea that offers individuals, organizations, and nations an alternative funding source for activities that are environmentally friendly and carbon-free. Businesses as members of society, have obligations to minimize carbon emissions and assist the government in doing so by implementing "green financing" for sustainable growth. Hence the chapter, examine the body of knowledge already in existence about green finance and Indian bank initiatives to support green financing.

DOI: 10.4018/979-8-3693-1388-6.ch011

INTRODUCTION

The COVID-19 pandemic in 2020 caused countless damage to the world's finances, humanity, and the planet in addition to financial institutions (Seale and Mirza,2020), which had a range of effects like fluctuations in markets, depreciating assets, and difficulties with company financing (Li et al., 2023). Environmental conservation has grown even more important in the face of the pandemic (Lu et al., 2022). Greenhouse gas emissions, primarily from fossil fuels and nonrenewable energy sources, are to blame for the majority of ecological issues. These emissions cause socioeconomic hazards as well as health problems (Masri et al., 2021). Accordingly, it is necessary to take the required long-term steps to implement green policies and frameworks to sustain future growth. Among the most important measures adopted to stop environmental deterioration are the adoption of green banking and financing. According to Falcone (2020), "green finance" refers to the actions and investment decisions that banks and other financial institutions take to support a sustainable economy. People are more aware of the necessity of a healthy ecological environment for human survival, and as a result, there is broad support for green financing and peaceful cohabitation of humans and nature. The idea of "green finance" can significantly contribute to achieving the SDGs, particularly objectives 11, 12, and 13. Green finance is more specifically the allocation of capital and financial system investments in environmentally friendly or ecological projects (Mehta et al., 2023). The increasing popularity of green finance has drawn interest from many nations and regions. It was also highly publicized and discussed at the G-20 nation's summit. According to Akomea-Frimpong et al. (2022), "green finance" is also known as "sustainable finance," "environmental finance," "climate finance," and "green investment." Furthermore, poor nations are at a turning point since they are more vulnerable to climate change and rely heavily on existing global climate funds for funding their programs for climate protection and mitigation. With enormous opportunities for capital, expansion, and financial dominance in the years to come, India is viewed as among the world's upcoming emerging nations. The environmental implications of rising temperatures, however, are proving to be a challenge for emerging economies like India. For example, it's believed that elevated sea levels have rendered India among the countries most vulnerable to climate change, which has led to the deterioration of biological diversity and worsening financial challenges for the populace. They have therefore implemented several strategies to decrease the risks and damaging consequences of environmental change on the ecology. This includes promoting sustainable development and stopping the destruction of the environment through structured, managed green finance consistent with global norms. Campiglio et al. (2018) also stated that green banking or green finance is one of the key components of sustainable economic development in a country like India. Green finance is an integral means of finance for any nation's sustainable economic development. In light of this, it can be claimed that green financing is crucial to any nation's efforts to combat climate change and achieve the Sustainable Development Goals (SDGs).

In addition, current technical developments have hastened the expansion of green finance. According to Giudici et al. (2019), financial technology (Fintech) has a significant impact on enhancing the commercial sector. Fintech can be used by fusing big data and artificial intelligence to increase financial sustainability. According to Lu et al. (2022), the combination of traditional financial tools with fintech lessens the technological challenges and difficulties associated with green finance in the contemporary corporate environment. Green finance is an essential financial tool for every nation's long-term economic success. Huge amounts of funding are needed to make the shift to sustainable and net-zero company models (Zhang et al., 2022). According to Polzin et al. (2020), there is a large discrepancy between the supply and demand for green finance, necessitating the need for the creation of cutting-edge intermediation modes. The chapter thus aims to explain the definition, history, drivers, types, benefits, challenges, and promoters of green finance. The study also discusses the initiatives taken by Indian Banks to promote green finance. Further, the relationship between green finance and fintech; green finance, and environmental quality has been shown. Therefore this study will make a remarkable contribution to existing literature on green finance.

GREEN FINANCE

The phrase "green finance," which is also frequently called "green investment," is used in both academics and industry to denote a range of topics. Green finance is a new concept that lacks a precise and standardized definition. A broad term, "green finance," can refer to financial investments made in endeavors and programs for environmentally conscious development, green products, and policies that assist in the building of an economy with greater sustainability. Green financing, in its simplest form, is a loan or investment that supports environmentally friendly activities, such as the acquisition of eco-friendly products and services or the development of green infrastructure. The promotion of the green transition, which is gaining popularity in both rich and developing nations, depends on green finance. The market for financial services and the field of environmentalism are connected via green finance. Its goal is to encourage sustainable development or sustainable finance. To promote the goals of equitable development, it is possible to increase the amount of financial inflows from the business, government, and non-profit sectors through the use of green financing. A financial tool called "green finance" is used to transfer environmental risks and improve environmental quality. It is based on market research. Green financial services have taken over as the dominant trend in financial development as a way to encourage sustainable development. Green financing is defined as financial support for green growth that considerably lowers emissions of greenhouse gases (GHGs) and air pollutants. Three contemporary risks to the world economy—climate change, energy shortages, and financial crisis—can be addressed through green growth. According to Srivastava et al. (2022), "Green finance is commonly stated for the banks and another financial sector as the provision of loans and other services that take environmental considerations into account across the financing making choices, ex-ante evaluation, and risk mitigation procedures stipulated to encourage ecologically conscious investments and catalyze green technologies, initiatives occupations, and enterprises. Numerous conservation objectives, such as controlling carbon emissions, water cleanliness, or biodiversity preservation, are made possible through green financing. Green finance is becoming more commonplace as the risks associated with ecologically harmful goods and services increase. Hence, the goal of green finance is to promote long-term development by achieving a balance between the development of financial events, environmental stability, and ecological preservation.

HISTORICAL BACKGROUND OF GREEN FINANCE

To raise consciousness about the environmental concerns in the financial industry, the United Nations Environment Program (UNEP) and some banking organizations formed the UNEP Finance Initiative (UNEP FI) in 1992 (unep.org, 2022). It might be considered the source of green finance. Later, the initiative engages in comprehensive discussions with other financial institutions, such as investment and commercial banks, insurance firms, and investment managers, about how to integrate environmental protection and sustainable economic growth. It aims to incorporate environmental considerations into existing financial practices and services. The member entities to the UNEP FI statement also have the opportunity to learn from the network about the newest trends and methods for enhancing possibilities for green growth and promoting the cause of green finance.

THE EQUATOR PRINCIPLES

When the Equator Principles (EPs) were first introduced in 2003, several powerful international banks were favorable towards them. According to Chaudhary et al. (2018), it serves as "a framework of deliberate indicators for determining, analyzing, and supervising social and environmental risks in venture financing." To carry out their financing activities, Equator Principles Financial Institutions (EPFIs) develop their own unique social and ecological strategies, methodologies, and models. They also commit not to extend credit to projects where the borrowers disagree with the principles outlined in the EPs. Meanwhile, EPFIs have responsibilities to make sure that the borrowers are aware of the fundamentals of standards and to advise them on how to best incorporate standards into planned undertakings. Additionally, if their clients can continue to look for funding for the project in the future, they must indicate their intention to comply with EPs' criteria.

UN GLOBAL COMPACT

The UN Global Compact (UNGC) contains ten optional principles. The parties to the agreement promise to obey employment laws, protect nature, fight corruption, and not infringe basic rights. According to the UNGC (2011), firms should support "a cautious way of dealing with environmental challenges; endeavor efforts that promote more prominent ecological responsibility; and compel the enhancement and transmission of earth well-disposed advances" concerning the sector they are focusing on (unglobalcompact.org, 2011).

CARBON DISCLOSURE PROJECT

A not-for-profit company called the CDP encourages firms, financiers, and other entities to publish their greenhouse gas (GHG) emissions and assess their potential vulnerability to risks related to the effects of climate change. It provides members with insight into their climate impacts by utilizing a climate change monitoring system. Through this endeavor, it will be possible to calculate with accuracy how much greenhouse gas emissions occur from a bank's support of a company. The CDP (2021) does not, however, have specific exclusion parameters or standards to reduce the immediate impact of financing provided by banks to companies that do not declare their carbon output (cdn.cdp.net, 2021).

DRIVERS OF GREEN FINANCE

First, the preferences of investors, managers, shareholders, clients, and society at large have significantly shifted in favor of the Sustainable Development Goals in recent years. Given that COVID-19 adversely impacted the poor and disadvantaged, it may have long-term effects on stakeholders' and investors' preferences for investments that consider environmental, social, and governance issues.

Second, utilizing green finance enables businesses and investors to manage and reduce risks related to sustainability challenges, such as those related to the climate.

Third, utilizing green finance gives benefits akin to insurance against both firm-specific and market shocks such as large environmental litigation and pandemics. Building social capital or trust through corporate social responsibility helps businesses. Having a high degree of social capital enhances one's credibility in the eyes of customers, clients, managers, and staff.

TYPES OF GREEN FINANCE

- **Green Mortgages:** When a buyer agrees to make investments to improve a property's environmental performance or purchases a home with a high environmental sustainability rating, they enable lenders to offer better conditions to the buyer.
- **Green loans:** These loans are used to fund environmental projects including home solar panels, electric vehicles, energy efficiency programs, and more.
- **Green credit cards:** Every time a consumer uses a green credit card, like Aspirations' Zero card, a tree is planted. Customers can use them to direct their spending toward green financing to make a long-lasting difference in the environment.
- **Green banks:** Similar to typical banks in operation, green banks use government resources to encourage private investment in renewable energy and other ecologically friendly projects.
- **Green bonds:** The great majority of green funding is made up of green bonds. They include bond investments, the proceeds of which are used to fund a range of green programs, including conservation, clean transportation, and renewable energy, among others.

WHY IS GREEN FINANCING IMPORTANT

Due to its purported benefits, green financing is significant. According to Usman et al. (2021), green financing promotes the growth of smart cities over time. It has also been seen that investing in environmentally friendly technologies, such as renewable energy, may help to reduce costs and hasten the wider spread of new technologies. Green finance promotes balanced growth in the economy. Long- and short-term levels of carbon emissions can be reduced through spending on initiatives that promote sustainability (Li et al., 2023). A recent study found that governments that support green finance help protect their communities from a time when resources become scarce. Green finance will benefit large investors who participate in impact investing. Diversifying impacts of green finance can be advantageous for participants in the business sector. By raising green funds, energy-intensive enterprises that threaten both humanity and our climate can be less financially supported. Various authors have found that by enhancing and making their participation in green finance more visible, companies, organizations, and corporations can increase the value of their portfolios (Reboredo, 2018). Thus, they can provide their company a competitive edge in the green market and entice more environmentally conscious customers and investors.

CHALLENGES OF GREEN FINANCE

According to Campiglio et al. (2018), there are several barriers to green finance. Ecological consequences, informative imbalances, a dearth of expertise in analysis, a vague understanding of "green" in green finance, an inconsistent wisdom between long-term and short-term investment decisions, the somewhat constrained short-term time horizon of consumers and financiers, an ineffective synergy among finances and environmental initiatives, and ambiguity over the extent of government backing are only a handful among the concerns. Falcone (2020) discusses further barriers to green finance. This includes (i) a dearth of transparency concerning laws and regulations, (ii) a shortage of encouragement from policymakers to support the marketing of unique breakthroughs, (iii) a lack of involvement of financial institutions with the different industries (iv) the short-term focus of financial instruments, (v) an insufficient awareness regarding funding alternatives, (vi) a lack of expertise. A few problems with green financing for enterprises were also mentioned by Gilchrist et al. in 2021. There are many challenges, including the inability to analyze green finance consistently, the paucity of green data, the uncertainty surrounding the specific definition of economic greenness, and the lack of consensus on how to grade a company's level of sustainability. In nations that have modest or intermediate incomes, organizational, financial, and political barriers are accountable for the unexplored green markets. According to Usman, et al. (2021), one reason why environmentally conscious entities have failed to increase green investment is because of the expensive transaction fees for eco-certification and supervision. It is because of the sector's poor institutional layout, that participants in the area of renewable energy have misaligned incentive structures. They also looked at the possibilities of security tokens built on the blockchain to help with failures of the market in green financing. Software threats, the unpredictability of regulations, and a fragile investment ecosystem were a few of the challenges they listed.

PROMOTERS OF GREEN FINANCE

The main drivers promoting the creation and expansion of green finance are banking institutions, large investors, scientific groups, agencies of government, fiscal authorities, regulatory bodies for global financial institutions, and academia (Ozili, 2022). Sharma et al. (2022) show how important private enterprises like banking institutions and venture capitalists are in improving green finance. In this regard, the European Investment Bank (EIB) is essential to finance renewable energy and energy-efficient activities in Europe, whereas national governments in these countries often focus on establishing laws and regulations that are conducive to these kinds of programs.

GREEN FINANCE IN INDIA

India is constantly incorporating sustainable development into its business behaviors. According to Vedanta, even if the business is lawful and crucial to humanity, its main objective should be to create prosperity for the general populace by using moral economic practices. The Vedic phrase "Sarvalokahitam" refers to "partner prosperity." This implies that ethical as well as environmentally accountable principles must guide all business dealings. Green finance enables the Bank to actively target and invest in ecologically responsible businesses that engage in green initiatives, which significantly aids in the shift to a carbon-neutral economy. Additionally, this will encourage the development of carbon-efficient technology and more sustainable supply chains, having a good effect on the environment. The Indian Banks are taking several steps to broaden their exposure to climate-friendly industries. By steadily greening its business activities, infrastructure, and operations, Indian Banks are dedicated to advancing the goal of a green globe. The Banks have committed to support India's NDC aim of reducing the GDP's carbon intensity by 33% to 35% from 2005 levels by 2030. The banks are also enthusiastic about furthering SDG 13 (Action on Climate Change) by engaging in green financing and establishing a variety of new initiatives that will green their internal operations to aid in the process of transitioning. To reduce paper usage, the banks are encouraging their retail banking clients to migrate to e-statements. The Bank additionally urges clients to use their online banking services to cut down on emissions from transportation and huge branch operations. Furthermore, Indian Banks are providing funding for green building programs with equivalents of LEED, GRIHA, and IGBC certifications. It also provides funding for the conversion of conventional structures into green structures. An important component of the bank's green finance effort is renewable energy. Renewable energy sources, such as sun, wind, and hydropower, are used to produce electricity. A dedicated clean energy Finance team with broad industry expertise has been established inside the project finance team. To make sure that the bank can effectively seize the opportunity and has a thorough awareness of the risks, this team communicates with a variety of stakeholders in the clean and green energy ecosystem, including lawmakers, administrators, and the holders of assets. The bank prioritizes funding and assisting ventures with a focus on environmental sustainability. Among them are forest restoration, sanitation, and water. To enhance the positive environmental impact, the bank has chosen to venture into EV finance and develop products around the full EV value chain. The banks are holding workshops to spread awareness of, emphasize the value of, and include sustainability and energy conservation. Indian Banks are aware of extreme weather events, irregular rainfall patterns, heat waves, and droughts, which are also seen as a long-term threat to the integrity of the financial system. The Bank is integrating its actions with the recommendations provided by the TCFD (Task Force on Climate-related Financial Disclosures) in recognition of the financial consequences of risks associated with climate change. The Bank is raising the bar through these disclosures to address any potential challenges related to climate risk.

GREEN FINANCE AND ENVIRONMENT QUALITY

The seeming rapid rise in global GF may be related to EQ (environmental quality). GF raises EQ and resource efficiency. GF places a greater emphasis on environmental preservation, sustainable development, and green industry than traditional finance does. According to Tao and Chao (2023), GF has a favorable effect on EQ and corporate social responsibility. Furthermore, Wang et al. (2022) claimed that an organization's environmental performance enhances its image and credibility. It demonstrates that environmental issues, such as climate change, pollution, and the energy crisis, among others, present business organizations with both opportunities and challenges. Green credit could generate financial support for sustainable development if it complies with environmental requirements. Findings demonstrate that GF and technical advancements lower CO2 levels (Kaur, 2023).

FINTECH AND GREEN FINANCE

The Financial Stability Board defines fintech as a "technology-driven invention in financial services that may open the door for new business models, applications, or methods with a concurrent profound impact on the financial services supply." Fintech can be defined more broadly as any innovation that helps businesses by enhancing the provision, usage, and process of financial services. These technologically advanced models have the potential to completely alter the financial industry (Nenavath, 2022). The financial sector is crucial for reforming the economy and guiding it towards a sustainable future. According to earlier research on the subject, there is a good correlation between the adoption of fintech and banks' performance in terms of sustainability and green finance claim that fintech has a big impact on lending. Additionally, it demonstrates the direct link between green financing and economic growth (Yan et al., 2022). According to Wang et al. (2021), fintech has a variety of characteristics. Supporting green finance may help the fintech markets develop sustainably as a whole. Awawdeh et al.'s study found that technical advancements and green funding greatly enhance a company's environmental performance, enhances sustainability by accelerating the development of cutting-edge energy technology. Fintech accelerates trade and boosts value generation. Green finance gains popularity thanks to fintech, which also lowers investment costs and increases user numbers.

CONCLUSION

The adoption of an environmental strategy that incorporates GF is required at both the national and international levels to properly manage societal concerns (such as climate change, resource depletion, etc.). This necessitates an ongoing, transparent discussion about potential, obstacles, and GF implementation objectives in all nations. The current research has examined the potential and criticalities influencing GF within this conceptual structure. To achieve the aims of sustainable development goals that consider ecological development, green money is therefore essential. Balanced sustainable development can be achieved by using accessible green funding, which contributes to lowering vulnerability to and raising adaptability to the adverse consequences of environmental degradation. It is generally agreed that monetary authorities are pioneers in the financial industry when it comes to formulating green finance legislation. Intending to deliver the necessary financial support for consumers facing volatile environmental conditions, banking institutions have a responsibility to encourage green products in deposits, loans, insurance coverage, monetary transfers, and emerging online distribution platforms. Although the concept of green finance is widely acknowledged, it is still in its early stages and requires a thorough evaluation mechanism. A greener approach to investing is also required to achieve the Sustainable Development Goals (SDGs), particularly SDG 1 (no poverty), SDG 7 (affordable and clean energy), and SDG 13 (climate action), all of which deliberately foster sustainable economic development. In the past couple of years, green investments have risen quickly across a range of sectors, especially in sustainable energy, solar power, and manufacturing capacity. The research undertaken emphasized how green finance will lead to significantly lower emissions of greenhouse gases. It can be claimed that India has an enormous opportunity to develop the ecologically sound infrastructure necessary for green financing by removing the barriers and increasing corporate citizens' awareness of the need for more sustainable growth. Shortly, all socioeconomic classes are willing to embrace green funding.

REFERENCES

Akomea-Frimpong, I., Adeabah, D., Ofosu, D., & Tenakwah, E. J. (2022). A review of studies on green finance of banks, research gaps and future directions. *Journal of Sustainable Finance & Investment*, *12*(4), 1241–1264. doi:10.1080/20430795.2020.1870202

Campiglio, E., Dafermos, Y., Monnin, P., Ryan-Collins, J., Schotten, G., & Tanaka, M. (2018). Climate change challenges for central banks and financial regulators. *Nature Climate Change*, *8*(6), 462–468. doi:10.103841558-018-0175-0

Chowdhury, A., Naz, A., Bhattacharyya, S., & Sanyal, P. (2018). Cost–benefit analysis of 'Blue Carbon'sequestration by plantation of few key mangrove species at Sundarban Biosphere Reserve, India. *Carbon Management*, *9*(6), 575–586. doi:10.1080/17583004.2018.1518105

Falcone, P. M. (2020). Environmental regulation and green investments: The role of green finance. *International Journal of Green Economics*, *14*(2), 159–173. doi:10.1504/IJGE.2020.109735

Giudici, P., Hochreiter, R., Osterrieder, J., Papenbrock, J., & Schwendner, P. (2019). AI and financial technology. *Frontiers in Artificial Intelligence*, *2*, 25. doi:10.3389/frai.2019.00025 PMID:33733114

Kaur, G. (2023). Biodiversity Financing: A Strategy Towards Sustainability. In Digital Transformation, Strategic Resilience, Cyber Security and Risk Management (Vol. 111, pp. 143-151). Emerald Publishing Limited. doi:10.1108/S1569-37592023000111B010

Li, C., Faridi, M. Z., & Nazar, R. (2023). *How does green finance asymmetrically affect greenhouse gas emissions? Evidence from the top-ten green bond issuer countries*. Borsa Istanbul Review. doi:10.1016/j.bir.2023.03.002

Lu, Q., Farooq, M. U., Ma, X., & Iram, R. (2022). Assessing the combining role of public-private investment as a green finance and renewable energy in carbon neutrality target. *Renewable Energy*, *196*, 1357–1365. doi:10.1016/j.renene.2022.06.072

Masri, S., LeBrón, A. M., Logue, M. D., Valencia, E., Ruiz, A., Reyes, A., & Wu, J. (2021). Risk assessment of soil heavy metal contamination at the census tract level in the city of Santa Ana, CA: Implications for health and environmental justice. *Environmental Science. Processes & Impacts*, *23*(6), 812–830. doi:10.1039/D1EM00007A PMID:33954329

Mehta, K., Sharma, R., & Jalotra, S. (2023). A Bibliometric Analysis of Green Banking: Present State and Future Directions. In *Perspectives on Blockchain Technology and Responsible Investing* (pp. 159–176). IGI Global. doi:10.4018/978-1-6684-8361-9.ch007

Nenavath, S. (2022). Impact of fintech and green finance on environmental quality protection in India: By applying the semi-parametric difference-in-differences (SDID). *Renewable Energy*, *193*, 913–919. doi:10.1016/j.renene.2022.05.020

Ozili, P. K. (2022). Green finance research around the world: A review of literature. *International Journal of Green Economics*, *16*(1), 56–75. doi:10.1504/IJGE.2022.125554

Polzin, F., Sanders, M., & Serebriakova, A. (2021). Finance in global transition scenarios: Mapping investments by technology into finance needs by source. *Energy Economics*, *99*, 105281. doi:10.1016/j.eneco.2021.105281

Reboredo, J. C. (2018). Green bond and financial markets: Co-movement, diversification and price spillover effects. *Energy Economics*, *74*, 38–50. doi:10.1016/j.eneco.2018.05.030

Seale, M., & Mirza, R. (2020). The coin of love and virtue: Academic libraries and value in a global pandemic. *Canadian Journal of Academic Librarianship*, *6*, 1–30. doi:10.33137/cjal-rcbu.v6.34457

Sharma, C., Sakhuja, S., & Nijjer, S. (2022). Recent trends of green human resource management: Text mining and network analysis. *Environmental Science and Pollution Research International*, *29*(56), 84916–84935. doi:10.100711356-022-21471-9 PMID:35790632

Srivastava, A. K., Dharwal, M., & Sharma, A. (2022). Green financial initiatives for sustainable economic growth: A literature review. *Materials Today: Proceedings*, *49*, 3615–3618. doi:10.1016/j.matpr.2021.08.158

Tao, Z., & Chao, J. (2023). A bibliometric and visualized analysis of research on green finance and energy in a global perspective. *Research in Globalization*, 100156.

Usman, M., Makhdum, M. S. A., & Kousar, R. (2021). Does financial inclusion, renewable and non-renewable energy utilization accelerate ecological footprints and economic growth? Fresh evidence from 15 highest emitting countries. *Sustainable Cities and Society*, *65*, 102590. doi:10.1016/j.scs.2020.102590

Wang, K. H., Zhao, Y. X., Jiang, C. F., & Li, Z. Z. (2022). Does green finance inspire sustainable development? Evidence from a global perspective. *Economic Analysis and Policy*, *75*, 412–426. doi:10.1016/j.eap.2022.06.002

Yan, C., Siddik, A. B., Yong, L., Dong, Q., Zheng, G. W., & Rahman, M. N. (2022). A two-staged SEM-artificial neural network approach to analyze the impact of FinTech adoption on the sustainability performance of banking firms: The mediating effect of green finance and innovation. *Systems*, *10*(5), 148. doi:10.3390ystems10050148

Zhang, H., Wu, C., Zhang, Z., Zhu, Y., Lin, H., Zhang, Z., & Smola, A. (2022). Resnest: Split-attention networks. In *Proceedings of the IEEE/CVF conference on computer vision and pattern recognition* (pp. 2736-2746). https://www.unep.org/explore-topics/green-economy/what-we-do/finance-initiative,2022. https://unglobalcompact.org/what-is-gc/mission/principles

Chapter 12
ESG Performance in Relationship With the Board of Directors, Sustainability Incentives, and CSR

Ali Ahmadi
https://orcid.org/0000-0002-2170-941X
Higher Institute of Business Administration of Gafsa, Tunisia

Tijani Amara
Higher Institute of Business Administration of Gafsa, Tunisia

ABSTRACT

This chapter seeks to address the ESG performance gap in the literature by examining the impact of board size, board independence, women on the board, incentive compensation in terms of sustainability, and CSR committee on the ESG performance. Using one of the largest datasets to date, consisting of an unbalanced dataset of 313 constant year observations from MENA region, spanning an eleven-year period (2007-2017), these results are several. First, the results indicate that board size is positively correlated with ESG performance. Also, the authors show that board independence and the percentage of women in the board are positively correlated with ESG performance.

1. INTRODUCTION

The performance of the company depends mainly on the board of directors (Ajaz et al., 2020), since it is responsible for approving and supervising the implementation of the strategic objectives, the system of governance and the creation of the corporate culture (Alessandrini & Jondeau, 2021). An effective board will also emphasize business ethics and corporate responsibility (Arayssi et al., 2020). A growing body of research has found a strong positive relationship between a company's sustainability performance and its profitability: companies with high sustainability scores significantly outperform their peers in market

DOI: 10.4018/979-8-3693-1388-6.ch012

value and book performance (Baraibar-Diez et al., 2019) . Based on these considerations, this study aims to identify the characteristics of the board of directors that improve the performance of environmental social governance. According to current literature (Arayssi et al., 2020), (Birindelli et al., 2018) our analysis examines the effect of board characteristics (gender diversity, size, activity, compensation, and ESG disagreements) on ESG performance in a sample of 313 MENA observers spanning a period from 2007 to 2017 To illustrate a company's sustainability performance, we use the Thomson Reuters ESG Asset Score 4, a broad and reliable measure of CSR performance adopted by researchers for both non-financial companies.

Our main empirical evidence shows that there is a linear relationship between the characteristics of the board of directors, the remuneration policy, the CSR committee and the ESG performance of the company. Interestingly, the correlation between the dependent and independent variables is linear, confirming that the characteristics of the board of directors, the remuneration policy and the CSR committee positively influence the ESG performance of the company.

We therefore support the critical theory of strict corporate sense, which means that after achieving a large board size, a high level of board independence, an increased presence of female directors on the board, the adoption of incentive compensation in terms of sustainable development, establishment of the CSR Committee have a positive impact on ESG (Arayssi et al., 2020), (Castellanos & George, 2020). The rest of the paper is organized as follows. Section 2 presents the research hypotheses. Section 3 discusses sampling procedures and the measurement of variables. Section 4 explains and discusses the results, and finally Section 5 presents the conclusions.

2. HYPOTHESES DEVELOPMENT

The variables most frequently used in the literature to describe the effect of board size, gender diversity, board independence, sustainability incentive compensation and performance of the CSR committee on ESG performance and we develop below our hypotheses for each of these characteristics of corporate governance (Harjoto & Wang, 2020), (Merendino & Melville, 2019), (Ng et al., 2020), (Peng, 2020), (Qa'dan & Suwaidan, 2019).

hypothesis 1. the size of the plaque favorably affects ESG performance.

hypothesis 2. the independence of the board positively affects the performance of the ESG. hypothesis 3. a high level of gender diversity positively affects ESG performance. executive compensation and carbon performance

hypothesis 4: ceteris paribus, large companies adopt sustainable ESG remuneration incentives, which are more important for process-oriented ESG performance.

hypothesis 5. the establishment of a CSR sustainability committee has a positive impact on ESG performance.

3. RESEARCH METHODOLOGY

Selection of Samples and Data Sources

our initial sample was based on the availability of ESG data in the thomson reuters asset4 and thomson reuters eikon databases. our final sample is based on an unbalanced dataset of 313 consistent year observations from 64 MENA listed companies, spanning an 11-year period (2007-2017). table 1 shows the distribution of the sample by country. we used the asset4 dataset and thomson reuters eikon to collect ESG data and corporate governance data. the thomson reuters asset4 database is used in our research because it is easily accessible to many investors and researchers.

Table 1. Sample distribution

Panel A. Distribution of the Sample by Country		
Firms	**Number of Observations per Country**	**Percent (%) per Country**
Bahrain	*6*	*2%*
Egypt	*73*	*23%*
Jordan	*9*	*3%*
Kuwait	*49*	*16%*
Morocco	*18*	*6%*
Oman	*20*	*6%*
Qatar	*36*	*12%*
Saudi Arab	*67*	*21%*
United Arab Emirates	*35*	*11%*
Total	*313*	*100%*

Table 2. Variables measurement and the expected relationship with ESGSCORE

Variable	Measurement	Expected Sign
ESG performance (ESGSCORE)	This score is based on three dimensions: environmental, social and corporate governance	Dependent variable
Board size (BOARDS)	Total number of directors on the bank's board	Positive
Board independence (BINDEP)	Percentage of independent board members as reported by the company (variable Independent Board Members)	Positive
Gender diversity (GENDERD)	Total number of women on the board of directors divided by the total number of board members	Positive
Sustainable Compensation incentives (SCINCENTIVES)	Dummy variable (yes = 1/no = 0) responding either the question "Does the frim apply extra-compensation policy" or "Is the senior executive's compensation linked to CSR Sustainability target".	Positive
CSR sustainability committee (CSRSUSTCOMM)	Dummy variable (yes = 1/no = 0) responding the question "Does the company have a CSR Sustainability committee or team?"	Positive

Dependent Variable

The next section will test the hypotheses regarding the effect of the board characteristics on the ESG SCORE, using panel data analysis. We estimate the following model:

ESGSCORE it = $\beta 0$ + $\beta 1$ BOARDS +$\beta 2$ BINDEP +$\beta 3$ GENDERD +$\beta 4$ SCINCENTIVES + $\beta 5$ CSRSUSTCOMM + ε

Empirical Results and Discussion

Descriptive Statistics

Table 3 shows the descriptive statistics for the dependent and independent variables. The average ESG performance level (ESG SCORE) of the analyzed company is 38.80%, with a maximum of 76.6%. This reveals that the companies' sustainability performance for the period 2007-2017 was very satisfactory according to the scoring criteria. Board size is 10.5 with a minimum of 3 members for eighteen directors. Likewise, average board independence seems insufficient, given that some boards do not have an independent director (maximum 100% with a minimum value of 0%).

Likewise, the mass of women (the proportion of women on the board) reaches an average value (6.6%) and a maximum value of 52.7%, and it appears to be still low, but it indicates that ``there are companies whose board members are all women. . Similarly, the average adoption of sustainable compensation incentives appears to be low given that 1.6% of our observations have a sustainable compensation incentive. In addition, about 26% of companies have adopted the Sustainable CSR Committee.

Table 3. Summary statistics of ESG SCORE and explanatory variables

Variable	Obs	Mean	Std. Dev.	Min	Max
esgscore	313	38.80111	15.29801	10.83474	76.59603
board_size	313	9.571885	2.438101	3	18
bindep	313	25.13203	26.63696	0	100
genderd	313	6.650018	9.334408	0	52.77778
scincentives	313	.0159744	.1255772	0	1
csrsustcomm	313	.2555911	.4368914	0	1

This table shows the summary statistics of ESG SCORE and explanatory variables. The number of firm-year observations is 313 for all the variables. Data source: Thomson Reuters Asset4 and Datastream.

Regression Results and Discussion

Table 4 shows the estimation results that could answer our hypotheses regarding the effect of board composition, activity and reward on ESG performance for a sample of 313 observations from the MENA region. In our model, BOARDS are important and positively associated with ESG performance. When it comes to interactions, the final sign of the predictor's effect is immediately readable from the grading table. Large boards are more likely to be served by managers with different skills and attitudes, including those with a strong tendency to embrace a culture of sustainability. Therefore, this result supports Hypothesis 1.

Hypothesis 2 predicts a relationship between the independent number of board meetings and ESG performance, even if the score is certain. Our results show a positive relationship: the coefficient associated with BINDEP is positive and significant. This result is consistent with studies (Arayssi et al., 2020), (Shahbaz et al., 2020). A large number of board meetings are likely to act as improvement elements that increase the performance of the company's ESG. Therefore, this result supports hypothesis 2.

Hypothesis 3 predicts a positive relationship between gender diversity and ESG performance. In this case, the hypothesis appears to have been confirmed. Therefore, the econometric model indicates that higher proportions of women on the board are associated with better sustainability performance. This positive effect is largely consistent with the results of (Zhang et al., 2020). Therefore, this result supports Hypothesis 3.

Contrary to the expectation of our hypothesis 4, the results show a positive but not significant coefficient of the SCINCENTIVES variable. We argue that in the presence of sustainable compensation, incentives may be in a better position to assess the company's carbon risks in order to design a more effective executive compensation plan that can improve the company's performance in the ESG. H4 is not supported.

Finally, premise 5 is very strong: the establishment of a CSR committee appears to have a positive impact on the company's ESG performance. Regarding this variable (see Table 4), in line with several studies, it is interesting to emphasize that it has a positive and significant effect on ESG performance. These results show that better sustainability performance is achieved especially by the largest and most profitable companies (Arayssi et al., 2020).

This table shows the results regression for all set of a sample of 313 observation and those by geographic areas. Data source: Thomson Reuters Asset4 and Datastream. Significant coefficients are indicated by the usual significance levels: ***, 1%; **, 5%; *, 10%

Table 4. Results of regression models of ESG SCORE

ESGSCORE	Coef.	t	P>t
BOARD_SIZE	.4990464*	1.76	0.081
BINDEP	.0336106*	2.31	0.090
GENDERD	.4301542***	5.91	0.000
SCINCENTIVES	5.978273	1.12	0.264
CSRSUSTCOMM	20.57513***	13.18	0.000
N. Obs	313		
F(6, 307)	43.83		
Prob > F	0.0000		
R-squared	0.4165		
Adj R-squared	0.4070		

CONCLUSION

Building on previous literature demonstrating that boards play a key supervisory role in financial institutions, this study examines the relationship between board composition (size, activity, gender diversity, and compensation) and ESG performance in a sample of 313 observations of 64 listed companies in the MENA region for the period 2002-2017. The main findings reveal that size, autonomy, gender balance, wages, and CSR committee have a positive impact on company performance in the ESG for all regression models for the entire sample, that is, for each geographic region. For this reason, we support a critical perspective that emphasizes board characteristics, such as board size, share of board independence, share of women on the board, executive pay on sustainability issues and a CSR committee are Important to improve ESG performance.

DECLARATIONS

Competing interests

I declare that we have no known competing financial interests or personal relationships that could have appeared to influence the work reported in this paper.

Funding

Not applicable.

REFERENCES

Ajaz, A., Shenbei, Z., & Sarfraz, M. (2020). Delineating the influence of boardroom gender diversity on corporate social responsibility, financial performance, and reputation. *LogForum, 16*(1).

Alessandrini, F., & Jondeau, E. (2021). Optimal strategies for ESG portfolios. *Journal of Portfolio Management*, *47*(6), 114–138. doi:10.3905/jpm.2021.1.241

Arayssi, M., Jizi, M., & Tabaja, H. (2020). *The impact of board composition on the level of ESG disclosures in GCC countries*. Sustainability Accounting, Management and Policy Journal. doi:10.1108/SAMPJ-05-2018-0136

Baraibar-Diez, E., Odriozola, M. D., & Fernández Sánchez, J. L. (2019). Sustainable compensation policies and its effect on environmental, social, and governance scores. *Corporate Social Responsibility and Environmental Management*, *26*(6), 1457–1472. doi:10.1002/csr.1760

Birindelli, G., Dell'Atti, S., Iannuzzi, A. P., & Savioli, M. (2018). Composition and activity ofthe board ofdirectors: Impact on ESG performance in the banking system. *Sustainability (Basel)*, *10*(12), 4699. doi:10.3390u10124699

Castellanos, J. D., & George, B. (2020). Boardroom leadership: The board of directors as a source of strategic leadership. *Economics and Business Review*, *6*(1), 103–119. doi:10.18559/ebr.2020.1.5

Harjoto, M. A., & Wang, Y. (2020). Board of Directors Network Centrality and Environmental, Social and Governance (ESG) Performance. *Corporate Governance: An International Journal of Business in Society*.

Merendino, A., & Melville, R. (2019). The board of directors and firm performance: empirical evidence from listed companies. *Corporate Governance: The international journal of business in society*.

Ng, T., Lye, C., Chan, K., Lim, Y., & Lim, Y. (2020). Sustainability in Asia: The roles of financial development in environmental, social and governance (ESG) Performance. *Social Indicators Research*, *150*(1), 1–28. doi:10.100711205-020-02288-w

Peng, C. (2020). The role of business strategy and CEO compensation structure in driving corporate social responsibility: Linkage towards a sustainable development perspective. *Corporate Social Responsibility and Environmental Management*, *27*(2), 1028–1039. doi:10.1002/csr.1863

Qa'dan, M. B. A., & Suwaidan, M. S. (2019). Board composition, ownership structure and corporate social responsibility disclosure: The case of Jordan. *Social Responsibility Journal*.

Shahbaz, M., Karaman, A. S., Kilic, M., & Uyar, A. (2020). Board attributes, CSR engagement, and corporate performance: What is the nexus in the energy sector? *Energy Policy*, *143*, 111582. doi:10.1016/j.enpol.2020.111582

Zhang, X., Zhou, C., & Zhang, S. (2020). The Environmental, Social and Governance (ESG) Responsibilities of Landscape Architecture Firms. In *E3S Web of Conferences* (*Vol. 143*, p. 02045). EDP Sciences.

Chapter 13
Sustainable Disclosure of Receivables in the Enterprise's Integrated Reports

Mariya Shygun
Kyiv National Economic University Named After Vadym Hetman, Ukraine

Hryhorii Mukhomor
Kyiv National Economic University Named After Vadym Hetman, Ukraine

ABSTRACT

The possibility of investment and movement of capital between the countries, and the simplification of tax and customs regulations for the expansion of business boundaries strengthen the role and value of non-financial information for stakeholders. The study examines global trends in non-financial reporting, its regulation, and the nature of its use among large and medium-sized enterprises. During the research, it was concluded that the Integrated Report is the most relevant report for a wide range of stakeholders, as evidenced by the active growth in demand for it. At the same time, the Integrated Report should be filled with relevant understandable information and answer key stakeholders` questions. Our research proves that accounts receivable is the important indicator, that makes possible to get an answer about the nature of the enterprise interaction with all types of capital.

OVERVIEW

Sustainable development of enterprises requires cooperation with society, especially in the area of the environment, economic stability, social protection. All these factors are highlighted in non-financial reporting, which determines the relevance of this research. The possibility of investment and movement of capital between the countries, and the simplification of tax and customs regulations for the expansion of business boundaries strengthen the role and value of non-financial information for stakeholders. Including the Integrated Report, it stands out as one that is able to show the process of value creation, but it remains promising for research to correctly fill it in accordance with information needs of users.

DOI: 10.4018/979-8-3693-1388-6.ch013

The chapter will be useful to representatives of medium and large businesses and other interested parties, who are considering or interested in preparing a non-financial report in general and an integrated one in particular. Since an Integrated Report is one of the reliable way to reveal the state of sustainable development in an enterprise.

Aim: The purpose of this study is to prove the importance of receivables in the Integrated Report and the possibility of filling information about receivables in different sections of this report.

Method: The study examines global trends in non-financial reporting, its regulation, and the nature of its use among large and medium-sized enterprises. To obtain thorough results, we used regulatory acts, including laws and recommendations. Also, study offers an analysis of statistical information to emphasize relevance of non-financial reporting, about the state of overdue receivables in the countries of Eastern Europe. We used the conclusions of key audit firms regarding the spread of integrated reporting, the main requirements of stakeholders. This study used economic, accounting concepts and methods of handling information.

Findings: During the research, it was concluded that the Integrated Report is the most relevant report for a wide range of stakeholders, as evidenced by the active growth in demand for it. At the same time, the Integrated Report should be filled with relevant understandable information and answer key stakeholders` questions. Our research proves that accounts receivable is the important indicator, that makes possible to get an answer about the nature of the enterprise interaction with all types of capital.

Originality and Value: The analysis shows that it had sufficient validity, significance, and accuracy.

INTRODUCTION

The expansion of enterprise activities, the development of competition, the entry of companies into new markets, and the attraction of investments form the need to establish relations with stakeholders. Financial reporting provides important indicators that allow you to quantitatively assess the real financial state of companies' activities but does not provide data for the analysis of qualitative parameters of activity, which include reasons, motives, prospects, risks, competitive advantages, etc. Accordingly, the requests of users to supplement financial statements with non-financial indicators are increasing and, as a result, the submission of non-financial statements by companies is spreading.

The preparation of non-financial statements is carried out using various formats, one of which is the format of integrated reporting according to the requirements of the IIRC. The reporting of this format could qualitatively and quantitatively reveal data on various aspects of the company's activity, revealing the environment of activity, social and managerial relations, as well as parameters of settlement management, including accounts receivable.

Separate disclosure in the Integrated Report of data on receivables and their management, in our opinion, complements a comprehensive understanding of the enterprise's activities, successes, risks, and threats and helps identify other important signals for decision-making by stakeholders. In this study, we consider the Integrated Report as one of the key types of non-financial reports and provide arguments in favor of displaying information on receivables and their management in the Integrated Report. Non-financial disclosure of accounts receivable provides additional information by stakeholder requests, which allows for more balanced and more informed decisions.

Research in the area of non-financial reporting allows to implement the foundations of sustainable development at the enterprise, when it is possible to evaluate the activity not only from the economic, but also from the social, ethical and non-financial side to various market participants.

LITERATURE REVIEW

The issues of non-financial reporting preparation are of increasing interest to scientists. In particular, Olivier Adam, the permanent coordinator of the UN in Ukraine, notes that after the adoption of the UN Global Compact, about 90% of all non-financial reports are created by the companies that signed the contract (Olivier & Vorobei, 2010). This agreement provides for the preparation by companies of non-financial reporting with the disclosure of the progress of their fulfillment of 17 global goals.

Global processes gave a significant impetus to the further development of scientific research in the field of non-financial reporting, which finds its expression in the articles of various authors. In the study on the role of non-financial reporting in non-state pension funds, Agaverdiyeva (2016) concludes that the fact of forming non-financial reporting is a signal to society about the social responsibility of the enterprise, that is, it is actually part of the sustainable development of the enterprise and connection with society. Pavelko and Harapko (2021) reveals the role of non-financial reporting as a source of information for stakeholders, analyzes the dynamics of the development of non-financial reporting, and highlights the important role of integrated reporting for users. Khomulyak (2015) emphasizes the need to form integrated reporting by medium and large enterprises.

Integrated Report

An important role in non-financial reporting is assigned to the use of integrated reporting by Partyn and Zagorodnii (2017), who attests to the broad informational possibilities of such reporting and provides recommendations on the development of the structure of such a report and its content in the composition of various economic indicators. Shakhvedryan and Karpushenko (2019) investigate the possibility of using an integrated report when determining the value of an enterprise, pay attention to other formats of non-financial reporting, and reveal their advantages and disadvantages.

Velt (2022) focuses special attention on the statistical analysis of correlations between the main reasons for the increase in the value of the enterprise in the case of drawing up integrated reporting. Desi and de Villiers (2019) conduct a comprehensive study of readiness for integrated reporting in Indonesia and Sri Lanka and also studies the reasons for the slow processes in the implementation of such reporting in the economic environment. Mihalski (2008) proves the importance and role of receivables as one of the key indicators for investors and its impact on the value of the enterprise, which emphasizes the importance of disclosing such indicators in non-financial statements of companies.

In general, research in the field of non-financial reporting can be characterized as overview and theoretical, which makes it possible to analyze the degree of spread of non-financial reporting, weaknesses of each type of non-financial reporting, and potential opportunities. But in addition to that, there are few practical recommendations for enterprises in the existing research on the formation and filling of the content of a non-financial report (in particular, an integrated one) so that it would give the enterprise economic and social advantages over competitors. Therefore, enterprises, as a rule, form only those non-financial statements that are required by law and have methodical recommendations for their preparation. We can recommend conducting further research in terms of filling the report with practical indicators, considering their expediency and effectiveness for different groups of users.

RESEARCH METHODOLOGY

The object of our research is the non-financial reporting of enterprises, in particular integrated reporting and the search for the possibility of improving the disclosure of information in it, using receivables in various sections of the integrated report in accordance with the request of stakeholders.

The article examines the issue of the main types of non-financial reporting, based on the reports of leading audit companies, its role in the success of enterprises, considers the issue of key interests of stakeholders, which are reflected in non-financial reporting in general and integrated reporting in particular. An important role is played by the analysis of the importance of receivables for the enterprises of Europe and Ukraine, by using statistical information during the last 5 years. Accordingly, our research makes it possible to form a hypothesis about the role of accounts receivable in an integrated report and to give impetus to further research in terms of a better display of information in the report, so that it meets the criteria of expediency and truthfulness, and informs about key risks and advantages, both economic and social. Such research, in our opinion, significantly optimizes the sustainable development of medium and large enterprises.

The Place of Non-Financial Reporting in the Structure of Enterprise Reporting

Every modern enterprise provides users with reports that have both financial and non-financial formats. Non-financial reporting, as a rule, concerns large enterprises, banks, and insurance companies, which are subjects of public importance. Financial statements are prepared according to national or international reporting standards. Different countries have different requirements for non-financial reporting regarding its format and presentation. For example, in Ukraine, the main format of non-financial reporting today is the Management Report, which, according to the requirements of the law, must include information on financial results of activities, management, environmental components, social interaction, investment, and other non-financial information (Methodological recommendations, 2018). The main users of the Management Report are owners, employees, shareholders.

In the EU, the preparation and submission of non-financial reporting was regulated by Directive 2014/95/EC, which stipulated requirements for the preparation of non-financial reporting by large companies and disclosure of such elements as information on company policy, environmental protection, employment, etc.

On January 5, 2023, the Directive (EU) 2022/2464 as regards corporate sustainability reporting entered into force, which applies to large enterprises and other entities of public importance and generally covers about 50,000 different companies. According to the Directive (EU) 2022/2464, companies must submit their first 2024 reports for 2023.

Today, non-financial reporting is becoming more and more widespread and reveals the issue of sustainable development by the vast majority of the largest enterprises of both the world (G250) and each state separately (N100 - 100 companies of each state with the largest revenues). According to the KPMG study, 96% of the G250 report on ESG (environmental, social, governance) indicators, and 71% of the N100 define ESG indicators as significant (Big shifts, 2022).

Research by Pavelko and Harapko (2021) allows to compare the main types of non-financial reporting, which is most often prepared by companies:

1. **Composed in an arbitrary form.**
2. **Compiled based on a comprehensive report using the method**:
   a) triple bottom line, where information on economic, environmental, and social aspects of activity is highlighted;
   b) London group of comparative analysis (charity, social investments, commercial initiatives, core activity);
   c) Corporate Social Citizenship – groups of corporate citizenship, where activities related to social responsibility are described.
3. **Standardized reporting**:
   a) GRI (Global Reporting Initiative) standards, where standardization, requirements, and principles for the preparation of non-financial reporting are applied. More than 4,000 companies in the world are preparing it as of 2022 (GRI Standards, 2022);
   b) AA-1000 (standard for the organization and implementation of the goals of sustainable development of the enterprise and the construction of its reporting) (Accountability standard, 2020);
   c) SA-8000 (social issues of labor protection, overtime work, discrimination in the workplace, etc.) (Standard for Social Responsibility, 2020);
   d) International <IR> Framework – a comprehensive report that provides information about the enterprise as a whole, and reveals the chain of value creation through interaction with six types of capital, social, and other issues by the above principles) (<IR> Framework, 2021).

In the practice of drawing up non-financial reporting, companies also use other formats, the task of which is to highlight various aspects of conducting business, increasing the level of socially responsible investing (SRI). As noted by Khomulyak (2015), leading sources of investment information (Bloomberg, Thomson Reuters) testify to the important role of non-financial information for effective investment decision-making. Accordingly, the size of SVI grows steadily every year and becomes a basic requirement of leading investment funds.

Interests of Stakeholders in Non-Financial Reporting

Based on the essence of the information presented in non-financial reporting, each group of users is interested in its different categories. For example, the state needs data on tax payment, rational use of natural resources, social stability, shareholders - on profitability, stability, and business prospects; society - cleanliness and preservation of the environment, working conditions of employees, and compliance with legal rules; commercial agents - stability of payment on payables and receivables, product quality, stability of activity, etc. (Pavelko and Harapko, 2021). A summary of the interests of key stakeholders' groups in various aspects of the company's activity is given in Table 1.

Table 1. Interests of the main stakeholders' groups regarding the company's activities

No	Stakeholders	Interests				
		Commercial	**Corporative management**	**Social security**	**Sustainability**	**Innovativeness**
1	2	3	4	5	6	7
1	**Owners (shareholders)**	Profit, stability, competition	Achieving maximum efficiency in corporate management, and productivity. Duration and quality of work with employees	Stability of income, reduction of uncertainty in the market	Long-term functioning, preservation of reputation	The need to maximize competitive advantage through innovation
2	**Management**	Salary, availability of non-financial benefits	Establishing social relationships to achieve maximum work efficiency	Social package, availability of additional benefits	Positioning of the enterprise on the market, stability	Innovation as a result of management efficiency and quality, is a tool of reputation. Innovation as a tool for attracting competitive advantages
3	**Workers**	Salary, additional benefits	Internal psychological and ethical situation, non-financial features of work (relation to overtime work)	Social package, insurance, non-financial benefits	The image of the company, its prospects, and the possibility of planning prospects, self-realization	Company image, working conditions
4	**Commercial agents**	Financial efficiency of cooperation, quality of execution of agreements, timeliness	Corporate success	Social success	Reputation, interest in lower transaction costs	Quality of execution of agreements, reputation during cooperation
5	**State**	Amount of tax revenues, timely payment of taxes, transparency of activity	Improvement of corporate culture, promotion of economic growth of the state, level of satisfaction of society	Payment of taxes, payroll deductions, interest in employee insurance, and occupational safety	Interest in continuous operation of the enterprise, full payment of taxes, reduction of harmful emissions into the environment, sustainable development,	Innovativeness and reduction of harmfulness of production, increase of innovativeness of the economy, accumulation of investments

Source: summarized by the authors based on (Pavelko and Harapko, 2021; Shakhvedryan and Karpushenko, 2019; Mihalski, 2008).

Each stakeholder expects to receive the information he needs, particularly, in Integrated Reporting. Each of the aspects of the enterprise's activity is important for users, including the state and management of receivables, which reflects the level of realization of goods (works, services), the quality of management in terms of optimizing its turnover, as well as the peculiarities of the accounting and contractual policy of the enterprise.

Integrated Report in the Structure of Non-Financial Reporting

The study of the practice of compiling non-financial reporting shows the use of different formats by companies, which significantly complicates the procedure for analyzing the activities of enterprises by different groups of stakeholders because the structure of the report, its form, and content differ in different organizations. In our opinion, companies can prepare an Integrated Report that can include both financial and non-financial information, which expands the circle of potential users.

The integrated report is actively spreading in the practice of reporting, however, according to the information of the official promoters of integrated reporting, the largest number of them are formed by European and Asian countries (26% and 44%, respectively) (The Integrated Reporting website, 2023). According to the KPMG study on the spread of Integrated Reporting on different continents among N100 enterprises, the results show that as of the end of 2022, 51% of enterprises in the Middle East will compile an Integrated Report, North America - 28%, Asia - 30%, Europe - 15%, Africa - 15% (Big shifts, 2022).

At the same time, as stated by Desi and de Villiers (2019), the lack of a properly developed methodology for compiling the Integrated Report in its parts (for example, the characteristics of operations related to implementation, the method of presenting information about it, etc.) inhibits the use of this type of reporting as the main type of non-financial reporting in Asian countries, in particular, Indonesia and Sri Lanka. Such a conclusion is relevant for most countries that do not have an appropriate methodological basis for the preparation of non-financial statements by companies.

The purpose of integrated reporting is to provide interested parties with information about the interaction of key types of company capital: financial, manufactural, human, social and reputational, intellectual and natural (<IR> Framework (2021). Through combination of financial and non-financial information, users have the opportunity to understand how the business is functioning, and how its value is created, predict the consequences of activity, its prospects, disadvantages and advantages of cooperation with the company, and make appropriate decisions.

Accounts receivable is one of the important indicators of the company's activity and is a key parameter for evaluating management policy. For stakeholders, accounts receivable is a qualitative indicator, understanding its changes, its formation, circulation, order of write-off, dynamics, and factors influencing the volume provides an opportunity to understand and predict the results of the enterprise in general. Accounts Receivable can provide valuable information to each group of potential users of Integrated Reporting, supporting their decisions and actions.

The presence of many user groups and a large amount of information makes it necessary to study how completely and in what sequence information should be disclosed in the report, the form of the report, requirements, and standardization issues. As noted by Velt (2022), accounts receivable is an element of economic activity and is related to management efficiency, which characterizes the company's position on the market.

Integrated reporting could most fully highlight the issues of creation, circulation, and repayment of receivables, and provide information on possible risks, achievements, accounting and contractual policies.

Accounts Receivable as a Tool for Disclosing Information About the Enterprise

The absence of specific rules for filling out the integrated report, as it is not mandatory, causes its use as such, which makes a certain advertisement for the enterprise. That is, the reader may have a false idea about the success and the possibility of sustainable development of the enterprise. This makes it necessary to establish certain mandatory rules for filling out the report, so that stakeholders have a better idea of the company's interaction with various types of capital. Our research shows that accounts receivable is an accounting and economic category that should be disclosed in almost all sections of the Integrated Report by user requests, which, in turn, can be radically different from each other. In particular, as Zymovets (2019) notes, before the start of the Russian-Ukrainian War in 2022-2023, there was a rather critical situation with the return of funds to creditors in cases of bankruptcy of Ukrainian enterprises, and only 8.9% of debts were returned. For comparison, the average indicator for the world is 36.6%, in European countries – 81.6% (Fig. 1). Such a situation makes it impossible for creditors to receive funds from bankrupt enterprises, despite the order and sequence of debt repayment clearly defined by legislation.

Figure 1. The share of receivables in non-financial organizations of Ukraine and Europe
Source: (Zymovets, 2019)

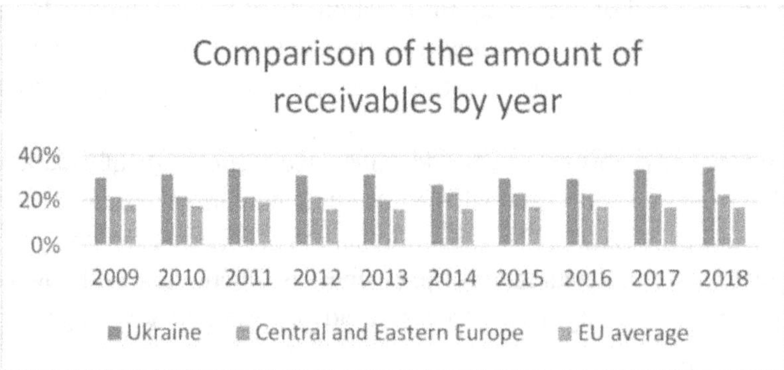

In times of crisis, as Zymovets (2019) emphasizes, small and medium-sized businesses in Ukraine receive support in the form of "dirty" funds, which are a significant part of enterprise financing. Such financing is often not used to support business but can be part of "money laundering". Such transactions are material and must be cleared to avoid a potential liquidity crisis.

One of the main reasons for the excessive increase in receivables is the difficulty of accessing capital, which inhibits the development of financial relations between enterprises. Accounts receivable is thus a mirror of transactions, and it is "shadow" transactions that may be the underlying cause of the excessive specific weight of accounts receivable in small and medium-sized enterprises.

In this regard, information on the state of receivables, their quality and structure, is not only a significant factor in the continuation of economic activity but is also a significant factor for the continuation of cooperation with counterparties. Therefore, it should be emphasized that receivables are a valuable source of information for counterparties in key aspects of their activities, accordingly, the main requests for information regarding receivables may include the following (Table 2).

Table 2. Requests for information about receivables by stakeholder

Stakeholders	Accounts receivable information is required
Owners (shareholders)	Dynamics of receivables by reporting periods, turnover, level of bad debts, effectiveness of receivables management, comparative information regarding other market participants
Management	The results of meeting the goals determined in previous reporting periods regarding receivables, the effectiveness of management by key indicators, turnover, statistical data on the results of the receivables management policy, analytical information on potential risks and benefits associated with the dynamics of receivables
Workers	Results of receivables management, debt level according to internal calculations, forecast data on receivables
Commercial counterparties	Accounting policy for debtors, an average level of delays, absolute and relative amounts of receivables, plans, expectations regarding amounts of receivables, contractual policy in general
State	The level of bad debts and its corresponding reasons, write-off of bad debts, receivables according to settlements with the budget

Source: The authors

The peculiarity of accounts receivable as an economic, legal, and psychological indicator is that it acts as a "pulse of economic activity", especially in the part of "business to business" (B2B) relations. When the enterprise has a confident position in the market, works with reliable counterparties, creates rational expectations, and has resources for business expansion, then there is a corresponding increase in the number of receivables, and the repayment period may increase, based on the growth of the enterprise's loyalty to the debtors.

When negative shifts begin in the market, uncertainty grows, which causes a corresponding reflection in commercial contracts in the direction of reducing the terms of repayment of receivables, the amount of overdue debts could symmetrically increase. If the market experiences a crisis and sudden changes in circumstances, sellers try to switch to prepayment, but this often results in overdue receivables.

Accounts receivable are thus a mirror of relations with counterparties, and the presence of its financial and non-financial parameters in the Integrated Report is a valuable source of data for business stakeholders to understand, but also a guarantee of reliable support of the company's reputation.

British resource "Atradius Collections" (2022) conducts systematic research and provides relevant statistics, including the "Atradius payment practices barometer". This indicator reflects the level of use of B2B consumer lending, and the terms of repayment of receivables, and tracks the reasons for changes in the amount of payments. In particular, for the year 2022, it was found that the countries of Eastern Europe are deeply uncertain about the growth or even the stability of the state economies, and the decrease in sales, the increase in the number of receivables in the manufacturing sector, and the manufacturing industry are also of particular concern. At the same time, there is an increase in sales in the field of retail and services. Data on consumer lending in 2021-2022 in the countries of Eastern Europe are shown in the table. 3.

Table 3. State of B2B receivables in Eastern Europe, comparison of 2021 and 2022

Indicator	2021	2022	Reasons for the change
Amount of transactions on postpaid terms	43%	44%	Steady efforts of enterprises to remain on the market, to occupy abandoned niches
Average number of credit days	40 days	42 days	The majority of surveyed enterprises want to move to markets weakened by external circumstances, create economic conditions for cashless payments, a state of active struggle for internal economies
Amount of overdue payments	43%	45%	The expected drop in B2B liquidity of buyers led to deliberate delays in payments
Bad debts	5%	6%	A drop in asset liquidity, a decrease in the economic activity of buyers, rational concerns
Cases of deterioration in the sale of goods (number of affirmative answers)	15%	48%	The general deterioration of the market situation and rational expectations created, including the war in Ukraine
The general state of affairs, description in words	Confidence in the growth of activity, little apprehension about risks	Deep insecurity	Inflation, energy crisis, geopolitical tension, and increases in production costs can hinder the development of the domestic economy of countries and enterprises

Source: generalized on the basis of the Atradius Collections (2022)

Table 3 shows examples of changes in receivables management policy in Eastern Europe, and in particular, reflects the ability of receivables to signal key parameters of activity, business condition, organization policy, tools for protecting market positions, development prospects, etc.

As noted by Lavery and Schmidt (2021), taking into account the degree of globalization, Eastern Europe is a new enclave of globalization growth, an increase in international transactions, the level of cooperation with foreign counterparties, and the growth of foreign direct investment by about 7% per year. Accordingly, accounts receivable is a key element in analyzing the company's activity and evaluating its effectiveness.

Accounts Receivable in the Company's Integrated Report

In Ukraine, the war had a significant impact on the level of direct investment, but the overall balance for 2022, according to the Ministry of Finance of Ukraine, generally remained positive (Direct investment page, 2023). After the end of the war, Ukraine will intensively recover, including at the expense of international support, which makes it necessary to increase the level of communications with economic partners, using integrated reporting and indicators that are of interest to potential stakeholders, in particular, regarding receivables, the level of foreign debt, the creditworthiness category of debtors, degree of debt insurance by internal and external institutions, etc.

Separate developments regarding the disclosure of data on receivables are presented in the study by Mihalski (2008). The author, in particular, proposes to use a group of financial and non-financial indicators when describing receivables, which may include the level of implementation of the marketing strategy for cooperation with markets, the relationship between receivables and profitability, the amount of future benefits and risks, the characteristics of the degree of confidence of the enterprise in the stability of its activities, the debtors characteristics, segregating categories according to various characteristics etc.

To ensure a reliable methodological basis for the preparation of Integrated reporting, we suggest considering a possible structure of data regarding receivables. Accounts receivable and changes in it are related to six types of capital, the disclosure of which is provided by the Integrated Report: financial, manufactural, intellectual, human, social and reputational, and natural capitals (Shygun & Muhomor, 2022). In addition, receivables show the company's ability to sell products (goods, services). This, in turn, reflects the presence of stable commercial relations, logistics, involvement in the production cycle of other enterprises.

Accordingly, various indicators regarding receivables should be presented in all sections of the Integrated Report, gradually forming in users an integrated view of the company's activities as a whole. We offer the following structure of indicators in the part of receivables, which can be disclosed in the key sections of the Integrated Report (Table 4).

Table 4. Disclosure of information about receivables in the Integrated Report of the company

Section of the Report	Information	Data source
1	2	3
Overview of the organization and external environment	Overview of the general economic situation on the market (recession, growth, etc.)	Information Report of the National Bank (in terms of inflation, currency volatility, discount rate, and rational expectations); Customs and tax legislation regarding goods and their sale
	Comparative performance indicators of competitors, distribution of market shares	Report of the Antimonopoly Committee; Marketing Report
	Features of goods (works, services) (life cycle, generally accepted form of implementation)	Notes to financial statements; Marketing Report
	Overview of the main forms of cooperation with counterparties (product, payment policy, statistics on the share of debtors, and other significant indicators)	Accounting Policies; Extract from accounting journals "Settlements with buyers and customers"
	Elements of the accounting policy (form of payment, method of cost formation, created reserves to cover debts, policy of encouraging early repayment)	Accounting Policies
	Analytical and statistical data in terms of absolute and relative amounts of receivables by groups of goods and counterparties (turnover, share of receivables in the Balance Sheet, in sales, information on average payment delays, etc.)	Balance Sheet; Report on Financial Results; Management reports
Management	Information about key persons involved in the company's product sales policy, their key results, and management methods (director and other key persons, time in office, work experience, key achievements, work principles)	Companys` Management Report
Business model	The place of receivables in the company's policy, clarification of the procedure for creating and repaying the debt, the features of the products and the order of payment for them, the quality of the receivables	Business plan of the Company; Accounting policy; Notes to Financial Statements; Companys` Management Report; Companys` development strategy

continues on following page

Table 4. Continued

Section of the Report	Information	Data source
Risks and opportunities	Information on the market situation, in particular, analytical data and forecasts regarding possible payment delays, changes in the market situation, demand for goods (works, services), changes in the accounting policy in the context of receivables, and the corresponding algorithm for working with new risks and opportunities	Information Report of the National Bank; Credit rating of the state, published on the website of the Ministry of Finance; Accounting rate and inflation rate (National Bank); Turnover and balance information for settlements with debtors; Financial Statements; Audit Report
Strategy and use of resources	Non-financial information that will make it possible to understand how the company operates on the market and the potential impact on the dynamics of receivables (strategy of actions on the market, market capture, policy of maintaining positions, clarification on the further strategy of behavior and appropriate use of resources in terms of markets)	Companys` Management Report; Business Plan of the Company; Marketing Report
Results of activity	Analysis of past accounts receivables goals. The results of using one or another strategy in the market, the level of effectiveness of managing receivables in comparison with alternatives. Disclosure of written-off receivables, relevant reasons, and comparison with other market participants in the same industry	Companys` Development Strategy; Business Plan of the Company; Financial Statements
Prospects	Forecasting the future amount of receivables, possible changes in the debts management policy, setting goals for future periods	Companys` Management Report
Basis for preparation and presentation	Standards for the preparation of financial statements in the part of accounts receivable data, Standards for non-financial statements used for the preparation of the Report	Data of the company's divisions, involved into the preparation of the Report

Source: the authors

Thus, accounts receivable as an element of the Integrated Report is a special system indicator and could be disclosed in details in various sections, providing relevant, essential and complex information about the company's activities. The content of information about receivables, which could be presented in Integrated Report, initiates further research in terms of the preparation of this type of reporting, filling it with financial and non-financial indicators, and providing recommendations for preparation by stakeholders` requests. Also of great scientific interest is the development of a methodology for disclosing information about receivables in the Integrated Report, which could ensure comparability of data for different enterprises within the field of activity and at the inter-industry level.

CONCLUSION

The conducted study of the role of non-financial reporting and its place in the reporting system of enterprises allowed us to emphasize the significant information provision of key groups of stakeholders through the preparation of the Integrated Report. This report comprehensively demonstrates information on the impact of key types of capital on the company's activities and the environment, which contributes to an integrated understanding by stakeholders of business features, and cause-and-effect relationships, and helps to make appropriate decisions. The integrated report could be considered a high-quality tool for dialogue with society regarding the sustainable development of the enterprise, therefore there is a need to research ways of qualitative information coverage in the report.

Providing information about receivables to interested parties is an important stage of communication with stakeholders that could increase the investment opportunities of the enterprise, and establish relations with counterparties, the state, and the public. At the same time, integrated reporting provides an opportunity to consistently and comprehensively disclose the policy, strategy, and features of the creation and write-off of receivables, to provide analytical information, possible risks, prospects, and forecasts.

The preparation of the Integrated Report with proper disclosure of sufficient information about receivables should comply with the principles and requirements of the International <IR> Framework, be presented consistently, following the sections of the report, be comparable with past periods, contain both financial and non-financial data, including operational features of the enterprise, the markets, the chosen strategy and accounting policies, forming an integrated understanding of the enterprise's value creation.

Further research in the area of disclosure of accounts receivable indicators in non-financial reporting should include proper methodological ways of accumulating information about accounts receivable, presenting it in a historical context based on the principles of data comparability, including basic indicators that would be regulated and used by other entities.

For countries in which non-financial reporting is just gaining popularity, it is especially necessary to create appropriate methodological recommendations for the construction of an Integrated Report, using clear indicators, methods, and algorithms, while providing an opportunity for enterprises to disclose essential information. Such methodological recommendations should be developed taking into account the basic elements of activity, covering issues of implementation, amounts of receivables, sustainable development, social component, and prospects (risks) of the activity. These and other questions form the current directions of further research in the part of integrated reporting and requirements for its preparation.

REFERENCES

AccountAbility. (2020). *Assurance Standard (AA-1000)*. AccountAbility. URL:https://www.accountability.org/static/3ff15429033873cdc775212ca63572fb/aa1000as_v3_final.pdf

Agaverdiyeva, H. F. (2016). Technologies of implementing non-financial reporting as a tool for regulating the social responsibility of a non-state pension fund in the conditions of European integration. *Economics and Finances*. *3*. 4-14. URL: http://repository.hneu.edu.ua/handle/123456789/11962

Atradius Collections. (2022). *Database of statistical data*. United Kingdom. https://atradiuscollections.com/global/reports/payment-practices-barometer-b2b-payment-practices-trends-western-europe-2022.html

Desi, A., & de Villiers, C. (2019). Integrated reporting: perspectives of corporate report preparers and other stakeholders. *Sustainability Accounting, Management and Policy Journal,*. *10*(1), 126-156. https://www.emerald.com/insight/content/doi/10.1108/SAMPJ-02-2018-0043/full/html

Europa. (2014). Directive of the European Parliament and the Council No. 2014/95/EC. Europa. https://eur-lex.europa.eu/legal-content/EN/TXT/?uri=celex:32014L0095

Europa. (2022). *Directive (EU) 2022/2464 of the European Parliament and of the Council.* Europa. https://eur-lex.europa.eu/legal-content/EN/TXT/?uri=CELEX:32022L2464

GRI Standards. (2022). *Standards.* Global reporting initiative. https://www.globalreporting.org/standards/

Integrated Reporting. (2023). *Home.* Integrated Reporting. https://www.integratedreporting.org/the-iirc-2/

International Framework. (2021The International Integrated Reporting Council. https://www.integratedreporting.org/resource/international-ir-framework/

Khomulyak, T. I. (2015). *The need for Integrated reporting, as in a new reporting format for business // Financial and credit activity: problems of theory and practice.* NBUV. http://nbuv.gov.ua/UJRN/Fkd_2015_1_23

KPMG. (2022). Big shifts, small steps Survey of Sustainability Reporting 2022. KPMG. https://assets.kpmg.com/content/dam/kpmg/xx/pdf/2023/04/big-shifts-small-steps.pdf

Lavery, S., & Schmidt, D. (2021, September). European Integration and the New Global Disorder. *Journal of Common Market Studies, 59*(5), 1322–1338. https://onlinelibrary.wiley.com/doi/full/10.1111/jcms.13184. doi:10.1111/jcms.13184

Mihalski, G. (2008). Operational risk in current assets investment decisions: Portfolio management approach in accounts receivable. *Agricultural Economics, 54*, 12-19. https://papers.ssrn.com/sol3/papers.cfm?abstract_id=1562672

Ministry of Finance. (2018). *On the approval of Methodological recommendations for drawing up a management report.* Ministry of Finance of Ukraine. https://zakon.rada.gov.ua/rada/show/v0982201-18#Text

Ministry of Finance. (2023). *Direct investment page.* Ministry of Finance. https://index.minfin.com.ua/ua/economy/fdi/

Olivier, A., & Vorobei, I. (2010). *Non-financial reporting: a tool of socially responsible business.* Global compact network Ukraine, Kyiv. https://www.ppv.net.ua/uploads/work_attachments/Non-Financial_Reporting__UA_.pdf

Partyn, G. O., & Zagorodnii, A. H. (2017). Taking into account the interests of stakeholders in the process of forming integrated enterprise reporting. *Bulletin.* Lviv Polytechnic National University. http://nbuv.gov.ua/UJRN/VNULPM_2017_862_31

Pavelko, O. V., & Harapko, N. I. (2021). Integrated enterprise reporting as a key source of information for stakeholders. Bulletin of the National University of Water Management and Nature Management. *Economic sciences, 1*(93). http://nbuv.gov.ua/UJRN/Vnuvgp_ekon_2021_1_16

Shakhvedryan, D. S., & Karpushenko, M. Yu. (2019). Integrated reporting as a source of assessment of the company's activity. *Business-Inform Magazine 3.* http://www.irbis-nbuv.gov.ua/ cgi-bin/ irbis_nbuv/cgiirbis_64. exe?I21DBN = LINK & P21DBN = UJRN & Z21ID = &S21REF = 10&S21CNR = 20&S21STN = 1&S21FMT = ASP_meta & C21COM = S&2_S21P03 = FILA= & 2_S21STR = binf_2019_3_38

Shygun, M. M., & Muhomor, G. V. (2022). Possibilities of assessing receivables in the integrated reporting of the enterprise. *Proceedings of the 10th International Scientific and Practical Conference "Perspectives for the Development of Accounting and Analysis in the Context of European Integration,* (pp. 102-103). HNEU. http://repository.hneu.edu.ua/bitstream/ 123456789/ 27522/1/ %D0%A2%D0 %B5%D0%B7%D0%B8%20-%D0%92%D0%BD%D1%83%D0%BA%D0%BE%D0%B2%D0%B0%20 %D0%9D%D0 %9C_%D0%9A %D0%B0%D0 %BD%D0%B8 %D0%B3%D1 %96%D0%BD %20 _%D0%A1 %D0% 9C.pdf

Standard for Social Responsibility (SA-8000). (2020). *Law.* Rada. https://zakon.rada.gov.ua/laws/show/n0015697-07#Text

Velt, P. (2022). *Archival research on integrated reporting: a systematic review of main drivers and the impact of integrated reporting on firm value // Journal of Management and Governance, No. 26.* URL., doi:10.100710997-021-09582-w

Zymovets, V. (2019). The excessive receivables of the enterprises: causes and consequences for the financial system of Ukraine. *Economy and Forecasting,* 5-18. http://econ-forecast.org.ua/docs/EP_19_2_05_en.pdf

Chapter 14
The Role of the Central Bank in Greening the Nigerian Financial System

Peterson K. Ozili
https://orcid.org/0000-0001-6292-1161
Central Bank of Nigeria, Nigeria

ABSTRACT

The chapter explores the role of the central bank of Nigeria in greening the financial system. The author explores the ways in which the central bank can green the financial system. Some of the offered suggestions include disclosure requirements, establishing green finance labs, creating a green bank, and the use of differentiated cash reserve requirement based on environmental impact. The insights offered in this chapter are useful to bank supervisors and the monetary authority in understanding how financial and monetary decisions affect the environment.

1. INTRODUCTION

Many central banks around the world have expanded their role beyond price and monetary stability in an attempt to mitigate non-economic exogenous shocks that affect the macro economy in unprecedented ways. For example, many central banks used unconventional monetary policy tools to respond to the COVID-19 induced health crisis (Mosser, 2020; Ozili and Arun, 2020). Some central banks have also responded to climate change by requiring regulated banks to disclose the impact of climate risk on their business (Campiglio et al, 2018). Other monetary authorities have responded to gender inequality issues in the banking sector to reduce gender inequality and the risk of social activism (Braunstein and Heintz, 2008; Ozili, 2023). These are few examples of how central banks are expanding their roles beyond their traditional function in order to address emerging non-economic issues and exogenous shocks.

An important emerging issue in the global economy is the effect of unfavourable climate change on the global economy and central banks are being pressured to respond to climate change (Dikau and Volz, 2021). In response to this, some central banks have begun to assess the potential effect of climate

DOI: 10.4018/979-8-3693-1388-6.ch014

change related risk on the banking sector. The outcome of such assessment can offer insights to central banks on how best to mitigate climate change related risk, and also offer some insights on how to make the financial system more resilient to environmental and climate change shocks.

One way to prepare the financial system to withstand climate change shocks in Nigeria is to embark on an aggressive green finance program for the financial system. Green finance is financing that yields economic benefits while protecting the environment. Wang and Zhi (2016) define green finance as finance that protects the environment while pursuing economic profits. These two definitions show that green finance promotes the financing of projects and activities while being mindful of any damage to the environment to ensure that firms do not damage the environment in the pursuit of profits.

Given this backdrop, this chapter offers some ideas on how the CBN can green the Nigerian financial system. The chapter contributes to the existing financial stability literature by showing that green finance offers a possible solution to mitigate or dampen the effect of climate change on the financial system. The chapter also adds to the finance literature by offering insights on how innovative finance, in this case green finance, can be used to promote a sustainable financial system.

The remainder of the chapter is categorized as follows. The related literature is discussed in section 2 while the ways in which the CBN can support the greening of the financial system are discussed in section 3. Finally, the concluding remark is presented in Section 4.

2. LITERATURE REVIEW

The literature show that green financing has several benefits. For instance, green financing can help to construct smart cities (He et al, 2020). Scaling green finance may significantly decrease funding for activities that harm the environment (Sachs et al 2019a). Green finance can also reduce CO2 emission (Li et al, 2021). Existing studies identified a number of innovative green financing instruments e.g., green bonds, (Ozili, 2021; Lindenberg, 2014); community-based green funds (Sachs et al, 2019b); green bond grant scheme (Chang et al, 2019), green blended finance instruments (Mehta, 2017) and central bank digital currency (Ozili, 2022). Berensmann and Lindenberg (2016) suggest three strategies to increase funding for green activities. They include (i) develop better standards and disclosure rules, (ii) encourage green financing and investments by providing incentives, and (iii) improve policy coordination. Tu et al (2020) show that a green bond market would need a low interest rate, favorable monetary policy and a sound legal framework. Taghizadeh-Hesary and Yoshino (2019) showed that private participation in green financing could increase by creating green credit guarantee schemes and by offering tax rebate to green investors. Some studies examine the role of a central bank in green financing. Ozili (2021) suggests the use of a capital surcharge, adjusted tier 2 capital, prohibiting lending to businesses that harm the environment, and requiring banks to move their critical infrastructure to a safer location, while Volz (2017) suggests that central banks should use policy instruments e.g., capital and interest rate controls. Other studies identify the challenges of greening the financial system. Berensmann and Lindenberg (2016) show that there is no clarity about the term 'green' in green finance and it leaves room for multiple interpretations, and there is an unwholesome short-term-ism among investors in green projects. Gilchrist et al (2021) and Falcone and Sica (2019) identify policy uncertainty about green finance, the short-term orientation of financial instruments and the unavailability of data as major challenges.

3. ROLE OF CENTRAL BANK OF NIGERIA IN GREENING THE NIGERIAN FINANCIAL SYSTEM

Greening the financial system should be considered by the CBN for two reasons. One, unfavourable climate change events can impede the productive capacity of the Nigerian economy and weaken its ability to generate employment and income. Two, greening the financial system can support the central bank's efforts to diversify the economy away from its dependence on carbon-laden crude oil products. It can help to grow the non-oil sector of the economy.

3.1. Issue Green Bonds to Support Green Finance

A 'green bond' is used to raise financing for green projects (Dikau and Volz, 2021). It has positive environmental and/or climate benefits. It raises funds from investors and the realized funds are used to fund activities that protect the environment from man-made activities that damage the environment.

3.2. Introduce an Environment Protection Strategy (EPS) Disclosure Requirement

This approach will require the CBN to introduce some disclosure requirement. CBN can require banks to ensure that corporate borrowers provide a comprehensive 'environment protection strategy (EPS)' documentation. The EPS is a documentation that require corporate borrowers to disclose the measures they have put in place to ensure that their corporate activities do not create any man-made risk to the environment and the climate. Such documentation requirement will ensure that borrowers' activities do not harm the environment where they operate.

3.3. Establish Green Finance Labs or Climate Regulatory Sandboxes

CBN can establish green finance labs that would develop innovative green financing products that incorporate ESG considerations into traditional and non-traditional financing instruments. This would ensure the development of financing instruments that (i) integrates ESG factors, (ii) lead to better long-term returns for investors, and (iii) generate positive benefits for society (Shaydurova et al, 2018; Cerqueti et al, 2023).

3.4. Establish a Green Bank

The CBN may consider creating a green bank. A green bank is a financial institution that offer loans only for green projects or projects that have sizeable benefits for the environment and society. The need for a green bank arises when traditional financial institutions are unwilling to issue loans for green projects primarily because green investments often have very low return on investment.

3.5. Use Differentiated Cash Reserve Requirement as an Incentive to Lenders

Under this approach, banks that give out substantial loans to green project and activities will be required to keep a lower cash reserve ratio with the CBN so that they can have more money to give out as loan for green projects and for green investment (Volz, 2017), while banks that do not lend to green projects and activities will be required to keep a higher cash reserve ratio with the CBN.

3.6. Green Central Banking

The CBN should incorporate environmental considerations into its core policymaking activities. This will require the CBN to take into account environmental factors in its monetary policy, financial stability and development finance decision making. This will not only ensure that the central bank leads by example in the financial sector but will also ensure that the CBN exclude fossil fuels from its development finance programs so that the central bank is not seen as contributing to climate change risk by encouraging lending to businesses involved in fossil fuel activities (Şimandan and Păun, 2021).

4. CONCLUSION

This article discussed the role of the CBN in greening the financial system. Five approaches were suggested, which includes: issuing the EPS disclosure requirements, establishing green finance labs, creating a green bank, and the use of differentiated cash reserve requirement based on environmental impact. The CBN should ensure that financial institutions lend to activities that promote a sustainable financial system while protecting the environment. Green finance offers an innovative approach to achieve this goal. The CBN should ensure that the lending decisions of financial institutions take into account environmental considerations when lending to corporate borrowers. It is recommended that the CBN should encourage financial institutions to increase lending to economic agents that seek loans for green projects and activities. It is also recommended that the Bankers committees together with the CBN should develop collective initiatives for greening the financial system. It is also recommended that the CBN should solicit the support of all stakeholders and the Bankers committee towards greening the financial sector.

One limitation of this study is that it did not use empirical data to suggest ways to dampen the effect of climate change. Another limitation of the study is that it focuses only on central banks. These limitations present a fruitful area for further research. Future research can extend this study by exploring ways to mitigate climate change risk and the role of CBN in mitigating such risk. Future research can explore how to regulate green finance in the banking sector.

REFERENCES

Berensmann, K., & Lindenberg, N. (2016). Green finance: actors, challenges and policy recommendations. *German Development Institute/Deutsches Institut für Entwicklungspolitik (DIE) Briefing Paper, 23.*

Braunstein, E., & Heintz, J. (2008). Gender bias and central bank policy: Employment and inflation reduction. *International Review of Applied Economics, 22*(2), 173–186. doi:10.1080/02692170801889643

Campiglio, E., Dafermos, Y., Monnin, P., Ryan-Collins, J., Schotten, G., & Tanaka, M. (2018). Climate change challenges for central banks and financial regulators. *Nature Climate Change, 8*(6), 462–468. doi:10.103841558-018-0175-0

Cerqueti, R., Deffains-Crapsky, C., & Storani, S. (2023). Green finance instruments: Exploring minibonds issuance in I taly. *Corporate Social Responsibility and Environmental Management*, *30*(4), 1965–1986. doi:10.1002/csr.2467

Chang, Y. (2019). Green finance in Singapore: Barriers and solutions. ADBI Working Paper 915. Dikau, S., & Volz, U. (2021). Central bank mandates, sustainability objectives and the promotion of green finance. *Ecological Economics*, *184*, 107022.

Falcone, P. M., & Sica, E. (2019). Assessing the opportunities and challenges of green finance in Italy: An analysis of the biomass production sector. *Sustainability (Basel)*, *11*(2), 517. doi:10.3390u11020517

Gilchrist, D., Yu, J., & Zhong, R. (2021). The Limits of Green Finance: A Survey of Literature in the Context of Green Bonds and Green Loans. *Sustainability (Basel)*, *13*(2), 478. doi:10.3390u13020478

He, Z., Liu, Z., Wu, H., Gu, X., Zhao, Y., & Yue, X. (2020). Research on the Impact of Green Finance and Fintech in Smart City. *Complexity*, *2020*, 2020. doi:10.1155/2020/6673386

LindenbergN. (2014). Definition of green finance. Lindenberg, Nannette, Definition of Green Finance. SSRN. https://ssrn.com/abstract=2446496

Mehta, A. (2017). *Catalyzing green finance: A concept for leveraging blended finance for green development*. Asian Development Bank.

Mosser, P. C. (2020). Central bank responses to COVID-19. *Business Economics (Cleveland, Ohio)*, *55*(4), 191–201. doi:10.105711369-020-00189-x PMID:33204040

Ozili, P. K. (2021). Managing Climate Change Risk: The Policy Options for Central Banks. In *New Challenges for Future Sustainability and Wellbeing*. Emerald Publishing Limited. doi:10.1108/978-1-80043-968-920211016

Ozili, P. K. (2022). Circular economy and central bank digital currency. *Circular Economy and Sustainability*, *2*(4), 1501–1516. doi:10.100743615-022-00170-0 PMID:35434721

Ozili, P. K. (2023). Effect of gender equality on financial stability and financial inclusion. *Social Responsibility Journal*. doi:10.1108/SRJ-12-2022-0565

OziliP. K.ArunT. (2020). Spillover of COVID-19: impact on the Global Economy. Available at SSRN 3562570. doi:10.2139/ssrn.3562570

Sachs, J., Woo, W. T., Yoshino, N., & Taghizadeh-Hesary, F. (2019a). Importance of green finance for achieving sustainable development goals and energy security. Handbook of green finance: Energy security and sustainable development. University of California.

Sachs, J. D., Woo, W. T., Yoshino, N., & Taghizadeh-Hesary, F. (2019b). *Why Is Green Finance Important?* (ADBI Working Paper 917). ADBI.

Shaydurova, A., Panova, S., Fedosova, R., & Zlotnikova, G. (2018). Investment attractiveness of "green" financial instruments. *Journal of Reviews on Global Economics*, *7*(Special Issue), 710–715. doi:10.6000/1929-7092.2018.07.65

Şimandan, R., & Păun, C. (2021). The costs and trade-offs of green central banking: A framework for analysis. *Energies*, *14*(16), 5168. doi:10.3390/en14165168

Taghizadeh-Hesary, F., & Yoshino, N. (2019). The way to induce private participation in green finance and investment. *Finance Research Letters*, *31*, 98–103. doi:10.1016/j.frl.2019.04.016

Tu, C. A., Rasoulinezhad, E., & Sarker, T. (2020). Investigating solutions for the development of a green bond market: Evidence from analytic hierarchy process. *Finance Research Letters*, *34*, 101457. doi:10.1016/j.frl.2020.101457

Volz, U. (2017). *On the role of central banks in enhancing green finance*. UN Environment Inquiry/ CIGI Research Convening.

Wang, Y., & Zhi, Q. (2016). The role of green finance in environmental protection: Two aspects of market mechanism and policies. *Energy Procedia*, *104*, 311–316. doi:10.1016/j.egypro.2016.12.053

Chapter 15
Impact of Green Finance on Sustainability in India's Commercial Banks

Munish Gupta
https://orcid.org/0000-0002-1982-4136
Chandigarh University, India

Pawan Kumar
https://orcid.org/0000-0003-4892-6374
Chandigarh University, India

Sachin Ghai
Graphic Era University (Deemed), India

ABSTRACT

Green finance and responsible investment are gaining importance within the scope of sustainable development goals (SDGs). This chapter explores how important green finance is to improving the sustainability performance of Indian commercial banks. The study looks at how social, economic, and environmental aspects of green finance, such as green financing techniques, environmental risk management, and economic characteristics, affect sustainability performance. Information is acquired from primary sources through surveying and interviewing influential figures in the financial sectors with 392 respondents in New Delhi using a sampling (non-probabilistic) approach. The results highlight the possibility for financial institutions to promote favorable environmental outcomes while guaranteeing long-term economic viability, shedding light on the considerable impact of green finance's social, economic, and environmental components on sustainability performance.

DOI: 10.4018/979-8-3693-1388-6.ch015

INTRODUCTION

Environmental degradation and climate change are among the most pressing challenges the global community faces in the modern era. These issues have profound implications for the well-being of the planet, its ecosystems, and all living beings, including human societies. Environmental degradation is the deterioration of the environment's natural components - namely, air, water, soil, and ecosystems, due to various human activities(Singh & Singh, 2017). Throughout history, human civilizations have altered their environments to cater to their needs for food, shelter, and economic development. However, with the emergence of industrialization and technological advancements, the magnitude and intensity of human impact on the environment have accelerated dramatically. Activities such as burning fossil fuels, industrial emissions, and intensive agricultural practices have led to pollution and contributed to climate change(Smith et al., 2016). While climate change is a natural progression throughout Earth's history, the contemporary pace of change is unprecedented and predominantly caused by human conduct. The impacts of climate change are not confined to specific regions or economies; they affect the entire planet, with varying degrees of severity across different regions. Developed countries, with extensive industrialization, urbanization, and consumption, have historically been major contributors to greenhouse gas emissions. Developing countries, while often contributing less to global greenhouse gas emissions, tend to be more vulnerable to the adverse effects of climate change due to their socio-economic characteristics(Ahmed et al., 2023). Many of these nations heavily rely on climate-sensitive sectors like agriculture, fisheries, and forestry for livelihoods and economic growth.

As people become more conscious of the need to protect the planet, they demand that their financial institutions adopt environmentally responsible practices and investments. Growing public awareness of environmental issues and the rise of environmental movements and activism have pressured governments and financial institutions to take meaningful action(Tillotson et al., 2023). By integrating green finance principles, institutions responding to this demand can enhance their reputation and attract environmentally conscious customers. The United Nations' Sustainable Development Goals (SDGs) have emphasized the importance of environmental sustainability as one of the core pillars for achieving a more equitable and prosperous world by 2030(Camodeca & Almici, 2021). Other international agreements, such as the Paris Agreement, have set ambitious targets for global climate action. The agreement's objective to limit global warming well below 2 degrees Celsius and pursue efforts to limit it to 1.5 degrees Celsius has compelled countries and financial institutions to align their strategies with these goals(Sachs, 2020). Governments and financial regulators increasingly integrate environmental considerations into their policies and regulations. These measures include disclosure requirements for climate-related risks, tax incentives for green investments, or guidelines on sustainable finance practices. Investments in renewable energy, clean technologies, and sustainable infrastructure are leading to profitable ventures while contributing to environmental objectives. Financial institutions actively adopt environmentally responsible policies and incorporate environmental risk assessments into their investment decisions to promote sustainable practices.

In a world where the urgency to tackle climate change and other environmental issues is gaining widespread recognition, financial institutions are playing an ever more crucial role in advocating sustainable practices and allocating resources towards eco-friendly initiatives(George et al., 2021). The global spotlight on environmental preservation, climate change mitigation efforts, and the pursuit of the Sustainable Development Goals (SDGs) by 2030 has significantly heightened the significance of green finance. As climate change emerges as a pressing global crisis, there is an increasing sense of urgency to take immediate action to address its far-reaching impacts(Jangir et al., 2023; Rajmil et al., 2022).

India, a densely populated nation with a rapidly growing economy, faces heightened vulnerability to the repercussions of climate change due to its diverse geography and socio-economic challenges. The country is witnessing a gradual rise in average temperatures, resulting in more frequent and intense heat waves. Climate change has disrupted the traditional monsoon patterns, leading to uneven distribution of rainfall(Panda, 2016; V. Sharma, Jangir, et al., 2023). Consequently, this irregular rainfall has significant implications for agriculture, water resources, and overall food security.

India's expansive coastal geography makes it inherently vulnerable to the consequences of elevated sea levels. Coastal erosion, flooding, and saltwater intrusion into freshwater sources pose substantial threats to communities and infrastructure along the coastal regions. Acknowledging the urgency of the situation, the Indian government and various stakeholders robustly participate in global climate negotiations, contributing to global efforts in combating climate change(Behal & Gupta, 2022; Torvanger et al., 2019). The nation has pledged to reduce greenhouse gas emissions intensity, amplify renewable energy capacity, and enhance climate resilience.

To address these challenges, India has instituted a suite of multiple initiatives and policies to promote sustainable development and climate resilience. The National Action Plan on Climate Change (NAPCC), the International Solar Alliance (ISA), and the Smart Cities Mission are among the key endeavors aimed at achieving these goals(Leal-Arcas et al., 2022; Tagger & Gupta, 2020). One critical approach is the concept of green finance, which offers a viable pathway to align fiscal resources with climate-related objectives, such as reducing greenhouse gas emissions and transitioning to renewable energy modalities.

Green finance pertains to the strategic deployment of financial instruments to fund ecologically sustainable activities, including investments in renewable energy, energy efficiency, and other green technologies(Gupta et al., 2023; Zhang et al., 2022). Commercial banks in India are increasingly recognizing the importance of green finance and its role in promoting sustainable practices and environmental conservation. By integrating environmental considerations into their fiscal strategies, risk mitigation practices, and investment decisions, these banks can contribute to positive environmental outcomes while ensuring long-term economic robustness(P. Sharma et al., 2023; Zhang et al., 2022).

Adopting green finance principles enables commercial banks to align their operations with global sustainability goals and meet the rising demands of environmentally conscious customers and investors. As India strives to mitigate the impacts of climate change and foster a greener economy, the adoption of green finance practices emerges as a linchpin in paving the way for a more sustainable future(V. Sharma, Gupta, et al., 2023; Srimannarayana et al., 2023).

Commercial banks in India are issuing green bonds for raising capital exclusively for projects with positive environmental impacts, focusing on incorporating environmental risk assessment into their lending and investment decisions, publishing sustainability reports disclosing their green financing activities, and demonstrating their commitment to responsible banking, introducing a suite of green financial products offerings that include green savings accounts, green mortgages, and green investment funds that prioritize environmentally friendly projects and collaborate with environmental organizations, government agencies, and international initiatives to support green finance projects and promote sustainable development.

REVIEW OF LITERATURE

The burgeoning awareness of environmental issues, such as climate change and resource depletion, has spurred interest in the role that financial institutions, particularly commercial banks, can play in fostering sustainable development (Zheng, Siddik, Masukujjaman, & Fatema, 2021). This literature review examines the various aspects of green finance and its impact on enhancing the sustainability performance of commercial banks. Green finance is defined as financial investments flowing into sustainable development projects and initiatives, which consider both environmental and social aspects (K. H. Wang et al., 2022). (Stanković et al., 2021) elaborate on sustainability performance as a multidimensional construct, encompassing economic, environmental, and social dimensions, often summarized as the Triple Bottom Line. Organizations are accountable to multiple stakeholders, such as shareholders, employees, and the environment. Studies such as (Stanković et al., 2021) and (Pham et al., 2021) find a positive correlation between green finance initiatives and financial performance metrics like Return on Assets (ROA) and Return on Equity (ROE). Research by (Chopra & Gupta, 2023; M. Sharma & Choubey, 2022) indicates that green financial products, such as green mortgages and green bonds, contribute to increased customer loyalty and reputation enhancement for commercial banks.

The literature reveals a consensus on the importance of green finance in enhancing the sustainability performance of commercial banks. This chapter critically analyzes the influence of green finance on the sustainability performance of commercial banks operating in India. The research revealed that the integration of green finance practices can have a considerable impact on the sustainability outcomes of commercial banks. The research findings also hold significant significance for politicians and regulators. The proposal recommends the establishment of a conducive framework for green finance, which entails offering tax exemptions and additional incentives to encourage banks to embrace environmentally sustainable operations. This would help to accelerate the transition to a more sustainable financial system.

HYPOTHESES DEVELOPMENT

Economic Dimension of Green Finance and Sustainability Performance

The pecuniary facets of green financing include supporting green economic growth, gaining competitive advantages, creating economic value through environmentally friendly projects, and considering the financial implications of government policies related to climate change (Taneja et al., 2022). Green financing involves providing funds to those projects and activities that have positive environmental impacts (Lee, 2020). It supports projects that create jobs, stimulate economic activity, and contribute to both ecological and financial well-being. The governments may provide incentives, regulations, or funding that influence the financial feasibility of green projects. The provision of financial support to ecologically sustainable initiatives, such as solar and alternative energy ventures, stands to amplify the competitive prowess of banks and concurrently foster the advancement of a nation's economic landscape (V. Sharma, 2022; Udeagha & Ngepah, 2023). The economic dimension inherent in green finance is delineated as the allocation of funds to projects harmonious with environmental preservation. It contributes to various economic benefits, including the generation of more revenues, lowering overall risk, and improving the sustainability performance of commercial banks(Lekakis & Kousis, 2013). Hence, it can be argued that the banking sector should adopt sustainable banking practices to fund environmentally friendly projects and to improve its social and environmental performance of the banking sectors and to attain the aforementioned economic benefits, the banking sector should adopt sustainable banking to finance projects that are compatible with environmental conservation. Research hypotheses were formulated based on the preceding discussions.

H1. The economic dimensions positively influence the societal extent of green finance.
H2. The economic dimensions positively influence the ecological scope of green finance.
H3. The economic dimensions positively influence the commercial banks' sustainability performance.

Social Dimension of Green Finance and Sustainability Performance

Green Finance's social aspects refer to the ways in which traditional financial institutions, like banks, participate in eco-friendly or environmentally sustainable projects for the sake of broader societal gains(Y. Sun et al., 2023). Private sector interests drive the social dimension of green investment, which integrates environmental and economic considerations to alter the employment composition of a community and encourage the development of residential and mixed-use properties. Maintaining an association with sustainability and environmental responsibility can strengthen a financial institution's reputation, thereby increasing its allure for both customers and investors(Lei et al., 2023). People are more likely to trust banks that are seen as actively contributing to a better and more sustainable future. Banks that are actively involved in eco-friendly projects often use these initiatives as part of their branding and marketing strategies. This not only raises awareness about their commitment to sustainability but also attracts customers who align with these values. The goal of social sustainability is to create an equitable environment in which individuals' multifaceted needs, including social, economic, and psychological dimensions, are adequately met (Lami & Mecca, 2020). This aims to create a societal framework that not only promotes equitable access to resources and opportunities but also emphasizes the strength of social institutions and the population's psychological well-being. The ultimate goal is to build a resilient society capable of meeting current and future challenges while allowing individuals to reach their full potential(Seddon et al., 2021). Social sustainability assesses how a company's business processes affect society and rural development(Seddon et al., 2021). Conversely, a company's social performance encompasses its interactions with the communities in which it operates(Barauskaite & Streimikiene, 2021), including aspects such as employee relationships, safety, and health measures, adequate wages to cover living expenses, non-discriminatory practices, employee turnover, education, and career advancement opportunities, among others. Research hypotheses were formulated based on the preceding discussions.

H4. The social dimension positively influences the commercial banks' sustainability performance.
H5. The social dimensions positively influence the environmental dimensions of green finance.

Environmental Dimension of Green Finance and Sustainability Performance

The environmental dimension of green finance is crucial in steering global capital towards sustainable projects and practices. Green finance prioritizes the funding of environmentally beneficial projects. This includes renewable energy ventures, waste management solutions, water conservation systems, and more(G. D. Sharma et al., 2022). These projects aim to reduce carbon footprints and environmental degradation and positively influence sustainability performance. With the rise of green finance, there's been an increased demand for transparency in environmental reporting(Al Hawaj & Buallay, 2022). Companies are expected to disclose their environmental, social, and governance (ESG) performance. Such transparency can drive better sustainability performance as companies are held accountable by stakeholders. As more investors seek to align their portfolios with sustainable objectives, there's a marked shift away from polluting and unsustainable industries towards greener alternatives(Och, 2020). Green finance often emphasizes stakeholder engagement. As financial institutions become more focused on sustainability, they engage with companies in their portfolios to drive better environmental practices, thus influencing sustainability performance at the operational level(Weston & Nnadi, 2023). By promoting environmentally sustainable projects and practices, green finance plays a role in creating more resilient communities and economies(S. Wang et al., 2022). This means reduced vulnerability to climate-related risks and other environmental disruptions.

H6. The environmental dimension positively influences commercial banks' sustainability performance.

Figure 1. Conceptual framework of study
Source: Author's Compilation

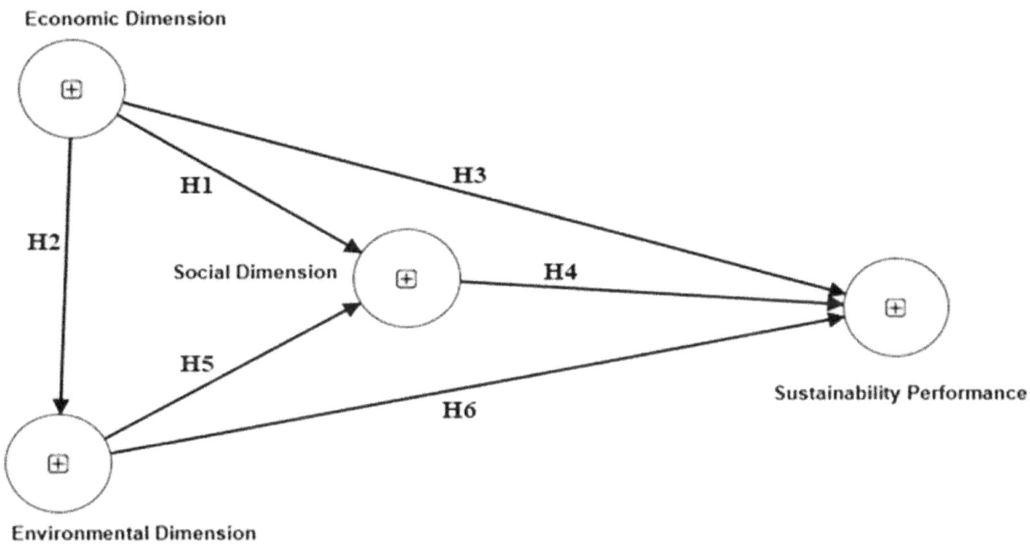

METHODOLOGY

Measures and Study Design

The objective of this study is to assess the fundamental elements of green finance and their influence on the sustainability outcomes of banks that primarily cater to commercial activities in India, with a specific focus on the city of New Delhi. This study is predicated on an extensive examination of 392 collections of primary survey data in New Delhi, which were obtained through surveys and interviews conducted with important stakeholders in the financial sectors. The poll utilized a Likert scale consisting of seven points to assess the opinions of the participants. The scale ranged from '1' indicating strong disagreement, to '7' representing strong agreement. The data collection period extended from March to June 2023 and focused on a self-administered questionnaire of 12 statements classified into four separate categories, as presented in Table 2. The validity and reliability of the questionnaire were assessed by a preliminary pilot research that included a sample of 90 individuals. The obtained Cronbach's alpha coefficient of 0.843 indicated a substantial level of reliability for the questionnaire. The coefficient in question serves to highlight the degree of internal consistency exhibited by the questions within the questionnaire with respect to their ability to measure the desired constructs accurately. The Smart PLS 4-variate-based partial least squares approach (PLS-SEM) was chosen as the analytical strategy for this study. The nonparametric structural modeling technique known as Partial Least Squares Structural Equation Modeling, as proposed by (Fornell & Larcker, 1981), was chosen due to its capacity to examine causal links by integrating both quantitative data and qualitative causal assumptions. This methodology facilitates the evaluation of the hypotheses formulated for the study. The objective of this study is to improve the understanding of the connections between various elements of green finance and the sustainability outcomes of banks focused on commerce in the Indian setting. The foundational elements of Green Finance, specifically the financial, societal, and environmental dimensions, have been derived from prior scholarly investigations. A survey instrument consisting of separate components was utilized to assess the elements mentioned above and measure the sustainability performance of commercial banks in India.

Table 1 provides a comprehensive overview of the participant's demographic characteristics. The data revealed that 81.1% of the respondents identified as males, whereas 18.9% identified as females. In terms of age distribution, the study found that 51.0% of the participants were categorized as middle-aged, and a smaller fraction, specifically 7.3%, were aged above 50. This indicates that a significant proportion of banking professionals in India can be classified as middle-aged. Turning to the educational backgrounds of respondents, the analysis indicated that 1.6% of the respondents held a doctorate, while the majority, accounting for 60.5%, possessed master's degrees. Additionally, 32.5% held undergraduate degrees, and a minor proportion, comprising 5.4%, held Secondary Higher Education Certificates. Notably, the empirical findings highlighted a positive correlation between higher levels of educational attainment and a greater willingness to adopt the principles of green banking and green financing.

Regarding work experience, 58.3% of the respondents reported having more than six years of professional experience. A further 20.9% indicated a tenure of three to six years, while the remaining 20.8% had less than three years of experience. This distribution of work experience indicates a considerable level of industry knowledge and exposure among the surveyed bankers. Considering the income levels, the research showed that 65.9% of the bankers earned a monthly income ranging between Rs. 40,001 and Rs. 50,000. Furthermore, 18.2% fell within the income bracket of Rs. 30,001 to Rs. 40,000. The collective data portrays a consistent pattern where the income per month on average for those surveyed is positioned between Rs. 40,000 and Rs. 50,000 per month.

Measures and Study Design

"The study aimed to examine the relationship between green finance and the sustainability performance of banks in India. Green finance refers to the financial activities that support the environmental improvement of projects or businesses. Sustainability performance measures how well an organization balances its economic, social, and environmental impacts. The researchers developed a questionnaire based on previous literature that identified three dimensions of green finance: social, economic, and environmental.

Each dimension had a section in the questionnaire with several items that asked the respondents to rate their agreement or disagreement with statements related to that dimension on a seven-point Likert scale. The questionnaire also included a section on bank sustainability, with nine items using the same scale.

Table 1. Descriptive analysis

Variable	Description	Frequency	Percentage (%)
Gender	Male	318	81.1
	Female	74	18.9
Age in Years	18-25	19	4.8
	25-30	83	21.2
	31-40	200	51.0
	41-50	54	15.7
	51 and Above	29	7.3
Educational Qualification	Secondary higher education	21	5.4
	Undergraduate Degree	127	32.5
	Master's degree	237	60.5
	PhD	6	1.6
Working experience	Less than one year	13	3.2
	"1–3 years" (mdpi.com)	69	17.6
	"3–6 years" (mdpi.com)	82	20.9
	Above six years	229	58.3
Monthly income (amount in INR)	Upto 20,000	25	6.4
	20,001–30,000	32	8.2
	30,001–40,000	71	18.2
	40,001–50,000	258	65.9
	50,001 and above	5	1.3

Source: Author's Compilation

In addition, survey participants were asked to rate the contribution of green financing in the expansion of India's banking industry using a series of yes/no questions. Table 3 summarizes the key features of green finance and their impact on long-term success. A pilot examination of 90 people confirmed the questionnaire's consistency and dependability, as evidenced by a Cronbach's alpha value of 0.823. A partial least squares structural equation model (PLS-SEM) with four independent variables was used to test and validate the hypotheses. As proposed by Fornell and Larcker (981), this nonparametric method for structural modeling combines qualitative assumptions about causality with quantitative data. The adoption of PLS was further justified by the non-normal distribution of some data points, as proven by the Kolmogorov-Smirnov test, and Smart PLS's capacity to handle data regardless of distribution. According to research from (Ghasemy et al., 2020), PLS-SEM is an appropriate technique for studying causal linkages in the setting of social and behavioral sciences. As a consequence, Smart PLS 4 was used to investigate the correlations between the variables in the theoretical framework.

Table 2. Measurement model

Item	Definition	Source
EcoD1	Developing a stronger edge over rivals	(Zahir Raihan, 2019; Zheng, Siddik, Masukujjaman, Fatema, et al., 2021)
EcoD2	Enhanced fiscal contribution to the governmental treasury	
EcoD3	Creation of supplementary economic value (economic value added)	
SD1	Improvement of the bank's reputation	(Neruja & Arulrajah, 2021; Zheng, Siddik, Masukujjaman, Fatema, et al., 2021)
SD2	Stakeholder involvement strategies	
SD3	Increased employee benefits provision	
EnvD1	Energy consumption of goods and amenities	(Zheng, Sidiki, Masukujjaman, Fatema, et al., 2021)
EnvD2	Energy utilization outside the organization	
EnvD3	Decrease in carbon secretions from funding events.	
SP1	Green support suggestively increases our bank's proceeds and market share.	(Khan & Quaddus, 2015; Zahir Raihan, 2019)
SP2	Green financing has helped our bank save a lot of paper and energy.	
SP3	Green financing substantially reduces our bank's operational spending.	

Source: Author's Compilation

RESULTS

Measurement Model Assessment

The analytical framework employed a measurement model to scrutinize convergent validity, as delineated in Table 3, in addition to discriminant legitimacy and core consistency reliability, presented in Table 4. The reliability of the indicators for each construct was validated using Cronbach's alpha and composite reliability metrics. According to established guidelines by Hair et al. (2014), Average Variance Extracted (AVE) values exceeding 0.50 were interpreted as evidence of satisfactory convergent validity across all constructs. Our findings corroborate that the constructs account for a minimum variance of 51% in their corresponding indicators(Henseler et al., 2015).

Moreover, Cronbach's alpha and composite reliability metrics for each construct surpassed the threshold value of 0.70, as recommended by (Hair et al., 2014)and (Nunnally, 1978), thereby affirming a high degree of reliability. "Particularly noteworthy is the elevated Cronbach's alpha values—exceeding 0.90—for constructs such as EcoD, EnvD, SD, and SP. These elevated values underscore a robust inter-item correlation within each variable, signifying that the items cohesively measure congruent facets of the respective constructs. This internal coherence amplifies the overarching reliability and internal consistency of the variables in question.

Results are comprehensively outlined in Table 5 for the evaluation of discriminant validity. Discriminant validity was assessed by employing the HTMT ratio (Hair et al., 2019)with the resulting ratios falling below the 0.85 benchmark. Additionally, the Fornell-Larcker criterion was invoked to validate further discriminant validity, wherein AVE values were juxtaposed against squared correlation coefficients between pertinent factors. Our analysis substantiated that the AVE values for each construct surpassed their relevant correlation coefficients, thereby affirming discriminant validity.

Table 3. Factor loadings

	Outer loading			
	Economic Dimension	**Environmental Dimension**	**Social Dimension**	**Sustainability Performance**
EcoD1	0.958			
EcoD2	0.967			
EcoD3	0.953			
EnvD1		0.976		
EnvD2		0.974		
EnvD3		0.972		
SD1			0.974	
SD2			0.973	
SD3			0.966	
SP1				0.971
SP2				0.973
SP3				0.918

Source: Author's Compilation

Table 4. Construct validity and reliability

Construct Reliability & Validity	Cronbach's alpha	Composite reliability (rho_a)	Average variance extracted (AVE)
Economic Dimension	0.957	0.958	0.92
Environmental Dimension	0.973	0.973	0.949
Social Dimension	0.969	0.969	0.942
Sustainability Performance	0.951	0.956	0.911

Structural Model Assessment

The study's structural model is illustrated in Figure 2, showing the relationships between various factors and constructs. Table 7 reveals that green finance positively influences sustainability performance within India's banking sector. Specifically, the economic dimension of green finance, referred to as EcoD, has a significant positive impact on both sustainable development (SD) (H1: $\beta = 0.277$, $p < 0.05$) and environmental development (EnvD) (H2: $\beta = 0.703$, $p < 0.05$). Additionally, EcoD's impact on sustainability performance (SP) is statistically significant and positive (H3: $\beta = 0.204$, $p > 0.05$). Likewise, the SD dimension significantly boosts SP (H4: $\beta = 0.28$, $p < 0.05$), and the EnvD dimension enhances SD (H5: $\beta = 0.47$, $p < 0.05$). Finally, EnvD also positively impacts SP (H6: $\beta = 0.47$, $p < 0.05$). The result shows that all three dimensions of green finance—social, economic, and environmental—contribute positively and significantly to the sustainability performance of banks in India.

Table 5. Discriminant validity

	Economic Dimension	Environmental Dimension	Social Dimension	Sustainability Performance
	HTMT Ratio			
Economic Dimension				
Environmental Dimension	0.728			
Social Dimension	0.653	0.717		
Sustainability Performance	0.745	0.838	0.762	
	Fornell–Lacker Criterion			
Economic Dimension	0.959			
Environmental Dimension	0.703	0.974		
Social Dimension	0.630	0.696	0.971	
Sustainability Performance	0.710	0.807	0.735	0.954

Source: Author's Computation via Smart PLS

Table 6. Evaluation of the structural framework

	Path Coefficient	β	M	STDEV	t-Statistics	*p*-Values
H1	EcoD → SD	0.277	0.291	0.085	3.244	0.001*
H2	EcoD → EnvD	0.703	0.704	0.053	13.289	0.000*
H3	EcoD → SP	0.204	0.203	0.042	4.855	0.000*
H4	SD → SP	0.28	0.276	0.074	3.785	0.000*
H5	EnvD → SD	0.501	0.488	0.091	5.524	0.000*
H6	EnvD → SP	0.47	0.474	0.07	6.715	0.000*

Source: Author's Computation via Smart PLS

DISCUSSION AND CONCLUSION

The main objective of this chapter is to scrutinize the various dimensions of green finance and their impact on the sustainability practices of commercial banks in India. Over the long term, enhanced sustainability performance can yield manifold benefits for a bank, including bolstering its reputation, boosting profitability, and contributing to overall stability. To understand how these green finance dimensions affect the sustainability performance of Indian commercial banks, we gathered first-hand information from industry experts. Structural equation modeling (SEM) was strategically used to examine the connections between the relevant factors. Using structural equation modeling (SEM), we can examine intricate hypotheses concerning the interconnected effects of many different factors. We also employed descriptive statistics, growth rate analysis, and visual depictions to give you a full picture of green financing in the commercial banking industry today.

Figure 2. A framework for the green finance dimensions impact on sustainability performance
Source: Author's Computation via Smart PLS

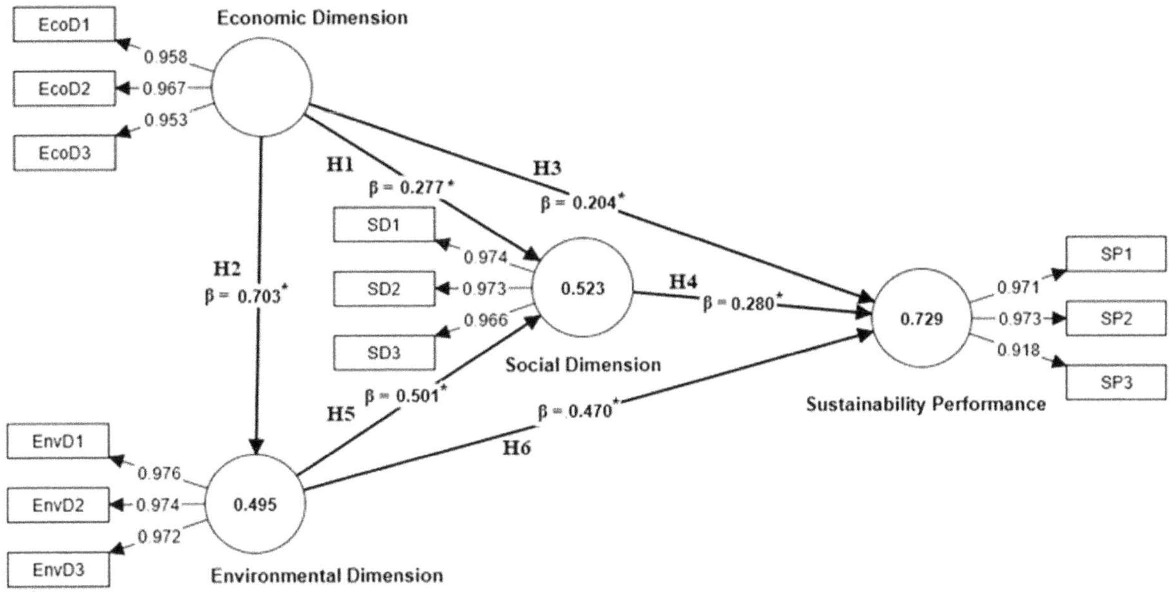

By providing empirical evidence in support of several hypotheses related to the dimensions of green finance and the sustainability performance of banks, this study integrates the existing literature. The first hypothesis (H1) is supported by the data, which demonstrates a positive and statistically significant connection between the economic aspect of green finance and its social dimension. Economic gains from investing in environmentally friendly projects are positively correlated with social gains like better stakeholder relations, customer loyalty, employee satisfaction, and corporate social responsibility, according to this finding. A theory by (Zhou et al., 2022) proclaims the economic component of green finance positively and significantly affects the environmental component. Financial incentives for investing in environmentally beneficial initiatives could lead to a variety of positive environmental results, including less carbon emissions, increased energy efficiency, better waste management, and the preservation of biodiversity. These results show the interdependence between the three pillars of green finance—social, economic, and environmental—and the Sustainable Development Goals (SDGs), which are frequently used by banks and other financial institutions to measure their sustainability performance. These results are in line with earlier research in this field and demonstrate the usefulness of these green finance dimensions for banks and other financial institutions seeking to enhance their sustainability performance by investing in initiatives that benefit the environment both financially and non-financially (Guang-Wen & Siddik, 2022). H3 is supported by the finding that there is a positive correlation between the economics of green finance and banks' sustainability performance. This point of view contends that the economic factor, which has a significant impact on how well banks perform in terms of sustainability and is linked to the social and environmental aspects of green financing, is a crucial quality for businesses. By supporting green initiatives, financial institutions like banks can boost their market share and competitiveness, which has an effect on the economy(H. Sun et al., 2020). Additionally, we find evidence supporting H4, demonstrating that the social dimension of green finance does, in fact, influence banks' sustainability performance for the better. As a result, the bank's reputation improves, trust is established, stakeholder engagement is facilitated, customer satisfaction is raised, employee perks are provided, and the bank's overall sustainability performance improves. When banks and other financial institutions invest in environmentally friendly projects, they demonstrate social responsibility and ethical values; this is good for the institutions' reputations and draws customers(Park & Kim, 2020). We also find substantial support for H5, as the research demonstrates a positive correlation between the social and environmental dimensions of green finance in the context of commercial banks in India. This is in line with previous research (Rabbanee et al., 2022)emphasizing the importance of the social dimension in resolving environmental problems, such as carbon emissions and energy consumption, within and outside of organizations. Financial institutions can cultivate a culture of environmental stewardship and innovation if their employees are encouraged to invest in projects that benefit society on a social level. H6 is also supported by the data, showing that the environmental aspect of green finance has a significant impact on the sustainability performance of banks by encouraging them to finance environmentally beneficial projects. This result is consistent with the study conducted by (Ning et al., 2023), which highlighted the direct impact of environmental factors on the sustainability performance of the Sri Lankan banking sector. Financial institutions can benefit from investing in environmentally friendly projects to mitigate environmental risks and costs, which is reflected in the environmental dimension.

The research underscores the interconnectedness and significance of the social, economic, and environmental dimensions of green finance in shaping the sustainability performance of commercial banks in India. These findings provide valuable insights for banks and financial institutions, emphasizing the importance of environmentally friendly investments in improving their sustainability performance.

LIMITATIONS AND FUTURE SCOPE OF THE STUDY

The present study offers valuable empirical insights, but it also comes with a number of limitations that must be acknowledged for a well-rounded understanding of its findings. The first limitation is the study's focus solely on commercial banks within the Indian context. By concentrating only on this specific financial sector, the study inadvertently excludes non-banking financial companies (NBFCs) from the scope of its analysis. NBFCs are crucial to India's financial ecosystem, often serving as complementary or alternative options to banks. Their omission from the study may overlook the contributions, challenges, or opportunities they might offer in terms of green financing and sustainability. Secondly, the study relies on primary data that captures the views of bankers regarding green financing and sustainability performance. While this offers an internal perspective on these issues, it lacks the breadth that could be provided by incorporating views from other stakeholders, such as clients or owners of the financial institutions. Their perspectives may offer a different but equally vital lens through which to assess the effectiveness of green financing initiatives and their impact on overall sustainability. A related concern is that the bankers themselves might not be fully informed on the intricate details of green financing, which is a relatively specialized and rapidly evolving field. Consequently, their opinions may be limited, skewed, or even incorrect. This can compromise the reliability of the data and, subsequently, the conclusions that are drawn from it. Lastly, the study's findings are simplified to fit the specific context of the banking industry, limiting the generalizability of its results to other sectors. Given that banks are just one part of a broader financial and industrial landscape, this limitation is noteworthy. Banks do have a role to play in reducing environmental pollution through green financing, but their strategies and performance can't be considered in isolation from the wider ecosystem. Given these limitations, future research endeavors could broaden the scope by including diverse financial institutions like NBFCs and by sourcing data from various stakeholders like clients and owners. This could provide a more holistic view of green financing initiatives. Additionally, future studies could delve deeper into the specific factors that influence the success of green financing and how it impacts organizational profitability.

REFERENCES

Ahmed, M., Shuai, C., & Ahmed, M. (2023). Analysis of energy consumption and greenhouse gas emissions trend in China, India, the USA, and Russia. *International Journal of Environmental Science and Technology*, *20*(3), 2683–2698. doi:10.100713762-022-04159-y

Al Hawaj, A. Y., & Buallay, A. M. (2022). A worldwide sectorial analysis of sustainability reporting and its impact on firm performance. *Journal of Sustainable Finance & Investment*, *12*(1), 62–86. doi: 10.1080/20430795.2021.1903792

Barauskaite, G., & Streimikiene, D. (2021). Corporate social responsibility and financial performance of companies: The puzzle of concepts, definitions and assessment methods. *Corporate Social Responsibility and Environmental Management*, *28*(1), 278–287. doi:10.1002/csr.2048

Behal, V., & Gupta, M. (2022). Reporting of Corporate Social Responsibility Practices: An Evidence from Indian BSE-Listed Companies. *Prabandhan: Indian Journal of Management*, *15*(3), 42–58. doi:10.17010/pijom/2022/v15i3/165633

Camodeca, R., & Almici, A. (2021). Digital Transformation and Convergence toward the 2030 Agenda's Sustainability Development Goals: Evidence from Italian Listed Firms. *Sustainability 2021, 13*(21), 11831. doi:10.3390/su132111831

Chopra, P., & Gupta, M. (2023). Fuzzy Logic and ANN in an Artificial Intelligent Cloud: A Comparative Study. In *Intelligent Communication Technologies and Virtual Mobile Networks* (pp. 559–570). Springer Nature Singapore Singapore. doi:10.1007/978-981-99-1767-9_41

Fornell, C., & Larcker, D. F. (1981). *Structural equation models with unobservable variables and measurement error: Algebra and statistics*. Sage Publications Sage CA.

George, G., Merrill, R. K., & Schillebeeckx, S. J. D. (2021). Digital Sustainability and Entrepreneurship: How Digital Innovations Are Helping Tackle Climate Change and Sustainable Development. *Entrepreneurship Theory and Practice*, *45*(5), 999–1027. doi:10.1177/1042258719899425

Ghasemy, M., Teeroovengadum, V., Becker, J. M., & Ringle, C. M. (2020). This fast car can move faster: a review of PLS-SEM application in higher education research. *Higher Education 2020 80:6, 80*(6), 1121–1152. doi:10.1007/s10734-020-00534-1

Guang-Wen, Z., & Siddik, A. B. (2022). Do Corporate Social Responsibility Practices and Green Finance Dimensions Determine Environmental Performance? An Empirical Study on Bangladeshi Banking Institutions. *Frontiers in Environmental Science*, *10*, 890096. doi:10.3389/fenvs.2022.890096

Gupta, M., Taneja, S., Sharma, V., Singh, A., Rupeika-Apoga, R., & Jangir, K. (2023). Does Previous Experience with the Unified Payments Interface (UPI) Affect the Usage of Central Bank Digital Currency (CBDC)? *Journal of Risk and Financial Management*, *16*(6), 286. doi:10.3390/jrfm16060286

Hair, J. F., Risher, J. J., Sarstedt, M., & Ringle, C. M. (2019). When to use and how to report the results of PLS-SEM. *European Business Review*, *31*(1), 2–24. doi:10.1108/EBR-11-2018-0203

Hair, J. F., Sarstedt, M., Hopkins, L., & Kuppelwieser, V. G. (2014). Partial least squares structural equation modeling (PLS-SEM): An emerging tool in business research. *European Business Review*, *26*(2), 106–121. doi:10.1108/EBR-10-2013-0128

Henseler, J., Ringle, C. M., & Sarstedt, M. (2015). A new criterion for assessing discriminant validity in variance-based structural equation modeling. *Journal of the Academy of Marketing Science*, *43*(1), 115–135. doi:10.100711747-014-0403-8

Jangir, K., Sharma, V., Taneja, S., & Rupeika-Apoga, R. (2023). The Moderating Effect of Perceived Risk on Users' Continuance Intention for FinTech Services. *Journal of Risk and Financial Management*, *16*(1), 21. doi:10.3390/jrfm16010021

Khan, E. A., & Quaddus, M. (2015). Development and Validation of a Scale for Measuring Sustainability Factors of Informal Microenterprises – A Qualitative and Quantitative Approach. *Entrepreneurship Research Journal*, *5*(4), 347–372. doi:10.1515/erj-2014-0017

Lami, I. M., & Mecca, B. (2020). Assessing Social Sustainability for Achieving Sustainable Architecture. *Sustainability 2021, 13*(1), 142. doi:10.3390/su13010142

Leal-Arcas, R., Al Zarkani, M., Jbara, L., Margaritidou, M., & Mubwana, R. M. (2022). The BRIC and Climate Change Mitigation. *International Trade and Sustainability: Perspectives from Developing and Developed Countries*, 229–280. https://doi.org/ doi:10.1007/978-3-031-14068-6_6/COVER

Lee, J. W. (2020). Green Finance and Sustainable Development Goals: The Case of China. *Journal of Asian Finance. Economics and Business*, *7*(7), 577–586. doi:10.13106/jafeb.2020.vol7.no7.577

Lei, N., Miao, Q., & Yao, X. (2023). Does the implementation of green credit policy improve the ESG performance of enterprises? Evidence from a quasi-natural experiment in China. *Economic Modelling*, *127*, 106478. doi:10.1016/j.econmod.2023.106478

Lekakis, J. N., & Kousis, M. (2013). Economic Crisis, Troika and the Environment in Greece. *South European Society & Politics*, *18*(3), 305–331. doi:10.1080/13608746.2013.799731

Neruja, S., & Arulrajah, A. A. (2021). The Impact of Environmental Knowledge and Awareness on Sustainability Performance of Organizations: The Mediating Role of Employee Green Behaviour. *International Business Research*, *14*(9), 1–68. https://ideas.repec.org/a/ibn/ibrjnl/v14y2021i9p68.html

Ning, Y., Cherian, J., Sial, M. S., Álvarez-Otero, S., Comite, U., & Zia-Ud-Din, M. (2023). Green bond as a new determinant of sustainable green financing, energy efficiency investment, and economic growth: A global perspective. *Environmental Science and Pollution Research International*, *30*(22), 61324–61339. doi:10.100711356-021-18454-7 PMID:34993809

Nunnally, J. C. (1978). An Overview of Psychological Measurement. *Clinical Diagnosis of Mental Disorders*, 97–146. doi:10.1007/978-1-4684-2490-4_4

Och, M. (2020). Sustainable Finance and the EU Taxonomy Regulation – Hype or Hope? SSRN *Electronic Journal*. https://doi.org/ doi:10.2139/SSRN.3738255

Panda, A. (2016). Exploring climate change perceptions, rainfall trends and perceived barriers to adaptation in a drought affected region in India. *Natural Hazards*, *84*(2), 777–796. doi:10.100711069-016-2456-0

Park, H., & Kim, J. D. (2020). Transition towards green banking: role of financial regulators and financial institutions. *Asian Journal of Sustainability and Social Responsibility*, *5*(1), 1–25. doi:10.1186/s41180-020-00034-3

Pham, D. C., Do, T. N. A., Doan, T. N., Nguyen, T. X. H., & Pham, T. K. Y. (2021). The impact of sustainability practices on financial performance: Empirical evidence from Sweden. *Cogent Business & Management*, *8*(1), 1912526. doi:10.1080/23311975.2021.1912526

Rabbanee, K., Hassan, K., Taufique, M. R., Shafiullah, G. M., Dewan, A., Dai, X., Siddik, A. B., & Tian, H. (2022). Corporate Social Responsibility, Green Finance and Environmental Performance: Does Green Innovation Matter? *Sustainability*, *14*(20), 13607. doi:10.3390/su142013607

Raihan, Z. Dr. M. (2019). *Sustainable Finance For Growth And Development Of Banking Industry In Bangladesh: An Equity Perspective*. DSpace. http://dspace.mist.ac.bd:8080/xmlui/handle/123456789/496

Rajmil, D., Morales, L., Aira, T., & Cardona Valles, M. (2022). Afghanistan: A Multidimensional Crisis. *Peace Review*, *34*(1), 41–50. doi:10.1080/10402659.2022.2023428

Sachs, N. M. (2020). The Paris agreement in the 2020s: Breakdown or breakup. *Ecology Law Quarterly*, *46*(3), 865–909. doi:10.15779/Z38H708140

Seddon, N., Smith, A., Smith, P., Key, I., Chausson, A., Girardin, C., House, J., Srivastava, S., & Turner, B. (2021). Getting the message right on nature-based solutions to climate change. *Global Change Biology*, *27*(8), 1518–1546. doi:10.1111/gcb.15513 PMID:33522071

Sharma, G. D., Verma, M., Shahbaz, M., Gupta, M., & Chopra, R. (2022). Transitioning green finance from theory to practice for renewable energy development. *Renewable Energy*, *195*, 554–565. doi:10.1016/j.renene.2022.06.041

Sharma, M., & Choubey, A. (2022). Green banking initiatives: A qualitative study on Indian banking sector. *Environment, Development and Sustainability*, *24*(1), 293–319. doi:10.100710668-021-01426-9 PMID:33967597

Sharma, P., Sharma, V., Jangir, K., Gupta, M., & Pathak, N. (2023). Unfolding the Emerging Trends in Non-performing Assets with Special Reference to the Energy Sector in Banking Industry. *Renewable Energy Optimization, Planning and Control: Proceedings of ICRTE 2022*, (pp. 411–422). IEEE.

Sharma, V. (2022). A Pragmatic Study on Management with Autocratic Approach and Consequential Impact on Profitability of the Organization. *Lecture Notes in Electrical Engineering*, *860*, 121–130. doi:10.1007/978-981-16-9488-2_10

Sharma, V., Gupta, M., Jangir, K., Chopra, P., & Pathak, N. (2023). The Impact of Post-Use Consumer Satisfaction on Smart Wearables Repurchase Intention in the Context of AI-Based Healthcare Information. In *Enhancing Customer Engagement Through Location-Based Marketing* (pp. 77–101). IGI Global. doi:10.4018/978-1-6684-8177-6.ch007

Sharma, V., Jangir, K., Chowhan, S. S., & Pathak, N. (2023). *Key Factors Influencing Electric Vehicle Purchase Decisions by Consumers: An Empirical Study of Indian Consumers*. 449–464. doi:10.1007/978-981-19-8963-6_40

Singh, R. L., & Singh, P. K. (2017). Global Environmental Problems. *Principles and Applications of Environmental Biotechnology for a Sustainable Future*, 13–41. doi:10.1007/978-981-10-1866-4_2

Smith, P., House, J. I., Bustamante, M., Sobocká, J., Harper, R., Pan, G., West, P. C., Clark, J. M., Adhya, T., Rumpel, C., Paustian, K., Kuikman, P., Cotrufo, M. F., Elliott, J. A., Mcdowell, R., Griffiths, R. I., Asakawa, S., Bondeau, A., Jain, A. K., & Pugh, T. A. M. (2016). Global change pressures on soils from land use and management. *Global Change Biology*, *22*(3), 1008–1028. doi:10.1111/gcb.13068 PMID:26301476

Srimannarayana, G., Lakshmi, V. V., Dondapati, A. S., Ratnakar, T., Dhanunjay, P., & Satyanarayana, P. (2023). Legal Blueprint For Clean Air: The Air (Prevention And Control Of Pollution) Act, 1981 In India. *Journal of Namibian Studies : History Politics Culture*, *35*, 691–712. doi:10.59670/JNS.V35I.3565

Stanković, J. J., Marjanović, I., Papathanasiou, J., & Drezgić, S. (2021). Social, Economic and Environmental Sustainability of Port Regions: MCDM Approach in Composite Index Creation. *Journal of Marine Science and Engineering 2021, 9*(1), 74. doi:10.3390/jmse9010074

Sun, H., Rabbani, M. R., Ahmad, N., Sial, M. S., Guping, C., Zia-Ud-din, M., & Fu, Q. (2020). CSR, Co-Creation and Green Consumer Loyalty: Are Green Banking Initiatives Important? A Moderated Mediation Approach from an Emerging Economy. *Sustainability, 12*(24), 10688. doi:10.3390/su122410688

Sun, Y., Guan, W., Jiang, H., & Yang, J. (2023). How does green economic recovery impact social and financial performance? *Economic Change and Restructuring*, *56*(2), 859–878. doi:10.100710644-022-09453-w

Tagger, S. S., & Gupta, M. (2020). A study of the relationship between total quality management and business performance in the banking sector. *International Journal of Business Competition and Growth*, *7*(2), 118. doi:10.1504/IJBCG.2020.111943

Taneja, S., Kaur, S., & Özen, E. (2022). Using green finance to promote global growth in a sustainable way. *International Journal of Green Economics*, *16*(3), 246. doi:10.1504/IJGE.2022.128930

Tillotson, P., Slade, R., Staffell, I., & Halttunen, K. (2023). Deactivating climate activism? The seven strategies oil and gas majors use to counter rising shareholder action. *Energy Research & Social Science*, *103*, 103190. doi:10.1016/j.erss.2023.103190

Torvanger, A., Dejonckheere, S., Singh, T., & Pruthi, A. (2019). The state of tracking financial flows under the Paris Agreement - A primer for policy makers in India. *22*. https://pub.cicero.oslo.no/cicero-xmlui/handle/11250/2618660

Udeagha, M. C., & Ngepah, N. (2023). The drivers of environmental sustainability in BRICS economies: Do green finance and fintech matter? *World Development Sustainability*, *3*, 100096. doi:10.1016/j.wds.2023.100096

Wang, K. H., Zhao, Y. X., Jiang, C. F., & Li, Z. Z. (2022). Does green finance inspire sustainable development? Evidence from a global perspective. *Economic Analysis and Policy*, *75*, 412–426. doi:10.1016/j.eap.2022.06.002

Wang, S., Sun, L., & Iqbal, S. (2022). Green financing role on renewable energy dependence and energy transition in E7 economies. *Renewable Energy*, *200*, 1561–1572. doi:10.1016/j.renene.2022.10.067

Weston, P., & Nnadi, M. (2023). Evaluation of strategic and financial variables of corporate sustainability and ESG policies on corporate finance performance. *Journal of Sustainable Finance & Investment*, *13*(2), 1058–1074. Advance online publication. doi:10.1080/20430795.2021.1883984

Zhang, X., Wang, Z., Zhong, X., Yang, S., & Siddik, A. B. (2022). Do Green Banking Activities Improve the Banks' Environmental Performance? The Mediating Effect of Green Financing. *Sustainability 2022*, *14*(2), 989. doi:10.3390/su14020989

Zheng, G. W., Siddik, A. B., Masukujjaman, M., & Fatema, N. (2021). Factors Affecting the Sustainability Performance of Financial Institutions in Bangladesh: The Role of Green Finance. *Sustainability 2021*, *13*(18), 10165. doi:10.3390/su131810165

Zheng, G. W., Siddik, A. B., Masukujjaman, M., Fatema, N., & Alam, S. S. (2021). Green Finance Development in Bangladesh: The Role of Private Commercial Banks (PCBs). *Sustainability 2021*, *13*(2), 795. doi:10.3390/su13020795

Zhou, G., Zhu, J., & Luo, S. (2022). The impact of fintech innovation on green growth in China: Mediating effect of green finance. *Ecological Economics*, *193*, 107308. doi:10.1016/j.ecolecon.2021.107308

Chapter 16
Achieving Sustainable Investment Practices Through Green Finance:
Challenges and Opportunities

Mohammad Kashif
https://orcid.org/0000-0002-4940-8264
Graphic Era University (Deemed), India

Syed Noorul Shajar
https://orcid.org/0000-0002-0042-0190
Vellore Institute of Technology, India

Nikita Singhal
https://orcid.org/0000-0002-0700-8086
IIMT University, Meerut, India

Puneet Kumar
IIMT University, Meerut, India

ABSTRACT

There is a positive trend in the substantial extension of green credit tools. These include climate bonds and numerous universal establishments. Although challenges are posed, there are numerous opportunities in this field. The environmental protection industry demands substantial upfront investment capital and often involves a lengthy payback period, necessitating a unique financing approach. Green finance policies can address government financing challenges through financial innovation and reform. Green bond issuance initially gained traction in Europe, but more communal and individual concerns in Asia are now adopting such device to support their unceasing growth objectives. The present chapter highlights challenges faced by sustainable investment practices through green finance and opportunities available globally for this particular area.

DOI: 10.4018/979-8-3693-1388-6.ch016

1. INTRODUCTION

Green finance represents the convergence of financial and business sectors with environmentally responsible practices, involving a diverse range of stakeholders, including individual and corporate consumers, manufacturers, investors, and financial institutions (Olubunmi et al., 2016; Sarangi, 2019; Zheng et al., 2021). The motivations for participating in green finance can vary, encompassing financial incentives, a commitment to environmental preservation, Unlike Historical commercial undertakings, sustainable economics gives greater importance to biological interests & atmosphere conservation gives priority to industry (Gabay et al., 2014; Ojo-Fafore et al., 2018).

Eco-efficiency is poised to have an additional significant role in navigating sustainable and high-quality economic growth. While India has made efforts to promote power preservation, hygiene development, reverse logistics, and sustainable utilization in recent years, it faces substantial challenges (Lee et al., 2020). The expensive costs of biodegradable items, often resulting from a lack of revolution in eco mechanism, have caused to heavy reliance on government subsidies for renewable energy. Substantial innovation in green technologies is necessary to achieve value advantages on non-atmosphere friendly profitable schemes (Berry & Junkus, 2013; Oguntuase & Windapo, 2021).

The global goal of achieving barometrical impartiality is energetic and necessitates consistent government policies, collaboration among state zone and economic ownership, & promoting from natives to combat global heating. It also involves shifting funds from excessive coal contributions to nil graphite & ecological acceptable design, which will require various forms of innovation, including financial products. The greening of funds is critical, with executives working on procedures to redirect investments from high-coal to zero coal schemes. Extensive assets are required for weather acclimatization, necessitating collaboration between executive & the investment zone (Darko et al., 2017).

One positive trend in the infrastructure resources business is the substantial extension of green credit tools. These include climate bonds and numerous universal establishments. Although the challenges posed by COVID-19, global green bond issuance reached USD 522 billion by the end of 2021, there is a 9% increase every year. In 2020, the majority of green bond issues were allocated to the Energy, Buildings, and Transport sectors, making up 85% of the total (Gabay et al., 2014; Gutierrez, 2016).

2. ROLE OF GREEN FINANCE IN SUSTAINABLE INVESTMENT

The environmental protection industry demands substantial upfront investment capital and often involves a lengthy payback period, necessitating a unique financing approach. Green finance policies can address government financing challenges through financial innovation and reform. These policies comprise three key aspects:

2.1 Innovation and Reform of Financial Tools

This involves exploring fiscal policies and feasible ways to raise funds for the development of green finance. It focuses on adapting and innovating existing financial tools to support environmental initiatives.

Figure 1. Green bond issuance
Source: Climate Bonds Initiative

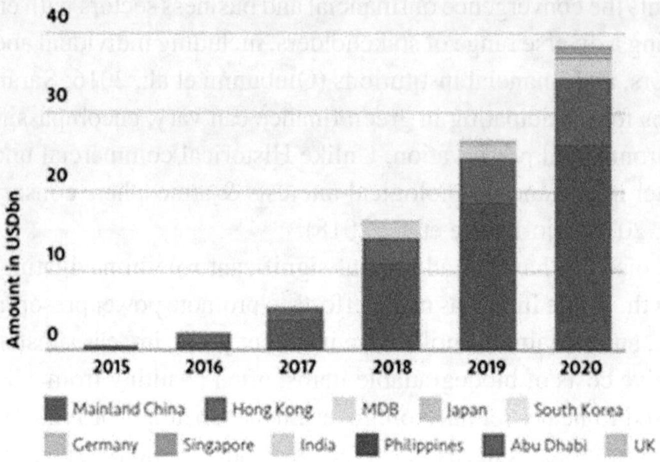

2.2 Reform of Fiscal Revenue Management and Distribution Policies

This entails improving the efficiency and direction of fiscal fund utilization, ensuring that funds are allocated effectively to support green finance projects.

2.3 Impact of Green Bonds on Environmental Protection

Financial instruments play a crucial role in implementing green finance in practical scenarios. The global green bond market has experienced significant growth. Green bonds combine the characteristics of traditional bonds with a focus on environmental sustainability (Lee et al., 2020; Ojo-Fafore et al., 2018). They share the fundamental features of regular bonds, offering advantages like low capital issuance costs, pre-tax interest charges, reduced investment risks, and the ability to raise funds for long-term projects, making them suitable for large-scale infrastructure initiatives. These bonds are accessible to various financing entities, including governments, financial institutions, and businesses. Investors find them appealing due to their potential for higher profitability, liquidity, and stability compared to bank deposits, as well as the flexibility provided by bond markets in terms of managing liquidity and exiting investments (Darko et al., 2017; Gutierrez, 2016; Oguntuase & Windapo, 2021).

3. CHALLENGES IN ACHIEVING SUSTAINABLE INVESTMENT THROUGH GREEN FINANCE

This study delves into the financial hurdles confronted by green technology enterprises, which can be summarized as follows:

3.1 Challenges in Securing Funding From Conventional Sources

Small and medium-sized private green technology innovators often face difficulties due to their limited assets, which make it hard to use as collateral for bank loans. Additionally, the extended investment timelines for green technology projects clash with the shorter growing of conventional bank debt in China, compounding the challenge of obtaining adequate funding through these avenues.

3.2 Access to Financing via Investment Capital and Risk Capital

These should be key fountainhead of external financing for technology firms, many green technology companies encounter obstacles due to underdeveloped economic paradigm, restricted merchandise potential, and relatively cheap returns on their projects. Furthermore, differing risk appetites among investors in China further complicate financing options for these green technology enterprises.

3.3 Unique Industry Risks in Green Projects

Green technology initiatives often come with distinctive technical risks, such as uncertainties related to factors like sunlight hours and wind power in photovoltaic and geothermal power projects. In green architecture, there's the probability of mechanism not meeting power and aqua protection quality. Additionally, biodiversity & power effective apparatus may experience performance instability. The absence of appropriate risk management tools can deter demand and impede the adoption of green technologies.

3.4 Insufficient Guidelines Inducement for Environmental Mechanism Funding

To foster innovation in green revolution and help the growth of green tech companies, policy incentives, such as fiscal incentives and tax breaks, assume a crucial role. These incentives not only directly help the growth of sustainable apparatus but also sign to the business, encouraging individual & communal money to invest in this sector. Such policies effectively leverage finite executive assets to attract substantial business wealth, thus facilitating the growth of green innovation venture.

4. OPPORTUNITIES FOR ADVANCING SUSTAINABLE INVESTMENT THROUGH GREEN FINANCE

4.1 Innovative Green Finance Instruments

A successful approach to promoting sustainable investment is the issuance of green bonds, which are dedicated to funding projects that contribute to climate and environmental sustainability. Over the last decade, the annual issuance of green bonds has seen substantial growth, increasing by over 100-fold in total value. Starting at 1.5 billion USD in 2007, it reached 167 billion USD in 2018.

Significantly, Asian share owners have embraced this approach. For instance, China, which had not issued any green bonds in 2015, represented 40.9% of worldwide green shares allocation in 2016, subsequently 24.6% in 2017. India also utilized green bonds from public institutions and corporations to finance segment of its 2022 continual power points (Gallagher & Muehlegger, 2011; Nenonen et al., 2019).

Table 1. Assessment of instruments for sustainable finance

Financial Instrument	Year of first application	Sustainability impact via	Use of Proceeds	ICMA/LMA Guidelines	Total Issuance 2021 (USD)	Market Share (2021)
Green Bond	2007	Usage of Proceeds	Green	Green Bond Principles	372.2 billion	71.2%
Sustainability Bond	2014	Usage of Proceeds	Green and Social	Sustainability Bond Guidelines	27.4 billion	5.2%
Social Bond	2015	Usage of Proceeds	Social	Social Bond Principles	21.7 billion	4.2%
Green Loan	2016	Usage of Proceeds	Green	Green Loan Principles	13.8 billion	2.6%
Sustainability-Linked Loan	2017	Sustainability performance	General Corporate Purposes*	Sustainability Linked Loan Principles	87.6 billion	16.8%
	Total				522.7 billion	100%

Source: Authors calculations based upon data provided by Climate Bonds Initiative.

Bank of America Merrill Lynch, the largest underwriter of green bonds globally, anticipates that Asia's entire climate bonds disbursement will reach around USD 600 billion in the next 5 years. Additionally, Christina Figures, the former head of the UNFCCC purposes to achieve a global total of USD 1 trillion in green bond issuance by 2025.

Green bond issuance initially gained traction in Europe, but more communal & individual concerns in Asia are now adopting such device to support their unceasing growth objectives.

Figure 2. Global comparison of green bond issuance
Climate Bond Issue (2014-2018)

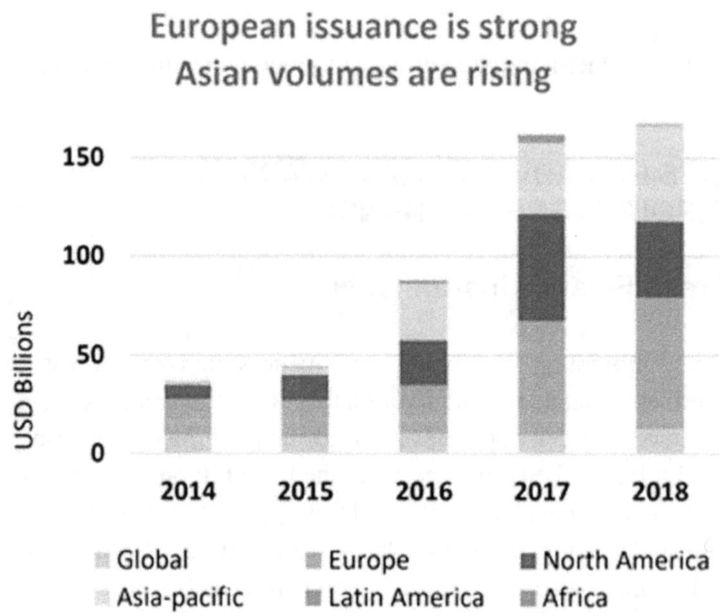

4.1.1 Introduction of Sustainable Debt Instruments

International Capital Markets Association introduced the Green Bond Principles (GBPs), offering guidance for issuing green bonds in 2014. These principles have become a widely recognized reference point used by regulators and issuers worldwide. They cover aspects like the utilization of revenues, scheme preferences & consideration, proceeds administration, and describing (Adabre & Chan, 2019; Andenæs et al., 2018; Xue et al., 2020).

However, the sustainable debt market in Asia has expanded beyond green bonds. It has not only grown significantly in size, with a 26% increase among 2017-2018 and 57% in 2021, resulting in \$522.7 billion wealth of sustainable debt product allotment but has varied. Four instruments have emerged:

4.1.2 Sustainability Bond

Introduced in 2014, these bonds allocate their proceeds exclusively to capitalize a merger of climate & communal schemes, meaning schemes with understandable atmosphere & community advantageous.

4.1.3 Social Bonds

These bonds direct their proceeds solely to finance or refinance social projects with evident socio-economic advantages.

4.1.4 Green Loan

These loans are earmarked for environmentally responsible activities, similar to green bonds.

4.1.5 Sustainability-Linked Loans

These loans tie loan terms to the borrower's performance on predefined viable elements like surroundings, communal & executives.

Figure 3. Increasing trend of sustainable bonds

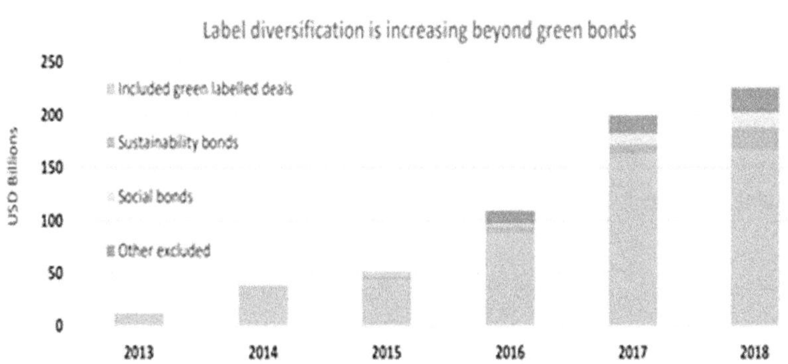

4.2 Collaboration and Partnerships

Partnerships are crucial for driving accountable, overall, and continuous extension. They can label business defeat, administration gaps, and faith represents that hinder market engagement in climate growth. Partnerships help as platforms to coordinate actions among various stakeholders and build connections among distinct section & climate extension aims (Agyekum et al., 2022; An & Pivo, 2020; Kennedy et al., 2016).

4.2.1 Coca-Cola's Supplier Engagement Program

Supplier Engagement Program (SEP) in backing of Coca-Cola Company's aim to sustainably was established by 2020. This program assists suppliers in complying with the company's Sustainable Agriculture Guiding Principles which align with several SDGs. It's a structured framework that provides information, guidance, assessments, audits, progress measurement, and validation to help suppliers qualify for sustainability certification.

4.2.2 Abraaj Group's Growth Markets Health Fund

Launched in 2016, this is a $1 billion equity fund devoted to investing in sustainable health ecosystems in select cities of Africa and South Asia. It involves collaboration with various investors, including Phillips, Medtronic, the IFC and Merck.

4.2.3 International Council on Mining and Metals

This alliance consists of 23 top mining companies and 34 regional associations that are liable for a substantial portion of international metals and minerals production. Their focus is on enlightening sustainable development in mining sector. Members commit to 10 Sustainable Development Principles and practices.

4.2.4 Electronic Industry Citizenship Coalition (EICC)

EICC was formed in 2004 by 8 companies to develop/implement Code of Conduct to improve environmental, social and ethical aspects in supply chain of the electronics. With over 110 member companies in various sectors, it focuses on workers' rights and addresses perplexing problems in value chain.

4.2.5 Global Agribusiness Alliance

Founded in 2016, this alliance involves 36 companies involved in agribusiness of Africa, Asia, and Middle East. They commit to supporting SDGs and addressing social and environmental issues in supply chains agricultural commodities.

4.2.6 Equator Principles

Co-convened by the IFC in 2006, this framework involves a group of banks aiming to recognize and arrange environmental and social risks. It has been accepted by 84 financial institutions. It covers more than 70 percent of international debt (Project Finance) in emerging markets.

4.2.7 SAI Platform

stablished in 2002, SAI Platform (Sustainable Agriculture Platform) includes seven major food and drinks companies focusing on sustainable manufacturing and agricultural raw materials. It works on six working groups to share knowledge and generate solutions impacting farmers' lives.

4.2.8 Smart Cities Council

This council brings together over 20 companies specializing in construction, digital technology and industrial design, along with inputs from laboratories, universities, and standards bodies. They support local governments to improve sustainability workability, and livability in cities.

4.3 Technological Advancements

Sustainable mechanisms are innovative solutions that lessen power utilization, contamination, and carbon costs while improving ecological conditions. These technologies cover various fields, including energy conservation, upright production, virtuous power, recyclable presentation, infrastructure, ecological agriculture, and more (Agyekum et al., 2022; Li et al., 2020; Wang et al., 2021).

Key actors in the green mechanism involves organizations, research Centre, the executive, & credit union. organizations drive innovation and implement green technologies, while research institutions provide intellectual support. Collaboration between these stakeholders is crucial, and the government incentivizes and benefits from green technology innovation through policies and mechanisms (Peskett et al., 2011).

5. STRATEGIES FOR OVERCOMING CHALLENGES:

5.1 Encouraging Banking and Financial Institutions to Support Green Technology Innovation

Traditional banks, which manage a substantial portion of financial resources and serve risk-averse clients, often hesitate to invest in more uncertain technology-based projects, including green technologies. To advance green technologies, it is advisable to encourage banks to initiate pilot funds-lending enterprise in the green technology segment. This entails establishing partnerships between banks and experienced private equity (PE) or venture capital (VC) funds or equity investment subsidiaries within a banking era. The PE/VC fund can provide equity financing, while the bank can offer matching loans (Peskett et al., 2011; Ren et al., 2020).

5.2 Supporting Banks to Invest in Green Funds Under Basel III Regulations on a Pilot Basis

At present, banks hold considerable capital within the financial system but have been relatively passive in mechanism funds, particularly in green technology finance. This is largely due to traditional banking regulations that have restricted banks from engaging in equity investments. It is recommended to support and facilitate banks in investing in green funds, especially under the new Basel III rule.

5.3 Promoting and Developing Green Private Equity and Venture Capital Institutions

A significant hurdle in green technology funds in China is the absence of specialized management institutions focusing on green private equity (PE) and venture capital (VC) funds. While there are over 500 funds registered under the banner of green technology, most of them invest in established firms and venture using growing strategy. Some investments in China concentrate on sustainable, clear, or surrounding apparatus. As global climate change strategies intensify and China's climate growth procedure deepens, owners are likely to see more inducements for climate and low-coal schemes in the future. Encouraging the growth of green PE/VC funds is essential to support green technology innovation (Hafner et al., 2020).

5.4 Encouraging Long-Term investments to Invest in Green PE/VC Funds

Green technology projects might have slightly longer payback periods compared to projects in other industries, often due to the development of newer technologies and the time required to establish a market. Incentives for carbon-reducing enterprises may also be short-term, but the benefits of carbon sinks are more likely to materialize in the long term. Some green projects necessitate larger initial investments compared to non-green schemes in the exact business, & returns on funds may initially be lower before increasing.

These strategies are aimed at removing barriers and facilitating investments in green technology, fostering sustainable and environmentally friendly innovations.

REFERENCES

Adabre, M. A., & Chan, A. P. C. (2019). Critical success factors (CSFs) for sustainable affordable housing. *Building and Environment*, *156*, 203–214. doi:10.1016/j.buildenv.2019.04.030

Agyekum, K., Opoku, A., Oppon, A. J., & Opoku, D. G. J. (2022). Obstacles to green building project financing: An empirical study in Ghana. *International Journal of Construction Management*, *22*(15), 2922–2930. doi:10.1080/15623599.2020.1832182

An, X., & Pivo, G. (2020). Green Buildings in Commercial Mortgage-Backed Securities: The Effects of LEED and Energy Star Certification on Default Risk and Loan Terms. *Real Estate Economics*, *48*(1), 7–42. doi:10.1111/1540-6229.12228

Andenæs, E., Kvande, T., Muthanna, T. M., & Lohne, J. (2018). Performance of blue-green roofs in cold climates: A scoping review. *Buildings*, *8*(4), 55. Advance online publication. doi:10.3390/buildings8040055

Berry, T. C., & Junkus, J. C. (2013). Socially Responsible Investing: An Investor Perspective. *Journal of Business Ethics*, *112*(4), 707–720. doi:10.100710551-012-1567-0

Bloomberg. (2019) *Sustainable Debt Market Sees Record Activity in 2018.* BNEF. https://about.bnef.com/blog/sustainable-debt-market-sees-record-activity-2018/

Climate Bonds Initiative. (2018). *India Ranks 8th in World for Climate Aligned Bond Issuance*. Climate Bonds Initative. https://www.climatebonds.net/resources/press-releases/2018/10/climate-bonds-state-market-report-points-huge-india-green-growth

Darko, A., Zhang, C., & Chan, A. P. C.Climate Bonds Initiative. (2021). *ASEAN Green Finance: State of the Market 2018*. London, UK: Darko, A., Zhang, C., & Chan, A. P. C. (2017). Drivers for green building: A review of empirical studies. *Habitat International*, *60*, 34–49. doi:10.1016/j.habitatint.2016.12.007

European Investment Bank. (2018). *EIB Issues First Sustainability Awareness Bond.* EIB. https://www.eib.org/en/infocentre/press/releases/all/2018/2018-223-eib-issues-first-sustainability-awareness-bond.htm

Gabay, H., Meir, I. A., Schwartz, M., & Werzberger, E. (2014). Cost-benefit analysis of green buildings: An Israeli office buildings case study. *Energy and Building*, *76*, 558–564. doi:10.1016/j.enbuild.2014.02.027

Gallagher, K. S., & Muehlegger, E. (2011). Giving green to get green? Incentives and consumer adoption of hybrid vehicle technology. *Journal of Environmental Economics and Management*, *61*(1), 1–15. doi:10.1016/j.jeem.2010.05.004

Gutierrez, A. V. (2016). Green banking: A proposed model for green housing loan. *ICIMSA 2016 - 2016 3rd International Conference on Industrial Engineering, Management Science and Applications*. IEEE. 10.1109/ICIMSA.2016.7504011

Hafner, S., Jones, A., Anger-Kraavi, A., & Pohl, J. (2020). Closing the green finance gap – A systems perspective. *Environmental Innovation and Societal Transitions*, *34*, 26–60. doi:10.1016/j.eist.2019.11.007

International Capital Market Association. (2018). *Green Bond Principles*. ICMA.

International Institute of Green Finance. (2018). *China Green Bond Market Development Report 2018*. IIGF.

Investment and Pensions Europe. (2018). *Bank analysts estimate $600bn of green bonds from Asia by 2023*. IPE. https://www.ipe.com/news/asset-allocation/bank-analysts-estimate-600bn-of-green-bonds-from-asia-by-2023/www.ipe.com/news/asset-allocation/bank-analysts-estimate-600bn-of-green-bonds-from-asia-by-2023/10024890.fullarticle

Kennedy, C., Zhong, M., & Corfee-Morlot, J. (2016). Infrastructure for China's Ecologically Balanced Civilization. *Engineering (Beijing)*, *2*(4), 414–425. doi:10.1016/J.ENG.2016.04.014

Lee, H. Y., So, G., Tang, E., Lam, T., & Cheng, V. (2020). Green finance performance and role of sustainability engineers in the greater bay Area. *IOP Conference Series. Earth and Environmental Science*, *588*(2), 022063. doi:10.1088/1755-1315/588/2/022063

Li, Q., Long, R., Chen, H., Chen, F., & Wang, J. (2020). Visualized analysis of global green buildings: Development, barriers and future directions. *Journal of Cleaner Production*, *245*, 118775. doi:10.1016/j.jclepro.2019.118775

Nenonen, S., Koski, A., Lassila, A. P., & Lehikoinen, S. (2019). Towards low carbon economy - Green bond and asset development. *IOP Conference Series. Earth and Environmental Science*, *352*(1), 012028. doi:10.1088/1755-1315/352/1/012028

Oguntuase, O. J., & Windapo, A. (2021). Green Bonds and Green Buildings: New Options for Achieving Sustainable Development in Nigeria. *Advances in 21st Century Human Settlements*, 193–218. doi:10.1007/978-981-33-4424-2_11

Ojo-Fafore, E. M., Aigbavboa, C., Thwala, W., & Remaru, P. (2018). *Green Finance for Sustainable Global Growth*. 244–269. doi:10.4018/978-1-5225-7808-6.ch010

Olubunmi, O. A., Xia, P. B., & Skitmore, M. (2016). Green building incentives: A review. *Renewable & Sustainable Energy Reviews*, *59*, 1611–1621. doi:10.1016/j.rser.2016.01.028

Peskett, L., Schreckenberg, K., & Brown, J. (2011). Institutional approaches for carbon financing in the forest sector: Learning lessons for REDD+ from forest carbon projects in Uganda. *Environmental Science & Policy*, *14*(2), 216–229. doi:10.1016/j.envsci.2010.10.004

Ren, X., Shao, Q., & Zhong, R. (2020). Nexus between green finance, non-fossil energy use, and carbon intensity: Empirical evidence from China based on a vector error correction model. *Journal of Cleaner Production*, *277*, 122844. doi:10.1016/j.jclepro.2020.122844

Sarangi, G. K. (2019). Green Finance in India: Barriers and Solutions. Handbook of Green Finance, 1–18. doi:10.1007/978-981-10-8710-3_4-1

Wang, W., Tian, Z., Xi, W., Tan, Y. R., & Deng, Y. (2021). The influencing factors of China's green building development: An analysis using RBF-WINGS method. *Building and Environment*, *188*, 107425. doi:10.1016/j.buildenv.2020.107425

Xue, Y., Temeljotov-Salaj, A., Engebø, A., & Lohne, J. (2020). Multi-sector partnerships in the urban development context: A scoping review. *Journal of Cleaner Production*, *268*, 122291. doi:10.1016/j.jclepro.2020.122291

Zerbib, O. D. (2019). The effect of pro-environmental preferences on bond prices: Evidence from green bonds. *Journal of Banking & Finance*, *98*, 39–60. doi:10.1016/j.jbankfin.2018.10.012

Zheng, G. W., Siddik, A. B., Masukujjaman, M., Fatema, N., & Alam, S. S. (2021). Green finance development in Bangladesh: The role of private commercial banks (PCBs). *Sustainability (Basel)*, *13*(2), 1–17. doi:10.3390u13020795

Chapter 17
From Tradition to Innovation:
The Role of Artificial Intelligence in Transforming the Hospitality Industry

Simran Jewandah
Chandigarh University, India

Padam Bhushan
Chandigarh University, India

Ercan Ozen
Usak University, Turkey

Sachin Ghai
Graphic Era University (Deemed), India

ABSTRACT

Artificial intelligence's ability to do traditionally human assignments at any time of day is driving its rising relevance in the hospitality sector. This implies that hotel owners may save a lot of money, eliminate human error, and offer the highest level of service. Its different perspectives on complicated issues have piqued academics' curiosity. AI-driven analytics and predictive modeling have optimized revenue management, enabling data-driven decisions and dynamic pricing strategies. Operational processes have been streamlined through AI, leading to improved efficiency and resource allocation. Furthermore, AI algorithms have leveraged guest data to deliver highly personalized experiences and customized offers, enhancing guest satisfaction and loyalty. In order to track the development of AI in the hotel industry, a bibliometric approach was used in this research. The study also seeks to pinpoint the crucial directions for further investigation. A systematic analysis of how artificial intelligence is changing the hotel business is offered as a perspective.

DOI: 10.4018/979-8-3693-1388-6.ch017

INTRODUCTION

The integration of Artificial Intelligence (AI) in the hospitality industry has gained significant momentum in recent years, bringing about transformative changes in how businesses operate and cater to guest needs. AI refers to the simulation of human intelligence in machines that can analyze data, make informed decisions, and perform tasks traditionally requiring human intelligence.

The hospitality industry is renowned for its commitment to exceptional service and personalized experiences, relying on traditional practices to meet guest needs and desires. One of the biggest and fastest expanding industries in the world is international tourism and hospitality. The hospitality industry is set to witness significant expansion, with an expected rise in its overall value from $3,952.87 billion in 2021 to $4,548.42 billion in 2022, driven by a compound annual growth rate (CAGR) of 15.1%. By 2026, it is projected to reach $6,715.27 billion, growing at a CAGR of 10.2%. Almost every facet of travel and tourism has adopted artificial intelligence (AI). Robots, conversational systems, intelligent travel agents, prediction and forecasting systems, language translation software, customization and recommendation systems, and speech recognition and AI technology systems are a few examples. Recent advancements in large data, algorithms, and computing power have significantly accelerated AI development.

However, with the rapid advancements in technology, particularly the integration of Artificial Intelligence (AI), the industry is undergoing a profound transformation. AI has emerged as a powerful force, revolutionizing the hospitality landscape and propelling it from tradition to innovation. This introduction aims to explore the role of AI in transforming the hospitality industry, highlighting its impact on various aspects of operations, guest experiences, and strategic decision-making(Bhatnagar et al., 2022a, 2022b,2023a, 2023b; Dangwal et al., 2022a, 2022b; Kumar et al., 2023a, 2023b; Özen et al., 2022, Singh et al., 2021; Taneja et al., 2022a, 2022b; 2023a, 2023b, 2023c, 2023d, 2023e 2023f; Gupta et al. 2023; Dahiya 2023; Bansal 2023; Reepu 2023;).

Traditionally, the hospitality industry has thrived on human interactions, with hotel staff using their expertise and intuition to anticipate guest needs and provide personalized services. While the human touch remains invaluable, AI has introduced a new dimension of efficiency, personalization, and operational excellence to the industry. Through the integration of AI technologies, hospitality businesses are embracing innovative approaches to enhance guest satisfaction, optimize revenue, streamline operations, and deliver personalized experiences that surpass traditional expectations.

Artificial intelligence (AI) is essential to both the industrial and service sectors' digital transformation. (Mariani and Borghi, 2019) and has a significant impact on how businesses develop and extract value (Huang and Rust, 2020). More precisely, AI technologies are transforming the services industry (Huang and Rust, 2018; 2020), changing both service interactions and operations (Wirtz et al., 2018). Personal travel assistants, robotics, prediction and forecasting systems, language translation software, speech recognition and natural language processing systems, and robots are among the AI applications now being researched and tested in the travel and tourist sector.

As customers grow more aware of the danger of contracting an infectious illness via human contact as a result of the Covid-19 outbreak, the use of service robots in the hospitality sector has increased. The use of service robots may indicate a lack of human interactions and a reduction in perceived risk of virus transmission, which may boost visit intention (Wan, Chan, & Luo, 2020). Due to their worries about safety, customers choose hotels with robot employees over those with human staff (Kim et al., 2021; Shin & Kang, 2020). It is anticipated that between 2020 and 2024, the market for service robots in the healthcare and hospitality industries would increase by 942 million USD (Technavio, 2020). . Through nudging,

AI may also successfully alter human behaviour, including that of visitors (Tussyadiah & Miller, 2019; Wagner, 2021b). Interest in the use of robotization and artificial intelligence in tourism and hospitality has grown over the last several years (Cain et al., 2019; Ivanov & Webster, 2019; Samala et al., 2020).

The primary goal of this research is to thoroughly examine how the hotel industry has changed as a result of the integration of artificial intelligence and to pinpoint the major effects of AI on the sector. It is suggested to conduct a thorough assessment of previous research using bibliometric analysis in order to achieve this goal.

LITERATURE REVIEW

The hotel business is among the many that artificial intelligence (AI) is influencing. AI is often seen as a supporting tool rather than as a substitute for people, gathering and analysing massive amounts of data to improve customer-focused processes. In reality, the case for using AI seems to be supported by its potential to boost organisational performance and expedite the achievement of strategic objectives. Robotics has concentrated on the mechanical aspects of AI, but AI was initially envisioned as a means to integrate observation, reasoning, and actuation with an emphasis on algorithms (virtual). 2020; Belanche, D., et al. Robotics and Intelligent services driven by AI (such as chatbots, cobots, and maidbots) are used to augment human cognitive and physical abilities, allowing service innovation in the delivery of personalised services. 2019 (Cain et al.; Zlatanov and Popesku; Belias and Varelas; Ivanov and Webster). In the hotel industry, utilising AI to offer services has a significant influence on staff performance but not on attrition, according to Prentice et al. (2019), suggesting that AI may increase employee productivity. Some of the major benefits of artificial intelligence are increased cost-effectiveness, greater resource utilisation, more accurate demand forecasting, better quality control, better process management, and the elimination of human error. 2019 (Ivanov and Webster). People may be able to shift their attention from regular jobs that an AI can do more efficiently to ones that take more time and effort as automation advances. Because artificial intelligence (A.I.) can quickly manage the tedious and time-consuming aspects of the assignment, most workers find it to be very desirable as an alternative to the slower, more taxing experience a person would go through while doing the same job. (Mamula,2019).

Facilitating consumers interactive virtual and physical assistance as well as real-time language translation tools to engage with overseas clientele. Consolidating services, allowing defect reduction, improving decision-making and service speed. using face recognition technology to recognise guests by name. Cain et al., 2019; Ivanov and Webster, 2019; Prentice et al., 2020; OECD, 2018; Ivanov and Webster, 2017;

To enhance our understanding of how AI technologies can affect service quality and customer satisfaction in the hospitality industry through employee-related outcomes (including employee engagement, retention, productivity, and service quality), it is imperative to thoroughly investigate their impact (Prentice-Hall, 2020).

Client Experience: Customers have varied expectations, requirements, and desires since they come from different backgrounds. Market segmentation is a technique used by every business, including the hospitality sector, to guarantee that each customer's demand is satisfied in accordance with their likes and preferences. There are several groups that make up the full consumer spectrum, and each has expectations and wants that are somewhat similar. The client spectrum may be divided into exceedingly tiny groups and subgroups that have never been observed before thanks to artificial intelligence. This strategy improves customer satisfaction and service by ensuring a more sustainable business.

Figure 1. Key driving factors of AI in hospitality
(Authors complication)

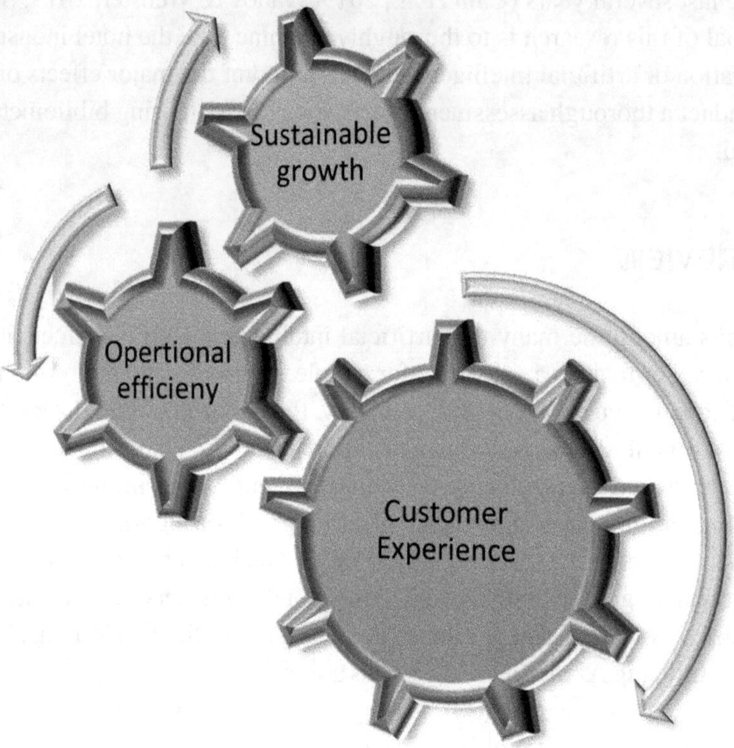

Operational Effectiveness: Responding to client calls, front desk visits, and online guest inquiries simultaneously is no longer a burdensome problem. Artificial intelligence (AI) reduces the need for workers to be under strict performance requirements and behave robotically, which leads to subpar service quality. Using chatbots to help several visitors at once has proven to be both a lifesaver and a gift. All online questions from prospective consumers are handled by chatbots, enabling front-desk employees to assist clients promptly and effectively. This improves hotel operations without sacrificing client satisfaction.

Sustainable Growth: Hotels all around the globe have adopted green practises to save energy by employing renewable energy sources and recycling garbage. Customers' trust in hotels increases as their sustainability increases, and as a consequence of their increased loyalty, the hotels are seen as being ecologically friendly. Regardless of location, a range of different hotels may simply adopt green practises as they have been researched and used in other hotels throughout the globe.

Optimizing demand forecasting: Hotel owners are always ready for demand since they are aware of the cyclical nature of the tourist business. They are capable of making swift adjustments in the event of any unanticipated events. The development of machine learning and big data has improved hotel operators' ability to forecast visitor demand. This programme offers in-the-moment analysis and dynamically refreshes its data in response to occurrences.

METHODOLOGY

An technique to the systematic review and synthesis of results from many research known as "narrative synthesis" largely focuses on the use of words and text to summarise and explain the synthesis's results. A narrative synthesis has been used in this essay. Additionally, a thorough assessment of the literature was conducted to investigate how the incorporation of artificial intelligence has changed the hospitality sector. The literature and data were found on EBSCO, Google Scholar, Scopus, Web of Science, and Science Direct in a variety of books and research publications. Studies that clearly specified how the hotel business changed with the application of artificial intelligence, were published, were written in English, and had through peer review all met the inclusion requirements. A list of keywords relating to AI in the hotel sector was selected for the data base search. Artificial intelligence, AI, adoption, technology, big data, and the hospitality sector were the keywords found. Conducting qualitative, systematic assessments using content analysis is a complete data analysis strategy. Additionally, to accommodate material that is by definition highly organized and contextualized, content analysis approaches should be modified or adjusted by qualitative systematic reviewers who aim to advance knowledge and theory (Finfgeld-Connett, 2014). As a consequence, a qualitative content analysis was employed in this review paper.

FINDINGS

Numerous facets of the tourism and hospitality industries, including the hotel and food and beverage industries have already been taken over by artificial intelligence (AI). Following a comprehensive examination of the previously published research, some of the areas where AI has revolutionized the hotel industry are mentioned below.

Fraud Detection: Payment fraud, which involves con artists using credit cards that have been reported stolen to make bookings or pay for their own housing, is the most common sort of fraud done by people. Some scam artists even demand a chargeback by claiming the card has been stolen. The travel and hospitality sectors created a customized machine learning model and employed AI technology to detect and foresee fraud.

Enhancing customer experience by using robots to give various experiences, intuitively comprehend consumer wants, and deliver top-notch customer service. A positive connection and high client retention are facilitated by personalizing the customer experience. The widespread integration of AI is altering our daily routines. You may quickly adopt a personal touch with AI to draw customers to your business and create sophisticated, individualised client loyalty.

Brand Reputation: Virtually every area of the hotel sector, including customer service, brand reputation, booking, staffing, and price optimization, has the potential to be transformed by AI. With continued development and experience, AI is moving toward improving employee accessibility and usability. Being hospitable allows you to provide visitors an experience that stands apart. As a result, reputation management is crucial in this industry. It matters what others say and think about your company. Customers may benefit from user-friendly intelligent services by integrating the capabilities of AI and virtual assistants.

Rate optimization and demand forecasting: By modifying daily pricing and following trends, AI enables you to compete in the market. It is simple to comprehend the occupancy patterns and take the appropriate action to optimise your income if you are aware of market demand and pricing trends. Machine learning powered by large amounts of data enables AI systems to continuously enhance pricing and advertising suggestions. Authorities now have the chance to concentrate on making strategic choices.

Intelligent AI chatbots are designed to allow quick and effective interactions between humans and machines. Our consumers benefit greatly from these chat bots' availability, quick service, and useful information since they are available around-the-clock. The needed request is sent to the guest relation by the chat bot, and the answer is stored in the database for future use. Chat bots become smarter, foresee problems, provide answers, help users on websites, social media, and messaging applications, and take on additional duties thanks to machine learning skills.

Purposed Model

An alignment model for AI in hospitality has been developed based on research and the literature that is already accessible. The following actions might be made in order to add AI into the model:

Information gathering: The data that AI gathers enables you to identify the details that are absent from the digital conversations you have with your clients. It draws attention to the holes that must be addressed. A business may answer the inquiries of potential clients live on its website by gathering real-time data. AI can evaluate data, spot patterns and trends, and provide suggestions about how to enhance the company's operations. For instance, AI can analyze booking data to identify busy hours and days, which may assist company owners in properly staffing their operations. AI can filter through a variety of customer evaluations, ratings, and online polls to provide a clear picture of consumer opinion in real-time, which enables businesses to enhance their products. Observing customer behaviour in relation to

Offering customization: AI technologies may assist in customizing interactions and experiences to specific visitors, hence providing personalization. By using data on customer preferences, satisfaction levels, purchase trends, likes and dislikes that is obtained from social media, professional networks, and other sources, AI may unleash customization. Artificial intelligence may be used to optimize hyper-individualized advertising to boost client retention and revenues. Additionally, ML may make it feasible to gather predictive data, identify trends in huge datasets, and comprehend client behaviour to facilitate customization.

Booking: Without the need for human intervention, AI can help companies provide customers a quick delivery service, round-the-clock availability, and booking services with a variety of customizable choices. Thanks to the combination of user data and appropriately tuned algorithms, every customer may profit from a tailored and extremely accessible experience that is fast, simple, and always improving. Voice assistants with AI capabilities may be developed to aid customers with simple booking, accurate pricing, etc. The gap between robots and humans can be filled by voice assistants.

Delivery: AI-enabled mobile applications may be created to make it easier for clients to stay, giving them the option to use their smart phones to unlock their rooms, adjust the temperature and operate the curtains, and buy refreshments. Chatbots with AI capabilities will improve the client experience. Visitors can interact with chatbots using the hotels' specialised mobile devices to carry out a variety of tasks, such as suggesting special dishes, ordering meals and drinks, responding to urgent questions, recommending nearby attractions, scheduling dinner or lunch, managing evening reservations, and adjusting the temperature and lighting in their rooms.

Experience: Using historical data, artificial intelligence can automatically and properly arrange the room. IoT devices update rooms with customised music, temperature, and lighting settings, anticipate room service requests and demand for specialised information, and might draw guests' attention to any hotel or outside service or activity. Determine the level and achieve favourable results. feedback. To determine the best time to send invitations and notifications via email, direct messages, or mobile apps, you can customise these services and activities.

Reflecting/Feedback: Artificial intelligence (AI) systems, such as digital concierges, can intelligently determine when it is appropriate to solicit feedback or reviews. Hotels can use machine learning tools to automatically gather, store, and analyse review data from various online sources. By encouraging brand loyalty, virtual concierges may encourage repeat business. Additionally, it may assist visitors in taking control of their hotel experience, ensuring that they get the most out of their stay and want to return again and again.

Figure 2. AI in hospitality
(Author's Model Suggested)

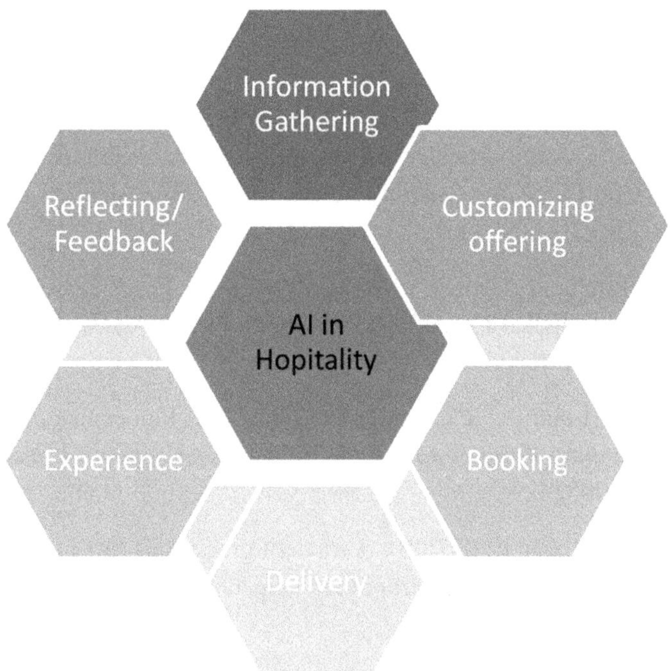

CONCLUSION

The integration of AI has ushered in a new era of transformation in the hospitality industry, propelling it from tradition to innovation. AI technologies have significantly impacted guest service and experience management, revenue optimization, operational efficiency, and personalization. This review article will provide an insight into how artificial intelligence is being used in the hotel industry and how it is changing it. As a result, the paper will help managers in the hotel sector and marketers in the sector better understand and put into practice effective strategies to satisfy the requirements and expectations of both consumers and staff via the use of AI. The use of AI and robots in tourism marketing will result in a positive and improved change that will improve the entire experience of visitors. The travel, tourism, and hospitality sectors may effectively employ chatbots, virtual reality, language translators, and other emerging technology.

A relatively new and immensely potent idea, artificial intelligence. It is necessary to do further study on the AI concept and its use in the hotel industry. Additional investigation will be done to shed light on the potential issues that using AI technology in the tourist sector might cause (Dirican, 2015). By effectively leveraging AI, hospitality businesses can achieve new levels of service quality, operational excellence, and guest satisfaction, paving the way for an innovative future in the industry. As hospitality businesses embrace AI, they navigate opportunities and challenges, ensuring responsible and ethical integration to maximize benefits for guests, employees, and the industry. Leveraging AI technologies effectively unlocks new levels of service quality, operational excellence, and guest satisfaction, redefining the future of hospitality.

REFERENCES

Bansal, N., Bhatnagar, M., & Taneja, S. (2023). Balancing Priorities Through Green Optim000ism: A Study Elucidating Initiatives, Approaches, and Strategies for Sustainable Supply Chain Management. In *Handbook of Research on Designing Sustainable Supply Chains to Achieve a Circular Economy* (pp. 60–81). IGI Global. doi:10.4018/978-1-6684-7664-2.ch004

Bhatnagar, M., Özen, E., Taneja, S., Grima, S., & Rupeika-Apoga, R. (2022a). The Dynamic Connectedness between Risk and Return in the Fintech Market of India: Evidence Using the GARCH-M Approach. *Risks*, *10*(11), 209. doi:10.3390/risks10110209

Bhatnagar, M., Taneja, S., Kumar, P., & Özen, E. (2023a). Does Financial Education Act as a Catalyst for SME Competitiveness. *International Journal of Education Economics and Development*, *1*(1), 1. doi:10.1504/IJEED.2023.10053629

Bhatnagar, M., Taneja, S., & Özen, E. (2022b). A wave of green start-ups in India—The study of green finance as a support system for sustainable entrepreneurship. *Green Finance*, *4*(2), 253–273. doi:10.3934/GF.2022012

Bhatnagar, M., Taneja, S., & Rupeika-Apoga, R. (2023b). Demystifying the Effect of the News (Shocks) on Crypto Market Volatility. *Journal of Risk and Financial Management*, *16*(2), 136. doi:10.3390/jrfm16020136

Buhalis, D., & Leung, R. (2018). Smart hospitality—Interconnectivity and interoperability towards an ecosystem. *International Journal of Hospitality Management*, *71*, 41–50. doi:10.1016/j.ijhm.2017.11.011

Dahiya, K., Taneja, S., & Özen, E. (2023). To Analyse the Impact of Multi-Media Technology on the Rural Entrepreneurship Development. In Contemporary Studies of Risks in Emerging Technology, Part A (pp. 221-240). Emerald Publishing Limited. doi:10.1108/978-1-80455-562-020231015

Dangwal, A., Kaur, S., Taneja, S., & Taneja, S. (2022a). A Bibliometric Analysis of Green Tourism Based on the Scopus Platform. In J. Kaur, P. Jindal, & A. Singh (Eds.), *Developing Relationships, Personalization, and Data Herald in Marketing 5.0* (Vol. i, pp. 1–327). IGI Global. doi:10.4018/978-1-6684-4496-2.ch015

Dangwal, A., Taneja, S., Özen, E., Todorovic, I., & Grima, S. (2022b). Abridgement of Renewables: It's Potential and Contribution to India's GDP. *International Journal of Sustainable Development and Planning*, *17*(8), 2357–2363. doi:10.18280/ijsdp.170802

Gretzel, U., Sigala, M., Xiang, Z., & Koo, C. (2015). Smart tourism: Foundations and developments. *Electronic Markets*, *25*(3), 179–188. doi:10.100712525-015-0196-8

Gupta, M., Arora, R., & Taneja, S. (2023). Bibliometric Analysis on Employee Engagement and Human Resource Management. In *Enhancing Customer Engagement Through Location-Based Marketing* (pp. 185–205). IGI Global. doi:10.4018/978-1-6684-8177-6.ch013

Huang, Y., & Zhang, Y. (2021). Artificial intelligence and robotics in the hospitality and tourism industry: A state-of-the-art review. *Journal of Travel Research*, 00472875211006404.

Ivanov, S., & Webster, C. (2017). *Adoption of robotics, artificial intelligence automation by travel, tourist and hospitality companies: a cost-benefit study*. Contemporary Tourism: Traditions and Innovations, an International Scientific Conference, Sofia University.

Kumar, P., Taneja, S., Özen, E., & Singh, S. (2023b). Artificial Intelligence and Machine Learning in Insurance: A Bibliometric Analysis. In Smart Analytics, Artificial Intelligence and Sustainable Performance Management in a Global Digitalised Economy (pp. 191-202). Emerald Publishing Limited. doi:10.1108/S1569-37592023000110A010

Kumar, P., Verma, P., Bhatnagar, M., Taneja, S., Seychel, S., Todorović, I., & Grim, S. (2023). The financial performance and solvency status of the indian public sector banks: A CAMELS rating and Z index approach. *International Journal of Sustainable Development and Planning*, *18*(2), 367–376. doi:10.18280/ijsdp.180204

Lai, C. H., & Huang, C. H. (2020). Artificial intelligence, big data, and virtual reality applications in the hospitality and tourism industry. In *Handbook of Research on Applied Data Science and Artificial Intelligence in Business and Industry* (pp. 57–82). IGI Global.

Neuhofer, B., Buhalis, D., & Ladkin, A. (2015). Technology as a catalyst of change: Enablers and barriers of the tourist experience and their consequences. The Routledge Handbook of Transport, Tourism and Hospitality, 51-70. Routledge.

Özen, E., & Sanjay, T. (2022a). Empirical Analysis of the Effect of Foreign Trade in Computer and Communication Services on Economic Growth in India. *Journal of Economics and Business Issues*, *2*(2), 24–34.

Reepu, R., Taneja, S., Ozen, E., & Singh, A. (2023). A Globetrotter to the Future of Marketing: Metaverse. In *Cultural Marketing and Metaverse for Consumer Engagement* (pp. 1–11). IGI Global. doi:10.4018/978-1-6684-8312-1.ch001

Rodriguez, R. V., Bellamkonda, R. S., Katkam, B. S., and Samala, N. (2020). A crucial insight regarding the effects of AI and robotics on the tourism industry. *Tourism Futures Journal.* . doi:10.1108/JTF-07-2019-0065

Sigala, M. (2020). Artificial intelligence in hospitality and tourism: Applications, challenges, and future research agenda. *Journal of Hospitality Marketing & Management*, *29*(7), 821–826.

Singh, V., Taneja, S., Singh, V., Singh, A., & Paul, H. L. (2021). Online advertising strategies in Indian and Australian e-commerce companies: A comparative study. *Big Data Analytics for Improved Accuracy, Efficiency, and Decision Making in Digital Marketing,* (pp. 124–138). IGI Global. doi:10.4018/978-1-7998-7231-3.ch009

Taneja, S., Bhatnagar, M., Kumar, P., & Grima, S. (2023c). A panel analysis of the effectiveness of the asset management in Indian agricultural companies. *International Journal of Sustainable Development and Planning*, *18*(3), 653–660. doi:10.18280/ijsdp.180301

Taneja, S., Bhatnagar, M., Kumar, P., & Rupeika-apoga, R. (2023b). India ' s Total Natural Resource Rents (NRR) and GDP : An Augmented Autoregressive Distributed Lag (ARDL) Bound Test. *Journal of Risk and Financial Management*, *16*(2), 91. doi:10.3390/jrfm16020091

Taneja, S., Gupta, M., Bhushan, P., Bhatnagar, M., & Singh, A. (2023f). Cultural Marketing in the Digital Era. In *Cultural Marketing and Metaverse for Consumer Engagement* (pp. 109–122). IGI Global. doi:10.4018/978-1-6684-8312-1.ch008

Taneja, S., Jaggi, P., Jewandah, S., & Ozen, E. (2022b). Role of Social Inclusion in Sustainable Urban Developments: An Analyse by PRISMA Technique. *International Journal of Design & Nature and Ecodynamics*, *17*(6), 937–942. doi:10.18280/ijdne.170615

Taneja, S., Kaur, S., & Özen, E. (2022a). Using green finance to promote global growth in a sustainable way. *International Journal of Green Economics*, *16*(3), 246–257. doi:10.1504/IJGE.2022.128930

Taneja, S., & Özen, E. (2023a). To analyse the relationship between bank's green financing and environmental performance. *International Journal of Electronic Finance*, *12*(2), 163–175. doi:10.1504/IJEF.2023.129919

Taneja, S., & Ozen, E. (2023d). Impact of the European Green Deal (EDG) on the agricultural carbon (CO2) emission in Turkey. *International Journal of Sustainable Development and Planning*, *18*(3), 715–727. doi:10.18280/ijsdp.180307

Taneja, S., & Sharma, V. (2023e). Role of Beaconing Marketing in Improving Customer Buying Experience. In *Enhancing Customer Engagement Through Location-Based Marketing* (pp. 176–184). IGI Global. doi:10.4018/978-1-6684-8177-6.ch012

Thomas, J. H., M. Alonso Jr., and L. N. Cain (2019). The state of robotics and AI in the hospitality sector: from science fiction to science fact. *Journal of Hospitality and Tourism Technology, 10*(4), 624-650.

Xiang, Z., Du, Q., Ma, Y., Fan, W., & Li, X. (2017). A comparative analysis of major online review platforms: Implications for social media analytics in hospitality and tourism. *Tourism Management*, *58*, 51–65. doi:10.1016/j.tourman.2016.10.001

Xu, F., Buhalis, D., & Weber, J. (2017). Serious games and the gamification of tourism. *Tourism Management*, *60*, 244–256. doi:10.1016/j.tourman.2016.11.020

Zhang, H., & Li, X. (2021). Artificial intelligence, robots, and service automation in hospitality and tourism. *Journal of Hospitality Marketing & Management*, *30*(1), 78–82.

Zhang, M., Li, X., & Hsu, C. H. (2021). Leveraging artificial intelligence for smart tourism destination marketing. *Journal of Travel Research*, 00472875211005936.

Chapter 18
Exploration of Opportunities and Challenges in Green Finance:
A Journey of Sustainable Development

Swati Gupta
Chitkara University, India

Gurloveleen Kaur
Chitkara University, India

Inu Kumari
Chitkara University, India

Dixit Kalra
Chandigarh University, India

ABSTRACT

Sustainability and green finance both are totally intertwined. As the economies are developing, they are forgetting the basic purpose of sustainable development. To curb this, many regulatory institutions have framed the policies which are mandatory for the companies to oblige. The present study tried to explore the opportunities available in promoting green finance and challenges involved with it. Long term vision, technological risks, market and demand, reputational and social risks, and alignment with global trends are observed as the key working parameters to attain sustainable development with green finance. Disclosures for financial institutions to assess the risks assessing the actual and proposed vulnerability analysis for various sectors, stress testing, regulatory measures, and initiatives planned and implemented by the Indian regulators are considered. Research models are framed after understanding and observing the data. Market exploration for green products and services, carbon agenda 2070 are the few other challenges to be sorted by regulators for effective execution of green finance.

DOI: 10.4018/979-8-3693-1388-6.ch018

1. INTRODUCTION

A well-defined financial activity formed to provide improved outcomes for the environment is green finance. As per the World Economic Forum, the trading value of green bonds will hit the target of $2.36 trillion in 2023. The US, China, and France are leading the world, as they have secured the position of issuing the top-most traded green bond countries. European Central Bank involvement in green finance is highly appreciated. If we talk about the proportion of green bonds trading in the Indian market from 2018 to 2020, it was just 0.7%, but this value was higher than the contribution made by developed nations such as the US, UK, and Australia.

The evolution of green bonds was remarkable in India, where six billion-dollar distributions were made. The country needs to invest $10,103 trillion to accomplish its goal of being carbon neutral by 2070. This goal is achieved through two strategies: switching coal to another renewable energy source and investing in green energy technology. The emblematic projects involved in green finance and sustainable development are related to renewable and efficient energy, the prevention and control of pollution, conservative biodiversity, initiatives for a circular economy, and the justifiable use of natural resources and land.

The giant renewable Indian energy companies, for instance, Adani Power Finance Co., distributed green bonds with a maturity period of 10 years, and the World Bank itself invested in Indian green bonds many times.

The following charts one and two provide information about global ESG funds, their classification, holdings distribution, and share of equity investment in ESG and non-ESG funds.

Figure 1. Charts one and two

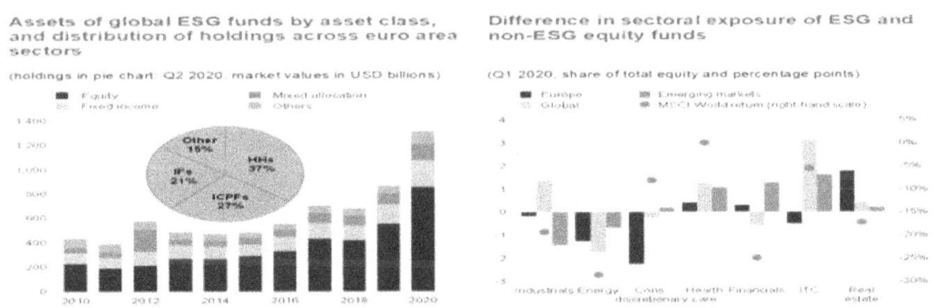

ESG holdings in equity, fixed income, mixed allocation, and others have raised up to US$1,400 in 2020 from US$400 in 2010, especially in Euro zones. Renewable energy and energy efficiency, biodiversity conservation, pollution prevention and control, sustainable use of natural resources and land, and circular economy initiatives are a few projects that fall under the umbrella of green finance. It embraces a range of debt assets, loans, their mechanisms, and investment ways that motivate investors to put energy into these green fiancé resources and try to nullify the impact of selected projects on the climate.

Long-term institutional investors can help with rebalancing and redistributing climate-related risks and maintaining financial stability. Hedging instruments (e.g., catastrophe bonds, indexed insurance) help insure against increasing natural disaster risk, and other financial instruments (e.g., green stock indices, green bonds, voluntary de-carbonization initiatives) can help re-allocate investment to "green" sectors (imf.org).

2. LITERATURE REVIEW

Ashta (2023) provided insights to others regarding the role of fintechs in climate improvement. Varied cases were discussed; large-cap firms like Ant Group, Mastercard, Adyen Fiserv, and Paypal were observed tackling the low use of paper within organizations, initiating green projects, managing unsettling innovation, and trying to make a balance with the environment through plantations, ecological preservation, and rebuilding. Brahmi et al. (2023) tried to ensure the intersection point where green innovations with financial inclusion can ensure sustainable development. Advanced technological novelties have a positive effect on mitigating carbon trading, which was confirmed in the research work. Kashi and Shah (2023) investigated the trajectory of sustainable finance literature in the Scopus repository employing qualitative and quantitative measures for bringing the bibliometric approach together in an analytical way that offers recommendations for future research possibilities. Similarly, Lin et al. (2023) investigated the sources of carbon emissions in 25 Chinese shires. Expansion of green finance, green credit progress, interest of energy-intensive companies, their consumption of energy, green securities issued, share and consumption in the stock market, share of investment in saving the environment, controlling pollution, and green agriculture insurance, income, and output were considered.

Sustainability initiatives are of interest to the business community as a whole since they may be included into banks operational strategies and are thought to have the potential to increase performance (Saluja et al., 2022). The thing that has piqued curiosity is the possibility of increased efficiency. "Sustainable Banking," a novel and inventive approach to banking, asserts that its use may concurrently encourage adherence to the principles of sustainable development, generate revenue from clients, and provide value to the full chain of operations. The term "sustainable banking" was initially introduced by the World Economic Forum in 2002, according to Sharma et al. (2023). Revisions and amplifications in the rudimentary plan of vulnerability evaluation were proposed by Turner et al. (2003) so that the human approach can be molded towards the environment. Root causes, unhealthy conditions, excess pressure, disaster occurrences, and hazardous factors were put into the PAR framework for vulnerability analysis. Furthermore, as Sideri (2021) points out, the use of sustainability tracking has made it possible for companies everywhere to effectively include corporate social responsibility (CSR) into their encompassing future planning. Yan et al. (2023) opined on the influences of digitalization and green finance on the sustainable growth of North and Middle Eastern African nations. Multinational companies' role in sustaining renewable and unrenewable energy, public growth, foreign direct investment, and the progress of the economy was assessed with a developed model. The BP neural grid technology to examine the role of green finance in supply chain management was analyzed. To assess the sustainable natural atmosphere, this network technique is moderately developed in terms of network theory and performance (Zhao, 2023).

3. RESEARCH METHODOLOGY

The official websites of the Securities and Exchange Board of India, the Reserve Bank of India, the Council on Energy, Environment, and Water, the Annual Reports of Sustainable Development, the National Oceanic and Atmospheric Administration, and others are used for the collection of secondary data. The study shared the Indian journey of green finance and its taxonomy for sustainability. The models proposed in the study provide information about that about factors to consider in Vulnerability Analysis, Regulatory Actions to Achieve Sustainable Development with Green Finance, Challenges to Achieving Sustainability through Green Finance and Opportunities to Foster Green Finance. It also gives data related to climate change and vulnerability analyses of the same. Five top and bottom Indian states achieving SDGs in the India Index are highlighted.

4. DATA DISCUSSION

A journey of green finance in India started dated back and entered in 2023 with the abundance of changes. India has the commitment to achieve the green deal initiated with neutrality of carbon until 2070. The Indian Government has identified its key focus areas: developing a transparent taxonomy that leads towards the progress of green projects with minimization of transaction costs; formulating a plan to price carbon with special emphasis on the cost of climate change due to mitigation and variation in strategies. The firm use of 'Green Infrastructure Investment Trusts 'in national investment policies comprises bond markets and instruments.

The proper guidelines, rules and regulations, practices, and frameworks are finalized at the end of regulators' time. The structured way to handle the issues related to climate harm and work on them is by guiding the companies and addressing the multiple risks involved in that. The IMF is aiding to endorse green finance widely and evolve climate-oriented stress techniques with the collaboration of varied central banks and institutions. Prominently, including water management, safety of biodiversity and its diversification, prevention, controlling, and compensating the indemnities to the environment, financial assistance to draft public strategies that help in the mitigation of damage caused to the environment, and picking eco-friendly projects and activities.

India got a rank of 112 in overall performance, a 63.4 country score, and a 67.2 regional score, given by the SDG index for 2023. The following two tables describe the SDG 7 and 13 achievements by India in 2019, 2020, and 2021.

Table 1. SDG7: Affordable and clean energy

SDG 7	Value (%)	Year
Population with access to electricity	99.0	2020
Population with access to clean fuels and technology for cooking	67.9	2020
CO2 emissions from fuel combustion per total electricity output	1.5	2019

Source: Sustainable Development Report, 2023

Table 2. SDG 13: climate action

SDG 7	Value (%)	Year
Renewable energy share in total final energy consumption	15.9	2019
CO2 emissions from fossil fuel combustion and cement production (tCO2/capita)	1.9	2021
CO2 emissions embodied in imports (tCO2/capita)	0.1	2018

Source: Sustainable Development Report, 2023

Almost electricity access is provided to 99% Indian population by 2020. The CO2 emissions from the combustion of fossil fuels and cement production were also down to 1.9% in 2021.

Regulatory Measures and Disclosures

The Indian financial sector, specifically its banking sector, has been at the forefront of developing the phenomenon of green finance. RBI dispensed the notice embarking on the role, significance, and need to attain sustainable development by banks in 2007. In light of this, the Equator Principles were consulted, providing a framework for identifying, managing, and assessing the environmental and social risks of monetizing projects. RBI in collaboration with UNEP published a report in 2016 stating the different aspects of the financial system in India and its prime role in promoting growth.

RBI has braced loans for spin-off projects of varied entities up to the limit of Rs. 15 crores, and for individuals, the range is decided up to Rs. 10,000,000. RBI became a member of the Network for Greening the Financial System (NGFS) in 2021, a group of nationalized banks that support the transition to a green economy through activities involving financial and climatic risks.

The Companies Act 2013 requires large corporations to contribute 2% of their annual profits to corporate social responsibility (CSR) programs that include environmental sustainability, protection of the environment, healthcare, rural expansion and edification. Carbon trading has been incorporated into the national policy framework through the "Perform Achieve and Trade" program. The governmental so emphasizes the development of the industry, especially the renewable energy sector, in the mission of transitioning to green energy.

Securities and Exchange Board of India (SEBI) is in the process of repeatedly publishing the various reporting standards for sustainability. The first reporting framework is the "annual corporate responsibility report" based on national voluntary principles. The core principle elements include the development of a company's environmental management system that can prevent damage to the environment during official activities.

Business Responsibility Reporting is one more framework added with the purpose of conducting entities' activities for the environment. This annual framework offers the model that companies can use to monitor their roles in the required areas. Eight guidelines and principle models are defined here that the institution must follow, consisting of: recyclable material percentage, total consumption of energy, use of energy-saving methods and the amount of energy saved, the amount of water consumed and the amount of water saved and recycled, emissions and greenhouse gas mitigation, pre-discharge water treatment and biodiversity restoration.

In the chain of development, SEBI took a giant leap forward and introduced the "Business Sustainability and Responsibility Report" (BRSR) to improve disclosure in Environmental, Social and Governance standards. treatment (ESG) in 2021. It is applicable to the first thousand companies and compulsory from the financial year 2022–23. The BRSR outline uses international ESG values like the Global Reporting Initiative (GRI) along with qualitative and quantitative presentation of data. It is estimated that the ESG data in the NIFTY 50 in that 40% of private companies have a favorable record. The SDG India Index determines goal-wise scores for each state and union territory on the 16 SDGs. In order to assess the sub-national unit's overall performance across the 16 SDGs, overall state and UT scores are created using goal-wise scores. These scores range from 0-100, and if a state or UT receives a 100, it means it has met the 2030 targets. The closer a state or UT comes to achieving its goal, the higher its score.

States and Union Territories are classified as below based on their SDG India Index score:

Aspirant: 0–49
Performer: 50–64
Front-Runner: 65–99
Achiever: 100
(Source: pib.gov.in)

The above-mentioned states and UTs numbers of aspirant, performer, frontrunner, and achiever were fetched from the below given information.

Figure 2. Chart three
Source: pib.gov.in

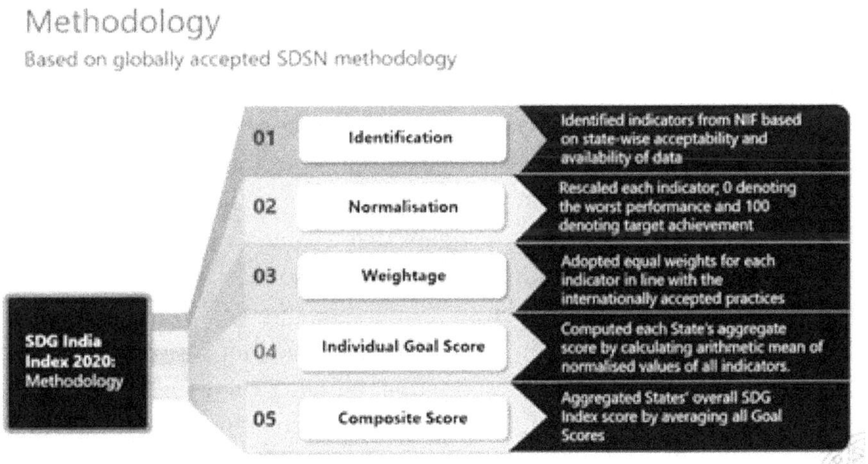

From 60 in 2019 to 66 in 2020–21, the nation's overall SDG score increased by 6 points. The country's outstanding performance in Goals 6 (Clean Water and Sanitation) and 7 (Affordable and Clean Energy), where the composite goal scores are 83 and 92, respectively, is largely responsible for this forward movement toward meeting the targets.

Figure 3. Chart four: Top five and bottom five states in SDG India Index (2020–21)
Source: pib.gov.in

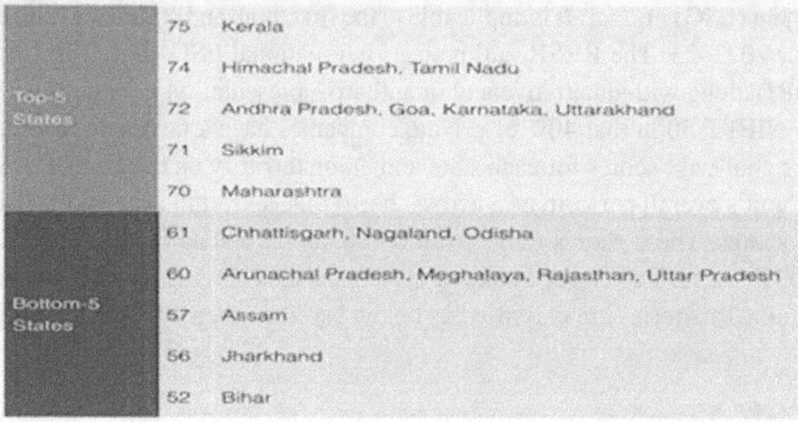

The top states promoting sustainability with green finance were Kerala, HP, TN, AP, Goa, Karnataka, Uttarakhand, Sikkim, and Maharashtra. Contrary to this, Chhattisgarh, Nagaland, Odisha, AP, Meghalaya, Rajasthan, UP, Assam, Jharkhand, and Bihar were detected in the lowline.

Data Related to Climate Risk and Vulnerability Analysis

During last year's COP26 brainstorming session in Glasgow, Indian Prime Minister Narendra Modi committed to achieving net-zero emissions by 2070. He also outlined an ambitious goal for India to develop 500 GW of energy from non-fossil sources by 2030 and cut carbon intensity to 45% as part of the five-pronged "Panchamrit" pledge. In addition, the Prime Minister committed to reducing anticipated carbon emissions by 1 billion tons between 2021 and 2030.

According to the Council on Energy, Environment, and Water (CEEW), achieving net-zero emissions by 2070 will necessitate investments in excess of $10 trillion. These investments would aid in the decarbonization of India's power, industrial, and transportation sectors. According to the CEEW, India's net-zero aim might result in a $3.5 trillion investment gap. Banks would and should play a critical role in attaining these investment targets and filling any gaps that may arise. Furthermore, banking is a sector on the frontlines of climate change, with the financial services industry accounting for a huge 72% of the entire potential financial effect of the change.

Today, technology plays a critical role in the net-zero transition for various sectors and is fast evolving. Some examples include electrifying transportation, building energy-efficient structures, reducing GHG emissions from the industrial and agricultural sectors, remaking the power grid to supply clean electricity, hydrogen fuel cells, and expanding carbon capture, use, and storage—all of which require a significant financial boost of up to US $2 trillion to accelerate the transition to net-zero emissions.

Figure 4. Charts five and six: Projected annual global carbon emissions and projected global temperatures
Source: The National Oceanic and Atmospheric Administration (NOAA), USA, 2021

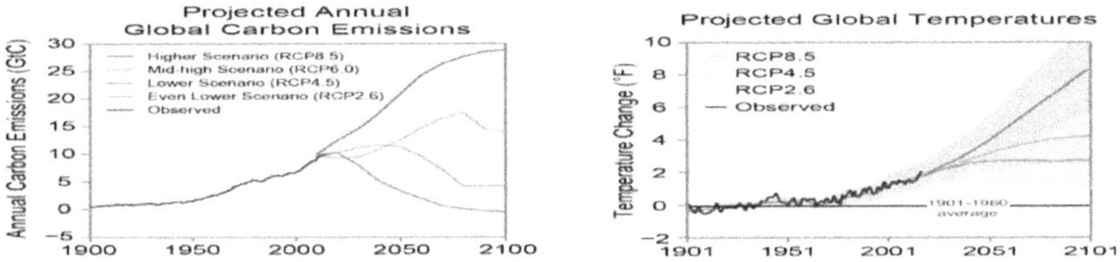

The above image provides information about projected annual global carbon emissions and projected global temperatures. As per the Swiss Re Institute, the global GDP is anticipated to be wiped out by 10% of its current value and as much as 18% by 2050. Germanwatch, an environment think tank, released its report in 2021 stating the most vulnerable climate change nations, and India got the 5th rank in the same. Germanwatch is an independent environmental body that actually works for sustainable growth and development at the international level.

Its importance as a primary force in minimizing the effects of climate change cannot be overstated. It is critical for financial institutions to support the country's transition to net-zero emissions by continuing to fund green infrastructure. Although banks do not have a big direct role in climate change, they do play a backend role as lenders to sectors.

Analyzing vulnerability in the context of green finance and sustainable development entails evaluating possible obstacles and threats that could impede the realization of environmental sustainability and the objectives of green finance projects. This examination plays a vital role in pinpointing regions requiring interventions to strengthen adaptability and secure the enduring triumph of sustainable development endeavors. Below are the essential stages and factors to consider when performing a vulnerability assessment within this framework:

Initiate the process by recognizing the primary stakeholders engaged in green finance and sustainable development, encompassing governmental bodies, financial institutions, corporations, non-governmental organizations (NGOs), and local communities. This might be covered in Identification of Key Stakeholders. Further, clearly delineate the objectives and aspirations underpinning green finance and sustainable development endeavors. What specific environmental and societal outcomes are being pursued? Defining these goals meticulously is pivotal for a thorough vulnerability assessment.

Environmental risk assessment in the form of climate change and biodiversity can be done, evaluating the susceptibility of projects and initiatives to the impacts of climate change, encompassing factors such as escalating temperatures, extreme weather events, and sea-level elevation. Consider both the physical and transitional risks linked to climate change. Furthermore, scrutinizing the potential consequences of projects on biodiversity and ecosystems, Identify regions where conservation endeavors may be exposed to the influence of development activities.

Social risk and financial risk Appraisal through Community Engagement, Labor and Human Rights, Market Risks, and Regulatory Risks: These variables involve gauging the extent of community involvement and social approval for sustainable development projects. Point out potential sources of conflict and risks associated with social unrest. Examine labor and human rights concerns within supply chains and project locales, pinpointing vulnerabilities linked to labor exploitation or violations. Also, assess market-related risks connected to investments in green finance, including shifts in consumer preferences, technological advancements, and policy alterations. Evaluate regulatory risks tied to evolving environmental regulations and incentives, as well as potential policy modifications that might impact the viability of green initiatives.

Figure 5. Factors to consider in vulnerability analysis
Source: Author's own work

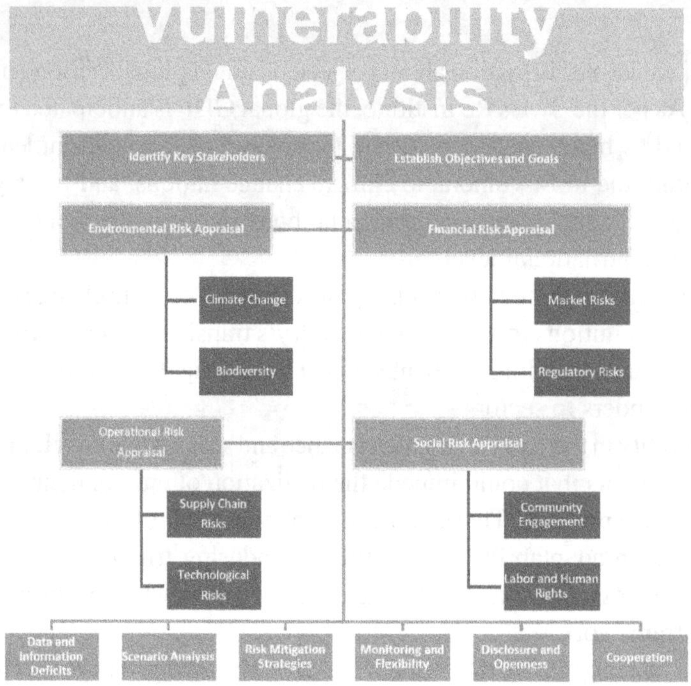

Supply chain risks and technological risks are part of the operational risk appraisal. Here, the vulnerabilities are analyzed in the supply chain, encompassing dependencies on critical resources that could be susceptible to shortages or price fluctuations. Recognizing technological risks, such as the obsolescence of sustainable technologies or cybersecurity threats, is also crucial.

The determination of gaps in data and information is essential because it impedes the accurate evaluation of vulnerability. Address the deficiencies through data collection and research. Conduct scenario analyses to model potential future developments and their implications for green finance and sustainable development goals. This may encompass various climate scenarios, policy alterations, or economic shifts. Next, formulate strategies to mitigate the identified vulnerabilities. This might involve diversifying investments, enhancing resilience measures, improving community engagement, and integrating risk management into project planning. Proper monitoring and flexibility in data establish a resilient system for monitoring and assessing the efficiency of risk mitigation measures, and be prepared to adjust strategies when necessary. Ongoing evaluation and adaptability are vital for sustaining efforts over the long term.

Sharing the results of the vulnerability assessment and efforts to mitigate risks with stakeholders in a transparent manner promotes trust and accountability within the green finance and sustainable development sectors. Encourage collaboration among stakeholders to exchange expertise, best practices, and resources for collectively addressing vulnerabilities.

Assessing vulnerability in the context of green finance and sustainable development is a continuous endeavor that should be seamlessly incorporated into project decision-making and planning. This practice serves to guarantee that investments possess the capacity to withstand environmental and societal hurdles, thereby playing a pivotal role in advancing the attainment of sustainable development objectives.

Regulatory measures have a pivotal role in advancing green finance and sustainable development by establishing a conducive framework that fosters environmentally conscious investments and behaviors. These rules and regulations aim to harmonize financial systems with sustainability objectives, address risks tied to environmental and social concerns, and stimulate investments in eco-friendly ventures. Here are several essential regulatory actions pertaining to green finance and sustainable development:

Regulatory measures have a pivotal role in advancing green finance and sustainable development by establishing a conducive framework that fosters environmentally conscious investments and behaviors. These rules and regulations aim to harmonize financial systems with sustainability objectives, address risks tied to environmental and social concerns, and stimulate investments in eco-friendly ventures. Here are several essential regulatory actions pertaining to green finance and sustainable development:

Figure 6. Regulatory actions to achieve sustainable development with green finance
Source- Author's own work

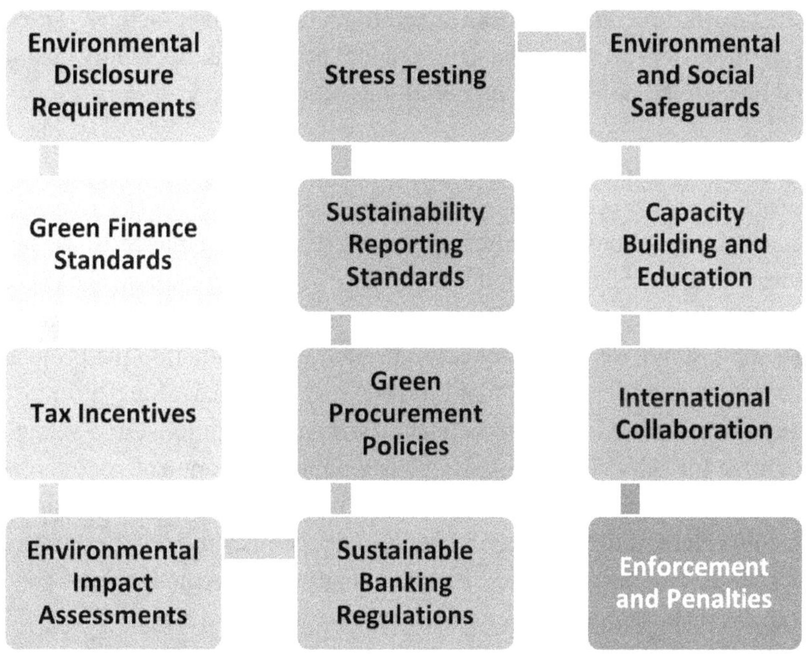

Compulsory reporting mandates that companies and financial institutions divulge their environmental impacts, carbon emissions, and sustainability practices, fostering transparency and enabling stakeholders and investors to make well-informed choices. Environmental Bonds: Create and enforce guidelines for green bonds to guarantee that the funds are directed towards environmentally beneficial endeavors such as renewable energy, energy efficiency, and sustainable infrastructure. Encourage the utilization of sustainability-linked loans, where the interest rate is linked to sustainability performance metrics, motivating borrowers to meet environmental and social goals. Provide tax incentives or deductions to individuals and businesses engaged in eco-friendly activities, such as renewable energy generation, energy-efficient construction, or the development of green technologies. Institute mechanisms for carbon pricing, such as carbon taxes or cap-and-trade systems, to internalize the cost of carbon emissions and incentivize reductions in emissions. Urge financial institutions to embrace responsible banking principles that incorporate environmental and social considerations into their lending and investment decisions.

Climate Stress Testing: Require financial institutions to conduct stress tests related to climate to assess the resilience of their portfolios against climate-related risks, ensuring preparedness for potential climate shocks. Enforce ESIA requirements for projects with potential environmental and social impacts, ensuring alignment with international standards. Invest in training programs and educational initiatives to enhance knowledge and skills among regulators, financial professionals, and the public regarding green finance and sustainable development concepts and practices.

Harmonization: Collaborate with international organizations and other nations to harmonize green finance regulations and facilitate cross-border investments in sustainable projects. Establish penalties for non-compliance with green finance and sustainability regulations to ensure that companies and financial institutions take their responsibilities seriously.

Efficient regulatory actions aimed at promoting green finance and sustainable development establish a conducive atmosphere for investments that contribute positively to both the environment and society. Simultaneously, they work to reduce the risks linked to unsustainable practices. The specific nature of these measures can differ depending on the geographical area and is frequently customized to address particular national or regional objectives and conditions.

Challenges for Green Finance

One of the most significant issues in analyzing the risks of green finance is the lack of established criteria for measuring project environmental effects. Due to varying approaches and criteria, it can be difficult for financial institutions to analyze and evaluate different green initiatives. It is foremost a constraint to establish some standards and to set certain criteria for evaluating the project's environmental consequences. Lack of standardization, availability, and quality of data, long-term vision, Political and legal risks, Technological risks Market and demand risks and reputational and social risks are the few challenges to overcome for achieving the goals of sustainable development.

It is a very apparent prerequisite for any form of study concerning challenges and opportunities and interpreting the results. Here, it is extremely difficult to get precise and reliable statistics on project environmental performance and sustainability. Financial institutions require robust and trustworthy data to properly analyze the risks and opportunities associated with green projects.

Many environmentally friendly investments, such as renewable energy infrastructure, have lengthy payback times. The risk increases with the increase in uncertainty, and uncertainty increases with the increase in time horizon. This creates uncertainty about future legislative changes, technological improvements, and market demands, which may have an impact on the project's financial sustainability.

Now, far and wide in the world, the emphasis is on green finance, environmental sustainability, or what one might call a green revolution in finance. The regulatory environment for green financing is swiftly changing not only in Bharat but in the whole business world as well. Environmental policies, carbon pricing mechanisms, and other regulations can all have an impact on the financial sustainability of green initiatives. We are in the world of the digital age. Emerging technologies are frequently used in green initiatives, which might pose technical and operational concerns. Financial institutions must scrutinize these technologies' availability and dependability. Technology is a great facility but also a challenge. The green products and services market may not develop as planned.

Figure 7. Challenges to achieving sustainability through green finance
Source: Author's own work

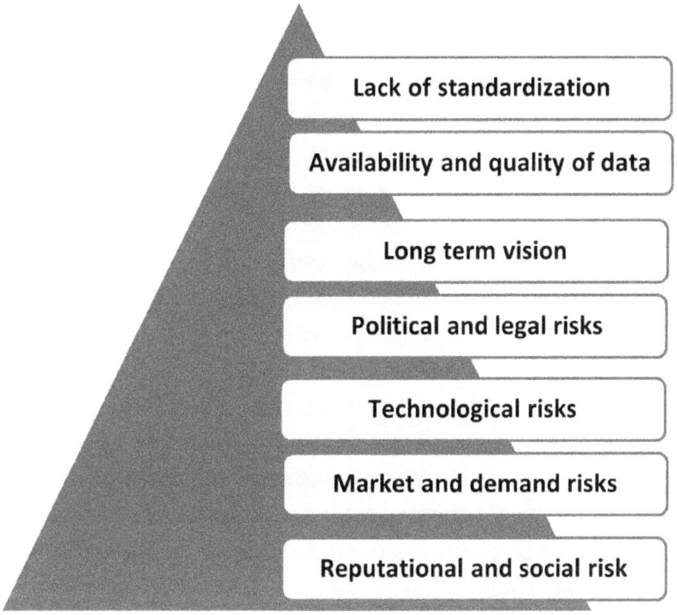

Financial institutions must consider potential changes in consumer tastes and behaviors that may have an impact on the success of green projects. Green projects can have a negative impact on a company's reputation and financing institutions if not implemented carefully and strategically. One should be mindful of the potential consequences if the projects fail to be deemed truly ecologically beneficial.

Opportunities Available for Realizing Sustainability

Financial institutions that identify and manage green financial risks effectively might position themselves as leaders in sustainable finance. This could attract eco-conscious investors and customers.

Green financing allows for the diversification of an investment portfolio, lowering exposure to traditional carbon-intensive assets. This has the potential to improve long-term resilience while also generating attractive returns.

The green finance industry has been geared for revolution. New financial products, risk management initiatives, and investment vehicles tailored to green projects can provide a competitive advantage. Participating in green finance may strengthen a financial institution's brand image and reputation. It displays an ongoing commitment to sustainability and ethical business practices.

As the entire world shifts toward sustainability, financial institutions that employ green finance may correspond with global trends, determining investment and international cooperation. Because of the growing interest in green investing, financial institutions that concentrate on green projects have improved access to funding sources such as green bonds and sustainable investment funds. India has set high standards for renewable energy and sustainable development. Financial institutions are able to contribute towards national goals while potentially profiting from government incentives by promoting green projects.

Figure 8. Opportunities to foster green finance
Source: Author's own work

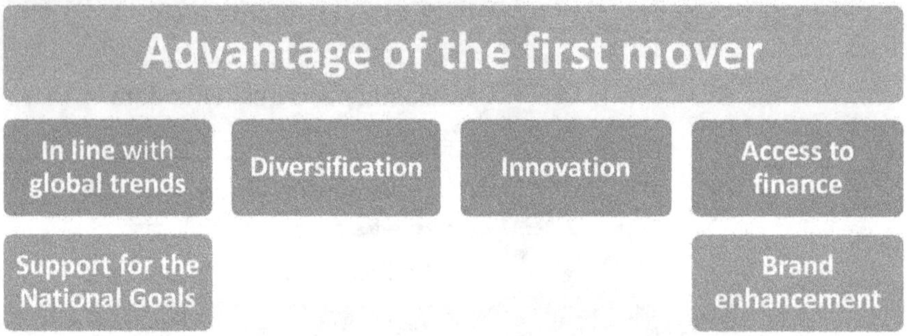

As of March 2020, the Reserve Bank of India's published data indicated that the total outstanding bank loans provided to the non-conventional energy sector amounted to approximately 365.43 billion rupees, equivalent to approximately $4.8 billion. This constituted approximately 7.9% of the total outstanding bank credit extended to the power generation sector.

CONCLUSION

With the regulations for large corporations to contribute 2% of their annual profits to Corporate Social Responsibility (CSR), in the Companies Act 2013, the movement toward green resources and environmental protection has grown significantly. Based on the analysis of numerous data and publications, it is encouraging to know that India is already working on it and has reached certain milestones. Green bonds have thrived in India, with $6 billion distributed, yet the nation must invest $10.1 trillion to achieve carbon neutrality by 2070. This hinges on shifting from coal to renewable and green technology. It is further observed that by sharing vulnerability assessment results transparently, fostering trust and accountability in green finance will also encourage stakeholder collaboration to reduce collective risk. Four models are proposed in the study, describing the factors to be considered for vulnerability analysis, Regulatory actions are required to foster sustainable development with green finance. Challenges must be overcome to achieve sustainable growth, and opportunities are available for companies to grow along with green finance. Though the Indian government has developed a taxonomy for promoting green initiatives within the country and set its own sustainable targets. The paper also provides useful insights on Environmental risk, Financial risk, social risk, operational risk appraisal and disclosure, and openness practices by companies. Several regulatory actions, like green procurement policies, sustainable banking regulations, international collaboration, etc., are to be built for better achievement of green finance. There is a dire need for proper long-term vision, the availability of qualitative data, and so many other factors to accomplish the set targets of sustainable development. Based on research into opportunities and challenges as well as database analysis, it is concluded that even though we have made significant progress toward achieving sustainable development goals, we are still far short of what is required. The road ahead for green finance is still very long and never-ending due to the deluge of environmental challenges.

REFERENCES

Ashta, A. (2023). How Can Fintech Companies Get Involved in the Environment? *Sustainability (Basel)*, *15*(10675), 1–18. doi:10.3390u151310675

Brahmi, M., Esposito, L., Parziale, A., Dhayal, K. S., Agrawal, S., Giri, A. K., & Loan, N. T. (2023). The Role of Greener Innovations in Promoting Financial Inclusion to Achieve Carbon Neutrality. *International Review of Economics*, *11*(194), 1–18. doi:10.3390/economies11070194

Kashi, A., & Shah, E. M. (2023). Bibliometric Review on Sustainable Finance. *Sustainability (Basel)*, *15*(7119), 1–30. https://www.mdpi.com/journal/sustainability. doi:10.3390u15097119

Lin, Z., Wang, H., Li, W., & Chen, M. (2023). Impact of Green Finance on Carbon Emissions Based on a Two-Stage LMDI Decomposition Method. *Sustainability (Basel)*, *15*(12808), 1–28. doi:10.3390u151712808

Saluja, S., Aggarwal, A., & Mittal, A. (2022). Understanding the fraud theories and advancing with integrity model. *Journal of Financial Crime*, *29*(4), 1318–1328. doi:10.1108/JFC-07-2021-0163

Sharma, R., Mehta, K., & Ahuja, S. (2023). A bibliometric analysis of green finance: Present state and future directions. *Advances in Finance, Accounting, and Economics*, *2023*, 135–154. doi:10.4018/978-1-6684-8624-5.ch009

Sideri, L. (2021). Leveraging CSR for Sustainability: Assessing Performance Implications of Sustainability Reporting in a National Business System. *Sustainability (Basel)*, *13*(1), 5987. doi:10.3390u13115987

Taneja, S., Bhatnagar, M., Kumar, P., & Rupeika-Apoga, R. (2023). India's Total Natural Resource Rents (NRR) and GDP:An Augmented Autoregressive Distributed Lag (ARDL) Bound Test. *Journal of Risk and Financial Management*, *16*(2), 91. doi:10.3390/jrfm16020091

Taneja, S., & Ozen, E. (2023, March). Impact of the European Green Deal (EDG) on the Agricultural Carbon (CO2) Emission in Turkey[[Journal homepage:]. *International Journal of Sustainable Development and Planning*, *18*(3), 715–727. https://iieta.org/journals/ijsdp. doi:10.18280/ijsdp.180307

Turner, B. L., & Roger, E. (2022). A framework for vulnerability analysis in sustainability science. *Proceedings of the National Academy of Sciences of the United States of America*, *14*(100), 8074–8079.

Yan, Y., Ibrahim, L. R., Al-Faryan, M. A. S., & Oke, D. M. (2023). Embracing Eco-Digitalization and Green Finance Policies for Sustainable Environment: Do the Engagements of Multinational Corporations Make or Mar the Target for Selected MENA Countries? *Sustainability (Basel)*, *15*(12046), 1–18. doi:10.3390u151512046

Zhao, H. (2023). Risk Management of Supply Chain Green Finance Based on Sustainable Ecological Environment. *Sustainability (Basel)*, *15*(7707), 1–15. https://www.mdpi.com/journal/sustainability. doi:10.3390u15097707

Chapter 19
Adoption Potential and Challenges of Artificial Intelligence in Banking

Arvinder Kaur
https://orcid.org/0000-0001-7360-5674
Chandigarh University, India

Anita Tanwar
Chitkara University, India

ABSTRACT

The proliferation of artificial intelligence (AI) evolved new business models through disruptive innovations. Recent technology developments and quicker data accessibility have moved it closer to commercial applications in financial industries. The study focused on exploring the significance and emergence of AI in the banking industry. This chapter depicting the adoption of AI in the banking sector also discusses the ground-level challenges in its large-scale implementation. Exploratory research was undertaken to examine the applications and factors that support and hinder the effective adoption of AI in the banking industry. Conventional banks are adopting AI due to the emergence of FinTech start-ups in their operations to improve productivity and customer services. The findings suggest that organizational resistance due to the high cost of implementation, skill, and lack of regulatory framework creates hurdles in its fuller adoption, and trust in financial technology is the critical indicator from the user's perspective.

1. INTRODUCTION TO ARTIFICIAL INTELLIGENCE

Implementation of artificial intelligence is a boon for finance sector and fostering sustainable finance alternatives. AI is pioneering in niche segmentation consistently enhancing customer experiences by catering personalized services, chat-bot based virtual assistant, risk management, fraud detention, novel and accurate credit risk assessment. Optimization of operational efficiency of financial institutions are achieved through automation of repetitive nature of tasks, cost reduction, real-time analytics and predic-

DOI: 10.4018/979-8-3693-1388-6.ch019

tive insights are gained by AI. Furthermore, AI set benchmark by integrating environment, social and governance integration by automation of reporting and compliance, along with the identification sustainable investment. With all these endeavors, AI in banking is expected to expand upto 64.03 billion USD by 2030 with a compounded annual growth rate of 32.6% from 2021 to 2030. According to Deloitte, by implementing Generative AI, the front operations departments of the 14 largest international investment banks can increase their efficiency by 27% to 35% by adopting generative AI. By 2026, this would add an average of US$3.5 million in income per front-desk worker. The capacity of robots to mimic or improve human intelligence, such as reasoning and experience-based learning, is known as artificial intelligence (AI) (Kumar & Kaur, 2022). The widespread adoption of artificial intelligence (AI) has resulted in developing novel business models brought about by disruptive actions. Recent technological advancements and manifold increases in data collection and assessment speed have brought it closer to commercial applications of AI in the financial industry. Numerous traditional industries like pharmaceutical, manufacturing, supply chain, media, traveling and financial sectors are starting to reshape their business models with the emergence of AI (Abu Daqar et al., 2020), cloud computing, the internet of things, and machine learning (ML) (Jagtiani & Lemieux, 2019; Janiesch et al., 2021). Conventional businesses, including well-established and new digital start-ups, are forced to respond strategically. Advanced AI technology enables corporate computational intelligence and integrates analytics into apps to support organizational tasks. This includes speedier data processing, more reliable data outputs, and high-level staff actions. Recently, AI-based technologies have been beneficial and practical. But company leaders lack AI strategy knowledge. As per research by (Ransbotham et al., 2017) 85% company executives recognized AI as a crucial tool for creating a sustainable competitive advantage, but only 39% had a strategic AI plan due to an absence of AI application competence (Huang et al., 2020). It is simple to overlook that artificial intelligence is not a recent science because of how much attention it has received. Depending on whether the goal was to demonstrate logical theorems or use neurology to replicate human mind, AI has gone through a number of distinct phases (Sharma et al., 2017). The application of digital technology may present fresh chances for productivity improvements, close client relationships, and development. This requires adapting new digital practices by introducing structural changes and a positive mindset to gain competitive advantage and value. Nowadays, it becomes necessary to equip themselves with these disruptive technologies in the digital era. AI and blockchain are deployed in the financial sector for investment purposes, stock trading, wealth management, risk management, automation of banking operations through verification of large-scale data, alternative ways of credit evaluation by tracking mobile phone data through digital footprint and personalized banking through virtual voice control assistant and chatbots.

Recent years have seen a boom in the use of ML and AI in banking and other financial institutions. These organizations have capitalized on their full potential by providing commercial models for public dealing operations and back-end operations to boost. This article will outline how financial institutions are making use of AI to enhance the way they operate. It will deliver an assessment of these technologies' value to various departments. Fintech companies, which embraced AI for a long time, contribute their innovation to financial intelligence, while conventional financial institutions are rapidly keeping up with artificial intelligence techniques with services like Chatbot. It is safe to state that AI innovations are taking over the banking industry, and we have no choice but to accept this. The following figure 1 is depicting the usage methods of AI in banking.

Figure 1. Adoption and Benefits of AI in Banking
Source: Businessinsider.in

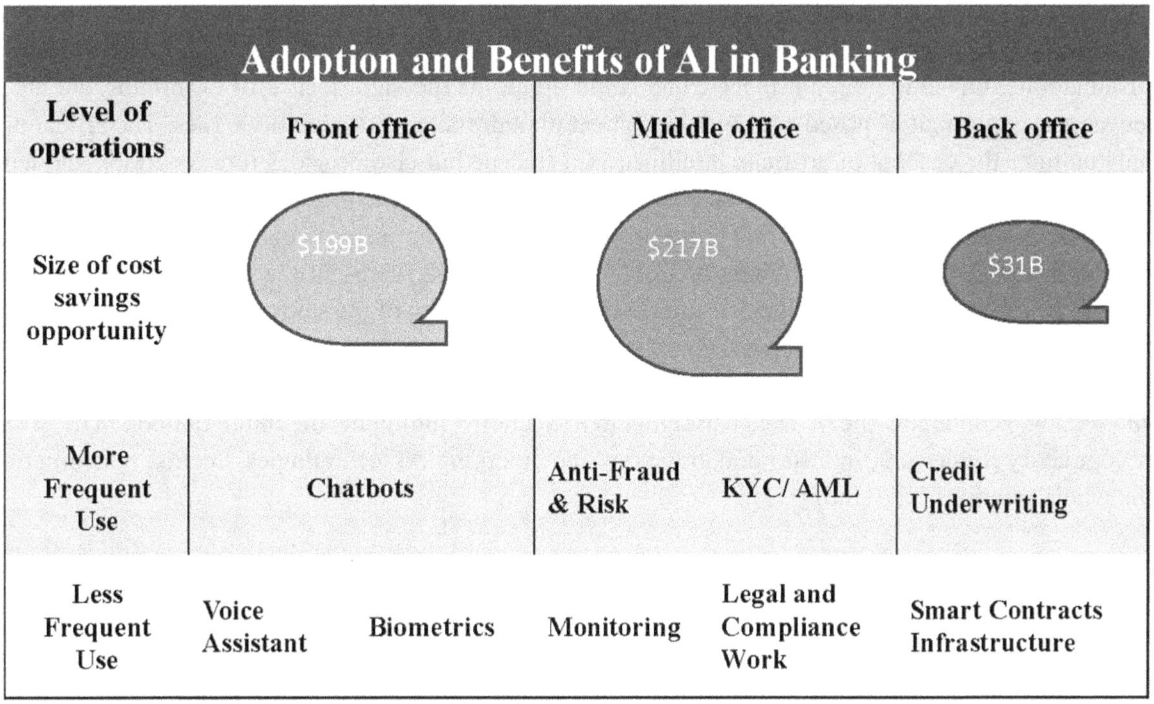

Nearly 80% of banks, according to Business Insider research, are aware of the potential advantages AI may bring to their industry. According to another estimate, deploying AI apps is expected to help banks save $447 billion by 2023. Figure 1 shows that, in order to increase effectiveness, productivity, and profitability while lowering costs, the banking and financial industry is moving quickly toward AI. Banks save $447 billion by using AI in official and client services as explained in above figure.

Existing financial institutions face a plethora of risks, but AI offers numerous chances for disruption in the FinTech sector through gathering information, assessment, security, and process optimization. This study is one of the first to investigate the potential advantages and disadvantages of utilizing artificial intelligence (AI) in banking services and to identify the factors that have the most significant impact on the possibility of its implementation. The policymakers of the financial industry can use the information gleaned from this study to better prepare for the problems posed by artificial intelligence (AI) adoption. Important indicators of clients' intentions to implement AI in banks are also provided. With this information, policymakers may develop plans to promote the widespread use of artificial intelligence. Based on the findings, it is clear that AI is a crucial component in the fight against fraud and other security threats. Adopting AI presents considerable hurdles, including legislative standards, confidentiality and safety of information, and a lack of required skills and IT infrastructure.

Novelty and Outline of Article

Explore a broad variety of activities that investigate the existence of AI in ESG and sustainable finance by assisting bank managers, investors, and creditors in making the right decisions for long-term financial sustainability. Given the circumstances, one could argue for the significance of examining the challenges and opportunities posed by AI in the context of addressing sustainability issues. The article not only outlines the concept of artificial intelligence in finance but also provides future outlook and new perspectives of AI business models and applications. It emphasizes the importance of AI for sustainable investments and its value beyond that of a simple problem-solving instrument.

The article is divided into various sections where section 2 represent the literature based on the theme and identified problem related to subject matter and the aim of the study and section 3 represents methodology, section 4 shows about the application of AI in the banking and finance industry, as well as how this technology is revolutionizing customer service thanks to its amazing advantages in section 5 and section 6 containing the barriers pertaining to it. Section 7 highlights the future outlook in the form of regulatory framework, industry collaborations and emerging AI technologies. Section 8 summaries the whole essence of the study.

2. LITERATURE REVIEW

With diversified market needs and changing trends to satisfy customers, contemporary financial institutions demand digital technology. AI has disrupted banking methods, products, and services such as ATMs, web-based banking, cellular banking, check visualization, speech detection, and chatbots. The rapid adoption of artificial intelligence and machine learning tools in banking organizations for performing critical jobs across the globe suggests that the COVID-19 pandemic will positively impact the growth rate of AI in the banking market. Banks can benefit from digitization thanks to AI, and AI also helps them compete with FinTech firms. Regarding gaining an edge in the marketplace, AI techniques like automated forecasting, automatic speech recognition, and various related tools are being used by approximately 32% of banks by 2020, according to a study performed jointly by the National Business Study Institute and Narrative Science.

The underlying concept of AI, what makes human intellect unique from other creatures: our capacity to learn from our mistakes and apply what we have learned to new circumstances. The credit goes to John McCarthy, who founded AI in 1956, which can mimic humans (McCarthy et al., 1956). The dot-com boom led AI to Web 2.0 in 2005, and information proliferation spurred the creation of AI. The idea of artificial intelligence has been around since the 19th century when Alan Turing first suggested an "imitation game" to measure machine intelligence. However, it was not until recent years that it became practical to reach upto its fuller potential due to the increased accessibility of computing power and data to train AI systems. Think about. This will help you grasp We can accomplish this because we have a highly developed brain with more neurons than other animal species. When computer pioneers like Alan Turing and John von Neumann first began looking into how machines might "think," artificial intelligence was first being studied. This was in the late 1940s. The 1956 discovery that a computer could answer any issue if given infinite memory, however, marked a critical turning point in the field of artificial intelligence. As a result, the General Problem Solver software was created (GPS).

AI development has been the primary force behind the digital revolutions occurring across a number of sectors (Holmes et al., 2019; Jatoba et al., 2019; Soni, 2020). The amount of money invested in artificial intelligence (AI) has increased dramatically during the previous four years (Kaur et al., 2023a; Kaur et al., 2023b). According to a Gartner analysis from 2016, the real use of AI only 9% of firms had invested in technology at the time, but three years later, in 2019, that percentage had risen to 25%, with the Enterprise Digital Research predicting that the growth rate will double over the next five years (Cosma et al., 2023). Additionally, it is now the most effective strategic technology for businesses. AI is becoming a key component of digital transformations, leveraging networking advancements and increased data processing for sustainable practices. In practically every sector, including banking and finance, artificial intelligence has become a significant disruptor. By boosting productivity and making judgements based on data that would be impossible for a human agent to comprehend, AI-based systems can assist banks in cutting expenses (Manoharan et al., 2023). Additionally, clever algorithms can identify false information in a couple of seconds and fraud detection providing the foundation of ESG norms. Banks and other financial organizations employ AI due to user acceptability, regulatory transformation, and technical development and capable of leading banking system with environment, social and governance parameters. However, security, privacy, compliance, and unemployment difficulties prevent its broad acceptance, and the main obstacle is the expense of implementation (Taplin, 2023). A study by Lee et al. (2023) show that the desire to embrace AI in mobile banking is highly influenced by perceived utility, trust, attitude towards AI, and subjective norms. However, perceived ease of use does not affect its adoption intention. Conventional businesses, including well-established and new digital start-ups, are forced to respond strategically (Gupta & Biswas, 2023). Although it has long been employed in computer programs, artificial intelligence is now used in various goods and services. For instance, in insurance sector some digital cameras use artificial intelligence algorithms to identify the objects in an image. AI-enabled personalized traveling suggestions show the cost and date beneficial for any tour and traveling planning (Mohammad, 2020). Additionally, it analyses supply and demand and balances prices and sales thus increase the performance of the organization. Experts also anticipate that artificial intelligence will be used in smart energy grids and many more novel applications. The use of AI in claim settlement through image processing is fruitful and relieves the customer by saving time and effort (Acemoglu & Restrepo, 2018). To answer real-world issues, AI employs methods from probability theory, economics, and algorithm design (Anshari et al., 2021). In addition, computer science, mathematics, psychology, and linguistics are all used in the AI discipline. Mathematics gives methods for modeling and resolving the ensuing optimization issues, whereas computer science offers tools for creating and constructing algorithms.

Investment banking has long made use of AI and automated processes, thus becoming pioneer in green and sustainable investment. Automating trades, updating managing hazards, and conducting research into investments are all areas that have significantly benefited from the application of natural language processing (NLP), blockchain, and ML algorithms. Contrast, despite making considerable investments in automating the different parts of the transaction life cycle, many jobs still need more human resources (Rjoub et al., 2023). However, numerous work may be automated using large language models (LLMs), saving money and boosting employee productivity. It might also liberate funds to encourage creativity and let front-desk workers devote extra time to engage with customers helpfully.

Artificial intelligence, through its innovations, brought phenomenal changes in business operations and fundamentals. It has revolutionized the way of managing and handling personal finances and corporate wealth management. Cost saving and customer friendly services by banks by implementing AI applications in their official and client-related services are the major motivator of its adoption. User acceptance, the regulatory transition towards AI and technological advancement are the key drivers for adopting AI by banks and other financial institutions. Nevertheless, certain issues become the hurdle in its fullest adoption, including security concerns, privacy issue, compliance, and unemployment and the biggest among them is the cost involved in implementing.

Gaps and Research Questions

Literature review reveals the following gaps: no study has demonstrated how AI applications promote green, sustainable, and environmentally friendly, responsible banking through innovative technology-based practices. Moreover, an obstacle exists regarding the implementation of AI in banking systems. To shed light on the potential benefits, risks, and obstacles in its broader implementation, the current paper compiles all the specific topics evolved along the path of adoption of AI in the banking business. Accordingly, the following research questions for the study is framed as shown below:

- What type of applications of artificial intelligence equip banking industry for sustainable financial practices?
- How financial institutions embrace their performance and gain competitive edge by attracting environmentally aware clientele through the adoption of AI in the context of sustainable finance?
- What kind of base-level obstacles faced by banking industry through the adoption of AI?
- What would be the future regulatory trends, industry and research collaborations in the same context?

3. METHODOLOGY

Research methodology gives the insight about the practical approach of research study. It answers how the data can be collected and what type of data analysis tools will be used. Quantitative, qualitative, exploratory and experimental are types of research methodology adopted to conduct research. As far as data collection is concerned, it's totally depends upon the type of research area we want to continue with, like for doing social and scientific research the data will be gathered from individual basis, so for that case we can use primary data sources. However in case of pursuing econometric research we generally utilize secondary data which is already published by companies, government and other agencies. For current study the exploratory research is instrumental. It contains the secondary information and data pertaining to research article, news, depositories and reports regarding the implementation and adoption of artificial intelligence in financial services.

4. APPLICATION OF AI IN THE BANKS FOR SUSTAINABLE FINANCE

AI assist banks, businesses and government agencies in better educated decision making and ecologically accountable choices. Additionally artificial intelligence in banking can significantly contribute to the advancement of sustainable finance. The following are several approaches that artificial intelligence can support sustainable finance:

4.1 Analytics of Data and ESG Score

Today, data analytics are utilized to forecast next developments and trends. AI is capable of analyzing enormous volumes of information to evaluate the ESG risks connected to investment funds and loans. This assists financial institutions in identifying possible sustainability-related risks and making better-informed decisions. Artificial intelligence (AI) can generate ESG scores for projects and businesses, offering a consistent method to assess their sustainability performance. Banking institutes also invest into such projects after going through these rankings to assess the social and environmental effect of their loans. In regular banking operations also data analytics is very helpful since it allows them to forecast future events and quickly identify patterns in consumer behavior. As a result, banks may reach out to the consumer with the appropriate product at the appropriate moment. For instance, when a customer last visited the bank, when they completed their transactions, and which websites they are now browsing. Together, all of this data may enable banks to develop distinctive client relationships. As a result, data analytics allows for the observation of future trends, which will aid banks in effectively up-selling and cross-selling.

4.2 Chatbots

AI-powered chatbots and virtual assistants may teach clients about ESG investing, trustworthy spending, and sustainable finance. In essence, conversational chatbots are used by banks to improve the client experience across all digital banking channels. Banking chatbots can increase client interaction and simplify antiquated operations in today's hectic, fast-paced world. For raising queries, the chatbots will revert you to the desired officer and authority on 24/7 access to financial services. This elevates the problems of call centers and saves costs for the organization. Chatbots in banking brings the following advantages:

- Cost-effectiveness
- Involving and keeping consumers
- Rationalizing banking procedures
- Increasing general effectiveness

4.3 Robotic Process Automation (RPA)

Automation of processes linked to sustainability norms like certifications, adherence to rules and complying reporting standards can be facilitated by artificial intelligence tools knowns as robotic process automation (RPA). As a result, financial institutions have fewer administrative responsibilities to do and can guarantee fast and accurate reporting.

Robotic process automation (RPA) software technology capable of building, deploying, and managing software robots that mimic human interaction with digital systems (Villar & Khan, 2021). Like humans, software robots can understand what is displayed on a screen, make the proper keystrokes, navigate computer systems, locate and extract data, and carry out various predefined tasks. However, software robots are faster and more reliable than people performing the same task without the need to stand up and stretch or take a coffee break.

Robotic process automation is being implemented in various sectors, including healthcare, manufacturing, and insurance. The market for RPA was estimated to be worth $1.57 billion globally, and it is anticipated to grow at a CAGR of 32.8% from 2021 to 2028. According to Gartner, 80% of financial sector leaders already utilize RPA in some capacity.

The banking industry is using RPA as a tool today. Because of the intense rivalry in the sector, each bank must work to keep expenses to a minimum while maximizing efficiency to maintain its position. However, the banks also need help maintaining the required security level. RPA is the only option, therefore, for all questions (Marek et al., 2019; Mehrotra & Menon, 2021). A few instances of banks that have embraced RPA include the following: RPA was first broadly implemented by ICICI Bank in India. As of today, 750 software robots handling 20 lakh transactions per day were deployed by the bank in 2016, which had 200 software robotics programmes (Published on the official website of ICICI Bank on 8 September 2016). Another illustration is Yes Bank, which has also utilized RPA for corporate to make export and import business operations easier. They have introduced a "Digital Export and Import" payments solution based on robots (Published on the official website of Yes Bank on 15 March 2018). Like Axis Bank and Deutsche Bank, additional banks are planning to deploy RPA. Therefore, one might reduce labour expenses and improve operational efficiency by implementing RPA.

4.4 Fraud Management and Detection

The ultimate goal of every business is to reduce the risks that are related to it. This assertion would apply to banking and financial institutions as well. Machine learning and deep learning techniques are critical in detecting financial crimes or dishonest financial practices like money laundering and corruption, which can jeopardize attempt for sustainable finance. Banks and other financial institutions must be prompt when collecting and disbursing interest on deposits and dividends because they deal with deposits and payments. This is why banking and financial institutions view fraud as a serious problem and use AI-enabled technologies to prevent financial pollution which was critical in conventional banking system (Kaur, 2020). The best technology for fraud and security detection is artificial intelligence (Jakhiya et al., 2020; Suryono et al., 2021).

AI enabled fraud detection mechanism works on customer's spending, payment and receipt transaction, which buzz the alarm of security mechanism when any sort of change and contradiction in pre-established pattern and location found.

4.5 Automated Virtual Personal Assistants for Risk Management

Users can make effective and efficient decisions regarding financial-related activities with the help of AI-powered financial experts and advisers. Implementation of artificial intelligence can optimize portfolios of securities to promote environmentally and environment-friendly assets. It may recommend ESG-aligned investments based on current and past information. This process takes into consideration watching the stock and bond market trends in accordance with the user's investment affordability and portfolio, which will help them make decisions about buying and selling stocks and bonds (Flavián et al., 2022). The use of these advisers, which are sometimes referred to as "Robo-Advisors," has grown thanks to well-known financial institutions and Fintech startups (Gomber et al., 2018; Paul & Sadath, 2021).

These are capable of analyzing and fast processing of structured data like companies financial information and excel sheet also unstructured data like information on the social media sites and news (Kaur et al., 2022a). Quick Processing of data means quicker transaction decision (Fratrič et al., 2022). Prediction of stock prices through intelligent trading system is generally more accurate as it test and validate all information before processing it (Kumar & Kaur, 2022). The recent innovation named as Alpaca Forecast AI Prediction Matrix in this regard.

4.6 Climate Risk Assessments and Energy Efficient Trading

By modeling and forecasting climate-related risks, artificial intelligence (AI) can assist banks in determining how global warming will affect their portfolios of securities and enable them to make more informed investments. Implementing AI in banking facilities holds promise for energy optimization, which could result in reduced carbon emissions and the promotion of sustainability goals.

4.7 Customer Perceptions for Green Investment and Lending

Banks can enhance their ability to meet customer demands for sustainable financing and environmental, social, and governance initiatives by employing AI to analyze user information to derive observations regarding their funding inclinations.

The usage of AI can aid lending organizations in the identification and evaluation of environmentally sustainable enterprises and ventures which satisfy the criteria for ecological loans. Artificial intelligence can assist financial institutions in adhering to evolving sustainability and reporting regulations.

4.8. Claims Treatment

AI-enabled technologies gather proof and intelligently analyze the data to guarantee the calibre of outcomes. AI-enabled technologies learn users' or customers' behavioral patterns to identify unusual behavior. activities and send out alerts for any unusual transactions or incidents (Thakor, 2020). These technologies have a significant impact on claims administration; in particular, machine learning techniques make it possible to skip over a number of steps in the claim settlement process (Taneja et al., 2023). AI-powered technologies efficiently streamline the data management process. It manages a large volume of data in a short amount of time, allowing insurers to settle claims electronically.

5. ARGUMENTS IN FAVOR OF ARTIFICIAL INTELLIGENCE

The use of AI technology has the calibre to cut costs drastically. An Accenture study discovered that financial institutions might improve their trading volume by 2.5 times while utilizing AI banking solutions to maintain this same headcount. Additionally, businesses that provide banking products are ideally situated to benefit from AI (Brewer, 2018). Without data, there is no AI in banking. However, the financial system gathers much data during normal company operations.

Admittedly, using artificial intelligence and machine learning in the financial sector and for banking services is nothing new. Already, dubious credit card activity has been discovered by artificial intelligence. The sector needs to use the appropriate technologies to safeguard its clients and reduce its risk while cybercrime, including data breach and privacy issue, also increasing.

AI enables better internal operations, minimizes the human error rate, and smooths customer services. Seamless and customer-friendly experience is the key motive of AI in financial and other sectors. An intelligent Decision Management System decreases the frequency of mistakes and shortens the time required to utilize users' data and perform operations and thus turn efficient in maintaining compliance. However, a thorough assessment of AI in banking and financial services would fall short if it skipped over certain common misconceptions about the technology. For instance, it is a misconception that machine learning can match human intelligence. Although AI seems to be superior than human, such as when analysing many variables to anticipate a result, the costs frequently outweigh the advantages.

Figure 2. Business Value derived worldwide
Source: Statista.com

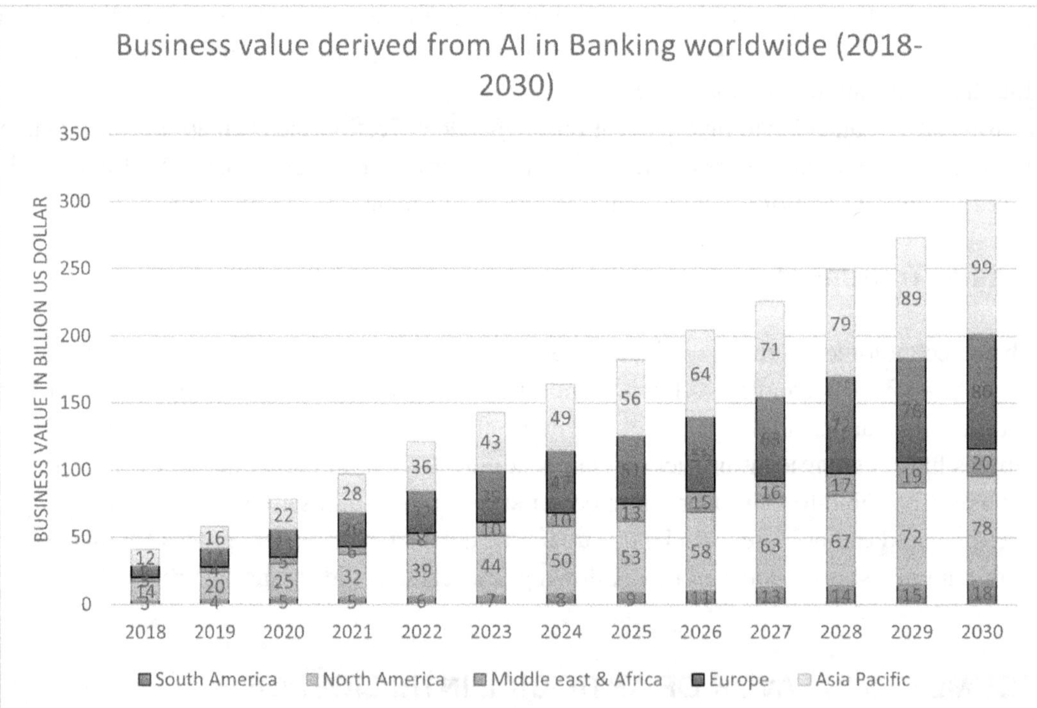

The forecast of business value derived worldwide during 2018-2030 is depicted in (Figure 2). It showed that Asia Pacific is gaining highest value by attaining progressive rate of benefits at 12 Billion USD in 2018 and bid to achieve 99 billion USD in 2030. However, Europe is at level 2 with minimal difference of achievement rate. North America is also shown a good gain of business value showing 14 billion UDS in 2018 to 78 billion USD in 2030As far as Middle East is concerned is stating a deserted view in terms of gain of business value. South America is shown least gain in business value derived.

5.1 Detecting Fraud and Adhering to Regulations

The banking sector has a chequered history that has cost investors millions. Companies violating the rules face severe fines under the laws. Consequently, when it is feasible, other financial institutions should streamline regulation.

A decision management system enables thorough audit evidence and rapid fraudulent identification (Leo et al., 2019; Yoon & Jun, 2019). Daily operations are hindered during the manual audit process when one is asked to provide certain information by sparing extra time. Information entered into the system will be accurate thanks to the right software and machine learning, and mistakes will be promptly detected and corrected.

Financial institutions' increased awareness causes scammers to change their tactics. Malicious actors have trained to operate in sums just below the detection threshold since high amount transfers are reported for inquiry. Despite achieving the rules, illicit conduct may only be noticed with a thorough analysis. In this particular field, artificial intelligence outperforms human intelligence. Large volumes of data are examined by AI, which identifies questionable transactions. Errors occur when such trades are manually analysed. The AI-enabled fraud detection mechanism is preventing money laundering and financing illicit operations.

5.2 Better Investment Appraisal

One aspect of raising funds is interest income. As a result, banks are constantly looking for profitable prospects to engage in and generate a profit. The asset allocation technology can offer investment strategies that suit these organizations' tolerance for risk (Mavlutova et al., 2021; Nagimova, 2022). Additionally, considering it is frequently challenging to interpret business facts, they can assess customer fundraising offers appropriately.

Create knowledge and still make investment decisions. Technology for stock valuation streamlines the procedure and allows for additional variables. Getting information may take a while if the institution has interests outside its national borders. While evaluating a new setting can be difficult, the correct AI software can speed up the procedure.

5.3 AI in Personalized Banking

DARQ facilitates organizations with improved outcomes; through personalized banking, it treats each bank customer as a segment (Gigante & Zago, 2022). DARQ comprises Distributed Ledger Technology (DLT) (Ante, 2020; Schulz & Feist, 2021), Artificial Intelligence, Extended Reality, and Quantum Computing Technique (Ding et al., 2019; Elsheikh, 2022) which offers the record of all types of electronic transactions and data collection. DLT is the basic technology that works to exchange cryptocurrency and blockchain applications (Chiu, 2017; Martin Kim, 2017). Also, it improves the automation of business processes add simplifies algorithm and computational processes. Extended Reality encompasses you with the virtual learning capable of bringing fun and thrill.

5.4 More Accurate Loan and Facility Evaluation

It frequently depends on inaccurate data, out-of-date data, and misrepresentation to qualify for funding employing credit ratings and scores (Klafft, 2008; Wu et al., 2022). Nevertheless, there is now a wealth of information online that can provide a more accurate portrait of the individual or company being assessed. If individuals have minimal historical banking transactions and financial data, an AI-based system can provide acceptance or refusal suggestions by considering additional factors (Kaur et al., 2022b).

The problematic element is that the technology's recommendations could be more obvious as to why they are made. No concerns are raised following the approval of a request. The organization owes the client an explanation if a request is turned down (Jagtiani & Lemieux, 2019; Mi et al., 2018).

Machines can exhibit prejudice despite being intended to be impartial. This is because configurations are only as excellent as their creators. Luckily, the majority of budget allocations that institutions get are comparable, and individuals are aware of institutional prejudice. As a result, programmers are now in a stronger place to choose the right variables when creating new apps and upgrades.

5.5 Reduced Risks and Costs of Operations

As much as we value interpersonal relationships, there is one huge disadvantage. Errors happen frequently and have detrimental effects (Leo et al., 2019). The wrong keystroke could expose the institution to a lawsuit and harm its reputation beyond repair, even when experienced professionals are in charge.

By incorporating logical processes into data gathering and utilizing prescriptive and predictive methods to address business issues, decision control systems lower this threat. Use onboarding as an illustration. Employing DMS, you may build up some rules based on the customer's bio-data or company data, showing them what kinds of accounts they can open.

The sort of account a customer can open depends on their age and source of income if they do it online. In that circumstance, minors cannot create accounts in their names, and overdraft protection is not available for personal savings accounts. As a result, you will need fewer personnel to interact with customers, saving your labor costs. Due to greater accuracy, the organization also needs fewer individuals to evaluate transactions and activities. Additionally, there is an advantage to staff wellness. For instance, a DMS speeds up information entry, allowing your staff to innovate and concentrate on important company activities more.

The value of a handshake cannot be replaced by artificial intelligence, notwithstanding its benefits. However, financial institutions can shift their focus from data entry to business development with savings from investing in AI technologies.

5.6 More Customer Satisfaction

Ease and accessibility are a continual priority for consumers. Even when the banks are closed, access to ATMs for banking transactions is the essential thing the customers require for the successful acceptance and implementation of technology (Dash & Chakraborty, 2021). Inventions and innovations are the key drivers responsible for spurring the degree of ease and accessibility. Smartphones, through app installation, provides the ease of opening bank account and doing transactions at their place of convenience.

The KYC norms compliance can be done quickly with the help of a Decision Management System (DMS) (Ozili, 2020), with more efficiency and reduced errors. Organizational choices can be made and applied quickly with the right technology and application.

Timely availability of new items and seasonal financial offers is possible. Fresh company choices and tariff adjustments can also be included in the framework. Computerized eligibility means customers who do not qualify will feel satisfied after going through the process only to be turned away. Despite having a diverse consumer base, this kind of technology creates the appearance of a personalized connection (Vyas & Raitani, 2014).

By speeding up response, institutions can gain the trust and confidence of their customers. Also, automate the approval process for facilities. Account limits were often imposed on customer accounts due to bank workers opening accounts incorrectly. For a client, that can be extremely aggravating. A seamless consumer journey is guaranteed by precise data collection and proper account activation. More the satisfaction of customer more market size of AI based industry. The (figure 3) shows a forecast of rise in market size of AI-enabled industry which could shows an emerging need to transform the business model to stay competitive in market and capture untraced market too.

Figure 3. Market size of AI from 2022-32
Source: Precedence Research

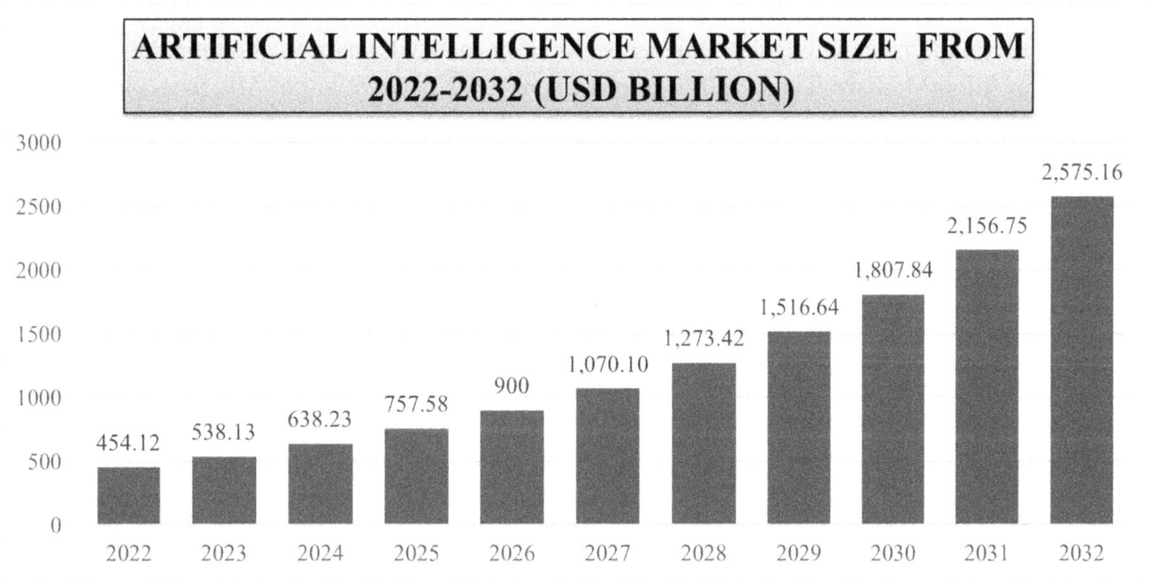

6. BARRIER TO ADOPTION OF ARTIFICIAL INTELLIGENCE

There are certainly real-world examples that show the implementation of artificial intelligence and Machine learning in the financial sector, illustrated as follows:

- Numerous banks use Optical Character Recognition to expedite their documentation and other processes.
- Machine learning programs are utilized to identify fraudulent activities.
- Predictive machine learning techniques streamline the buying policy and related activities.

However the implementation of AI is still at its infancy stage. As per the report on ML by Bank of England only 13% of industrial organizations have adopted AI in its majority of operations in true sense. The following are the obstacle in the pathway of its fuller adoption:-

6.1 The Nascent and Dispersed Technological Environment

An extremely new and scattered digital landscape is one of the turbulent times that the developing discipline of ML faces as it develops (Lu et al., 2022; Ruffolo, 2022). On average, firms currently take two to three months to implement ML techniques into production manufacturing. The lengthy preparation time is a sign of the dearth of developed pattern recognition operationalization technologies. Nevertheless, considering the speed at which Machine learning operationalized programs are evolving, it is only a matter of time before tooling catches up.

6.2 A Dearth of Skilled Personnel

A group of data experts, including data engineers, scientists, and ML analysts, is required to implement AI initiatives fully (Muthaiyah et al., 2021). Consequently, the deployment of ML across industries—including the banking sector—continues to be hampered by a paucity of analytical experts. According to a Deloitte poll, 23% of the most experienced AI users cited a serious shortage of talent skilled in implementing AI. A targeted approach for upskilling and reskilling and for particular skills is required to close this skill gap (Patnaik et al., 2016).

6.3 Low Level of Trust and Confidence in ML

It might be challenging to understand or justify the assumptions made by sophisticated ML algorithms. The end-users struggle to embrace the outcomes of black-box models because they do not comprehend how they work. IBM Watson is one example. Its black-box design failed to gain the trust of its end users, despite being once hailed as the healthcare industry's future. These doctors correctly chose not to leave choices about mortality and life up to a mysterious AI system. Similarly, black-box models are hard for financial services authorities to trust when making critical choices like fraud detection. This is especially true when achieving reporting requirements and preventing discrimination, unfair outcomes depend on transparency. The challenge of interpretability can transit into a greater level of skepticism about the suitability of an AI approach."

Additionally, customer trends and requirements shift, particularly those of digital users and Z-generation. FinTech has moved established business methods to mobile apps that can be far more convenient, accessible, and quick. Apps run on mobile have emerged as the primary support system for financial developments and serve as a conduit for the delivery of Mobile banking that crosses all geographic and temporal boundaries, enhancing economic inclusivity (Dawood et al., 2022). A key element in the financial technology environment is perceived trust or confidence in adopting financial business models via mobile technology. Trust has a mediating influence on the intention and acceptance of various fintech models.

6.4 Scarcity of Quality Data Availability

The adoption of national data protection laws in the United States and Europe shows that authorities closely examine how businesses handle relevant information and dataset (Protopappas et al., 2020). Furthermore, trans-national transnational data sharing is still somewhat restricted because of regional variations in information protection legislation. Due to these regulations, there is a dearth of information on which algorithms for machine learning may be trained and projections made.

6.5 The Final Phase of Operationalization

The last constraint, or the difficulty of delivering outcomes to the appropriate individuals at the appropriate moment, also affects ML programs. Subscribers of mobile apps, in contrast, would not be happy to discover that a specific tip takes ten minutes to load if they were anticipating instant satisfaction. The user experience in speeding up the installation process should be simplified and fast.

6.6 Micro and Macro Level Risks

Through the advent of digital disruption, Industry 4.0 innovations have been transforming the financial sector over the past few decades. Stablecoin, an AI-enabled payment driver, is an example of digital currency that offers a more efficient, stable, cost-effective money transfer alternative and is environment-friendly (Singhal et al., 2022). These disruptive technologies have also created a new monetary taxonomy called "digital currencies." Nevertheless, its widely used form of payment presents distinct threats to the financial system, endangering the nation's economy. Several significant risk categories keep stablecoins from being widely used payment methods. The technological risk was considered the prime barrier to preventing its widespread usage. Next comes up about macro-level risk, including regulatory (Kunhibava & Muneeza, 2019; Mahalle et al., 2021), legal threats (Arner et al., 2015), terror funding, database risk, wealth concentration issues, bank fraud, money laundering, illegal activities, privacy and information theft risk (Kruglova & Dolbezhkin, 2019).

7. FUTURE OUTLOOK OF AI IN BANKING INDUSTRY

Banking organizations are becoming more cognizant of the potential benefits of AI in addressing environmental, social, and governance (ESG) challenges. The emergence of AI technologies in the banking sector is promising for sustainable finance. Take into account these significant industrial policies, collaborations, partnerships and regulatory perspectives:

7.1 Industry Partnerships

Banks can collaborate with AI-focused FinTech startups to access innovative sustainable finance solutions. These collaborations can assist institutions in swiftly implementing AI ESG reporting and analysis capabilities. Financial institutions require dependable and up-to-date data for AI-powered sustainability evaluations from data providers, particularly those that offer comprehensive environmental, social, and governance (ESG) data. Financial and academic research institutions can collaborate to create AI models and tools that address sustainability concerns, such as measuring impact and assessing climate risks. Banks can form partnerships with green technology and renewable energy companies to provide funding for sustainable projects. AI enables the identification of potential partnership opportunities that can be advantageous. Experienced AI service providers in the financial industry can assist in developing sustainable finance solutions. These agreements may involve ESG-related customer service AI platforms, chatbots, and virtual assistants.

7.2 Emerging AI Technologies

Financial institutions can gain valuable insights into sustainability trends and market sentiment by utilizing natural language processing to extract and analyze informal environmental, social, and governance information from social media platforms, reports, and news sources. Understanding AI (XAI) will ensure full disclosure, accountability and adherence to regulatory requirements. XAI will highlight the importance of ESG considerations by enabling banks to provide justifications for AI-powered decisions. Financial institutions will utilize AI technology to develop cutting-edge green financial products that cater to the needs of environmentally conscious customers and financiers. We will provide options for green mortgages, ESG funds, and sustainable bonds.

7.3 Regulatory Trends

Regulatory authorities are anticipated to enhance ESG reporting requirements to promote sustainable financial transparency and standardization. It is essential for banks to incorporate AI into their data gathering, investigating, examining and reporting processes to meet these criteria. Regulators may require climate stress testing to assess financial firms' climate-related risks. Banks will utilize AI computations to evaluate and handle these risks. Establishing Ethical AI Frameworks: Financial authorities can establish ethical norms for AI to promote transparency, explain ability, and fairness in its implementation. These frameworks play a crucial role in the widespread adoption of AI in the industry. AI can effectively quantify the concrete outcomes of sustainable investments by automating the process of measuring their impact. This will enable financial institutions to report their achievements in sustainable financing.

8. CONCLUSION

The development of artificial intelligence in the banking sector is facilitated by the enhancement of amassing information technologies among banks. The global market is expanding because of bank spending on artificial intelligence to promote sustainable finance, ecological lending and leading with ESG norms. However, market expansion is stymied by obstacles, including the high implementation price for AI, more sophisticated machine learning, and a dearth of qualified workers. However, throughout the time frame anticipated, prospects to grow AI in the banking industry are likely to be lucrative due to the rising popularity of new banking software applications.

To better manage the large amount of information that is produced for pertinent knowledge and more accurate choices, the remedy sector is likely to capture a sizable part of the AI in the banking market during the time frame being forecast. Artificial intelligence (AI) and advanced machine learning algorithms are becoming more popular across sectors as businesses place a premium on developing new avenues for expansion and profit with adoption of sustainable financial practices. Today, data analytics are utilized to forecast next developments and trends. AI is capable of analyzing enormous volumes of information to evaluate the ESG risks connected to investment funds and loans. This assists financial institutions in identifying possible sustainability-related risks and making better-informed decisions. By modeling and forecasting climate-related risks, artificial intelligence (AI) can assist banks in determining how global warming will affect their portfolios of securities and enable them to make more informed investments. As the demand for cloud-based AI services from end users continues to rise, the provider category is predicted to increase at the fastest rate over the projection period. Financial Conduct Authority has captured the effect of AI on the financial industry and services. Approximately 72% of the UK financial industry players either using or developing machine learning in their top management decision formulation and in day-to-day operations. The financial sector is evolving quickly. Financial institutions must adopt new technology to keep up with the rapidly evolving sector. AI is one such technical achievement, the adoption benefits the organizations by reduced fraud, better decisions, and improved consumer experiences. New, influential technologies are driving futuristic innovation and digital transformations. The platform allows companies to respond to subscriber needs and requirements. The evolution of AI in the banking sector not only simplifies the business process and brings transition but also helps reduce costs. The performance of the banking sector by integrating AI in their operations can be measured through the time used to serve the bank's customer application, the total number of customer applications served, the cost involved in the processing, and the financial resources saved in serving clients. Through e-signature, e-KYC and e-authentication processes, AI expands the accessibility of financial services and makes them available on a 24*7 basis (Wang et al., 2020).

Nevertheless, employees' productivity increased by assimilating AI techniques and saving time and money. But the drawbacks like employee resistance, labor unemployment, and theft of personal information. For banks to fully profit from AI, limitations must be removed. The significant barriers to the growth and invention of AI are illustrated as a shortage of experienced people, regulations, data that is not readily available, poor quality, and a lack of knowledge. The technological risk was considered the prime barrier to preventing its widespread usage. Next comes up about macro-level risk, including regulatory and legal threats. From the users' viewpoint, trust is investigated as a fundamental aspect of adopting AI in banking. Through the DARQ technique, the Distributed Ledger, artificial intelligence, extended reality, and quantum computing significantly impact the business's productivity and improve customer experience in the financial sector.

Considering the adoption level in the private and public sectors, up to this point, the private sector has mostly been responsible for driving AI-based applications, which have primarily focused on consumer goods. It is essential for policymakers in the government to pay attention due to the innovation's expansive scope and implications. Open and private finance options are available for AI research that India should consider from early AI achievements in the United States, China, South Korea, and other countries. The sequential arrangement of training and employment is outmoded in the current economic climate as the concept of jobs evolves swiftly, and aptitudes become significant and outdated in only years. The obstacles on the checklist listed above can be overcome with enough time and effort. The advantages of AI in banking are numerous and difficult to overlook. According to the Forbes Report,

65% of top management is expected to have a positive outcome from its implementation (Aitken, 2018). By solving these issues, the financial sector would have been one step closer to reaping the benefits of AI implementation.

Several applications of AI could assist the banking industry in integrating sustainable practices into its business and financial decisions more efficiently. Ultimately, this can promote ethical banking procedures, increase financing for green initiatives, and reduce exposure to sustainability risks, all of which contribute to a more ecologically conscious world market and equitable finance.

AI can effectively quantify the concrete outcomes of sustainable investments by automating the process of measuring their impact. This will enable financial institutions to report their achievements in sustainable financing.

By automating the procedure for assessing the effects of sustainable investments, AI is capable of precisely quantifying the tangible results. Financial institutions will be empowered to disclose their accomplishments in the realm of sustainable financing.Ultimately, the banking industry's adoption of AI technologies for sustainable finance will be characterized by careful regulatory oversight, strategic partnerships, and continuous improvement of AI capabilities. By providing ethical and environmentally conscious financial services, banks in this context can fulfil the increasing need for sustainable finance.

REFERENCES

Abu Daqar, M. A. M., Arqawi, S., & Karsh, S. A. (2020). Fintech in the eyes of Millennials and Generation Z (the financial behavior and Fintech perception). *Banks and Bank Systems*, *15*(3), 20–28. doi:10.21511/bbs.15(3).2020.03

Acemoglu, D., & Restrepo, P. (2018). *Artificial Intelligence, Automation and Work*. NBER. https://www.nber.org/papers/w24196

Aitken, R. (2018). Global Financial Services Bullish On AI, The "Disruptive Tech" Frontrunner. *Forbes*. https://www.forbes.com/sites/rogeraitken/2018/11/28/global-financial-services-bullish-on-ai-the-disruptive-tech-frontrunner/?sh=7366b0d82311

Anshari, M., Almunawar, M. N., Masri, M., & Hrdy, M. (2021). Financial Technology with AI-Enabled and Ethical Challenges. *Society*, *58*(3), 189–195. doi:10.100712115-021-00592-w

Ante, L. (2020). A place next to Satoshi: foundations of blockchain and cryptocurrency research in business and economics. *Scientometrics 124*(2), 1305–1333. doi:10.1007/s11192-020-03492-8

Arner, D. W., Barberis, J. N., & Buckley, R. P. (2015). The Evolution of Fintech: A New Post-Crisis Paradigm? SSRN *Electronic Journal*. doi:10.2139/ssrn.2676553

Brewer, J. (2018). Exploring paths to a more accessible digital future. *ASSETS 2018 - Proceedings of the 20th International ACM SIGACCESS Conference on Computers and Accessibility*, (pp. 1–2). ACM. 10.1145/3234695.3243502

Chiu, I. H.-Y. (2017). A new era in fintech payment innovations? A perspective from the institutions and regulation of payment systems. *Law, Innovation and Technology*, *9*(2), 190–234. doi:10.1080/17579961.2017.1377912

Cosma, S., Rimo, G., & Torluccio, G. (2023). Knowledge mapping of model risk in banking. *International Review of Financial Analysis*, *89*, 102800. doi:10.1016/j.irfa.2023.102800

Dash, G., & Chakraborty, D. (2021). Digital transformation of marketing strategies during a pandemic: Evidence from an emerging economy during covid-19. *Sustainability (Basel)*, *13*(12), 6735. doi:10.3390u13126735

DawoodH. M.LiewC. Y.LauT. C. (2022). Mobile perceived trust mediation on the intention and adoption of FinTech innovations using mobile technology: A systematic literature review. *F1000Research, 10*. doi:10.12688/f1000research.74656.2

Ding, H., Liu, H., & Yang, K. (2019). A method of capturing and transferring customer value in product service system. *Mathematical Problems in Engineering*, *2019*, 1–16. doi:10.1155/2019/8717386

Elsheikh, A. S. (2022). Blockchain Analytics Reference Architecture for FinTech-A Positioning Paper Advancing FinTech with Blockchain, Data Analytics, and Enterprise Architecture. *ACM International Conference Proceeding Series*, (pp. 1–7). ACM. 10.1145/3531056.3531068

Flavián, C., Pérez-Rueda, A., Belanche, D., & Casaló, L. V. (2022). Intention to use analytical artificial intelligence (AI) in services – the effect of technology readiness and awareness. *Journal of Service Management*, *33*(2), 293–320. doi:10.1108/JOSM-10-2020-0378

Fratrič, P., Sileno, G., Klous, S., & van Engers, T. (2022). Manipulation of the Bitcoin market: an agent-based study. *Financial Innovation, 8*(1), 1–29. doi:10.1186/s40854-022-00364-3

Gigante, G., & Zago, A. (2022). *DARQ technologies in the financial sector: artificial intelligence applications in personalized banking*. Qualitative Research in Financial Markets., doi:10.1108/QRFM-02-2021-0025

Gomber, P., Kauffman, R. J., Parker, C., & Weber, B. W. (2018). On the Fintech Revolution: Interpreting the Forces of Innovation, Disruption, and Transformation in Financial Services. *Journal of Management Information Systems*, *35*(1), 220–265. doi:10.1080/07421222.2018.1440766

Gupta, S., & Biswas, S. (2023). The confluence of smart computing and traditional businesses to foster productivity, profitability, and prosperity. In *Artificial Intelligence Techniques in Human Resource Management*. Apple Academic Press. https://www.scopus.com/inward/record.uri?eid=2-s2.0-85162263500&partnerID=40&md5=9f2b5b2a95e6c83f85318541dcf27e5e

Holmes, W., Bialik, M., & Fadel, C. (2019). *Artificial Intelligence In Education Promises and Implications for Teaching and Learning*. AIED. http://bit.ly/AIED-

Huang, J., Chai, J., & Cho, S. (2020). Deep learning in finance and banking: A literature review and classification. *Frontiers of Business Research in China*, *14*(13), 13. doi:10.118611782-020-00082-6

Jagtiani, J., & Lemieux, C. (2019). The roles of alternative data and machine learning in fintech lending: Evidence from the LendingClub consumer platform. *Financial Management*, *48*(4), 1009–1029. doi:10.1111/fima.12295

Jakhiya, M., Mittal Bishnoi, M., & Purohit, H. (2020). Emergence and growth of mobile money in modern india: A study on the effect of mobile money. *2020 Advances in Science and Engineering Technology International Conferences, ASET 2020*. Bitly. 10.1109/ASET48392.2020.9118375

Janiesch, C., Zschech, P., & Heinrich, K. (2021). Machine learning and deep learning. *Electronic Markets, 31*(3), 685–695. doi:10.100712525-021-00475-2

Jatoba, M., Gutierriz, I. E., Fernandes, P. O., Teixeira, J. P., & Moscon, D. (2019). Artificial intelligence in the recrutment & selection: innovation and impacts for the human resources management. *43rd International Scientific Conference on Economics and Social Development*, (pp. 96–104). Biblioteca Digital. https://bibliotecadigital.ipb.pt/handle/10198/21703

Kaur, A. (2020). Banking Fraud : A Conceptual Framework Of Dredging Up Various Banking Scams, Causes And Preventive Role Of Law. *PALARCH JOURNAL, 17*(6), 2003–2021.

Kaur, A., Kumar, P., & Sharma, V. (2022a). Probabilistic Assessment To Measure Insolvency Risk of Indian Public. *Madhya Pradesh Journal of Social Sciences A Biannually Journal of M. P. Institute of Social Science Research, 27*(11), 59–72.

Kaur, A., Tanwar, A., Kaur, H., & Singh, J. (2023a). IOP Conference Series: Earth and Environmental Science A Study on Linkage between Global Warming Indicators and Climate Change Expenditure. *IOP Conference Series. Earth and Environmental Science, 1110*(1), 1–19. doi:10.1088/1755-1315/1110/1/012059

Kaur, H., Singh, K., Kumar, P., & Kaur, A. (2022b). Assessing the environmental sustainability corridor : An empirical study of Renewable energy consumption in BRICS nation Assessing the environmental sustainability corridor : An empirical study of Renewable energy consumption in BRICS nation. *IOP Conference Series. Earth and Environmental Science, 1110*(1), 12053. doi:10.1088/1755-1315/1110/1/012053

Kaur, H., Singh, K., Kumar, P., & Kaur, A. (2023b). Assessing the environmental sustainability corridor : An empirical study of Renewable energy consumption in BRICS nation Assessing the environmental sustainability corridor : An empirical study of Renewable energy consumption in BRICS nation. *IOP Conference Series: Earth and Environmental Science PAPER*, 1–10. 10.1088/1755-1315/1110/1/012053

Klafft, M. (2008). *Peer to Peer Lending: Auctioning Microcredits over the Internet*. SSRN. https://papers.ssrn.com/abstract=1352383

Kruglova, I. A., & Dolbezhkin, V. A. (2019). Objective Barriers to the Implementation of Blockchain Technology in the Financial Sector. *Proceedings - 2018 International Conference on Artificial Intelligence: Applications and Innovations, IC-AIAI 2018*, (pp. 47–50). IEEE. 10.1109/IC-AIAI.2018.8674451

Kumar, P., & Kaur, A. (2022). Exploring the Role of Artificial Intelligence in Changing Business Dimension. *International Conference on Scientific Computing in Innovation*, (pp. 621–625). IEEE.

Kunhibava, S., & Muneeza, A. (2019). Regulating fintech businesses: The malaysian experience. In *Impact of Financial Technology (FinTech) on Islamic Finance and Financial Stability*. IGI Global. doi:10.4018/978-1-7998-0039-2.ch008

Lee, J.-C., Tang, Y., & Jiang, S. (2023). Understanding continuance intention of artificial intelligence (AI)-enabled mobile banking applications: An extension of AI characteristics to an expectation confirmation model. *Humanities & Social Sciences Communications*, *10*(1), 333. doi:10.105741599-023-01845-1

Leo, M., Sharma, S., & Maddulety, K. (2019). Machine Learning in Banking Risk Management: A Literature Review. *Risks 2019, 7*(1), 29. doi:10.3390/risks7010029

Lu, Y., Sheng, Z., Zhang, K., & Duan, Q. (2022). Predicting P2P lenders' decisions: The prospect theory approach. *International Journal of Electronic Business*, *17*(1), 1–12. doi:10.1504/IJEB.2022.119935

Mahalle, A., Yong, J., & Tao, X. (2021). Regulatory Challenges and Mitigation for Account Services Offered by FinTech. *Proceedings of the 2021 IEEE 24th International Conference on Computer Supported Cooperative Work in Design, CSCWD 2021*, (pp. 280–287). IEEE. 10.1109/CSCWD49262.2021.9437631

Manoharan, H., Yuvaraja, T., Kuppusamy, R., & Radhakrishnan, A. (2023). Implementation of explainable artificial intelligence in commercial communication systems using micro systems. *Science Progress*, *106*(3), 00368504231191657. doi:10.1177/00368504231191657 PMID:37533330

Marek, J., Blümlein, K., Neubauer, J., & Wehking, C. (2019). Ditching labor-intensive paper-based processes: Process automation in a Czech insurance company. In R. M. vom Brocke J. Mendling J. (Ed.), *CEUR Workshop Proceedings* (*Vol. 2428*, pp. 16–24). CEUR-WS. https://www.scopus.com/inward/record.uri?eid=2-s2.0-85071386197&partnerID=40&md5=bc8c6591e8905c17d01c71da748d3c76

Martin Kim, M. H. (2017). Blockchain technology and the fintech revolution. *Turkish Online Journal of Educational Technology, 2017*(December Special Issue ITEC), 77–82. https://www.scopus.com/inward/record.uri?eid=2-s2.0-85057640853&partnerID=40&md5=ca1ec6c72648da0d865cdc30b2529f3e

Mavlutova, I., Volkova, T., Spilbergs, A., Natrins, A., Arefjevs, I., & Verdenhofs, A. (2021). The role of fintech firms in contemporary financial sector development. *WSEAS Transactions on Business and Economics*, *18*, 411–423. doi:10.37394/23207.2021.18.42

McCarthy, J., Minsky, M. L., & Rochester, N. (1956). *Artificial Intelligence (AI) Coined at Dartmouth | Artificial intelligence: past, present, and future*. Dartmouth. https://home.dartmouth.edu/about/artificial-intelligence-ai-coined-dartmouth

Mehrotra, A., & Menon, S. (2021). Second round of FinTech - Trends and challenges. *Proceedings of 2nd International Conference on Computation, Automation and Knowledge Management, ICCAKM 2021*, (pp. 243–248). IEEE. 10.1109/ICCAKM50778.2021.9357759

Mi, J. J., Hu, T., & Deer, L. (2018). User Data Can Tell Defaulters in P2P Lending. *Annals of Data Science*, *5*(1), 59–67. doi:10.100740745-017-0134-z

Mohammad, S. M. (2020). Artificial Intelligence in Information Technology. SSRN *Electronic Journal*. https://doi.org/ doi:10.2139/SSRN.3625444

MuthaiyahS.PhangK.SembakuttiS. (2021). Bridging skill gaps and creating future ready accounting and finance graduates: An exploratory study. *F1000Research, 10*. doi:10.12688/f1000research.72880.1

Nagimova, A. Z. (2022). Islamic Fintech: Digitalization Of Global Islamic Finance. *World Economy and International Relations*, *66*(5), 50–58. doi:10.20542/0131-2227-2022-66-5-50-58

Ozili, P. K. (2020). Financial inclusion research around the world: A review. *The Forum for Social Economics.* doi:10.1080/07360932.2020.1715238

Patnaik, B. C. M., Satpathy, I., & Rachayeeta, P. (2016). Issues of Micro, Small and Medium Enterprises (MSME) in India. *International Journal of Innovative Research and Development*, *5*(6), 1–5.

Paul, L. R., & Sadath, L. (2021). A systematic analysis on fintech and its applications. *Proceedings of International Conference on Innovative Practices in Technology and Management, ICIPTM 2021*, (pp. 131–136). IEEE. 10.1109/ICIPTM52218.2021.9388371

Protopappas, L., Sideridis, A. B., & Yialouris, C. P. (2020). Implementation issues of cross border e-government systems and services. In K. S. Vlontzos G. (Ed.), *CEUR Workshop Proceedings* (Vol. 2761, pp. 155–166). CEUR-WS. https://www.scopus.com/inward/record.uri?eid=2-s2.0-85097525958&partnerID=40&md5=58405b2ec67c1e363d90c737bafad930

Ransbotham, S., Kiron, D., Gerbert, P., & Reeves, M. (2017). Reshaping Business With Artificial Intelligence: Closing the Gap Between Ambition and Action. *MIT Sloan Management Review*, *59*(1). https://store.hbr.org/product/reshaping-business-with-artificial-intelligence-closing-the-gap-between-ambition-and-action/SMR625

Rjoub, H., Adebayo, T. S., & Kirikkaleli, D. (2023). Blockchain technology-based FinTech banking sector involvement using adaptive neuro-fuzzy-based K-nearest neighbors algorithm. *Financial Innovation*, *9*(1), 65. doi:10.118640854-023-00469-3 PMID:36919101

Ruffolo, M. (2022). The Role of Ethical AI in Fostering Harmonic Innovations that Support a Human-Centric Digital Transformation of Economy and Society. *Lecture Notes in Networks and Systems*, *282*, 139–143. doi:10.1007/978-3-030-81190-7_15

Schulz, K., & Feist, M. (2021). Leveraging blockchain technology for innovative climate finance under the Green Climate Fund. *Earth System Governance*, *7*, 100084. doi:10.1016/j.esg.2020.100084

Sharma, S. K., Govindaluri, S. M., Muharrami, S. M., & Tarhini, A. (2017). A multi-analytical model for mobile banking adoption: A developing country perspective. *Review of International Business and Strategy*, *27*(1), 133–148. doi:10.1108/RIBS-11-2016-0074

Singhal, A., Dube, P., & Jain, V. K. (2022). Modelling barriers of artificial intelligence in banking sectors using total interpretive structural modelling. *International Journal of Applied Decision Sciences*, *15*(3), 311–335. doi:10.1504/IJADS.2022.122649

Soni, V. D. (2020). Emerging Roles of Artificial Intelligence in E-Commerce. *International Journal of Trend in Scientific Research and Development*, *4*(5), 223–225. doi:10.1201/9780429282829-12

Suryono, R. R., Budi, I., & Purwandari, B. (2021). Detection of fintech P2P lending issues in Indonesia. *Heliyon*, *7*(4), e06782. doi:10.1016/j.heliyon.2021.e06782 PMID:33981873

Taneja, S., Bhatnagar, M., Kumar, P., & Rupeika-Apoga, R. (2023). India’s Total Natural Resource Rents (NRR) and GDP: An Augmented Autoregressive Distributed Lag (ARDL) Bound Test. *Journal of Risk and Financial Management 2023, 16*(2), 91. doi:10.3390/jrfm16020091

Taplin, R. (2023). Artificial intelligence, intellectual property, cyber risk and robotics: A new digital age. In *Artificial Intelligence, Intellectual Property, Cyber Risk and Robotics: A New Digital Age*. Taylor and Francis. doi:10.4324/9780367857561

Thakor, A. V. (2020). Fintech and banking: What do we know? *Journal of Financial Intermediation*, *41*(November), 100833. doi:10.1016/j.jfi.2019.100833

Villar, A. S., & Khan, N. (2021). Robotic process automation in banking industry: a case study on Deutsche Bank. *Journal of Banking and Financial Technology 2021*, *5*(1), 71–86. doi:10.1007/s42786-021-00030-9

Vyas, V., & Raitani, S. (2014). Drivers of customers' switching behaviour in Indian banking industry. *International Journal of Bank Marketing*, *32*(4), 321–342. doi:10.1108/IJBM-04-2013-0033

Wang, Y., Kim, D.-K., & Jeong, D. (2020). A Survey of the Application of Blockchain in Multiple Fields of Financial Services. *Journal of Information Processing Systems*, *16*(4), 935–958. doi:10.3745/JIPS.04.0185

Wu, P.-C., Liu, S.-Y., & Huang, C.-W. (2022). The Impact of FinTech Index on P2P Lending Rate. *Review of Integrative Business and Economics Research*, *11*(2), 79–94. https://www.scopus.com/inward/record.uri?eid=2-s2.0-85130418723&partnerID=40&md5=350c589f0a8bf47b93da12c42aa01617

Yoon, K.-S., & Jun, J. (2019). Liability And Antifraud Investment In Fintech Retail Payment Services. *Contemporary Economic Policy*, *37*(1), 181–194. doi:10.1111/coep.12281

Chapter 20
Green Finance 2.0:
Pioneering Pathways for Sustainable Development and Health Through Future Trends and Innovations

Jaspreet Kaur
Chandigarh University, India

ABSTRACT

The need for the global community to address important issues including climate change, biodiversity loss, and public health concerns is growing. The idea of 'green finance 2.0' has evolved as a potent paradigm for lining up financial systems with sustainable development and health outcomes in response to these linked problems. This chapter examines the rapidly changing field of green finance, highlighting significant developments and trends that are laying the foundation for a more sustainable and healthy future. By extending its scope and ambition, green finance 2.0 builds upon the guiding principles of the first version. It recognises the need for a comprehensive strategy for sustainability and includes a wider range of environmental, social, and governance (ESG) factors.

INTRODUCTION

Climate change, sustainable development, and the complicated relationship between environmental issues and public health make "Green Finance 2.0" a potent force in a fast-changing world. This new financial system paradigm could lead the global economy towards sustainability and create a healthy, ecologically sound world. This essay will examine the complex relationship between green finance, sustainable development, and public health and demonstrate the transformative power of innovative financial instruments and policies (Rolffs et al.,2015).

DOI: 10.4018/979-8-3693-1388-6.ch020

Green Finance Promotes Sustainability

Green money, sometimes known as "sustainable finance," promotes ecologically friendly, socially responsible, and economically viable enterprises. It is more than a slogan—it is a vital answer to environmental issues. Traditional financial institutions have caused environmental deterioration by investing in fossil fuels, deforestation, and polluting industries. In contrast, green money invests in environmental, climate change, and sustainability projects (Rolffs et al., 2015).

Sustainable Development-Public Health Nexus

The UN Sustainable Development Goals (SDGs) represent a global commitment to solving humanity's biggest problems. These aims include poverty reduction, gender equality, inexpensive and renewable energy, and climate action. These aims are interdependent. Human health is threatened by air and water pollution, deforestation, and climate change. Sustainable development is about improving public health (Rolffs et al., 2015).

Green Finance 2.0: The Future

Green finance 2.0 is the next sustainable financing step. It adapts to new trends and advances. Capital flows are changing rapidly due to new technology and investment instruments. Blockchain technology can improve supply chain transparency, ensuring environmental responsibility. Sustainable bonds, green bonds, and impact investment fund renewable energy, clean transportation, and conservation projects. These technologies demonstrate how green finance 2.0 advances public health and sustainable development (Manaswi et al., 2023). Green financing 2.0 is crucial. It outlines solutions to global issues like climate change and public health. Benefits are widespread:

Green finance improves resilience against environmental threats and climate change by diverting investments from polluting businesses to sustainable practises. This benefits the environment and mitigates economic and health concerns. Green financing may boost renewable energy, sustainable agriculture, and eco-friendly technology, creating jobs. Green financing also reduces air pollution and climate-related health hazards. Additionally, it builds healthcare infrastructure.

Moreover, as ethical and sustainable investments become more important, investors are given ways to match their values with financial decisions. This empowers people and guides the private sector towards sustainability. Green finance promotes worldwide cooperation on environmental and health issues. It unites a divided planet (Manaswi et al., 2023).

"Green Finance 2.0: Pioneering Pathways for Sustainable Development and Health through Future Trends and Innovations" is a key shift in the making. It links finance, sustainability, and public health to show how novel financial tools and methods may create a greener, healthier future. Governments, businesses, investors, and civic society must lead these paths forward. The future of our planet and its inhabitants is at stake. Green finance 2.0 is a call to action to create a sustainable and healthy future. It's a chance to connect money with our aspirations of a healthy planet and better lives (Manaswi et al., 2023).

Finance Rethought for Sustainability. A significant change in the financial sector has been brought about by the growth of green finance and its critical role in advancing sustainable development. It entails reevaluating conventional financial models to give environmental and social objectives top priority. Here is a look at this evolution as depicted in figure 1:

Figure 1. Finance rethought for sustainability

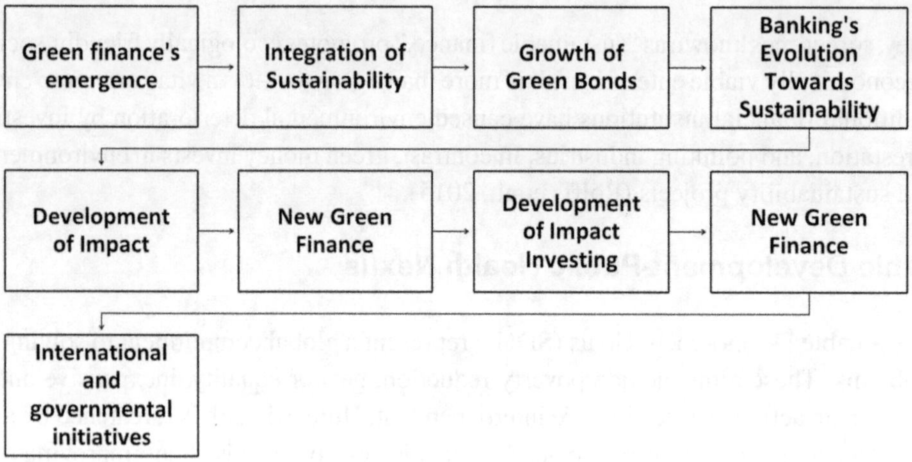

Green finance's emergence:

Early Environmental Concerns: In reaction to escalating environmental worries, notably those involving climate change, pollution, and resource depletion, the idea of green finance began to take off.

First Wave of Green Finance: The primary sources of funding for environmental projects during the first wave of green finance were benevolent endeavours and government-sponsored efforts. It wasn't widely used in conventional finance (Ahmad et al., 2023).

Integration of Sustainability

Awareness and Regulation: As social and environmental issues gained more attention; regulatory entities began to intervene. Companies and financial institutions were forced to take these concerns into account by the implementation of environmental rules, disclosure requirements, and sustainability reporting frameworks.

Integration of ESG Criteria: Environmental, Social, and Governance (ESG) criteria are becoming more and more popular as a framework for evaluating the sustainability performance of investments. When making investing selections, investors started taking ESG concerns into account in addition to financial returns.

ESG criteria (environment) assess a company's environmental impact. Investors can use these parameters to evaluate a company's sustainability efforts and goods. Investors can assess a company's climate change and environmental responsibility by assessing carbon emissions, resource utilisation, and environmental policies. Investors can discover environmentally responsible organisations and analyse their long-term sustainability with this information.

ESG standards (social) evaluate a company's relationships with employees, customers, suppliers, and communities. Social criteria assist investors assess a company's human capital management, diversity and inclusion, fair labour practises, product safety, and community engagement. Investors can promote sustainability and equity while decreasing social impact risks by prioritising investments in firms with high social performance.

ESG criteria of governance consider a company's internal structures and policies, which affect sustainability. These criteria consider board independence, executive compensation, shareholder rights, openness, and anti-corruption. Governance factors assist investors evaluate a company's leadership's integrity and responsibility. Strong governance helps companies overcome problems and develop sustainably (Ahmad et al.,2023).

Investors can encourage sustainability by using ESG criteria to make investments:

Risk Mitigation: ESG criteria can identify and reduce environmental, social, and governance risks, lowering financial losses.

Long-Term Performance: ESG-focused companies are more resilient and adaptive to shifting social and market expectations, making them better positioned for long-term success.

Aligning with Values: ESG-focused investing lets people and institutions invest in social and environmental change.

Investment in ESG-conscious companies can encourage others to improve their sustainability performance, promoting industry-wide transformation.

Strong ESG performance can improve a company's reputation, brand, customer loyalty, and capital availability. Since ESG ratings and assessments vary by rating agency and source, comprehensive due diligence is needed when employing ESG factors in investing decisions. Investors should match their ESG goals with their financial goals and consider the ESG criteria that matter most to them, bearing in mind that sustainable investment is evolving (Ahmad et al.,2023).

Growth of Green Bonds

Debt market innovation: Green bonds have become a ground-breaking financial tool. These bonds are specifically issued to finance green initiatives like sustainable agriculture, clean transportation, and renewable energy.

Certification and Transparency: The Green Bond Principles and Climate Bonds Initiative were formed as certification and reporting criteria to guarantee the legitimacy of green bonds. These guidelines aid investors in determining how their investments may affect the environment (Gollwitzer et al., 2018).

Banking's Evolution Towards Sustainability

Sustainable Banking Principles: Banks began to include ESG factors into their lending and investment choices as part of sustainable banking principles. They also started assessing their clients' sustainable practises.

Innovative Financial Products: Banks offered green loans, which offer advantageous terms to companies undertaking environmentally friendly projects (Gollwitzer et al., 2018).

Development of Impact Investing

Investing for Positive Impact: As interest in opportunities that produce favourable social and environmental effects in addition to financial gains increased, impact investing gained traction.

Impact measuring techniques have made it possible for investors to calculate the economic, social, and environmental returns on their investments (Cantele and Zardini, 2018).

New Green Finance

Sustainability on a holistic level: Green Finance 2.0 is a more thorough approach to sustainability, requiring financial institutions to take a wider range of environmental, social, and health-related concerns into account when making decisions.

Innovation and technology are improving decision-making by changing how financial institutions evaluate sustainability risks and possibilities. This includes breakthroughs in fintech and regtech (Cantele and Zardini, 2018).

International and Governmental Initiatives

The Paris Climate Change Agreement, which was ratified by several nations, was essential in setting the direction of green financing. It sets challenging goals for cutting carbon emissions and urges increasing spending on sustainable infrastructure and clean energy.

Global Sustainability Goals: The Sustainable Development Goals (SDGs) of the United Nations offer a framework for tackling a variety of sustainability-related challenges globally, highlighting the significance of matching financial flows with sustainable goals (Elkington, 2018).

Significance of the Study

This study is crucial for understanding how green finance may address global sustainable development issues like poverty, renewable energy, and ecological restoration.

Public Health Benefits: By studying the interaction between environment, finance, and health, the study can find ways to reduce environmental health risks and promote well-being.

Economic Resilience: Green financing reduces environmental risk and creates new opportunities in renewable energy, green technologies, and sustainable agriculture.

Investor Guidance: The study can help investors make informed decisions that support environmental and health goals while potentially earning high profits.

Policy Development: This study can help policymakers create green finance legislation and incentives to accelerate the transition to a sustainable and health-conscious financial sector.

Innovation and Technology: The study can inspire finance, sustainability, and health breakthroughs by analysing emerging trends and innovations like blockchain for transparent supply chains.

Global Collaboration: The study can promote international cooperation by emphasising environmental and health concerns' global dimension and the need for coordination.

The "Green Finance 2.0" study is crucial to addressing climate change, public health, and sustainable development. It shows how creative financing methods can make the globe more sustainable and healthier for future generations.

Opportunities and Challenges

The necessity for standardised reporting, consistent measurement techniques, and overcoming scepticism about greenwashing are among the challenges in the development of green finance.

Opportunities: The change to green financing offers a variety of economic benefits, including the development of jobs in the renewable energy sector, a reduction in long-term climate risks, and enhanced public health results (Backstrand, 2006; Fairclough, 2002)

In conclusion, the transformation of green finance from a cutting-edge idea to an established strategy is essential for advancing sustainable development. As people become more aware of the connections between societal, environmental, and financial well-being, traditional financial models are evolving to incorporate these factors. As green finance develops, it will become more and more important in tackling urgent global issues and pursuing sustainable development objectives.

Problem Statements

- Climate change, deforestation, and pollution are causing an environmental crisis. These challenges endanger humans and the environment.
- Environmental issues like air and water pollution, harsh weather, and biodiversity loss affect public health directly and indirectly. The intensity and complexity of these repercussions are rising.
- Insufficient Sustainable Financing: Despite increased environmental and health awareness, sustainable development projects lack money. Climate action, conservation, and healthcare infrastructure sometimes lack funding.
- Sustainability is not inherent in traditional financial systems. Investments in fossil fuels and other polluting industries are slow to move, hindering the greener and healthier future.
- Innovative Finance Solutions: These interrelated issues require imaginative financial solutions. Some solutions include green bonds, impact investing, and ESG considerations in investment decisions.

RESEARCH METHODOLOGY

Literature Review

First, the literature on green finance, sustainable development, public health, and new trends in these disciplines has been examined to grasp current research, identify knowledge gaps and analyse academic articles, reports, books, and policy documents.

Collecting Data

The study involved gathering data from financial reports, health statistics, environmental indicators, and green finance case studies.

Case Studies

Case studies that demonstrate green finance's successful integration into sustainable development and public health have been analysed for best practises, challenges, and lessons.

Analysis of Policy

The study assessed how green finance and sustainability initiatives affected public health to find policy gaps and improvements.

Assessing Innovation

Blockchain, impact investing, and sustainable bonds are green finance examined to see how these ideas are altering sustainable development and healthcare.

Interdisciplinary Framework

The study created an interdisciplinary framework that integrates money, sustainability, and health to better comprehend the relationship between sustainable development and health promotion with green funding.

The "Green Finance 2.0" study is crucial to addressing climate change, public health, and sustainable development. It shows how creative financing methods can make the globe more sustainable and healthier for future generations.

SOPHISTICATED AND ALL-ENCOMPASSING PERSPECTIVE OF SUSTAINABLE FINANCE APPROACHED WITH THE RISE OF GREEN FINANCE 2.0

New Financial Instruments

Financial Product Diversification: Green Finance 2.0 presents cutting-edge financial instruments beyond conventional green bonds. These could include impact investment funds, green securitization, green mortgages, and sustainability-linked loans.

It promotes blended finance approaches in which the public and private sectors work together to finance sustainable initiatives. These business models make use of public funding to draw private capital, particularly for initiatives in poor nations (Agbemabiese et al., 2018).

Extensive Impact Measurement

Improved Reporting and Disclosure: Green Finance 2.0 places a greater emphasis on accurate impact measurement and open reporting. Companies and financial organisations are required to provide thorough information on the results of their investments in the areas of the environment, society, and health.

Technology is used to increase impact measurement efficiency and accuracy. Examples include blockchain and artificial intelligence. The verification of project milestones and impact measures can be automated using smart contracts.

Standardisation: The creation of uniform impact measurement frameworks and reporting requirements guarantees the comparability and consistency of impact data across various investments (Agbemabiese et al., 2018).

A Comprehensive Strategy for Sustainability

Environmental, Social, and Health Considerations: Green Finance 2.0 broadens its emphasis to encompass social and health aspects of sustainability in addition to environmental issues. It acknowledges that in order to address complicated global concerns, a comprehensive strategy is required.

Environmental, social, and governance (ESG) factors are taken into account while making investment decisions. In order to do this, it is necessary to evaluate not just the environmental impact but also social and governance factors like diversity, labour practises, and corporate ethics.

Stakeholder Participation: A wider range of parties are actively involved in the decision-making process, such as communities, consumers, and civil society organisations. Their advice contributes to ensuring that investments reflect local values and requirements (Lucaci, 2022).

Risk Reduction

Green Finance 2.0 lays a lot of attention on evaluating the risks associated with climate change and sustainability in investment portfolios. Investors can foresee and reduce potential financial losses linked to these risks by using this proactive approach to risk management.

Transition Finance: It aids in financing the shift to a sustainable, low-carbon economy. Transition financing strives to ease this transition while acknowledging that some industries may need assistance on their path to sustainability (Khanchel et al., 2023).

Support for Regulations and Policies

Government Incentives: Policymakers and regulatory organisations are providing more and more incentives for environmentally friendly and sustainable investments. This covers financial incentives, subsidies, and special consideration for environmentally friendly enterprises.

Regulations are being created to make sure that businesses and financial institutions report their sustainability practises and risks. ESG factor reporting is increasingly being made mandatory (Khanchel et al., 2023).

Market Development and Demand

Investor Demand: Sustainable and ethical investment options are in greater demand from investors. Financial institutions and companies are adapting to match this enthusiasm, which is fueling the expansion of Green Finance 2.0.

Integration into the Mainstream: Green Finance 2.0 reflects this transition by offering a wide choice of options for investors wishing to align their portfolios with their values and long-term objectives. Sustainability issues are increasingly being taken into account when making investment decisions (Khanchel et al., 2023).

International Cooperation

International Collaboration: Green Finance 2.0 emphasises the value of cross-border cooperation in addressing sustainability issues. For the purpose of funding significant sustainable projects and solving global concerns like climate change, cross-border initiatives and collaborations are essential.

In conclusion, Green Finance 2.0 is a more advanced and sophisticated method of financing sustainability. It integrates cutting-edge financial tools, exact effect measurement, and a comprehensive approach to sustainability that takes into account factors affecting the environment, society, and health. This evolution is a result of the rising understanding that investing in and managing finances demands a thorough and integrated approach (Owen et al., 2023).

Healthy Sustainable Development

The complex relationships between sustainability and health highlight the crucial link between environmental sustainability and human population health (Malik et al., 2014). To create a more sustainable and healthy future, it is essential to comprehend how environmental deterioration affects public health and how sustainable practises might reduce these dangers as depicted in figure 2 below.

Figure 2. Impact of environment deterioration on human health

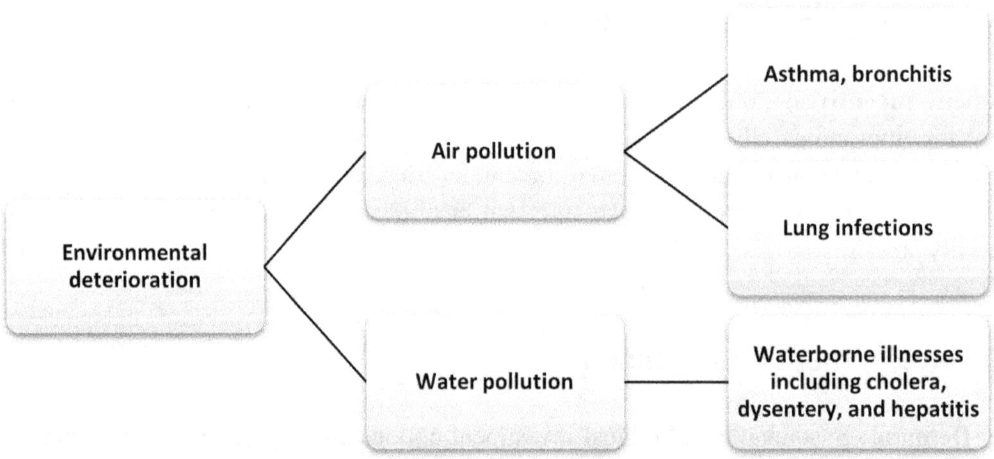

Respiratory conditions including asthma, bronchitis, and lung infections are brought on by environmental deterioration, particularly air pollution brought on by the combustion of fossil fuels and industrial activity. PM2.5, as well as pollutants like sulphur dioxide (SO2) and nitrogen dioxide (NO2), can have detrimental impacts on one's health. Sustainable practises for mitigating climate change include switching to clean and renewable energy sources, boosting energy efficiency, and promoting the use of electric vehicles and public transportation. These efforts lead to better outcomes for respiratory health because they lower air pollution and enhance air quality (Tyagi et al., 2014).

Waterborne illnesses including cholera, dysentery, and hepatitis can result from water pollution, which is frequently brought on by industrial discharge, agricultural runoff, and poor sanitation. Water supplies that are contaminated present a serious health danger, especially in developing areas.

Sustainable water management practises include safeguarding water sources, effectively treating wastewater, and encouraging ethical farming and land usage. For the sake of public health, having access to clean, safe drinking water is essential.

Also, as a result of environmental deterioration and greenhouse gas emissions, climate change has significant negative effects on human health. It can aggravate ailments brought on by the heat, accelerate the development of vector-borne illnesses (such as malaria and dengue), impair water and food supply, and result in hunger and foodborne illnesses (Tyagi et al., 2014).

Sustainable actions to address climate change include adopting renewable energy sources to reduce carbon emissions, enhancing energy efficiency, and establishing low-carbon economies. By lowering the frequency and severity of health risks associated to climate change, these initiatives not only defend against climate change but also protect the public's health.

The prevalence and distribution of infectious diseases may change as a result of the loss of biodiversity brought on by habitat destruction and ecosystem degradation. As observed with diseases like COVID-19, decreased biodiversity can result in an increase in the transmission of zoonotic diseases from animals to people. Sustainable practises include adopting responsible land-use methods, conserving and repairing ecosystems, and protecting wildlife habitats. The danger of new infectious diseases arising is decreased by preserving biodiversity and supporting the maintenance of natural disease control mechanisms (Iwejingi, 2011).

Unsustainable farming methods, such as overuse of pesticides, monoculture farming, and soil deterioration, can jeopardise nutrition and food security. Malnutrition, obesity, and health problems linked to diet can come from this. Chemical input reduction, crop diversity, and soil health are the top priorities of sustainable agriculture practises such organic farming, agroecology, and regenerative agriculture. By encouraging the development of wholesome, sustainable foods, these practises enhance public health. Stress, anxiety, and depression can be exacerbated by unsustainable urbanisation, which is characterised by overcrowding, a lack of green space, and insufficient access to public services (Iwejingi, 2011).

Green and liveable cities with plenty of green space, effective public transportation, and community involvement are the goals of sustainable urban design. These programmes improve mental health and lessen the burden of mental illness. As a result of the complex relationships between sustainability and health, it is imperative to adopt sustainable behaviours in order to safeguard both the environment and public health. The concept of sustainable development acknowledges the close relationship between human well-being and ecosystem health. We can reduce health risks, foster resilience, and create a better and more sustainable future for all by tackling environmental degradation through sustainable practises (Iwejingi, 2011).

Case Examples and Research Results Demonstrate How Responsible Agriculture, Clean Energy Transitions, and Sustainable Urban Planning have the Potential to Improve Health Outcomes

The potential for sustainable urban planning, clean energy transitions, and ethical agriculture to greatly improve health outcomes has undoubtedly been continuously shown by case studies and study results. These good effects are illustrated by the following examples:

Urban Sustainability and Public Health

Brazil's Curitiba is frequently used as an example of sustainable urban planning. The city established a thorough public transit network with designated bus lanes, large green areas, and thoughtful urban planning. According to research, these actions lowered air pollution, increased physical activity as a result of walkable neighbourhoods, and enhanced general public health.

Research Finding: According to a study that appeared in the "The Lancet" journal, urban neighbourhoods that are compact, well-planned, and have access to green spaces and public transportation had reduced incidences of obesity, cardiovascular disease, and mental health problems. Healthy lifestyles are encouraged through sustainable urban planning that places a high priority on green infrastructure and active transportation (Liu et al., 2022).

Transitions to Clean Energy and Air Quality

Case Study: Denmark's Transition to Wind Energy: Denmark's switch to wind energy is a well-known illustration of a sustainable energy transition. Utilising wind energy instead of fossil fuels decreased reliance on them and considerably improved air quality. According to studies, this transformation will result in a decline in respiratory illnesses and the associated medical expenses.

Research Finding: The Global Burden of Disease Study has demonstrated that lowering air pollution through the use of renewable energy sources and the transition to clean energy can have significant positive effects on public health, including a decrease in the number of avertible deaths from cardiovascular and respiratory diseases (Liu et al., 2022).

Responsible Food and Agriculture

Case Study: Organic Farming in Uganda in recent years, organic farming methods have become more prevalent in Uganda. Responsible land management and minimal use of pesticides and chemical fertilisers are key components of organic farming. According to research, eating organic foods can lessen one's exposure to pesticide residues and enhance nutrition in general.

Findings from the research: A study that appeared in the "British Journal of Nutrition" indicated that using organic farming methods can increase the amount of nutrients in organic crops, which may improve health outcomes. Additionally, a lower risk of pesticide-related health problems is linked to reduced pesticide exposure (Schroeder et al., 2019).

Transportation Alternatives and Exercise

Case Study: Bogotá, Colombia Bogotá is known for its cutting-edge sustainable mobility programmes, such as the Ciclova programme, which allows bikes and pedestrians access to streets on Sundays and other holidays. According to research, this programme has helped inhabitants become more physically active and the prevalence of diseases like obesity and heart disease has decreased.

Research Finding: A study in the journal "Preventive Medicine" showed that inhabitants in communities with bike-friendly infrastructure and active transportation programmes typically engage in more physical activity, have lower obesity rates, and have better cardiovascular health.

In conclusion, these case studies and research findings show how ethical farming, clean energy transitions, and sustainable urban planning can all result in observable improvements in public health. In addition to addressing environmental issues, these practises encourage healthier lifestyles, lessen exposure to contaminants, and improve general wellbeing. The likelihood of having a beneficial impact on health grows as sustainability is given more importance by governments and communities (Edenhofer et al., 2011).

Innovations in Green Finance, From Social Impact Bonds Aimed at Healthcare Infrastructure to Block Chain-based Transparent Supply Chain Financing

Green finance innovations are essential for advancing sustainability and solving societal and environmental problems (Nassiry, 2018). Here are some noteworthy advancements in green finance, like social impact bonds for healthcare infrastructure and transparent supply chain financing based on blockchain as depicted in figure 3 below:

Figure 3. Advancements in green finance

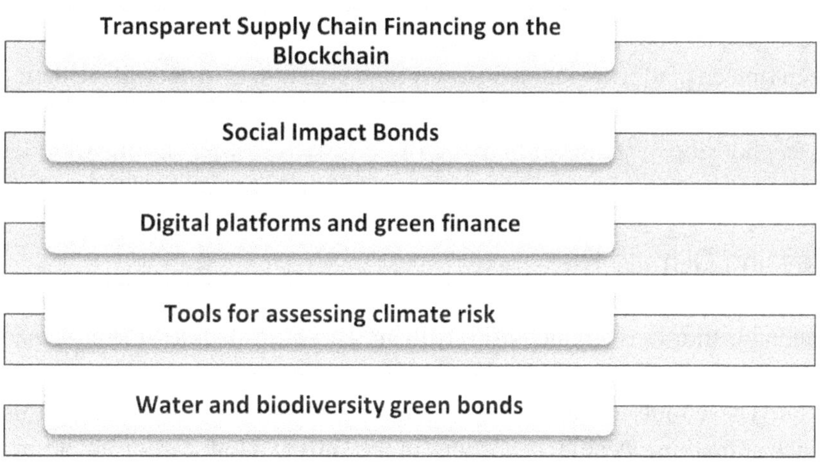

Transparent Supply Chain Financing on the Blockchain

Overview: Supply chains are becoming more transparent and traceable thanks to blockchain technology, especially in sectors like electronics and agriculture that have intricate worldwide supply lines.

How It Works: The blockchain enables safe, unchangeable records of business dealings and goods movements. This technology can be applied to supply chain financing to trace the origin of goods and confirm their conformity to sustainability requirements.

Impact: This innovation encourages ethical production and sourcing. It guarantees that goods marked as sustainable or environmentally friendly actually satisfy the required standards. Additionally, by enabling suppliers to access funding based on their adherence to sustainability criteria, it facilitates supply chain finance for sustainable practises (Rana et al., 2021).

Healthcare Infrastructure Targeted by Social Impact Bonds (SIBs)

Overview: Pay-for-Success contracts, commonly referred to as Social Impact Bonds (SIBs), are financial tools that combine funding from the public and private sectors to address social and environmental issues.

How It Works: Investors provide up-front funding through SIBs to finance social or environmental initiatives like enhancing hospital infrastructure. If predetermined social or environmental results are reached, the government gives investors a return on their investment.

Impact: SIBs encourage private investment in important initiatives that might not have funding otherwise. In terms of healthcare infrastructure, SIBs can finance the building or remodelling of health-care facilities, improving access to healthcare, improving health outcomes, and lowering government healthcare spending (Campbell, 2023).

Digital Platforms and Green Finance

Overview: The fintech industry is embracing sustainability by creating digital tools and software that let people and organisations make more environmentally friendly financial decisions.

How It Works: Green fintech platforms offer data and instruments to evaluate the social and environmental effects of financial, banking, and spending decisions. They frequently include carbon footprint tracking, ESG research, and opportunities for sustainable investments.

Impact: Green fintech platforms enable investors and consumers to coordinate their financial actions with environmental objectives. They give people the knowledge and resources they need to make wise decisions, such as choosing sustainable banking options or investing in renewable energy initiatives (Campbell, 2023).

Tools for Assessing Climate Risk

Overview: Financial institutions are increasingly using climate risk assessment techniques and models to identify the possible financial hazards linked to climate change.

How It Works: These tools evaluate the potential effects on investments and portfolios of climate-related events, such as extreme weather conditions or the shift to a low-carbon economy. They shed light on the financial opportunities and risks associated with climatic change.

Impact: Financial institutions can create plans for risk mitigation and adaptation by recognising climate-related hazards and using that information to make better investment decisions. This promotes investment protection and strengthens the financial systems' resilience (Arnone, 2022).

Water and Biodiversity Green Bonds

Overview: Originally intended for climate-related projects, green bonds are now being used to fund water conservation and biodiversity preservation initiatives.

How It Works: Projects to protect and restore ecosystems, conserve water resources, and address water-related issues including water scarcity and pollution are funded through green bonds for water and biodiversity.

Impact: These bonds direct funding towards vital environmental initiatives that protect ecosystems and guarantee access to clean water. Beyond climate change, they address urgent sustainability-related challenges.

These new developments in green finance show inventive ways to link economic actions to sustainability objectives. By encouraging responsible investment and fostering beneficial environmental and social effects, they fill the gap between the financial sector and environmental and social objectives (Arnone, 2022).

How Technology is Transforming the Financial Sector to Promote Sustainability Goals, Such as Fintech and Regtech

A revolutionary role is being played by technology, particularly fintech (financial technology) and regtech (regulatory technology), in transforming the financial landscape to promote sustainability goals. Here are some ways that these technologies are promoting financial sustainability:

Superior Data Analytics

Fintech: To examine environmental, social, and governance (ESG) aspects, fintech solutions use big data analytics and artificial intelligence. They give investors important information about how well businesses and investments perform in terms of sustainability.

Financial institutions may quickly gather, analyse, and publish ESG data using regtech solutions to meet regulatory requirements. This guarantees that data on sustainability is easily accessible for reporting and decision-making (Alt et al., 2018).

ESG Risk Evaluation

Fintech: Fintech platforms analyse investment-related ESG risks using predictive analytics and machine learning. They assist investors in identifying potential social and environmental hazards that could have an impact on financial profits.

Regtech: By enabling real-time monitoring and reporting capabilities, regtech systems help financial institutions assess and manage ESG-related risks. This makes proactive risk reduction possible (Alt et al., 2018).

Platforms for Sustainable Investment

Fintech: ESG-compliant assets, such as green bonds or socially conscious funds, can be found and purchased using user-friendly sustainable investment platforms.

Regtech platforms help financial institutions ensure that investments adhere to sustainability norms and standards, lowering compliance costs and promoting ethical investing (Arner et al., 2016).

Sustainable Digital Payment and Banking

Fintech: More and more digital banking and payment apps are providing features that encourage sustainable consumption. Users can keep tabs on their expenditure, carbon footprint, and support environmentally friendly companies.

Regtech: Regulatory technology plays a role in ensuring that online banking and payment services adhere to ethical and sustainable business practises. This includes keeping an eye on transactions to ensure they adhere to moral banking standards (Arner et al., 2016).

Transparency in the Supply Chain

Fintech: By tracing the origin and travel of products, blockchain technology, which is frequently employed in fintech applications, can increase supply chain transparency. Consumers may choose more sustainably thanks to this transparency, which also makes businesses responsible for their supply chain procedures.

Regtech: Regulatory technology supports the tracking and reporting of supply chain practises to guarantee that they adhere to ethical and sustainable norms. It makes it easier to follow laws pertaining to ethical sourcing (Anagnostopoulos, 2018).

Crowdfunding and Green Loans

Fintech: Platforms for this industry are enabling green financing and crowdfunding for environmentally friendly initiatives. They link investors to green activities including sustainable agriculture and renewable energy projects.

Green loans and crowdfunding initiatives are in compliance with sustainability and ethical finance laws thanks to regulatory technology, which also promotes transparency and investor protection (Anagnostopoulos, 2018).

Sustainability Disclosure and Reporting

Fintech: By automating data gathering and reporting, fintech solutions make the process of sustainability reporting for businesses simpler. As a result, more companies are motivated to share their ESG performance.

Financial institutions and companies can use regtech solutions to meet reporting obligations for sustainability, assuring accountability and transparency.

In conclusion, by offering tools and solutions for ESG data analysis, risk assessment, investment, and regulatory compliance, fintech and regtech play a critical role in advancing sustainability in the financial sector. These technologies permit people to match their financial actions with their sustainability aspirations, as well as financial institutions, to make more sustainable investment decisions (Anagnostopoulos, 2018).

Examining How Governments and International Organisations are Pushing Sustainability and Green Money

It evaluates the effects of regional initiatives and policy frameworks like the Paris Agreement. In order to address the world's environmental concerns, the role of governments and international organisations in promoting green financing and sustainability is crucial. Regional initiatives and policy frameworks like the Paris Agreement have a big influence on how sustainable finance develops. Here is a breakdown of their contributions and effects (Polonsky, 2008):

Governments' Function

Policy and Regulation: Through the development and implementation of policies and regulations, governments play a crucial role in supporting green finance. These regulations may include mandates for sustainable investments, tax incentives, and subsidies.

Market Development: By fostering an environment that is favourable to sustainable investments, governments may promote the growth of green financial markets. To lower investment risks, they can create national green banks, promote the issuing of green bonds, and offer guarantees.

Environmental Goals: Governments establish regional and national environmental objectives, such as targets for renewable energy and emissions reduction. These goals foster market incentives for environmentally friendly investments and encourage the development of sustainable technologies.

Governments frequently support research and development projects targeted at promoting green technologies, which can result in inventions that draw funding from the private sector.

Impact Assessment: Companies and financial institutions may be required by governments to evaluate and disclose the environmental and social impacts of their operations and investments. For well-informed green finance decision-making, this transparency is essential (Polonsky, 2008).

Role of International Bodies

Global Coordination: International organisations that promote global coordination and collaboration on sustainability concerns include the United Nations, the World Bank, and the World Economic Forum. They encourage the exchange of knowledge and the sharing of best practises.

Standardisation: These groups work to establish international norms and regulations for sustainable finance, including standards for green bonds, ESG disclosure, and impact assessment. In the green financing sector, standardisation improves comparability and transparency.

Growing Capacity: To help developing nation's access and incorporate green money, international organisations promote growing capacity in those nations. Technical know-how, education, and financial support for sustainable project development all fall under this aid.

International organisations promote sustainability and green finance on a global scale through advocacy and public education. They promote understanding of the significance of sustainable development and aid in coordinating national policies with international sustainability objectives (Chygryn et al., 2019).

Policy Frameworks' Effects

The Paris Agreement, which was ratified in 2015, has significantly impacted green financing. Investments in renewable energy, energy efficiency, and climate adaptation are encouraged by the binding targets it sets for nations to reduce global warming. Now, a lot of financial institutions match the objectives of the agreement with their portfolios.

Regional Initiatives: Regional initiatives offer regional frameworks for improving sustainability, such as the European Green Deal and the Sustainable Development Goals (SDG) initiative of the Asian Development Bank. Within particular regions, they encourage the use of renewable energy, sustainable investments, and the development of green infrastructure.

Financial institutions must evaluate and disclose the environmental impact of their investments under regulations like the Sustainable Finance Disclosure Regulation (SFDR) of the European Union. This has an impact on investment choices and promotes the allocation of funding for sustainable initiatives.

Market Development: The issuance of green bonds and prospects for sustainable investment have significantly increased as a result of policy frameworks. They have drawn a wider variety of investors and strengthened the green finance ecosystem.

In conclusion, through establishing policy frameworks, stimulating market growth, standardising procedures, and fostering global coordination, governments and international organisations play crucial roles in improving green finance and sustainability. The shift to a more sustainable and resilient global economy is facilitated by the impact of regional initiatives and regulations like the Paris Agreement (Scheyvens, 2007).

Overcoming Regulatory Obstacles to Establishing a Favourable Environment for Sustainable Financing

It requires overcoming a number of regulatory obstacles to create an environment that supports sustainable finance. The development of sustainable finance markets may be hampered by these issues, which may also make it more difficult to link financial activity to ESG (environmental, social, and governance) goals. The following are some significant regulatory issues that need to be resolved:

Lack of Standardisation: When it comes to sustainability-related information, investors and businesses may become perplexed in the absence of standardised terminology, reporting systems, and disclosure standards. It makes it challenging to evaluate the sustainability performance of investments and complicates the comparability of ESG data.

Misrepresentation and Greenwashing: Greenwashing is the practise of representing financial items or investments as being more environmentally or socially responsible than they actually are. The trust in sustainable finance markets can be weakened by deceptive claims and representations made possible by lax regulatory scrutiny.

Regulatory Fragmentation: When sustainability laws vary throughout countries, it can result in regulatory fragmentation. A complicated network of regional, national, and international sustainability regulations may be difficult for businesses and financial institutions to understand.

Inconsistent Tax and Subsidy Policy: Tax and subsidy policies have a big impact on investment choices. The flow of capital into sustainable projects may be deterred by inconsistent tax treatment of sustainable investments vs traditional ones (Rizos et al., 2016).

Reporting Burden: It can be time-consuming and expensive for organisations to comply with the many sustainability reporting standards set forth by various regulators. This problem can be solved by harmonising reporting requirements and streamlining reporting procedures.

Focus on the Short Term and Quarterly Reporting: Traditional financial reporting frequently places an emphasis on the Short Term, which may deter Long Term Sustainable Investments. To encourage sustainability, regulatory adjustments that support longer-term reporting and financial planning are required.

Lack of Data Quality and Verification: For making wise investment decisions, sustainability data must be accurate and reliable. Standards and regulatory control are required to guarantee the accuracy and validity of ESG data (Painuly, 2001).

Fiduciary Duty Interpretation: The obligation of financial professionals to act in their clients' best interests is referred to as fiduciary duty. ESG considerations in investment decisions may be discouraged under some interpretations of fiduciary obligation. Fiduciary responsibility must be made clear in the perspective of sustainability.

Risk Assessment and Disclosure: Regulatory frameworks frequently place a strong emphasis on financial risk assessment, but they may fall short in taking ESG-related issues, such climate risk, into account. Regulations must be changed to call for thorough risk evaluations and disclosures that take ESG issues into account.

Smaller businesses and investors may have difficulty accessing the sustainable finance markets because of regulatory limitations or a lack of financial solutions that are specifically suited to their needs. Broader participation may be encouraged by developing more welcoming regulatory regimes.

Green Bonds and Green Finance Certification: To guarantee that green bonds and sustainable financial instruments actually fund sustainable initiatives, rigorous criteria and oversight are needed for the certification and verification of these products.

While sustainable finance focuses on fresh green investments, moving established sectors to sustainability can be difficult due to a lack of legal backing and unambiguous transition finance frameworks (Fisher et al., 2008).

Collaboration between governments, financial institutions, and international organisations is necessary to address these regulatory difficulties. A more favourable and enabling environment for sustainable finance can be produced by initiatives to harmonise standards, enhance data quality, and explain regulatory expectations. Additionally, regulatory organisations must change and adapt to keep up with the quickly evolving sustainable finance ecosystem.

Developing Themes That Are Expected to Influence the Direction of Sustainable Development and Green Finance

Future developments in green finance and sustainable development are expected to be influenced by a number of new themes. The interconnection of environmental, social, and governance (ESG) elements and their influence on financial decision-making are becoming increasingly recognised, as shown by these trends (Fisher et al., 2008). The possibilities of circular economies, impact investing, and the incorporation of ESG factors into investment decisions are discussed below:

The Circular Economy

Overview: Circular economies develop goods, materials, and systems with the intention of reusing, remanufacturing, and recycling in order to reduce waste and maximise resource use.

Potential for green financing: Initiatives to promote the circular economy demand significant investments in infrastructure, technology, and innovation. By providing funds for the study, creation, and implementation of sustainable, closed-loop systems, green finance can play a critical role in assisting circular economy initiatives.

Impact on Sustainability: Circular economies limit the use of resources, the production of waste, and the emission of greenhouse gases. These behaviours support sustainability objectives and increase economic and environmental resilience (Bai, 2022).

Influence Investing

Overview: Impact investment aims to produce quantifiable environmental and social benefits in addition to financial gains. It includes financial backing for initiatives and businesses that benefit people and the environment.

Potential for Green Finance: Impact investment has accelerated significantly as a result of investors looking for ways to address urgent global issues including poverty, inequality, and climate change. Green finance invests money in projects that have a positive social or environmental impact, such as those that promote clean water, sustainable agriculture, and renewable energy.

Sustainability Impact: Impact investing uses indicators other than typical financial ones to gauge its success. It is a potent tool for furthering sustainability since it promotes investments in initiatives and businesses that have a good social and environmental impact (Ante, 2021).

Including ESG Criteria

Overview: The evaluation of a companies or investment's environmental, social, and governance performance as part of the investment analysis is the integration of ESG factors into investment decisions.

Potential for Green Finance: It is already common practise to consider ESG factors when making investment decisions. When building portfolios and determining risk, financial institutions and asset managers are increasingly taking ESG aspects into account. Green finance products are becoming more and more well-liked, such as ESG-focused funds and green bonds.

Impact on Sustainability: Better corporate responsibility, risk management, and long-term value development are a result of ESG integration. Businesses that place a high priority on ESG performance are frequently better equipped to handle sustainability-related difficulties and seize chances for sustainable growth (Hardianto et al., 2021).

Instruments for Sustainable Debt

Overview: Sustainable debt products, such as green bonds, social bonds, and sustainability-linked loans, are financial services intended to finance initiatives that are both socially and environmentally responsible.

Green finance potential: The market for environmentally friendly financing instruments is growing quickly. These securities offer investors transparency and certainty about how the revenues will be used while also giving issuers a mechanism to collect money for sustainability activities.

Impact on Sustainability: Financial resources are allocated to projects with direct advantages for sustainability through the use of sustainable financing instruments. In order to help reduce carbon emissions, green bonds, for instance, finance renewable energy, energy-efficient, and clean transportation projects (Hardianto et al., 2021).

Technological Advancements

Overview: The way financial institutions evaluate sustainability risks and possibilities is changing as a result of technological advancements like blockchain, artificial intelligence, and data analytics.

Green finance potential: Technology makes it possible to collect and analyse ESG data with greater accuracy, which makes it simpler for investors to find sustainable assets and evaluate risk. Blockchain can improve sustainable product certification and supply chain transparency.

Impact on Sustainability: Technological advancements boost the effectiveness and efficiency of sustainable financial practises. They improve effect measurement, lessen fraud and greenwashing, and aid in the selection of sustainable investments (Hardianto et al., 2021).

In conclusion, a change towards all-encompassing, impact-oriented strategies will define the future of green finance and sustainable development. The incorporation of ESG criteria into investment decisions, circular economies, and impact investing are key themes that support ethical and sustainable financial behaviour while supporting environmental and social well-being. Undoubtedly, international case studies and viewpoints from many areas provide helpful insights into how green finance is being embraced globally. These instances highlight the various strategies and programmes that various nations and regions are using to advance sustainable finance and address environmental issues. The following are some prominent examples and viewpoints:

The European Green Deal

Overview: The European Green Deal is the EU's (European Union) comprehensive strategy to achieve climate neutrality by 2050. Initiatives to mobilise sizable investments in green finance and make the switch to a more sustainable economy are included.

Impact: As a result of the European Green Deal, green bonds were issued, a sustainable finance taxonomy was created, and the EU Sustainable Finance Action Plan was established. Investments in sustainable infrastructure, energy-efficient technologies, and renewable energy sources are being stimulated by these policies (Fetting, 2020).

Green Finance Initiatives in China

Overview: Through its policies and activities to promote sustainability, China has made significant advancements in the field of green finance. Green finance development has been outlined in recommendations by the People's Bank of China, and green bonds have grown in popularity.

Impact: As a result of China's efforts in green financing, investments in renewable energy, electric vehicles, and environmentally friendly infrastructure have expanded. The nation actively promotes both internal and international sustainable development by participating in the global green bond market (Fetting, 2020).

Sustainable Investing Growth in the United States

Overview: Asset managers and financial institutions are incorporating ESG factors into their investment strategies as sustainable investing has gained popularity in the United States. For instance, California actively promotes green financing and sustainable infrastructure initiatives.

Impact: There has been a significant increase in sustainable investing assets in the United States, which reflects growing interest in coordinating investments with social and environmental objectives. Investments in programmes for community development, affordable housing, and renewable energy are being driven by this trend (Muganyi et al., 2021).

Africa: Financing for Renewable Energy

Overview: A number of African nations, including Kenya and South Africa, have worked hard to entice green financing for renewable energy projects. Funds for the development of renewable energy are to be raised through initiatives like the African Renewable Energy Fund (AREF).

Impact: These initiatives have expanded financial support for hydro, wind, and solar energy projects all over Africa, which has improved energy access, created new jobs, and cut carbon emissions (Schueth, 2003).

Finance for Sustainable Agriculture in Latin America

Overview: Through programmes in green financing, Latin American nations like Brazil and Colombia are tackling issues with agricultural sustainability. They advocate for ethical land usage and sustainable agricultural methods.

Impact: Sustainable agricultural financing in Latin America supports initiatives that lessen deforestation, safeguard biodiversity, and enhance rural populations' standard of living (Asongu at al., 2021; Holt, 2006).

Investments in Renewable Energy in the Middle East

Overview: In order to diversify their economies and lessen their dependency on fossil fuels, Gulf Cooperation Council (GCC) nations like Saudi Arabia and the United Arab Emirates are investing in renewable energy projects.

Impact: Investments in renewable energy have helped the Middle East create large-scale wind and solar farms, boosting energy sustainability and opening up new business opportunities (Aslani et al., 2012).

Asia: Development of Sustainable Infrastructure

Overview: A lot of Asian nations, including Singapore and Japan, are emphasising sustainable infrastructure development. They are incorporating green finance into initiatives involving urban planning, transportation, and water management.

Impact: By making these investments, Asian cities will enjoy higher living standards, lessen environmental damage, and experience faster economic expansion (Adetola et al., 2011).

These case studies and regional viewpoints emphasise the international scope of green financing and the variety of strategies being used to advance sustainability. They emphasise how crucial global innovation, collaboration, and regulatory support are to improving green finance.

To fully realise the benefits of green finance in promoting sustainability, it is essential to address the barriers to its widespread adoption. The need for improved risk assessment and a distinct taxonomy for sustainable investments are a couple of the major obstacles. Overcoming these obstacles has major economic and societal advantages, such as improved public health, climate change resilience, and job creation (Cui et al., 2020; Akomea et al., 2022).

In conclusion, resolving issues with green finance adoption, such as risk assessment and taxonomy clarity, is crucial for achieving the societal and economic advantages of sustainability. Green Finance 2.0 plays a critical role in driving the shift to a more sustainable and resilient global economy, ultimately benefiting both the present and future generations by enhancing openness, lowering risk perception, and encouraging innovation (Akomea et al., 2022).

This chapter demonstrates how conventional financial models are changing to match with environmental and social aims throughout its examination of the development of green finance, from its early origins to its current condition. With the rise of novel financial products like green bonds and the expansion of impact investment, it highlights the shift from niche charity endeavours to mainstream inclusion of sustainability considerations. The book also emphasises how important national and international programmes like the Paris Agreement and the Sustainable Development Goals are in influencing the development of the green finance industry.

The advent of Green Finance 2.0, characterised by innovative investment tools, meticulous effect measurement, and a comprehensive approach to sustainability, serves as a beacon of progress. It denotes the development of sustainable finance, with a wider selection of financial goods and services created to handle difficult global issues. Financial institutions are further empowered by the incorporation of cutting-edge technology, such as blockchain and artificial intelligence, to evaluate sustainability risks and possibilities with previously unheard-of accuracy and effectiveness (Akomea et al., 2022).

The genuine potential of Green Finance 2.0, however, shines in the acceptance of difficulties and the pursuit of possibilities. The document emphasises the need of overcoming obstacles like risk assessment and taxonomy clarity and the advantages these actions will have for society and the economy. The practical benefits of a world committed to sustainable finance include increased public health, resilience to climate change, and job growth in sustainable sectors (Wang et al., 2022).

"Green Finance 2.0" advocates for a time when business and sustainability are intrinsically intertwined and every financial choice helps to create a society that is more sustainable, just, and healthy. It highlights the importance of cutting-edge financial strategies, strong legislative frameworks, and international cooperation in paving the road for this revolutionary vision. By adopting Green Finance 2.0, we set out on a path to a more sustainable and healthy future for all—a future in which finance is not only a tool for profit but also a force for long-term, good change in the world.

CONCLUSION

This chapter concluded that Green Finance 2.0 is crucial to sustainable development and public health in the face of environmental issues. This chapter's main lessons include how financial institutions, environmental sustainability, and public health are interconnected. Environmental deterioration brings health and economic problems, but green finance can alleviate them.

Climate Action: Climate change is a worldwide catastrophe that requires immediate action. Green money helps fund climate mitigation and adaptation, supporting global goals like the Paris Agreement.

Innovation and technology: This chapter covered blockchain, impact investment, and green bonds in green finance. These technologies improve sustainable investment efficiency and effectiveness.

Policy and Regulation: Strong and consistent regulatory frameworks are crucial. Governments and international entities must collaborate to promote green financing and sustainable development.

Investor Engagement and Education: Investors shape green financing. Education and transparency in sustainable investment are needed as more people and institutions seek it. The chapter concludes by emphasising worldwide collaboration. Environmental concerns are global and require international cooperation in financing, sustainability, and health.

These conversations show that Green Finance 2.0 is a promising topic. Integrating finance, sustainability, and health can lead to a more resilient, impartial, and healthy future. However, problems remain, and governments, businesses, investors, and civil society must collaborate to maximise Green Finance 2.0's potential. The findings from this chapter will lay the groundwork for the exciting discussions ahead as we learn about and design finance for sustainable development and health." This conclusion summarises the chapter's important ideas and prepares for future study.

REFERENCES

Adetola, A., Goulding, J., & Liyanage, C. (2011). Collaborative engagement approaches for delivering sustainable infrastructure projects in the AEC sector: a review. *International Journal of Construction supply chain management, 1*(1), 1-24.

Agbemabiese, L., Nyangon, P. D., Lee, J. S., & Byrne, J. (2018). *Enhancing climate finance readiness: A review of selected investment frameworks as tools of multilevel governance*. University of Delaware, Center for Energy & Environmental Policy.

Ahmad, H., Yaqub, M., & Lee, S. H. (2023). Environmental-, social-, and governance-related factors for business investment and sustainability: A scientometric review of global trends. *Environment, Development and Sustainability*, 1–23. doi:10.100710668-023-02921-x PMID:36714213

Akomea-Frimpong, I., Adeabah, D., Ofosu, D., & Tenakwah, E. J. (2022). A review of studies on green finance of banks, research gaps and future directions. *Journal of Sustainable Finance & Investment, 12*(4), 1241–1264. doi:10.1080/20430795.2020.1870202

Alt, R., Beck, R., & Smits, M. T. (2018). FinTech and the transformation of the financial industry. *Electronic Markets, 28*(3), 235–243. doi:10.100712525-018-0310-9

Anagnostopoulos, I. (2018). Fintech and regtech: Impact on regulators and banks. *Journal of Economics and Business*, *100*, 7–25. doi:10.1016/j.jeconbus.2018.07.003

Ante, L. (2021). The scope of green finance research: Research streams, influential works and future research paths. In *25th FMM Conference 2021 Macroeconomics of Socio-Ecological Transition* (*Vol. 36*).

Arner, D. W., Barberis, J., & Buckey, R. P. (2016). FinTech, RegTech, and the reconceptualization of financial regulation. *Nw. J. Int'l L. & Bus.*, *37*, 371.

Arnone, G. (2022). BLOCKCHAIN AND CRYPTOCURRENCY INNOVATION FOR A SUSTAINABLE FINANCIAL SYSTEM. *International Journal of Information Management*, *15*(1), 1–16.

Aslani, A., Naaranoja, M., & Zakeri, B. (2012). The prime criteria for private sector participation in renewable energy investment in the Middle East (case study: Iran). *Renewable & Sustainable Energy Reviews*, *16*(4), 1977–1987. doi:10.1016/j.rser.2011.12.015

Asongu, S. A., & Odhiambo, N. M. (2021). Inequality, finance and renewable energy consumption in Sub-Saharan Africa. *Renewable Energy*, *165*, 678–688. doi:10.1016/j.renene.2020.11.062

Bäckstrand, K. (2006). Multi-stakeholder partnerships for sustainable development: Rethinking legitimacy, accountability and effectiveness. *European Environment*, *16*(5), 290–306. doi:10.1002/eet.425

Bai, X. (2022). Exploring the Sustainable Development Path of a Green Financial System in the Context of Carbon Neutrality and Carbon Peaking: Evidence from China. *Sustainability (Basel)*, *14*(23), 15710. doi:10.3390u142315710

Campbell-Verduyn, M. (2023). Conjuring a cooler world? Imaginaries of improvement in blockchain climate finance experiments. *Environment and Planning C: Politics and Space*. Sage.

Cantele, S., & Zardini, A. (2018). Is sustainability a competitive advantage for small businesses? An empirical analysis of possible mediators in the sustainability–financial performance relationship. *Journal of Cleaner Production*, *182*, 166–176. doi:10.1016/j.jclepro.2018.02.016

Chygryn, O., Pimonenko, T., Luylyov, O., & Goncharova, A. (2019). Green bonds like the incentive instrument for cleaner production at the government and corporate levels: Experience from EU to Ukraine. *Journal of Environmental Management and Tourism*, *9*(7), 1443–1456. doi:10.14505//jemt.v9.7(31).09

Cui, H., Wang, R., & Wang, H. (2020). An evolutionary analysis of green finance sustainability based on multi-agent game. *Journal of Cleaner Production*, *269*, 121799. doi:10.1016/j.jclepro.2020.121799

Edenhofer, O., Pichs-Madruga, R., Sokona, Y., Seyboth, K., Kadner, S., Zwickel, T., & Matschoss, P. (Eds.). (2011). *Renewable energy sources and climate change mitigation: Special report of the intergovernmental panel on climate change*. Cambridge University Press. doi:10.1017/CBO9781139151153

Elkington, J. (2018). 25 years ago I coined the phrase "triple bottom line." Here's why it's time to rethink it. *Harvard Business Review*, *25*, 2–5.

Fairclough, J. (2002). *Rethinking construction innovation and research-a review of the government's R&D policies and practices*.

Fetting, C. (2020). The European green deal. *ESDN report, 53*. ESDN.

Fisher, B., Turner, K., Zylstra, M., Brouwer, R., De Groot, R., Farber, S., Ferraro, P., Green, R., Hadley, D., Harlow, J., Jefferiss, P., Kirkby, C., Morling, P., Mowatt, S., Naidoo, R., Paavola, J., Strassburg, B., Yu, D., & Balmford, A. (2008). Ecosystem services and economic theory: Integration for policy-relevant research. *Ecological Applications*, *18*(8), 2050–2067. doi:10.1890/07-1537.1 PMID:19263897

Gollwitzer, L., Ockwell, D., Muok, B., Ely, A., & Ahlborg, H. (2018). Rethinking the sustainability and institutional governance of electricity access and mini-grids: Electricity as a common pool resource. *Energy Research & Social Science*, *39*, 152–161. doi:10.1016/j.erss.2017.10.033

Hardianto, A., Marimin, M., Adrianto, L., & Fahmi, I. (2021, December). Sustainable Financing for Instrastructure Development to Support Tourism Connectivity: A Systematic Literature Review. In Conference Towards ASEAN Chairmanship 2023 (TAC 23 2021) (pp. 74-80). Atlantis Press.

Holt-Giménez, E. (2006). *Campesino a campesino: voices from Latin America's farmer to farmer movement for sustainable agriculture*. Food first books.

Iwejingi, S. F. (2011). Population growth, environmental degradation and human health in Nigeria. *Pakistan Journal of Social Sciences*, *8*(4), 187–191.

Khanchel, I., Lassoued, N., & Bargaoui, I. (2023). Pollution control bonds and environmental performance in energy utility firms: is there an incantation effect?. *International Journal of Energy Sector Management*.

Liu, H., Alharthi, M., Atil, A., Zafar, M. W., & Khan, I. (2022). A non-linear analysis of the impacts of natural resources and education on environmental quality: Green energy and its role in the future. *Resources Policy*, *79*, 102940. doi:10.1016/j.resourpol.2022.102940

Lucaci, B. (2022). *The Renewed Promise of Disclosure: an EU Approach to Sustainable Finance*. Sage.

Malik, A., Grohmann, E., & Akhtar, R. (2014). Environmental deterioration and human health. *Springer Dordrecht*, *10*, 978–994.

Manaswi, K., Singh, A., & Gupta, V. (2023). Building a Better Future with Sustainable Investments: Insights from Recent Research. *Indian Journal of Human Development*, *0*(0), 320–343. doi:10.1177/09737030231194836

Muganyi, T., Yan, L., & Sun, H. P. (2021). Green finance, fintech and environmental protection: Evidence from China. *Environmental Science and Ecotechnology*, *7*, 100107. doi:10.1016/j.ese.2021.100107 PMID:36160697

Nassiry, D. (2018). *The role of fintech in unlocking green finance: Policy insights for developing countries (No. 883)*. (ADBI working paper). ADBI.

Owen, R., Botelho, T., Mac an Bhaird, C., Hussain, J. G., Pierrakis, Y., Scott, J. M., & Lodh, S. (2023). Editorial entrepreneurial finance for green innovative SMEs. *IEEE Transactions on Engineering Management*, *70*(3), 942–949. doi:10.1109/TEM.2022.3224870

Painuly, J. P. (2001). Barriers to renewable energy penetration; a framework for analysis. *Renewable Energy*, *24*(1), 73–89. doi:10.1016/S0960-1481(00)00186-5

Polonsky, M. J. (2008). An introduction to green marketing. *Global Environment: Problems and Policies*, *2*(1), 1–10.

Rana, R. L., Tricase, C., & De Cesare, L. (2021). Blockchain technology for a sustainable agri-food supply chain. *British Food Journal*, *123*(11), 3471–3485. doi:10.1108/BFJ-09-2020-0832

Rizos, V., Behrens, A., Van der Gaast, W., Hofman, E., Ioannou, A., Kafyeke, T., Flamos, A., Rinaldi, R., Papadelis, S., Hirschnitz-Garbers, M., & Topi, C. (2016). Implementation of circular economy business models by small and medium-sized enterprises (SMEs): Barriers and enablers. *Sustainability (Basel)*, *8*(11), 1212. doi:10.3390u8111212

Rolffs, P., Ockwell, D., & Byrne, R. (2015). Beyond technology and finance: Pay-as-you-go sustainable energy access and theories of social change. *Environment & Planning A*, *47*(12), 2609–2627. doi:10.1177/0308518X15615368

Scheyvens, R. (2007). Exploring the tourism-poverty nexus. *Current Issues in Tourism*, *10*(2-3), 231–254. doi:10.2167/cit318.0

Schroeder, P., Anggraeni, K., & Weber, U. (2019). The relevance of circular economy practices to the sustainable development goals. *Journal of Industrial Ecology*, *23*(1), 77–95. doi:10.1111/jiec.12732

Schueth, S. (2003). Socially responsible investing in the United States. *Journal of Business Ethics*, *43*(3), 189–194. doi:10.1023/A:1022981828869

Tyagi, S., Garg, N., & Paudel, R. (2014). Environmental degradation: Causes and consequences. *European researcher, 81*(8-2), 1491.

Wang, K. H., Zhao, Y. X., Jiang, C. F., & Li, Z. Z. (2022). Does green finance inspire sustainable development? Evidence from a global perspective. *Economic Analysis and Policy*, *75*, 412–426. doi:10.1016/j.eap.2022.06.002

Compilation of References

Abbas, Q., Nurunnabi, M., Alfakhri, Y., Khan, W., Hussain, A., & Iqbal, W. (2020). The role of fixed capital formation, renewable and non-renewable energy in economic growth and carbon emission: A case study of Belt and Road Initiative project. *Environmental Science and Pollution Research International*, *27*(36), 45476–45486. doi:10.100711356-020-10413-y PMID:32794094

Abroms, L. C., & Maibach, E. W. The Effectiveness of Mass Communication to Change Public Behavior. *Annual Reviews*. https://www.annualreviews.org/doi/pdf/10.1146/annurev.publhealth.29.020907.090824

Abu Daqar, M. A. M., Arqawi, S., & Karsh, S. A. (2020). Fintech in the eyes of Millennials and Generation Z (the financial behavior and Fintech perception). *Banks and Bank Systems*, *15*(3), 20–28. doi:10.21511/bbs.15(3).2020.03

AccountAbility. (2020). *Assurance Standard (AA-1000)*. AccountAbility. URL:https://www.accountability.org/static/3ff15429033873cdc775212ca63572fb/aa1000as_v3_final.pdf

Acemoglu, D., & Restrepo, P. (2018). *Artificial Intelligence, Automation and Work*. NBER. https://www.nber.org/papers/w24196

Adabre, M. A., & Chan, A. P. C. (2019). Critical success factors (CSFs) for sustainable affordable housing. *Building and Environment*, *156*, 203–214. doi:10.1016/j.buildenv.2019.04.030

Adetola, A., Goulding, J., & Liyanage, C. (2011). Collaborative engagement approaches for delivering sustainable infrastructure projects in the AEC sector: a review. *International Journal of Construction supply chain management, 1*(1), 1-24.

Adu, E., Zhang, Y. D., Liu, D., & Tontiwachwuthikul, P. (2020). Parametric process design and economic analysis of post-combustion CO2 capture and compression for coal-and natural gas-fired power plants. *Energies*, *13*(10), 2519. doi:10.3390/en13102519

Afif, N., & Purwantini, A. H. (2022, December). The Paradox of Perceived Risk and Trust on Intention to Use Fintech Payment: Evidence in MSMEs. In *3rd Borobudur International Symposium on Humanities and Social Science 2021 (BIS-HSS 2021)* (pp. 645-648). Atlantis Press.

Agaverdiyeva, H. F. (2016). Technologies of implementing non-financial reporting as a tool for regulating the social responsibility of a non-state pension fund in the conditions of European integration. *Economics and Finances*. *3*. 4-14. URL: http://repository.hneu.edu.ua/handle/123456789/11962

Agbemabiese, L., Nyangon, P. D., Lee, J. S., & Byrne, J. (2018). *Enhancing climate finance readiness: A review of selected investment frameworks as tools of multilevel governance*. University of Delaware, Center for Energy & Environmental Policy.

Aggarwal, K. K., & Aggarwal, S. (2021). Is Green banking an Adequate Initiative for Environment Sustainability. In New India: Emerging Trends in Indian Business Scenario (Vol. 1, pp. 87–97). Notion Press.

Agrawal, B., Awad, R., & Banerjee, S. (2019). Construction of α Resolvable 2-Associates PBIB Designs. *International Journal of Applied Social Science*, *6*(1), 166–170.

Agyekum, K., Opoku, A., Oppon, A. J., & Opoku, D. G. J. (2022). Obstacles to green building project financing: An empirical study in Ghana. *International Journal of Construction Management*, *22*(15), 2922–2930. doi:10.1080/15623599.2020.1832182

Ahiabenu, K. (2022). A Critical Analysis of the Regulatory Framework for the Financial Technology (FinTech) Sector in Ghana. *African Journal of Business & Economic Research*, *17*(2), 109–128. doi:10.31920/1750-4562/2022/v17n2a5

Ahmad, H., Yaqub, M., & Lee, S. H. (2023). Environmental-, social-, and governance-related factors for business investment and sustainability: A scientometric review of global trends. *Environment, Development and Sustainability*, 1–23. doi:10.100710668-023-02921-x PMID:36714213

Ahmed, M., Shuai, C., & Ahmed, M. (2023). Analysis of energy consumption and greenhouse gas emissions trend in China, India, the USA, and Russia. *International Journal of Environmental Science and Technology*, *20*(3), 2683–2698. doi:10.100713762-022-04159-y

Aitken, R. (2018). Global Financial Services Bullish On AI, The "Disruptive Tech" Frontrunner. *Forbes*. https://www.forbes.com/sites/rogeraitken/2018/11/28/global-financial-services-bullish-on-ai-the-disruptive-tech-frontrunner/?sh=7366b0d82311

Ajaz, A., Shenbei, Z., & Sarfraz, M. (2020). Delineating the influence of boardroom gender diversity on corporate social responsibility, financial performance, and reputation. *LogForum*, *16*(1).

Akanbi, A., & Adeyeye, C. (2011). The Association between Advertising and Sales Volume. *Journal of Emerging Trends in Economic and Management Sciences*. www.jetems.scholarlinkeresearch.org

Akhlaq, A., & Ahmed, E. (2015). Digital commerce in emerging economies: Factors associated with online shopping intentions in Pakistan. *International Journal of Emerging Markets*.

Aklilu, Y. T., & Ding, J. (2021). Survey on blockchain for smart grid management, control, and operation. *Energies*, *15*(1), 193. doi:10.3390/en15010193

Akomea-Frimpong, I., Adeabah, D., Ofosu, D., & Tenakwah, E. J. (2022). A review of studies on green finance of banks, research gaps and future directions. *Journal of Sustainable Finance & Investment*, *12*(4), 1241–1264. doi:10.1080/20430795.2020.1870202

Al Hawaj, A. Y., & Buallay, A. M. (2022). A worldwide sectorial analysis of sustainability reporting and its impact on firm performance. *Journal of Sustainable Finance & Investment*, *12*(1), 62–86. doi:10.1080/20430795.2021.1903792

Al-Dmour, H., Ra'ed Masa'deh, A. S., Al-Dmour, R., & Abuhashesh, M. (2022). The Role of Mass Media Interventions on Promoting Public Health Knowledge and Behavioral Social Change Against COVID-19 Pandemic in Jordan. *SAGE Open*, *12*(1). doi:10.1177/21582440221082125

Aleksić, J., Alvarez, E. A., Antonelli, L. A., Antoranz, P., Asensio, M., Backes, M., Barrio, J. A., Bastieri, D., González, J. B., & Bednarek, W. (2012). Performance of the MAGIC stereo system obtained with Crab Nebula data. *Astroparticle Physics*, *35*(7), 435–448. doi:10.1016/j.astropartphys.2011.11.007

Alessandrini, F., & Jondeau, E. (2021). Optimal strategies for ESG portfolios. *Journal of Portfolio Management*, *47*(6), 114–138. doi:10.3905/jpm.2021.1.241

Alexandri, M. B., Usman, I., Narimawati, U., & Taryana, A. (2023). Unraveling the Fintech Landscape: A Systematic Mapping Study on the Impact of Financial Technology Innovation on Investment Decision-Making in ASEAN Banking. *Khazanah Sosial*, *5*(1), 113–124. doi:10.15575/ks.v5i1.24555

AlHajjaj, H. Z., & Ahmad, A. M. K. (2022). Drivers Of the Consumers Adoption Of FinTech Services. *Interdisciplinary Journal of Information, Knowledge, and Management*, *17*, 259–285. doi:10.28945/4971

Alharbi, S. S., Al Mamun, M., Boubaker, S., & Rizvi, S. K. A. (2023). Green finance and renewable energy: A worldwide evidence. *Energy Economics*, *118*, 106499. doi:10.1016/j.eneco.2022.106499

Ali, J., & Ghildiyal, A. K. (2023). Socio-economic characteristics, mobile phone ownership and banking behaviour of individuals as determinants of digital financial inclusion in India. *International Journal of Social Economics*, *50*(10), 1375–1392. doi:10.1108/IJSE-10-2022-0673

Allen, F., Gu, X., & Jagtiani, J. (2021). A survey of fintech research and policy discussion. *Review of Corporate Finance*, *1*(3-4), 259–339. doi:10.1561/114.00000007

Almousa, M. (2011). Perceived risk in apparel online shopping: A multi-dimensional perspective. *Canadian Social Science*, *7*(2), 23–31.

Alparslan, A., & Saner, T. (2020). The Influence of Sustainable Talent Management on Job Satisfaction and Organizational Commitment: Moderating Role of In-Service Training. *Revista de Cercetare si Interventie Sociala*, *69*(June), 96–121. doi:10.33788/rcis.69.6

Alt, R., Beck, R., & Smits, M. T. (2018). FinTech and the transformation of the financial industry. *Electronic Markets*, *28*(3), 235–243. doi:10.100712525-018-0310-9

Anagnostopoulos, I. (2018). Fintech and regtech: Impact on regulators and banks. *Journal of Economics and Business*, *100*, 7–25. doi:10.1016/j.jeconbus.2018.07.003

Andenæs, E., Kvande, T., Muthanna, T. M., & Lohne, J. (2018). Performance of blue-green roofs in cold climates: A scoping review. *Buildings*, *8*(4), 55. Advance online publication. doi:10.3390/buildings8040055

Aneja, R., Kappil, S. R., Das, N., & Banday, U. J. (2023). Does the green finance initiatives transform the world into a green economy? A study of green bond issuing countries. *Environmental Science and Pollution Research International*, *30*(14), 42214–42222. doi:10.100711356-023-25317-w PMID:36645606

Anlesinya, A., & Amponsah-Tawiah, K. (2020). Towards a Responsible Talent Management Model. *European Journal of Training and Development*, *44*(2/3), 279–303. doi:10.1108/EJTD-07-2019-0114

Annur, C.M. (2019). *APJII Survey: Internet user penetration in Indonesia reaches 64.8%.* Datadata. co. en.

Ansari, M., & Joloudar, E. (2011). An investigation of TV advertisement effects on customers' purchasing and their satisfaction. *International Journal of Marketing Studies*, *3*(4), 175.

Anshari, M., Almunawar, M. N., Masri, M., & Hrdy, M. (2021). Financial technology with ai-enabled and ethical challenges. *Society*, *58*(3), 189–195. doi:10.100712115-021-00592-w

Ante, L. (2020). A place next to Satoshi: foundations of blockchain and cryptocurrency research in business and economics. *Scientometrics 124*(2), 1305–1333. doi:10.1007/s11192-020-03492-8

Ante, L. (2021). The scope of green finance research: Research streams, influential works and future research paths. In *25th FMM Conference 2021 Macroeconomics of Socio-Ecological Transition* (*Vol. 36*).

An, X., & Pivo, G. (2020). Green Buildings in Commercial Mortgage-Backed Securities: The Effects of LEED and Energy Star Certification on Default Risk and Loan Terms. *Real Estate Economics*, *48*(1), 7–42. doi:10.1111/1540-6229.12228

An, Y. J., Choi, P. M. S., & Huang, S. H. (2021). Blockchain, cryptocurrency, and artificial intelligence in finance. In *Fintech with artificial intelligence, big data, and blockchain* (pp. 1–34). Springer Singapore. doi:10.1007/978-981-33-6137-9_1

Arayssi, M., Jizi, M., & Tabaja, H. (2020). *The impact of board composition on the level of ESG disclosures in GCC countries*. Sustainability Accounting, Management and Policy Journal. doi:10.1108/SAMPJ-05-2018-0136

Ardichvili, A., & Zavyalova, E. (2019). TALENT MANAGEMENT AND DEVELOPMENT IN THE RUSSIAN FEDERATION. In K. M. Dirani, F. M. Nafukho, and B. J. Irby (eds.) Global Issues And Talent Development: Perspectives From Countries Around The World, 41–56. International Higher Education.

Ariffin, S. K., Mohan, T., & Goh, Y. N. (2018). Influence of consumers' perceived risk on consumers' online purchase intention. *Journal of Research in Interactive Marketing*.

Arlinghaus, J. (2015). Imp*acts of Carbon Prices on Indicators of Competitiveness: A Review of Empirical Findings.* (OECD Environment Working Papers, No. 87). OECD Publishing, Paris. doi:10.1787/19970900

Arner, D. W., Barberis, J., & Buckey, R. P. (2016). FinTech, RegTech, and the reconceptualization of financial regulation. *Nw. J. Int'l L. & Bus.*, *37*, 371.

Arner, D. W., Barberis, J., & Buckley, R. P. (2015). The evolution of Fintech: A new post-crisis paradigm. *SSRN*, *47*, 1271. doi:10.2139srn.2676553

Arnold, J., & Toledano, P. (2021). *Corporate Net-Zero Pledges: The Bad and the Ugly*. Columbia Centre on Sustainable Investment.

Arnone, G. (2022). BLOCKCHAIN AND CRYPTOCURRENCY INNOVATION FOR A SUSTAINABLE FINANCIAL SYSTEM. *International Journal of Information Management*, *15*(1), 1–16.

Asayama, S. (2021). The Oxymoron of Carbon Dioxide Removal: Escaping Carbon Lock-In and yet Perpetuating the Fossil Status Quo? *Frontiers in Climate*, *3*, 673515. doi:10.3389/fclim.2021.673515

Ashta, A. (2023). How Can Fintech Companies Get Involved in the Environment? *Sustainability (Basel)*, *15*(10675), 1–18. doi:10.3390u151310675

Asif, M., Khan, M. N., Tiwari, S., Wani, S. K., & Alam, F. (2023). The Impact of Fintech and Digital Financial Services on Financial Inclusion in India. *Journal of Risk and Financial Management*, *16*(2), 122. doi:10.3390/jrfm16020122

Aslani, A., Naaranoja, M., & Zakeri, B. (2012). The prime criteria for private sector participation in renewable energy investment in the Middle East (case study: Iran). *Renewable & Sustainable Energy Reviews*, *16*(4), 1977–1987. doi:10.1016/j.rser.2011.12.015

Asongu, S. A., & Odhiambo, N. M. (2021). Inequality, finance and renewable energy consumption in Sub-Saharan Africa. *Renewable Energy*, *165*, 678–688. doi:10.1016/j.renene.2020.11.062

Atradius Collections. (2022). *Database of statistical data.* United Kingdom. https://atradiuscollections.com/global/reports/payment-practices-barometer-b2b-payment-practices-trends-western-europe-2022.html

Awotunde, J. B., Adeniyi, E. A., Ogundokun, R. O., & Ayo, F. E. (2021). Application of big data with fintech in financial services. In *Fintech with Artificial Intelligence, Big Data, and Blockchain* (pp. 107–132). Springer Singapore. doi:10.1007/978-981-33-6137-9_3

Ayanwale. (2005). The Influence of Advertising on Consumer Brand Preference. *Journal of Social Science*, *10*(1), 9–16.

Ayesha, Meryem, M., Vaneeza, R., & Anjum. (2020). *Role of Mass Media and Public Health Communications in the COVID-19 Pandemic*. doi:10.7759/cureus.10453

Baber, H. (2017). Risk mitigation practices in banking: A study of hdfc bank. In Risk and Contingency Management: Breakthroughs in Research and Practice (pp. 453–468). IGI Global. doi:10.4018/978-1-5225-3932-2.ch023

Bäckstrand, K. (2006). Multi-stakeholder partnerships for sustainable development: Rethinking legitimacy, accountability and effectiveness. *European Environment*, *16*(5), 290–306. doi:10.1002/eet.425

Badgley, G., Chay, F., Chegwidden, O., Hamman, J., Freeman, J., & Cullenward, D. (2022). California's forest carbon offsets buffer pool is severely undercapitalized. *Frontiers in Forests and Global Change*, *5*, 930426. doi:10.3389/ffgc.2022.930426

Badugu, D., & Chanhan, S. (2011). Understanding the Indian Rural Market Potential. *International Journal of Multidisciplinary Research*, *1*(6), 68–82. https://www.researchgate.net/publication/312161872_UNDERSTANDING_THE_INDIAN_RURAL_MARKET_POTENTIAL

Bai, X. (2022). Exploring the Sustainable Development Path of a Green Financial System in the Context of Carbon Neutrality and Carbon Peaking: Evidence from China. *Sustainability (Basel)*, *14*(23), 15710. doi:10.3390u142315710

Banna, H., Hassan, M. K., Ahmad, R., & Alam, M. R. (2022). Islamic banking stability amidst the COVID-19 pandemic: The role of digital financial inclusion. *International Journal of Islamic and Middle Eastern Finance and Management*, *15*(2), 310–330. doi:10.1108/IMEFM-08-2020-0389

Bansal, N., Bhatnagar, M., & Taneja, S. (2023). Balancing priorities through green optimism: A study elucidating initiatives, approaches, and strategies for sustainable supply chain management. In *Handbook of Research on Designing Sustainable Supply Chains to Achieve a Circular Economy*. IGI Global., doi:10.4018/978-1-6684-7664-2.ch004

Baraibar-Diez, E., Odriozola, M. D., & Fernández Sánchez, J. L. (2019). Sustainable compensation policies and its effect on environmental, social, and governance scores. *Corporate Social Responsibility and Environmental Management*, *26*(6), 1457–1472. doi:10.1002/csr.1760

Barauskaite, G., & Streimikiene, D. (2021). Corporate social responsibility and financial performance of companies: The puzzle of concepts, definitions and assessment methods. *Corporate Social Responsibility and Environmental Management*, *28*(1), 278–287. doi:10.1002/csr.2048

Barnosky, A. D., Brown, J. H., Daily, G. C., Dirzo, R., Ehrlich, A. H., Ehrlich, P. R., Eronen, J. T., Fortelius, M., Hadly, E. A., Leopold, E. B., Mooney, H. A., Myers, J. P., Naylor, R. L., Palumbi, S., Stenseth, N. C., & Wake, M. H. (2014). Introducing the scientific consensus on maintaining humanity's life support systems in the 21st century: Information for policy makers. *The Anthropocene Review*, *1*(1), 78–109. doi:10.1177/2053019613516290

Behal, V., & Gupta, M. (2022). Reporting of Corporate Social Responsibility Practices: An Evidence from Indian BSE-Listed Companies. *Prabandhan: Indian Journal of Management*, *15*(3), 42–58. doi:10.17010/pijom/2022/v15i3/165633

Belozyorov, S. A., & Xie, X. (2021). China's green insurance system and functions. *E3S Web of Conferences*, *311*, 3001.

Ben Bouheni, F., Tewari, M., Sidaoui, M., & Hasnaoui, A. (2023). An econometric understanding of Fintech and operating performance. *Review of Accounting and Finance*, *22*(3), 329–352. doi:10.1108/RAF-10-2022-0290

Benitez-Amado, J., Llorens-Montes, F., & Fernandez-Perez, V. (2015). IT Impact on Talent Management and Operational Environmental Sustainability. *INFORMATION TECHNOLOGY\& MANAGEMENT*, *16*(3), 207–20. . doi:10.1007/s10799-015-0226-4

Benjaafar, S., Li, Y., & Daskin, M. (2013). Carbon footprint and the management of supply chains: Insights from simple models. *IEEE Transactions on Automation Science and Engineering*, *10*(1), 99–116. doi:10.1109/TASE.2012.2203304

Berensmann, K., & Lindenberg, N. (2016). Green finance: actors, challenges and policy recommendations. *German Development Institute/Deutsches Institut für Entwicklungspolitik (DIE) Briefing Paper, 23.*

Bernadette, J. & Goddard, C. (2002), *Australian Institute of Family Studies.* AIFS. https://aifs.gov.au/resources/policy-and-practice-papers/role-mass-media-facilitating-community-education-and-child

Berry, T. C., & Junkus, J. C. (2013). Socially Responsible Investing: An Investor Perspective. *Journal of Business Ethics*, *112*(4), 707–720. doi:10.100710551-012-1567-0

Bhastary, M. D., Lubis, A. R., Utami, S., & Meldi Kesuma, T. (2023). Implementation Of Talent Management as An Effort to Realize Sustainable Performance of The Palm Oil Industry in Indonesia. *Quality - Access to Success*, *24*(195), 255–262. doi:10.47750/QAS/24.195.30

Bhatnagar, A., Misra, S., & Rao, H. R. (2000). On risk, convenience, and Internet shopping behavior. *Communications of the ACM*, *43*(11), 98–105. doi:10.1145/353360.353371

Bhatnagar, M., Özen, E., Taneja, S., Grima, S., & Rupeika-Apoga, R. (2022). The Dynamic Connectedness between Risk and Return in the Fintech Market of India: Evidence Using the GARCH-M Approach. *Risks*, *10*(11), 209. doi:10.3390/risks10110209

Bhatnagar, M., Pathak, N., & Taneja, S. (2023). Tech-Optimists and Financial Education - A Research on the Efficacy of Communication Mediums of Government Economic Policies. *International Journal of Sustainable Development and Planning*, *18*(7), 2245–2252. doi:10.18280/ijsdp.180729

Bhatnagar, M., Taneja, S., Kumar, P., & Özen, E. (2023a). Does Financial Education Act as a Catalyst for SME Competitiveness. *International Journal of Education Economics and Development*, *1*(1), 1. doi:10.1504/IJEED.2023.10053629

Bhatnagar, M., Taneja, S., & Özen, E. (2022b). A wave of green start-ups in India—The study of green finance as a support system for sustainable entrepreneurship. *Green Finance*, *4*(2), 253–273. doi:10.3934/GF.2022012

Bhatnagar, M., Taneja, S., & Rupeika-Apoga, R. (2023). Demystifying the Effect of the News (Shocks) on Crypto Market Volatility. *Journal of Risk and Financial Management*, *16*(2), 136. Advance online publication. doi:10.3390/jrfm16020136

Bhattacharyya, M., Chaudhary, A., & Yadav, G. (2008). Conditional VaR estimation using Pearson's type IV distribution. *European Journal of Operational Research*, *191*(2), 386–397. doi:10.1016/j.ejor.2007.07.021

Bhukya, R., & Singh, S. (2015). The effect of perceived risk dimensions on purchase intention: An empirical evidence from Indian private labels market. *American Journal of Business*, *30*(4), 218–230. doi:10.1108/AJB-10-2014-0055

Birindelli, G., Dell'Atti, S., Iannuzzi, A. P., & Savioli, M. (2018). Composition and activity ofthe board ofdirectors: Impact on ESG performance in the banking system. *Sustainability (Basel)*, *10*(12), 4699. doi:10.3390u10124699

Blanco, C. (2020). (Forthcoming). A Classification of Carbon Abatement Opportunities of Global Firms. *Manufacturing & Service Operations Management.*

Blanco, C., Caro, F., & Corbett, C. (2020). Do carbon abatement opportunities become less profitable over time? A global firm-level perspective using CDP data. *Energy Policy*, *138*, 111–252. doi:10.1016/j.enpol.2020.111252

Blaufelder, C., Levy, C., Mannion, P., & Dickon, P. (2021). *A blueprint for scaling voluntary carbon markets to meet the climate challenge*. McKinsey and Company.

Bloomberg. (2019) *Sustainable Debt Market Sees Record Activity in 2018.* BNEF. https://about.bnef.com/blog/sustainable-debt-market-sees-record-activity-2018/

Blum, P., Helmcke, S., Heuss, R., Hundertmark, T., Marlier, S., Somers, K., & Pinner, D. (2021). *Net zero or bust: Beating the abatement cost curve for growth.* McKinsey and Company. https://www.mckinsey.com/capabilities/operations/our-insights/net-zero-or-bust-beating-the-abatement-cost-curve-for-growth

Bourlakis, M., Papagiannidis, S., & Fox, H. (2008). E-consumer behaviour: Past, present and future trajectories of an evolving retail revolution. [IJEBR]. *International Journal of E-Business Research*, *4*(3), 64–76. doi:10.4018/jebr.2008070104

Bragdon, J. H., & Marlin, J. A. T. (1972). Is pollution profitable? *Risk Management*, *19*(4), 9–18.

Brahmi, M., Esposito, L., Parziale, A., Dhayal, K. S., Agrawal, S., Giri, A. K., & Loan, N. T. (2023). The Role of Greener Innovations in Promoting Financial Inclusion to Achieve Carbon Neutrality. *International Review of Economics*, *11*(194), 1–18. doi:10.3390/economies11070194

Brammer, S., & Millington, A. (2008). Does it pay to be different? An analysis of the relationship between corporate social and financial performance. *Strategic Management Journal*, *29*(12), 1325–1343. doi:10.1002mj.714

Braunstein, E., & Heintz, J. (2008). Gender bias and central bank policy: Employment and inflation reduction. *International Review of Applied Economics*, *22*(2), 173–186. doi:10.1080/02692170801889643

Brewer, J. (2018). Exploring paths to a more accessible digital future. *ASSETS 2018 - Proceedings of the 20th International ACM SIGACCESS Conference on Computers and Accessibility*, (pp. 1–2). ACM. 10.1145/3234695.3243502

Broekhoff, D., Gillenwater, M., Colbert-Sangree, T., & Cage, P. (2019). Securing Climate Benefit: A Guide to Using Carbon Offsets. Stockholm Environment Institute & Greenhouse Gas Management Institute. Busch,P.,Kendall,A.,Murphy ,C.W., Miller,S.A. (2022). Literature Review on policies to mitigate GHG emissions for cement and concrete. *Resources, Conservation and Recycling*, *182*, 106278.

Bu, D., Hanspal, T., Liao, Y., & Liu, Y. (2022). Cultivating self-control in FinTech: Evidence from a field experiment on online consumer borrowing. *Journal of Financial and Quantitative Analysis*, *57*(6), 2208–2250. doi:10.1017/S0022109021000314

Buenestado-Fernández, M., Ramírez-Montoya, M. S., Ibarra-Vazquez, G., & Patiño, A. (2023). Digital competency as a key to the financial inclusion of young people in complex scenarios: A focus groups study. *Citizenship. Social and Economics Education*, *22*(1), 48–62. doi:10.1177/14788047231170083

Buhalis, D., & Leung, R. (2018). Smart hospitality—Interconnectivity and interoperability towards an ecosystem. *International Journal of Hospitality Management*, *71*, 41–50. doi:10.1016/j.ijhm.2017.11.011

Bukhari, S. A. A., Hashim, F., & Amran, A. (2021). Green banking: A conceptual framework. *International Journal of Green Economics*, *15*(1), 59. doi:10.1504/IJGE.2021.117682

Burke, T. J., & Segrin, C. (2014). Examining diet-and exercise-related communication in romantic relationships: Associations with health behaviors. *Health Communication*, *29*(9), 877–887. doi:10.1080/10410236.2013.811625 PMID:24295060

Busch, T., Bassen, A., Lwandowski, S., & Sump, F. (2022). Corporate Carbon and Financial Performance Revisited. *Organization & Environment*, *35*(1), 154–171. doi:10.1177/1086026620935638

Camodeca, R., & Almici, A. (2021). Digital Transformation and Convergence toward the 2030 Agenda's Sustainability Development Goals: Evidence from Italian Listed Firms. *Sustainability 2021, 13*(21), 11831. doi:10.3390/su132111831

Campbell-Verduyn, M. (2023). Conjuring a cooler world? Imaginaries of improvement in blockchain climate finance experiments. *Environment and Planning C: Politics and Space*. Sage.

Campiglio, E., Dafermos, Y., Monnin, P., Ryan-Collins, J., Schotten, G., & Tanaka, M. (2018). Climate change challenges for central banks and financial regulators. *Nature Climate Change*, *8*(6), 462–468. doi:10.103841558-018-0175-0

Canham, C. (2021). *Rethinking forest carbon offsets. Cary Institute of Ecosystem Studies*. Cary Institute. https://www.caryinstitute.org/news-insights/feature/rethinking-forest-carbon-offsets

Cantele, S., & Zardini, A. (2018). Is sustainability a competitive advantage for small businesses? An empirical analysis of possible mediators in the sustainability–financial performance relationship. *Journal of Cleaner Production*, *182*, 166–176. doi:10.1016/j.jclepro.2018.02.016

Cao, K., Xu, X., Wu, Q., & Zhang, Q. (2017). Optimal production and carbon emission reduction level under cap-and-trade and low carbon subsidy policies. *Journal of Cleaner Production*, *167*, 505–513. doi:10.1016/j.jclepro.2017.07.251

Cardwell, H. (2022). *Govt unlikely to prevent pine and exotic forest owners from earning under ETS*. Radio New Zealand. https://www.rnz.co.nz/news/national/471839/govt-unlikely-to-prevent-pine-and-exotic-forest-owners-from-earning-under-ets

Carton, W., Lund, F. J., & Dooley, K. (2021). Undoing Equivalence: Rethinking Carbon Accounting for Just Carbon Removal. *Frontiers in Climate*, *3*, 664130. doi:10.3389/fclim.2021.664130

Carver, T., Dawson, P., & Kerr, S. (2017). *Including Forestry in an Emissions Trading Scheme: Lessons from New Zealand.* (Motu Working Paper 17-11). Motu Economic and Public Policy Research.

Castellanos, J. D., & George, B. (2020). Boardroom leadership: The board of directors as a source of strategic leadership. *Economics and Business Review*, *6*(1), 103–119. doi:10.18559/ebr.2020.1.5

Census of India. (2011). *Uttar Pradesh*. CDN. https://cdn.s3waas.gov.in/s34c5bde74a8f110656874902f07378009/uploads/2016/09/2018022381.pdf

Cerqueti, R., Deffains-Crapsky, C., & Storani, S. (2023). Green finance instruments: Exploring minibonds issuance in I taly. *Corporate Social Responsibility and Environmental Management*, *30*(4), 1965–1986. doi:10.1002/csr.2467

Challenges in Rural Communication . (2018-23). Brainkart. https://www.brainkart.com/article/Challenges-in-Rural-Communication_6095/

Chan, C.-S., Chang, T. C., & Liu, Y. (2022). Investigating Creative Experiences and Environmental Perception of Creative Tourism: The Case of PMQ (Police Married Quarters) in Hong Kong. *Journal of China Tourism Research*, *18*(2), 223–244. doi:10.1080/19388160.2020.1812459

Chang, Y. (2019). Green finance in Singapore: Barriers and solutions. ADBI Working Paper 915. Dikau, S., & Volz, U. (2021). Central bank mandates, sustainability objectives and the promotion of green finance. *Ecological Economics*, *184*, 107022.

Chen, L., Tong, T. W., Tang, S., & Han, N. (2022). Governance and design of digital platforms: A review and future research directions on a meta-organization. *Journal of Management*, *48*(1), 147–184. doi:10.1177/01492063211045023

Chen, L., & Yang, X. (2018). Using EPPM to evaluate the effectiveness of fear appeal messages across different media outlets to increase the intention of breast self-examination among Chinese women. *Health Communication*. PMID:30080982

Chen, M. (2020). Beyond donation: China's policy banks and the reshaping of development finance. *Studies in Comparative International Development*, *55*(4), 436–459. doi:10.100712116-020-09310-9

Chen, Z., Mirza, N., Huang, L., & Umar, M. (2022). Green Banking—Can Financial Institutions support green recovery? *Economic Analysis and Policy*, *75*, 389–395. doi:10.1016/j.eap.2022.05.017 PMID:35694019

Chien, F. (2023). The Impact of Green Investment, Eco-Innovation, and Financial Inclusion on Sustainable Development: Evidence from China. *The Engineering Economist*, *34*(1), 17–31. doi:10.5755/j01.ee.34.1.32159

Childs, P. D., Ott, S. H., & Triantis, A. J. (1998). Capital Budgeting for Interrelated Projects: A Real Options Approach. *Journal of Financial and Quantitative Analysis*, *33*(3), 305–334. doi:10.2307/2331098

Chin, W. W. (1998). The partial least squares approach to structural equation modeling. *Modern Methods for Business Research*, *295*(2), 295–336.

Chithra, V., & Kothai, S. (2015). Television viewing behavior of consumers and television advertisement's impact on consumer purchase decision. *International Journal of Research in Commerce & Management*, *6*(10).

Chiu, C. M., Wang, E. T., Fang, Y. H., & Huang, H. Y. (2014). Understanding customers' repeat purchase intentions in B2C e-commerce: The roles of utilitarian value, hedonic value and perceived risk. *Information Systems Journal*, *24*(1), 85–114. doi:10.1111/j.1365-2575.2012.00407.x

Chiu, I. H.-Y. (2017). A new era in fintech payment innovations? A perspective from the institutions and regulation of payment systems. *Law, Innovation and Technology*, *9*(2), 190–234. doi:10.1080/17579961.2017.1377912

Choi, Y., & Qi, C. (2019). Is South Korea's Emission Trading Scheme Effective? An Analysis Based on the Marginal Abatement Cost of Coal-Fueled Power Plants. *Sustainability (Basel)*, *11*(9), 2504. doi:10.3390u11092504

Chopra, P., & Gupta, M. (2023). Fuzzy Logic and ANN in an Artificial Intelligent Cloud: A Comparative Study. In *Intelligent Communication Technologies and Virtual Mobile Networks* (pp. 559–570). Springer Nature Singapore Singapore. doi:10.1007/978-981-99-1767-9_41

Chowdhary, R., Jore, S., & Khandewal, S. (2013). Income Consumption Relationship in Indore City, An Application of Engel's Law. *PRERNA: Journal of Management Thought and Practice*, *5*(1), 1–13.

Chowdhury, A., Naz, A., Bhattacharyya, S., & Sanyal, P. (2018). Cost–benefit analysis of 'Blue Carbon'sequestration by plantation of few key mangrove species at Sundarban Biosphere Reserve, India. *Carbon Management*, *9*(6), 575–586. doi:10.1080/17583004.2018.1518105

Chygryn, O., Pimonenko, T., Luylyov, O., & Goncharova, A. (2019). Green bonds like the incentive instrument for cleaner production at the government and corporate levels: Experience from EU to Ukraine. *Journal of Environmental Management and Tourism*, *9*(7), 1443–1456. doi:10.14505//jemt.v9.7(31).09

Clean Development Mechanism. (2022). *CDM Executive Board 114th meeting: meeting report*. United Nations Framework Convention on Climate Change.

Clement, J. (2019). E-commerce worldwide-Statistics & Facts. *Statista. Recuperado el, 5.*

Climate Bonds Initiative. (2018). *India Ranks 8th in World for Climate Aligned Bond Issuance*. Climate Bonds Initative. https://www.climatebonds.net/resources/press-releases/2018/10/climate-bonds-state-market-report-points-huge-india-green-growth

Climate Change Commission. (2022). *Advice on NZ ETS unit limits and price control settings for 2023-2027.* CCC. https://ccc-production-media.s3.ap-southeast-2.amazonaws.com/public/ETS-advice-July-22/PDFs/NZ-ETS-settings-2023-2027-final-report-web-27-July-2022.pdf

Climate Change Committee. (2022). *Voluntary Carbon Markets and Offsetting.* Climate Change Committee, United Kingdom. https://www.theccc.org.uk/publication/voluntary-carbon-markets-and-offsetting/

Coffie, C. P. K., Hongjiang, Z., Mensah, I. A., Kiconco, R., & Simon, A. E. O. (2021). Determinants of FinTech payment services diffusion by SMEs in Sub-Saharan Africa: Evidence from Ghana. *Information Technology for Development, 27*(3), 539–560. doi:10.1080/02681102.2020.1840324

Cosma, S., Rimo, G., & Torluccio, G. (2023). Knowledge mapping of model risk in banking. *International Review of Financial Analysis, 89*, 102800. doi:10.1016/j.irfa.2023.102800

Cotton, C., & Babb, M. (1978). Consumer Response to Promotional Deals. *Journal of Marketing, 42*(3), 109–113. doi:10.2307/1250544

Cui, H., Wang, R., & Wang, H. (2020). An evolutionary analysis of green finance sustainability based on multi-agent game. *Journal of Cleaner Production, 269*, 121799. doi:10.1016/j.jclepro.2020.121799

Cumming, D., Johan, S., & Reardon, R. (2023). Global fintech trends and their impact on international business: A review. *Multinational Business Review, 31*(3), 413–436. doi:10.1108/MBR-05-2023-0077

Customer's Perception towards Promotional Tools of IMC. Retrieved from https://www.academia.edu/38955514/Customers_Perception_towards_Promotional_Tools_of_IMC

Cutler, Z., Huizenga, T., Kuvshinikov, M., & Westney, R. (2022). *Transforming capital projects to deliver net-zero emissions.* McKinsey & Company. https://www.mckinsey.com/capabilities/operations/our-insights/global-infrastructure-initiative/voices/transforming-capital-projects-to-deliver-net-zero-emissions

Dahiya, K., Taneja, S., & Özen, E. (2023). *To Analyse the Impact of Multi-Media Technology on the Rural Entrepreneurship Development. Contemporary Studies of Risks in Emerging Technology, Part A.* Emerald Group Publishing Ltd., doi:10.1108/978-1-80455-562-020231015

Damert, M., Paul, A., & Baumgartner, R. (2017). Exploring the determinants and long-term performance outcomes of corporate carbon strategies. *Journal of Cleaner Production, 160*, 123–138. doi:10.1016/j.jclepro.2017.03.206

Dangwal, A., Kaur, S., Taneja, S., & Taneja, S. (2022). A Bibliometric Analysis of Green Tourism Based on the Scopus Platform. In J. Kaur, P. Jindal, & A. Singh (Eds.), *Developing Relationships, Personalization, and Data Herald in Marketing 5.0* (Vol. i, pp. 1–327). IGI Global., doi:10.4018/978-1-6684-4496-2.ch015

Dangwal, A., Taneja, S., Özen, E., Todorovic, I., & Grima, S. (2022). Abridgement of Renewables: It's Potential and Contribution to India's GDP. *International Journal of Sustainable Development and Planning, 17*(8), 2357–2363. doi:10.18280/ijsdp.170802

Darko, A., Zhang, C., & Chan, A. P. C.Climate Bonds Initiative. (2021). *ASEAN Green Finance: State of the Market 2018.* London, UK: Darko, A., Zhang, C., & Chan, A. P. C. (2017). Drivers for green building: A review of empirical studies. *Habitat International, 60*, 34–49. doi:10.1016/j.habitatint.2016.12.007

Dash, G., & Chakraborty, D. (2021). Digital transformation of marketing strategies during a pandemic: Evidence from an emerging economy during covid-19. *Sustainability (Basel), 13*(12), 6735. doi:10.3390u13126735

Daud, S. N. M., & Ahmad, A. H. (2023). Financial inclusion, economic growth and the role of digital technology. *Finance Research Letters, 53*, 103602. Advance online publication. doi:10.1016/j.frl.2022.103602

Daugaard, D. (2019). Emerging new themes in environmental, social and governance investing: A systematic literature review. *Accounting and Finance, 60*(2), 1501–1530. doi:10.1111/acfi.12479

Davis, F. D. (1985). *A technology acceptance model for empirically testing new end-user information systems: Theory and results.* [Unpublished doctoral dissertation, Massachusetts Institute of Technology].

Davis, K., Maddock, R., & Foo, M. (2017). Catching up with Indonesia's fintech industry. *Law and Financial Markets Review, 11*(1), 33–40. doi:10.1080/17521440.2017.1336398

DawoodH. M.LiewC. Y.LauT. C. (2022). Mobile perceived trust mediation on the intention and adoption of FinTech innovations using mobile technology: A systematic literature review. *F1000Research, 10*. doi:10.12688/f1000research.74656.2

de Carvalho Ferreira, M. C. R., Sobreiro, V. A., Kimura, H., & de Moraes Barboza, F. L. (2016). A systematic review of literature about finance and sustainability. *Journal of Sustainable Finance \& Investment, 6*(2), 112–147. doi:10.1080/20430795.2016.1177438

de Kandavel. (2013). Green Banking Initiatives of Commercial Banks in India. *SIT Journal of Management, 3*(2), 213–225.

Dechezleprêtre, A., Nachtigall, D., & Venmans, F. (2018). The joint impact of the European Union emissions trading system on carbon emissions and economic performance. (OECD Economics Department Working Papers, No. 1515). OECD Publishing, Paris. doi:10.1787/18151973

Delmas, M., & Montiel, I. (2009). Greening the supply chain: When is customer pressure effective? *Journal of Economics & Management Strategy, 18*(1), 171–201. doi:10.1111/j.1530-9134.2009.00211.x

Delmas, M., Nairn-Brich, N., & Lim, J. (2015). Dynamics of environmental and financial performance: The case of greenhouse gas emissions. *Organization & Environment, 28*(4), 374–393. doi:10.1177/1086026615620238

Department of Official Language. (n.d.). *Languages Included in the Eighth Schedule of the Indian Constitution.* Ministry of Home Affairs GoI. https://rajbhasha.gov.in/en/languages-included-eighth-schedule-indian-constitution

Department of the Environment. (2016). *Modelling and analysis of Australia's abatement opportunities. Government of Australia.* DCCEEW. https://www.dcceew.gov.au/sites/default/files/documents/modelling-and-analysis-australias-2030-abatement-opportunities.pdf

Desalegn, G., & Tangl, A. (2022). Enhancing Green Finance for Inclusive Green Growth: A Systematic Approach. *Sustainability (Basel), 14*(12), 7416. doi:10.3390u14127416

Desi, A., & de Villiers, C. (2019). Integrated reporting: perspectives of corporate report preparers and other stakeholders. *Sustainability Accounting, Management and Policy Journal,. 10*(1), 126-156. https://www.emerald.com/insight/content/doi/10.1108/SAMPJ-02-2018-0043/full/html

Despotović, A., Parmaković, A., & Miljković, M. (2023). Cybercrime and Cyber Security in Fintech. In *Digital Transformation of the Financial Industry: Approaches and Applications* (pp. 255–272). Springer International Publishing. doi:10.1007/978-3-031-23269-5_15

Deters, J. (2019). Global leadership talent selection as an integrated acquisition process. Advances in Global Leadership. Emerald Group Publishing LTD. doi:10.1108/S1535-120320180000011003

Diallo, M. F., & Siqueira, J. R. Jr. (2017). How previous positive experiences with store brands affect purchase intention in emerging countries: A comparison between Brazil and Colombia. *International Marketing Review, 34*(4), 536–558. doi:10.1108/IMR-07-2014-0224

Ding, H., Liu, H., & Yang, K. (2019). A method of capturing and transferring customer value in product service system. *Mathematical Problems in Engineering, 2019*, 1–16. doi:10.1155/2019/8717386

Dobbs, R., Manyika, J., & Woetzel, J. (2016). No ordinary disruption: The four global forces breaking all the trends. Hachette UK.

Dong, C., Wu, H., Zhou, J., Lin, H., & Chang, L. (2023). Role of renewable energy investment and geopolitical risk in green finance development: Empirical evidence from BRICS countries. *Renewable Energy*, *207*, 234–241. doi:10.1016/j.renene.2023.02.115

Dormady, N., & Englander, G. (2016). Carbon allowances and the demand for offsets: A comprehensive assessment of imperfect substitutes. *Journal of Public Policy*, *36*(1), 139–167. doi:10.1017/S0143814X14000336

Dörry, S., & Schulz, C. (2018). Green financing, interrupted. Potential directions for sustainable finance in Luxembourg. *Local Environment*, *23*(7), 717–733. doi:10.1080/13549839.2018.1428792

Dou, D., & Li, L. (2022). *Does sustainable financial inclusion and energy efficiency ensure green environment? Evidence from B.R.I.C.S. countries*. Economic Research-Ekonomska Istrazivanja., doi:10.1080/1331677X.2022.2032785

Ducas, E., & Wilner, A. (2017). The security and financial implications of blockchain technologies: Regulating emerging technologies in Canada. *International Journal (Toronto, Ont.)*, *72*(4), 538–562. doi:10.1177/0020702017741909

Dutot, V., Bhatiasevi, V., & Bellallahom, N. (2019). Applying the technology acceptance model in a three- countries study of smartwatch adoption. *The Journal of High Technology Management Research*, *30*(1), 1–14. doi:10.1016/j.hitech.2019.02.001

Du, Y., & Wang, W. (2023). The role of green financing, agriculture development, geopolitical risk, and natural resource on environmental pollution in China. *Resources Policy*, *82*, 103440. doi:10.1016/j.resourpol.2023.103440

Edenhofer, O., Pichs-Madruga, R., Sokona, Y., Seyboth, K., Kadner, S., Zwickel, T., & Matschoss, P. (Eds.). (2011). *Renewable energy sources and climate change mitigation: Special report of the intergovernmental panel on climate change*. Cambridge University Press. doi:10.1017/CBO9781139151153

Elgin, B. (2022). This Timber Company Sold Millions of Dollars of Useless Carbon Offsets. *Bloomberg News*. https://www.bloomberg.com/news/articles/2022-03-17/timber-ceo-wants-to-reform-flawed-carbon-offset-market?leadSource=uverify%20wall

Elkington, J. (2018). 25 years ago I coined the phrase "triple bottom line." Here's why it's time to rethink it. *Harvard Business Review*, *25*, 2–5.

Elsaid, H. M. (2021). *A review of literature directions regarding the impact of fintech firms on the banking industry*. Qualitative Research in Financial Markets. doi:10.1108/QRFM-10-2020-0197

Elsheikh, A. S. (2022). Blockchain Analytics Reference Architecture for FinTech-A Positioning Paper Advancing FinTech with Blockchain, Data Analytics, and Enterprise Architecture. *ACM International Conference Proceeding Series*, (pp. 1–7). ACM. 10.1145/3531056.3531068

Environment and Finance. (2022). *Transparency, liquidity and integrity in the voluntary carbon market.* Field Gibson Media. https://www.environmental-finance.com/content/analysis/transparency-liquidity-and-integrity-in-the-voluntary-carbon-market.html

ETV Bharat. (2021). *India's active Internet population to hit 900M by 2025: Report*. ETV Bharat National. https://www.etvbharat.com/english/national/science-and-technology/indias-active-internet-population-to-hit-900m-by-2025-report/na20210606053027467

Europa. (2014). Directive of the European Parliament and the Council No. 2014/95/EC. Europa. https://eur-lex.europa.eu/legal-content/EN/TXT/?uri=celex:32014L0095

Europa. (2022). *Directive (EU) 2022/2464 of the European Parliament and of the Council*. Europa. https://eur-lex.europa.eu/legal-content/EN/TXT/?uri=CELEX:32022L2464

European Investment Bank. (2018). *EIB Issues First Sustainability Awareness Bond.* EIB. https://www.eib.org/en/info-centre/press/releases/all/2018/2018-223-eib-issues-first-sustainability-awareness-bond.htm

Fairclough, J. (2002). *Rethinking construction innovation and research-a review of the government's R&D policies and practices*.

Falcone, P. M. (2020). Environmental regulation and green investments: The role of green finance. *International Journal of Green Economics*, *14*(2), 159. doi:10.1504/IJGE.2020.109735

Falcone, P. M., & Sica, E. (2019). Assessing the opportunities and challenges of green finance in Italy: An analysis of the biomass production sector. *Sustainability (Basel)*, *11*(2), 517. doi:10.3390u11020517

Fang, T. (2019). A Tale of Two Strategies: Economic Growth Strategy and Talent Management Strategy in China. In H Wang and L Miao (eds.) Handbook On China And Globalization, 393–412. Edward Elgar Publishing LTD.

Federal Communications Commission, Broadcast Station Totals as of September 30, 2016, on the internet retrieved from https://apps.fcc.gov/edocs_public/attachmatch/DOC-341807A1.pdf

Fetting, C. (2020). The European green deal. *ESDN report, 53*. ESDN.

Fisher, B., Turner, K., Zylstra, M., Brouwer, R., De Groot, R., Farber, S., Ferraro, P., Green, R., Hadley, D., Harlow, J., Jefferiss, P., Kirkby, C., Morling, P., Mowatt, S., Naidoo, R., Paavola, J., Strassburg, B., Yu, D., & Balmford, A. (2008). Ecosystem services and economic theory: Integration for policy-relevant research. *Ecological Applications*, *18*(8), 2050–2067. doi:10.1890/07-1537.1 PMID:19263897

Flavián, C., Pérez-Rueda, A., Belanche, D., & Casaló, L. V. (2022). Intention to use analytical artificial intelligence (AI) in services – the effect of technology readiness and awareness. *Journal of Service Management*, *33*(2), 293–320. doi:10.1108/JOSM-10-2020-0378

Florin, M. V., & Bürkler, M. T. (2017). *Introduction to the IRGC risk governance framework* (No. REP_WORK). EPFL.

Fornell, C., & Larcker, D. F. (1981). *Structural equation models with unobservable variables and measurement error: Algebra and statistics*. Sage Publications Sage CA.

Fornell, C., & Larcker, D. F. (2012). Equation algebra unobservable error: Variables. *JMR, Journal of Marketing Research*, *18*(3), 382–388. doi:10.1177/002224378101800313

Fratrič, P., Sileno, G., Klous, S., & van Engers, T. (2022). Manipulation of the Bitcoin market: an agent-based study. *Financial Innovation, 8*(1), 1–29. doi:10.1186/s40854-022-00364-3

Fu, Y., & Yi, Z. (2023). Multi-province comparisons of digital financial inclusion performance in China: A group ranking method with preference analysis. *China Economic Review*, *80*, 102014. Advance online publication. doi:10.1016/j.chieco.2023.102014

Gabay, H., Meir, I. A., Schwartz, M., & Werzberger, E. (2014). Cost-benefit analysis of green buildings: An Israeli office buildings case study. *Energy and Building*, *76*, 558–564. doi:10.1016/j.enbuild.2014.02.027

Gajanad, A. & Karthik. (2017). *Role of traditional media in rural development*. BioTech Articles. https://www.biotecharticles.com/Agriculture-Article/Role-of-Traditional-Media-in-Rural-Development-4099.html

Gallagher, K. S., & Muehlegger, E. (2011). Giving green to get green? Incentives and consumer adoption of hybrid vehicle technology. *Journal of Environmental Economics and Management*, *61*(1), 1–15. doi:10.1016/j.jeem.2010.05.004

Gallego-Alvarez, I., Segura, L., & Matinez-Ferrero, J. (2015). Carbon emission reduction: The impact on the financial and operational performance of international companies. *Journal of Cleaner Production*, *103*, 149–159. doi:10.1016/j.jclepro.2014.08.047

Gangwani, N. (2022). How Rural Communication Has Evolved: The Journey of Media In Rural India. *Rural Marketing Association of India (RMAI).* https://armworldwide.com/how-rural-communication-has-evolved-the-journey-of-media-in-rural-india/

Gao, Q., Liu, Y., Ayub, B., & Hussain, M. (2022). Does Health Crises Effect Tourism: Role of Financial Inclusion for Green Financial Development. *Frontiers in Public Health*, *10*, 896894. doi:10.3389/fpubh.2022.896894 PMID:35719629

Gardas, B. B., Mangla, S. K., Raut, R. D., Narkhede, B., & Luthra, S. (2019). Green Talent Management to Unlock Sustainability in the Oil and Gas Sector. *Journal of Cleaner Production*, *229*(August), 850–862. doi:10.1016/j.jclepro.2019.05.018

Garg, D. K., & Singh, G. P. (2011). Construction of Three and Four Associate Class PBIB Designs using Method of Duality. *International Journal of Agricultural and Statistics Sciences*, *7*(2), 579–587.

Garg, D. K., & Singh, G. P. (2014). Construction of Three Associate Class PBIB Designs using Method of Juxtapositions. *Indian Journal of Research*, *4*(5), 616–618.

Garner, S. J. (1986). Perceived risk and information sources in services purchasing. *The Mid-Atlantic Journal of Business*, *24*(2), 49–58.

Gefen, D., & Straub, D. (2005). A practical guide to factorial validity using PLS-Graph: Tutorial and annotated example. *Communications of the Association for Information Systems*, *16*(1), 5. doi:10.17705/1CAIS.01605

George, G., Merrill, R. K., & Schillebeeckx, S. J. D. (2021). Digital Sustainability and Entrepreneurship: How Digital Innovations Are Helping Tackle Climate Change and Sustainable Development. *Entrepreneurship Theory and Practice*, *45*(5), 999–1027. doi:10.1177/1042258719899425

Ghachem L. (2011). *Communications of the IBIMA*. IBIMA Publishing. . doi:10.5171/2011.489627

Ghasemy, M., Teeroovengadum, V., Becker, J. M., & Ringle, C. M. (2020). This fast car can move faster: a review of PLS-SEM application in higher education research. *Higher Education 2020 80:6, 80*(6), 1121–1152. doi:10.1007/s10734-020-00534-1

Ghozali, I. (2013). *Multivariate Analysis Application with IBM and SPSS Programs* (5th ed.). BP Universitas Dipenogoro.

Gibson, E. (2022). *Government proposes banning pine carbon farms from the ETS*. Stuff. https://www.stuff.co.nz/environment/climate-news/127946385/government-proposes-banning-pine-carbon-farms-from-the-ets?rm=a

Gigante, G., & Zago, A. (2022). *DARQ technologies in the financial sector: artificial intelligence applications in personalized banking*. Qualitative Research in Financial Markets., doi:10.1108/QRFM-02-2021-0025

Giglio, F. (2022). Fintech: A literature review. *International Business Research*, *15*(1), 80–85. doi:10.5539/ibr.v15n1p80

Gilchrist, D., Yu, J., & Zhong, R. (2021). The limits of green finance: A survey of literature in the context of green bonds and green loans. *Sustainability (Basel)*, *13*(2), 478. doi:10.3390u13020478

Gillenwater, M., & Seres, S. (2011). *The Clean Development Mechanism: A review of the first international offset program*. Pew Centre on Global Climate Change.

Giudici, P., Hochreiter, R., Osterrieder, J., Papenbrock, J., & Schwendner, P. (2019). AI and financial technology. *Frontiers in Artificial Intelligence*, *2*, 25. doi:10.3389/frai.2019.00025 PMID:33733114

Goldstein, A., & Ruef, F. (2016). State of Forest Carbon Finance 2016 - View from the Understory. *Ecosystem Marketplace, Forest Trends*. https://www.forest-trends.org/publications/view-from-theunderstory/

Gollwitzer, L., Ockwell, D., Muok, B., Ely, A., & Ahlborg, H. (2018). Rethinking the sustainability and institutional governance of electricity access and mini-grids: Electricity as a common pool resource. *Energy Research & Social Science*, *39*, 152–161. doi:10.1016/j.erss.2017.10.033

Gomber, P., Kauffman, R. J., Parker, C., & Weber, B. W. (2018). On the fintech revolution: Interpreting the forces of innovation, disruption, and transformation in financial services. *Journal of Management Information Systems*, *35*(1), 220–265. doi:10.1080/07421222.2018.1440766

Gopalan, S., & Rajan, R. S. (2022). Does digital financial inclusion moderate or exacerbate output volatility? *Applied Economics Letters*, *29*(19), 1804–1809. doi:10.1080/13504851.2021.1963400

Gottschalk, P. (2010). Categories of financial crime. *Journal of Financial Crime*, *17*(4), 441–458. doi:10.1108/13590791011082797

Goulder, L. H., Parry, I. W. H., Williams, R. C. III, & Burtraw, D. (1999). The cost-effectiveness of alternative instruments for environmental protection in a second-best setting. *Journal of Public Economics*, *72*(3), 329–360. doi:10.1016/S0047-2727(98)00109-1

Gretzel, U., Sigala, M., Xiang, Z., & Koo, C. (2015). Smart tourism: Foundations and developments. *Electronic Markets*, *25*(3), 179–188. doi:10.100712525-015-0196-8

GRI Standards. (2022). *Standards*. Global reporting initiative. https://www.globalreporting.org/standards/

Griffin, J. M., Kruger, S., & Mahajan, P. (2023). Did fintech lenders facilitate PPP fraud? *The Journal of Finance*, *78*(3), 1777–1827. doi:10.1111/jofi.13209

Guang-Wen, Z., & Siddik, A. B. (2022). Do Corporate Social Responsibility Practices and Green Finance Dimensions Determine Environmental Performance? An Empirical Study on Bangladeshi Banking Institutions. *Frontiers in Environmental Science*, *10*, 890096. doi:10.3389/fenvs.2022.890096

Guiso, L. (2010). *A trist-driven financial crisis. implications for the future of financial markets.*

Gujrati (2016). An emerging Indian rural market: Challenges and opportunities. *International Journal of Multidisciplinary Research and Development*, *3*(7) 334-340 https://www.researchgate.net/publication/333131633_An_emerging_Indian_rural_market_Challenges_and_opportunities

Gunasegaran, M., Basiruddin, R., Abdul Rasid, S. Z., & Mohd Rizal, A. (2018). The case studies of fraud prevention mechanisms in the Malaysian medium enterprises. *Journal of Financial Crime*, *25*(4), 1024–1038. doi:10.1108/JFC-05-2017-0034

Guo, J., Gu, F., Liu, Y., Liang, X., Mo, J., & Fan, Y. (2020). Assessing the impact of ETS trading profit on emission abatements based on firm-level transactions. *Nature Communications*, *11*(1), 2078. doi:10.103841467-020-15996-1 PMID:32350279

Gupta, S., & Biswas, S. (2023). The confluence of smart computing and traditional businesses to foster productivity, profitability, and prosperity. In *Artificial Intelligence Techniques in Human Resource Management*. Apple Academic Press. https://www.scopus.com/inward/record.uri?eid=2-s2.0-85162263500&partnerID=40&md5=9f2b5b2a95e6c83f85318541dcf27e5e

Gupta, M., Arora, K., & Taneja, S. (2023). Bibliometric analysis on employee engagement and human resource management. In *Enhancing Customer Engagement Through Location-Based Marketing*. IGI Global. doi:10.4018/978-1-6684-8177-6.ch013

Gupta, M., Taneja, S., Sharma, V., Singh, A., Rupeika-Apoga, R., & Jangir, K. (2023). Does Previous Experience with the Unified Payments Interface (UPI) Affect the Usage of Central Bank Digital Currency (CBDC)? *Journal of Risk and Financial Management*, *16*(6), 286. doi:10.3390/jrfm16060286

Gupta, T. (2012). Rural Marketing: Looking Ahead. *International Journal of Management Research and Review*, *2*(1), 186–191. https://www.proquest.com/scholarly-journals/rural-marketing-looking-ahead/docview/1418665021/se-2

Gutierrez, A. V. (2016). Green banking: A proposed model for green housing loan. *ICIMSA 2016 - 2016 3rd International Conference on Industrial Engineering, Management Science and Applications*. IEEE. 10.1109/ICIMSA.2016.7504011

Hafner, S., Jones, A., Anger-Kraavi, A., & Pohl, J. (2020). Closing the green finance gap – A systems perspective. *Environmental Innovation and Societal Transitions*, *34*, 26–60. doi:10.1016/j.eist.2019.11.007

Haigh, M. (2012). Publishing and defining sustainable finance and investment. *Journal of Sustainable Finance & Investment*, *2*(2), 88–94. doi:10.1080/20430795.2012.688797

Hailiang, Z., Chau, K. Y., & Waqas, M. (2023). Does green finance and renewable energy promote tourism for sustainable development: Empirical evidence from China. *Renewable Energy*, *207*, 660–671. doi:10.1016/j.renene.2023.03.032

Hair, J. F., Risher, J. J., Sarstedt, M., & Ringle, C. M. (2019). When to use and how to report the results of PLS-SEM. *European Business Review*, *31*(1), 2–24. doi:10.1108/EBR-11-2018-0203

Hair, J. F., Sarstedt, M., Hopkins, L., & Kuppelwieser, V. G. (2014). Partial least squares structural equation modeling (PLS-SEM): An emerging tool in business research. *European Business Review*, *26*(2), 106–121. doi:10.1108/EBR-10-2013-0128

Hamrick, K., & Gallant, M. (2017a). Fertile Ground - State of Forest Carbon Finance 2017. *EcosystemMarketplace, Forest Trends.* https://www.forest-trends.org/publications/fertile-ground/

Hamrick, K., & Gallant, M. (2017b). Unlocking Potential - State of the Voluntary Carbon Markets 2017. *Ecosystem Marketplace, Forest Trends.* https://www.forest-trends.org/publications/unlockingpotential/

Han Oh, J., Hoon Kim, S., Kang, J. Y., Hee Oh, C., & Gong, H. S. (2010). Effect of age on functional and structural outcome after rotator cuff repair. *The American Journal of Sports Medicine*, *38*(4), 672–678. doi:10.1177/0363546509352460 PMID:20357401

Ha, N. (2020). The impact of perceived risk on consumers' online shopping intention: An integration of TAM and TPB. *Management Science Letters*, *10*(9), 2029–2036. doi:10.5267/j.msl.2020.2.009

Han, M. C., & Kim, Y. (2017). Why consumers hesitate to shop online: Perceived risk and product involvement on Taobao. com. *Journal of Promotion Management*, *23*(1), 24–44. doi:10.1080/10496491.2016.1251530

Hardianto, A., Marimin, M., Adrianto, L., & Fahmi, I. (2021, December). Sustainable Financing for Instrastructure Development to Support Tourism Connectivity: A Systematic Literature Review. In Conference Towards ASEAN Chairmanship 2023 (TAC 23 2021) (pp. 74-80). Atlantis Press.

Harjoto, M. A., & Wang, Y. (2020). Board of Directors Network Centrality and Environmental, Social and Governance (ESG) Performance. *Corporate Governance: An International Journal of Business in Society.*

Hassan, N. (2019). *Ransomware revealed*. Apress. doi:10.1007/978-1-4842-4255-1

He, L., Liu, R., Zhong, Z., Wang, D., & Xia, Y. (2019). Can green financial development promote renewable energy investment efficiency? A consideration of bank credit. *Renewable Energy*, *143*, 974–984. doi:10.1016/j.renene.2019.05.059

Henseler, J., Ringle, C. M., & Sarstedt, M. (2015). A new criterion for assessing discriminant validity in variance-based structural equation modeling. *Journal of the Academy of Marketing Science*, *43*(1), 115–135. doi:10.100711747-014-0403-8

Hernandez, Y., Zatarain, R., & Barron, L. (2019). A Talent Management Model for Innovation and Competitiveness in Complex Domains: A Case Study in the Latin American Energy Sector. In G. Cortes-Robles, J. L. Garcia-Alcaraz, and G. Alor-Hernandez (eds.) Managing Innovation In Highly Restrictive Environments: Lessons From Latin America And Emerging Markets. Springer. doi:10.1007/978-3-319-93716-8_6

He, Z., Liu, Z., Wu, H., Gu, X., Zhao, Y., & Yue, X. (2020). Research on the Impact of Green Finance and Fintech in Smart City. *Complexity*, *2020*, 2020. doi:10.1155/2020/6673386

Hodžić, S., Šikić, T. F., & Dogan, E. (2023). Green environment in the EU countries: The role of financial inclusion, natural resources and energy intensity. *Resources Policy*, *82*, 103476. doi:10.1016/j.resourpol.2023.103476

Holmes, W., Bialik, M., & Fadel, C. (2019). *Artificial Intelligence In Education Promises and Implications for Teaching and Learning*. AIED. http://bit.ly/AIED-

Holt-Giménez, E. (2006). *Campesino a campesino: voices from Latin America's farmer to farmer movement for sustainable agriculture*. Food first books.

Hřebíček, J., Soukopová, J., Štencl, M., & Trenz, O. (2011). Integration of economic, environmental, social and corporate governance performance and reporting in enterprises. *Acta Universitatis Agriculturae et Silviculturae Mendelianae Brunensis*, *59*(7), 157–177. doi:10.11118/actaun201159070157

Huang, J., Chai, J., & Cho, S. (2020). Deep learning in finance and banking: A literature review and classification. *Frontiers of Business Research in China*, *14*(13), 13. doi:10.118611782-020-00082-6

Huang, Y., & Zhang, Y. (2021). Artificial intelligence and robotics in the hospitality and tourism industry: A state-of-the-art review. *Journal of Travel Research*, 00472875211006404.

Hua, S. Y. (2016). Logistic suppliers' decarbonization practices and prioritization. *International Journal of Environmental, Cultural, Economic and Social Sustainability*, *12*(1), 1–16. doi:10.18848/1832-2077/CGP/1-16

Hua, X., & Huang, Y. (2021). Understanding China's fintech sector: Development, impacts and risks. *European Journal of Finance*, *27*(4-5), 321–333. doi:10.1080/1351847X.2020.1811131

Hu, D., Fang, X., & DiGiovanni, Y. M. (2023). Technological progress, financial constrains, and digital financial inclusion. *Small Business Economics*. doi:10.100711187-023-00745-7

Hugé, J., Waas, T., Dahdouh-Guebas, F., Koedam, N., & Block, T. (2013). A discourse-analytical perspective on sustainability assessment: Interpreting sustainable development in practice. *Sustainability Science*, *8*(2), 187–198. doi:10.100711625-012-0184-2

Hu, Z., Ding, S., Li, S., Chen, L., & Yang, S. (2019). Adoption intention of fintech services for bank users: An empirical examination with an extended technology acceptance model. *Symmetry*, *11*(3), 340. doi:10.3390ym11030340

Indian Express. (2018). More than 19,500 mother tongues spoken in India: Census. *Indian Express*. https://indianexpress.com/article/india/more-than-19500-mother-tongues-spoken-in-india-census-5241056/

Integrated Reporting. (2023). *Home*. Integrated Reporting. https://www.integratedreporting.org/the-iirc-2/

Intergovernmental Panel on Climate Change. (2022). Climate Change 2022: Mitigation of Climate Change. *IPCC Sixth Assessment Report. Intergovernmental Panel on Climate Change 2022*. IPCC. https://report.ipcc.ch/ar6/wg3/IPCC_AR6_WGIII_Full_Report.pdf

International Capital Market Association. (2018). *Green Bond Principles*. ICMA.

International Framework. (2021The International Integrated Reporting Council. https://www.integratedreporting.org/resource/international-ir-framework/

International Institute of Green Finance. (2018). *China Green Bond Market Development Report 2018*. IIGF.

Investment and Pensions Europe. (2018). *Bank analysts estimate $600bn of green bonds from Asia by 2023*. IPE. https://www.ipe.com/news/asset-allocation/bank-analysts-estimate-600bn-of-green-bonds-from-asia-by-2023/www.ipe.com/news/asset-allocation/bank-analysts-estimate-600bn-of-green-bonds-from-asia-by-2023/10024890.fullarticle

Irimia-Diéguez, A., Velicia-Martín, F., & Aguayo-Camacho, M. (2023). Predicting FinTech innovation adoption: The mediator role of social norms and attitudes. *Financial Innovation*, *9*(1), 1–23. doi:10.118640854-022-00434-6 PMID:36687792

Islam, K., Akhther, N., & Seeger, M. W. (2023). Variability in Media Content of Public Health Outbreak Coverage: A Crisis Communication Approach. *Communication Studies*, *74*(2), 113–130. doi:10.1080/10510974.2023.2183516

Ivanov, S., & Webster, C. (2017). *Adoption of robotics, artificial intelligence automation by travel, tourist and hospitality companies: a cost-benefit study*. Contemporary Tourism: Traditions and Innovations, an International Scientific Conference, Sofia University.

Iwata, H., & Okada, K. (2011). How does environmental performance affect financial performance? Evidence from Japanese manufacturing firms. *Ecological Economics*, *70*(9), 1691–1700. doi:10.1016/j.ecolecon.2011.05.010

Iwejingi, S. F. (2011). Population growth, environmental degradation and human health in Nigeria. *Pakistan Journal of Social Sciences*, *8*(4), 187–191.

Jagtiani, J., & Lemieux, C. (2019). The roles of alternative data and machine learning in fintech lending: Evidence from the LendingClub consumer platform. *Financial Management*, *48*(4), 1009–1029. doi:10.1111/fima.12295

Jain, A. (2012). Brand Awareness and Customer Preferences for FMCG Products in Rural Market of Garhwal Region. *VSRD-IJBMR*, *2*(8), 434-443. https://www.scribd.com/document/142534349/Brand-Awareness-Consumer-Preference

Jain, S. (2020). Financing India's Green Transition. *Observer Research Foundation, 338*.

Jain, A., & Rathod, R. (2005). Distribution and Retailing Trends in Rural Markets - A Study in Villages of Gujarat. *Indian Journal of Marketing*, *35*(9), 1–10. https://www.indianjournalofmarketing.com/index.php/ijom/article/view/34243/0

Jakhiya, M., Mittal Bishnoi, M., & Purohit, H. (2020). Emergence and growth of mobile money in modern india: A study on the effect of mobile money. *2020 Advances in Science and Engineering Technology International Conferences, ASET 2020*. Bitly. 10.1109/ASET48392.2020.9118375

James, E., & Rabbi, F. (2023). Fortifying the IoT Landscape: Strategies to Counter Security Risks in Connected Systems. *Tensorgate Journal of Sustainable Technology and Infrastructure for Developing Countries*, *6*(1), 32–46.

Jangir, K., Sharma, V., Taneja, S., & Rupeika-Apoga, R. (2023). The Moderating Effect of Perceived Risk on Users' Continuance Intention for FinTech Services. *Journal of Risk and Financial Management*, *16*(1), 21. doi:10.3390/jrfm16010021

Jang-Jaccard, J., & Nepal, S. (2014). A survey of emerging threats in cybersecurity. *Journal of Computer and System Sciences*, *80*(5), 973–993. doi:10.1016/j.jcss.2014.02.005

Janiesch, C., Zschech, P., & Heinrich, K. (2021). Machine learning and deep learning. *Electronic Markets, 31*(3), 685–695. doi:10.100712525-021-00475-2

Jarvenpaa, S. L., Tractinsky, N., & Vitale, M. (2000). Consumer trust in an Internet store. *Information Technology and Management, 1*(1), 45–71. doi:10.1023/A:1019104520776

Jatoba, M., Gutierriz, I. E., Fernandes, P. O., Teixeira, J. P., & Moscon, D. (2019). Artificial intelligence in the recrutment & selection: innovation and impacts for the human resources management. *43rd International Scientific Conference on Economics and Social Development*, (pp. 96–104). Biblioteca Digital. https://bibliotecadigital.ipb.pt/handle/10198/21703

Jha, N., & Bhome, S. (2013). A study of green banking trends in India. *International Monthly Referred Journal of Research in Management and Technology*, 2, 127–132.

Ji, J., Zhang, Z., & Yang, L. (2017). Carbon emission reduction decisions in the retail-/dual-channel supply chain with comsumers' preference. *Journal of Cleaner Production, 141*, 852–867. doi:10.1016/j.jclepro.2016.09.135

Julie, T. (2019). The Role of Newspapers in Rural Minnesota. *Rural Minnesota.* https://www.ruralmn.org/the-role-of-newspapers-in-rural-minnesota/

Kafetzopoulos, D., Psomas, E., & Bouranta, N. (2022). The Influence of Leadership on Strategic Flexibility and Business Performance: The Mediating Role of Talent Management. *Management Decision, 60*(9), 2532–2551. doi:10.1108/MD-10-2021-1310

Kakkad, R. (2016). A study on effect of newspaper advertisement on consumer buying behavior of two wheelers. *Philica, 2*, 35.

Kang, L., Wang, J., Zhang, Y., Kou, Z., & Gao, S. (2009). iPS cells can support full-term development of tetraploid blastocyst-complemented embryos. *Cell Stem Cell, 5*(2), 135–138. doi:10.1016/j.stem.2009.07.001 PMID:19631602

Kantrowitz, T. M. (2019). Applying Adaptive Approaches to Talent Management Practices. In R. N. Landers (ed.) Cambridge Handbook Of Technology And Employee Behavior. Cambridge Univ Press.

Kashi, A., & Shah, E. M. (2023). Bibliometric Review on Sustainable Finance. *Sustainability (Basel), 15*(7119), 1–30. https://www.mdpi.com/journal/sustainability. doi:10.3390u15097119

Kashyap, P. (2012). *Rural Marketing. Pearson* (3rd ed.).

Kaur, A., Kumar, P., & Sharma, V. (n.d.). *Probabilistic Assessment To Measure Insolvency Risk Of Indian Public Sector Banks For Sustainable Financial Health.* Research Gate.

Kaur, G. (2023). Biodiversity Financing: A Strategy Towards Sustainability. In Digital Transformation, Strategic Resilience, Cyber Security and Risk Management (Vol. 111, pp. 143-151). Emerald Publishing Limited. doi:10.1108/S1569-37592023000111B010

Kaur, H., Sood, K., Yadav, U. S., & Grima, S. (2023). Sustainable Solutions for Insurance and Risk Management. *The Impact of Climate Change and Sustainability Standards on the Insurance Market*, 359.

Kaur, A. (2020). Banking Fraud : A Conceptual Framework Of Dredging Up Various Banking Scams, Causes And Preventive Role Of Law. *PALARCH JOURNAL, 17*(6), 2003–2021.

Kaur, A., Kumar, P., & Sharma, V. (2022a). Probabilistic Assessment To Measure Insolvency Risk of Indian Public. *Madhya Pradesh Journal of Social Sciences A Biannually Journal of M. P. Institute of Social Science Research, 27*(11), 59–72.

Kaur, A., Tanwar, A., Kaur, H., & Singh, J. (2023a). IOP Conference Series: Earth and Environmental Science A Study on Linkage between Global Warming Indicators and Climate Change Expenditure. *IOP Conference Series. Earth and Environmental Science*, *1110*(1), 1–19. doi:10.1088/1755-1315/1110/1/012059

Kaur, H., Singh, K., Kumar, P., & Kaur, A. (2023). Assessing the environmental sustainability corridor: An empirical study of Renewable energy consumption in BRICS nation. *IOP Conference Series. Earth and Environmental Science*, *1110*(1), 012053. doi:10.1088/1755-1315/1110/1/012053

Kaur, P., & Garg, D. K. (2020). Construction of Tm – type and Tm – Assisted PBIB Designs. *Revista de Statistica.*

Kediehor, O. & Chimezie. (2019). The Effectiveness of Rural Communication Modes on Modern Mass Media. *Transatlantic Journal of Rural Research*, *1*(3), 1-16. https://www.transatlanticj.com/tjrr/. doi:10.5281/zenodo.3402105

Kennedy, C., Zhong, M., & Corfee-Morlot, J. (2016). Infrastructure for China's Ecologically Balanced Civilization. *Engineering (Beijing)*, *2*(4), 414–425. doi:10.1016/J.ENG.2016.04.014

Keohane, N., & Seymour, F. (2021). *Forests and International Carbon Markets: Climate and Forests 2030.* The Climate and Land Use Alliance. https://www.climateandforests2030.org/app/uploads/2021/10/CARBON-MARKETS_Forests-and-International-Carbon-Markets_KeohaneSeymour.pdf

Khan, A. G., Banik, S., Uddin, M. A., & Moudud-Ul-Huq, S. (2021). Unlocking the Relationship Between Talent Management Practices and Performance Sustainability in the Sports Industry. *International Journal of Asian Business and Information Management*, *12*(3), 366–380. doi:10.4018/IJABIM.20210701.oa22

Khanchel, I., Lassoued, N., & Bargaoui, I. (2023). Pollution control bonds and environmental performance in energy utility firms: is there an incantation effect?. *International Journal of Energy Sector Management.*

Khan, E. A., & Quaddus, M. (2015). Development and Validation of a Scale for Measuring Sustainability Factors of Informal Microenterprises – A Qualitative and Quantitative Approach. *Entrepreneurship Research Journal*, *5*(4), 347–372. doi:10.1515/erj-2014-0017

Khan, E., Mubarik, M. S., & Shahid, Z. A. (2021). In the Pursuit of Green in COVID-19: Harnessing the Existing Talent to Pursue Green Corporate Entrepreneurship. *Frontiers in Psychology*, *12*(October), 751961. Advance online publication. doi:10.3389/fpsyg.2021.751961 PMID:34759871

Khan, M. A., & Salah, K. (2018). IoT security: Review, blockchain solutions, and open challenges. *Future Generation Computer Systems*, *82*, 395–411. doi:10.1016/j.future.2017.11.022

Khan, Z., Badeeb, R. A., Zhang, C., & Dong, K. (2023). Financial inclusion and energy efficiency: Role of green innovation and human capital for Malaysia. *Applied Economics*, 1–16. doi:10.1080/00036846.2023.2206109

Kharade, M. (2021). *Green Finance for Sustainable Development- study on the Indian context, 18*(10), 2459–2466.

Khomulyak, T. I. (2015). *The need for Integrated reporting, as in a new reporting format for business // Financial and credit activity: problems of theory and practice.* NBUV. http://nbuv.gov.ua/UJRN/Fkd_2015_1_23

Kim, J. S. (2016). An extended technology acceptance model in behavioral intention toward hotel tablet apps with moderating effects of gender and age. *International Journal of Contemporary Hospitality Management*, *28*(8), 1535–1553. doi:10.1108/IJCHM-06-2015-0289

King, A., & Lenox, M. (2002). Exploring the Locus of Profitable Pollution Reduction. *Management Science*, *48*(2), 289–299. doi:10.1287/mnsc.48.2.289.258

Klafft, M. (2008). *Peer to Peer Lending: Auctioning Microcredits over the Internet.* SSRN. https://papers.ssrn.com/abstract=1352383

Ko, H., Jung, J., Kim, J., & Shim, S. W. (2004). Cross-cultural differences in perceived risk of online shopping. *Journal of Interactive Advertising*, *4*(2), 20–29. doi:10.1080/15252019.2004.10722084

Konou, C. M. (2023). Entrepreneurial Risk and Digital Financial Inclusion: A Cross-Country Analysis. *Economic Papers*, *42*(3), 267–281. doi:10.1111/1759-3441.12399

Kothari, C. R. (2020). *Research Methodology* (2nd ed.). New Age International Publishers.

Kouladoum, J.-C., Wirajing, M. A. K., & Nchofoung, T. N. (2022). Digital technologies and financial inclusion in Sub-Saharan Africa. *Telecommunications Policy*, *46*(9), 102387. doi:10.1016/j.telpol.2022.102387

KPMG. (2022). Big shifts, small steps Survey of Sustainability Reporting 2022. KPMG. https://assets.kpmg.com/content/dam/kpmg/xx/pdf/2023/04/big-shifts-small-steps.pdf

Krahnen, J., Rocholl, J., & Thum, M. (2023). A Primer on Green Finance: From Wishful Thinking to Marginal Impact. *Review of Economics*, *74*(1), 1–19. doi:10.1515/roe-2023-0019

Kruglova, I. A., & Dolbezhkin, V. A. (2019). Objective Barriers to the Implementation of Blockchain Technology in the Financial Sector. *Proceedings - 2018 International Conference on Artificial Intelligence: Applications and Innovations, IC-AIAI 2018*, (pp. 47–50). IEEE. 10.1109/IC-AIAI.2018.8674451

Kumar & Dangi. (2013). Rural Marketing in India: Challenges and Opportunities, International. *Journal of Management and Social Sciences Research*, *2*(8), 93–100. https://citeseerx.ist.psu.edu/viewdoc/download?doi=10.1.1.403.7838&rep=rep1&type=pdf

Kumar, P., & Taneja, S. Mukul, & Ozen, E. (2023). Digital transformation of the insurance industry - a case of the Indian insurance sector. In The Impact of Climate Change and Sustainability Standards on the Insurance Market. Wiley.

Kumar, P., Taneja, S., Özen, E., & Singh, S. (2023b). Artificial Intelligence and Machine Learning in Insurance: A Bibliometric Analysis. In Smart Analytics, Artificial Intelligence and Sustainable Performance Management in a Global Digitalised Economy (pp. 191-202). Emerald Publishing Limited. doi:10.1108/S1569-37592023000110A010

Kumar, P., & Kaur, A. (2022). Exploring the Role of Artificial Intelligence in Changing Business Dimension. *International Conference on Scientific Computing in Innovation*, (pp. 621–625). IEEE.

Kumar, P., Khurana, A., & Sharma, S. (2021). Performance evaluation of public and private sector banks. *World Review of Entrepreneurship, Management and Sustainable Development*, *17*(2–3), 306–322. doi:10.1504/WREMSD.2021.114436

Kumar, P., Mukul, Kaur, D., & Kaur, A. (2023). Green Infrastructure- A Roadmap Towards Sustainable Development. *IOP Conference Series. Earth and Environmental Science*, *1110*(1), 012060. doi:10.1088/1755-1315/1110/1/012060

Kumar, P., Özen, E., & Vurur, S. (2023). Adoption of blockchain technology in the financial sector. In *Contemporary Studies of Risks in Emerging Technology, Part A*. Emerald Group Publishing Ltd., doi:10.1108/978-1-80455-562-020231018

Kumar, P., Verma, P., Bhatnagar, M., Taneja, S., Seychel, S., Todorović, I., & Grim, S. (2023). The Financial Performance and Solvency Status of the Indian Public Sector Banks: A CAMELS Rating and Z Index Approach. *International Journal of Sustainable Development and Planning*, *18*(2), 367–376. doi:10.18280/ijsdp.180204

Kunal, & Sharma, T. (2022). An empirical study of customer satisfaction and customer loyalty intentions for payment banks. In *Digital Marketing Outreach: the Future of Marketing Practices*. Taylor and Francis. doi:10.4324/9781003315377-4

Kunhibava, S., Ling, S. T. Y., Rahman, N. F. A., & Ruslan, M. K. (2019). Green banking frameworks in Asia with an in-depth focus on Bangladesh and China. *Asia Pacific Journal of Environmental Law*, *22*(1), 93–116. doi:10.4337/apjel.2019.01.05

Kunhibava, S., & Muneeza, A. (2019). Regulating fintech businesses: The malaysian experience. In *Impact of Financial Technology (FinTech) on Islamic Finance and Financial Stability*. IGI Global. doi:10.4018/978-1-7998-0039-2.ch008

Lai, C. H., & Huang, C. H. (2020). Artificial intelligence, big data, and virtual reality applications in the hospitality and tourism industry. In *Handbook of Research on Applied Data Science and Artificial Intelligence in Business and Industry* (pp. 57–82). IGI Global.

Lami, I. M., & Mecca, B. (2020). Assessing Social Sustainability for Achieving Sustainable Architecture. *Sustainability 2021, 13*(1), 142. doi:10.3390/su13010142

Lan, J., Wei, Y., Guo, J., Li, Q., & Liu, Z. (2023). The effect of green finance on industrial pollution emissions: Evidence from China. *Resources Policy*, *80*, 103156. doi:10.1016/j.resourpol.2022.103156

Laroche, M., Yang, Z., McDougall, G. H., & Bergeron, J. (2005). Internet versus bricks-and-mortar retailers: An investigation into intangibility and its consequences. *Journal of Retailing*, *81*(4), 251–267. doi:10.1016/j.jretai.2004.11.002

Larsen, M. L. (2022). Driving global convergence in green financial policies: China as policy pioneer and the EU as standard setter. *Global Policy*, *13*(3), 358–370. doi:10.1111/1758-5899.13105

Lavery, S., & Schmidt, D. (2021, September). European Integration and the New Global Disorder. *Journal of Common Market Studies*, *59*(5), 1322–1338. https://onlinelibrary.wiley.com/doi/full/10.1111/jcms.13184. doi:10.1111/jcms.13184

Leal-Arcas, R., Al Zarkani, M., Jbara, L., Margaritidou, M., & Mubwana, R. M. (2022). The BRIC and Climate Change Mitigation. *International Trade and Sustainability: Perspectives from Developing and Developed Countries*, 229–280. https://doi.org/ doi:10.1007/978-3-031-14068-6_6/COVER

Lee, C.-C., Wang, F., & Lou, R. (2022). Digital financial inclusion and carbon neutrality: Evidence from non-linear analysis. *Resources Policy*, *79*, 102974. doi:10.1016/j.resourpol.2022.102974

Lee, H. Y., So, G., Tang, E., Lam, T., & Cheng, V. (2020). Green finance performance and role of sustainability engineers in the greater bay Area. *IOP Conference Series. Earth and Environmental Science*, *588*(2), 022063. doi:10.1088/1755-1315/588/2/022063

Lee, J. W.LEE. (2020). Green Finance and Sustainable Development Goals: The Case of China. *The Journal of Asian Finance. Economics and Business*, *7*(7), 577–586. doi:10.13106/jafeb.2020.vol7.no7.577

Lee, J.-C., Tang, Y., & Jiang, S. (2023). Understanding continuance intention of artificial intelligence (AI)-enabled mobile banking applications: An extension of AI characteristics to an expectation confirmation model. *Humanities & Social Sciences Communications*, *10*(1), 333. doi:10.105741599-023-01845-1

Lee, K. S., & Tan, S. J. (2003). E-retailing versus physical retailing: A theoretical model and empirical test of consumer choice. *Journal of Business Research*, *56*(11), 877–885. doi:10.1016/S0148-2963(01)00274-0

Lee, K.-H., Min, B., & Yook, K.-H. (2015). The impacts of carbon (CO2) emissions and environmental research and development (R&D) investment on firm performance. *International Journal of Production Economics*, *167*, 1–11. doi:10.1016/j.ijpe.2015.05.018

Lee, Y. H., Hsieh, Y. C., & Hsu, C. N. (2011). Adding innovation diffusion theory to the technology acceptance model: Supporting employees' intentions to use e-learning systems. *Journal of Educational Technology & Society*, *14*(4), 124–137.

Lei, N., Miao, Q., & Yao, X. (2023). Does the implementation of green credit policy improve the ESG performance of enterprises? Evidence from a quasi-natural experiment in China. *Economic Modelling*, *127*, 106478. doi:10.1016/j.econmod.2023.106478

Lekakis, J. N., & Kousis, M. (2013). Economic Crisis, Troika and the Environment in Greece. *South European Society & Politics*, *18*(3), 305–331. doi:10.1080/13608746.2013.799731

Leo, M., Sharma, S., & Maddulety, K. (2019). Machine Learning in Banking Risk Management: A Literature Review. *Risks 2019*, *7*(1), 29. doi:10.3390/risks7010029

Leong, C., Tan, B., Xiao, X., Tan, F. T. C., & Sun, Y. (2017). Nurturing a FinTech ecosystem: The case of a youth microloan startup in China. *International Journal of Information Management*, *37*(2), 92–97. doi:10.1016/j.ijinfomgt.2016.11.006

Liao, Z., & Wong, W. K. (2008). The determinants of customer interactions with internet-enabled e-banking services. *The Journal of the Operational Research Society*, *59*(9), 1201–1210. doi:10.1057/palgrave.jors.2602429

Li, C., Faridi, M. Z., & Nazar, R. (2023). *How does green finance asymmetrically affect greenhouse gas emissions? Evidence from the top-ten green bond issuer countries*. Borsa Istanbul Review. doi:10.1016/j.bir.2023.03.002

Li, G., Lv, X., & Han, X. (2023). Digital financial inclusion and household debt in China. *Applied Economics Letters*, *30*(19), 2862–2866. doi:10.1080/13504851.2022.2110560

Li, J., Wang, J., Wangh, S., & Zhou, Y. (2019). Mobile payment with alipay: An application of extended technology acceptance model. *IEEE Access : Practical Innovations, Open Solutions*, *7*, 50380–50387. doi:10.1109/ACCESS.2019.2902905

Lindenberg, N. (2014). *Definition of green finance*. SSRN.

LindenbergN. (2014). Definition of green finance. Lindenberg, Nannette, Definition of Green Finance. SSRN. https://ssrn.com/abstract=2446496

LinH.-J. (2010). Why Should Managers Like Payback Period? SSRN. https://ssrn.com/abstract=1688730

Linnenluecke, M., Marrone, M., & Singn, A. (2020). Conducting systematic literature reviews and bibliometric analyses. *Australian Journal of Management*, *45*(2), 175–194. doi:10.1177/0312896219877678

Lin, Z., Wang, H., Li, W., & Chen, M. (2023). Impact of Green Finance on Carbon Emissions Based on a Two-Stage LMDI Decomposition Method. *Sustainability (Basel)*, *15*(12808), 1–28. doi:10.3390u151712808

Li, Q., Long, R., Chen, H., Chen, F., & Wang, J. (2020). Visualized analysis of global green buildings: Development, barriers and future directions. *Journal of Cleaner Production*, *245*, 118775. doi:10.1016/j.jclepro.2019.118775

Liu, H., Alharthi, M., Atil, A., Zafar, M. W., & Khan, I. (2022). A non-linear analysis of the impacts of natural resources and education on environmental quality: Green energy and its role in the future. *Resources Policy*, *79*, 102940. doi:10.1016/j.resourpol.2022.102940

Liu, X., & Wei, K. K. (2003). An empirical study of product differences in consumers' E-commerce adoption behavior. *Electronic Commerce Research and Applications*, *2*(3), 229–239. doi:10.1016/S1567-4223(03)00027-9

Liu, Z., Zheng, S., Zhang, X., & Mo, L. (2023). The Impact of Green Finance on Export Technology Complexity: Evidence from China. *Sustainability (Basel)*, *15*(3), 2625. doi:10.3390u15032625

Livemint. (2016). *Television viewership in India up by 12% since: Barc study*. Live Mint. https://www.livemint.com/Consumer/mHADAtpTFzfZ3UnC54oyDI/Television-viewership-in-India-up-by-12-since-2016-Barc-st.html

Li, X.-F., Li, Q.-K., Cheng, J., Liu, L., Yan, Q., Wu, Y., Zhang, X.-H., Wang, Z.-Y., Qiu, Q., & Luo, Y. (2016). Conversion of dinitrogen to ammonia by FeN3-embedded graphene. *Journal of the American Chemical Society*, *138*(28), 8706–8709. doi:10.1021/jacs.6b04778 PMID:27383680

Lohse, G. L., & Spiller, P. (1998). Electronic shopping. *Communications of the ACM*, *41*(7), 81–87. doi:10.1145/278476.278491

Lucaci, B. (2022). *The Renewed Promise of Disclosure: an EU Approach to Sustainable Finance*. Sage.

Lu, M., Xu, H., & Wang, X. (2021). Impact of carbon markets on industrial competitiveness: An analysis of selected industries in Beijing. *Energy Reports*, *7*, 1601–1611. doi:10.1016/j.egyr.2021.09.063

Lu, Q., Farooq, M. U., Ma, X., & Iram, R. (2022). Assessing the combining role of public-private investment as a green finance and renewable energy in carbon neutrality target. *Renewable Energy*, *196*, 1357–1365. doi:10.1016/j.renene.2022.06.072

Lu, X., Lai, Y., & Zhang, Y. (2023). Digital financial inclusion and investment diversification: Evidence from China. *Accounting and Finance*, *63*(S2), 2781–2799. doi:10.1111/acfi.13043

Lu, Y., Sheng, Z., Zhang, K., & Duan, Q. (2022). Predicting P2P lenders' decisions: The prospect theory approach. *International Journal of Electronic Business*, *17*(1), 1–12. doi:10.1504/IJEB.2022.119935

Macarthy, E. & McDaniel, C. (2000). *Basic Marketing*. University Book Stall.

Macfarlane, M. (2022). Assessing the State of the Voluntary Carbon Market in 2022. *Carbon Direct Blog*. https://www.carbon-direct.com/insights/assessing-the-state-of-the-voluntary-carbon-market-in-2022

Madaleno, M., Dogan, E., & Taskin, D. (2022). A step forward on sustainability: The nexus of environmental responsibility, green technology, clean energy and green finance. *Energy Economics*, *109*, 105945. doi:10.1016/j.eneco.2022.105945

Mahalle, A., Yong, J., & Tao, X. (2021). Regulatory Challenges and Mitigation for Account Services Offered by FinTech. *Proceedings of the 2021 IEEE 24th International Conference on Computer Supported Cooperative Work in Design, CSCWD 2021*, (pp. 280–287). IEEE. 10.1109/CSCWD49262.2021.9437631

Malik, A., Grohmann, E., & Akhtar, R. (2014). Environmental deterioration and human health. *Springer Dordrecht*, *10*, 978–994.

Mallou, V., Boubeta, R., & Tobío, B. (2001). Consumer Preferences and Brand Equity Measurement of Spanish National Daily Newspapers: A Conjoint Analysis Approach. *The Spanish Journal of Psychology*, *4*(1), 48–54. doi:10.1017/S1138741600005643 PMID:11705342

Manaswi, K., Singh, A., & Gupta, V. (2023). Building a Better Future with Sustainable Investments: Insights from Recent Research. *Indian Journal of Human Development*, *0*(0), 320–343. doi:10.1177/09737030231194836

Manero, A., Taylor, K., Nikolakis, W., Adamowicz, W., Marshall, V., Spencer-Cotton, A., Nguyen, M., & Grafton, Q. (2022). A systematic literature review of non-market valuation of Indigenous peoples' values: Current knowledge, best-practice and framing questions for future research. *Ecosystem Services*, *54*, 101–147. doi:10.1016/j.ecoser.2022.101417

Manley, B. (2013). Deforestation Survey 2012. *MPI Technical Paper 2013/02*. Ministry for Primary Industries.

Manley, B. (2014). Deforestation Survey 2013, Final Report. *MPI Technical Paper 2014/02*. Ministry for Primary Industries. https://www.mpi.govt.nz/document-vault/4131

Manley, B. (2015). Deforestation Survey 2014. *MPI Technical Paper 2015/02*. Ministry for Primary Industries. https://www.mpi.govt.nz/document-vault/6355

Manley, B. (2016a). *Afforestation Responses to Carbon Price Changes and Market Certainties*. University of Canterbury School of Forestry. https://www.mfe.govt.nz/publications/climatechange/afforestation-responses-carbon-price-changes-and-market-certainties

Manley, B. (2016b). *Deforestation Intentions Survey 2015*. Ministry for Primary Industries. https://www.mpi.govt.nz/document-vault/11776

Manley, B. (2019). *Impacts of carbon prices on forest management*. Ministry for Primary Industries. https://www.mpi.govt.nz/dmsdocument/46561-Impacts-of-carbon-prices-on-forest-management

Manley, B. (2021). *Afforestation and Deforestation Intentions Survey 2021*. Ministry for Primary Industries. https://www.mpi.govt.nz/dmsdocument/52405-Afforestation-and-Deforestation-Intentions-Survey-2021

Manoharan, H., Yuvaraja, T., Kuppusamy, R., & Radhakrishnan, A. (2023). Implementation of explainable artificial intelligence in commercial communication systems using micro systems. *Science Progress*, *106*(3), 00368504231191657. doi:10.1177/00368504231191657 PMID:37533330

Mao, F., Wang, Y., & Zhu, M. (2023). Digital financial inclusion, traditional finance system and household entrepreneurship. *Pacific-Basin Finance Journal*, *80*, 102076. doi:10.1016/j.pacfin.2023.102076

Marek, J., Blümlein, K., Neubauer, J., & Wehking, C. (2019). Ditching labor-intensive paper-based processes: Process automation in a Czech insurance company. In R. M. vom Brocke J. Mendling J. (Ed.), *CEUR Workshop Proceedings* (*Vol. 2428*, pp. 16–24). CEUR-WS. https://www.scopus.com/inward/record.uri?eid=2-s2.0-85071386197&partnerID=40&md5=bc8c6591e8905c17d01c71da748d3c76

Marketplace, E. (2022). *The art of integrity- state of the voluntary carbon markets 2022 Q3*. Forest Trends.

Markusson, N., McLaren, D., & Tyfield, D. (2018). Towards a cultural political economy of mitigation deterrence by negative emissions technologies (NETs). *Global Sustainability*, *1*(e10), 1–9. doi:10.1017us.2018.10

Marron, D. B., & Steel, D. G. (2000). Which countries protect intellectual property? The case of software piracy. *Economic Inquiry*, *38*(2), 159–174. doi:10.1111/j.1465-7295.2000.tb00011.x

Martin Kim, M. H. (2017). Blockchain technology and the fintech revolution. *Turkish Online Journal of Educational Technology, 2017*(December Special Issue ITEC), 77–82. https://www.scopus.com/inward/record.uri?eid=2-s2.0-85057640853&partnerID=40&md5=ca1ec6c72648da0d865cdc30b2529f3e

MartinssonG.StrombergP.SajtosL.ThomannC. (2022). *Carbon Pricing and Firm-Level CO2 Abatement: Evidence from a Quarter of a Century-Long Panel.* (Finance Working Paper No. 842) European Corporate Governance Institute. https://ssrn.com/abstract=4206508 or doi:10.2139/ssrn.4206508

Masri, S., LeBrón, A. M., Logue, M. D., Valencia, E., Ruiz, A., Reyes, A., & Wu, J. (2021). Risk assessment of soil heavy metal contamination at the census tract level in the city of Santa Ana, CA: Implications for health and environmental justice. *Environmental Science. Processes & Impacts*, *23*(6), 812–830. doi:10.1039/D1EM00007A PMID:33954329

Mather-Gratton, Z. J., Larsen, S., & Bentsen, N. S. (2021). Understanding the sustainability debate on forest biomass for energy in Europe: A discourse analysis. *PLoS One*, *16*(2), e0246873. doi:10.1371/journal.pone.0246873 PMID:33596217

Mavlutova, I., Volkova, T., Spilbergs, A., Natrins, A., Arefjevs, I., & Verdenhofs, A. (2021). The role of fintech firms in contemporary financial sector development. *WSEAS Transactions on Business and Economics*, *18*, 411–423. doi:10.37394/23207.2021.18.42

Mayer, R. C., & Davis, J. H. (1999). The effect of the performance appraisal system on trust for management: A field quasi-experiment. *The Journal of Applied Psychology*, *84*(1), 123–136. doi:10.1037/0021-9010.84.1.123

McCarthy, J., Minsky, M. L., & Rochester, N. (1956). *Artificial Intelligence (AI) Coined at Dartmouth | Artificial intelligence: past, present, and future*. Dartmouth. https://home.dartmouth.edu/about/artificial-intelligence-ai-coined-dartmouth

McKenney, B. A., & Kiesecker, J. M. (2010). Policy Development for Biodiversity Offsets: A Review of Offset Frameworks. *Environmental Management*, *45*(1), 165–176. doi:10.100700267-009-9396-3 PMID:19924472

McLaren, D. (2016). Mitigation deterrence and the "moral hazard" of solar radiation management. *Earth's Future*, *4*(12), 596–602. doi:10.1002/2016EF000445

Mclaren, D. (2020). Quantifying the potential scale of mitigation deterrence from greenhouse gas removal techniques. *Climatic Change*, *162*(4), 2411–2428. doi:10.100710584-020-02732-3

McLaren, D., Willis, R., Szerszynski, B., Tyfield, D., & Markusson, N. (2021). Attractions of delay: Using deliberative engagement to investigate the political and strategic impacts of greenhouse gas removal technologies. *Environment and Planning. E, Nature and Space*, *0*(0).

McMullen, J. S., & Warnick, B. J. (2016). Should we require every new venture to be a hybrid organization? *Journal of Management Studies*, *53*(4), 630–662. doi:10.1111/joms.12150

Media, S. (2022). Planting Forests That Are Good For Nature, Climate, And The Economy. *Scoop News Website*. https://www.scoop.co.nz/stories/PA2210/S00032/planting-forests-that-are-good-for-nature-climate-and-the-economy.htm

Mehrban, S., Nadeem, M. W., Hussain, M., Ahmed, M. M., Hakeem, O., Saqib, S., & Khan, M. A. (2020). Towards secure FinTech: A survey, taxonomy, and open research challenges. *IEEE Access: Practical Innovations, Open Solutions*, *8*, 23391–23406. doi:10.1109/ACCESS.2020.2970430

Mehrotra, A., & Menon, S. (2021). Second round of FinTech - Trends and challenges. *Proceedings of 2nd International Conference on Computation, Automation and Knowledge Management, ICCAKM 2021*, (pp. 243–248). IEEE. 10.1109/ICCAKM50778.2021.9357759

Mehta, A. (2017). *Catalyzing green finance: A concept for leveraging blended finance for green development*. Asian Development Bank.

Mehta, K., Sharma, R., & Jalotra, S. (2023). A Bibliometric Analysis of Green Banking: Present State and Future Directions. In *Perspectives on Blockchain Technology and Responsible Investing* (pp. 159–176). IGI Global. doi:10.4018/978-1-6684-8361-9.ch007

Meitei, K. K. S. (2015). Doubly Linked Block Association Schemes. *International Journal of Innovative Research in Engineering & Management (IJIREM) ISSN: 2350-0557*, *2*(6), 101- 104.

Merendino, A., & Melville, R. (2019). The board of directors and firm performance: empirical evidence from listed companies. *Corporate Governance: The international journal of business in society*.

Meryl, P., & Roger, A. (1984). Consumer Response to Promotions: Some New Perspectives. Advances in Consumer Research, 11, 420-425. Agro- Economic Research Centre University of Allahabad.

Mihalski, G. (2008). Operational risk in current assets investment decisions: Portfolio management approach in accounts receivable. *Agricultural Economics, 54*, 12-19. https://papers.ssrn.com/sol3/papers.cfm?abstract_id=1562672

Mi, J. J., Hu, T., & Deer, L. (2018). User Data Can Tell Defaulters in P2P Lending. *Annals of Data Science*, *5*(1), 59–67. doi:10.100740745-017-0134-z

Mills, E. (2009). A global review of insurance industry responses to climate change. *The Geneva Papers on Risk and Insurance. Issues and Practice*, *34*(3), 323–359. doi:10.1057/gpp.2009.14

Milne, P. (2021). The potential for using forestry offsets to meet University of Canterbury's net-zero carbon emissions targets: a case study. [Unpublished Dissertation. New Zealand School of Forestry].

Ministry for Primary Industries. (2021). *National Exotic Forest Description*. MPI. https://www.mpi.govt.nz/dmsdocument/43540/direct

Ministry for Primary Industries. (2022). *Managing exotic afforestation incentives: A discussion document on proposals to change forestry settings in the New Zealand Emissions Trading Scheme*. (MPI Discussion Paper No:2022/02). MPI. https://www.mpi.govt.nz/dmsdocument/50206-Managing-exotic-afforestation-incentives-Proposals-to-change-forestry-settings-in-the-NZ-Emissions-Trading-Scheme

Ministry for the Environment. (2018). *Emissions pricing impact on innovation and competitiveness*. Wellington: Ministry for the Environment. https://environment.govt.nz/assets/Publications/Files/Innovation-and-competitiveness-review-FINAL.pdf

Ministry for the Environment. (2020). *Guidance for voluntary carbon offsetting –updated and extended until 31 December 2021*. Wellington: Ministry for the Environment. https://environment.govt.nz/assets/Publications/Files/guidance-for-voluntary-carbon-offsetting-updated-and-extended-until-31-December-2021.pdf

Ministry for the Environment. (2020). *Marginal abatement cost curves analysis for New Zealand: Potential greenhouse gas mitigation options and their costs*. Cabinet Briefing, Wellington: Ministry for the Environment. https://environment.govt.nz/assets/publications/Cabinet-papers-briefings-and-minutes/2020-b-06369-publication-of-marginal-abatement-cost-curves-report.pdf

Ministry for the Environment. (2020). *Marginal abatement cost curves analysis for New Zealand: Potential greenhouse gas mitigation options and their costs*. Wellington: Ministry for the Environment. https://environment.govt.nz/assets/Publications/Files/marginal-abatement-cost-curves-analysis_0.pdf

Ministry of Agriculture and Forestry. (2012). *Interaction between the voluntary carbon market, New Zealand's accounting under the Kyoto Protocol and the New Zealand Emissions Trading Scheme*. Wellington: Ministry for Agriculture and Forestry. https://www.mpi.govt.nz/dmsdocument/5140/direct

Ministry of Finance. (2018). *On the approval of Methodological recommendations for drawing up a management report*. Ministry of Finance of Ukraine. https://zakon.rada.gov.ua/rada/show/v0982201-18#Text

Ministry of Finance. (2023). *Direct investment page*. Ministry of Finance. https://index.minfin.com.ua/ua/economy/fdi/

Mirza, N., Afzal, A., Umar, M., & Skare, M. (2023). The impact of green lending on banking performance: Evidence from SME credit portfolios in the BRIC. *Economic Analysis and Policy*, *77*, 843–850. doi:10.1016/j.eap.2022.12.024

Mirza, N., Elhoseny, M., Umar, M., & Metawa, N. (2023). Safeguarding FinTech innovations with Machine Learning: Comparative Assessment of Various Approaches. *Research in International Business and Finance*, *66*, 102009. doi:10.1016/j.ribaf.2023.102009

Misani, N., & Pogutz, S. (2015). Unraveling the effects of environmental outcomes and processes on financial performance: A non-linear approach. *Ecological Economics*, *109*, 150–160. doi:10.1016/j.ecolecon.2014.11.010

Mishra, (2015). An empirical analysis of the marketing of services in rural Uttar Pradesh. *IMPACT: International Journal of Research in Business Management, 3*(2), 23-34 https://citeseerx.ist.psu.edu/viewdoc/download?doi=10.1.1.684.600&rep=rep1&type=pdf

Mishra, B. (2003). *Rural Non-Farm Employment in Uttar Pradesh*. Agro- Economic Research Centre University of Allahabad. https://allduniv.ac.in/ckfinder/userfiles/files/Rural_Non-Farm_Employment_in_Uttar_Pradesh.pdf

Mohammad, S. M. (2020). Artificial Intelligence in Information Technology. SSRN *Electronic Journal*. https://doi.org/doi:10.2139/SSRN.3625444

Mohd, S., & Kaushal, V. K. (2018). Green finance: A step towards sustainable development. *MUDRA: Journal of Finance and Accounting*, *5*(1), 59–74. doi:10.17492/mudra.v5i01.13036

Money Life. (2010). Digital TV growth in India driven by the rural market. *Money Life*. https://www.moneylife.in/article/digital-tv-growth-in-india-driven-by-rural-market/5287.html

Morgan, P. J. (2022). Assessing the risks associated with green digital finance and policies for coping with them. In *Green Digital Finance and Sustainable Development Goals* (pp. 51–68). Springer Nature Singapore. doi:10.1007/978-981-19-2662-4_3

Morton, J. (2021). Covering climate now: is NZ getting forestry right? *New Zealand Herald*. https://www.nzherald.co.nz/nz/covering-climate-now-is-nz-getting-forestry-right/5J2IA4YVDQO2K4YEEIFKHBCQIQ/

Mosser, P. C. (2020). Central bank responses to COVID-19. *Business Economics (Cleveland, Ohio)*, *55*(4), 191–201. doi:10.105711369-020-00189-x PMID:33204040

Mousa, M., & Ayoubi, R. M. (2019). Inclusive/Exclusive Talent Management, Responsible Leadership and Organizational Downsizing A Study of Academics in Egyptian Public Business Schools. *Journal of Management Development*, *38*(2), 87–104. doi:10.1108/JMD-11-2018-0325

Mozib Lalon, R. (2015). Green Banking: Going Green. *International Journal of Economics. Finance and Management Sciences*, *3*(1), 34. doi:10.11648/j.ijefm.20150301.15

Mpinganjira, M. (2016). An investigation of customer attitude towards online stores. *African Journal of Science, Technology, Innovation and Development*, *8*(5), 447–456. doi:10.1080/20421338.2016.1222752

Muganyi, T., Yan, L., & Sun, H. P. (2021). Green finance, fintech and environmental protection: Evidence from China. *Environmental Science and Ecotechnology*, *7*, 100107. doi:10.1016/j.ese.2021.100107 PMID:36160697

Mukul, & Pathak, N. (2021a). Are the financial inclusion schemes of India developing the nation sustainably? *E3S Web of Conferences, 296*, 06011. doi:10.1051/e3sconf/202129606011

Mukul, S. Taneja, E. Özen, R. Plaha, M., & Zammit, L. (2023). *Banking, Fintech, BigTech: Emerging Challenges for Multimedia Adoption. Intelligent Multimedia Technologies for Financial Risk Management: Trends, Tools and Applications*. Institution of Engineering and Technology.

Mukul, T. S., Özen, E., Plaha, R., & Zammit, M. L. (2023). Banking, Fintech, BigTech: Emerging challenges for multimedia adoption. In Intelligent Multimedia Technologies for Financial Risk Management: Trends, Tools and Applications. Institution of Engineering and Technology.

Muncy, J. A., & Wilkie, W. (1987). Consumer behavior. In *Journal of Marketing, 51(3)*. Dryden. doi:10.2307/1251656

MuthaiyahS.PhangK.SembakuttiS. (2021). Bridging skill gaps and creating future ready accounting and finance graduates: An exploratory study. *F1000Research, 10*. doi:10.12688/f1000research.72880.1

Nagimova, A. Z. (2022). Islamic Fintech: Digitalization Of Global Islamic Finance. *World Economy and International Relations*, *66*(5), 50–58. doi:10.20542/0131-2227-2022-66-5-50-58

Najaf, K., Schinckus, C., & Yoong, L. C. (2020). VaR and market value of fintech companies: An analysis and evidence from global data. *Managerial Finance*, *47*(7), 915–936. doi:10.1108/MF-04-2020-0169

Nassiry, D. (2018). *The role of fintech in unlocking green finance: Policy insights for developing countries (No. 883).* (ADBI working paper). ADBI.

Nathan, J., & Jacobs, B. (2020). Blockchain consortium networks: Adding security and trust in financial services. *Journal of Corporate Accounting & Finance*, *31*(2), 29–33. doi:10.1002/jcaf.22428

Naucler, T., & Enkvist, P. (2009). *Pathways to a Low-Carbon Economy: Version 2 of the Global Greenhouse Gas Abatement Cost Curve*. Mckinsey & Company.

Nawaz, M. A., Seshadri, U., Kumar, P., Aqdas, R., Patwary, A. K., & Riaz, M. (2021). Nexus between green finance and climate change mitigation in N-11 and BRICS countries: Empirical estimation through difference in differences (DID) approach. *Environmental Science and Pollution Research International*, *28*(6), 6504–6519. doi:10.100711356-020-10920-y PMID:32997248

Nayak, K., & Shah, B. (2015). The effectiveness of newspaper prints ads. *Indian Journal of Applied Research*, *5*(2), 328–331.

Ndubisi, N., & Moi, C. (2005). Customers behavioral responses to sales promotion: The role of fear of losing face. *Asia Pacific Journal of Marketing and Logistics*, *17*(1), 32–49. https://www.researchgate.net/publication/241699350_Customers_behaviourial_responses_to_sales_promotion_The_role_of_fear_of_losing_face. doi:10.1108/13555850510672278

Nedopil, C., Dordi, T., & Weber, O. (2021). The Nature of Global Green Finance Standards—Evolution, Differences, and Three Models. *Sustainability (Basel)*, *13*(7), 3723. doi:10.3390u13073723

Nelson, O., & Salawu, A. (2016). Effective Use of Media Awareness Campaigns for Breast Cancer Care among Women: A Comparative Study. *Journal of International Women's Studies*, *17*(4), 160–173. https://vc.bridgew.edu/jiws/vol17/iss4/12

Nenavath, S. (2022). Impact of fintech and green finance on environmental quality protection in India: By applying the semi-parametric difference-in-differences (SDID). *Renewable Energy*, *193*, 913–919. doi:10.1016/j.renene.2022.05.020

Nenonen, S., Koski, A., Lassila, A. P., & Lehikoinen, S. (2019). Towards low carbon economy - Green bond and asset development. *IOP Conference Series. Earth and Environmental Science*, *352*(1), 012028. doi:10.1088/1755-1315/352/1/012028

Neruja, S., & Arulrajah, A. A. (2021). The Impact of Environmental Knowledge and Awareness on Sustainability Performance of Organizations: The Mediating Role of Employee Green Behaviour. *International Business Research*, *14*(9), 1–68. https://ideas.repec.org/a/ibn/ibrjnl/v14y2021i9p68.html

Neuhofer, B., Buhalis, D., & Ladkin, A. (2015). Technology as a catalyst of change: Enablers and barriers of the tourist experience and their consequences. The Routledge Handbook of Transport, Tourism and Hospitality, 51-70. Routledge.

New Zealand Forest Service. (2022). *Emissions Trading Scheme for Forestry as at 30 June 2022*. Ministry for Primary Industries. https://www.mpi.govt.nz/dmsdocument/45232-Emissions-Trading-Scheme-for-Forestry-land-statistics-

New Zealand Productivity Commission. (2018). *Low-emissions economy: Final report*. New Zealand Productivity Commission. www.productivity.govt.nz/low-emissions

Ng, A. W., & Kwok, B. K. (2017). Emergence of Fintech and cybersecurity in a global financial centre: Strategic approach by a regulator. *Journal of Financial Regulation and Compliance*, *25*(4), 422–434. doi:10.1108/JFRC-01-2017-0013

Ng, E., & Pan, S. L. (2022). Competitive strategies for ensuring Fintech platform performance: Evidence from multiple case studies. *Information Systems Journal*, isj.12406. doi:10.1111/isj.12406

Ng, E., Tan, B., Sun, Y., & Meng, T. (2023). The strategic options of fintech platforms: An overview and research agenda. *Information Systems Journal*, *33*(2), 192–231. doi:10.1111/isj.12388

Ng, T., Lye, C., Chan, K., Lim, Y., & Lim, Y. (2020). Sustainability in Asia: The roles of financial development in environmental, social and governance (ESG) Performance. *Social Indicators Research*, *150*(1), 1–28. doi:10.100711205-020-02288-w

Nguyen, T. T., Quynh, M. P., Van, H. N., Le Thi, H., Van, L. N., Nguyen, T. D., & Van, D. N. (2023). The Role of Availability of Financial Institutions and Financial Innovation on the Financial Inclusion: Does Digital Finance Moderate this Linkage? *Cuadernos de Economía (Santiago, Chile)*, *46*(130), 11–20. doi:10.32826/cude.v1i130.1002

Ning, Y., Cherian, J., Sial, M. S., Álvarez-Otero, S., Comite, U., & Zia-Ud-Din, M. (2023). Green bond as a new determinant of sustainable green financing, energy efficiency investment, and economic growth: A global perspective. *Environmental Science and Pollution Research International*, *30*(22), 61324–61339. doi:10.100711356-021-18454-7 PMID:34993809

Niu, G., Jin, X., Wang, Q., & Zhou, Y. (2022). Broadband infrastructure and digital financial inclusion in rural China. *China Economic Review*, *76*, 101853. doi:10.1016/j.chieco.2022.101853

Nobin, E. (2016). *Exploring community newspapers and brand building in the digital age* [Doctoral dissertation, The IIE].

Noreen, U., & Imran, R. (2021). Impact of Talent Management Practices on Financial Performance: Evidence from GCC Banking Sector. *Middle East Journal Of Management*, *8*(2–3), 113–124. doi:10.1504/MEJM.2021.113977

Nunnally, J. C. (1978). An Overview of Psychological Measurement. *Clinical Diagnosis of Mental Disorders*, 97–146. doi:10.1007/978-1-4684-2490-4_4

Och, M. (2020). Sustainable Finance and the EU Taxonomy Regulation – Hype or Hope? SSRN *Electronic Journal*. https://doi.org/ doi:10.2139/SSRN.3738255

Oduntan, T. (2021). Proliferation of radio stations. *Daily Trust*. https://dailytrust.com/proliferation-of-radio-stations-social-impacts-and-need-for-rededication

Oguntuase, O. J., & Windapo, A. (2021). Green Bonds and Green Buildings: New Options for Achieving Sustainable Development in Nigeria. *Advances in 21st Century Human Settlements*, 193–218. doi:10.1007/978-981-33-4424-2_11

Ojo-Fafore, E. M., Aigbavboa, C., Thwala, W., & Remaru, P. (2018). *Green Finance for Sustainable Global Growth*. 244–269. doi:10.4018/978-1-5225-7808-6.ch010

Olatunji, O., Akinlabi, S. A., Ayo, O., Madushele, N., Adedeji, P. A., & Fatoba, S. O. (2019). Drivers and barriers to competitive carbon footprint reduction in manufacturing supply chain: A brief review. *Procedia Manufacturing*, *35*, 992–1000. doi:10.1016/j.promfg.2019.06.047

Olivier, A., & Vorobei, I. (2010). *Non-financial reporting: a tool of socially responsible business*. Global compact network Ukraine, Kyiv. https://www.ppv.net.ua/uploads/work_attachments/Non-Financial_Reporting__UA_.pdf

Olubunmi, O. A., Xia, P. B., & Skitmore, M. (2016). Green building incentives: A review. *Renewable & Sustainable Energy Reviews*, *59*, 1611–1621. doi:10.1016/j.rser.2016.01.028

Osei-Assibey Bonsu, M., Wang, Y., & Guo, Y. (2023). Does fintech lead to better accounting practices? Empirical evidence. *Accounting Research Journal*, *36*(2/3), 129–147. doi:10.1108/ARJ-07-2022-0178

Othman, H. (2020). Ambient Ads as Unconventional Media Approach. *International Design Journal*, *10*(2), 269-278. https://idj.journals.ekb.eg/article_81142.html doi:10.21608/idj.2020.81142

Owen, R., Botelho, T., Mac an Bhaird, C., Hussain, J. G., Pierrakis, Y., Scott, J. M., & Lodh, S. (2023). Editorial entrepreneurial finance for green innovative SMEs. *IEEE Transactions on Engineering Management*, *70*(3), 942–949. doi:10.1109/TEM.2022.3224870

Özen, E., Taneja, S., & Makalesi, A. (2022b). Critical Evaluation of Management of NPA / NPL in Emerging and Advanced Economies : a Study in Context of India GelişenveGelişmişEkonomilerde NPA / NPL YönetiminEleştirelDeğerlendirmesi : HindistanBağlamında Bir Çalışma. *YalovaSosyalBilimlerDergisi, 12*(2), 99–111.

Özen, E., & Sanjay, T. (2022a). Empirical Analysis of the Effect of Foreign Trade in Computer and Communication Services on Economic Growth in India. *Journal of Economics and Business Issues*, *2*(2), 24–34.

Ozili, P. K. (2020). Financial inclusion research around the world: A review. *The Forum for Social Economics*. doi:10.1080/07360932.2020.1715238

Ozili, P. K. (2021). Managing Climate Change Risk: The Policy Options for Central Banks. In *New Challenges for Future Sustainability and Wellbeing*. Emerald Publishing Limited. doi:10.1108/978-1-80043-968-920211016

Ozili, P. K. (2022). Circular economy and central bank digital currency. *Circular Economy and Sustainability*, *2*(4), 1501–1516. doi:10.100743615-022-00170-0 PMID:35434721

Ozili, P. K. (2022). Green finance research around the world: A review of literature. *International Journal of Green Economics*, *16*(1), 56–75. doi:10.1504/IJGE.2022.125554

Ozili, P. K. (2023). Effect of gender equality on financial stability and financial inclusion. *Social Responsibility Journal*. doi:10.1108/SRJ-12-2022-0565

OziliP. K.ArunT. (2020). Spillover of COVID-19: impact on the Global Economy. Available at SSRN 3562570. doi:10.2139/ssrn.3562570

Painuly, J. P. (2001). Barriers to renewable energy penetration; a framework for analysis. *Renewable Energy*, *24*(1), 73–89. doi:10.1016/S0960-1481(00)00186-5

Panda, A. (2016). Exploring climate change perceptions, rainfall trends and perceived barriers to adaptation in a drought affected region in India. *Natural Hazards*, *84*(2), 777–796. doi:10.100711069-016-2456-0

Pande. (2022). Rural Marketing: Problems & Strategies. *International Journal For Administration in Management, Commerce and Economics*, 123-128, https://www.researchgate.net/publication/361901564_Rural_Marketing_Problems_Strategies

Panos, G. A., & Wilson, J. O. (2020). Financial literacy and responsible finance in the FinTech era: Capabilities and challenges. *European Journal of Finance*, *26*(4-5), 297–301. doi:10.1080/1351847X.2020.1717569

Pappas, I. O., Kourouthanassis, P. E., Giannakos, M. N., & Chrissikopoulos, V. (2017). Sense and sensibility in personalized e-commerce: How emotions rebalance the purchase intentions of persuaded customers. *Psychology and Marketing*, *34*(10), 972–986. doi:10.1002/mar.21036

Park, H., & Kim, J. D. (2020). Transition towards green banking: role of financial regulators and financial institutions. *Asian Journal of Sustainability and Social Responsibility, 5*(1), 1–25. doi:10.1186/s41180-020-00034-3

Partyn, G. O., & Zagorodnii, A. H. (2017). Taking into account the interests of stakeholders in the process of forming integrated enterprise reporting. *Bulletin*. Lviv Polytechnic National University. http://nbuv.gov.ua/UJRN/VNULPM_2017_862_31

Parvadavardini, S., & Nagarajan, V. (2015). A study on the agricultural value chain financing in India. *Zemedelská Ekonomika*, *61*(2), 31–38. doi:10.17221/38/2014-AGRICECON

Patnaik, B. C. M., Satpathy, I., & Rachayeeta, P. (2016). Issues of Micro, Small and Medium Enterprises (MSME) in India. *International Journal of Innovative Research and Development*, *5*(6), 1–5.

Paul & Christo. (2022). *Central Uttar Pradesh Region.* Encuclopedia. https://encyclopedia.adventist.org/article?id=AJB2#:~:text=Territory%3A%20The%20following%20districts%20in,Bareli%2C%20Sitapur%2C%20and%20Unnao

Paul, L. R., & Sadath, L. (2021). A systematic analysis on fintech and its applications. *Proceedings of International Conference on Innovative Practices in Technology and Management, ICIPTM 2021*, (pp. 131–136). IEEE. 10.1109/ICIPTM52218.2021.9388371

Pavelko, O. V., & Harapko, N. I. (2021). Integrated enterprise reporting as a key source of information for stakeholders. Bulletin of the National University of Water Management and Nature Management. *Economic sciences, 1*(93). http://nbuv.gov.ua/UJRN/Vnuvgp_ekon_2021_1_16

Pavlou, P. A. (2003). Consumer acceptance of electronic commerce: Integrating trust and risk with the technology acceptance model. *International Journal of Electronic Commerce*, *7*(3), 101–134. doi:10.1080/10864415.2003.11044275

Pavlou, P. A., & Featherman, M. S. (2003). Predicting e-services adoption: A perceived risk facets perspective. *International Journal of Human-Computer Studies*, *59*(4), 451–474. doi:10.1016/S1071-5819(03)00111-3

Peng, C. (2020). The role of business strategy and CEO compensation structure in driving corporate social responsibility: Linkage towards a sustainable development perspective. *Corporate Social Responsibility and Environmental Management*, *27*(2), 1028–1039. doi:10.1002/csr.1863

Pentury, F. (2023). The Role Of Knowledge and Penetration Of FinTech Services In Improving Msmes Of Fishermen And Marine Farmers In Remote Small Islands Region. *Jurnal Manajemen Teori Dan Terapan [Journal of Theory and Applied Management], 1*(16), 23-37. doi:10.20473/jmtt.v16i1.43743

Peong, K. K. & Tan, K. (2021). Behavioural Intention Of Commercial Banks' Customers Towards Financial Technology Services. *GATR Journal of Finance and Banking Review, 5*(4), 10-27. doi:10.35609/jfbr.2021.5.4(2)

Peskett, L., Schreckenberg, K., & Brown, J. (2011). Institutional approaches for carbon financing in the forest sector: Learning lessons for REDD+ from forest carbon projects in Uganda. *Environmental Science & Policy*, *14*(2), 216–229. doi:10.1016/j.envsci.2010.10.004

Pham, D. C., Do, T. N. A., Doan, T. N., Nguyen, T. X. H., & Pham, T. K. Y. (2021). The impact of sustainability practices on financial performance: Empirical evidence from Sweden. *Cogent Business & Management*, *8*(1), 1912526. doi:10.1080/23311975.2021.1912526

Pinkse, J., & Busch, T. (2013). The emergence of corporate carbon norms: Strategic directions and managerial implications. *Thunderbird International Business Review*, *55*(6), 633–645. doi:10.1002/tie.21580

Pinnington, A., Alshamsi, A., Karatas-Ozkan, M., Nicolopoulou, K., Ozbilgin, M., Tatli, A., & Vassilopoulou, J. (2015). Early Organizational Diffusion of Contemporary Policies: Narratives of Sustainability and Talent Management. In E. Gimzauskiene, K. Duoba, X. Pavie, A. Pinnington, & M. Vilka, 20th International Scientific Conference - Economics And Management. Elesvier. doi:10.1016/j.sbspro.2015.11.480

Pires, P. J. (2006). Winning through innovation: A practical guide to leading organizational change and renewal. *RAC. Revista de Administração Contemporânea*, *10*(1), 177–177. doi:10.1590/S1415-65552006000100013

Polonsky, M. J. (2008). An introduction to green marketing. *Global Environment: Problems and Policies*, *2*(1), 1–10.

Polzin, F., Sanders, M., & Serebriakova, A. (2021). Finance in global transition scenarios: Mapping investments by technology into finance needs by source. *Energy Economics*, *99*, 105281. doi:10.1016/j.eneco.2021.105281

Poonam, & Aggarwal, K. K. (2023). Analysis of the impact of COVID-19 on the stock market and capability of investing strategies. *AIP Conference Proceedings, 2782*. doi:10.1063/5.0154174

Pournader, M., Shi, Y., Seuring, S., & Koh, S. L. (2020). Blockchain applications in supply chains, transport and logistics: A systematic review of the literature. *International Journal of Production Research*, *58*(7), 2063–2081. doi:10.1080/00207543.2019.1650976

Prayag, G. (2009). Tourists' evaluations of destination image, satisfaction, and future behavioral intentions-The case of Mauritius. *Journal of Travel & Tourism Marketing*, *26*(8), 836–853. doi:10.1080/10548400903358729

Preston, L. E., & O'Bannon, D. P. (1997). The Corporate Social-Financial Performance Relationship: A Typology and Analysis. *Business & Society*, *36*(4), 419–429. doi:10.1177/000765039703600406

Protopappas, L., Sideridis, A. B., & Yialouris, C. P. (2020). Implementation issues of cross border e-government systems and services. In K. S. Vlontzos G. (Ed.), *CEUR Workshop Proceedings* (Vol. 2761, pp. 155–166). CEUR-WS. https://www.scopus.com/inward/record.uri?eid=2-s2.0-85097525958&partnerID=40&md5=58405b2ec67c1e363d90c737bafad930

Psychogios, A., & Prouska, R. (2019). Human Resource Management Practices in SMEs. In Managing People In Small And Medium Enterprises In Turbulent Contexts. Routledge. doi:10.4324/9781315102610-2

Qa'dan, M. B. A., & Suwaidan, M. S. (2019). Board composition, ownership structure and corporate social responsibility disclosure: The case of Jordan. *Social Responsibility Journal.*

Qadri, R. A., Nabilah, I., & Ambarwati, R. D. (2022). Black-or-White of Online Lending in Indonesia: Conventional Platform or Sharia Scheme (A Netnography Study). *Jurnal Ilmiah Akuntansi dan Bisnis, 17*(2), 184-200.

Qin, M., Zhang, X., Li, Y., & Badarcea, R. M. (2023). Blockchain market and green finance: The enablers of carbon neutrality in China. *Energy Economics*, *118*, 106501. doi:10.1016/j.eneco.2022.106501

Rabbanee, K., Hassan, K., Taufique, M. R., Shafiullah, G. M., Dewan, A., Dai, X., Siddik, A. B., & Tian, H. (2022). Corporate Social Responsibility, Green Finance and Environmental Performance: Does Green Innovation Matter? *Sustainability, 14*(20), 13607. doi:10.3390/su142013607

Raihan, Z. Dr. M. (2019). *Sustainable Finance For Growth And Development Of Banking Industry In Bangladesh: An Equity Perspective*. DSpace. http://dspace.mist.ac.bd:8080/xmlui/handle/123456789/496

Rajmil, D., Morales, L., Aira, T., & Cardona Valles, M. (2022). Afghanistan: A Multidimensional Crisis. *Peace Review*, *34*(1), 41–50. doi:10.1080/10402659.2022.2023428

Raju, A., & Devi, S. (2012). Means of advertisement impact on consumer buying behavior with reference to health drinks in Kuppam. *International Journal of Management and Social Sciences Research*, *1*(2), 31–35.

Ramalingam, V., Palaniappan, B., Panchnatham, N., & Palanivel, S. (2006). Measuring Advertising Effectiveness - A Neural Network Approach. *Journal of Business Research*, *31*, 159–160.

Rana, R. L., Tricase, C., & De Cesare, L. (2021). Blockchain technology for a sustainable agri-food supply chain. *British Food Journal*, *123*(11), 3471–3485. doi:10.1108/BFJ-09-2020-0832

Ransbotham, S., Kiron, D., Gerbert, P., & Reeves, M. (2017). Reshaping Business With Artificial Intelligence: Closing the Gap Between Ambition and Action. *MIT Sloan Management Review*, *59*(1). https://store.hbr.org/product/reshaping-business-with-artificial-intelligence-closing-the-gap-between-ambition-and-action/SMR625

Reboredo, J. C. (2018). Green bond and financial markets: Co-movement, diversification and price spillover effects. *Energy Economics*, *74*, 38–50. doi:10.1016/j.eneco.2018.05.030

Reddy, A. S. B. (2018). Green Finance-Financial Support for Sustainable Development. *International Journal of Pure and Applied Mathematics*, *118*(20), 645–652.

Reepu, R., Taneja, S., Ozen, E., & Singh, A. (2023). A globetrotter to the future of marketing: Metaverse. In *Cultural Marketing and Metaverse for Consumer Engagement*. IGI Global. doi:10.4018/978-1-6684-8312-1.ch001

Rehman, A. U., Zakar, R., Zakar, M. Z., Hani, U., Wrona, K. J., & Fischer, F. (2021). Role of the Media in Health-Related Awareness Campaigns on Perception of COVID-19: *A Pre-post Study in the General Population of Pakistan. Frontiers in Public Health*, *9*, 779090. doi:10.3389/fpubh.2021.779090 PMID:34869191

Ren, X., Shao, Q., & Zhong, R. (2020). Nexus between green finance, non-fossil energy use, and carbon intensity: Empirical evidence from China based on a vector error correction model. *Journal of Cleaner Production*, *277*, 122844. doi:10.1016/j.jclepro.2020.122844

Ren, X., Shi, Y., & Jin, C. (2022). Climate policy uncertainty and corporate investment: Evidence from the Chinese energy industry. *Carbon Neutrality*, *1*(1), 14. doi:10.100743979-022-00008-6

Richardson-Barlow, C., Pimm, A., Taylor, P., & Gale, W. (2022). Policy and pricing barriers to steel industry decarbonization: A UK case study. *Energy Policy*, *168*, 1–12. doi:10.1016/j.enpol.2022.113100

Ringe, W. G., & Christopher, R. U. O. F. (2020). Regulating Fintech in the EU: The Case for a Guided Sandbox. *European Journal of Risk Regulation*, *11*(3), 604–629. doi:10.1017/err.2020.8

Rizos, V., Behrens, A., Van der Gaast, W., Hofman, E., Ioannou, A., Kafyeke, T., Flamos, A., Rinaldi, R., Papadelis, S., Hirschnitz-Garbers, M., & Topi, C. (2016). Implementation of circular economy business models by small and medium-sized enterprises (SMEs): Barriers and enablers. *Sustainability (Basel)*, *8*(11), 1212. doi:10.3390u8111212

Rjoub, H., Adebayo, T. S., & Kirikkaleli, D. (2023). Blockchain technology-based FinTech banking sector involvement using adaptive neuro-fuzzy-based K-nearest neighbors algorithm. *Financial Innovation*, *9*(1), 65. doi:10.118640854-023-00469-3 PMID:36919101

Roberts, L. D., Indermaur, D., & Spiranovic, C. (2013). Fear of cyber-identity theft and related fraudulent activity. *Psychiatry, Psychology and Law*, *20*(3), 315–328. doi:10.1080/13218719.2012.672275

Rodriguez, R. V., Bellamkonda, R. S., Katkam, B. S., and Samala, N. (2020). A crucial insight regarding the effects of AI and robotics on the tourism industry. *Tourism Futures Journal*. . doi:10.1108/JTF-07-2019-0065

Rolffs, P., Ockwell, D., & Byrne, R. (2015). Beyond technology and finance: Pay-as-you-go sustainable energy access and theories of social change. *Environment & Planning A*, *47*(12), 2609–2627. doi:10.1177/0308518X15615368

Roszkowska, P. (2021). Fintech in financial reporting and audit for fraud prevention and safeguarding equity investments. *Journal of Accounting & Organizational Change*, *17*(2), 164–196. doi:10.1108/JAOC-09-2019-0098

Rudd, M. D., Mitchell, J. W., & Klein, S. (1990). Use of building thermal mass to offset cooling loads. *1990 Annual Meeting of the American Society of Heating, Refrigerating and Air-Conditioning Engineers, Technical and Symposium Papers, Conference Proceedings*. NREL.

Ruffolo, M. (2022). The Role of Ethical AI in Fostering Harmonic Innovations that Support a Human-Centric Digital Transformation of Economy and Society. *Lecture Notes in Networks and Systems*, *282*, 139–143. doi:10.1007/978-3-030-81190-7_15

Rural Energy Access. (2021). Reach the World. https://www.reachtheworld.org/karans-journey-india/nations/rural-energy-access)

Ryu, H. (2018). Understanding Benefit and Risk Framework Of FinTech Adoption: Comparison Of Early Adopters And Late Adopters. *Proceedings of the 51st Hawaii International Conference on System Sciences*. Scholar Space. 10.24251/HICSS.2018.486

Ryu, H. S. (2018). *Understanding benefit and risk framework of fintech adoption: Comparison of early adopters and late adopters.*

Sachs, J. D., Woo, W. T., Yoshino, N., & Taghizadeh-Hesary, F. (2019b). *Why Is Green Finance Important?* (ADBI Working Paper 917). ADBI.

Sachs, J., Woo, W. T., Yoshino, N., & Taghizadeh-Hesary, F. (2019a). Importance of green finance for achieving sustainable development goals and energy security. Handbook of green finance: Energy security and sustainable development. University of California.

Sachs, N. M. (2020). The Paris agreement in the 2020s: Breakdown or breakup. *Ecology Law Quarterly*, *46*(3), 865–909. doi:10.15779/Z38H708140

Saluja, S., Aggarwal, A., & Mittal, A. (2022). Understanding the fraud theories and advancing with integrity model. *Journal of Financial Crime*, *29*(4), 1318–1328. doi:10.1108/JFC-07-2021-0163

Sama, R. (2019). Impact of Media Advertisements on Consumer Behavior. *Journal of Creative Communications*, *14*(1), 54–68. doi:10.1177/0973258618822624

Sapuric, S., Kokkinaki, A., & Georgiou, I. (2022). The relationship between Bitcoin returns, volatility and volume: Asymmetric GARCH modeling. *Journal of Enterprise Information Management*, *35*(6), 1506–1521. doi:10.1108/JEIM-10-2018-0228

Sarangi, G. K. (2019). Green Finance in India: Barriers and Solutions. Handbook of Green Finance, 1–18. doi:10.1007/978-981-10-8710-3_4-1

Schaltegger, S., & Wagner, M. (2011). Sustainable entrepreneurship and sustainability innovation: Categories and interactions. *Business Strategy and the Environment*, *20*(4), 222–237. doi:10.1002/bse.682

Scheyvens, R. (2007). Exploring the tourism-poverty nexus. *Current Issues in Tourism*, *10*(2-3), 231–254. doi:10.2167/cit318.0

Schierz, P. G., Schilke, O., & Wirtz, B. W. (2010). Understanding consumer acceptance of mobile payment services: An empirical analysis. *Electronic Commerce Research and Applications*, *9*(3), 209–216. doi:10.1016/j.elerap.2009.07.005

Schroeder, P., Anggraeni, K., & Weber, U. (2019). The relevance of circular economy practices to the sustainable development goals. *Journal of Industrial Ecology*, *23*(1), 77–95. doi:10.1111/jiec.12732

Schueth, S. (2003). Socially responsible investing in the United States. *Journal of Business Ethics*, *43*(3), 189–194. doi:10.1023/A:1022981828869

Schulz, K., & Feist, M. (2021). Leveraging blockchain technology for innovative climate finance under the Green Climate Fund. *Earth System Governance*, *7*, 100084. doi:10.1016/j.esg.2020.100084

Seale, M., & Mirza, R. (2020). The coin of love and virtue: Academic libraries and value in a global pandemic. *Canadian Journal of Academic Librarianship*, *6*, 1–30. doi:10.33137/cjal-rcbu.v6.34457

Seddon, N., Smith, A., Smith, P., Key, I., Chausson, A., Girardin, C., House, J., Srivastava, S., & Turner, B. (2021). Getting the message right on nature-based solutions to climate change. *Global Change Biology*, *27*(8), 1518–1546. doi:10.1111/gcb.15513 PMID:33522071

Seeberg-Elverfeldt, C. (2010). *Carbon finance possibilities for agriculture, forestry and other land use projects in the smallholder context.* Natural Resources Management and Environment Department, Food and Agriculture Organization.

Shahbaz, M., Karaman, A. S., Kilic, M., & Uyar, A. (2020). Board attributes, CSR engagement, and corporate performance: What is the nexus in the energy sector? *Energy Policy*, *143*, 111582. doi:10.1016/j.enpol.2020.111582

Shakhvedryan, D. S., & Karpushenko, M. Yu. (2019). Integrated reporting as a source of assessment of the company's activity. *Business-Inform Magazine 3.* http://www.irbis-nbuv.gov.ua/ cgi-bin/ irbis_nbuv/ cgiirbis_64. exe?I21DBN = LINK & P21DBN = UJRN & Z21ID = &S21REF = 10&S21CNR = 20&S21STN = 1&S21FMT = ASP_meta & C21COM = S&2_S21P03 = FILA= & 2_S21STR = binf_2019_3_38

Shang, Y., Zhu, L., Qian, F., & Xie, Y. (2023). Role of green finance in renewable energy development in the tourism sector. *Renewable Energy*, *206*, 890–896. doi:10.1016/j.renene.2023.02.124

Sharma, V., Jangir, K., Chowhan, S. S., & Pathak, N. (2023). *Key Factors Influencing Electric Vehicle Purchase Decisions by Consumers: An Empirical Study of Indian Consumers*. 449–464. doi:10.1007/978-981-19-8963-6_40

Sharma, V., Jangir, K., Chowhan, S. S., & Pathak, N. (2023). Key Factors Influencing Electric Vehicle Purchase Decisions by Consumers: An Empirical Study of Indian Consumers. In *Renewable Energy Optimization, Planning and Control: Proceedings of ICRTE 2022* (pp. 449–464). Springer.

Sharma, C., Sakhuja, S., & Nijjer, S. (2022). Recent trends of green human resource management: Text mining and network analysis. *Environmental Science and Pollution Research International*, *29*(56), 84916–84935. doi:10.100711356-022-21471-9 PMID:35790632

Sharma, G. D., Verma, M., Shahbaz, M., Gupta, M., & Chopra, R. (2022). Transitioning green finance from theory to practice for renewable energy development. *Renewable Energy*, *195*, 554–565. doi:10.1016/j.renene.2022.06.041

Sharma, K. & Garg, D. K. (2017). Construction of Three Associate PBIB Designs using Some Sets of Initial Blocks. [IJASS]. *International Journal of Agricultural and Statistics Sciences*, *13*(01), 55–60.

Sharma, M., & Choubey, A. (2022). Green banking initiatives: A qualitative study on Indian banking sector. *Environment, Development and Sustainability*, *24*(1), 293–319. doi:10.100710668-021-01426-9 PMID:33967597

Sharma, M., & Kumar, P. (2021). *Adoption of Blockchain Technology: A Case Study of Walmart. Blockchain Technology and Applications for Digital Marketing*. IGI Global, doi:10.4018/978-1-7998-8081-3.ch013

Sharma, P., Sharma, V., Jangir, K., Gupta, M., & Pathak, N. (2023). In A. Khosla & M. Kolhe (Eds.), *Unfolding the Emerging Trends in Non-performing Assets with Special Reference to the Energy Sector in Banking Industry BT - Renewable Energy Optimization, Planning and Control* (pp. 411–422). Springer Nature Singapore.

Sharma, P., Sharma, V., Jangir, K., Gupta, M., & Pathak, N. (2023). Unfolding the Emerging Trends in Non-performing Assets with Special Reference to the Energy Sector in Banking Industry. *Renewable Energy Optimization, Planning and Control: Proceedings of ICRTE 2022*, (pp. 411–422). IEEE.

Sharma, R., Mehta, K., & Ahuja, S. (2023). A bibliometric analysis of green finance: Present state and future directions. *Advances in Finance, Accounting, and Economics*, *2023*, 135–154. doi:10.4018/978-1-6684-8624-5.ch009

Sharma, S. K., Govindaluri, S. M., Muharrami, S. M., & Tarhini, A. (2017). A multi-analytical model for mobile banking adoption: A developing country perspective. *Review of International Business and Strategy*, *27*(1), 133–148. doi:10.1108/RIBS-11-2016-0074

Sharma, V. (2022). A Pragmatic Study on Management with Autocratic Approach and Consequential Impact on Profitability of the Organization. In P. K. Mallick, A. K. Bhoi, A. González-Briones, & P. K. Pattnaik (Eds.), *Electronic Systems and Intelligent Computing* (pp. 121–130). Springer Nature Singapore. doi:10.1007/978-981-16-9488-2_10

Sharma, V., Gupta, M., Jangir, K., Chopra, P., & Pathak, N. (2023). The Impact of Post-Use Consumer Satisfaction on Smart Wearables Repurchase Intention in the Context of AI-Based Healthcare Information. In *Enhancing Customer Engagement Through Location-Based Marketing* (pp. 77–101). IGI Global. doi:10.4018/978-1-6684-8177-6.ch007

Shaydurova, A., Panova, S., Fedosova, R., & Zlotnikova, G. (2018). Investment attractiveness of "green" financial instruments. *Journal of Reviews on Global Economics*, *7*(Special Issue), 710–715. doi:10.6000/1929-7092.2018.07.65

Shen, H., Luo, T., Gao, Z., Zhang, X., Zhang, W., & Chuang, Y.-C. (2023). Digital financial inclusion and the urban–rural income gap in China: Empirical research based on the Theil index. *Ekonomska Istrazivanja*, *36*(3), 2156575. doi:10.1080/1331677X.2022.2156575

Shikweni, S., Schurink, W., & van Wyk, R. (2019). Talent Management in the South African Construction Industry. *SA Journal of Human Resource Management*, *17*(May). doi:10.4102ajhrm.v17i0.1094

Shrestha, A., Eshpeter, S., Li, N., Li, J., Nile, J. O., & Wang, G. (2022). Inclusion of forestry offsets in emission trading schemes: Insights from global experts. *Journal of Forestry Research*, *33*(1), 279–287. doi:10.100711676-021-01329-5

Shygun, M. M., & Muhomor, G. V. (2022). Possibilities of assessing receivables in the integrated reporting of the enterprise. *Proceedings of the 10th International Scientific and Practical Conference "Perspectives for the Development of Accounting and Analysis in the Context of European Integration*, (pp. 102-103). HNEU. http://repository.hneu.edu.ua/bitstream/ 123456789/ 27522/1/ %D0%A2%D0 %B5%D0%B7 %D0%B8%20- %D0%92%D0 %BD%D1%83 %D0%BA%D0%BE%D0%B2%D0%B0%20%D0%9D%D0%9C_%D0%9A%D0%B0%D0%BD%D0%B8%D0%B3%D1 %96%D0%BD %20_%D0%A1 %D0% 9C.pdf

Siddiqui, S., Johri, A., Shoeb, A., Saxena, K., Siddiqui, J. H., & Usmani, K. (2021). A study on the influence and impact of advertising to consumer purchase behavior in rural areas of India. *Academy of Strategic Management Journal*, *20*(5), 1–22.

Sideri, L. (2021). Leveraging CSR for Sustainability: Assessing Performance Implications of Sustainability Reporting in a National Business System. *Sustainability (Basel)*, *13*(1), 5987. doi:10.3390u13115987

Sigala, M. (2020). Artificial intelligence in hospitality and tourism: Applications, challenges, and future research agenda. *Journal of Hospitality Marketing & Management*, *29*(7), 821–826.

Şimandan, R., & Păun, C. (2021). The costs and trade-offs of green central banking: A framework for analysis. *Energies*, *14*(16), 5168. doi:10.3390/en14165168

Singh, N., Bathla, G., & Sharma, V. (2022). Task Scheduling Algorithm Based on Load Balancing and Activity based Costing Method in Cloud Computing. *2022 11th International Conference on System Modeling & Advancement in Research Trends (SMART)*, 429–432.

Singh, R. L., & Singh, P. K. (2017). Global Environmental Problems. *Principles and Applications of Environmental Biotechnology for a Sustainable Future*, 13–41. doi:10.1007/978-981-10-1866-4_2

Singh, V., Taneja, S., Singh, V., Singh, A., & Paul, H. L. (2021). Online advertising strategies in Indian and Australian e-commerce companies:: A comparative study. *Big Data Analytics for Improved Accuracy, Efficiency, and Decision Making in Digital Marketing*, 124–138. doi:10.4018/978-1-7998-7231-3.ch009

Singh, A., Sharma, S., Singh, A., Unanoğlu, M., & Taneja, S. (2023a). Cultural Marketing and Metaverse for Consumer Engagement. In *Cultural Marketing and Metaverse for Consumer Engagement*. IGI Global. doi:10.4018/978-1-6684-8312-1

Singhal, A., Dube, P., & Jain, V. K. (2022). Modelling barriers of artificial intelligence in banking sectors using total interpretive structural modelling. *International Journal of Applied Decision Sciences*, *15*(3), 311–335. doi:10.1504/IJADS.2022.122649

Singh, G. P., & Garg, D. K. (2022). Modified Partially Balanced Incomplete Block Designs Having Higher Associate Classes by using the Literals of K-Maps. *Far East Journal of Theoretical and Applied Sciences*, *1*, 25–32.

Singh, J. P. (2019). Development finance 2.0: Do participation and information technologies matter? *Review of International Political Economy*, *26*(5), 886–910. doi:10.1080/09692290.2019.1616600

Singh, S., & Srivastava, S. (2018). Moderating effect of product type on online shopping behaviour and purchase intention: An Indian perspective. *Cogent Arts & Humanities*, *5*(1), 1495043. doi:10.1080/23311983.2018.1495043

Smith, P., House, J. I., Bustamante, M., Sobocká, J., Harper, R., Pan, G., West, P. C., Clark, J. M., Adhya, T., Rumpel, C., Paustian, K., Kuikman, P., Cotrufo, M. F., Elliott, J. A., Mcdowell, R., Griffiths, R. I., Asakawa, S., Bondeau, A., Jain, A. K., & Pugh, T. A. M. (2016). Global change pressures on soils from land use and management. *Global Change Biology*, *22*(3), 1008–1028. doi:10.1111/gcb.13068 PMID:26301476

Sobti, N., Sharma, V., & Khanna, K. (2023). A Systematic Literature Review on Factors Affecting Customer Engagement in Mobile Applications. *Cultural Marketing and Metaverse for Consumer Engagement*, 12–25.

Soni, V. D. (2020). Emerging Roles of Artificial Intelligence in E-Commerce. *International Journal of Trend in Scientific Research and Development*, *4*(5), 223–225. doi:10.1201/9780429282829-12

Soro, K., & Senou, M. M. (2023). Digital financial inclusion and income inequality in WAEMU: What causality for what heterogeneity? *Cogent Economics & Finance*, *11*(2), 2242662. doi:10.1080/23322039.2023.2242662

Soundarrajan, P., & Vivek, N. (2016). Green finance for sustainable green economic growth in India. [Zemědělská Ekonomika]. *Zemedelská Ekonomika*, *62*(1), 35–44. doi:10.17221/174/2014-AGRICECON

Spiller, P. (2021). *Making supply-chain decarbonization happen*. McKinsey and Company. https://www.mckinsey.com/capabilities/operations/our-insights/making-supply-chain-decarbonization-happen

Srimannarayana, G., Lakshmi, V. V., Dondapati, A. S., Ratnakar, T., Dhanunjay, P., & Satyanarayana, P. (2023). Legal Blueprint For Clean Air: The Air (Prevention And Control Of Pollution) Act, 1981 In India. *Journal of Namibian Studies : History Politics Culture*, *35*, 691–712. doi:10.59670/JNS.V35I.3565

Srinvasrao, G. (2002). *Rural Marketing in India- A Case Study*. Anmol Publication P. Ltd.

Srivastava, A. K., Dharwal, M., & Sharma, A. (2022). Green financial initiatives for sustainable economic growth: A literature review. *Materials Today: Proceedings*, *49*, 3615–3618. doi:10.1016/j.matpr.2021.08.158

Standard for Social Responsibility (SA-8000). (2020). *Law*. Rada. https://zakon.rada.gov.ua/laws/show/n0015697-07#Text

Stanković, J. J., Marjanović, I., Papathanasiou, J., & Drezgić, S. (2021). Social, Economic and Environmental Sustainability of Port Regions: MCDM Approach in Composite Index Creation. *Journal of Marine Science and Engineering 2021, 9*(1), 74. doi:10.3390/jmse9010074

Stats, I.W. (2015). *Internet usage statistics: World internet users and population stats.*

Stewart, H., & Jürjens, J. (2018). Data security and consumer trust in FinTech innovation in Germany. *Information and Computer Security*, *26*(1), 109–128. doi:10.1108/ICS-06-2017-0039

Stojanović, B., Bozic, J., Hofer-Schmitz, K., Nahrgang, K., Weber, A., Badii, A., Sundaram, M., Jordan, E., & Runevic, J. (2021). Follow the Trail: Machine Learning For Fraud Detection In FinTech Applications. *Sensors (Basel)*, *5*(21), 1594. doi:10.339021051594 PMID:33668773

Sultana. (2018). Analyzing the Impact of Social Media. *Global Journal of Management and Business Research: E Marketing, 18*(2), 1-9 https://www.researchgate.net/profile/Nahida-Sultana-3/publication/326327402_Analyzing_the_Impact_of_Social_Media_A_Study_on_Online_Shoppers_of_Apparel_Companies_in_Bangladesh/links/5b46146a458515b4f663dd84/Analyzing-the-Impact-of-Social-Media-A-Study-on-Online-Shoppers-of-Apparel-Companies-in-Bangladesh.pdf

Sun, H., Rabbani, M. R., Ahmad, N., Sial, M. S., Guping, C., Zia-Ud-din, M., & Fu, Q. (2020). CSR, Co-Creation and Green Consumer Loyalty: Are Green Banking Initiatives Important? A Moderated Mediation Approach from an Emerging Economy. *Sustainability, 12*(24), 10688. doi:10.3390/su122410688

Sunil, A., & Momany, M. T. (2020). Impact of green finance on the economy of developing countries. [IJM]. *International Journal of Management, 11*(8), 1112–1120.

Sun, Y., Guan, W., Jiang, H., & Yang, J. (2023). How does green economic recovery impact social and financial performance? *Economic Change and Restructuring, 56*(2), 859–878. doi:10.100710644-022-09453-w

Sun, Y., Zhang, J., Xiong, Y., & Zhu, G. (2014). Data Security and Privacy in Cloud Computing. *International Journal of Distributed Sensor Networks, 10*(7), 190903. doi:10.1155/2014/190903

Suryono, R. R., Budi, I., & Purwandari, B. (2021). Detection of fintech P2P lending issues in Indonesia. *Heliyon, 7*(4), e06782. doi:10.1016/j.heliyon.2021.e06782 PMID:33981873

Swailes, S., Downs, Y., & Orr, K. (2014). Conceptualising Inclusive Talent Management: Potential, Possibilities and Practicalities. *Human Resource Development International, 17*(5), 529–544. doi:10.1080/13678868.2014.954188

Tagger, S. S., & Gupta, M. (2020). A study of the relationship between total quality management and business performance in the banking sector. *International Journal of Business Competition and Growth, 7*(2), 118. doi:10.1504/IJBCG.2020.111943

Taghizadeh-Hesary, F., & Yoshino, N. (2019). The way to induce private participation in green finance and investment. *Finance Research Letters, 31*, 98–103. doi:10.1016/j.frl.2019.04.016

Taghizadeh-Hesary, F., & Yoshino, N. (2020). Sustainable Solutions for Green Financing and Investment in Renewable Energy Projects. *Energies, 13*(4), 788. doi:10.3390/en13040788

Talukder, M., Kabir, F., Muhsina, K., & Das, I. R. (2023). Emerging Concepts of Artificial Intelligence in the Hotel Indusatry: A Conceptual Paper. *International Journal of Research Publication and Reviews.*

Talukder, M. B. (2021). An assessment of the roles of the social network in the development of the Tourism Industry in Bangladesh. *International Journal of Business, Law, and Education, 2*(3), 85–93. doi:10.56442/ijble.v2i3.21

Talukder, M. B., Kumar, S., Sood, K., & Grima, S. (2023). Information Technology, Food Service Quality and Restaurant Revisit Intention. *International Journal of Sustainable Development and Planning, 18*(1), 295–303. doi:10.18280/ijsdp.180131

Taneja, S., Bhatnagar, M., Kumar, P., & Grima, S. (2023). A Panel Analysis of the Effectiveness of the Asset Management in Indian Agricultural Companies. *International Journal of Sustainable Development and Planning, 18*(3), 653–660. doi:10.18280/ijsdp.180301

Taneja, S., Bhatnagar, M., Kumar, P., & Rupeika-Apoga, R. (2023). India's Total Natural Resource Rents (NRR) and GDP: An Augmented Autoregressive Distributed Lag (ARDL) Bound Test. *Journal of Risk and Financial Management, 16*(2), 91. doi:10.3390/jrfm16020091

Taneja, S., Grima, S., Kumar, P., & Ozen, E. (2023). Special Issue: 'Green Asset and Risk Management for Promoting Sustainable Entrepreneurship in the Building of the Green Economy.'. *International Journal of Technology Management & Sustainable Development*, *22*(2), 127–130. doi:10.1386/tmsd_00071_7

Taneja, S., Gupta, M., Bhushan, P., Bhatnagar, M., & Singh, A. (2023). Cultural marketing in the digital era. In *Cultural Marketing and Metaverse for Consumer Engagement*. IGI Global. doi:10.4018/978-1-6684-8312-1.ch008

Taneja, S., Jaggi, P., Jewandah, S., & Ozen, E. (2022). Role of Social Inclusion in Sustainable Urban Developments: An Analyse by PRISMA Technique. *International Journal of Design & Nature and Ecodynamics*, *17*(6), 937–942. doi:10.18280/ijdne.170615

Taneja, S., Kaur, S., & Özen, E. (2022). Using green finance to promote global growth in a sustainable way. *International Journal of Green Economics*, *16*(3), 246–257. doi:10.1504/IJGE.2022.128930

Taneja, S., & Ozen, E. (2023). Impact of the European Green Deal (EDG) on the Agricultural Carbon (CO2) Emission in Turkey. *International Journal of Sustainable Development and Planning*, *18*(3), 715–727. doi:10.18280/ijsdp.180307

Taneja, S., & Özen, E. (2023). To Analyse the Relationship between Bank's Green Financing and Environmental Performance. *International Journal of Electronic Finance*, *12*(2), 163–175. doi:10.1504/IJEF.2023.129919

Taneja, S., & Sharma, V. (2023). Role of beaconing marketing in improving customer buying experience. In *Enhancing Customer Engagement Through Location-Based Marketing*. IGI Global. doi:10.4018/978-1-6684-8177-6.ch012

Tang, T., Ran, G., & Ran, X. (2023). Analyzing the effect of digital financial inclusion on urban private sector employment in China. *Applied Economics Letters*, 1–5. doi:10.1080/13504851.2023.2206614

Tao, Z., & Chao, J. (2023). A bibliometric and visualized analysis of research on green finance and energy in a global perspective. *Research in Globalization*, 100156.

Taplin, R. (2023). Artificial intelligence, intellectual property, cyber risk and robotics: A new digital age. In *Artificial Intelligence, Intellectual Property, Cyber Risk and Robotics: A New Digital Age*. Taylor and Francis. doi:10.4324/9780367857561

Taylor, M. R. (2012). Innovation under cap-and-trade programs. *Proceedings of the National Academy of Sciences of the United States of America*, *109*(13), 4804–4809. doi:10.1073/pnas.1113462109 PMID:22411797

Taylor, S., & Todd, P. A. (1995). Understanding information technology usage: A test of competing models. *Information Systems Research*, *6*(2), 144–176. doi:10.1287/isre.6.2.144

Thakor, A. V. (2020). Fintech and banking: What do we know? *Journal of Financial Intermediation*, *41*(November), 100833. doi:10.1016/j.jfi.2019.100833

Thalladi. (2022). Rural Communication. *International Journal of Research*, *9*(2), 371-389. https://www.ijrjournal.com/index.php/ijr/article/view/377

Thomas, J. H., M. Alonso Jr., and L. N. Cain (2019). The state of robotics and AI in the hospitality sector: from science fiction to science fact. *Journal of Hospitality and Tourism Technology, 10*(4), 624-650.

Tillotson, P., Slade, R., Staffell, I., & Halttunen, K. (2023). Deactivating climate activism? The seven strategies oil and gas majors use to counter rising shareholder action. *Energy Research & Social Science*, *103*, 103190. doi:10.1016/j.erss.2023.103190

Torvanger, A., Dejonckheere, S., Singh, T., & Pruthi, A. (2019). The state of tracking financial flows under the Paris Agreement - A primer for policy makers in India. *22*. https://pub.cicero.oslo.no/cicero-xmlui/handle/11250/2618660

Tu, C. A., Rasoulinezhad, E., & Sarker, T. (2020). Investigating solutions for the development of a green bond market: Evidence from analytic hierarchy process. *Finance Research Letters*, *34*, 101457. doi:10.1016/j.frl.2020.101457

Tufail, M., Song, L., Umut, A., Ismailova, N., & Kuldasheva, Z. (2022). Does financial inclusion promote a green economic system? Evaluating the role of energy efficiency. *Ekonomska Istrazivanja*, *35*(1), 6780–6800. doi:10.1080/1331677X.2022.2053363

Turner, B. L., & Roger, E. (2022). A framework for vulnerability analysis in sustainability science. *Proceedings of the National Academy of Sciences of the United States of America*, *14*(100), 8074–8079.

Tvaronavičienė, M. (2023). Towards Renewable Energy: Opportunities and Challenges. *Energies*, *16*(5), 2269. doi:10.3390/en16052269

Tyagi, S., Garg, N., & Paudel, R. (2014). Environmental degradation: Causes and consequences. *European researcher*, *81*(8-2), 1491.

U.S. Securities and Exchange Commission. (2022). *Factsheet: Enhancement and Standardization of Climate-Related Disclosures*. US Securities and Exchange Commission.

Udeagha, M. C., & Muchapondwa, E. (2023). Green finance, fintech, and environmental sustainability: Fresh policy insights from the BRICS nations. *International Journal of Sustainable Development and World Ecology*, *30*(6), 1–17. doi:10.1080/13504509.2023.2183526

Udeagha, M. C., & Ngepah, N. (2023). The drivers of environmental sustainability in BRICS economies: Do green finance and fintech matter? *World Development Sustainability*, *3*, 100096. doi:10.1016/j.wds.2023.100096

Ulrich, S., Trench, A., & Steffen, H. (2022). Gold mining greenhouse gas emissions, abatement measures, and the impact of a carbon price. *Journal of Cleaner Production*, *340*, 130851. doi:10.1016/j.jclepro.2022.130851

Una, B. K., & Prabowo, H. Y. (2022). Fintech lending fraud prevention strategy: A case study. *Journal of Contemporary Accounting*, 37-52.

Unruh, G. C. (2000). Understanding carbon lock-in. *Energy Policy*, *28*(12), 817–830. doi:10.1016/S0301-4215(00)00070-7

Usman, M., Makhdum, M. S. A., & Kousar, R. (2021). Does financial inclusion, renewable and non-renewable energy utilization accelerate ecological footprints and economic growth? Fresh evidence from 15 highest emitting countries. *Sustainable Cities and Society*, *65*, 102590. doi:10.1016/j.scs.2020.102590

Vadrale, S. K. (2016). *Green Banking Initiatives By Indian Public and Private Sector Banks*. *9*(February), 1–14. https://www.researchgate.net/publication/305547284

Valavan, M., & Rita, S. (2023). Predictive-Analysis-based Machine Learning Model for Fraud Detection with Boosting Classifiers. *Computer Systems Science and Engineering*, *45*(1), 231–245. doi:10.32604/csse.2023.026508

Valentin, M. A., & Valentin, C. (2019). TALENT MANAGEMENT BEST PRACTICES Harnessing the Dragon for Competitive Advantage. In K M Dirani, F M Nafukho, and B J Irby, (eds.) Global Issues And Talent Development: Perspectives From Countries Around The World. Information Age Publishing.

Van Kien, P., Ou, J. P., Sadiq, D. M., Nguyen, T. T. H., Huy, P. Q., & Tran, T. K. (2023). What role financial inclusion, green trade and natural resources utilization play in ASEAN economic growth: Evidence from post COVID era. *Resources Policy*, *85*, 103884. doi:10.1016/j.resourpol.2023.103884

van Kooten, C., & Johnston, C. (2016). The Economics of Forest Carbon Offsets. *Annual Review of Resource Economics*, *8*(1), 227–2246. doi:10.1146/annurev-resource-100815-095548

Varma, P., Nijjer, S., Sood, K., Grima, S., & Rupeika-Apoga, R. (2022). Thematic Analysis of Financial Technology (Fintech) Influence on the Banking Industry. *Risks*, *10*(10), 186. doi:10.3390/risks10100186

Velt, P. (2022). *Archival research on integrated reporting: a systematic review of main drivers and the impact of integrated reporting on firm value // Journal of Management and Governance, No. 26.* URL., doi:10.100710997-021-09582-w

Ventre, I., & Kolbe, D. (2020). The impact of perceived usefulness of online reviews, trust and perceived risk on online purchase intention in emerging markets: A Mexican perspective. *Journal of International Consumer Marketing*, *32*(4), 287–299. doi:10.1080/08961530.2020.1712293

Verma, A. K., Dash, R. R., & Bhunia, P. (2012). A review on chemical coagulation/flocculation technologies for removal of colour from textile wastewaters. *Journal of Environmental Management*, *93*(1), 154–168. doi:10.1016/j.jenvman.2011.09.012 PMID:22054582

Villar, A. S., & Khan, N. (2021). Robotic process automation in banking industry: a case study on Deutsche Bank. *Journal of Banking and Financial Technology 2021, 5*(1), 71–86. doi:10.1007/s42786-021-00030-9

Villarini, G., Smith, J. A., Serinaldi, F., & Ntelekos, A. A. (2011). Analyses of seasonal and annual maximum daily discharge records for central Europe. *Journal of Hydrology (Amsterdam)*, *399*(3–4), 299–312. doi:10.1016/j.jhydrol.2011.01.007

Visvizi, A. (2022). Sustainability in International Business: Talent Management, Market Entry Strategies, Competitiveness. *Sustainability (Basel)*, *14*(16), 10191. Advance online publication. doi:10.3390u141610191

Volz, U. (2017). *On the role of central banks in enhancing green finance*. UN Environment Inquiry/CIGI Research Convening.

Vyas, V., & Raitani, S. (2014). Drivers of customers' switching behaviour in Indian banking industry. *International Journal of Bank Marketing*, *32*(4), 321–342. doi:10.1108/IJBM-04-2013-0033

Wagner Mainardes, E., de Almeida, C. M., & de-Oliveira, M. (2019). e-Commerce: An analysis of the factors that antecede purchase intentions in an emerging market. *Journal of International Consumer Marketing*, *31*(5), 447–468. doi:10.1080/08961530.2019.1605643

Wakefield, A., Loken, B., & Hornik, C. (2014). *Use of mass media campaigns to change health behavior*. NCBI. https://www.ncbi.nlm.nih.gov/pmc/articles/PMC4248563/

Wakelin, S., Paul, T., & Manley, B. (2021). *The potential contribution from increased sequestration in pre1990 forests to New Zealand's Paris Agreement 2030 target.* (MPI Technical Paper No: 2021/28). Ministry for Primary Industries. https://www.mpi.govt.nz/dmsdocument/47980-The-potential-contribution-from-increased-sequestration-in-pre-1990-forests-to-New-Zealands-Paris-Agreement-2030-target

Wang, C., Nie, P., Peng, D., & Li, Z. (2017). Green insurance subsidy for promoting clean production innovation. *Journal of Cleaner Production*, *148*, 111–117. doi:10.1016/j.jclepro.2017.01.145

Wang, K. H., Zhao, Y. X., Jiang, C. F., & Li, Z. Z. (2022). Does green finance inspire sustainable development? Evidence from a global perspective. *Economic Analysis and Policy*, *75*, 412–426. doi:10.1016/j.eap.2022.06.002

Wang, L., Li, S., & Gao, S. (2014). Do greenhouse gas emissions affect financial performance? An empirical examination of Australian public firms. *Business Strategy and the Environment*, *23*(8), 505–519. doi:10.1002/bse.1790

Wang, S., Sun, L., & Iqbal, S. (2022). Green financing role on renewable energy dependence and energy transition in E7 economies. *Renewable Energy*, *200*, 1561–1572. doi:10.1016/j.renene.2022.10.067

Wang, W., Tian, Z., Xi, W., Tan, Y. R., & Deng, Y. (2021). The influencing factors of China's green building development: An analysis using RBF-WINGS method. *Building and Environment*, *188*, 107425. doi:10.1016/j.buildenv.2020.107425

Wang, Y. S., Wu, S. C., Lin, H. H., Wang, Y. M., & He, T. R. (2012). Determinants of user adoption of web''Automatic Teller Machines': An integrated model of'Transaction Cost Theory and Innovation Diffusion Theory'. *Service Industries Journal*, *32*(9), 1505–1525. doi:10.1080/02642069.2010.531271

Wang, Y., Kim, D.-K., & Jeong, D. (2020). A Survey of the Application of Blockchain in Multiple Fields of Financial Services. *Journal of Information Processing Systems*, *16*(4), 935–958. doi:10.3745/JIPS.04.0185

Wang, Y., Wu, Z., & Zhang, G. (2022). Firms and climate change: A review of carbon risk in corporate finance. *Carbon Neutrality*, *1*(1), 6. doi:10.100743979-022-00005-9

Wang, Y., & Zhi, Q. (2016). The Role of Green Finance in Environmental Protection: Two Aspects of Market Mechanism and Policies. *Energy Procedia*, *104*, 311–316. doi:10.1016/j.egypro.2016.12.053

Wang, Z., Yao-Ping Peng, M., Anser, M. K., & Chen, Z. (2023). Research on the impact of green finance and renewable energy on energy efficiency: The case study E−7 economies. *Renewable Energy*, *205*, 166–173. doi:10.1016/j.renene.2022.12.077

Wannan, O. (2022). Start-up CarbonCrop pauses new carbon offsets after questions raised. *Stuff*. https://www.stuff.co.nz/environment/climate-news/129091128/startup-carboncrop-pauses-new-carbon-offsets-after-questions-raised?rm=a

Wanyama, D., & Mwikya, J. (2022). *Internal Control Measures On Fraud Detection and Prevention in Fintech Companies in Kenya*. Kirinyaga University

Weber, O., Fenchel, M., & Scholz, R. W. (2008). Empirical analysis of the integration of environmental risks into the credit risk management process of European banks. *Business Strategy and the Environment*, *17*(3), 149–159. doi:10.1002/bse.507

Wei, Y., Zhu, R., & Tan, L. (2022). Emission trading scheme, technological innovation, and competitiveness: Evidence from China's thermal power enterprises. *Journal of Environmental Management*, *320*, 115874. doi:10.1016/j.jenvman.2022.115874 PMID:35947908

Weston, P., & Nnadi, M. (2023). Evaluation of strategic and financial variables of corporate sustainability and ESG policies on corporate finance performance. *Journal of Sustainable Finance & Investment*, *13*(2), 1058–1074. Advance online publication. doi:10.1080/20430795.2021.1883984

Wronka, C. (2023). Financial crime in the decentralized finance ecosystem: New challenges for compliance. *Journal of Financial Crime*, *30*(1), 97–113. doi:10.1108/JFC-09-2021-0218

Wu, P.-C., Liu, S.-Y., & Huang, C.-W. (2022). The Impact of FinTech Index on P2P Lending Rate. *Review of Integrative Business and Economics Research*, *11*(2), 79–94. https://www.scopus.com/inward/record.uri?eid=2-s2.0-85130418723&partnerID=40&md5=350c589f0a8bf47b93da12c42aa01617

Xiang, Z., Du, Q., Ma, Y., Fan, W., & Li, X. (2017). A comparative analysis of major online review platforms: Implications for social media analytics in hospitality and tourism. *Tourism Management*, *58*, 51–65. doi:10.1016/j.tourman.2016.10.001

Xue, Y., Temeljotov-Salaj, A., Engebø, A., & Lohne, J. (2020). Multi-sector partnerships in the urban development context: A scoping review. *Journal of Cleaner Production*, *268*, 122291. doi:10.1016/j.jclepro.2020.122291

Xu, F., Buhalis, D., & Weber, J. (2017). Serious games and the gamification of tourism. *Tourism Management*, *60*, 244–256. doi:10.1016/j.tourman.2016.11.020

Yan, C., Siddik, A. B., Yong, L., Dong, Q., Zheng, G. W., & Rahman, M. N. (2022). A two-staged SEM-artificial neural network approach to analyze the impact of FinTech adoption on the sustainability performance of banking firms: The mediating effect of green finance and innovation. *Systems*, *10*(5), 148. doi:10.3390ystems10050148

Yang, L., & Geng, Z. (2022). Impact of Digital Financial Inclusion on Optimization of Employment Structure: Evidence from China. *Applied Economics*, *54*(57), 6625–6638. doi:10.1080/00036846.2022.2078779

Yan, Y., Ibrahim, L. R., Al-Faryan, M. A. S., & Oke, D. M. (2023). Embracing Eco-Digitalization and Green Finance Policies for Sustainable Environment: Do the Engagements of Multinational Corporations Make or Mar the Target for Selected MENA Countries? *Sustainability (Basel)*, *15*(12046), 1–18. doi:10.3390u151512046

Yoon, K.-S., & Jun, J. (2019). Liability And Antifraud Investment In Fintech Retail Payment Services. *Contemporary Economic Policy*, *37*(1), 181–194. doi:10.1111/coep.12281

Zerbib, O. D. (2019). The effect of pro-environmental preferences on bond prices: Evidence from green bonds. *Journal of Banking & Finance*, *98*, 39–60. doi:10.1016/j.jbankfin.2018.10.012

Zhang, H., Wu, C., Zhang, Z., Zhu, Y., Lin, H., Zhang, Z., & Smola, A. (2022). Resnest: Split-attention networks. In *Proceedings of the IEEE/CVF conference on computer vision and pattern recognition* (pp. 2736-2746). https://www.unep.org/explore-topics/green-economy/what-we-do/finance-initiative,2022. https://unglobalcompact.org/what-is-gc/mission/principles

Zhang, X., Wang, Z., Zhong, X., Yang, S., & Siddik, A. B. (2022). Do Green Banking Activities Improve the Banks' Environmental Performance? The Mediating Effect of Green Financing. *Sustainability 2022, 14*(2), 989. doi:10.3390/su14020989

Zhang, X., Zhou, C., & Zhang, S. (2020). The Environmental, Social and Governance (ESG) Responsibilities of Landscape Architecture Firms. In *E3S Web of Conferences* (*Vol. 143*, p. 02045). EDP Sciences.

Zhang, A., Wang, S., & Liu, B. (2022). How to control air pollution with economic means? Exploration of China's green finance policy. *Journal of Cleaner Production*, *353*, 131664. doi:10.1016/j.jclepro.2022.131664

Zhang, D., Mohsin, M., Rasheed, A. K., Chang, Y., & Taghizadeh-Hesary, F. (2021). Public spending and green economic growth in BRI region: Mediating role of green finance. *Energy Policy*, *153*, 112256. doi:10.1016/j.enpol.2021.112256

Zhang, H., & Li, X. (2021). Artificial intelligence, robots, and service automation in hospitality and tourism. *Journal of Hospitality Marketing & Management*, *30*(1), 78–82.

Zhang, M., Li, X., & Hsu, C. H. (2021). Leveraging artificial intelligence for smart tourism destination marketing. *Journal of Travel Research*, 00472875211005936.

Zhang, S., Xu, C., Larrimore, K. E., & Ng, D. T. (2017). Slp1-Emp65: A guardian factor that protects folding polypeptides from promiscuous degradation. *Cell*, *171*(2), 346–357. doi:10.1016/j.cell.2017.08.036 PMID:28919078

Zhang, X. (2014). Reference-dependent electric vehicle production strategy considering subsidies and consumer trade-offs. *Energy Policy*, *67*, 422–430. doi:10.1016/j.enpol.2013.12.028

Zhao, H. (2023). Risk Management of Supply Chain Green Finance Based on Sustainable Ecological Environment. *Sustainability (Basel)*, *15*(7707), 1–15. https://www.mdpi.com/journal/sustainability. doi:10.3390u15097707

Zheng, G. W., Siddik, A. B., Masukujjaman, M., & Fatema, N. (2021). Factors Affecting the Sustainability Performance of Financial Institutions in Bangladesh: The Role of Green Finance. *Sustainability 2021, 13*(18), 10165. doi:10.3390/su131810165

Zheng, G.-W., Siddik, A. B., Masukujjaman, M., Fatema, N., & Alam, S. S. (2021). Green Finance Development in Bangladesh: The Role of Private Commercial Banks (PCBs). *Sustainability (Basel)*, *13*(2), 795. doi:10.3390u13020795

Zhou, B., & Zhang, C. (2023). When green finance meets banking competition: Evidence from hard-to-abate enterprises of China. *Pacific-Basin Finance Journal*, *78*, 101954. doi:10.1016/j.pacfin.2023.101954

Zhou, G., Zhu, J., & Luo, S. (2022). The impact of fintech innovation on green growth in China: Mediating effect of green finance. *Ecological Economics*, *193*, 107308. doi:10.1016/j.ecolecon.2021.107308

Zymovets, V. (2019). The excessive receivables of the enterprises: causes and consequences for the financial system of Ukraine. *Economy and Forecasting*, 5-18. http://econ-forecast.org.ua/docs/EP_19_2_05_en.pdf

About the Contributors

Sanjay Taneja is an Associate Professor at DOMS, Graphic Era Deemed to be University, Dehradun, India. He received his PG degrees in Management (Gold Medalist) (Finance) from Chaudhary Devi University, Sirsa, India in 2012. He earned his Doctor of Philosophy (Sponsored By ICSSR) in Banking and Finance entitled "An Appraisal of financial performance of Indian Banking Sector: A Compartative study of Public, Private and Foreign banks in 2016 from Chaudhary Devi University, Sirsa, India. Before joining Chandigarh University in Oct. 2021, Sanjay had served three organisations with a total experience of 9+ yrs. He has published various articles in various journals and presented papers at various international conferences. His research mainly focuses on regulations, Banking and Finance in insurance, insurance management, economics and management of innovation in insurance. She has edited 3 books with international and national publishers. He has over 30 publications in his account, and his research works have been published in reputed journals, i.e. Springer, Elsevier, Taylor & Francis, Hindawi and IGI Global, with high impact factor and SCI/SCIE/Scopus/WoS indexing.

Pawan Kumar has academic experience of 15 years and have done hus phd from Kurukshetra university, Kurukshetra.He have done 20 publications in national and international journals and had presented papers in 15 National & International seminars and confrences.

Simon Grima, is the the Deputy Dean of the Faculty of Economics, Management and Accountancy, Associate Professor and the Head of the Department of Insurance and Risk Management. Simon is also a Professor at the University of Latvia, Faculty of Business, Management and Economics. He is the President of the Malta Association of Risk Management (MARM) and President of the Malta Association of Compliance Officers (MACO). Moreover, he chairs the Scientific Education Committee of the Public Risk Management Organization (PRIMO) and the Federation of European Risk Managers (FERMA). He has over 30 years of experience varied between Financial Services, academia and public entities. He has acted as co-chair and is a member of the scientific program committee on some international conferences and is a chief editor, editor and review editor of some Journals and Book Series. He has been awarded outstanding reviewer for Journal of Financial Regulation and Compliance in the 2017 and 2022 Emerald Literati Awards. Moreover, Simon acts as an Independent Director sits on Committees and carries out duties as a Compliance Officer, Internal Auditor and Risk Manager.

Ercan Özen is working as Asso. Prof in Department of Finance and Banking, USAK University, Turkey

Kiran Sood is a professor at Chitkara Business School, Chitkara University, Punjab, India. She is also an affiliate professor at the University of Malta. She received her undergraduate and postgraduate degrees in commerce from Panjab University, respectively, in 2002 and 2004. She earned her Master of Philosophy degree in 2008 and Doctor of Philosophy in Commerce with a concentration on Product Portfolio Performance of General Insurance Companies in 2017 from Panjabi University, Patiala, India. Before joining Chitkara University in July 2019, Kiran had served four organisations with a total experience of 19 years. She has published various articles in various journals and presented papers at various international conferences. She serves as an Editor of the refereed journal, particularly the IJBST International Journal of BioSciences and Technology, the International Journal of Research Culture Society and The Journal of Corporate Governance, Insurance, and Risk Management (JCGIRM), 2021. Her research mainly focuses on regulations, marketing and finance in insurance, insurance management, economics and management of innovation in insurance. She has edited more than ten books with various international publishers such as Emerald, CRC, Taylors & Francis, AAP, WILEY scrivener, IET, Rivers Publishers, and IEEE.

* * *

Kapil Kumar Aggarwal is an Associate Professor of Finance at the University School of Business, Chandigarh University. He has earned PhD, M. Phil, MFC, MBA & M. Com. He has more than 16 years of teaching and research experience. His research experience is inclusive of 18 research papers published in National journals, International Journals, Edited Books, ABDC-listed journals, Scopus Indexed, Web of Sciences and Peer Reviewed journals, 32 research papers presented in National/International conferences and two books published in his account. His teaching interest is primarily focused on finance, management sciences, quantitative techniques, business mathematics, and business statistics. He is the reviewer of the International Journal of Educational Development Journal, indexed in Scopus Elsevier, Social Sciences Citation Index and Educational and Information Technologies Journal indexed in SCOPUS, Social Science Citation Index, and UGC-CARE List (India) and Editorial Board member of International Journal of Accounting, Finance and Risk Management (IJAFRM). He is also a pioneer in the field of SPSS and R and has delivered multiple lectures and workshops on the same, which has helped in the training of fellow colleagues and professors. He is a lifetime member of the Indian Commerce Association. Dr. Kapil also has excellent management knowledge, networking skills, and the ability to build strong professional relationships with both students and colleagues. He has also been instrumental in supervising, advising, and mentoring research scholars, teaching assistants, and graduate and post-graduate students.

Mukul Bhatnagar is an accomplished academic professional with five years of invaluable experience in the field of commerce and finance. As an esteemed academician, his dedication to research and his commitment to promoting sustainable business practices are evident in his extensive body of work. Mr. Bhatnagar's prolific research journey has resulted in the publication of twelve indexed papers in reputable databases such as SCOPUS, Web of Science (WOS), and ABDC. Additionally, his contributions have been recognized by UGC-CARE with three publications, further establishing his research prowess. His insightful work extends beyond the academic realm, with four other publications to his name. In the realm of innovation, Mr. Bhatnagar boasts two published patents, demonstrating his ability to bridge theory and practical application. His dedication to staying at the forefront of industry trends is evidenced by his attainment of two Google certifications and thirteen Elsevier certifications. Mukul Bhatnagar is not only a prolific researcher but also an engaging educator. He has presented his research findings at both national and international levels, with an impressive tally of five national and thirteen international paper presentations. His expertise extends to the publication of three book chapters and two books, making his knowledge accessible to a wide audience. Beyond academia, Mukul Bhatnagar has also ventured into the digital realm with his YouTube channel, "MUKUL BHATNAGAR," which has garnered an impressive 4,15,000 footprints, showcasing his commitment to knowledge dissemination. In terms of scholarly impact, Mr. Bhatnagar's citations reflect the significance of his contributions, with 44 citations since 2018. His h-index of 4 and i10-index of 2 underline his influence in his field. As a dynamic and forward-thinking academic, Mukul Bhatnagar continues to inspire and drive innovation in the world of commerce and finance. His dedication to research, commitment to education, and passion for sustainable practices make him a valuable asset to the academic community and beyond. His role as an Editor at the "International Journal of Economics, Finance, and Management Sciences" further solidifies his standing in the scholarly world.

Padam Bhushan is an Associate Professor, Chandigarh University, Punjab.

Chandan Gupta is Sr. Assistant Professor, Department of Commerce, Graphic Era Deemed to be University, Dehradun, India. He holds a master degree in commerce and management and earned his Doctorate in management. He has also qualified UGC NET in Commerce. He has been teaching marketing, accounting and finance in several universities and has gained an experience of 12 years in academics and teaching. He is supervising 3 Ph.D. research scholars under him, he has published several research papers and Book chapter in the leading journals and conferences. Dr. Gupta also has industry experience and having worked in marketing and insurance sector. He is appreciated to translate academic research into practical applications.

Priya Jindal is currently working as an Associate Professor at Chitkara Business School, Chitkara University, Punjab, India and holds a master degree in commerce and economics. She earned her doctorate in management. She has contributed more than 16 years in teaching. She supervised four Ph.D. research scholars and two M.Phil candidates.There are numerous research papers to her credit in leading journals among them seven research paper has been published in Scopus Indexed Journal. Her areas of research included Banking, Finance and insurance. She has filed more than 21 patents and one copyright. She is the editor of two books under IGI publications and the book got indexed in Scopus.

Firoj Kabir is an accomplished author, researcher and Lecturer of the Department of "Tourism and Hospitality Management" of Daffodil Institute of IT (DIIT) with a strong academic background in Tourism and Hospitality Management in Bangladesh. His passion lies in exploring the intersection of travel and culture. His diverse areas of interest include Archaeological tourism, Sustainable tourism, and the unique characteristics of Generation Z travelers. Through his extensive research and insightful writing, He sheds light on the intricate connections between historical sites, responsible tourism, and the evolving preferences of the next generation of travelers. His work not only enriches the field of tourism but also inspires readers to engage with the world around them in meaningful and responsible ways.

Fahmida Kaiser is a distinguished academic figure in the field of tourism and hospitality management. As a Lecturer at the Department of Tourism and Hospitality Management at Daffodil Institute of IT, she has dedicated her career to advancing knowledge in the intersection of tourism and sustainability. With a passion for exploring the multifaceted relationship between tourism and sustainable practices, Her research has not only contributed to the academic community but also holds significant implications for the global tourism industry. Her commitment to shedding light on the importance of responsible and eco-conscious tourism practices has garnered recognition from both peers and students alike.

Preet Kanwal has been teaching the students of post-graduation for the last 2 decades. After completing her Ph.D. from IK Gujral PTU, India, she joined the School of Management, University of Quebec in Montreal, Canada as a Post Doctoral Fellow. She has also international experience of teaching to students of MBA from Victoria University, Australia, and Sunway University, Malaysia.

Mohammad Kashif is assistant professor in the area of finance, economics and research. He has several publications indexed in WoS, Scopus and ABDC. He authored a book titled Financial Management for undergraduate students. He is guiding PhD scholars in his area of expertise. Besides he is a member of several professional bodies at university level. He has been awarded research and innovation award by IIMT University, India.

Jaspreet Kaur is currently working as an Assistant Professor in University Business School, Chandigarh University, Mohali, Punjab. She is a post graduate (MBA-H.R) from Panjab University, Chandigarh. She has also qualified UGC NET JRF in Human Resource Management/Labour and Social Welfare and is currently pursuing PhD in Business Management from Chandigarh University, Mohali. She has over 8 years of experience in academic and administrative assignments. She also received 'Best Teacher of the Department Award' in the year 2019 and 2021 in the field of imparting quality education. Her research interests include Employee Engagement, Management of Organizational Change and Organization Development. She has published several research papers and articles in reputed international and national journals and has presented papers in various national and international conferences. She also contributed one edited book and 10 book chapters on various topics.

Rumit Kaur is a Research Scholar of Management at Chandigarh University, Mohali. She holds a Master's in MBA (Finance and Marketing) from Punjabi University, Patiala. With almost 4 years 9 Months of experience in the Industrial Sector and 5 years 2 Months of teaching experience at an A+ Accredited (NAAC) Institute, her research interests include (but not limited to) Finance and Marketing.

Sanjeev Kumar is an accomplished expert in Food and Beverage. He currently holds the positions of Professor at the Lovely Professional University, Punjab, India. With over a decade of experience in the field, food Service Industry, his research focuses on Alcoholic beverages, Event management and Sustainable Management Practices, Metaverse and Artificial Intelligence. He has published more than 35 research papers, articles and chapters in Scopus Indexed, UGC Approved and peer reviewed Journals and books. Dr. Sanjeev Kumar participated and acted as resource person in various National and International conferences, seminars, research workshops and industry talks and his work has been widely cited.

K. K. Mishra is working as a Professor of Marketing at the University School of Business, Chandigarh University, Chandigarh. He has published 26 national and international research papers including three in Scopus-indexed journals and presented 26 papers at national and international conferences. He has 23 years of teaching and research experience. He did his PhD in Strategy formulation for marketing of services in rural Uttar Pradesh from Uttar Pradesh Rajarshi Tandon University, Allahabad. He has qualified for UGC – NET in Management twice.

Amar Kumar Mishra has done PhD in HR, MBA (OB & HR), M.Com from the University of Burdwan (West Bengal). Besides he has qualified UGC NET in Management, Commerce and HR. Dr. Mishra has got experience of more than 20 years in academics. At present Dr. Mishra is rendering his services to Graphic Era (Deemed to be) University. Dehradun as Professor in the Department of Commerce. Dr. Mishra has published more than 100 papers in various journals including 22 research articles in Scopus indexed journals; An expert in SPSS and AMOS, Dr. Mishra has conducted more than three dozen workshops on Research Methodology in various colleges and universities across India such as Delhi University, Lucknow Central University, Punjabi University, Patyala, JIS University, Kolkata, IMS Ghaziabad to name a few. He has also conducted two MDP at Petronet LNG, Dahej, Gujrat. Dr. Mishra has guided two scholars for PhD and is presently guiding 8 scholars for PhD.

Hryhorii Mukhomor is a PhD student of the Accounting and Consulting Department Kyiv National Economic University named after Vadym Hetman, Kyiv, Ukraine.

Nitin Pathak is working as Head of Commerce Department of Chandigarh University.

Andre Poyser is currently pursing doctoral studies at the University of Otago. A native of Jamaica, Andre's research has focused on indigenous finance, sustainability and climate finance. Andre holds a Master of Applied Finance from the Auckland University of Technology.

Syed Noorul Shajar is an Assistant Professor in the department of Commerce, under School of Social Sciences and languages at Vellore Institute of Technology, Vellore.

Mariya M. Shygun is Doctor of Science in Economics (Accounting, Analysis and Audit), Professor, Auditor of Ukraine and Professor of the Accounting and Consulting Department at the Kyiv National Economic University named after Vadym Hetman (Kyiv, Ukraine). She is an author of more than 240 publications. Leader and participant in more than 12 research on accounting, auditing and taxation. Has been awarded for CIMA Employability Excellence Award 2021 – Regional Champion (Europe) and for Distinguished Contribution 2020 "Conceptual Changes in Accounting" for the CIMA Research Excellence Award, presented by the CGMA Global University and Academic Center of Excellence. Awarded as a recognized expert in the field of audit by the "Honor of the Audit Chamber of Ukraine" (2016). Research interests: theory and methodology of accounting and auditing; modeling of accounting.

Mohammad Badruddoza Talukder is an Assistant Professor & Head of the Department, Department of Tourism and Hospitality Management, Daffodil Institute of Information Technology (at the National University), Dhaka, Bangladesh. Presently, he is pursuing PhD in Hotel Management, School of Hotel Management and Tourism, Lovely Professional University, India. He holds a bachelor's and a master's degree in Hotel Management from India. He has been teaching various courses in the Department of Tourism and Hospitality at various universities in Bangladesh since 2009. His research areas include tourism management, hotel management, hospitality management, food & beverage management, and accommodation management, where he has published research papers in well-known journals in Bangladesh and abroad. Mr. Talukder is one of the executive members of the Tourism Educators Association of Bangladesh. He has led training and counseling for a wide range of hospitality organizations in Bangladesh. As an administrator, Mr. Talukder served as a debate advisor at the University, coordinator for courses and exams in the Department of Tourism and Hotel Management. He has experience as a manager in various business class hotels in Bangladesh. He is one of the certified trainers for the food and beverage service department of the SIEP project from Bangladesh. He just become an honorary facilator at Bangladesh Tourism Board's Bangabandhu international tourism and hospitality training institution.

Index

A

B

C

D

E

F

G

H

I

J

L

M

N

O

P

Q

R

S

T

U

V

www.ingramcontent.com/pod-product-compliance
Lightning Source LLC
LaVergne TN
LVHW080631011026
849160LV00014B/1176
* 9 7 9 8 3 6 9 3 4 7 9 3 5 *